ICT as Innovator Between Tourism and Culture

Célia M.Q. Ramos
University of Algarve, Portugal

Silvia Quinteiro
University of Algarve, Portugal

Alexandra R. Gonçalves
University of Algarve, Portugal

A volume in the Advances in Business Strategy
and Competitive Advantage (ABSCA) Book Series

Published in the United States of America by
IGI Global
Business Science Reference (an imprint of IGI Global)
701 E. Chocolate Avenue
Hershey PA, USA 17033
Tel: 717-533-8845
Fax: 717-533-8661
E-mail: cust@igi-global.com
Web site: http://www.igi-global.com

Copyright © 2022 by IGI Global. All rights reserved. No part of this publication may be reproduced, stored or distributed in any form or by any means, electronic or mechanical, including photocopying, without written permission from the publisher. Product or company names used in this set are for identification purposes only. Inclusion of the names of the products or companies does not indicate a claim of ownership by IGI Global of the trademark or registered trademark.

Library of Congress Cataloging-in-Publication Data

Names: Ramos, Célia M. Q., editor. | Quinteiro, Sílvia, editor. | Gonçalves, Alexandra Rodrigues, editor.
Title: ICT as innovator between tourism and culture / Célia M.Q. Ramos, Sílvia Quinteiro, and Alexandra Goncalves, editor.
Description: Hershey PA : Business Science Reference, [2022] | Includes bibliographical references and index. | Summary: "This book provides relevant theoretical frameworks and the latest empirical research findings for professionals who want to improve their understanding of all facets of ICT as innovator between tourism and culture, and providing original viewpoints and/or innovative empirical research"-- Provided by publisher.
Identifiers: LCCN 2021024366 (print) | LCCN 2021024367 (ebook) | ISBN 9781799881650 (hardcover) | ISBN 9781799881667 (paperback) | ISBN 9781799881674 (ebook)
Subjects: LCSH: Tourism--Information technology. | Culture and tourism. | Social media--Influence.
Classification: LCC G156.5.I5 I37 2022 (print) | LCC G156.5.I5 (ebook) | DDC 910.285--dc23
LC record available at https://lccn.loc.gov/2021024366
LC ebook record available at https://lccn.loc.gov/2021024367

This book is published in the IGI Global book series Advances in Business Strategy and Competitive Advantage (ABSCA) (ISSN: 2327-3429; eISSN: 2327-3437)

British Cataloguing in Publication Data
A Cataloguing in Publication record for this book is available from the British Library.

All work contributed to this book is new, previously-unpublished material. The views expressed in this book are those of the authors, but not necessarily of the publisher.

For electronic access to this publication, please contact: eresources@igi-global.com.

Advances in Business Strategy and Competitive Advantage (ABSCA) Book Series

Patricia Ordóñez de Pablos
Universidad de Oviedo, Spain

ISSN:2327-3429
EISSN:2327-3437

Mission

Business entities are constantly seeking new ways through which to gain advantage over their competitors and strengthen their position within the business environment. With competition at an all-time high due to technological advancements allowing for competition on a global scale, firms continue to seek new ways through which to improve and strengthen their business processes, procedures, and profitability.

The **Advances in Business Strategy and Competitive Advantage (ABSCA) Book Series** is a timely series responding to the high demand for state-of-the-art research on how business strategies are created, implemented and re-designed to meet the demands of globalized competitive markets. With a focus on local and global challenges, business opportunities and the needs of society, the **ABSCA** encourages scientific discourse on doing business and managing information technologies for the creation of sustainable competitive advantage.

Coverage

- Differentiation Strategy
- Small and Medium Enterprises
- Globalization
- Core Competencies
- Strategy Performance Management
- Co-operative Strategies
- Business Models
- Competitive Strategy
- Foreign Investment Decision Process
- Resource-Based Competition

IGI Global is currently accepting manuscripts for publication within this series. To submit a proposal for a volume in this series, please contact our Acquisition Editors at Acquisitions@igi-global.com or visit: http://www.igi-global.com/publish/.

The Advances in Business Strategy and Competitive Advantage (ABSCA) Book Series (ISSN 2327-3429) is published by IGI Global, 701 E. Chocolate Avenue, Hershey, PA 17033-1240, USA, www.igi-global.com. This series is composed of titles available for purchase individually; each title is edited to be contextually exclusive from any other title within the series. For pricing and ordering information please visit http://www.igi-global.com/book-series/advances-business-strategy-competitive-advantage/73672. Postmaster: Send all address changes to above address. Copyright © 2022 IGI Global. All rights, including translation in other languages reserved by the publisher. No part of this series may be reproduced or used in any form or by any means – graphics, electronic, or mechanical, including photocopying, recording, taping, or information and retrieval systems – without written permission from the publisher, except for non commercial, educational use, including classroom teaching purposes. The views expressed in this series are those of the authors, but not necessarily of IGI Global.

Titles in this Series

For a list of additional titles in this series, please visit: www.igi-global.com/book-series

Leadership and Followership in an Organizational Change Context
Sajjad Nawaz Khan (Iqra University, Pakistan)
Business Science Reference • ©2022 • 361pp • H/C (ISBN: 9781799828075) • US $225.00

Emerging Ecosystem-Centric Business Models for Sustainable Value Creation
Xenia Ziouvelou (National Centre for Scientific Research "Demokritos", Greece & University of Southampton, UK) and Frank McGroarty (University of Southampton, UK)
Business Science Reference • ©2022 • 237pp • H/C (ISBN: 9781799848431) • US $195.00

Impact of Disruptive Technologies on the Sharing Economy
Ford Lumban Gaol (Bina Nusantara University, Jakarta, Indonesia) Natalia Filimonova (Vladimir State University, Russia) and Chandan Acharya (College of Staten Island, City University of New York, USA)
Business Science Reference • ©2021 • 269pp • H/C (ISBN: 9781799803614) • US $245.00

Global Corporate Social Responsibility Initiatives for Reluctant Businesses
Syed Abdul Rehman Khan (School of Management and Engineering, Xuzhou University of Technology, Xuzhou, China & Department of Business Administration, ILMA University, Karachi, Pakistan & Beijing Key Laboratory of Urban Spatial Engineering, Beijing, China) Zhang Yu (Chang'an University, China) Mirela Panait (Petroleum-Gas University of Ploiesti, Romania & Institute of National Economy, Bucharest, Romania) Laeeq Razzak Janjua (Poznan University of Economics and Business, Poland) and Adeel Shah (Institute of Business Management, Pakistan)
Business Science Reference • ©2021 • 280pp • H/C (ISBN: 9781799839880) • US $195.00

Impacts and Implications for the Sports Industry in the Post-COVID-19 Era
Armand Faganel (University of Primorska, Slovenia) Igor Rižnar (University of Primorska, Slovenia) and Arne Baruca (Texas A&M University San Antonio, USA)
Business Science Reference • ©2021 • 304pp • H/C (ISBN: 9781799867807) • US $215.00

Computational Thinking for Problem Solving and Managerial Mindset Training
Luisa Dall'Acqua (University of Bologna, Italy & LS TCO, Italy)
Business Science Reference • ©2021 • 293pp • H/C (ISBN: 9781799871262) • US $225.00

Bioentrepreneurship and Transferring Technology Into Product Development
Swati Agarwal (Banasthali University, India) Sonu Kumari (Banasthali University, India) and Suphiya Khan (Banasthali University, India)
Business Science Reference • ©2021 • 335pp • H/C (ISBN: 9781799874119) • US $245.00

701 East Chocolate Avenue, Hershey, PA 17033, USA
Tel: 717-533-8845 x100 • Fax: 717-533-8661
E-Mail: cust@igi-global.com • www.igi-global.com

Editorial Advisory Board

João Albino Silva, *Universidade do Algarve, Portugal*
Graham Busby, *University of Plymouth, UK*
Evrim Çeltek, *Tokat Gaziosmanpaşa Üniversitesi, Turkey*
Cihan Cobanoglu, *University of South Florida, United States of America*
Carlos Costa, *Universidade de Aveiro, Portugal*
Nancy Duxbury, *University of Coimbra, Portugal*
Carlos Fernandes, *Polytechnic Institute of Viana do Castelo, Portugal*
Ulrike Gretzel, *University of Southern California, USA*
Charlie Mansfield, *University of Plymouth, UK*
Ana Maria Molina-Casado, *University of Málaga, Spain*
Maria de Lourdes Netto Simões, *Universidade Estadual de Santa Cruz (DLA/Uesc), Brazil*
Vanessa Ratten, *La Trobe University, Australia*
Mike Robinson, *University of Birmingham, UK*
Lindy Stiebel, *University of KwaZulu-Natal, South Africa*
Nicola Watson, *Open University, UK*

Table of Contents

Preface xvi

Acknowledgment xxi

Section 1
Technology, Tourism, and Culture

Chapter 1
The Contribution of Spatial Augmented Reality to the Synergy of Special and Alternative Forms
of Tourism in Greece 1
    Stylianos Bouzis, University of the Aegean, Greece
    Panoraia Poulaki, University of the Aegean, Greece

Chapter 2
The Use of ICT in Tourist and Educational Literary Routes: The Role of the Guide 15
    Jordi Chumillas, University of Vic, Spain
    Mia Güell, University of Vic, Spain
    Pere Quer, University of Vic, Spain

Chapter 3
Importance of ICT Advancement and Culture of Adaptation in the Tourism and Hospitality
Industry for Developing Countries 30
    Tanvir Abir, International University of Business, Agriculture, and Technology (IUBAT),
        Bangladesh
    Md Yusuf Hossein Khan, International University of Business, Agriculture, and Technology
        (IUBAT), Bangladesh

Chapter 4
ICT as an Acculturative Agent and Its Role in the Tourism Context: Introduction, Acculturation
Theory, Progress of the Acculturation Theory in Extant Literature 42
    Yakup Kemal Özekici, Adıyaman University, Turkey

Chapter 5
Role of Technology on Religious Tourism in Turkey 67
    Muhammad Farooq, Yasar University, Turkey
    Volkan Altintas, Izmir Katip Celebi University, Turkey

Chapter 6
ICT and PB Learning Combined for the Advancement of Intercultural Education: The Case of the MIEC Virtual Exhibition 81
    Sara Cerqueira Pascoal, ISCAP, Polytechnic Institute of Porto, Portugal
    Laura Tallone, ISCAP, Polytechnic Institute of Porto, Portugal
    Marco Furtado, ISCAP, Polytechnic Institute of Porto, Portugal

Section 2
Technology and Tourism

Chapter 7
Technology Use and Innovation Strategies in Event Tourism 104
    Tuba Türkmendağ, Atatürk University, Turkey
    Zafer Türkmendağ, Atatürk University, Turkey

Chapter 8
Virtual Tourism and Challenges in a Post-Pandemic Context 122
    Carla Sousa Martins, Polytechnic Institute of Cávado and Ave, Portugal
    Ana Carvalho Ferreira, Polytechnic Institute of Cávado and Ave, Portugal
    Catarina Silva Pereira, Polytechnic Institute of Cávado and Ave, Portugal
    Bruno Barbosa Sousa, Polytechnic Institute of Cávado and Ave, Portugal & CiTUR, Portugal

Chapter 9
Relationship Between ICT and Tourism: The Case of Mediterranean Countries 138
    Selman Bayrakcı, Necmettin Erbakan University, Turkey
    Ceyhun Can Özcan, Necmettin Erbakan University, Turkey

Chapter 10
Digital Detox, Trends, and Segmentation in Tourism 155
    Beatriz Juncal, Polytechinc Institute of Cávado and Ave, Portugal
    Gabriela Vides, Polytechinc Institute of Cávado and Ave, Portugal
    Pedro Matos, Polytechinc Institute of Cávado and Ave, Portugal
    Bruno Barbosa Sousa, Polytechnic Institute of Cávado and Ave, Portugal & CiTUR, Portugal

Chapter 11
Innovation Dynamics Through the Encouragement of Knowledge Spin-Off From Touristic Destinations 170
    Sofia Vairinho, University of the Algarve, Portugal & Facultad de Derecho, Universidad de Huelva, Spain

Section 3
Social Media and Tourism

Chapter 12
Tourist Social Media Engagement: Conceptualization and Indicators 192
    Rayane Ruas, University of Aveiro, Portugal
    Belem Barbosa, University of Porto, Portugal

Chapter 13
The Role of Social Media Marketing in the Tourism and Hospitality Industry: A Conceptual
Study on Bangladesh 213
    Md Yusuf Hossein Khan, International University of Business, Agriculture, and Technology
        (IUBAT), Bangladesh
    Tanvir Abir, International University of Business, Agriculture, and Technology (IUBAT),
        Bangladesh

Chapter 14
Social Media's Influence on Destination Image: The Case Study of a World Heritage City 230
    Maria Angeles Garcia-Haro, University of Castilla-La Mancha, Spain
    Maria Pilar Martinez-Ruiz, University of Castilla-La Mancha, Spain
    Ricardo Martinez-Cañas, University of Castilla-La Mancha, Spain
    Pablo Ruiz-Palomino, University of Castilla-La Mancha, Spain

Chapter 15
Determination of Guest Satisfaction by Text Mining: Case of Turkey Hotels 247
    Ozan Çatir, Usak University, Turkey

Compilation of References 270

About the Contributors 311

Index 316

Detailed Table of Contents

Preface xvi

Acknowledgment xxi

Section 1
Technology, Tourism, and Culture

Chapter 1
The Contribution of Spatial Augmented Reality to the Synergy of Special and Alternative Forms of Tourism in Greece 1
    Stylianos Bouzis, University of the Aegean, Greece
    Panoraia Poulaki, University of the Aegean, Greece

This research investigates whether the evolution of augmented reality contributes to the combination of specific and alternative forms of tourism in Greece. More specifically, in the first stage, information and communication technologies and the new emerging perspectives that appear over time are described. Then, talking about special and alternative forms of tourism, the authors talk about cultural, gastronomic, and educational tourism, elements of which intersect in the light of spatial augmented reality (SAR). The main purpose of the chapter is to prove that SAR excels in the synergy of the three forms of tourism mentioned. Also, a successful example of the development of SAR in the Greek tourist area is given, with the presentation of a case study of a museum in Greece. Finally, the benefits provided by the combination of special forms of tourism with SAR are presented, and it is concluded that all ages have the opportunity to actively participate in such projects using SAR, without the informal exclusion of older people.

Chapter 2
The Use of ICT in Tourist and Educational Literary Routes: The Role of the Guide 15
    Jordi Chumillas, University of Vic, Spain
    Mia Güell, University of Vic, Spain
    Pere Quer, University of Vic, Spain

This chapter focuses on the use of ICT in literary routes and explores how technologies can influence the tour guides. It begins with a reflection on the key concept of literary routes (from both an educational and tourist perspective) and then considers the antecedents and components that define the guide. Finally, a survey of professionals and teachers with experience in the design and execution of literary routes is carried out in order to explore aspects such as (1) the actual use of ICT on the routes, (2) the synergies between the guide's skills and the use of ICT, and (3) to what extent the use of ICT leads to a change in the role of the guide.

Chapter 3
Importance of ICT Advancement and Culture of Adaptation in the Tourism and Hospitality
Industry for Developing Countries 30
    Tanvir Abir, International University of Business, Agriculture, and Technology (IUBAT),
        Bangladesh
    Md Yusuf Hossein Khan, International University of Business, Agriculture, and Technology
        (IUBAT), Bangladesh

The influence of ICT on tourism and hospitality is related to the facilitation of contact with stakeholders, acting as an effective distribution channel, and providing an effective forum for marketing, among other things. Tourism and hospitality are heavily reliant on information and communication technology in developing countries as well as in the developed nations. ICT has had a major effect on this market. The primary goal of this research is to identify the difference in ICT advancement and adaptation between developed and developing countries, as well as to determine how developing countries can benefit from it and make recommendations. This research was conducted using a qualitative approach. Using various types of literature such as research papers, articles, and books, this study highlights and scrutinizes the significance of ICT and how these actions contribute to the tourism and hospitality sector to raise awareness among academicians, researchers, tourism businesses, and government officials about the effectiveness of ICT applications in tourism and hospitality.

Chapter 4
ICT as an Acculturative Agent and Its Role in the Tourism Context: Introduction, Acculturation
Theory, Progress of the Acculturation Theory in Extant Literature 42
    Yakup Kemal Özekici, Adıyaman University, Turkey

ICTs have played a transformative role on the cultural components of all stratums of the society. This role has had a demand as well as supply-oriented reflection on the tourism system. In the scope of this chapter, the role of ICTs in the changing social structure is explained through the lens of acculturation. Beyond this, the acculturative process on the modern community's tourism-oriented reflections caused by ICTs were discussed through nine components (renting over owning, free-of-charge ownership, narcissism, connected loneliness, social capital, multiple realities, new identities, novel values, enculturation), and predictions were made with a futuristic perspective. In this context, it was explicated that the ICT-oriented digital acculturation process would add the concepts alternative tourism types, soft mass tourism, sharing economy-based tourism system, intense offline interactions between host and guests, multicultural destinations, virtual reality-based leisure, sharing as a novel pushing motivation, virtual demonstration effect, and diaspora to the future tourism system.

Chapter 5
Role of Technology on Religious Tourism in Turkey 67
    Muhammad Farooq, Yasar University, Turkey
    Volkan Altintas, Izmir Katip Celebi University, Turkey

The religious tourism sector is a booming industry and attracts a sizable number of tourists around the world. While several factors play an important role in increasing the number of tourists for religious purposes, technology plays a vital role in managing and boasting religious tourism in a country. The authors aim to see this in the context of Turkey, a country that is a bridge between East and West, possessing a number of religious touristic sites and attracting a large number of tourists. The profile of the country and the role of technology in increasing tourism in Turkey also suggest improvements in the technological landscape of the country to increase and facilitate the religious tourists.

Chapter 6
ICT and PB Learning Combined for the Advancement of Intercultural Education: The Case of the MIEC Virtual Exhibition 81
    Sara Cerqueira Pascoal, ISCAP, Polytechnic Institute of Porto, Portugal
    Laura Tallone, ISCAP, Polytechnic Institute of Porto, Portugal
    Marco Furtado, ISCAP, Polytechnic Institute of Porto, Portugal

This chapter intends to describe the case of the MIEC virtual exhibition as well as reflect upon the relevance of ICT, namely Google Arts and Culture, for the promotion of cultural heritage tourism. In this vein, the authors will first approach the issues of cultural tourism and ICT, exploring how virtual exhibitions and digitization have become an important tool to empower institutions and audiences. Secondly, the authors will present, discuss, and assess the project-based learning (PBL) activities, starting with the presentation of the platform, its advantages and disadvantages for learning and teaching. Then, the authors will analyze some of the results obtained from a pedagogical perspective by scrutinizing students' surveys and opinions. These results will also report on the research outcomes of the project, and an accountability of its marketing purposes will be proposed. The chapter will finally put forward the limitations of this ongoing project and intended future research, suggesting how similar projects can be implemented, managed, and assessed.

Section 2
Technology and Tourism

Chapter 7
Technology Use and Innovation Strategies in Event Tourism 104
    Tuba Türkmendağ, Atatürk University, Turkey
    Zafer Türkmendağ, Atatürk University, Turkey

Event tourism has undergone a serious change in the world with developing technology and innovations. In this respect, this chapter examines the direct, marketing, and management effects of technology on event tourism with a literature review. Studies in this field in the literature show that technologies such as artificial intelligence, big data, robots, decision support systems, internet of things, 5G cause behavioral changes in tourists; thus, event organizers use these technologies effectively to keep up with this change. In this context, academic studies in the field, new technologies, and methods used, innovation strategies are explained in detail in the book section, and a framework has been developed and presented to examine smart event tourism in detail. The results of the research are thought to contribute to the literature and offer managerial solutions.

Chapter 8
Virtual Tourism and Challenges in a Post-Pandemic Context 122
Carla Sousa Martins, Polytechnic Institute of Cávado and Ave, Portugal
Ana Carvalho Ferreira, Polytechnic Institute of Cávado and Ave, Portugal
Catarina Silva Pereira, Polytechnic Institute of Cávado and Ave, Portugal
Bruno Barbosa Sousa, Polytechnic Institute of Cávado and Ave, Portugal & CiTUR, Portugal

The role played by technologies of information and communication, ICT, has become increasingly important in the way of life of societies. As well as technologies to revolutionize or everyone's way of life, it also brings a sense of alertness to match. This chapter aims to present a reflection on the importance of virtual tourism in the pandemic scenario (new coronavirus) and the main challenges in the post-pandemic period. The tourist sector must continue to communicate with clients in order to retain them. In this way, several companies choose to enter into a partnership with digital influencers, seeing that they are presented as a link between the company and the customers. From an interdisciplinary perspective, the chapter presents contributions to marketing, (virtual) tourism, and pandemic management.

Chapter 9
Relationship Between ICT and Tourism: The Case of Mediterranean Countries 138
Selman Bayrakcı, Necmettin Erbakan University, Turkey
Ceyhun Can Özcan, Necmettin Erbakan University, Turkey

The relationship between tourism and information and communication technology (ICT) is called electronic tourism or e-tourism. The use of ICT makes markets from local to global and has a positive effect in increasing the market share of firms. Managing, planning, developing, and marketing tourism data through ICT increase the development and economic potential of tourism. ICT has provided the strategic management of all tourism-oriented companies and revolutionized the operations within the tourism distribution channel, causing tourism-related stakeholders to reassess their actions and positions. The purpose of this chapter is to reveal the relationship between ICT and tourism in the case of 14 Mediterranean countries from approximately 1995–2019. Dumitrescu and Hurlin Panel causality test was used for this analysis. The main findings indicate that ICT stimulates tourism that, in turn, boosts ICT even further in some countries (Algeria, Egypt, Morocco, Tunisia, and Turkey).

Chapter 10
Digital Detox, Trends, and Segmentation in Tourism 155
Beatriz Juncal, Polytechinc Institute of Cávado and Ave, Portugal
Gabriela Vides, Polytechinc Institute of Cávado and Ave, Portugal
Pedro Matos, Polytechinc Institute of Cávado and Ave, Portugal
Bruno Barbosa Sousa, Polytechnic Institute of Cávado and Ave, Portugal & CiTUR, Portugal

The chapter aims to demonstrate the growing importance of the concept of 'digital detox' as a segment of the tourism market to indicate the reasons and factors that encourage its demand, the diversity of establishments, the strategies employed by them, the limits, facilitating the adaptation to market conditions, and assisting in the development of marketing strategies that respond to customer needs. Through a content analysis of some research papers from the last 10 years and websites, as well as an interview with the founder from one of the establishments specialized in "disconnection with technologies" experiences, the "Offline House," this study presents inputs on marketing (digital), tourism (niches), and consumer behavior.

Chapter 11
Innovation Dynamics Through the Encouragement of Knowledge Spin-Off From Touristic Destinations 170
    Sofia Vairinho, University of the Algarve, Portugal & Facultad de Derecho, Universidad de Huelva, Spain

The present approach aims to explore the innovation dynamic that may lead to knowledge opportunities in a specific regional cluster characterized by a strong touristic positioning. The new technology-based companies, namely the spin-out created from university research, represent a possible and reliable approach to the economy stimulation. This said, it is mandatory to explore the topics that will allow a reflection on the networks associated with innovation processes, developed from the relations between the public universe (including universities and research centers), and the new technology or humanistic based companies. This chapter intends to be a contribution to the discussion of innovation clusters and sets the preliminary issues to discuss and implement an innovation ecosystem. This chapter explores and reflects the importance of regional innovation clusters dynamics, setting and describing the steps and specific strategical procedures in order to implement an innovation ecosystem, using as example a specific touristic territory.

Section 3
Social Media and Tourism

Chapter 12
Tourist Social Media Engagement: Conceptualization and Indicators 192
    Rayane Ruas, University of Aveiro, Portugal
    Belem Barbosa, University of Porto, Portugal

Social media are transforming relationships with customers for all sectors, including tourism. Since the search for information is a critical aspect of tourist purchase decision process, the importance of social media for tourism is evident. However, the presence of tourism brands in social media is not enough to have an impact on tourist purchase decisions: it is necessary to generate engagement. This chapter aims to conceptualize tourist engagement on social media and identify tourist engagement indicators. Tourist engagement was conceptualized through a literature review that identified four dimensions of engagement: popularity, commitment, virality, and post engagement. A set of indicators is proposed to measure tourist engagement in each of these dimensions. The proposed TSM engagement framework was validated through a mixed-method approach, using secondary data and interviews carried out with Brazilian tourist destinations.

Chapter 13
The Role of Social Media Marketing in the Tourism and Hospitality Industry: A Conceptual Study on Bangladesh... 213

 Md Yusuf Hossein Khan, International University of Business, Agriculture, and Technology (IUBAT), Bangladesh
 Tanvir Abir, International University of Business, Agriculture, and Technology (IUBAT), Bangladesh

Social networking is a series of Web 2.0-based applications that connect, communicate, and exchange ideas, views, perspectives, knowledge, and relationships among internet users worldwide. In the age of social media, businesses' marketing tactics have shifted from bringing products out to encouraging customers to buy things into their stores to foster a more engaging and mutually beneficial relationship. It is a significant player in the online tourism sector since it is a common and influential information source for tourists looking for destination-specific information. This study was conducted qualitatively, and this illustrates and discusses the role of social media marketing and how it works in the tourism and hospitality industries, with an emphasis on Bangladesh in particular, using a range of literature, including academic articles, journals, and books. This study would educate academics, researchers, politicians in tourism industries, and government officials about the importance of social media marketing.

Chapter 14
Social Media's Influence on Destination Image: The Case Study of a World Heritage City 230

 Maria Angeles Garcia-Haro, University of Castilla-La Mancha, Spain
 Maria Pilar Martinez-Ruiz, University of Castilla-La Mancha, Spain
 Ricardo Martinez-Cañas, University of Castilla-La Mancha, Spain
 Pablo Ruiz-Palomino, University of Castilla-La Mancha, Spain

Social media have become key tools for promoting and spreading the image of a tourist destination. In particular, these communication channels are critical for heritage destinations looking to boost awareness and attract a greater number of visitors. However, the tourism marketing literature has devoted limited attention to how these destinations project their image on social media. In order to cover this gap, this chapter focuses on analyzing the image projected by a specific heritage destination—Cuenca, a World Heritage City—on Facebook and Instagram. To this end, the chapter analyzes the posts, comments, and hashtags that have been published on the different tourism pages about Cuenca. The results of the analysis underscore the growing importance of the image projected by destinations on social networks. That said, there is a need to deepen our knowledge about the communication potential of these channels.

Chapter 15
Determination of Guest Satisfaction by Text Mining: Case of Turkey Hotels 247

 Ozan Çatir, Usak University, Turkey

The satisfaction of guests is of paramount importance to ensure the continuity and profitability of hotels. This study aims to determine guests' satisfaction with hotels by analyzing the online comments of guests. The text mining method has been utilized in this study. 58,193 Turkish comments about 5-star hotels in Turkey have been examined. These comments have been subjected to frequency and association analysis by models with Rapid Miner program. It may be stated that the guests are satisfied with 5-star hotel management in Turkey, and they are also satisfied with hotels in general and the services provided by hotels.

Compilation of References 270

About the Contributors 311

Index 316

Preface

Nowadays, tourists consider their mobile devices an essential accessory for the organization and realization of their travel, before, during and after the visit. Such devices allow them to search for information about points of interest, services, and/or products in real-time. Thus, mobile devices come to be considered essential tools to support decision-making regarding trips.

In the digital environment, tourists seek complementary information to consolidate knowledge about the destination, heritage, culture, customs, and traditions that make the visited place unique. Simultaneously, all that complementary information turns tourist experiences into a memory associated with travel, full of emotions and sensory impressions. These instruments also contribute to the sustainability of local populations, the reduction of inequalities, and the improvement of the quality of life of all involved (residents and tourists) because they facilitate the approximation to the community and to a wider and more diversified offer.

This book differs from others in the same areas insofar as it aims to place emphasis on and increase the bridge of knowledge linking ICT, tourism, and culture. The focus is on ICT as the main driver that creates the ecosystem that enables development and enhances the tourist experience in general, and in particular when linked to cultural heritage. ICT as a means to develop more sustainable and intelligent tourist destinations, aiming at the well-being of the local population and visitors.

The chapters of this volume offer a holistic vision that integrates ICT, Tourism and Culture, highlighting the potential of ICT to add value to products and tourist experiences, namely increasing authenticity, valuing heritage, and contributing to show and preserve the cultural identity of places.

Currently, and in a transversal way, ICT is a growing presence in the areas of tourism and culture. Hence the relevance of studying this relationship through the development of research in areas of culture such as gastronomy, religion, literature, education (of residents and tourists), natural, built, and intangible heritage, leisure activities, and support services.

In this book, researchers have studied topics that have been grouped into three categories: Technology, Tourism, and Culture; Technology and Tourism; Social Media and Tourism.

TECHNOLOGY, TOURISM, AND CULTURE

Information and communication technologies have been a powerful ally of all tourism activity in communication and information sharing. In addition to these potentials, new ones appeared, considering the use of emerging technologies to communicate, educate and provide new means to disseminate the culture associated with tourist destinations, such as augmented reality, digital guides, and virtual exhibitions.

Preface

In this context, new ways of communicating cultural tourism emerge, either in terms of creating new synergies for the emergence of new forms of tourism or developing cultural routes associated with a cultural dimension. The adaptation and synchronization of the development of the tourist destination focusing on its cultures, such as the religious dimension and cultural knowledge acquisition, enables the discovery of the authenticity of the places, of the residents' values and the traditions providing unexpected tourist experiences.

TECHNOLOGY AND TOURISM

Emerging technologies have been one of the main drivers in the development of tourism activity, boosting the emergence of innovation in this economic sector in terms of products, services, and decision support by the main and complementary companies in this industry.

Information and Communication Technologies applied to the tourism sector can contribute to the innovation of strategies applied to this activity, creation of virtual environments to contribute to the development of this activity, in a context of crisis such as a pandemic; to revolutionize the management and decision-making of activities with a view to optimizing the distribution of tourist information among all stakeholders; allowing the definition of new segmentation strategies; enabling the implementation of new dynamics that encourage the transfer of knowledge between academia and companies in the tourist region, which support tourist activity.

SOCIAL MEDIA AND TOURISM

Social media is widely used in the decision-making process of purchasing a trip. At any stage of the trip, tourists use platforms to look for official and other tourist information to identify opportunities and challenges at their destination. Social media now plays the role of tourist destination agents that are open 24 hours a day, 7 days a week, and have the testimonies of other travelers.

Social media is a marketing tool that marketers should use to define and enrich the relationship with their customers in order to increase their involvement in the tourist destination, contributing to improving the performance of the different components of the tourist product, with a focus on hotel management, which can be analyzed and driven through the management of indicators. On the other hand, social media influence the image of the destination, contributing to the rise the attention of future tourists, as well as allowing the analysis of tourist satisfaction through a customer satisfaction analysis using text mining techniques applied to comments generated on these platforms.

Social media increases the possibility of defining metrics to support business decision-makers on how to strategize for the future.

ORGANIZATION OF THE BOOK

The book is organized in 15 chapters. A brief description of each of the chapters follows:

Chapter 1 examines whether the evolution of augmented reality contributes to the combination of specific and alternative forms of tourism in Greece. More specifically, in the first stage, information and communication technologies and the new emerging perspectives that appear over time are described. Then, talking about special and alternative forms of tourism, it focuses on cultural, gastronomic, and educational tourism, elements intersected in the light of Spatial Augmented Reality.

Chapter 2 is about the use of ICT in literary routes, and explores how technologies can influence tour guides. It begins with a reflection on the key concept of literary routes (from both an educational and tourist perspective), and then considers the antecedents and components that define the guide. Finally, a survey of professionals and teachers with experience in the design and execution of literary routes is carried out in order to explore aspects such as the actual use of ICT on the routes; the synergies between the guide's skills and the use of ICT; and to what extent the use of ICT leads to a change in the role of the guide.

Chapter 3 focuses on how the influence of ICT on tourism and hospitality is related to the facilitation of contact with stakeholders, acting as an effective distribution channel, and providing an effective forum for marketing, among other things. The primary goal of this research is to identify the difference in ICT advancement and adaptation between developed and developing countries, as well as to determine how developing countries can benefit from it and make recommendations.

Chapter 4 examines how ICTs have played a transformative role in the cultural components of all social and economic groups of the society. This role has had a demand as well as supply-oriented reflection on the tourism system. In the scope of this chapter, the role of ICTs in the changing social structure is explained through the lens of acculturation. Beyond this, the acculturative process on the modern community tourism-oriented reflections caused by ICTs was discussed through nine components (renting over owning, free of charge ownership, narcissism, connected loneliness, social capital, multiple realities, new identities, novel values, enculturation), and predictions were made with a futuristic perspective.

Chapter 5 highlights the religious tourism sector. A booming industry that attracts a sizable number of tourists around the world. While several factors play an important role in increasing the number of tourists for religious purposes, technology plays a vital role in managing and boasting religious tourism in a country. We aim to see this in the context of Turkey, a country that bridges East and West and possesses a wide number of religious tourist sites, attracting numerous tourists.

Chapter 6 intends to describe the case of the MIEC virtual exhibition as well as to reflect upon the relevance of ICT, namely Google Arts & Culture, for the promotion of cultural heritage tourism. With this aim, it starts by approaching the issues of Cultural Tourism and ICT, exploring how virtual exhibitions and digitization have become important tools to empower institutions and audiences. Secondly, the authors present, discuss, and assess the Project-Based Learning (PBL) activities, starting with the presentation of the platform, its advantages and disadvantages for learning and teaching. Finally, the authors analyze some of the results obtained from a pedagogical perspective by scrutinizing students' surveys and opinions.

Chapter 7 studies the events in tourism that have undergone a serious change in the world with the development of technological innovations. Therefore, it examines the direct, marketing, and management effects of technology on event tourism with a literature review. Studies in this field show that technologies such as artificial intelligence, big data, robots, decision support systems, the Internet-of-Things, and 5G cause behavioral changes in tourists and, thus, event organizers use these technologies to keep up with this change.

Chapter 8 deals with the role played by Information and Communication Technologies and how it has become increasingly important in the way of life of societies. Technologies not only revolutionize ways of life it also brings a sense of alertness to match. This chapter aims to present a reflection on the

Preface

importance of virtual tourism in the pandemic scenario (new coronavirus) and the main challenges in the post-pandemic period. The tourist sector must continue to communicate with its clients in order to retain them.

Chapter 9 is focused on the relationship between Tourism and Information and Communication Technology (ICT), which is the so-called electronic tourism or e-tourism. The use of ICT transforms local markets into global ones and has a positive effect in increasing the market share of firms. The purpose of this chapter is to reveal the relationship between ICT and tourism in the case of 14 Mediterranean countries between 1995–2019.

Chapter 10 aims to demonstrate the growing importance of the concept of "Digital Detox" as a segment of the tourism market; to indicate the reasons and factors that encourage its demand, the diversity of establishments, the strategies employed by them, the limits; to facilitate the adaptation to market conditions and assist in the development of marketing strategies that respond to customer needs. Through a content analysis of some research papers from the last ten years and websites, as well as an interview with the founder from one of the establishments specialized in "disconnection with technologies" experiences - the "Offline House", this study presents inputs on marketing (digital), tourism (niches) and consumer behavior.

Chapter 11 presents an approach that aims to explore the innovation dynamics that may lead to knowledge opportunities in a specific regional cluster characterized by a strong tourist positioning. The new technology-based companies, namely the spin-out created from university research, represent a possible and reliable approach to economic stimulation. This chapter explores and reflects the importance of regional innovation clusters dynamics, setting and describing the steps and specific strategical procedures in order to implement an innovation ecosystem, using a specific touristic territory as an example.

Chapter 12 considers that Social Media are transforming relationships with customers for all sectors, including tourism. Since the search for information is a critical aspect of tourists' purchase-decision process, the importance of social media for tourism is evident. However, the presence of tourism brands in social media is not enough to have an impact on tourists' purchase decisions: it is necessary to generate engagement. This chapter aims to conceptualize tourist engagement on social media and identify tourist engagement indicators. The proposed TSM Engagement Framework was validated using a mixed-method approach, secondary data, and interviews done in Brazilian tourist destinations.

Chapter 13 discusses social networking as a series of Web 2.0-based applications that connect, communicate, and exchange ideas, views, perspectives, knowledge, and relationships among Internet users worldwide. This study was conducted qualitatively, and this illustrates and discusses the role of social media marketing and how it works in the tourism and hospitality industries, with an emphasis on Bangladesh in particular, also intend to present the potentialities to academics, researchers, politicians in tourism industries, and government officials about the importance of social media marketing.

Chapter 14 explores Social Media as a key tools for promoting and spreading the image of a tourist destination. In particular, these communication channels are critical for heritage destinations looking to boost awareness and attract a greater number of visitors. However, the tourism marketing literature has devoted limited attention to how these destinations project their image on social media. In order to cover this gap, this article focuses on analyzing the image projected by a specific heritage destination – Cuenca, a World Heritage City – on Facebook and Instagram.

Chapter 15 evaluates the satisfaction of hotels guests and its importance to ensure continuity and profitability. This study aims to determine guests' satisfaction with hotels by analyzing their online comments. The text mining method was utilized in this study based on 58.193 Turkish comments, that have been obtained from a TripAdvisor travel site about 5-star hotels in Turkey. These comments were subjected to frequency and association analysis by models with the Rapid Miner program. It may be stated that the guests are satisfied with 5-star hotel management in Turkey, and they are also satisfied with hotels and the services they provide in general.

Célia M. Q. Ramos
University of the Algarve, Portugal

Sílvia Quinteiro
University of the Algarve, Portugal

Alexandra R. Gonçalves
University of the Algarve, Portugal

Acknowledgment

The editors would like to acknowledge the help of all the people involved in this project and, more specifically, the authors and the reviewers that took part in the review process. Without their support, this book would not have become a reality.

The editors thank each one of the authors for their contributions. Our sincere gratitude goes to the authors of the chapters who contributed with their time and expertise to this book.

The editors would also like to thank the Research Centre for Tourism, Sustainability and Wellbeing (CinTurs) - Portuguese Foundation for Science and Technology (FCT) (project UIDB/04020/2020), and to the Center for Research in Communication Sciences and Arts (CIAC).

Célia M. Q. Ramos
University of the Algarve, Portugal

Sílvia Quinteiro
University of the Algarve, Portugal

Alexandra R. Gonçalves
University of the Algarve, Portugal

Section 1
Technology, Tourism, and Culture

Chapter 1
The Contribution of Spatial Augmented Reality to the Synergy of Special and Alternative Forms of Tourism in Greece

Stylianos Bouzis
University of the Aegean, Greece

Panoraia Poulaki
University of the Aegean, Greece

ABSTRACT

This research investigates whether the evolution of augmented reality contributes to the combination of specific and alternative forms of tourism in Greece. More specifically, in the first stage, information and communication technologies and the new emerging perspectives that appear over time are described. Then, talking about special and alternative forms of tourism, the authors talk about cultural, gastronomic, and educational tourism, elements of which intersect in the light of spatial augmented reality (SAR). The main purpose of the chapter is to prove that SAR excels in the synergy of the three forms of tourism mentioned. Also, a successful example of the development of SAR in the Greek tourist area is given, with the presentation of a case study of a museum in Greece. Finally, the benefits provided by the combination of special forms of tourism with SAR are presented, and it is concluded that all ages have the opportunity to actively participate in such projects using SAR, without the informal exclusion of older people.

DOI: 10.4018/978-1-7998-8165-0.ch001

The Contribution of Spatial Augmented Reality to the Synergy of Special and Alternative Forms of Tourism

INTRODUCTION

Augmented Reality technology (hereinafter referred to as AR) has become more and more common in recent decades in various business sectors. This is due to the supply and demand of smartphones and tablets nowadays. On the other hand, the appearance of special and alternative forms of tourism is quite upward, due to the rapid development of tourism activity. As early as the beginning of the 21st century, organized mass tourism seems to be lagging behind and special and alternative forms of tourism are emerging. According to them, there is a special incentive in the demand of tourists (e.g., sports, culture) and the development of a special infrastructure in the tourist destinations, thus aiming at the best possible service of each special form (Kokkosis, Tsartas, Grimba, 2011). Tourists, in this type of tourism, seek their autonomy regarding matters of organization and conduct of the trip. But how do these two emerging 21st century trends really come together?

Guided by the latest technology and the interest of tourists in alternative tourism, museums are claiming their place in this new venture. It is, perhaps, the top choice of space to establish once and for all the combination of technology and special tourism. The research questions posed in this chapter are also the objectives of completing the research. More specifically, the questions are answered: H1: To what extent has SAR evolved in the Greek tourist area and in what other sectors is it found? H2: How can SAR reach older tourists, without restricting the age target group by giving opportunities to all interested parties? H3: Does the project of the Museum of Natural History resonate with the general public after the integration of SAR inside? And what are his next actions? The philosophy is also adopted that the user should be the protagonist of the discovery and not just an observer. This is one of the goals of SAR for culture, that is, users, from passive receivers to become active observers, to interact with what they see, to assemble the pieces of history and thus discover for themselves the sights of the space they visit.

LITERATURE REVIEW

Spatial Augmented Reality

Despite the more intensive application of AR in recent years, it is worth mentioning the fact that the terminology of this imaging technique is not new. The term was introduced in 1992 by Tom Caudell and David Mizell, who worked for Boeing, helping workers lay cables on boats. Augmented reality is a technique that attempts the vivid and real-time depiction of an environment, which is even enriched with images and information in two (2D) or three-dimensional (3D) (Thomas, David, 1992). This information is usually audio, graphics, videos, location data, etc. Therefore, it is a process in which the real world is not only not degraded, but instead enhanced (augmented) by various virtual information (Marras, Nikolaidis, Mikrogeorgis, Lyroudia, & Pitas, 2008). Thus, the user has the ability to see the real world and the virtual objects that are displayed at the same time. This display follows the instructions of a digital database and is implemented with the help of various technological means/ tools. These tools are usually smart phones, which through the camera and GPS system provide information/ data for each Point of Interest (hereinafter referred to as POI). In addition, the viewing of virtual data can be achieved, in addition to screens of mobile devices, through special projection glasses.

According to Azuma (1997) AR is a variant of pre-existing virtual reality (VR) and individual virtual environments (Virtual Environments - VE). Specifically, AR is based on VR. Virtual Reality (VR) technologies, however, have the ability to completely "immerse" users in a purely virtual environment, in which the real world and the objects around them are not visible. In AR, on the other hand, as mentioned above, the virtual projection of objects in the real world is achieved, but they can be perceived. Therefore, AR complements reality and does not completely replace it. One of the most important differences between these two technologies is the fact that AR allows users to move both indoors and outdoors. With this feature, users, as they move, improve their overall experience, as they better understand the application, the game, or any other activity.

Depending on the technological means used and the goals set by AR technology, it is divided into four categories: index-based AR, index-free AR, projection-based AR, and superimposition-based AR. For the correct operation of each technology, of course, it is necessary to have an input system, an imaging device and detection sensors (compass, GPS). The whole process starts through the camera, which is the input system, and thus a picture from the real world is recorded, on which the virtual objects / information is added (augmented). Finally, the output system presents the result, which is perceived by users with the help of their senses.

However, with the passing of the decades and the increasing flourishing of technology, data display is taking on new dimensions and projector-based displays are becoming more and more popular since the early 1990s. Now AR provides virtual content combined with the real world not only through digital screens, but by displaying virtual digital objects in the natural environment through Spatial Augmented Reality (SAR) technology (Raskar, Welch, Fuchs, 1998). This is how SAR is displayed, which separates users from the necessary devices and presents digital objects and images in a real environment.

Unlike the first augmented reality systems, SAR achieves the projection of objects and information using projection systems and mapped projection. One of the most well-known projection systems is CAVE - a multi-faceted projection space. This and other similar spatial display techniques essentially "free" the user from the forced use of a screen and integrate it into the wider environment. It is an emerging technology that creates the feeling that real and virtual objects coexist in the same space at the same time (Thomas, Von Itzstein, Vernik, Porter, Marner, Smith, ... & Schumacher, (2011). a wide variety of spatial screens represent about 90% of all VR screens.

More specifically, the most basic AR imaging devices consist of three types (Carmigniani et al., 2010). First appears the Head-Mounted Display (HMD), a visual imaging device that adapts to the user's head and displays real or virtual objects. A second device is the Handheld Display, a small portable device that contains a screen and a camera, which the user holds in his hands, thus projecting an augmented video in real time. Finally, the Spatial Display (SAR), in which, as mentioned, mainly projection screens are used, but also other technologies for the display of graphical pop-up information on naturally existing objects. Part of this visualization is, among others, the projection systems technology (Projection Augmented Reality). Indicative areas of application of SAR are, among others, museum tours and the general tourism sector.

SPECIAL AND ALTERNATIVE FORMS OF TOURISM

A necessary condition for carrying out special activities is the existence of a special purpose, an incentive, which pushes the tourist to choose the specific type of vacation. For the development of these forms also, it is customary to support the basic principle of sustainability, which is achieved with respect for the environment, the local community and the culture.

In a country like Greece, with such a rich and developed cultural element, cultural tourism is presented as a special form of tourism in which abundant activities are included. An expanded range of theoretical concepts and thematic terms characterizes cultural tourism (Silberberg, 1995; Waitt, 2000). These terms are significantly different from those of mass tourism and have absolutely nothing to do with the common destinations characterized by "sun and sea". According to Asplet and Cooper (2000), cultural tourism can include as products the local language, gastronomy, technology and clothing of the past, leisure activities and various educational programs, always in the context of tourism. According to him, the way of life, history, art, architecture and religion of the local people also emerge (Borowiecki, Castiglione, 2014).

At the individual level, cultural tourism is considered as a method for enhancing residents' awareness, pride and national identity (Bachleitner and Zins, 1999; Taylor, 2001). It also promotes intercultural communication that can lead to understanding between the host and the visitor. This is in fact one of its biggest assets.

The main categories that govern cultural tourism are cultural heritage tourism, tradition tourism, religious tourism, which includes pilgrimage routes, creative tourism and special event / festival tourism. For each of these categories, there are some major points of interest from tourists with a highly developed cultural motivation. These points can be both the archeological sites themselves, as well as any other activity directly related to Greek culture. According to the Public Consultation of the Draft Joint Ministerial Decision in Greece, entitled "Special Framework for Spatial Planning and Sustainable Development for Tourism and the interconnected strategic environmental impact study" of the Ministry of Environment and Energy, the strengthening of the actions for the creation of multi-spaces of digital representation of historical, mythological and other cultural scenarios. This is a proposal that serves the connection of technological innovation and culture in Greece.

As a representation of the general culture of a country, its traditional food can undoubtedly be characterized (Yulia, Hasbullah, Nikmawati, Mubaroq, Abdullah, & Widiaty, 2018). Gastronomic tourism is often equated with experiences that focus on delicious food and drink. Nevertheless, gastronomic tourism is much more than this general assumption. Indicatively, then, gastronomy as a tourist product may also include participation in cooking classes, the purchase of typical local products, visiting food or beverage production environments, participation in gastronomic festivals, festivals and much more.

There is no doubt that most of the memories that a tourist from the countries he visits, at the end of his vacation, are inextricably linked to the gastronomic experiences and what he tasted in each of them. Especially when it comes to Greece, as everywhere in this country there are destinations where a cultural experience can be harmoniously combined with various local delicacies. It is also proven, according to financial data of the World Food Travel Association, that in 2019 in Greece from the 16 billion euros of tourist income, 4 billion came from gastronomic tourism. At the same time, according to a survey by the same organization in 2016, it was announced that 25% of tourists "spend significant amounts" on food and drink in the countries they visit. This result justifies the efforts of the bodies involved in gastronomic tourism and sets standards for the optimal development of this form of tourism.

On the other hand, talking about special forms of tourism that strengthen the Greek tourism package, educational tourism should also be mentioned, as it seems to actively participate in the offer of Greek tourism with the presence of several activities. Educational tourism means a trip to a destination with the aim of involving the interested party in any educational activity. Educational tourism includes, among other things, visits to special research and educational facilities, which have the appropriate attractions, as well as visits to participatory education and experiential tourism in relevant reception facilities. A typical example is the visit to archeological sites, through which the interested party combines his interest in culture and his desire for learning/ training.

A basic form of educational tourism is student tourism. The development environment of this form of tourism is determined according to the priorities set by the student/ tourist himself and the motivations that push him for education and tourism. With this in mind, in the environment of tourism is identified the common space/ place of tourism and education that distinguishes student tourism with four specific forms. Adult tourism, Edu tourism (ecotourism, cultural tourism, etc.) and student tourism. In Greece, the Ministry of Education is still used to characterize visits that last more than a day as "educational visits" and not "student tourism". Definition basis, as submitted by the World Tourism Organization (W.T.O.), should be defined as visits in the form of tourism "educational visits".

Some of the results of the strengthening of educational tourism are the stimulation of domestic student tourism, the reduction and effective treatment of the seasonality of tourism, the extension of the summer tourist season in certain destinations, the strengthening of the domestic tourism market and the stimulation of local businesses at an economic and social level.

ICT AND TOURISM - THE INCLUSION OF ICT IN MUSEUMS

New information and communication technologies (hereinafter referred to as ICT) appear in the last century to completely change the economic indicators and the way businesses operate. ICT provides companies and entities in various sectors with new and competitive ways to attract customers in order to maintain their customer base and gain a competitive advantage in the market. It is a very innovative idea for the tourism industry, as it provides the ability to provide information to customers in a fairly direct, economical and fast way. In fact, as many researchers argue, tourism should be treated as an information-intensive industry Schertler (1995).

There are several ICTs available, which influence and enhance all experiences in the tourism sector. More specifically, they are defined as a set of electronic tools, which facilitate business strategy and allow information management and interactive communication with stakeholders to achieve their mission and objectives (Keil, Pujol, Roussou, Engelke, Schmitt, Bockholt, & Eleftheratou, 2013). The fact that technology has changed not only human interactions and behaviors but also the role of people in society, affects the tourism industry itself, like any other industry, in terms of its competitiveness.

The faster growth of the tourism industry goes hand in hand with the equally rapid advancement of ICT with a high interest in the strategic exploitation of information management technologies and equally effective communication. This rapid technological development, therefore, means that the more powerful and complex ICT becomes, the more accessible and interesting it is to users. New screen trends are taking advantage of a number of large spatially aligned visuals, such as combinations of beams, holograms, and video projectors. In many cases, SAR displays go beyond the technological and ideological limitations of conventional AR systems.

Due to the reduced financial costs and the available technological projection tools (e.g., personal computers, projectors and graphic material) there is a growing interest in the adoption and exploitation of SAR systems in various fields such as universities, research centers, archeological sites, industries. and in the art world.

Focusing not only on the tourism sector, but also on archeological sites and more specifically on museums, it seems that there is a growing interest in utilizing the technological means/ possibilities in them. This is mainly due to the effort to upgrade the experience provided to the visitor, on the part of the museums, providing new technologies, so that they offer their best and innovative services. There are now many museums that, in addition to the natural collection of available objects, also create a corresponding digital museum space of exhibits (Falk, & Dierking, 2008).

Making a brief historical review of the integration of ICT in museums, it is clear that the gradual evolution of these archaeological sites has reached its zenith. So, it all starts in the 1960s, where an early interest begins to emerge with few applications. The changes appear in the next decade (1970), with the introduction of the first mini computers. Then the pressures for the proper management and proper registration of the cultural heritage increase (Waitt, 2000). Thus, the first two major cultural heritage registration programs are created, the Inventaire Général in France and the National Inventory Program in Canada.

In the 1980s computers in museums spread. Local networks are set up in museums and commercial electronic applications are adopted (mainly for archiving documentation). Reaching the 1990s, multimedia and the internet emerged. Museum websites, websites and the first virtual museums with developed graphics are being created. However, when the 2000s come to the fore, information spreads everywhere. Then interactivity and virtual reality appear. This 3D virtual world presents another life (true and false at the same time) and functions as the main link between archiving, librarianship and museology.

However, in order to better understand the fields of application of ICT in museums, an "artificial categorization" must be made in conventional and virtual museums. Conventional ones are those that have natural exhibits but are often presented to use new technologies in the front & back office. However, the applications that excite the visitors, concern the final service provided, namely the display of the exhibits.

Upgrading the museum experience is usually done in two ways. Initially, through the improvement of the existing experience (e.g., improvement of the conditions of the space, integration of systems for electronic tour, etc.). Second, a completely new, alternative and innovative experience can be offered. The use of media for the representation of digital exhibits, representations and emerging data/ information can contribute to this.

On the other side there are the virtual museums (Soren, & Canadian Heritage Information Network, 2005). These museums are based entirely on information systems and new technologies are used both for the display and promotion of exhibits and for the management of their content. Based on this division, modern museums can be classified into three categories, in terms of the exhibits they display and the rates of use of new technologies. In the first category are the museums that contain "real" and existing exhibits in a natural space, with or without the aforementioned technological upgrade of experience. Secondly, there are many museums that exhibit real objects with electronic representations, either through the internet or in specially designed spaces. Finally, the third category includes museums that offer electronic representations of non-existent exhibits, either via the internet or in specially designed spaces. In this case all the surrounding objects, even the exhibits, are artificial and made by computers.

Summarizing and taking into account the above, it is concluded that the integration of SAR in museums is admittedly a difficult process, especially when it is not framed by experts and operators. A positive omen, however, is the fact that this work finds fertile ground in Greece, as museums nowadays seem willing to participate in research programs/ experiments, which aim to introduce augmented reality technology in their rooms. But we need cost-effective, efficient and simple methods of creating exhibits based on the collection of 3D models. In addition, on the part of visitors it now tends to seem like an imperative, as the visitor and exhibit interface should be easier and more fun. Museums are now willing to participate in research projects or experiments (Abawi, Los Arcos, Haller, Hartmann, Huhtala, &

Träskbäck, 2004) that temporarily introduce augmented reality technology into their museum exhibits and halls. However, in most cases, the results of the project do not reach the permanent exhibition halls.

BENEFITS OF SAR IN TOURISM AND CULTURE

Turning to the benefits of SAR in the tourism sector and compared to device screens, headlights offer many advantages in terms of visual quality, such as e.g., the image resolution, the field of view, the focus, etc. Also, several technical issues are solved, such as the monitoring of objects and the special lighting of a room, while at the same time the human factor of inability to use is limited.

In practice, tools are more flexible when a single tool can perform multiple functions simultaneously. This also reduces the number of tools required to use the system. For example, in the case of a projection in a museum room, only one projection is required as a projection medium, through which a more intuitive environment is provided using a purely digital display.

In addition, users can interact from anywhere in the space, thus providing movement during the tour (in case of application of SAR in an archaeological site). It also allows people to interact with each other but also between them and objects.

In terms of imaging devices, the important advantage of SAR over HMD and Handheld Display is that the user is not required to hold and operate any type of device or general equipment. It can also be used by multiple users simultaneously. For example, in the field of tourism, by applying the SAR in a room of an archeological site, visitors will have the opportunity to "get in touch" with the exhibit at the same time. In this way, the delay of a museum tour is avoided and the modern service of many visitors is achieved at the same time. It is understood that this fact in itself is a strong advantage due to time constraints.

In addition, with the entry of SAR in its fields of application, it is possible to present different designs of a product similar to the real ones. That is, if, for example, a museum exhibit has a specific appearance, such as statues, it is possible, with the help of SAR, to make it more documentary. How is this going to be done; If projectors place virtual objects and / or information on the statue, such as various types of clothing that characterize human history over the centuries, historical information about the statue and more.

Finally, according to research by Neuhofer & Buhalis (2014), some additional benefits are recorded from the use of ICT in the field of cultural tourism for tourism companies. Easy and quick access to the exhibits and the services provided by the museum is one of them, as the tourist can now access a lot of information in a short time with the help of SAR. In addition, with the continuous development of technology, tourism companies are given the opportunity to check for a better understanding of the needs of their customers due to research based on available information. Finally, an additional advantage is the simplification and automation of business processes, as this leads to cost reduction and bureaucracy. Thus, in the above ways, the trust between customers / tourists and the respective business is established.

Culture, in particular, with the help of SAR seems to be becoming more accessible. This fact is proved when the younger ones realize the importance and significance of a work of art, of an ancient find, with the virtual and three-dimensional representation of scenes in any space. As a result, new art forms and new artists are coming closer to the general public. At this point, in fact, the phrase is added that "the user must be the protagonist of the discovery and not just a passerby". The goal of SAR, therefore, is for passive observer users to become active participants, to interact with what they see, to assemble pieces of history - to take part in learning activities and thus to discover the sights they visit.

From the point of view of entrepreneurs, the transfer of SAR to museums is admittedly a difficult endeavor. But once such an idea is put into practice, it only has benefits. Initially, as far as time is concerned, an exhibit captured with SAR needs less time to be watched by the visitor than another presented with simple VR or AR. This is because in SAR the means of projection of the electronic object is the projector, which already exists located in the space / room. So, it makes sense to be a faster tool, as it does not require visitors / tourists to use their own manual devices. This means that there is a given time for the display of each exhibit. On the other hand, most museum visitors get tired and / or unable to read extensive instructions for using another system, even when it is provided free of charge by the company.

This is where the age factor comes in. It is imperative, therefore, that the tourist and exhibit interface be easy, short and fun. The handling should be simple and ideally the tourist should look at the exhibit with virtual information and objects, but without being required to participate in any way. So, what is more ideal than SAR? No one is dealing with difficult and fragile monitoring devices or projection systems that require complex customization and do not need any preparation of the medium or reading specific instructions for use. At the same time, however, new technologies are used, information emerges in an interactive way and the tour acquires another rhythm with new images and interesting activities.

Museums, therefore, need efficient, cost-effective and simple methods of presenting exhibits based on the collection of 3D models. Users need to be able to interact with a SAR exhibit as easily and naturally as they can interact with museum objects in a real and non-virtual world.

CASE STUDY: MUSEUM OF NATURAL HISTORY AND MUSHROOMS, GREECE

Although there are many options for including AR in museums, it was chosen to present as an case study an effort that objectively brings together several advantages over others. This view stems from the fact that this area seems to make the most of ICT and in particular the SAR technique, aiming to attract more and more stakeholders.

For example, the most common way ARs are used by museums, which is also found in the present case study, is to display emerging information and explanations of exhibits. This way, visitors get even more information when they see the exhibits in the space using AR technology. In combination with this, museums can also use AR to digitally display the faces of the artists themselves, next to their works, which are exhibited in the surrounding area. These three-dimensional illustrations can then provide a narrative of key features or a more general description of the work.

There are already many museums around the world, which include AR in their premises. In Greece, however, the Meteora Museum of Natural History and the Mushroom Museum are a successful example of the integration of ICT in archaeological sites. Some of the exhibits of this museum now, with the presence of SAR, present something new and special from the other existing collections and clearly attract a wider audience.

Thus, AR is now proven to seem to completely change the overall experience of the visitor / tourist in the museums of Greece, by introducing a different interactive relationship that develops between the visitors and the exhibits. The information provided is now digitally enhanced with multiple and more tempting, for the senses, methods, such as the addition of various visual, acoustic and other somatosensory transformations within the Greek museum spaces.

In a nutshell, this is a new emerging interactive technology, which enables visitors to interact in the physical world by adding digital and virtual information to it each time. This is achieved both with the use of projection systems and with the technique of mapped projection. In this way, the use of individual projection systems by each visitor separately (e.g. screens from smartphones and tablets) is not required, as the SAR allows the cooperative and simultaneous interaction between all visitors. This is the main reason why SAR finds suitable ground worldwide and is preferred in several museum facilities, changing the way of group tour and the information received by each visitor.

More specifically, Interactive Light Designs (ILD) is the first company to bring SAR technology to Greece, with an original reference project taking place at the Meteora Museum of Natural History and the Mushroom Museum. ILD is a design company based in Larissa, which has applied to a new wing of the museum the new and innovative technology of "Spatial Augmented Reality". In fact, together they manage to win the "BRONZE" award at the Lighting Awards 2020 in the category "Cultural", the seventh, in a row, award of 2020. This is the first time that this emerging technology is used in a museum in Greece, which is based on color pixel mapping, but also in the projection of graphics on a multilevel surface through a projection machine (multiplayer projection mapping). In this way, the new wing of the Museum is highlighted through a feast of colors, which makes the museum experience unique and highly attractive.

The Museum of Natural History of Meteora and the Museum of Mushrooms have a variety of exhibits, a rich collection of birds and mammals, as well as a complete mushroom museum, the first mushroom museum in Greece. About 350 species of animals and 250 species of mushrooms are on display. The way the collections are presented through 3D illustrations, manages to represent with absolute accuracy, the natural environment in which the animals live and the mushrooms grow. The quality of the exhibits is excellent and they are placed in the museum space in separate thematic rooms. Therefore, all exhibits are distributed in the space depending on the type of ecosystem to which they belong.

An original way of presentation has been designed for the display of mushrooms, which includes the three phases of their development, thus providing a complete first image to the interested visitor. So, this new section, entitled "12 top edible and 12 top healing mushrooms", comes to highlight the contribution of mushrooms and strengthen the educational theme of the Mushroom Museum, combining text (in Greek and English), painting and sculpture with modern digital representation technologies. Specifically, in this area the coloring of the mushrooms is increased using 3D projection mapping in each mushroom sculpture separately. This makes all the color details visible from a long distance, both on the side of the top edibles and on the side of the top medicinal mushrooms.

This particular visualization technique guides the entire tour, emphasizing mainly the genre that is presented each time and focusing on the relevant text or the corresponding work of art. At the same time, with the help of laser technology (3D animation), the digital display and the connection of the valuable elements of each mushroom with the specific organs of the human body is achieved. Therefore, the interactive relationship of the visitor with innovative digital 3D imaging applications is supported, which makes the tour at least attractive.

Also, the activities of the Museum (mushroom festival, truffle hunting and truffle cooking), the mushroom collection process, the various research activities on the subject and some general references to the environment (geological phenomena, flora and fauna), are imprinted in various mural compositions. A striking example of these murals is the depiction of an eagle flying over the rocks, while the dance and the shadow theater at the mushroom festival below Meteora emphasize the heavy cultural heritage of the place.

FUTURE RESEARCH DIRECTIONS

The presentation of this case study showed that ICT contributes significantly to the combination of certain specific and alternative forms of tourism with each other. Specifically, according to the successful example of a Greek museum, it seemed that gastronomic, cultural and educational tourism are conceptually united with the help of SAR. Thus, tourists of all three forms of tourism are attracted to this archaeological site. This results in increased visits, revenue, and the development of the museum based on the demand. Interesting, however, would be a study, which would focus on other possible advanced actions on the part of museums. In particular, research on the 3D projection of objects and information outdoors and not indoors is considered important. This would be a rather innovative practice, which is rarely encountered. In addition, can SAR activate other senses besides vision? For example, could an audio system be integrated with various recorded messages (such as nature sounds)? Also, the addition of sensors that will emit odors from traditional food is an original action. These and many more could be key research features in a future research on the subject.

CONCLUSION

Tomorrow of the museums will not be the same as yesterday, since the data and the trends are constantly changing. More and more, new approaches are required and informally every ingenuity and creativity are required to strengthen the industry. However, the digital transformation of museums should be taken for granted. Whether it is virtual exhibitions or the presentation of digital virtual products.

The big question now is the balance between the real and digital world and to what extent the virtual reality of a museum can replace the physical presence of both exhibits and the public itself, since in the future there may be the possibility of a purely remote online museum tour.

At the same time, it's next that this digital shift must be based on very strong foundations, so that it becomes viable. Perhaps the strongest basis of these is this strategy, which presents the necessary training of staff in new skills and the use of new programs.

Regarding the research questions that were asked from the beginning, they are answered in the continuation of this section and give the impetus for future research. First, for the first question, it is worth mentioning that the SAR technique is beginning to be integrated in Greece in the last decade, so as it is understood, its evolution cannot be investigated at the moment it is now "born". Certainly, in addition to the tourism sector, SAR finds fertile ground in the science of medicine.

A positive omen, however, in the consolidation and development of SAR in museums and wider archaeological sites, is the answer to the second research question and specifically the universal approach of stakeholders. More specifically, in the case of SAR, a technique in which projection systems are used to display objects and information, it makes sense for participation to be enhanced and for older people to be able to participate, regardless of their basic technology skills. In contrast, in other cases, with the simple AR, where users are required to hold the media of an exhibit themselves, it follows that many of them cannot or do not know how to operate the device.

Finally, according to the boom of technology, SAR seems to be emerging rapidly, as it is very popular in the tourism sector - mainly in the form of simple AR - and besides, it now seems to be adopted by most companies. In this case, of the Museum of Natural History and Mushrooms, the response is proven to be huge both by the visitors of the museum and by the whole society. In fact, this is confirmed by the numerous awards and distinctions that the company constantly receives, just 1.5 years after the start of this technique.

ACKNOWLEDGMENT

This research received no specific grant from any funding agency in the public, commercial, or not-for-profit sectors.

REFERENCES

Asplet, M., & Cooper, M. (2000). Cultural designs in New Zealand souvenir clothing: The question of authenticity. *Tourism Management*, *21*(3), 307–312. doi:10.1016/S0261-5177(99)00061-8

Azuma, R., Baillot, Y., Behringer, R., Feiner, S., Julier, S., & MacIntyre, B. (2001). Recent advances in augmented reality. *IEEE Computer Graphics and Applications*, *21*(6), 34–47. doi:10.1109/38.963459

Azuma, R. T. (1997). A survey of augmented reality. *Presence (Cambridge, Mass.)*, *6*(4), 355–385. doi:10.1162/pres.1997.6.4.355

Bachleitner, R., & Zins, A. H. (1999). Cultural tourism in rural communities: The residents' perspective. *Journal of Business Research*, *44*(3), 199–209. doi:10.1016/S0148-2963(97)00201-4

Benko, H., Wilson, A. D., & Zannier, F. (2014, October). Dyadic projected spatial augmented reality. In *Proceedings of the 27th annual ACM symposium on User interface software and technology* (pp. 645-655). 10.1145/2642918.2647402

Bimber, O., & Raskar, R. (2005). *Spatial augmented reality: merging real and virtual worlds*. CRC Press. doi:10.1201/b10624

Bimber, O., & Raskar, R. (2019). *Spatial augmented reality: merging real and virtual worlds*. AK Peters / CRC Press.

Borowiecki, K. J., & Castiglione, C. (2014). Cultural participation and tourism flows: An empirical investigation of Italian provinces. *Tourism Economics*, *20*(2), 241–262. doi:10.5367/te.2013.0278

Burton, E. P., Frazier, W., Annetta, L., Lamb, R., Cheng, R., & Chmiel, M. (2011). Modeling Augmented Reality Games with Preservice. *Journal of Technology and Teacher Education*, *19*(3), 303–329.

Carmigniani, J., Furht, B., Anisetti, M., Ceravolo, P., Damiani, E., & Ivkovic, M. (2011). Augmented reality technologies, systems and applications. *Multimedia Tools and Applications*, *51*(1), 341–377. doi:10.100711042-010-0660-6

Cerqueira, C. S., & Kirner, C. (2012). Developing Educational Applications with a Non-Programming Augmented Reality Authoring Tool. *Proceedings of World Conference on Educational Multimedia, Hypermedia and Telecommunications*, 2816-2825.

Ciolfi, L. (2005). *Proceedings of the International Workshop Re-Thinking Technology in Museums: Towards a new understanding of people's experience in museums*. Academic Press.

Falk, J. H., & Dierking, L. D. (2008). Enhancing visitor interaction and learning with mobile technologies. *Digital technologies and the museum experience: Handheld guides and other media*, 19-33.

Hammady, R., Ma, M., Strathern, C., & Mohamad, M. (2020). Design and development of a spatial mixed reality touring guide to the Egyptian museum. *Multimedia Tools and Applications*, *79*(5), 3465–3494. doi:10.100711042-019-08026-w

Harrison, R., Byrne, S., & Clarke, A. (2013). *Reassembling the collection: ethnographic museums and indigenous agency*. SAR Press.

Keil, J., Pujol, L., Roussou, M., Engelke, T., Schmitt, M., Bockholt, U., & Eleftheratou, S. (2013, October). A digital look at physical museum exhibits: Designing personalized stories with handheld Augmented Reality in museums. In *2013 Digital Heritage International Congress (Digital Heritage)* (Vol. 2, pp. 685-688). IEEE. 10.1109/DigitalHeritage.2013.6744836

Kim, D. B., & Lee, K. H. (2011). Computer-aided appearance design based on BRDF measurements. *Computer Aided Design*, *43*(9), 1181–1193. doi:10.1016/j.cad.2011.04.015

Kokkossis, H., Tsartas, P., & Grimba, E. (2011). *Special and alternative forms of tourism*. Kritiki.

Kozhevnikov, M., & Thornton, R. (2006). Real-Time Data Display, Spatial Visualization Ability, and Learning Force and Motion Concepts. *Journal of Science Education and Technology*, *15*(1), 1. doi:10.100710956-006-0361-0

Krauß, M., & Bogen, M. (March 31, 2010). Conveying Cultural Heritage and Legacy with Innovative AR-based Solutions. In J. Trant & D. Bearman (Eds.), *Museums and the Web 2010: Proceedings*. Archives & Museum Informatics. Available at https://www.archimuse.com/mw2010/papers/krauss/krauss.html

Loureiro, S. M. C., Guerreiro, J., & Ali, F. (2020). 20 years of research on virtual reality and augmented reality in tourism context: A text-mining approach. *Tourism Management*, *77*, 104028. doi:10.1016/j.tourman.2019.104028

Marras, I., Nikolaidis, N., Mikrogeorgis, G., Lyroudia, K., & Pitas, I. (2008). A virtual system for cavity preparation in endodontics. *Journal of Dental Education*, *72*(4), 494–502. doi:10.1002/j.0022-0337.2008.72.4.tb04514.x PMID:18381855

Marty, P. F. (2008). Museum websites and museum visitors: Digital museum resources and their use. *Museum Management and Curatorship*, *23*(1), 81–99. doi:10.1080/09647770701865410

Neuhofer, B., & Buhalis, D. (2014). *Issues, challenges and trends of technology enhanced tourism experience. The Routledge Handbook of Tourism Marketing*.

Papalexandri, N., & Lymperopoulos, D. (2014). *Public Relations: The function of communication in modern organizations*. Benou.

Perez, P., Gonzalez-Sosa, E., Kachach, R., Ruiz, J., Benito, I., Pereira, F., & Villegas, A. (2019, March). Immersive gastronomic experience with distributed reality. In *2019 IEEE 5th Workshop on Everyday Virtual Reality (WEVR)* (pp. 1-6). IEEE. 10.1109/WEVR.2019.8809591

Polyzos, S. (2015). *Urban development*. Kritiki Publications.

Pujol-Tost, L. (2011). Integrating ICT in exhibitions. *Museum Management and Curatorship, 26*(1), 63–79. doi:10.1080/09647775.2011.540127

Raskar, R., Welch, G., Cutts, M., Lake, A., Stesin, L., & Fuchs, H. (1998). The office of the future: a unified approach to image-based modeling and spatially immersive displays. *SIGGRAPH 1998 Proceedings of the 25th Annual Conference on Computer Graphics and Interactive Techniques*, 179–188. 10.1145/280814.280861

Raskar, R., Welch, G., & Fuchs, H. (1998). Spatially augmented reality. *Proceeding of the First IEEE Workshop on Augmented Reality*, 63–72.

Schertler, G. F., & Hargrave, P. A. (1995). Projection structure of frog rhodopsin in two crystal forms. *Proceedings of the National Academy of Sciences of the United States of America, 92*(25), 11578–11582. doi:10.1073/pnas.92.25.11578 PMID:8524807

Silberberg, T. (1995). Cultural tourism and business opportunities for museums and heritage sites. *Tourism Management, 16*(5), 361–365. doi:10.1016/0261-5177(95)00039-Q

Soren, B. J. (2005). Best practices in creating quality online experiences for museum users. *Museum Management and Curatorship, 20*(2), 131–148. doi:10.1080/09647770500402002

Taylor, J. (2001). Authenticity and Sincerity in Tourism. *Annals of Tourism Research, 28*(1), 7–26. doi:10.1016/S0160-7383(00)00004-9

Thomas, B. H., Von Itzstein, G. S., Vernik, R., Porter, S., Marner, M. R., Smith, R. T., ... Schumacher, P. (2011, March). Spatial augmented reality support for design of complex physical environments. In *2011 IEEE International Conference on Pervasive Computing and Communications Workshops (PERCOM Workshops)* (pp. 588-593). IEEE. 10.1109/PERCOMW.2011.5766958

Thomas, P. C., & David, W. M. (1992). Augmented reality: An application of heads-up display technology to manual manufacturing processes. In Hawaii international conference on system sciences (pp. 659-669). Academic Press.

Waitt, G. (2000). Consuming heritage: Perceived historical authenticity. *Annals of Tourism Research, 27*(4), 835–862. doi:10.1016/S0160-7383(99)00115-2

Weking, A. N., & Santoso, A. J. (2020). A Development of Augmented Reality Mobile Application to Promote the Traditional Indonesian Food. *International Journal of Interactive Mobile Technologies, 14*(9), 248. doi:10.3991/ijim.v14i09.11179

Yovcheva, Z., Buhalis, D., & Gatzidis, C. (2013). Engineering augmented tourism experiences. In *Information and communication technologies in tourism 2013* (pp. 24–35). Springer. doi:10.1007/978-3-642-36309-2_3

Yulia, C., Hasbullah, H., Nikmawati, E. E., Mubaroq, S. R., Abdullah, C. U., & Widiaty, I. (2018). Augmented reality of traditional food for nutrition education. In *MATEC Web of Conferences* (Vol. 197, p. 16001). EDP Sciences.

KEY TERMS AND DEFINITIONS

ICT Integration in Museums: Is a new emerging trend, in which museums use the internet to display exhibits, as this offers multiple advantages in attracting interested visitors (Papalexandri & Lymperopoulos, 2014, pp. 289-291).

Spatial Augmented Reality: Is called the technological variant of simple augmented reality. It is a projection system, in which the development of virtual environments is carried out through projection systems and not mobile devices (Bimber & Raskar, 2019).

Special and Alternative Tourism: Is considered the set of integrated (or not) tourist services, which are addressed to a specialized public. They are based on mild and ecological activities, highlighting the natural resources of each area (Polyzos, 2015).

Chapter 2
The Use of ICT in Tourist and Educational Literary Routes:
The Role of the Guide

Jordi Chumillas
University of Vic, Spain

Mia Güell
University of Vic, Spain

Pere Quer
University of Vic, Spain

ABSTRACT

This chapter focuses on the use of ICT in literary routes and explores how technologies can influence the tour guides. It begins with a reflection on the key concept of literary routes (from both an educational and tourist perspective) and then considers the antecedents and components that define the guide. Finally, a survey of professionals and teachers with experience in the design and execution of literary routes is carried out in order to explore aspects such as (1) the actual use of ICT on the routes, (2) the synergies between the guide's skills and the use of ICT, and (3) to what extent the use of ICT leads to a change in the role of the guide.

INTRODUCTION

One of the most present and relevant specific fields in cultural tourism is that of literary tourism. This field generates a wide range of very different tourist products, all of them based on the experience of visiting spaces and places linked to literature and reliving the related texts in them. This type of experience is of great educational value for those who attend, and that is why literary routes are used as educational instruments to teach students at every level. Research on this subject, that of the use of literary routes as a didactic instrument, is one of the main lines of the Research Group «Textos literaris contemporanis»

DOI: 10.4018/978-1-7998-8165-0.ch002

(Contemporary literary texts) (TEXLICO) of the University of Vic – Central University of Catalonia and the project «Geografies Literàries 3.0» (Literary Geographies 3.0) (GEOLIT) of the University of Valencia (involving members of eight universities in the Catalan linguistic area), to which the authors of this chapter belong.

At the same time, ICT currently offers many possibilities of application to cultural tourism in general and to literary routes in particular, so that the user can access numerous resources that complement their experience. This phenomenon can also affect the role of the person who leads the route, given that the ICT can condition the way in which some of the components traditionally associated with this task develop. The chapter aims to identify what contributions ICT can make in components of the literary route guide's role and, as a consequence, what changes can occur in it. For that, it will be necessary to:

1. Establish how ICT is currently used in the routes and identify what would be the most desirable contribution of ICT to literary routes in the preparation, implementation and post-activity phases.
2. Identify which skills of the guide ICT can best interact and synergise with.
3. Verify to what extent there is awareness that the new possibilities provided by ICT to literary tourism activities lead to a change in the role of literary route guide.

BACKGROUND

The Concept of Literary Route: Distinction Between Educational and Tourist Routes

The chapter starts with the classic concept of the literary route as an itinerary that groups together visits to different places linked to literary works or authors to read related texts. The concepts of route and itinerary are used as synonyms, and it does not go into the relevant distinctions proposed by Quinteiro and Baleiro (2017) associated with their nature as tourist products differentiated according to their duration and complexity.

Having made this clarification, the authors of this chapter consider the literary route or itinerary an instrument, a construction that cannot exist apart from its pieces; that is, from the places that are connected by it: the content, the texts, are in the places. However, this instrumentalization of the route does not diminish its importance, quite the contrary, since the itinerary structures and gives meaning to the succession of places. In general, and as pointed out by Ramos and Prats (2019), the selection of places that make up the itinerary can give rise to two main types of literary route. On the one hand, those that focus on places with a direct relation to literary content, such as places linked to the biography of the author, locations where the author has performed his/her task, locations of the plot of a literary work, and so forth (Soldevila, 2009; Soldevila & San Eugenio, 2012). On the other hand, those that focus on a specific theme and associate literary texts to places related to the theme. In both cases, the selection and order of these places is essential for the route to be agile, so that an unnecessary back and forth between points or the inclusion of places that are too far apart are avoided, and the presence of rest points and refreshment options are ensured. An itinerary that is well-measured, balanced, organised and thematically cohesive thus ensures a large part of the success of any route. In this regard, tourist and educational routes are identical.

Taking into account what has been said so far, should a distinction be made between educational literary routes and tourist routes? Didactic literary rotes and tourist routes have a great deal in common, and it might even be thought that literary routes, regardless of their characteristics, are, in fact, concrete applications of tourist routes and itineraries in general, which in turn can be considered «structuring elements of the routes offered in a tourist destination» (Figueira, 2013, p. 25). Even so, the researchers of this chapter believe it is useful to distinguish between them because the didactic or educational routes (which can also be called «school», «teaching» or «formative» for greater precision) have less variety of formats and some characteristics that the others often do not.

Following Bataller (2011) and Soldevila (2010), in the case of didactic literary routes it is very important that what can be found in the places visited connects with the contents worked on (or that can be worked on) in the corresponding educational context: the educational literary route is prepared in the classroom and culminates in the street. If this does not occur, it loses educational efficiency and emotional power.

It could be said that any educational literary route has something touristy about it, since the fact of visiting certain places generates in the students an experience in which the cultural, heritage and tourist elements that these places have also converges. Can this statement be formulated the other way round? Are literary tourism itineraries educational? Do they have an educational aspect? It is true that the discovery of places also puts people in contact, and in an integrated way, with their literary and cultural values, and this act is educational and formative in itself. In this regard, literary tourism itineraries fit to the notion of «serious leisure» as defined by Stebbins (2001). According to Chappel and Brown (2006), «the potential consequences of travel, even when it is not focused on a directed study program, justify its description as a form of serious leisure» (p. 1765).

The educational effect of literary routes is usually achieved based on two parameters:

- That the proposed itinerary for the route encourages, respects and enhances the literary sense of the places that constitute it, beyond anecdote. For example, a text that describes how two marginalised characters get by in the centre of a city at the foot of an exuberant architectural monument could be part of a literary route on poverty and social marginalisation or in another on the artistic wealth of the same city. But in both their presence should be justified by the literary contribution they make to the route, and it would be fitting for the guide to appropriately highlight reflection on both viewpoints. This will be what makes the experience of reading the text in the related place educational, taking participants beyond anecdote.
- That there has been prior work that facilitates the connection between the places the participants visit and the knowledge or concepts shared by them. The ideal would be to be able to guarantee with this prior work a group experience, to achieve a certain group communion in the moment of the discovery of the whole formed by the text and the surroundings.

With regards to the second point, it is easier for educational than for tourist routes, since the former normally occur in homogenous environments of stable groups and within regulated educational programmes, at whatever level. This gives them a considerable advantage for the prior preparation of the route and its contents with the people who will participate in it: the students.

Another difference between educational literary routes and tourist literary routes is that, generally speaking, the latter are based on established authors that are already well-known, figures that are in some sense institutionalised and often even with houses-museums dedicated to them. In contrast, educational literary routes usually include places that are not so well established, sometimes not exploited for tourism, precisely because those who lead them can work on these places and their relation with literature in class beforehand. In other words, we could say that tourist literary routes usually work with a smaller canon of authors, more «first line» authors, and that educational routes are more able to expand this canon and include less well-known authors, perhaps local or county authors, something that allows them to take full advantage of the literature linked to the region, regardless of the critical success they might have had or their fame.

As Herbert (2001) points out, literary places (and, by extension, the routes) are still «social constructions, created, amplified, and promoted to attract visitors» (p. 313), be they tourists or students. Obviously, the actions that must be applied to make a certain place attractive to tourists or students will be different.

The ICT Component in Literary Routes

As stated at the beginning of the chapter, ICT currently offers many possibilities of application to cultural tourism in general and to literary routes in particular; in this regard, «there is little doubt that digital technologies have revolutionised scientific and public access to cultural heritage» (Alivizatou-Barakou et al., 2017, p. 130). However, when considering its application, we must take into account that fact that, according to Laporte (2013), guided tours are still the method of obtaining information preferred by users because, unlike others, it also offers the possibility of maintaining a dialogue.

In the specific case of literary tourism, Quinteiro (2020) identifies three possible applications of ICT: «as a way to list and make resources available; as an integral part of the product or experience of literary tourism; and as a form of communication/dissemination of products and experiences» (p. 384). Although it is possible to distinguish between various types of ICT applications, those that seek to replace real experience in the digital world (virtual museums, virtualised routes, 360° visits, and so forth) remain outside the focus of this study. Those who seek to give digital support to real experience and the dialogue associated with it are the ones that are taken into account. Specifically, the study focuses on applications that provide added value to the experience of visiting places of literary interest through the use of reproduction and storage of information or geolocation tools.

In this regard, the texlico research group of the university of vic – central university of catalonia maintains the portal http://endrets.cat of geolocated literary texts, within the project «endrets.cat: geografia literaria dels països catalans», directed by dr. llorenç soldevila. the portal is aimed at both cultural organisations and tourist companies and students, tourists, hikers and those who wish to know more about catalan literature and the heritage linked to the geography of the catalan linguistic area. currently, endrets.cat includes 1,136 authors and 9,225 texts linked to 4,727 locations.

As previously mentioned, one of the keys to the success of literary routes, of whatever type, is the possibility of working in advance on the text and content related to the places involved. Tools such as Endrets.cat, which applies geolocation technologies to a database of literary texts, can contribute decisively to ensure this, since with these tools the information related to the specific itinerary can be «prepared» and sent to the participants in the literary tourism routes, not only so that they can get to know it in advance, but also so that it can be consulted in situ during the route through mobile devices or the use of applications that allow the reality of the places visited to be amplified. All this can provide greater group cohesion during the itinerary.

Thus, from the perspective of the content of the routes, ICT support can be decisive if it is used properly. From the perspective of their educational and research activity, the authors of this chapter believe that the relationship between ICT and tourist routes should go beyond the mere availability of information about the site (read on the mobile phone what would be read on paper); neither should ICT only seek to replace real tourist experience. Therefore, the position defended in this chapter is that the contribution that ICT can make to literary routes must be analysed in terms of their capacity to complement and improve the literary routes (or, in general, the activities of literary tourism) and not in terms of what capacity they have «to replace» the people who lead the route of the visit. However, it is clear that the introduction of ICT fosters the redefinition of the functions of these people and forces them to «reflect upon their own added value from a tourist perspective» (Bryon, 2012, p. 30) or, generically, from the perspective of the user.

Change in the Role of the Person who Leads the Route

Considering that the introduction of ICT has clear implications in the role of the person (guide or teacher) that leads the route (in this case, literary), it is appropriate to examine the figure of the modern guide, his/her antecedents and evolution. According to Erik Cohen (1985), the origins of the modern guide go back to the seventeenth and eighteenth centuries (coinciding with the emergence of the *Grand Tour* and, later, with the beginnings of modern tourism) and two profiles associated with very different social roles: the pathfinder and the mentor. The role of the pathfinder is associated with that of the «geographical guide who leads the way through and environment in which his followers lack orientation or through a socially defined territory to which they have no access» (Cohen, 1985, p. 7). And the role of the mentor is most clearly seen in the figure of the tutor that guided his/her pupil (spiritually or geographically) during the educational and experiential journey of the *Grand Tour*.

Following the postulates of Cohen (1985), the role of the modern guide (which obviously includes the people who lead literary routes, whether educational or tourist), can be seen as the result of the combination (not necessarily harmonious) of both forerunners (pathfinder and mentor), and developed in two different spheres: those of leadership and mediation. In the leadership sphere (an extension of the figure of the pathfinder) the guide plays a key role from the moment they provide the group with privileged access to a region or context that they would not otherwise be able to access. And through the mediatory sphere (linked to the figure of the mentor), the guide becomes a model with regards to social and cultural mediation (between the group members and between the group and the setting/context). The two spheres of the guide's role consist in a series of internally and externally related elements outlined by Cohen as follows:

Table 1. Schematic Representation of the Principal Components of the Tourist Guide's Role

	Outer-Directed	Inner-Directed
(A) Leadership sphere	(1) Instrumental	(2) Social
(B) Mediatory sphere	(3) Interactionary	(4) Communicative

Source: (Cohen, 1985, 10)

Cohen (1985) links the (1) component of instrumental leadership of the modern guide with the adequate completion of the route and identifies elements in it like the spatio-temporal direction of the route, access to the different places (physical and social) and group control (safety or behavioural aspects). In turn, the (2) social leadership component affects the guide's responsibility with regard to the cohesion and morale of the group, and involves elements associated with conflict management between (or with) members of the group, their integration and their mood. With regards to the (3) interactive component of mediation, this affects the role of the guide as «middleman between his party and the local population, sites and institutions» (Cohen, 1985, 13), and involves representation of the group and, also, organization (mainly provision of services). Finally, the (4) communicative component of mediation can be measured by «the extent to which the guide interposes himself between the tourist and the sight as a 'culture broker'» (Cohen, 1985, 14), and involves crucial elements such as the selection of the content of the route, the information provided and the interpretation of this information, which, ultimately, is one of the most important tasks of the guide and most requested and valued by the users of the route. As Bryon (2012) points out, «since tourists in general are inquisitive, guides need to be interpretative and creative» (p. 30).

Beyond verifying that, in some way, the task of the guide involves a combination of components from both spheres, Cohen (1985) identifies different dynamics in the role of the tourist guide depending on the components that are prioritised: the original guide (focused on the instrumental component), the animator (specialised in the social component), the itinerary leader (focused on the interactive component), and, finally, the professional guide (focused on the communicative component). At the same time, he points to a trend in the modern guide that involves «the transition from the role of the Original Guide, concerned mainly with instrumental activities, to that of the Professional Guide, which focuses primarily on the communicative ones» (Cohen, 1985, p. 17), mainly on interpretative ones.

In a similar vein, Bryon (2012) analyses the different dynamics or topologies of the tourist guide, and proposes an alternative taxonomy based on four dimensions: the nature of the organisations where they work; the target groups that participate in the activities, the stories told, and the techniques used to create the experience. From these elements, he identifies (1) official guides, (2) alternative guides, (3) entrepreneurial guides, and (4) relational guides (independent, private and residential). In any case, and in a similar way to Cohen, he concludes that «interpretation has become more important than knowledge about the destination and the actual content of the guided tour» (Bryon, 2012, p. 41).

The emphasis on the communicative/interpretative component means that the guide must be prepared to help the participants interpret information that, on occasions, they can also obtain on their own. The person who leads the route must try to transform all this information into knowledge, highlighting the most important aspects, relating it to other cultural or social content that is connected with the elements of the route. In this regard, the role of the person who leads the route is more like that of teacher. This means that the robustness of a route proposal is no longer so focused on the specific place and but rather on the coherence of the storytelling that can be established for the itinerary, for the set of places. Such storytelling, moreover, is not innocent (Correia et al., 2016); it has its own purposes, and whoever leads the route and conducts this storytelling must be aware of its didactic, emotional and even ethical potentiality.

Therefore, if the routes (in this case, literary routes) are to prioritise an educational component based on interpretation of the texts and on a thematic approach to literary tourism, it is crucial to adequately combine what ICT offers in the different components of the guide's role with a change in the positioning of those who prepare and lead the routes that allows them to reflect on the added value that they can contribute to the users (Bryon, 2012) and, in consequence, prioritise the communicative and interpretative component of their role.

METHODOLOGY AND DATA COLLECTION TOOLS

In the context of this research, fieldwork is proposed that allows us to obtain as much information as possible about the reality studied: educational literary routes with ICT support and the role of those who lead them. To achieve the objectives set, and beyond the pertinent documental analysis, the main instrument used to collect data was a questionnaire aimed at people who lead and design literary routes. The anonymous survey was distributed among people who work in the linguistic area of Catalan language and who belong to groups or associations related to literary tourism and the teaching of language and literature. Specifically, a hundred people were directly asked to respond to the survey, and 66 responses were collected, 52 of which were complete and valid – and which were the ones used in the analysis of the results.

The questionnaire consisted of different sections that are listed below.

The first section collected personal and socio-professional data, the former being limited to sex and age, and the latter focusing on the professional profile, experience and the main and secondary type of route or activities that each participant engaged in.

The aim of the second section was to try to measure the use of ICT tools in the prepared routes, in different aspects. First, respondents were asked about the applicability of these tools in the different phases of the designed routes (preparation, execution and post-activity). Second, they were asked about the purpose to which ICT tools could be applied in literary routes, with an assessment of their usefulness for each of these purposes.

The third and final section enquired about the complementarity of the ICT tools and the role of the person who leads the literary route. The respondents were offered a selection of different functions of the route leader and they were asked to give their opinion on which of these functions they believed the ICT tools helped the most. They were also asked for which of these functions it was most necessary to develop new ICT tools or applications.

In addition to the survey described, some data were also taken from another survey that was prepared to collect assessments of people who participated in literary route activities. Reference will be made in some points of the present study to the results of this second survey, in order to complement, reinforcing or comparing, the results of the base survey. In this second survey, 75 people were consulted and 50 responses collected, 32 of which were complete and valid.

RESULTS OF THE SURVEY

Personal and Socio-Professional Data

With regards to gender, the sample was balanced, with slightly more responses from women (54% women; 44% men; 2% non-binary). With regards to age, there were three brackets: under 30 years (6%); between 30 and 50 years (37%); over 50 years (57%). As can be seen, and this was to be expected given the composition of the groups that were invited to respond to the survey, the sample represents people over 30, with a certain predominance of people over 50.

Regarding experience in designing and leading literary routes, respondents were asked how long they had been preparing routes. The options were: 5 or more years (27%); between 6 and 10 years (35%); and 11 or more years (38%). From these responses, it can be deduced that the people surveyed have considerable experience. From the crossing of these data with those of the age of those surveyed, it can be observed that there are more people with less experience than people with less age, from which we can infer that the field of literary routes is incorporating people that already have extensive professional experience in other activities.

For the socio-professional profiles, the varied response options have been organised into two large groups:

- **Teachers**, formed by people who design, organise, prepare and lead educational literary routes as didactic instruments within their regular teaching activity, which consists of many more teaching-learning activities. This group works in schools, institutes, universities and other teaching areas.
- **Professionals**, which refers to people whose professional activity involves the custody and dissemination of the legacy of literary authors and therefore organise and lead literary routes. This group works in house museums, interpretation centres, tourist companies or freelance activities, libraries and institutions, among others.

The professionals make up 54% of respondents, and the teachers 46%, so there is no pronounced bias between the two groups.

Finally, with regard to the main types of routes or activities carried out, the response options distinguished between (1) Literary routes based on authors or works; (2) Literary routes based on places, thematic routes or 'literaturised' routes; (3) Routes that take place within defined spaces (like house museums, interpretation centres, libraries, among others); and (4) Museumisation activities. In speaking of *literaturised* spaces or routes, we are following Soldevila (2009), Soldevila and San Eugenio (2012) and Ramos and Prats (2019), understanding that they occur when text and place are connected through a relation created by the designers of the route that did not clearly exist before the activity, thus establishing new significant relationships based on elements that can be connected with literary texts.

Thus, types (1) and (2) represent two different approaches to the routes: (1) that of creative individualisation (in authorship or work) and (2) that of spatial, thematic or conceptual generalisation. In the city of Barcelona, examples of type (1) would be the Mercè Rodoreda route (*Ruta Mercè Rodoreda. Ruta de arte y cultura*, n.d.) or *La sombra del viento* route (*Ruta de la Sombra del Viento. Ruta de arte y cultura*, n.d.), of Carlos Ruiz Zafón. Examples of type (2) would be a possible route on medieval Barcelona (spatial), a route on workers' revolutions and the Civil War (thematic) or the route on dragons (conceptual), which relates texts about these fantastic beings with architectural representations of them, from different periods and located in different parts of the city (Díaz-Plaja, Prats & Ramos, n.d.).

In this regard, the data collected show a trend of the group of teachers towards type (2) routes - that is, towards spatial, thematic and literaturised routes (for two thirds of them, these are their main activity) - and a trend of the group of professionals towards type (1) routes - that is, towards routes based on authors and works (for three quarters of them, these are their main activity). To complete these trends, it should be noted that when the people surveyed were asked about their secondary activities, in the teachers group they were mainly type (1), while in the professionals group type (3) and (4) predominated; that is, those that are carried out in defined spaces.

While expected, these trends are significant insofar as in the educational sector the routes are often an instrument to work on literary contents alongside other cultural aspects of context; and, on the other hand, in the professional tourist-cultural sector the purpose is limited more frequently to figures who already have their own appeal and are well-known to the public, as already mentioned. It can also be inferred that the teachers group work more frequently in open and non-defined spaces, and the professionals group work predominantly in defined spaces.

The Use of ICT Tools

The second section of the survey began with the question on whether literary routes allow the use of ICT tools, to which virtually all (96%) those surveyed responded affirmatively. It should be noted here that one of the comments collected in the observations section of the survey said that ICT tools are adequate for individual routes, but not for group ones.

They were then asked about what types of ICT tools were applicable. The responses mainly point to applications for the visual and audiovisual reproduction of texts in mobile devices (88% marked this possibility) and geolocation applications on maps, tracking and so forth (82%). Although with less support, the following tools were also seen as applicable: those for the evaluation of the participants in the activity (58%), those of participation, social networks and assessment of the route (46%) and, in last place, the applications of augmented reality (42%).

In considering the applicability of ICT tools, no particularly important trends between the groups of teachers and professionals stand out, and only two points need commenting on. First, the fact that the group of teachers see the tools of augmented reality as less applicable than the group of professionals. Second, the fact that both groups consider the applications for the evaluation of the participants in the routes applicable, which shows an interesting trend towards a greater «educational» involvement of such cultural tourism activities.

With regards to the respondents' age, no unexpected trend can be observed. In the over 50 years group, applicability is more focused on the tools of reproduction of texts and geolocation, while for those under 50 years, applicability of other types, such as participation, evaluation and augmented reality, is proportionally greater.

Regarding the phase in which the ICT tools are applied in the literary routes (preparation, execution or post- activity), as expected those of text reproduction and those of augmented reality are used mostly in the execution phase; those of geolocation in the preparation and execution phases; and those of evaluation of the participants and of participation, social networks and assessment of the route, in the post-activity phase. Despite this, it is interesting to observe that a fairly significant number of responses state that tools of evaluation or of participation, social networks or assessment are used during the actual activity. This could indicate an interesting trend towards the inclusion of ICT tools in the interaction between participants on the routes. Two contrasting comments that were recorded in the survey are pertinent here: one which states that the use of ICT tools during the routes could be much more dynamic and attractive; and one that states that ICT tools are useful for the preparation of the literary route but should not be used during the activity in order not to interfere with the interaction between the guide and the group.

On this point it is useful to bring up a result of the survey carried out with participants in literary routes, where it can be seen that the types of ICT tools used include those of geolocation in a very minor way, whereas according to the route organisers they are widely used. This leads us to think that for the organisers these applications are very useful in the preparation phase of the activity (hence their invisibility for the participants), but they use them much less during the actual activity than they state in their responses.

The survey continues with questions about the specific purposes for which the ICT tools used are applied. For convenience, we present in Table 2 the results in order of priority, with each specific purpose and the percentage of people who mentioned them.

Table 2. Specific purposes to which ICT tools are in literary routes

Order	Specific purpose	%
1	Texts to be heard on mobile devices	86.5%
2	Texts to be read on mobile devices	84.6%
3	GPS coordinates and location of places on maps	78.8%
4	Collection of evaluations of the participants about the route or activity	77%
5	Links to information related to the specific place or space (such as heritage description of monuments or natural spaces, music or gastronomy of the area)	73%
6a	Evaluation of the participants on specific aspects of the texts, in educational routes	59.6%
6b	Links to practical information about the place and the environment (such as schedule, prices, restaurants or accommodation)	59.6%
6c	Dossier of texts in PDF	59.6%
7	Augmented reality (such as recreations in video or photography, holograms or mapping)	55.7%

In fact, the ordering of applications for these specific purposes is broadly consistent with the preference of the types of tools. No significant trend is observed in these applications of the table either in the filtering by groups of teachers and professionals or in the analysis by age group.

Regarding the utility of these specific purposes, the vast majority of respondents point to texts to be read (2) and to be heard (1) on mobile devices, the collection of evaluations of the participants (4) and the evaluation of the participants on specific aspects of the texts (6a). Those that are seen as least useful are the dossier of texts in PDF (6c) and the links to practical information about the place and the environment (6b).

ICT Tools and the Role of the Person who Leads the Route

To extract information on how the people surveyed saw the relationship between the use of ICT and the role of the person who leads the route, they were asked about four functions, based on the components established by Cohen (1985) for the figure of the guide, already identified in preceding sections.
The four functions are:

- **Instrumental – Organisational:** These are the actions related to the organisation of the activity in order to carry out: registration, preparation of material or contacts.
- **Instrumental – Spatio-temporal leading:** These are the actions and information to correctly locate places, itineraries or travel.
- **Communicative – Informative:** These are the actions that serve to convey information about places, authors or texts to participants, so that they can follow the programmed route.

- **Communicative - Interpretative:** These are the actions aimed at offering those who participate in the route the interpretative keys of the texts, their relationship with the places, with the lives of the authors or with the topics discussed.

These functions (mainly communicative ones) play a decisive role in establishing the identity of places visited in a route and, in a way, they could be related to the internal place branding elements proposed by Zakarevičius and Lionikaitė (2013) and applied by Mansfield (2017) in his case study on Nantes.

As can be seen, two of the four functions belong to the instrumental component, in the sphere of leadership, and the other two belong to the communicative component, in the sphere of mediation. For the first two a distinction was made between an organisational function and a more situational one, of the spatio-temporal leading of the group throughout the route or itinerary. In those of the communicative component, an informative function was differentiated from a more interpretative one. Those surveyed were asked which of these functions of the guide they thought the ICT tools helped most. It was a question with a single answer, and the majority chose the communicative functions (60%), with far fewer choosing the instrumental ones (33%). The remaining 7% correspond to answers that either failed to choose any option because they considered that all of them helped equally, or because they thought none of them helped.

Within the communicative component, the informative function stands out with almost twice as many responses (39%) as the interpretative function (21%). And in the instrumental component, the function of spatio-temporal leading (19.5%) received more responses than the organisational one (13.5%). That is, the perception of those who organise and lead literary routes is that ICT tools help them in their communicative-informative functions much more than in their interpretative ones, and that they also help them in their instrumental functions, both in spatio-temporal leading functions and in organisational ones.

Filtering these responses according to socio-professional profile does show a clear trend. Within the responses that chose communicative functions, those of the group of teachers mostly chose informative over interpretative (nine versus three), much more than in the group of professionals (ten over eight). In other words, the teacher group finds it very difficult to see ICT tools helping the interpretative function of the person who leads the activity, whereas they do believe that they can help in the informative function. Within the responses that leaned towards instrumental functions, the teachers group were more or less evenly divided between the organisational and spatio-temporal leading functions (six versus four), while the professionals group opted more for the leading functions than the organisational ones (six versus one).

The next question asked respondents to indicate which of these functions would require the development of new ICT tools, and it allowed multiple answers. The function that received slightly more responses was the communicative-interpretative function (36.5%), closely followed by the communicative-informative (30.7%), the instrumental function of spatio-temporal leading (28.8%), the instrumental-organisational (28.8%), and other answers that failed to opt for any of them (3.8%). No significant trend in the responses of the teachers group and professionals group stands out. We understand that the slightly higher percentage of answers that consider it important to develop ICT tools to help the communicative-interpretative function can be interpreted as a reinforcement of the earlier perception on the fact that this is the function of the guide that is most difficult to replace. In spite of this, we should point out the opinion of one respondent who explicitly states that with the use of ICT tools there is no need for a person to lead the route, which contrasts clearly with the other opinions we have reported.

It is pertinent at this point to go back to the results of the survey that was made for the participants on the routes. In one of the questions, they were asked to order the functions discussed above from the most to the least important for the success of the activity. Here, the communicative functions also predominated, and most of the answers chose the communicative-interpretative function first, coinciding with the responses of main survey.

All of this supports the interpretation that the communicative-interpretative function is seen as the most genuine and is the one that really indicates the value of the work of those who lead the literary route. Some of the opinions that were expressed in the comments section of the survey express this more forcefully. For example:

Creiem que tant en les rutes literàries com les visites guiades l'important és la persona que les guia (formada, atenta, etcètera). En el nostre cas, les TIC poden complementar, però no traslladen l'emoció als visitants (ni en la recitació). No som partidaris de les TIC en les visites.

We believe that both in the literary routes and in the guided tours, the important thing is the person who guides them (well-prepared, attentive, etc.). In our case, ICTs can complement, but do not transmit emotion to the visitors (or in the recitation). We are not in favour of ICTs in visits.

Les TIC són perfectes per a la virtualitat, per resoldre aspectes logístics i per a complementar informació abans o després de la visita presencial. Per assaborir a fons el paisatge i la literatura, l'experiència ha de ser real, davant del paisatge i amb una bona lectura en directe.

ICTs are perfect for virtuality, to solve logistical aspects and to complement information before and after the face-to-face visit. To fully savour the landscape and the literature, the experience must be real, in front of the landscape and with a good live reading.

CONCLUSION

After the reflections expressed and the results of the survey, in this final section we revisit the objectives formulated at the beginning of the chapter to present some conclusions.

The use of ICT tools by people who lead literary routes is practically unanimous according to the results of the survey (96%), and in all the questions that refer to specific uses we saw that it occurs in all phases and for multiple purposes.

ICT tools are mainly applied to communicative-informative aspects; that is, to provide or reproduce information in multiple formats (audio, video, text and so forth) mainly during the execution phase of the route but also in the preparation phase, especially in educational routes. Thus, the use of ICT could be accentuated also in the preparation phase of tourist routes, since that could provide greater group cohesion, similar to that which occurs in educational routes, which would contribute to the success of the experience. The possibilities offered by the proximity of the educational and tourist routes are notable, and their numerous points of contact augurs good results and the sharing of good practices if they are treated in correlation. In this regard, in the results of the survey one can intuit a certain interest of the group of professionals toward the educational aspects of the visit, which could reflect a certain orientation of the tourist-cultural sector to make the tourist experience more educational.

The survey results show that in the instrumental aspects (organisational and spatio-temporal leading) the level of application of ICT tools can be increased, which would open up the possibility of greater specialisation of the guide in the communicative-interpretative aspects of their task. In fact, the results show a relative absence of ICT tools that help this function.

With all the above, it can be stated that there is an awareness among the people who lead literary routes of ICT's usefulness, and of the fact that its application in activities of literary tourism encourages a rethinking of their role as guides.

In line with these findings, the authors of this chapter conclude that in literary routes, it is difficult to replace the communicative-interpretative role of the person who leads them with ICT tools, and that it is the most important factor for the success of the activity. In fact, according to the perception obtained by the initial reflections and the evaluations and opinions of guides and participants, the change in the role of the guides would be more productively oriented incorporating more ICT tools into the other functions in order to focus on the added value that they can provide as interpreters of the realities visited.

Beyond certain differences in the various forms they can take, in the activities of literary tourism it is crucial, therefore, to reinforce complementarity between the contribution of the ICT tools and the non-transferable, communicative-interpretative skills of the guides. Leading a route involves above all the creation of a narrative that gives meaning to the set of places and texts selected in order to create in the participants a significant educational and lived experience. The activity's success depends on the extent to which this is achieved.

ACKNOWLEDGMENT

This research received no specific grant from any funding agency in the public, commercial, or not-for-profit sectors.

This study is registered in the work of the Research Group *Textos Literaris Contemporanis* (TEX-LICO) of the University of Vic – Central University of Catalonia.

We would like thank Paul Marshall for translating this chapter to English.

REFERENCES

Alivizatou-Barakou, M., Kitsikidis, A., Tsalakanidou, F., Dimitropoulos, K., Giannis, C., Nikolopoulos, S., Al Kork, S., Denby, B., Buchman, L., Adda-Decker, M., Pillot-Loiseau, C., Tillmane, J., Dupont, S., Picart, B., Pozzi, F., Ott, M., Erdal, Y., Charisis, V., Hadjidimitriou, S., ... Grammalidis, N. (2017). Intangible Cultural Heritage and New Technologies: Challenges and Opportunities for Cultural Preservation and Development. In M. Ioannides, N. Magneant-Thalmann, & G. Papagiannakis (Eds.), *Mixed Reality and Gamification for Cultural Heritage* (pp. 129–158). Springer. doi:10.1007/978-3-319-49607-8_5

Bataller, A. (2011). *La ruta literaria como actividad universitaria vinculada al territorio y al patrimonio*. Revista Asa-branca.

Bryon, J. (2012). Tour Guides as Storytellers – From Selling to Sharing. *Scandinavian Journal of Hospitality and Tourism*, *12*(1), 27–43. doi:10.1080/15022250.2012.656922

Chappel, S., & Brown, L. (2006). Literary Tourism Beyond the City. In P. A. Whitelaw & G. Barry O'Mahoney (Eds.), *CAUTHE 2006: To the City and Beyond* (pp. 1764–1772). Victoria University School of Hospitality, Tourism and Marketing.

Cohen, E. (1985). The Tourist Guide: The Origins, Structure and Dynamics of a Role. *Annals of Tourism Research*, *12*(1), 5–29. doi:10.1016/0160-7383(85)90037-4

Correia, A., Oliveira, M., Leal, M., Roque, M. I., Forte, M. J., & Rodrigues de Sousa, S. (2016). *The Mediating Role of Literary Tour Guides: Saramago versus Mafra's National Palace. In New Challenges and Boundaries in Tourism: Policies, Innovations and Strategies*. International Association of Tourism Policy.

Díaz-Plaja, A., Prats, M., & Ramos, J. M. (n.d.). *Dracs literaris*. https://sites.google.com/site/dracsliteraris/home

Figueira, L. M. (2013). *Manual para elaboração de roteiros de turismo cultural*. Instituto Politécnico de Tomar.

Herbert, D. (2001). Literary Places, Tourism and the Heritage Experience. *Annals of Tourism Research*, *28*(2), 312–333. doi:10.1016/S0160-7383(00)00048-7

Laporte, A. (2013). Estructuración, comercialización y comunicación de casas museo como productos de turismo cultural. In A. Cardona (Coord.), Casas museo: museología y gestión. Actas de los Congresos sobre Casas Museo (2006, 2007, 2008) (pp. 22-27). Ministerio de Educación, Cultura y Deporte.

Mansfield, C. (2017). Travel Writing in Place Branding. A Case Study on Nantes. *Journal of Tourism. Heritage & Services Marketing*, *3*(2), 1–7.

Quinteiro, S., & Baleiro, R. (2017). *Estudos em literatura e turismo*. Universidade de Lisboa. Faculdade de Letras. Centro de Estudos Comparatistas.

Quinteiro, S. (2020). Link up with Technology Application in Literary Tourism. In A. Hassan & A. Sharma (Eds.), *The Emerald Handbook of ICT in Tourism and Hospitality* (pp. 379–389). Emerald Publishing Limited. doi:10.1108/978-1-83982-688-720201024

Ramos, J. M., & Prats, M. (2019). Procés de creació d'un protocol d'anàlisi de rutes literàries des de la perspectiva de la recerca de didàctica de la literatura. *Didacticae*, *3*, 99–114.

Ruta la Sombra del Viento. Ruta de arte y cultura. (n.d.). https://www.catalunya.com/ruta-laposombra-del-vent-24-1-22?language=es

Ruta Mercè Rodoreda. Ruta de arte y cultura. (n.d.). https://www.catalunya.com/rutas-merce-rodoreda-barcelona-24-1-62?language=es

Soldevila, L. (2009). *Geografia literària: Comarques Barcelonines*. Pòrtic.

Soldevila, L. (2010). Les rutes literàries. Algunes pautes organitzatives i logístiques a tenir en compte. In G. Bordons (Ed.), *Manual de gestió del patrimoni literari de l'Alt Pirineu i Aran*. Garsineu – CAN.

Soldevila, L., & San Eugenio, J. (2012). Geografia literària dels Països Catalans. El cas de la comarca d'Osona. *AUSA*, *170*, 979–1001.

Stebbins, R. (2001). Serious Leisure. *Society, 38*(4), 53–57. doi:10.100712115-001-1023-8

Zakarevičius, P. & Lionikaitė, J. (2013). An Initial Framework for Understanding the Concept of Internal Place Branding. *Organizacijų vadyba: sisteminiai tyrimai, 67,* 143-160.

KEY TERMS AND DEFINITIONS

ICT Tools: A set of technological tools used, for example, to store, manage or communicate information.

Interpretative Role: In a literary route, a role of the guide consisting in offering those who participate in the route the interpretative keys of the texts, their relationship with the places, with the lives of the authors or with the topics discussed.

Literary Place: A place connected to writers, literary works or literary events.

Literary Route: An itinerary that groups together visits to different places linked to literary works or authors to read related texts.

Literary Tourism: A type of cultural tourism that deals with places linked to literary works or literary authors.

Storytelling: In a literary route, a narrative established by the guide for the itinerary to share information, knowledge and experiences with the participants.

Tourist Guide: A person who guides tourists in an area or who leads tourists on a tour/route.

Chapter 3
Importance of ICT Advancement and Culture of Adaptation in the Tourism and Hospitality Industry for Developing Countries

Tanvir Abir
International University of Business, Agriculture, and Technology (IUBAT), Bangladesh

Md Yusuf Hossein Khan
International University of Business, Agriculture, and Technology (IUBAT), Bangladesh

ABSTRACT

The influence of ICT on tourism and hospitality is related to the facilitation of contact with stakeholders, acting as an effective distribution channel, and providing an effective forum for marketing, among other things. Tourism and hospitality are heavily reliant on information and communication technology in developing countries as well as in the developed nations. ICT has had a major effect on this market. The primary goal of this research is to identify the difference in ICT advancement and adaptation between developed and developing countries, as well as to determine how developing countries can benefit from it and make recommendations. This research was conducted using a qualitative approach. Using various types of literature such as research papers, articles, and books, this study highlights and scrutinizes the significance of ICT and how these actions contribute to the tourism and hospitality sector to raise awareness among academicians, researchers, tourism businesses, and government officials about the effectiveness of ICT applications in tourism and hospitality.

DOI: 10.4018/978-1-7998-8165-0.ch003

Importance of ICT Advancement and Culture of Adaptation in the Tourism and Hospitality Industry

INTRODUCTION

According to the World Travel and Tourism Council's (WTTC) annual report, the total contribution of travel and tourism to GDP was 4.4 percent of total GDP in 2018, with this sector supporting 3.9 percent of total employment (24, 14,400 jobs) and visitor exports accounting for 0.8 percent of total exports (2018, WTTC). ICT is an abbreviation for information and communication technology used to improve any company or organization. Tourism and hospitality have emerged as one of the most exciting fields of work in recent years. Most tourism and hospitality companies are heavily reliant on information and communication technology (Khatri, 2019). ICT is used for a wide range of tasks, from customer recruitment to higher-level administrative tasks. As a result, there is a strong relationship between ICT and the tourism and hospitality industries. The performance has grown in significance, and it can now be seen as a model for developing countries. This remarkable success can be attributed mainly to implementing information and communication technology (Richard, 2013). Each year, significant capital is invested in developing goods and services and enhancing hotel operations (Paryani et al., 2010). Improving the efficiency of this sector's operation has emerged as one of the most pressing concerns in an increasingly volatile global market, with improvements in distribution channels, marketing services, and customer relationship management serving as critical components. For the hospitality industry, in particular, the Internet not only contributes significantly to the dissemination of information about the provided goods and services on the broadest possible scale, but it also facilitates their merchandising process.

The use of the Internet has brought new products and services, new ways of managing tourism operations and businesses in the region, and even today, determines a continuous optimization of the acquisition and promotion processes for tourism services. Tourism, leisure, hospitality, and the hotel industry all depend heavily on information and communication technology. The incorporation of ICT in the hotel industry is critical to the success of hotels (Bethapudi, 2013). Some academics agree that ICT will help nations grow economically (Aziz et al., 2012; Kamel, Rateb, & El-Tawil, 2009). American and European hotels have successfully integrated systems such as computer reservation system (CRS), customer relation management (CRM), enterprise resource planning (ERP), supply chain management (SCM), project management system (PMS), knowledge management system (KMS), and office automation system (OAS) and are reaping the intended benefits (Li, 2012). Most third-world countries continue to face challenges in effectively administering ICT to improve their industry's operational efficiency (Shereni, 2020). These include a lack of guidance and mechanisms for ICT implementation, a lack of modern ICTs, ineffective organizational methods, the influence of corruption, and unfeasible policies affecting industries such as the hotel sector (Makiwa, 2018). Based on these constraints, many modern hotels in most third-world countries have struggled to mature and contribute significantly to ICT adoption in tourism and HI (Harris, 2019).

BACKGROUND OF THE STUDY

Tourism and hospitality heavily rely on information and communication technology in developing countries (Firoiu & Croitoru, n.d.). Tourism and hospitality are becoming increasingly important in developing countries and have significantly affected this market. ICT has gradually developed a modern paradigm change, altering the market structure and opening up many new opportunities. Tourism and hospitality will only flourish if the government ultimately grows the country's ICT infrastructure

(Khan & Hossain, 2018). ICT enables users to identify, alter, and buy tourism goods, and it contributes to business globalization by offering resources for growing, controlling, and marketing (Bethapudi, 2013). ICT has significantly altered each player's position in the value-creation process in the tourism and hospitality industries. ICT advancement is critical for developing a country's tourism and hospitality industries (Khan & Hossain, 2018). This research aims to identify the difference in ICT advancement and adaptation between developed and developing countries, determine how developing countries can benefit, and make recommendations. This ICT chapter has the potential to transform the tourism and hospitality industries. Customers' satisfaction is increasing, so adoption is critical.

SIGNIFICANCE OF THE STUDY

The influence of ICT on tourism and hospitality includes the facilitation of contact with stakeholders, acting as an effective distribution mechanism, offering an effective forum for marketing, and other benefits ("ICT in Tourism and Hospitality Industry," 2014). Tourism and hospitality are significant and growing industries in Bangladesh. ICT has had a considerable influence on the travel and hospitality sectors. The majority of residential tourist businesses are yet to use ICT as a customer acquisition tool. In a developing world, there is a vast amount of work to be done. In the tourism and hospitality industries, information and communication technologies (ICTs) are becoming increasingly significant. Information and communication technology (ICT) is crucial for the sustained progress of emerging countries. Today, there is no question that the combination of technology and tourism is ideal. Some of the technical advancements that are currently promoting this industry are mentioned below. The use of technology in hospitality and tourism is a way to minimize costs, increase operational quality, and improve services. The idea of introducing ICT in tourism has the potential to be fruitful in developed countries.

OBJECTIVES OF THE STUDY

The primary goal of this study is to determine how developing countries might benefit from the proposed ICT adoption framework and make some recommendations.
This research will look at the following questions, in particular, to find out:

1. To recognize the importance of ICT in a developing country's tourism industry.
2. To determine how developing countries might benefit from the proposed ICT adoption framework
3. To make some relevant recommendations for the profitability in developing countries by introducing ICTs in tourism.

METHODOLOGY

The qualitative approach serves as the study's analytical foundation, allowing the researchers to obtain a more in-depth understanding of the usage of ICT applications in the tourism and hospitality sectors around the world. This study illustrates and scrutinizes the importance of ICT and how these activities relate to the Tourism and Hospitality sector by using different forms of literature such as research papers, journals, and books. This research also includes a critical analysis of the literature from a large established study in this field. Based on secondary research, the researchers hope to find the void and make a recommendation.

ICT in Tourism and Hospitality

Computers, networks, and information management systems are examples of ICT used in the hospitality industry for internal organizational reasons such as improved business practices and efficiencies. The reservation and booking services used by consumers through eTourism are the most important influence of ICT on the hotel industry today. The biggest business in tourism is accommodation providers (e.g. 12.3m rooms worldwide according to Cunill and Forteza, 2010).

The International Federation for IT and Travel and Tourism (IFITT) also shows an increasing degree and potential for e-commerce in the hotel industry, with tourism accounting for 22.5 percent of all eCommerce in the EU (Marcussen, 1999). The majority of accommodation providers are small and medium-sized enterprises (SMEs), with 95.5 percent of all organizations employing less than nine people (Cunill and Forteza, 2010). The majority of these organizations are hampered by their limited scale and lack of access to markets and technology. As a result, distribution channels are small.

Computer Reservation Systems (CRS) and Property Management Systems (PMS) allow for greater capacity management. A database is used in this case to get a sense of the customers. Getting a sense of the customers entails being sufficiently aware of the customer's profile and frequency of visits. Large hotel chains typically have their own CRS and PMS systems, while smaller hotels may have custom-

Figure 1. The use of CRS systems to interconnect with Global Reservation Systems
(Source: IFITT Report, 2013)

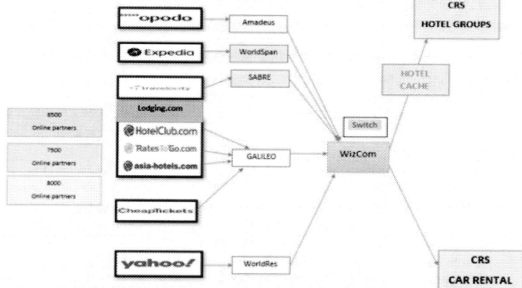

ized systems from software manufacturers such as Gastrodat. These systems are designed to receive and publicize bookings by connecting directly to the internet and other General Distribution Systems (e.g., Sabre, Amadeus, Gailileo and Worldspan). The hotel will have a Computer Reservation System (CRS) that will communicate with the GDS. More internal tasks, such as CRM, marketing, mailing, and reporting, can be handled by the CRS.

Many hotels use this framework when using Computer Reservation Systems (CRS) and Property Management Systems (PMS) to manage space and inventory. Many hotels are well-versed in the use of a website for marketing and Customer Relationship Management (CRM). It has provided a cooperative atmosphere for customers to pre-book or obtain customer review information. These types of measures allow a company to increase profits while also gaining a competitive advantage in the market (Hudson and Gilbert 2006).

Development in the sector of ICT in HI will include more direct selling to customers. There would be less third-party selling, as well as less interference from situational factors. Since we're discussing customer satisfaction, ICT requires direct access to product or service information. The importance of using ICT will lead to customer satisfaction and loyalty to specific goods. Furthermore, it offers up-to-date information about the facilities, since we know there are several places where we need to improve this HI. Many ICT techniques are being used in developing countries to provide better service to their customers. Voice Search and Voice Control, Robots, Contactless Payment, Virtual Reality, AI Chatbot, Internet of Things, Recognition Technology, Big Data, are some of the ICT tools that are currently being used in the tourism and hospitality industry and making a difference to this field (REVFINE, 2020).

The advancement of Internet technology, with its high accessibility and interactive existence, has resulted in shifts in customer behaviors and attitudes toward conventional tourism and hospitality service models. The adoption of the internet and networking has given many benefits to companies and has paved the way for globalization. Modern technology has challenged conventional business models in tourism and hospitality-related organizations (e.g., High Street Travel agents, Airlines and their restricted range of services, and traditional booking systems) (Khan & Hossain, 2018). According to Poon (1993), the introduction of innovations has produced a schism between traditional and modern tourism cultures. This is very remarkable for the countries that have used ICT in such a way that they are using their wealth while still taking care of an individual's income. In developed countries, information and communication technology (ICT) allows for greater management versatility. As can be shown, the use of ICT in hospitality and tourism in developing countries is minimal. There are several things to include. Many things are handled manually in developing countries, although we see a different picture in developed countries.

The use of ICT improves business productivity automatically. According to our findings, hotel management in developed countries is inefficient. As we all know, hotel management must run some front desk operations, and in developing countries, they use software to add a lot of versatility to keep things running smoothly. Gracesoft is one of the softwares (Capterra, 2021). It analyzes, secures, and stores the customer's data. Since hotel management no longer has to do it manually, this program has increased productivity. They can easily collect, enter, and analyze data whenever it is needed. It enables many online travel agencies (OTA) to communicate with them and have a smooth business operation such as costing, booking, and being updated about the availability of many services. It seamlessly extends the marketing campaign of travel agencies. It is critical in developing countries to ensure that their limited resources are used effectively. Businesses would do much better if we could guarantee E-tourism. Business-to-consumer (B2C) application is supported by e-tourism. Customers have the option of contacting the firm. They will have less work to do until their visit.

While ICT has many positive aspects but addressed many of the challenges related to integrating new technology. Hughes and Moso (2019) noted that it is generally a more limited field in scope. Since tourism is a people-based service industry, automating tasks like self-check-in and meal ordering, as well as e-booking, will reduce the interpersonal and spontaneous aspects of travel. A decline in emotional or personal interest may lead to dissatisfaction. Furthermore, privacy and security issues are a major concern for visitors nowadays, especially if the information is kept indefinitely. IoT and supporting Cloud technology, in particular, were heavily debated for collecting and storing data without individuals' knowledge or consent. Furthermore, identity protection, as well as the risk of network security and infiltration for criminal or terrorist purposes, are issued to be concerned about (Gubbi et al., 2013; Manyika et al., 2013). As technology advances, there is a possibility that people will be able to substitute augmented reality encounters for conventional travel. While this may mitigate some of the difficulties associated with dealing with tourists in fragile, remote, and/or overcrowded destinations, it may also generate new challenges in terms of attracting sufficient visitors to specific locations (Hughes and Moscardo, 2019). Similarly, tourists can become annoyed if they attempt to use modern technology and systems in places that do not assist them.

Importance of ICT in a Developing Country's Tourism Industry

A strong tourism business can be interpreted as reflecting a country's social development, evolution, and progression. Furthermore, due to globalization, more individuals are being urged to purchase touristic products from various countries. Because tourism is a major sector/industry in today's world, many countries compete to attract tourists through all means of communication. Such communication has become a major driver of touristic sectors around the world. Due to the fact that tourism is a significant sector in today's world, many countries compete for tourists through various modes of communication, and such communication has become a major driver of touristic sectors worldwide. The purpose of communication is to educate prospective tourists and to influence their choices of tourist destinations and tourist products.

Numerous countries have been successful in developing their tourism industries through the use of ICTs, specifically the internet. Malaysia, for example, have been extremely successful in attracting a large number of tourists via these methods (Mohsin 2005). On the other hand, countries such as Iran have struggled to increase their international visitor numbers, owing in large part to a lack of ICT and internet development (Salavati and Hashim 2015). Although Ethiopia is endowed with numerous natural, religious, historical, and cultural tourist attractions, tourism as a sector of the economy dates all the way back to the 1950s. In recognition of tourism's economic contribution to Ethiopia, the first tourism office was established during the imperial regime in 1962. (Ali 2017). During the military regime, the sector's contribution was significantly reduced, but tourism began to grow in the 1990s. Ethiopia has nine UNESCO world heritage sites among its fascinating tourist attractions (Ali 2017). However, the economic contribution and potential of the tourism sector are incomparable. According to research findings, it is impossible to increase visitor numbers unless a country promotes its tourist attractions to the rest of the world. As a result, integration of well-designed ICT solutions is required, and because we live in a digitized world, the tourism industry must rely on ICTs, particularly the internet, as a means of international communication.

Advantages of Adopting ICT in Tourism and Hospitality in Developing Countries

Thakur (2020) outlined some benefits of utilizing ICT in developing countries' tourist and hospitality businesses. The following are some of the critical advantages of using ICT:

Growth and boost in Economic Activities

Using ICT in hospitality and tourism opens up a plethora of possibilities for developing countries. There will be more positions available, with various paths to success. In this regard, an E-commerce platform can be used for, which can benefit developing countries in various ways (Shanker, 2008).

1. By providing local companies with access to global markets.
2. By ensuring new ways to export much of the local market's services.
3. If we use ICT to enhance our operation, we will increase internal firm performance. Economic development can be achieved by introducing ICT in hospitality and tourism.

Boost Wide-Scale Industry Revenues

There will be a wide range of industry revenues if we introduce ICT in tourism and hospitality. Many businesses would profit from this. The number of entrepreneurs will grow, and the industry will generate income by using the firms.

Infrastructure Development

The infrastructure will undergo adjustments. There will be many lifestyle changes as we consider economic growth. Implementing ICT allows for the implementation of new technologies and an increase in people's living standards.

Country's Improved Brand Image

Developing countries would have a positive face value. Applying ICT to the hospitality and tourism industries can quickly establish a positive brand image in developing countries. Tourists from developing countries interested in visiting will be able to do so, and they will be able to experience convenience and comfort at the same time by living there.

Source of Foreign Exchange Earnings

Adoption of ICT in the tourism and hospitality sectors will ensure foreign exchange earnings. There would be more foreign exchange earnings as there are more visitors from developing countries. As we all know, developing countries depend heavily on foreign exchange earnings. These earnings can be used to improve infrastructure and the living standards of people in developing countries.

Source of Employment Generation

There would be a source of income for the general public. ICT will advance the tourism industry, and by using it, more opportunities will be available in the labour market. The problem of unemployment is more severe in developing countries. The use of ICT in HI will aid in the resolution of the issue. People will get more work offers, which will help the whole economy.

Connectivity and Growth to Local, Regional, and Even the Remotest Areas

As ICT implementation connects more people, there will be fewer difficulties in visiting the place. The happiness of visitors would motivate more people to work and help a country grow. Development can occur both locally and regionally. Connection networks can be more adaptable and dependable.

Cultural Growth

ICT is getting people closer together by improving or maintaining better communication networks. People are being exposed to many different cultures as they have more opportunities to meet new people. People in developed countries are affected by these cultures, and by adopting them, they better themselves.

Introduction of New Technologies can be Implemented in Developing Countries

The adoption of ICT in hospitality and tourism worldwide, especially in developing countries, can lead to many new technological advances. Those who have adapted to modern technologies will see an immediate rise in their level of production. When an entire country adopts this method, it becomes more high-tech.

Figure 2. Proposed ICT Adoption Framework in Thailand (Sirirak 2015)

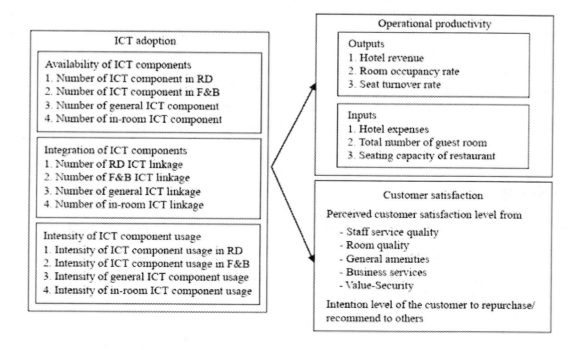

In our opinion, this is the proposed diagram for the tourism and hospitality industries in developing countries. This diagram (figure 01) addresses the dependability of information and communication technology in the hospitality and tourism industries. This integration promotes industry growth. It is seen that hotel performance is influenced by ICT. When it comes to resource efficiency, we can see a difference between traditional and modern management. This model was proposed for Thailand, and it has an impact on revenue gains and expenses. In business terms, we try to find strategies that can benefit the industry. This proposed model ensures resource management and concludes that this can be an intelligent step for developing countries. Even though this model focuses on Thailand and its tourism industry, we can find some parallels during implementation for Bangladesh and many developing countries because they have fewer cultural differences than Thailand.

The Internet is an example of a networked technology that has made significant contributions to various industries. There are several social media sites where we can see people sharing their views and learning from multiple sources. This can be a very profitable field to invest in for marketing purposes. If we look at the chart above, we can see that it discusses perceived consumer satisfaction, which is closely linked to post-purchase activity. ICT enables companies to conduct surveys to gain more loyal customers by offering better service.

CONCLUSION

Information and communication technology, as well as the tourism and hospitality industries, are inextricably linked. With the involvement of ICT, the tourism and hospitality industry is developing day by day. ICT has had a significant influence on the tourism and hospitality industries. In a developing world, the tourism and hospitality industry is critical to the development of financial capacity. Some sectors of the tourism and hospitality industry in developed countries need the product. They can rapidly improve in the Tourism and Hospitality Industry if they can easily interact with ICT. The proposed diagram (figure 02) depicts the entire process of introducing ICT and the result. The hotel income and turnover rate are both increasing. ICT enables hotel management to devise plans that are tailored to their specific needs. They also learn about the scopes that can be used. The tourism divide between developed and developing countries is defined here. Tourism as a whole must be incorporated with ICT. The effective use of ICT in hospitality and tourism will help to ensure the sector's long-term viability. This sector is also essential to the economy's strength. If developing countries do not attract more visitors, they will face problems in a variety of industries. They must draw visitors to improve their situation. This is only possible if they implement ICT in their tourism and hospitality sectors. This study proposes a blueprint for adapting to and staying ahead in the tourism industry.

REFERENCES

Ali, Y. (2017). *Challenge and prospect of ethiopian tourism policy*. Global J Manag Bus Res.

Annex 2. Tourism as an Economic Development Tool. (n.d.). Retrieved February 12, 2021, Retrieved From http://www.oas.org/dsd/publications/unit/oea78e/ch10.htm

Aziz, A. A., Bakhtiar, M., Syaquif, M., Kamaruddin, Y., & Ahmad, N. (2012). Information and communication technology application's usage in hotel industry. *Journal of Tourism, Hospitality, and Culinary Arts, 4*(2), 34–48.

Bethapudi, A. (2013). The role of ICT in tourism industry. *Journal of Applied Economics and Business, 1*(4), 67–79.

Capterra. (2021). *The 7 most popular hotel management software for hotel chains compared. Software Buying Tips and Advice for Businesses.* Retrieved from: https://blog.capterra.com/most-popular-hotel-management-software-for-hotel-chains/

Cunill, O. M., & Forteza, C. M. (2010). The franchise contract in hotel chains: A study of hotel chain growth and market concentrations. *Tourism Economics, 16*(3), 493–515.

Firoiu, D., & Croitoru, A. (2013). Tourism And Tourism Infrastructure From The Perspective Of Technological Changes. *Romanian Economic Business Review, Romanian-American University, 8*(2), 93–103.

Gubbi, J., Buyya, R., Marusic, S., & Palaniswami, M. (2013). Internet of things (IoT). *Future Generation Computer Systems, 29*(7), 1645–1660. doi:10.1016/j.future.2013.01.010

Hadad, S., Hadad, Y., Malul, M., & Rosenboim, M. (2012). The economic efficiency of the tourism industry: A global comparison. *Tourism Economics, 18*(5), 931–940. doi:10.5367/te.2012.0165

Hudson, S., & Gilbert, D. (2006). The Internet and small hospitality businesses: B&B marketing in Canada. *Journal of Hospitality & Leisure Marketing, 14*(1), 99–116. doi:10.1300/J150v14n01_06

Hughes, K., & Moscardo, G. (2019). ICT and the future of tourist management. *Journal of Tourism Futures, 5*(3), 228–240. doi:10.1108/JTF-12-2018-0072

Jeong, M., & Oh, H. (1998). Quality function deployment: An extended framework for service quality and customer satisfaction. *Journal on Information Systems in Developing Countries, 36*(1), 1–21.

Kamel, S., Rateb, D., & El-Tawil, M. (2009). The impact of ICT investments on economic development in Egypt. *The Electronic Journal on Information Systems in Developing Countries, 36*(1), 1–21. doi:10.1002/j.1681-4835.2009.tb00248.x

Khan, M. Y. H., & Hossain, A. (2018). *The Effect of ICT Application on the Tourism and Hospitality Industries in London.* doi:10.21272ec.4(2).60-68.2018

Khatri, I. (2019). Information Technology in Tourism & Hospitality Industry: A Review of Ten Years' Publications. *Journal of Tourism and Hospitality Education, 9*, 74–87. doi:10.3126/jthe.v9i0.23682

Li, Y. (2012). *ICT, the single greatest force affecting change in the hospitality industry.* Academic Press.

Manyika, J., Chiu, M., Bughin, J., Dobbs, R., Bisson, P., & Marrs, A. (2013). *Disruptive Technologies.* McKinsey Global Institute.

Makiwa, J. (2018). Developing and validating an ICT adoption framework for SMES in developing countries: A case of Zimbabwe. *Management Journal, 17*(1), 7–28.

Marcussen, C. (1999). *Internet Distribution of European Travel and Tourism Services*. Research Centre of Bornholm.

Mohsin, A. (2005). Tourist attitudes and destination marketing—The case of Australia's Northern Territory and Malaysia. *Tourism Management, 26*(5), 723–732. doi:10.1016/j.tourman.2004.03.012

Paryani, K., Masoudi, A., & Cudney, E. A. (2010). *QFD application in the hospitality industry: A hotel case study*. Quality.

Poon, A. (1993). *Tourism, Technology and Competitive Strategies*. CAB International.

REVFINE. (2020). *11 key technology trends emerging in the travel industry in 2020*. Retrieved From: https://www.revfine.com/technology-trends-travel-industry/

Richard, L. (2013). The role of ICT in the hospitality industry. *International Journal of Scientific Research, 2*(9), 49–51. doi:10.15373/22778179/SEP2013/17

Salavati, S., & Hashim, N. H. (2015). Website adoption and performance by Iranian hotels. *Tourism Management, 46*, 367–374. doi:10.1016/j.tourman.2014.07.017

Shereni, N. C., & Chambwe, M. (2020). Hospitality Big Data Analytics in Developing Countries. *Journal of Quality Assurance in Hospitality & Tourism, 21*(3), 361–369. doi:10.1080/1528008X.2019.1672233

Sirirak, S., Islam, N., & Khang, D. B. (2015). Does ICT adoption enhance hotel performance? *Journal of Hospitality and Tourism Technology, 2*(1). doi:10.1108/17579881111112403

Thakur, K. (2020). *Importance of Tourism & Economic Values*. Retrieved from: https://market-width.com/blogs/Importance-Tourism-Industry-Economic-Value.htm

WTTC. (2021). *Travel & Tourism*. Retrieved From: https://wttc.org/

KEY TERMS AND DEFINITIONS

Culture: Culture is a term that refers to the characteristics and knowledge of a particular group of people, and includes language, religion, cuisine, social habits, music, and the arts.

Developing Country: A developing country is one that has a less developed industrial base and a low Human Development Index when compared to other nations.

Hotel: A hotel, inn, tourist camp, tourist court, tourist cabin, motel, or any other place where rooms, lodgings, or accommodations are furnished to transients for a fee for short-term basis.

Information and Communication Technology: Information and communication technologies (ICTs) is a broader term for information technology (IT), which encompasses all communication technologies, such as the internet, wireless networks, cell phones, computers, software, middleware, video conferencing, social networking, and other media applications and services.

Marketing: Marketing is the activity, set of institutions, and processes involved in developing, communicating, delivering, and exchanging offerings that are valuable to customers, clients, partners, and society at large.

Tourism and Hospitality Industry: The tourism and hospitality industry encompasses a diverse range of businesses, including lodging, restaurants, tourism destinations and attractions, as well as airlines and other modes of transport. They not only stimulate economic activity, but also create jobs, generate revenue, and contribute significantly to development.

Tourism Development: Tourism development is the process of establishing and maintaining a tourism industry in a particular location. At its most fundamental level, tourism development can be defined as the process of developing strategies and plans to increase/develop/encourage tourism in a particular destination.

Chapter 4
ICT as an Acculturative Agent and Its Role in the Tourism Context:
Introduction, Acculturation Theory, Progress of the Acculturation Theory in Extant Literature

Yakup Kemal Özekici
Adıyaman University, Turkey

ABSTRACT

ICTs have played a transformative role on the cultural components of all stratums of the society. This role has had a demand as well as supply-oriented reflection on the tourism system. In the scope of this chapter, the role of ICTs in the changing social structure is explained through the lens of acculturation. Beyond this, the acculturative process on the modern community's tourism-oriented reflections caused by ICTs were discussed through nine components (renting over owning, free-of-charge ownership, narcissism, connected loneliness, social capital, multiple realities, new identities, novel values, enculturation), and predictions were made with a futuristic perspective. In this context, it was explicated that the ICT-oriented digital acculturation process would add the concepts alternative tourism types, soft mass tourism, sharing economy-based tourism system, intense offline interactions between host and guests, multicultural destinations, virtual reality-based leisure, sharing as a novel pushing motivation, virtual demonstration effect, and diaspora to the future tourism system.

INTRODUCTION

Today, the extent of enhancement for ICTs have tremendous effect on enabling communicating, therefore, exchanging ideas for diverse communities over the world. Nascent social networking sites and apparatus like smart technologies have facilitated this process (Yen & Dey, 2019) and lead cultural transformation

DOI: 10.4018/978-1-7998-8165-0.ch004

ICT as an Acculturative Agent and Its Role in the Tourism Context

process between communities to accelerate (Kizgin et al., 2018). Cultural transformation issue is discussed for centuries, however, its theoretical base has barely passed a century once acculturation theory was put forward (Berry, 1997; Redfield et al., 1936). Yet, conceptual structure is not adequate for explicating role of ICTs as an acculturative agent (Dey et al., 2020) compared to role of international migration (Berry, 1997) or globalisation (Cleveland & Laroche, 2007). Evaluation of ICTs as an acculturation agent has extended the mainstream acculturation perspective and bring multiculturalism in the extant literature (Dey et al., 2019). This extension has lead the more complex acculturation process such as adopting cultural attributes of a digital consumer culture through interacting over online world to be considered (Dey et al., 2019) through concepts such as digital acculturation (Dey et al., 2020), online acculturation (Kizgin et al., 2020) or remote acculturation (Ferguson & Bornstein, 2012). Such that, widely referred acculturation strategies for culture change in offline world (Berry, 1997) were re-evaluated and novel strategies were put forward for online world (Dey et al., 2020). Whatever it is called for, ICTs bring online communication opportunities and social networks into the community life and generate social capital due to the fact that they are conceived as tremendous means for communication and social networking (Sharma et al., 2013) as well as touch upon our values, norms, mind-set and culture in the general sense. Such communication platform has prompted in turn acculturation process to the virtual world. Such that, an individual may experience cultural transformation process without moving out his/her district and construct his/her identity according to the shared contents of online cultural groups (Lindridge et al., 2015). However, despite the tremendous importance of these technologies in context of cultural transformation in modern society structures; it is evident that the interplay between ICTs and cultural transformation concepts were not evaluated sufficiently (Kizgin et al., 2018, 2020; Yen & Dey, 2019).

The revolutionary transformation within modern community will precisely have repercussions on tourism system, which is accepted as the one of critical hubs for acculturation since "weekendismo" term was coined in 1960s (Berry, 2008; Burns, 1999; Nunez, 1963). Yet, recently emerging conceptual provision on addressing the culturally transformative role of ICTs (Dey et al., 2019; Dey et al., 2020) was not undertaken in context of tourism system to the knowledge of author. Even sociology literature lacks understanding on how social media or any other ICTs apparatus have the impact on acculturation outcomes of individuals or communities (Dey et al., 2020). It is therefore important to provide critical information regarding interplay between ICTs and acculturation within the scope of tourism, as the special characteristics of tourism system which owns a different framework and acculturation process than classical acculturation models were tested (Özekici & Ünlüönen, 2019c). Therefore, it is the aim of this chapter to bridge this gap and provide inspiring information on the relation between acculturation and ICTs. This chapter concerns the role of ICTs in context of acculturation phenomenon. In another words, it is the aim of this chapter and to reveal the permeating role of state of art technologies to spread acculturative cases across all strata of the community. In this context, it is explained that ICTs induced acculturation process creates a novel culture with nine cultural components (renting over owning, free of charge ownership, narcissism, connected loneliness, social capital, multiple realities, new identities, novel values, enculturation). Moreover, it is envisioned how these nine novel cultural components will affect the demand and supply structure of the tourism system. In that, fourteen projected outcomes as a result of digital acculturation process are expected to occur. These outcomes are as follows; democratized youth tourism, sharing economy integrated with tourism system, expanded recreation opportunities, robotic employees with hospitality industry, soft sense of mass tourism, physical interaction as a pulling motivation, augmented host-tourist interaction, multicultural destinations, virtual reality based leisure, image oriented travel motivation, virtual demonstration effect, getting likes as a travel motivation, alternative travel types, diaspora tourism. That is, main motivation of the chapter is to shed light on how digital/online/remote acculturation process touches the lives of tourists, hosts and employees. To do so, acculturation theory and its main components (premises, models, stages of its development in literature) as well as digital/online/remote acculturation phenomenon will be taken into consideration, then, endeavoured to explain the connection between this centenarian phenomenon and ICTs. Thereafter, anticipated output of this interplay will be explicated in context of tourism system covering tourism demand as well as supply aspects.

ACCULTURATION THEORY

Acculturation is defined as the change in the cultural structure or identity of counterparts as a result of unmediated interaction of different cultures (Redfield et al., 1936, p. 149). Identity is the main base of the acculturation psychology dimension within acculturation theory (J. Phinney, 2003). More specifically, it is the social identity being defined as the emotional and evaluative consequences of belonging to a specific group (Tajfel, 1982) that acculturation theory considers. One of the main focus of the theory is the cultural transformation of the social identity and interaction of the interlocutors (Berry et al., 2006), as can be understood from the definition. In this context, the acculturation process is about how the values, behaviours and identities of the individual or society are transformed or protected (Ward & Geeraert, 2016). Accordingly, acculturation phenomenon is a many-sided concept (C. Li et al., 2019), therefore involves numerous facts (e.g. cultural transformation, culture shock, acculturative stress, acculturative agent), models (one, two or three dimensional) and involved within mature disciplines such as anthropology (Jun et al., 2014), sociology (Ozer, 2013) and psychology (Berno & Ward, 2005). Orientation of relevant disciplines on acculturation theory has been a result of the reflection of revolutionary events that direct social life to literature. Therefore, the acculturation theory has played a role in the adoption of events that change the cultural context of the society by mature disciplines. The historical process has led to a change in this role of acculturation theory.

Progress of the Acculturation Theory in Extant Literature

When the trajectory of acculturation theory in the literature is examined, it can be said that the conditions of the age directly affect the scope of the acculturation theory. This situation is visualized in figure 1 as follows.

Accordingly, it can be said that the theory was included in the discipline of anthropology within the context of colonialism in the early periods, when imperialism was common (Choney et al., 1995). The reflection of these conditions in literature has been the emergence of the one dimensional or unidirectional model (Ward & Geeraert, 2016). Prototype of the one-dimensional model developed in 1920s posited that acculturation has taken place in a way that resembles exchanging cultural components in a bazaar. Subsequent approaches to the one-dimensional model has explicated how cultural alteration occurs in stages (Flannery et al., 2001). Gordon (1964)'s one dimensional assimilation model is the embodiment of this model. As the global migration waves have become at the center of the world agenda during the following periods, the reality of cultural interaction caused by immigration made the theory enter the field of sociology. The reflection of this situation in the acculturation literature emerged by upholding that both the host and heritage culture of immigrants could be adopted. Thus, the bidimensional acculturation model was developed (Berry, 1997; Berry et al., 1989). Bidimensional acculturation models are not limited with Berry. Because, there are some alternatives upholding similar ideas on acculturation process of ethnic groups (J. S. Phinney, 1990). With the spread of mass media and SNS in the following periods, the tendency of communal societies to individualism has led to the fact that the literature on acculturation theory gains importance in the psychology literature (Berry, 2008; Hwang & He, 1999). The reflection of this period in literature was in the form of updating bidimensional models. Also, instead of looking into group level acculturation process, individual level acculturation process were begun to be addressed as a result of effect that psychology discipline has on the acculturation theory (Sam & Berry, 2010). In addition, advancement of television and emerging opportunity towards dissemination of knowledge instantly led the development and operationalization of the remote acculturation concept (Ferguson et al., 2017; Ferguson & Bornstein, 2012) as well as acculturation to the global consumer culture model (Cleveland & Laroche, 2007) as two-dimensional models examining the global consumer culture specifically, mass media and the first version of SNS stand out as two important model oriented examples that can be given to the effect on the acculturation phenomenon. As a result of the tremendous technological advancement experienced in the last two decades, the increase in the impact coefficient of SNS platforms compared to classic mass media tools has had a determining effect on world cultures (Dey et al., 2019, 2020; Kizgin et al., 2020). On the other hand, a different branch dealing with classical acculturation process has developed an ABCD model within acculturation literature and argued that acculturation theory should be merged with psycho-social theories concerning identity to be enriched and to answer cultural alteration process of the communities (Ward & Szabo, 2019). Consequently, it is observed that technology studies show an orientation to acculturation theory (Dey et al., 2019, 2020; Kizgin et al., 2020). However, it is seen that a cutting edge acculturation model representing the current period process has not been developed. AR, VR and Hyper reality tech are thought to create extended self in societies, thus leading to new identities (Belk, 2014, 2016). Changes that will occur on identity will bring about acculturation oriented developments that will be caused by the new generation ICTs in the future. Thus, it is possible to put forward that as being an amalgam of sociology, psychology and technology fields; novel technologies will create hyper identity oriented acculturation in future researches.

Table 1. Progress of Acculturation as a Research Field

	First Period	**Second Period**	**Third Period**	**Fourth Period**	**Fifth Period**
Triggering factor	Colonialism	Global migration flows	Democratization of mass media	Social networking sites	Augmented reality, virtual reality and hyper reality
Reflection on extant knowledge	Integration of acculturation within anthropology discipline	Integration of acculturation within sociology discipline	Integration of acculturation within psychology discipline	Integration of acculturation within technology literature	
Output from acculturation field	One dimensional acculturation model	Bidimensional acculturation model	Remote acculturation model / Updating of bidimensional acculturation model	-	

ROLE OF MASS MEDIA ON ACCULTURATION PHENOMENON

Technology shapes our identity by presenting a new perception of the world (Gere, 2008). Developing technologies has utilized the current theory to explain technology oriented cultural transformation. At this context, television was accepted previously as a novel edge of diffusor for novel culture as globalization (Arnett, 2002), and television was seen as a mean to instill components from another culture (Hwang & He, 1999). During that period, the cultural codes of the core country which were sent through TV and cinema were imitated and internalized by the peripheral community (Arnett, 2002). It is possible to state that the vision of masses has expanded with the development of ICTs. Because, the reactions to the outside world take place after the experiences and impressions are processed. The development of ICTs, by providing the exchange of different experiences on the global scale between societies in virtual and real reality environments, made it possible for the realization of brain's experience process progress to a wider extent (Rosenfeld, 2015) and accelerated the globalization (Arnett, 2002). This will lead to differentiation of the individual identity formation from classic acculturation strategies phases. Hence, acculturation phenomenon regarded as a classic and primal style of cultural interaction has evolved into a novel phenomenon as technology democratize across the globe. This understanding may stem from the main focus of the theory being on host-immigration interaction and cultural transformational process (Berry et al., 1989).

In the following periods, content creation opportunities enabled by introducing web 2.0 technologies come up first with forums and this novel apparatus was seen to provide a sense of cohesion towards any identity an individual feels to belong himself/herself within that group (Ye, 2006). In this context, while acculturation was moved to online platforms, it has been a matter of fact that the acculturation process was performed with multiple media tools as a result of the unilateral content creation to maintain its effectiveness. This process, in which the cultural process takes place with multiple media tools, has been a means of exchanging cultural components in an interaction process other than face-to-face interaction. This process has been defined as "remote acculturation" in the literature (Ferguson et al., 2017; Ferguson & Bornstein, 2012), continuing the core-periphery model of world systems theory. The only factor changed was the dominance of media tools in the cultural interaction platform. After that, the internet and then the social networking sites have functioned as global culture spreaders. As being diffuser tools of SNS, particularly the channels with large number of followers served mass changes on the Z generation. Thus, a new generation digital acculturation process has come into play.

DIGITAL ACCULTURATION

Transformation by technologies in the media have changed how we envision ourselves, therefore, our mindset and culture (Gere, 2008). This happened within a process. In the first stage, the concentration of mediascape has achieved permeation for global culture by keeping global media tools superior to local media tools (Appadurai, 1990). In the following years, the structure of the media has changed and a transformation has taken place from a mass media model to a bottom-up media model. Thus, the society itself started to create content in media (youtube channels or etc) (Gere, 2008). As a result; similar, different, interesting and attractive aspects of societies have been made apparent to other societies. Therefore, in societies that have accessed technology; awareness and knowledge towards other societies has increased, different thinking and behaving patterns have been discovered, and component transfer such as cuisine, movies and fashion has reached a global level (Ozer, 2019). As postulated by Contact theory (Allport, 1954), the atmosphere in which interaction is established determines the quality of relation between groups. The contact opportunities, which emerged with the development of the Internet, enabled the realization of structural and unstructural intergroup contact. Thus, the 7 characteristics of online interaction (anonymity, control over physical exposure, control over interaction, finding similar others, high accessibility and availability, equality, fun) provided an advantage to intergroup interaction quality. These advantages have enabled different groups to decrease their prejudices against each other and increase their empathy (Amichai-Hamburger et al., 2015). This has ensured that the interaction requirement in providing acculturation is fulfilled. This whole process has enabled nations to think about their own learned culture components and to compare other nations with the similar cultural component. Thus, it is thought that the process of evaluating its own culture has started and the component that is perceived as superior in other culture is adopted and recoded specific to the individual of the core culture. Thus, the components specific to periphery culture also had the opportunity to penetrate into core culture (Ozer, 2019), and the chance of acculturation has increased (Cong Li & Tsai, 2015). This has led to development of the concepts of digital acculturation (Dey et al., 2020), online acculturation (Kizgin et al., 2020), virtual acculturation (C. Li et al., 2019). Therefore, it emerged as a digital acculturation case.

In this process, cutting edge technology tools (Netflix, Youtube, Spotify, Facebook etc), which play a role in the recoding of local culture, are thought to instill global consumer culture into local cultures. In this context, particularities specific to each culture were exhibited in a market with ICT tools and created a specific identity by combining the details requested by each individual (Cleveland & Bartsch, 2018). Therefore, it is possible to state that the mediascape subset of globalization (Appadurai, 1990) is experienced in today's societies. As a result, consumer groups owning almost same consumption preferences has emerged as nascent stratum of communities (Bartsch et al., 2016).

As another result of the digital acculturation process, glocal or croelized multiple identities and numerous consumption patterns have occurred due to the large number of feedback for GCC (Cleveland & Bartsch, 2018). Because the observation of the people's lives in their immediate environment has spread as a new culture. Thus; the perception, value, behaviour and culture of societies were transformed (Rosenfeld, 2015, p. 22). This situation can be considered as the new generational demonstration effect. Indeed, the spread of Hinduism (Chari, 2011) and Islam (Mistiaen, 2013) together with SNS platforms can be given as an example to this situation.

DIGITAL ACCULTURATION AND TOURISM NEXUS

Destinations are acknowledged as hubs throughout which multicultural interactions between guests and hosts occur simultaneously (MacLeod, 2004). These interactions involve the changes of identities. As tourists are generated from heterogeneous groups, destinations are regarded as a specific spots in terms of social identities (Pearce, 2013). Because there are various counterparts instilling and emulating numerous cultural components in the setting (Ward, 2008). Unique situation specific to the touristic destinations made specific theoretical base a necessity to explain how the transformation of identity in context of host-tourist interaction actualize (Carter & Beeton, 2008). Acculturation theory was seen as an eligible theory as it is able to explain the mediating role of tourism oriented demonstration effect for cultural transformation process (Fisher, 2004) and to explicate how interaction between core and periphery region yielded a novel culture context (Gjerald, 2008).

The fact that upheld acculturation theory as a convenient theoretical base for cultural transformation issue has attracted interest from diverse research fields including tourism (Özekici & Ünlüönen, 2019b). First decades of tourism-acculturation interaction have addressed mutual interaction between hosts and guests at destinations. The studies (e.g. Berno, 1999; Bojanic & Xu, 2006) in this period have approached tourism oriented acculturation process from the perspective of Berry (1997)'s two dimensional acculturation strategies in a way that ignores conditions specific to the tourism system and role of ICTs on acculturation process. Following years have yielded studies considering role of ICTs and compatible with up-to-date conditions for acculturation process (e.g. Ferguson & Bornstein, 2015; C. Li et al., 2019).

The cultural transformation process caused by ICTs tools has spawned a new generation of cultural context in today's societies. This context has specific characteristics and those characteristics have some reflections on the tourism system. These reflections can be considered nexus amongst factors such as ICT, tourism and acculturation phenomenon. As looking into how digitalization occurs for acculturation-tourism nexus, it can be argued that a heterogeneous process involving digital and classic (face-to-face) interactions plays a mutual role. During the process, global consumer culture promulgates the metropolises through the ICTs. After adopting GCC as a subject and deciding for travel, novel culture is instilled within destinations through cultural interaction between host and tourists. Therefore, diffusion of GCC through interaction with ICTs apparatuses and hosts triggers the promulgation of digital acculturation process in tourism context (Özekici & Ünlüönen, 2019a). Also, introduction of ICTs into communities has led a different aspect in acculturation process. Adaptation of SNS has shortened the learning process, ensured pre-visiting experience through sharings of others as well as made possible continuous contact with heritage culture (J. Kim & Fesenmaier, 2015). This in turn may probably hinder culture shock, pave the way for integration strategies to pervade for tourists as well as decelerate the classic vis-à-vis cultural exchange process between host and guest for tourists.

There are numerous instances which can be delineated as a repercussion of digital acculturation process on tourism system. It has been observed for instance in particular destinations within Turkey that western cuisine and values are adopted in rural places through both ICTs apparatus and tourism-oriented demonstration effect in the most remote geographies, where there has been no change in the cultural codes for centuries (Özekici, 2019). Also, SNS were seen to form pro-environmental norms amongst Chinese tourists and to catalyse a pro-environmental societal community (Han et al., 2018). Again, with emulating mass tourism experience developed with the western cultural background as an output of SNS usage, certain evidences were argued to emerge within Islamic community such as the development of halal tourism system (Jafari & Scott, 2014; Levitt, 1983). Therefore, realization of cultural interaction in the SNS of the core region show that the core region plays a major role in the cultural code transfer of technology.

COVID-19 as a pandemic has also deeply affect the mutual interaction between tourism system and ICTs as well as course of acculturation sequentially. In that, social distance leads robotic technology to take presence within hospitality industry, redefine interaction process between counterparts (S. Kim et al., 2021) which in turn, transforms (Zhang et al., 2021) weakens (Zeng et al., 2020) and standardizes (S. Kim et al., 2021) the interaction intensity amongst counterparts involving hosts and tourists. On the top of that lockdown process paves the way for replacing tourist experience in setting with extended reality (Kwok & Koh, 2020). All these development refer a deviation from classic acculturation trajectories upheld by background studies of the extant literature (Berry, 1997; Berry et al., 1989). The relevant deviation will result in transformation of the infused cultural components to some extent. At this context, it can be envisioned that culture which will be adopted in the near future will change from top to toe.

ICT as an Acculturative Agent and Its Role in the Tourism Context

One of the instance from this course can be explicated that the COVID-19 process has led hosts to view tourists as virus spreaders. This triggers xenophobia, (Wassler & Talarico, 2021). This can minimize the host-tourist interaction and start the enculturation process. Opposite side effects of digital acculturation process were observed as well. In this term, high level of interaction with ICTs gave rise to alternative tourism types as digital free tourism within which it is guaranteed that tourist disconnect from all digital devices during leisure experience (Egger et al., 2020)

METHODOLOGY

The main aim of the relevant study is to reveal the nexus between acculturation and ICTs in context of tourism system and to envision probable reflections of this nexus on the tourism system in a futuristic perspective. Fulfilling concerning aim makes cross-sectional, therefore, interdisciplinary evaluation on research fields towards acculturation, ICTs and tourism phenomenon's a prerequisite. Thus, a three staged design was initiated to reach the specific studies which resembles the intersection of three research fields (acculturation, ICTs and tourism). In the first phase, a pre-screen phase was conducted. During this process, basic keywords concerning related to two fields were searched out together. Some examples of them involve "acculturation and tourism", "acculturation and ICTs", "tourism and ICTs". The process yielded over thousand papers. These papers were evaluated to decide whether they were eligible to be involved within the main theme of the study through glancing their titles, keywords and abstracts. Pre-screening period has enabled more specific keywords to be acquired and paved the way for reaching directly relevant studies on the topic. In the second phase, more specific keywords such as "demonstration effect", "host-tourist interaction", "online acculturation", "digital acculturation", "hospitable artificial intelligence", "cultural change", "transformational learning with technology" reached during the pre-screening period were utilized to acquire more relevant studies. Searching out process at the platforms involving Web of Science, science direct, emerald, Taylor and Francis, Sage, Wiley and google scholar were initiated then in 2 February 2021 and lasted until 18 July 2021. Articles, book chapters, conference papers and dissertations were included within the scope of the study while grey literature were excluded. The process has yielded 112 Studies. In the third phase, all these studies were scrutinized in detail and full texts of them were read in detail. After detailed screening, 29 of them were regarded to be indirect or irrelevant with the main context of the study and excluded from the dataset. Remaining 83 studies were compiled, evaluated and relevant projections were conducted over information acquired from them. The relevant evaluation and subsequent projections are delineated under following chapters.

NOVEL CULTURE AS AN OUTCOME OF DIGITAL ACCULTURATION PROCESS AND ITS REPERCUSSION IN CONTEXT OF TOURISM SYSTEM

The mass migration movements to cities brought by capitalism, large-scale wars and the industrialization have led to - by making complex calculations - the development of tabulating machines where social control would be provided, cryptoanalysis methods that enable the breaking of passwords sent over radio frequencies and data storage technology required to make those analyses more rapidly, and thus the emergence of modern computers used in directing the atomic bomb technology (Gere, 2008). In other words, there was a monopolar relationship between technology and culture. In the following years, technology has started to be effective on culture as a result of the emergence of ICTs tools (Amichai-Hamburger et al., 2015).

Figure 1. Digital acculturation process and its reflections on novel culture and tourism system

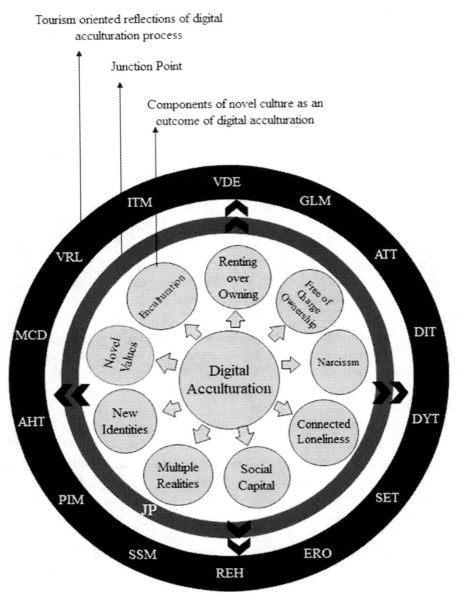

According to the constructivist theory, the tools we use affect our perceptions (Rosenfeld, 2015). Acculturation theory expresses the role of these tools on perception and then the change of cultural components with the concept of "acculturation agents" (Penaloza, 1994). Technology has changed the platform where the classical acculturation process takes place (Dey et al., 2020; Kizgin et al., 2020). This brought about a structural change in the cultural context of the society (Cleveland & Bartsch, 2018) and created a novel culture. Thus, whole acculturative process stemming from interplay between ICTs and cultural components of societies is believed to generate a novel digital culture on societal level which delineates itself on the online and offline world (Deuze, 2006; Dey et al., 2020). This culture can be characterized with purchase evaluation based on scoring, omnipresent feedbacks (through e-wom), real time surveillance, various profiles with different pseudonyms, lower level of concern towards privacy, etc. (Bauman & Lyon, 2013). It has been envisioned, explicated in next parts of the chapter and visualized on figure 1 that there are nine different aspects of this technology oriented acculturative process that leads to the novel culture in question. Also, demand and supply oriented aspects of this process on the tourism system constitutes fourteen factors.

Abbreviations: DYT: democratized youth tourism, SET: sharing economy integrated with tourism system, ERO: expanded recreation opportunities, REH: robotic employees with hospitality industry, SSM: soft sense of mass tourism, PIM: physical interaction as a pulling motivation, AHT: augmented host-tourist interaction, MCD: multicultural destinations, VRL: virtual reality based leisure, ITM: image oriented travel motivation, VDE: virtual demonstration effect, GLM: getting likes as a travel motivation, ATT: alternative travel types, DIT: diaspora tourism, JP: junction point.

In figure 1, digital acculturation process and outcomes of this novel culture as a result of digital acculturation process in terms of community culture components and projected tourism oriented reflections are delineated. Within the figure, central component titled as digital acculturation represents the digital acculturation process narrated in previous sections. Nine components bonded to digital acculturation shows the output of digital acculturation process in community level. Circle in the middle layer delineates the junction point between communal output and its reflection on tourism system. In other words, junction point represents the interplay process that community reflect its casual habits on its travel patterns. Lastly, circle ring in the outmost layer owns components. These components are tourism oriented reflections of digital acculturation process. In other words, these components may be accepted as supply and demand aspects of novel tourism system as a result of digital acculturation process. Components can be explicated as follows;

Renting over Owning

New technologies have created a culture of purchasing a product containing thousands of items instead of buying a product too much (Gere, 2008). Multiple demonstration effects are at the heart of this new culture due to its versatile information source. For this reason, the new culture encourages experiencing many things with the same budget, rather than sparing a significant portion of the budget to own one thing. The reflection of this culture component on consumption habits is the cultural component at the basis of sharing economy. Sharing economy is a system where personal commodities with monetary costs can be rented temporarily through technological platforms (Botsman, 2013). Sharing value, which underlies sharing economy, is to create value co-creation by connecting people, products and production processes (Lessig, 2008). This value co-creation makes renting prevalent. Thus, the opportunity to benefit from many things that renting provides has reduced the popularity of owning in digital culture (Hamari et al., 2016). The underlying factor for that is the novel culture created by digital acculturation. Hence, it becomes possible to exhibit multiple identities through renting and for individuals to project themselves as they wish with the consumption aspect (Durgee & Colarelli O'Connor, 1995). On the other hand, it is possible to state that the consuming culture, which emphasizes consuming itself as a need, being prevalent on a global scale (Firat & Venkatesh, 1995) constitutes the cultural background of this economic platform. The fact that the markets approach each other with shopping moving to the online platform has made it easier for almost everything to be shared and rented. This constitutes the technological background of the sharing economy (Hamari et al., 2016). In this context, for example Jain and Mishra (2020), as a result of their research on millennials; identified the social projection tendency as the strongest motivation factor in sharing economy preference for luxury fashion consumption.

When viewed from the tourism perspective, it is possible to state that the renting system is located inside tourism system. Thus, the fact that experience is the thing consumed within the scope of tourism experience, and that renting plays a predominant role instead of owning shows that the tourism system is in a form suitable for sharing economy. Nevertheless, it can be considered that the integration level of tourism system to sharing economy will expand in the future. Accordingly, it is thought that tourism experience platforms based on dues will emerge at first. Therefore, since many films can be accessed at the same time nowadays by paying dues to the film and TV series platforms, the same thing will be available for tourism oriented experience, too. In this context, it is considerable that various online platforms will develop and the opportunity to try a different destination each year will be met systematically through those platforms by making monthly payments. This may lead to transformation of the second home tourism sub-sector with a focus on renting rather than owning. In addition, job descriptions of tour operators may also be subject to transformation. Secondly, the expansion of car renting sector may be the reflection for sharing economy to become widespread in the tourism sector. Third, as a reflection of value co-creation in the tourism system, movements for the common use of transport vehicles, technological devices and other means brought along by tourists as well as the platforms that mediate these trends may emerge. And fourth, sharing economy's ability to consume the same product at low price will enable the democratization of youth tourism around the world.

Free of Charge Ownership

The novel self-extended areas caused by digital culture have changed the requirement to pay a financial price to own something. Because, objects that can be acquired online and free on digital platforms can create extended self of individuals (Belk, 2013). The reflection of this aspect of digital acculturation process has become open source movement with the widespread use of sharing economy. Indeed, Wikipedia and open source software can be listed among the examples for this (Hamari et al., 2016). In this context, the common production of people who do not know each other is seen as an ordinary or even optimum production condition (Lessig, 2008). The basis of this is to recode the sense of cooperation in the traditions of archaic societies with the sense of peer to peer technology (Gere, 2008). As a result of this recode process, the removal of borders in the virtual world, the open access format of SNS, and the spread of open education and open learning (Bozkurt et al., 2019) have brought a different direction to online cooperation. It can be observed that the response for cultural change on this issue is beginning to evolve in today's societies. Because, the fact that the public holiday sites and recreative experience areas are expected from municipalities as a service class are among the basic indicators of this situation. As a result of the spread of digital acculturation, it is thought that the expectation for the expansion and categorization of recreative areas will increase. On the other hand, tourism plans and policies will also be affected by this transformation. Because, it is thought that the announcement of beaches as a public space and the practices that are against the open platform such as beaches, forests that are private to the customers and closed to the public, etc. This will bring about a change in the statutes and regulations in the destination policy.

Narcissism

It is among the topics discussed in the literature that ICTs tools direct individuals to narcissism and selfishness (Mehdizadeh, 2010). As a matter of fact, it has been determined that digital activities such as online activity on SNS platforms (Ryan & Xenos, 2011), posting selfies (Stuart & Kurek, 2019) are related to narcissism. Accordingly, as a result of content creation being democratized, the need to attract attention has been transferred to the digital platform. This has encouraged motivation to get likes, share and attract attention (J. W. Kim & Chock, 2017; Van Ouytsel et al., 2016). As a result of all this desire and motivation, it is alleged that the content culture formed on the digital platform incited narcissism (Ryan & Xenos, 2011). Feeding the narcissism will bring along a change in consumption habits. With the development of robotic technology backed with artificial intelligence, it will be easier to serve society with developing narcissism in the hospitality industry. Because in classical tourism system, the services tailored according to individual requests required by narcissism could not be fulfilled due to limited budgets. Therefore, the combination of increasing narcissism and decreasing costs in robotic technology apparatus will encourage the use of this technology in tourism system. In this way, the humanoid robot technology supported by AI technology will enable the recording of information containing requests and preferences specific to each individual, processing this information by AI and operationalize tailored service understanding designed according to each individual's behaviour, state of motion, gesture and other factors by giving commands to humanoid robots. Thus, the sense of mass tourism will be relaxed and a soft sense of mass tourism tailored to the individual will develop.

Connected Loneliness

Novel ICTs have changed the nature of communication and provided real time interaction. Therefore, continuous and instantaneous communication has become possible with different tools (de Zúñiga et al., 2017). Yet, individuals who are connected by these communication tools are thought to feel lonelier (Belk, 2013). This situation was expressed with the concept of "networked individualism" in the early periods (Wellman, 2001). The first stage of online loneliness took place with SNSs playing a moderator role in the transition of societies from collectivism to individualism (Rosenfeld, 2015). The loneliness caused by individualism as an adapted novel cultural context has pushed people to use SNS (Ryan & Xenos, 2011). The dependence on SNS, which is caused by the increase in use, has also deepened the perception of loneliness (Gökçearslan et al., 2021; Tokunaga & Rains, 2010). In this process, it is thought that individuals will move away from real people more. Thus, it is predicted that the human-computer interaction process that starts with programmable robotic pets will evolve into a process that extends until robotic technology takes on the spouse role (Turkle, 2011). The deepening loneliness increases the desire to attach more to individuals through technology. This process turns the concept of connected loneliness, which is always online but has a sense of loneliness, into a social reality. For this reason, just as ecotourism and nature has turned into a motivation element after the destruction of nature (Kızılcık & Taştan, 2019), establishing physical interaction will also turn into a pulling motivation element for future generations. Thus, just as the blue flag is a reason for preference today, it is possible that the concepts of "only human" or "real interaction" can turn into criteria used in the service classification of the hospitality industry. On the other hand, it is thought that interaction equality will increase at a tremendous rate in the future as a result of the possibilities offered by technology, the availability of smartphones in almost every person and the improvement of translation applications (Amichai-Hamburger & Furnham, 2007). This will eliminate the intermediary role of acculturation agents in destinations, and direct host-tourist interaction will be possible. Thus, intense interaction between host and tourist, which is seen today in niche tourism segments such as backpacker, will enable every segment of the society to interact directly with tourists without language barriers in the future. Thus, digital elements will increase the quality of offline acculturation at destinations.

Social Capital

Social capital is defined as the summary of actual or virtual resources added to the individual or society through having a solid network (Bourdieu & Wacquant, 1992). Moving the social network to the online platform has made it possible to interact with different profiles and create a network as well as providing individuals with the opportunity to create an identity (Boyd & Ellison, 2007; Sharma et al., 2013). Therefore, the desire to enrich social capital increased the motivation of using SNS (Lin & Lu, 2011; Phua et al., 2017). Thus, SNS tools have started to complement or replace offline interaction in obtaining social capital. It is thought that the physical characteristic plays a critical role in this linear relationship of SNS usage and social capital. Because, the controllability of physical characteristics (Amichai-Hamburger et al., 2015) will also ensure that social capital consists of different outgroups. Therefore, the ability of person to control his/her physical appearance he/she reflects will reduce the possibility of the outgroup to develop a stereotype. For this reason, it can be considered that heterogeneous culture mosaic will be represented at a higher level in future destinations rather than homogeneous cultures. Thus, the effects of multidimensional cultures will be in question instead of the dominant cultures seen in destinations. This will turn destinations into global identity permeation centers.

Multiple Realities

Modern society individuals experience multiple realities. In this context; augmented reality, virtual reality and ultimately hyper reality are introduced, and a separate stage is set up in each of them in different dimensions of reality. The ubiquitous character of technology removes the distinction between real and virtual (Rosenfeld, 2015: 27). In this respect, the fun provided by VR can provide a more powerful synergy within interaction process than the interaction in RL (Amichai-Hamburger et al., 2015), even requests for tangible goods are replaced with virtual goods, a post materialist social structure is formed (Belk, 2013). Wearable technology is an important breaking point here. Because, real and virtual realities are intertwined with these tools.

Virtual reality was developed to increase the attractiveness of destinations (Williams & Hobson, 1995), and it was claimed to be able to substitute physical tourism experience (Williams & Hobson, 1995). Sustainability concern has increased the possibility of VR substitution (Tavakoli & Mura, 2015; Williams & Hobson, 1995). As a matter of fact, it is observed today that especially AR technology is used as an assistive element in the imagery of museums (Rosenfeld, 2015), that it meets leisure and social interaction necessity (Kampf & Cuhadar, 2015), transforms gifts into virtual (Belk, 2013) and facilitates the marketing activity of destinations. However, the fact that the digital acculturation process being the spreader of global consumer culture (Berry, 2008; Cleveland & Bartsch, 2018) has provided a basis to Williams and Hobson (1995)'s claim. Because, the limitations in real life are removed with Hyperreality (Rosenfeld, 2015: 11). Thus, a stage is created where the sense of eternity of needs instilled by the consuming culture is adopted and the hedonic digital culture citizens can meet their needs to live free of limitation. Accordingly, the spread of digital culture to the general public i.e. democratization of digital acculturation will make virtual reality-based leisure a competitor to physical leisure, and the demand aspect of VR based leisure will be formed. The first stage of this is Second life. On this platform, it offers a synchronous or asynchronous virtual leisure experience. It is thought that realistic interaction is experienced through this technology (Tavakoli & Mura, 2015). COVID-19 pandemic has accelerated the pace at which these tools are adopted among the tourists as an alternative for physical leisure experience (El-Said & Aziz, 2021). It is considered that these platforms will be enriched in the future and the conditions that prevent travel will make it easier to choose these platforms.

New Identities

In times when face to face interaction was the only option, messages for single identity were given through verbal symbols or gestures (Goffman, 1959). The fact that ICTs caused multiple identities (Cleveland & Bartsch, 2018) has led to the creation of new identities on virtual platforms. So when we want to send a message through any identity, the messages evoking that identity are transmitted (Rosenfeld, 2015: p.20). Therefore, the virtual identity that millenials set up in their minds is embodied through SNS accounts. This situation has become the reality of modern society (Turkle, 2011). The virtual identity fed in SNS is effective on the real life identity (Belk, 2013, 2016; Rosenfeld, 2015), and the avatar determined in VR transforms into the extended self of the person (Belk, 2016). Indeed, Dunne et al (2010) determined that presenting a specific identity is the main motivation in millennials' use of SNS. In this context, new identities constructed on SNS required to sustain this self-image (Amichai-Hamburger et al., 2015). Therefore, in whichever shape the propagated image is, the contents shared on SNS are also shaped accordingly (Dunne et al., 2010). In other words, real life identity is designed according to the identity created in VR. Because tourists are affected by the content and network in social media (Chunqing Li et al., 2019). This situation plays a decisive role in travel motivation. Also travel choice is affected by sharing inclination. As a matter of fact, the continuation of ecotourism motivation of a person who reflects the image of the world that he reflects sensitivity to the ecosystem on SNS platforms will create a new generation pressure element that the person feels on himself. Because if that person makes a different type of travel choice than the image he launched, this will cause his image not be credible on SNS platforms.

Novel Values

The adoption of bottom-up approach in terms of content creation in the media (Gere, 2008), and the tethering of people with high income levels in the world to SNS (Turkle, 2011) has led to the emergence of new norms and values. This is thought to be based on the social learning theory (C. Li et al., 2019). As a matter of fact, the level of exposure to the preferred media tool plays an important role in the development of an individual's belief about something (Kline & Liu, 2005). Therefore, as a result of SNS being the common communication tool in today's society, individuals enter a norm and value acquisition process with four stages (observing, choosing, acting and being rewarded) (Bandura, 2002; C. Li et al., 2019). At the end of the process, the masses have the acculturation footprint through digital platforms.

This process has had visible results in society. The first of these is the increase in sensitivity towards nature. As a result of the spread of SNS tools, ecological sensitivity has been adopted as a value in society (Ward & Geeraert, 2016) and pro-environmental sensitivity has emerged as a condition for touristic enterprises sequentially (Han et al., 2018). In addition, the rise of vanity and feminist understanding due to narcissism (Pham, 2015) and decreasing privacy concern (Turkle, 2011) are among the prominent new generation values. The reflection of these values on the tourism system will be in the form of joining the travel activity of groups that have experienced cultural transformation on online platforms at the first stage. In the second phase, those participating in travel activity will share their holiday experiences due to the increase in vanity and narcissism tendencies and the decrease in privacy concern. Being developed and promoted through pandemic conditions (Zeng et al., 2020), robotic technologies will encourage decreasing level of privacy concern. In the third stage, a virtual demonstration effect will appear. Thus, story on SNSs will be watched by the followers and encourage the holiday action. For those who share, the passion to get likes will turn into a travel motivation. In other words, the participation of people who have undergone a digital acculturation process to international travel activities causes different segments of the society to reflect their travel patterns and to be followed in other parts of the world in real time. The rise of values such as ecological sensitivity and feminism will also lead to the sharing of alternative tourism paths instead of mass tourism. Thus, alternative travel patterns will be embraced on a global scale. Just like the adoption of 3S tourism as a homogenous travel activity around the world, observing the travel activity of all stratums in societies today enables the adoption of travel flow in other countries, which has become widespread in one country. As an example, the development of sustainable tourism flow on a global scale as a result of the spread of global warming on a global scale can be provided. Accordingly, decreasing snowfalls and increasing winter tourism relation is another example. Lastly, instant communication and being able to come together on social media platforms will lead to the formation of their own hubs of this travel pattern.

Enculturation

Enculturation can be expressed as an increase in the level of adoption of one's own ingroup values (Weinreich, 2009). The tendency to adopt heritage culture components will increase in line with the individual's enculturation level. This will lead to the development of consumption behaviour of heritage culture and the strengthening of heritage identity (Kizgin et al., 2018). The internet allows the person to limit his / her interaction with the people in his / her cultural group. Also, joining groups with common characteristics is among the advantages of online platforms (Amichai-Hamburger et al., 2015). The time spent on online platforms can exceed face-to-face interaction in today's society. However, due to the fact that online interaction is more persistent compared to face-to-face interaction (Amichai-Hamburger et al., 2015), the development of in-group interaction level in online platforms (Amichai-Hamburger et al., 2015; Amichai-Hamburger & Furnham, 2007) will allow the enculturation level to increase. In other words, the number of individuals who prefer the separation strategy (Berry, 1997) will increase.

The first reflection of digital acculturation-enculturation association in the tourism system will be the spread of diaspora tourism. As a matter of fact, the online interaction with others in mainland provides the opportunity to re-establish the lost ties with mainland (Hiller & Franz, 2004). In this context, it is thought that the interaction established in SNS tools plays a role in the development of diaspora tourism (T. E. Li et al., 2020). Again, as a result of the consumption-oriented reflection of enculturation, it is possible to state that the leakage level in destinations will increase as a result of tourists demanding products produced in heritage regions. On the other hand, the interest in heritage culture will increase the demand for cultural tourism.

CONCLUSION

In this study, the role of ICTs on the changing social structure is explained through lens of acculturation. Beyond this, the acculturative process of the modern community's tourism oriented reflections caused by ICTs was discussed through nine components (renting over owning, free of charge ownership, narcissism, connected loneliness, social capital, multiple realities, new identities, novel values, enculturation) and predictions were made with a futuristic perspective. As a result of the widespread use of mass media, unilateral interplay between media source and audiences has enabled audiences to partially play a role in content creation with the development of web 1.0. By removing media channels from being an absolute media source, the later developed Web 2.0 technology and SNS platforms enabled audiences to create content and begin to interact with these contents,. Thus, it has led today's ICTs to take the moderator role in online interaction. This has turned ICTs into a new generation acculturation agent.

The increase in the level of interaction brought by technology and real time observation on our acquaintances has transformed the acculturation phenomenon from being a phenomenon for only specific groups into a dynamic of the social life. The fact that technology provides a weakened extended self (Belk, 2014) can be interpreted as digital acculturation will lead to a cultural transformation process with a relatively low qualification level compared to face-to-face interaction. This situation can be compared to situation of the marginalization strategy within bidimensional model. Because although this strategy is believed to exist theoretically, its representation in real life is relatively weak (Cheung-Blunden & Juang, 2008). However, it can be stated that novel technological devices and possessions have a specific aspect in terms of gaining a different dimension to life rather than qualification. In other words, technological opportunities can lead to a change in the culture of the society by changing the structure of dimensions that constitute the individual's identity or by increasing the weight ratios of these dimensions in the identity compared to the old generation people. On the other hand, in the acculturation literature review, despite the culturally transformative effect of ICTs in the community life, it is seen that scales that measure the classical, two-dimensional acculturation phenomenon are used in the acculturation literature to measure the digital acculturation phenomenon. Therefore, it is thought that future researches developing items that reflect the digital acculturation process instead of using scales that operationalize offline acculturation will contribute to literature. Because, due to the lack of a model representing digital acculturation, the development of a scale that measures this concept will fulfil a pioneering role for future research. Besides, testing the personality variables with scales operationalizing digital acculturation in a comparative way according to the x, y and z generation will provide information about the level of ICTs induced cultural transformation process in the society. Thus, foresight will be obtained in determining culture oriented policies. On the other hand, the examination of the nine aspects that are thought to have been created by the novel culture as a result of acculturation process through the quantitative or qualitative methods within the scope of acculturation theory will contribute to recognize the characteristic of the novel culture and thus to the development of management strategies in line with this culture. On the other hand, the cultural transformational process in society based on ICTs will lead to a revolutionary change in the organizational structure of the tourism system. Therefore, it will come to the fore as a need for hospitality businesses to redefine their organizational structures, subordinate relations and job descriptions that make up this relationship. Because, new generation technologies transform collectivist communities into individualists. It can be considered that this individualist community structure will contain its own global embeddedness, cosmopolitanism will become widespread and a kind of narcissism will find its place in the ordinary identity. In this type of society, it is thought that employees will prefer to define themselves as co-partners rather than an employed individual. Therefore, in the world of the future, it would be appropriate to consider this new cultural context in the process of coming to the forefront of competition by empowering internal customers. Measuring perceptions of consumers toward consumer responsibility strategies of tourism businesses actions in the field of marketing will provide useful information in re-designing the future marketing strategies because the cultural structure changed by the digital acculturation process can bring about a change in the marketing approach. In this respect, examining the moderating role of acculturation level in the influence of existing marketing strategies on purchasing intention will provide foresight information to the marketing department of enterprises in the tourism system. On the other hand, it is widely acknowledged on the field that there still exist a requirement for comprehensive and multi-disciplinary models (Juang & Syed, 2019) that meets the interdisciplinary structure of tourism field and explain how acculturation process evolve within destinations at which multiple cultural components penetrates

REFERENCES

Allport, G. (1954). *The nature of prejudice*. Addison-Wesley.

Amichai-Hamburger, Y., & Furnham, A. (2007). The Positive Net. *Computers in Human Behavior*, *23*(2), 1033–1045. doi:10.1016/j.chb.2005.08.008

Amichai-Hamburger, Y., Hasler, B. S., & Shani-Sherman, T. (2015). Structured and unstructured intergroup contact in the digital age. *Computers in Human Behavior*, *52*, 515–522. doi:10.1016/j.chb.2015.02.022

Appadurai, A. (1990). Disjuncture and difference in the global cultural economy. *Theory, Culture & Society*, *7*(2–3), 295–310. doi:10.1177/026327690007002017

Arnett, J. J. (2002). The psychology of globalization. *The American Psychologist*, *57*(10), 774–783. doi:10.1037/0003-066X.57.10.774 PMID:12369500

Bandura, A. (2002). Social cognitive theory in cultural context. *Applied Psychology*, *51*(2), 269–290. doi:10.1111/1464-0597.00092

Bartsch, F., Riefler, P., & Diamantopoulos, A. (2016). A Taxonomy and Review of Positive Consumer Dispositions toward Foreign Countries and Globalization. *Journal of International Marketing*, *24*(1), 82–110. doi:10.1509/jim.15.0021

Bauman, Z., & Lyon, D. (2013). *Liquid Surveillance: A Conversation*. John Wiley & Sons. https://www.wiley.com/en-us/Liquid+Surveillance%3A+A+Conversation-p-9780745662824

Belk, R. W. (2013). Extended Self in a Digital World. *The Journal of Consumer Research*, *40*(3), 477–500. doi:10.1086/671052

Belk, R. W. (2014). Digital consumption and the extended self. *Journal of Marketing Management*, *30*(11–12), 1101–1118. doi:10.1080/0267257X.2014.939217

Belk, R. W. (2016). Extended self and the digital world. In *Current Opinion in Psychology* (Vol. 10, pp. 50–54). Elsevier., doi:10.1016/j.copsyc.2015.11.003

Berno, T. (1999). When a guest is guest: Cook islanders view tourism. *Annals of Tourism Research*, *26*(3), 656–675. doi:10.1016/S0160-7383(99)00002-X

Berno, T., & Ward, C. (2005). Innocence abroad: A pocket guide to psychological research on tourism. *The American Psychologist*, *60*(6), 593–600. doi:10.1037/0003-066X.60.6.593 PMID:16173892

Berry, J. W. (1997). Immigration, acculturation, and adaptation. *Applied Psychology*, *46*(1), 5–34. doi:10.1111/j.1464-0597.1997.tb01087.x

Berry, J. W. (2008). Globalisation and acculturation. *International Journal of Intercultural Relations*, *32*(4), 328–336. doi:10.1016/j.ijintrel.2008.04.001

Berry, J. W., Kim, U., Power, S., Young, M., & Bujaki, M. (1989). Acculturation Attitudes in Plural Societies. *Applied Psychology*, *38*(2), 185–206. doi:10.1111/j.1464-0597.1989.tb01208.x

Berry, J. W., Phinney, J. S., Sam, D. L., & Vedder, P. (2006). Immigrant Youth: Acculturation, Identity, and Adaptation. *Applied Psychology*, *55*(3), 303–332. doi:10.1111/j.1464-0597.2006.00256.x

Bojanic, D., & Xu, Y. (2006). An investigation of acculturation and the dining-out behavior of Chinese living in the United States. *International Journal of Hospitality Management*, *25*(2), 211–226. doi:10.1016/j.ijhm.2005.06.002

Botsman, R. (2013). *The sharing economy lacks a shared definition*. http://www.collaborativeconsumption.com/2013/11/22/the-sharing-economy-lacks-a-shared-definition/

Bourdieu, P., & Wacquant, L. J. (1992). *An invitation to reflexive sociology*. University of Chicago Press.

boyd, d. m., & Ellison, N. B. (2007). Social Network Sites: Definition, History, and Scholarship. *Journal of Computer-Mediated Communication*, *13*(1), 210–230. doi:10.1111/j.1083-6101.2007.00393.x

Bozkurt, A., Koseoglu, S., & Singh, L. (2019). An analysis of peer reviewed publications on openness in education in half a century: Trends and patterns in the open hemisphere. *Australian Journal of Educational Technology*, *35*(4), 78–97. doi:10.14742/ajet.4252

Burns, P. M. (1999). *An Introduction to Tourism and Anthropology*. Routledge. https://books.google.com.tr/books?hl=tr&lr=&id=d9un9bkVkrkC&oi=fnd&pg=PP11&dq=an+introduction+to+tourism+anthropology&ots=ZWxleh-_RR&sig=_mDGSMKbUvWjSAvnmXlWUs_JuKo&redir_esc=y#v=onepage&q=anintroductiontotourismanthropology&f=false

Carter, R. W., & Beeton, R. J. S. (2008). Managing cultural change and tourism: A review and Perspective. In Cultural and heritage tourism in Asia and the Pacific. Routledge.

Chari, S. (2011). The Impact of Hinduism on the West. *India Currents*. https://indiacurrents.com/the-impact-of-hinduism-on-the-west/

Cheung-Blunden, V. L., & Juang, L. P. (2008). Strategies generalizable in a colonial context? Expanding acculturation theory: Are acculturation models and the adaptiveness of acculturation. *International Journal of Behavioral Development, 32*(1), 21–33. doi:10.1177/0165025407084048

Choney, S. K., Berryhill-Paapke, E., & Robbins, R. R. (1995). The acculturation of American Indians: developing frameworks for research and practice. In *Handbook of multicultural counseling* (pp. 73–92). Sage Publications.

Cleveland, M., & Bartsch, F. (2018). Global consumer culture: Epistemology and ontology. *International Marketing Review*. Advance online publication. doi:10.1108/IMR-10-2018-0287

Cleveland, M., & Laroche, M. (2007). Acculturation to the global consumer culture: Scale development and research paradigm. *Journal of Business Research, 60*(3), 249–259. doi:10.1016/j.jbusres.2006.11.006

de Zúñiga, H. G., Barnidge, M., & Scherman, A. (2017). Social Media Social Capital, Offline Social Capital, and Citizenship: Exploring Asymmetrical Social Capital Effects. *Political Communication, 34*(1), 44–68. doi:10.1080/10584609.2016.1227000

Deuze, M. (2006). Participation, remediation, bricolage: Considering principal components of a digital culture. *The Information Society, 22*(2), 63–75. doi:10.1080/01972240600567170

Dey, B. L., Alwi, S., Yamoah, F., Agyepong, S. A., Kizgin, H., & Sarma, M. (2019). Towards a framework for understanding ethnic consumers' acculturation strategies in a multicultural environment: A food consumption perspective. *International Marketing Review, 36*(5), 771–804. doi:10.1108/IMR-03-2018-0103

Dey, B. L., Yen, D., & Samuel, L. (2020). Digital consumer culture and digital acculturation. *International Journal of Information Management, 51*, 102057. doi:10.1016/j.ijinfomgt.2019.102057

Dunne, Á., Lawlor, M. A., & Rowley, J. (2010). Young people's use of online social networking sites - a uses and gratifications perspective. *Journal of Research in Interactive Marketing, 4*(1), 46–58. doi:10.1108/17505931011033551

Durgee, J. F., & Colarelli O'Connor, G. (1995). An exploration into renting as consumption behavior. *Psychology and Marketing, 12*(2), 89–104. doi:10.1002/mar.4220120202

Egger, I., Lei, S. I., & Wassler, P. (2020). Digital free tourism – An exploratory study of tourist motivations. *Tourism Management, 104098*, 1–10. doi:10.1016/j.tourman.2020.104098

El-Said, O., & Aziz, H. (2021). *Virtual Tours a Means to an End: An Analysis of Virtual Tours' Role in Tourism Recovery Post COVID-19*. Https://Doi.Org/10.1177/0047287521997567 doi:10.1177/0047287521997567

Ferguson, G. M., & Bornstein, M. H. (2012). Remote acculturation: The "Americanization" of Jamaican Islanders. *International Journal of Behavioral Development, 36*(3), 167–177. doi:10.1177/0165025412437066

Ferguson, G. M., & Bornstein, M. H. (2015). Remote acculturation of early adolescents in Jamaica towards European American culture: A replication and extension. *International Journal of Intercultural Relations, 45*, 24–35. doi:10.1016/j.ijintrel.2014.12.007 PMID:25709142

Ferguson, G. M., Tran, S. P., Mendez, S. N., & van de Vijver, F. J. R. (2017). Remote acculturation: Conceptualization, measurement, and implications for health outcomes. In S. J. Schwartz & J. B. Unger (Eds.), *The Oxford Handbook of Acculturation and Health*. Oxford University Press.

Firat, A. F., & Venkatesh, A. (1995). Liberatory Postmodernism and the Reenchantment of Consumption. *The Journal of Consumer Research*, *22*(3), 239. doi:10.1086/209448

Fisher, D. (2004). The Demonstration Effect Revisited. *Annals of Tourism Research*, *31*(2), 428–446. doi:10.1016/j.annals.2004.01.001

Flannery, W. P., Reise, S. P., & Yu, J. (2001). An Empirical Comparison of Acculturation Models. *Personality and Social Psychology Bulletin*, *27*(8), 1035–1045. doi:10.1177/0146167201278010

Gere, C. (2008). *Digital Culture* (2nd ed.). Reaktion Books.

Gjerald, O. (2008). *Sociocultural Impacts of Tourism: A Case Study from Norway*. Http://Dx.Doi.Org/10.1080/14766820508669095 doi:10.1080/14766820508669095

Goffman, E. (1959). *The presentation of self in everyday life*. Anchor Book.

Gökçearslan, Ş., Yildiz Durak, H., Berikan, B., & Saritepeci, M. (2021). Smartphone Addiction, Loneliness, Narcissistic Personality, and Family Belonging Among University Students: A Path Analysis. *Social Science Quarterly*, *102*(1), 1–18. doi:10.1111squ.12949

Gordon, M. (1964). *Assimilation in American Life: The Role of Race*. Religion and National Origin.

Hamari, J., Sjöklint, M., & Ukkonen, A. (2016). The sharing economy: Why people participate in collaborative consumption. *Journal of the Association for Information Science and Technology*, *67*(9), 2047–2059. doi:10.1002/asi.23552

Han, W., McCabe, S., Wang, Y., & Chong, A. Y. L. (2018). Evaluating user-generated content in social media: An effective approach to encourage greater pro-environmental behavior in tourism? *Journal of Sustainable Tourism*, *26*(4), 600–614. doi:10.1080/09669582.2017.1372442

Hiller, H. H., & Franz, T. M. (2004). New ties, old ties and lost ties: The use of the internet in diaspora. *New Media & Society*, *6*(6), 731–752. doi:10.1177/146144804044327

Hwang, B., & He, Z. (1999). Media Uses and Acculturation Among Chinese Immigrants in the USA. *Gazette (Leiden, Netherlands)*, *61*(1), 5–22. doi:10.1177/0016549299061001001

Jafari, J., & Scott, N. (2014). Muslim world and its tourisms. In Annals of Tourism Research (Vol. 44, Issue 1, pp. 1–19). Pergamon. doi:10.1016/j.annals.2013.08.011

Jain, S., & Mishra, S. (2020). Luxury fashion consumption in sharing economy: A study of Indian millennials. *Journal of Global Fashion Marketing*, *11*(2), 171–189. doi:10.1080/20932685.2019.1709097

Juang, L. P., & Syed, M. (2019). The Evolution of Acculturation and Development Models for Understanding Immigrant Children and Youth Adjustment. *Child Development Perspectives*, *13*(4), 241–246. doi:10.1111/cdep.12346

Jun, J. W., Ham, C.-D., & Park, J. H. (2014). Exploring the Impact of Acculturation and Ethnic Identity on Korean U.S. Residents' Consumption Behaviors of Utilitarian versus Hedonic Products. *Journal of International Consumer Marketing, 26*(1), 2–13. doi:10.1080/01924788.2013.848077

Kampf, R., & Cuhadar, E. (2015). Do computer games enhance learning about conflicts? A cross-national inquiry into proximate and distant scenarios in Global Conflicts. *Computers in Human Behavior, 52*, 541–549. doi:10.1016/j.chb.2014.08.008

Kim, J., & Fesenmaier, D. R. (2015). Sharing Tourism Experiences: The Posttrip Experience. *Journal of Travel Research, 56*(1), 28–40. doi:10.1177/0047287515620491

Kim, J. W., & Chock, T. M. (2017). Personality traits and psychological motivations predicting selfie posting behaviors on social networking sites. *Telematics and Informatics, 34*(5), 560–571. doi:10.1016/j.tele.2016.11.006

Kim, S., Kim, J., Badu-Baiden, F., Giroux, M., & Choi, Y. (2021). Preference for robot service or human service in hotels? Impacts of the COVID-19 pandemic. *International Journal of Hospitality Management, 93*, 102807. doi:10.1016/j.ijhm.2020.102795

Kizgin, H., Jamal, A., Dey, B. L., & Rana, N. P. (2018). The Impact of Social Media on Consumers' Acculturation and Purchase Intentions. *Information Systems Frontiers, 20*(3), 503–514. doi:10.100710796-017-9817-4

Kizgin, H., Jamal, A., Dwivedi, Y. K., & Rana, N. P. (2020). The impact of online vs. offline acculturation on purchase intentions: A multigroup analysis of the role of education. *Journal of Business Research*. Advance online publication. doi:10.1016/j.jbusres.2020.05.011

Kızılcık, O., & Taştan, H. (2019). Mağara turizminin motivasyon faktörlerinin belirlenmesi: Karaca Mağarası Örneği. *Çukurova Üniversitesi Sosyal Bilimler Enstitüsü Dergisi, 28*(3), 240–251.

Kline, S. L., & Liu, F. (2005). The influence of comparative media use on acculturation, acculturative stress, and family relationships of Chinese international students. *International Journal of Intercultural Relations, 29*(4), 367–390. doi:10.1016/j.ijintrel.2005.07.001

Kwok, A. O. J., & Koh, S. G. M. (2020). COVID-19 and extended reality (XR). *Current Issues in Tourism*, 1–6. doi:10.1080/13683500.2020.1798896

Lessig, L. (2008). *Remix: Making art and commerce thrive in the hybrid economy*. Penguin Press. doi:10.5040/9781849662505

Levitt, T. (1983). The globalization of markets. *Harvard Business Review, 61*(3), 92–102.

Li, C., Guo, S., Wang, C. L., & Zhang, J. (2019). Veni, vidi, vici: The impact of social media on virtual acculturation in tourism context. *Technological Forecasting and Social Change, 145*, 513–522. doi:10.1016/j.techfore.2019.01.013

Li, C., & Tsai, W.-H. S. (2015). Social media usage and acculturation: A test with Hispanics in the U.S. *Computers in Human Behavior, 45*, 204–212. doi:10.1016/j.chb.2014.12.018

Li, T. E., McKercher, B., & Chan, E. T. H. (2020). Towards a conceptual framework for diaspora tourism. *Current Issues in Tourism, 23*(17), 2109–2126. doi:10.1080/13683500.2019.1634013

Lin, K. Y., & Lu, H. P. (2011). Why people use social networking sites: An empirical study integrating network externalities and motivation theory. *Computers in Human Behavior, 27*(3), 1152–1161. doi:10.1016/j.chb.2010.12.009

Lindridge, A., Henderson, G. R., & Ekpo, A. E. (2015). (Virtual) ethnicity, the Internet, and well-being. *Marketing Theory, 15*(2), 279–285. doi:10.1177/1470593114553328

MacLeod, D. V. L. (2004). Tourism, globalisation and cultural change: an island community perspective. Channel View Publications.

Mehdizadeh, S. (2010). Self-Presentation 2.0: Narcissism and Self-Esteem on Facebook. *Cyberpsychology, Behavior, and Social Networking, 13*(4), 357–364. doi:10.1089/cyber.2009.0257 PMID:20712493

Mistiaen, V. (2013). Converting to Islam: British women on prayer, peace and prejudice. *The Guardian.* https://www.theguardian.com/world/2013/oct/11/islam-converts-british-women-prejudice

Nunez, T. A. (1963). Tourism, Tradition, and Acculturation: Weekendismo in a Mexican Village. *Ethnology, 2*(3), 352. doi:10.2307/3772866

Özekici, Y. K., & Ünlüönen, K. (2019a). Bir Küresel Tüketim Kültürü Aracı: Turizm. *Sosyal. Beşeri ve İdari Bilimler Dergisi, 2*(7), 508–524. doi:10.26677/TR1010.2019.196

Özekici, Y. K., & Ünlüönen, K. (2019b). Reflection of acculturation in tourism: A systematic literature review. In International Journal of Tourism Anthropology (Vol. 7, Issues 3–4, pp. 284–308). Inderscience Publishers. doi:10.1504/IJTA.2019.107322

Özekici, Y. K., & Ünlüönen, K. (2019c). Turizm Odaklı Kültürel Dönüşümü Açıklayıcı Bir Temel: Kültürleşme Teorisi. *Seyahat ve Otel İşletmeciliği Dergisi, 16*(3), 470–492. doi:10.24010oid.539666

Ozer, S. (2013). Theories and Methodologies in Acculturation Psychology: The Emergence of a Scientific Revolution? *National Academy of Psychology, 58*(3), 339–348. doi:10.100712646-013-0203-0

Ozer, S. (2019). Towards a Psychology of Cultural Globalisation: A Sense of Self in a Changing World. *Psychology and Developing Societies, 31*(1), 162–186. doi:10.1177/0971333618819279

Pearce, L. (2013). *The social psychology of tourist behaviour: International series in experimental social psychology*. Elsevier.

Penaloza, L. (1994). Atravesando Fronteras/Border Crossings: A Critical Ethnographic Exploration of the Consumer Acculturation of Mexican Immigrants. *The Journal of Consumer Research, 21*(1), 54. doi:10.1086/209381

Pham, M. H. T. (2015). "I click and post and breathe, waiting for others to see what i see": On #feministselfies, outfit photos, and networked vanity. *Fashion Theory, 19*(2), 221–241. doi:10.2752/175174115X14168357992436

Phinney, J. (2003). Ethnic identity and acculturation. In K. Chun, P. Organista, & G. Marin (Eds.), *Acculturation: Advances in theory, measurement, and applied research* (pp. 63–81). American Psychological Association Inc. doi:10.1037/10472-006

Phinney, J. S. (1990). Ethnic identity in adolescents and adults: Review of research. *Psychological Bulletin, 108*(3), 499–514. doi:10.1037/0033-2909.108.3.499 PMID:2270238

Phua, J., Jin, S. V., & Kim, J. (2017). Uses and gratifications of social networking sites for bridging and bonding social capital: A comparison of Facebook, Twitter, Instagram, and Snapchat. *Computers in Human Behavior, 72*, 115–122. doi:10.1016/j.chb.2017.02.041

Redfield, R., Linton, R., & Melville, J. H. (1936). Memorandum for the Study of Acculturation. *American Anthropologist, 38*(1), 149–152. doi:10.1525/aa.1936.38.1.02a00330

Rosenfeld, K. N. (2015). *Digital online culture, identity, and schooling in the twenty-first century*. Palgave Macmillan. doi:10.1057/9781137442604

Ryan, T., & Xenos, S. (2011). Who uses Facebook? An investigation into the relationship between the Big Five, shyness, narcissism, loneliness, and Facebook usage. *Computers in Human Behavior, 27*(5), 1658–1664. doi:10.1016/j.chb.2011.02.004

Sam, D. L., & Berry, J. W. (2010). *Acculturation: When Individuals and Groups of Different Cultural Backgrounds Meet*. Https://Doi.Org/10.1177/1745691610373075 doi:10.1177/1745691610373075

Sharma, G., Qiang, Y., Wenjun, S., & Qi, L. (2013). Communication in virtual world: Second life and business opportunities. *Information Systems Frontiers, 15*(4), 677–694. doi:10.100710796-012-9347-z

Stuart, J., & Kurek, A. (2019). Looking hot in selfies: Narcissistic beginnings, aggressive outcomes? *International Journal of Behavioral Development, 43*(6), 500–506. doi:10.1177/0165025419865621

Tajfel, H. (1982). *Social Psychology of Intergroup Relations*. Http://Dx.Doi.Org/10.1146/Annurev. Ps.33.020182.000245 doi:10.1146/annurev.ps.33.020182.000245

Tavakoli, R., & Mura, P. (2015). "Journeys in Second Life" - Iranian Muslim women's behaviour in virtual tourist destinations. *Tourism Management, 46*, 398–407. doi:10.1016/j.tourman.2014.07.015

Tokunaga, R. S., & Rains, S. A. (2010). An Evaluation of Two Characterizations of the Relationships Between Problematic Internet Use, Time Spent Using the Internet, and Psychosocial Problems. *Human Communication Research, 36*(4), 512–545. doi:10.1111/j.1468-2958.2010.01386.x

Turkle, S. (2011). *Alone Together: why we expect more from technology and less from each other*. Basic Books.

Van Ouytsel, J., Van Gool, E., Walrave, M., Ponnet, K., & Peeters, E. (2016). Exploring the role of social networking sites within adolescent romantic relationships and dating experiences. *Computers in Human Behavior, 55*, 76–86. doi:10.1016/j.chb.2015.08.042

Ward, C. (2008). Thinking outside the Berry boxes: New perspectives on identity, acculturation and intercultural relations. *International Journal of Intercultural Relations, 32*(2), 105–114. doi:10.1016/j.ijintrel.2007.11.002

Ward, C., & Geeraert, N. (2016). Advancing acculturation theory and research: The acculturation process in its ecological context. *Current Opinion in Psychology*, *8*, 98–104. doi:10.1016/j.copsyc.2015.09.021 PMID:29506811

Ward, C., & Szabo, A. (2019). Affect, behaviour, cognition and development: Adding to the alphabet of acculturation. In D. Matsumoto & H.-S. Hwang (Eds.), Handbook of culture and psychology (2nd ed., pp. 640–692). Oxford University Press.

Wassler, P., & Talarico, C. (2021). Sociocultural impacts of COVID-19: A social representations perspective. *Tourism Management Perspectives*, *38*(100813), 1–10. doi:10.1016/j.tmp.2021.100813

Weinreich, P. (2009). "Enculturation", not "acculturation": Conceptualising and assessing identity processes in migrant communities. *International Journal of Intercultural Relations*, *33*(2), 124–139. doi:10.1016/j.ijintrel.2008.12.006

Wellman, B. (2001). Physical Place and Cyberplace: The Rise of Personalized Networking. *International Journal of Urban and Regional Research*, *25*(2), 227–252. doi:10.1111/1468-2427.00309

Williams, P., & Hobson, J. P. (1995). Virtual reality and tourism: Fact or fantasy? *Tourism Management*, *16*(6), 423–427. doi:10.1016/0261-5177(95)00050-X

Ye, J. (2006). An Examination of Acculturative Stress, Interpersonal Social Support, and Use of Online Ethnic Social Groups among Chinese International Students. *The Howard Journal of Communications*, *17*(1), 1–20. doi:10.1080/10646170500487764

Yen, D. A., & Dey, B. L. (2019). Acculturation in the social media: Myth or reality? Analysing social-media-led integration and polarisation. *Technological Forecasting and Social Change*, *145*, 426–427. doi:10.1016/j.techfore.2019.04.012

Zeng, Z., Chen, P.-J. J., & Lew, A. A. (2020). From high-touch to high-tech: COVID-19 drives robotics adoption. *Tourism Geographies*, *22*(3), 724–734. doi:10.1080/14616688.2020.1762118

Zhang, C. X., Wang, L., & Rickly, J. M. (2021). Non-interaction and identity change in Covid-19 tourism. *Annals of Tourism Research*, *89*, 1–14. doi:10.1016/j.annals.2021.103211

KEY TERMS AND DEFINITIONS

Acculturation: Change in the cultural structure or identity of counterparts as a result of unmediated interaction of different cultures.

Connected Loneliness: A term used to delineate individuals who are connected by these communication tools are thought to feel lonelier.

Enculturation: An increase in the level of adoption of one's own ingroup values.

Remote Acculturation: Cultural process of exchanging cultural components in an interaction process other than face-to-face interaction.

Second Life: A virtual platform offering synchronous or asynchronous virtual leisure experience.

Sharing Economy: A system where personal commodities with monetary costs can be rented temporarily through technological platforms.

Social Capital: Summary of actual or virtual resources added to the individual or society through having a solid network.

Social Identity: Emotional and evaluative consequences of belonging to a specific group.

Chapter 5
Role of Technology on Religious Tourism in Turkey

Muhammad Farooq
Yasar University, Turkey

Volkan Altintas
Izmir Katip Celebi University, Turkey

ABSTRACT

The religious tourism sector is a booming industry and attracts a sizable number of tourists around the world. While several factors play an important role in increasing the number of tourists for religious purposes, technology plays a vital role in managing and boasting religious tourism in a country. The authors aim to see this in the context of Turkey, a country that is a bridge between East and West, possessing a number of religious touristic sites and attracting a large number of tourists. The profile of the country and the role of technology in increasing tourism in Turkey also suggest improvements in the technological landscape of the country to increase and facilitate the religious tourists.

INTRODUCTION

Religious tourism traces back to biblical times is one of the most common and practiced forms of tourism globally. The religious tourism industry is massive and continues to grow at an estimated compounded annual growth rate of 6%, the market size of USD 18 Billion, with 300 Million travelers. The visitors are usually triggered by religious motivations and faith to visit the holy sites (Buzinde et al 2014; Chou et al 2016). There is another motivation besides faith and religious ceremonial significance, instigating the religious tourists, including humanitarian causes, the destination`s perceived image, or traveling for the architectural beauty of a religious tourism site, like Hagia Sophia Mosque in Turkey or Vatican City in Italy where the number of visitors from different faiths also visit in large numbers for the architectural beauty, historical significance or destination travel (Tidbits, 2014). Celebrated countries for religious tourism are also capitalizing on their religious tourism potential besides solely labeling the country as a religious tourism site, and expanding the scope for the visitors. The Saudi Arabian Vision 2030 is the

DOI: 10.4018/978-1-7998-8165-0.ch005

depiction of the fact, where visitors are made familiar with the country's scope beyond religious tourism sites, developing special touristic places, the establishment of smart city, name as ''Neom'', (Thoblany, & Alyuosef 2021), Vatican City's tourists are also thrilled by Italian nonreligious touristic tourist destinations as well, and Italian government promotes the country beyond religious tourism site to draw more visitors (Kim,& Kim 2018). These approaches are supplemented by effective use of technology to raise the awareness, branding the destination, or in the field of facilitation of tourists who are visiting the country for religious tourism. Our aim in the chapter is to explore the role of technological aspects in religious tourism empathizing Turkey, a key religious tourism destination.

Turkey is ranked as one of the major sites for religious tourism, the country due to its unique geographical location and prestigious historical significance, is home to major religious touristic sites of Muslim, Christianity, and Judaism faiths (Nuray 2016). The country welcomes large numbers of tourists from all geographies, who have remarkable value for their religious sites.

In this chapter, it is aimed that the potential of the Turkish Tourism sector is seen in the context of technology to observe the influence of technology in the religious tourism sector. The chapter also explores the use of technology in religious tourism, the visitors' awareness about them, the impact on religious tourism in Turkey, being a famous religious tourism destination. We analyze the potential of Turkey as a hotspot destination for religious tourism and the use of technology currently in the tourism sector by the country, the future aspirations, and the suggestions that can help to further uplift the country's profile.

LITERATURE REVIEW

Religious tourism can be traced in previous studies from the 1980s (Cohen, 1984; Graburn, 1983). The evolution of the movement of pilgrimage across different religions led to the subsequent typology of religious tourism.

The previous literature shows that researchers have observed different aspects in the context of religious tourism including pilgrimage tourism Henderson, (2011); Abbate & Di Nuovo, (2013), secular pilgrimage Collins-Kreiner, (2016), Brown, (2016), sustainable tourism Murray & Graham, (1997); Gupta, (1999) heritage tourism (Shackley, 2002; Bond et al., 2015).

Consideration by the researchers to study different disciplines concerning tourism and inclusion sociology Murray & Graham, (1997); Eade, (1992); Andriotis, (2011) Management; Wong, McIntosh, & Ryan, (2016); Hung et al., (2017), Marketing Kruger & Saayman, (2016); Hughes et al., (2013) Economics Nethengwe, & Sumbana, (2017)); Dafuleya, Gyekye, Oseifuah, Nethengwe, & Sumbana, (2017) Globalisation aspects (Moaven et al. 2017). Some other notable studies on the topic include those of Henderson (2011) who studies the implementation of modern management of pilgrims at Hajj occasion, a religious ritual in Muslims' faith, considering the effective use of managerial and technological resources from the authorized. García et al (2018) discuss the socio-economic impact of religious tourism taking into consideration different aspects of tourism. Brown & Chalmers (2003) highlight the impact of mobile technologies on religious tourism, the ease in tourism due to the availability of content applications and services. Vukonic (1997) argues that religious tourists are influenced by all modern technology during and before their trip, they are utilizing electronic travel guides, useful mobile applications, interactive maps, social media, to make their travel experience more enriched and share about it with others.

Although the studies have covered the topic generally specific studies about the religious tourism sector, with the impact of technology and its influence on travelers' perceptions, its overall role on the tourism sector needs to be studied more in detail. With Turkey as the selected country in the chapter, we aim to explore how the Turkish religious tourism landscape is embracing the impact of technology on religious tourism and the suggestions to be made in that regard.

The Market of Religious Tourism

Religious tourism can be defined as a form of tourism in which a tourist or a pilgrimage, is motivated by specially or exclusively religious believes or associations, and undertakes the journey to fulfill those or perform a religious ritual (Rinschede 1992). Religious tourism can be more specified with the word Pilgrimage, which is mentioned as a journey resulting from religious causes externally to a holy site and internally for a spiritual purpose and internal understanding (Barber 1991)

The religious tourism market is tremendously sized. Three major religions in the world, Islam, constituting followers which are 23% and Christianity followers account for 31% of the 6.9 Billion of the world population and Judaism, sizes at 25 Million of the adherents. These major adherents constitute the majority of the religious tourism market (Kucuk 2013; NPR 2015). Data from World Tourism Organization UNWTO (2014), approximately 330 Million visitors visited religious sites globally, which constitutes 27% of total universal arrivals in the world, and 24% of the total tourists are interested in religious tourism.

Religious tourism accounts for a substantial portion of the economies of several countries. It is the second-largest industry in the Kingdom of Saudi Arabia, accounting for a revenue of USD 8 Billion. Numbering the visitors with two million foreigners, an additional 700,000 local pilgrims, usually travel for Hajj in the Kingdom. Europe is also a considerable region for religious tourism with an estimated five million visit Lourdes in France. India is also a hub of Hinduism religious touristic attractions, constituting 28 million Hindu pilgrims who visit the famous Ganges River, (Singh, 2006). Moreover, Spain and Portugal also are eminent, as Montserrat in Spain draws two million visitors, whereas Fatima in Portugal has an estimated four million visitors per annum (Saayman et al. 2013).

Turkey possesses some of the major religious tourism sites but, lags in this sector as compared to peer nations. Turkish statistics Institute's report shows that only 0.2 to 0.5 percent of the total visitors visited Turkey in the year 2012 (Turkstat 2012). According to the Ministry of Tourism, in 2015, 4.5% of international tourists came for religious tourism purposes. These statistics are much lesser for a country with such religious tourism potential. However, the visits were mostly because of archaeological and historical significance too rather than mere religious value. The country over the few decades has also marketed itself differently, with 3s tourism, sand, sun, and sea. The presence of a large number of shrines can be attached as complementary religious tourism. Keeping in view the change in visitors perceptions and trends, the Turkish

Considering the changing motivations of tourists and the importance of developing alternative types of tourism for the future of the tourism industry, the MoCT, (Ministry of Tourism and Culture), Turkey, has planned to focus more on religious tourism sites with the view of promoting more cities with religious sites. These sites are located mostly in the provinces of Hatay, Gaziantep, Şanlıurfa, Mardin, etc. (Türker 2016).

The tourism sector henceforth is a multidimensional field. The tendency of religious tourism in the medieval pilgrimage was just towards visiting the religious sites and uni-purpose tourism, but it kept evolving during the middle and modern ages. In the modern age, tourists are not confined to visiting just the touristic sites but they are more tentative towards exploring the other culture and other attractions (Abbate and Di Nuovo, 2013). Backed by Anthropologists who claim that in addition to spiritual motives the tourists are attracted to shrines and other religious tourist sites because of the cultural value and significate attached to those places (Vokonic 2002). We can ascertain that the religious tourism market is highly interrelated with cultural and other forms of truism and they complement each other.

Religious Tourism Potential in Turkey

Turkish economy banks on tourism sector substantially. It's a growing sector which accounted for 7.7 percent of total employment in the country, directly employing 2.2 million people, with the contribution to Gross Domestic Product at 3.8%. It has a whopping 51.9% percent share of the total services exports in 2018. (OECD, 2020)

The Anatolian region of turkey is dominated by shrines, temples, chapels, tombs, and sculptures that hold significant religious values and are known for hundreds of years, also synonymous with their architectural, aesthetic, and historical significance. It can be said that Mosques, Churches, Synagogues, Caves, and Mountains are a major part of Turkish cultural heritage (Okuyucu and Somuncu 2013).

Turkey has significant potential to develop religious tourism. Apart from these sites, the excavations of the areas in Göbeklitepe, Urfa, dates back to 10,000 years. The excavation in the Anatolian region has shown the remains of temples dating back to 11,000 years old (National Geographic 2011). Turkey

Figure 1. Distribution of the most important religious resources in Anatolia by major religions
Source Okuyucu and Somuncu (2013): 633.

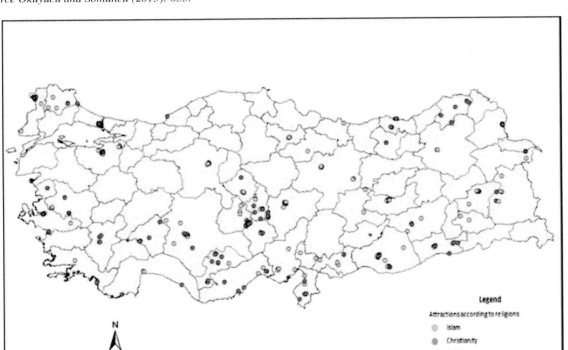

is one of the only few countries where Abrahamic religion had been present and coexisted (COE 2013). The presence of religious landmarks is also a testimony of the fact that Turkey has been a sacred site for all major religions.

Figure 1 shows the diversity of Turkey and possession of major religious cities across Turkey, showing the significance of the country for religious tourism for all three major religions.

Turkish government envisioned this from 1990 to enhance the tourism potential of the country and to enhance the projection of religious tourism sites. To support the related local communities and promote the religious tourism sites, the government planned to have more offseason tourists for the country, which usually experience a high volume of tourists in Summer, Specially for sand sea and summer tourism, to go beyond that image. The ministry of culture and tourism in Turkey, (MoCT) had worked extensively and listed 300 plus religious tourism sites to promote among the travelers who know Turkey mostly for summer tourism merely. The richness

The enhancement of this potential can further be accelerated by utilizing the effective use of technology. The current utilization of the technology by religious tourists is also consideration point of this chapter.

THE INTRODUCTION OF TECHNOLOGY INTO RELIGIOUS TOURISM

Technology and religious tourism have created a fruitful combination that does not only enhance but also facilitates the market and creates a convenient experience for travelers. Communication technology is arguably the most used tool for the religious tourism sector. It has become essential to create travel media, and advert campaigns through tools of modern communication like social media, apps, newspapers, radio, and TV to make visitors familiar with the locations, especially those located at far-off places. (Tavalaee, 2006).

The globalization of information and communication technologies (ICT), has helped people in different regions across the globe be aware of lifestyles, values, and norms of behavior. It would lead to reverse change or strengthen lifestyles, values, and norms (Khaje Nuri, 2014).

The role of technology is also very critical in not only the promotion but also the management of religious tourists. In the case of Saudi Arabia and Italy where the pilgrimage flock in great numbers every year, the use of many modern technologies to manage, track and assist the pilgrims are helping the authorities a great deal. (Raj, & Griffin, 2015). The application of Smart Media Technology by the Kingdom especially on Hajj occasions has proven to be a game-changer. Smart Media Technology or SMT, includes the technologies such as E-Bracelets for pilgrims, tracking the locations, identities, and health, availability of free high-speed WiFi, mobile charging services at dedicated points, dedicated websites, and social media channels specially created for the pilgrims. The public-private partnership has come into play resulting in huge investments and an increasing number of tourists, with higher satisfaction levels. (Qurashi and Sharpley2018).

The inclusion of modern technology in religious travel also helps to generate what is called, E-word of mouth, sharing the experiences electronically and encouraging others to also undertake the tourism experience. Religious tourism especially needs more guided experience, in that regard, the QR codes are now used to make the visitors familiar with the historical significance of the site, guided tours with audio equipment with native language support options, and virtual and augmented reality experiences, to see the place from historical perspectives. It also lets the pilgrims have digital access to their memorable experiences after the visit is over, back home, reliving the moments with digital catalogs and social media share tools. The online travel review platforms, OTRs, also play a significant role, where visitors share the experiences and learn about the services they had, paving ways for other potential travelers who aim to visit (Ascaniis, and Cantoni, 2016).

The example of Sacro Monte di Oropa in Italy which is now a UNESCO World Heritage site, was unknown unless references and experiences were shared by tourists using multiple media channels and technologies. It got later the attention of tourists and is now a sacred roman catholic touristic site (Cerutti and Piva 2016). Ndivo & Cantoni (2016) mentions a similar occurrence in Northern Africa, where the rock-hewn churches in Ethiopia which were also included in the UNESCO World Heritage site, also came to know with regular mentions in the media and technological channels. De Ascaniis, S., & Cantoni, L. (2016) mention relatedly the role of smartphones as a parameter of communication and experience share. They highlight the Catholic bishop Álvaro del Portillo, the festival held in Madrid Spain, in 201 which drew more than 250,000 people from 70 different nations. It was also a religious experience for the masses, such a big gathering was also a challenge for the local authorities to manage. The authorities develop a mobile application and communication channels using event website, WhatsApp messaging services support to facilitate the visitors and help them in the native language of their origin. This help to have a seamless experience and support for the visitors and they had positive feedback and appreciation for the event management.

Tourism and technology create a valuable mix and enhance the tourist`s experience and also help the related authority to manage the visitors and keep the databases, and to have easier future projections. It also assists in policy formations. Ramos et al (2016) mention different aspects related to tourism, mention the impact of technology on the experience shared by the tourist

post visits, using technological and social platforms. They mention the use of Augmented Reality, (AR) in the religious tourism industry. It allows the visitors to virtually experience the place using the seamless physical experience using sound and other sensory elements. They also discuss how gamification use in the religious tourism industry has changed the landscape and provided convenience to the travelers, with increased satisfaction. Technology has helped the religious tourism sector significantly as it has more sentimental values attached to it, and with modern technology usage, the creation of intelligent interfaces to further enhance the historical and cultural significance of the places too boasts the industry more.
We here, discuss the three biggest factors, that have a major influence currently on religious tourism.

E-Wom and Religious Tourism

Electronic word of mouth has gained importance in the modern digitalized and tech-run era. Breazeale (2009) identified nine main elements that constitute eWOM they are noted down as

- The sharing of one opinion with the others
- Leaders in opinion-making have a big role in transforming the opinion of the masses
- The online interaction through different platforms
- Network-based communication between related parties
- Information being directed to several people
- The nature of nitration is not time or space barred
- Communications can go anonymous
- Credibility issues are major concerns as every communication is online
- Currently massively impacting consumer decisions

Companies and individuals put special focus on electronic word of mouth i.e the opinions and experiences of people express online, E-WOM affects the tourism sector comprehensively. Researchers and practitioners belonging to the tourism sector admit the comprehensive role of E-WOM in destination and religious tourism (Jalilvand & Samiei, 2012). A chunk of over 50% US consumers read online reviews before deciding travel (Kristen, 2014).

(Jalilvand & Samiei, 2012). A report released by Pew research in 2014 showed that about 50% of US online users consider online reviews before making their decisions (Kristen, 2014). Kwahk and Ge (2012) reported that 70% of consumers visit social media websites such as message boards, social networking sites, and blogs to get information on a company, brand, or product and about 49% of these customers make a purchase decision based on information gathered from social media sites.

Iriobe, O., & Abiola-Oke, E. (2019) uses the theory of planned behavior to find the revisit intention of the tourists in religious tourist sites, and found huge support. They found that through the eWOM the tourists' revisit changes of about the visited place increase exceptionally.

The eWOM factor is, therefore, a major rising by-product of technology that has a substantial influence on the visits, and must be controlled and used to advantage by the governments, agencies, and related operatives.

Augmented Reality and Religious Tourism

Augmented reality and, mobile communication technologies are playing vital role in the promotion of tourism at present. The use of augmented and mobile tehonology are not confined to one sector but has spread multi domically and hence have cohesive impact on religious tourism sector Jung, T. H., & Han, D. I. (2014).

Several researchers have dissected the correlation between the use of technologies like mobile communication and augmented reality and religious tourism.

Husain, & Dih, L. Y. (2012). In their research argue the huge impact of augmented reality technologies and their impact on religious tourism, they propose personalize travel recommendation system (PLTRS) for the religious tourist, using the location based services, and to make their trip more interactive.

Augmented reality and mobile communication technologies are not merely confined to one singular technology, it entails several aspects covering wide ranging of technological applications and programs that assist the user. Kenteris, et al (2009), further spreading it, comes up with a ''Mytilene E-Guide, A mobile platform to guide the tourist's exemplar, showcase an approach which strives to achieve web to mobile model, that serves both online and offline, guide the tourists with seamless experiences of the religious sites they visit, and provide them with detailed guidance and historical background of the sites, using location based services.

Weking and Ndala, (2018) mentions the itourism, that is, a travel mobile buddy an application and augmented reality platform, that aims to provide assistance and guidance for religious tourists. This application and portal has greatly helped the religious tourism sector in Malaysia and beyond in the region. Not only has it ensured support and fatigue less travel experience but also it makes tourists to share their experiences which in result, attract millions of other religious tourists.

The case of East Flores in this regard is worth mention too, where the augmented reality, and mobile technology changed the landscape of religious tourist attraction. The tourists visiting Semana Santa processions, were comprising of locals and foreigners. The long occasion kept many tourists away y getting the updated and live information of many religious rituals performed. The problem was addressed by performing location based analysis, using the help of global positioning system, GPS, and connecting all the visitors together from their location, where using augmented reality and mobile application enabled them to see and get informed by the religious rituals. That was well appreciated by local and global devotees ((Weking, A. N., & Ndala, S. (2018)

Artificial Intelligence

Artificial intelligence has brought convenience and amazement in almost all aspect of life. From personal assistance to business decision, health to tourism, the impact has caused a paradigm change.

The technology like working for tourism is using working principle of K-Nearest Neighbour (K-NN), which enables the distance of nearest attraction to the user, based on his/her location and guides him to the spot, and provides logistical assistance. This has led to the development of the new religious tourist maps, based on the locations visited. Maps provides recommendations based on the past visits and experiences. These recommendations are not only helpful for the future of travelers but also for the decision making bodies (Wahyono et al 2020))

Artificial intelligence enable auto check-ins, lesser employees involvement and error free continuation of the process. The timeliness and prudence achieved in the tourism journey is a unique preposition that artificial intelligence devices bring. ((Ivanov, S., & Webster, C. 2019)

Specially in big religious gatherings, the sorting of visitors in sections, enabling smooth entrance and exits, and proving services to the areas otherwise not easily reachable is a great plus of artificial intelligence.

During the Muslim ritual of Hajj, Kingdom of Saudi Arabia massively use the article intelligence technology for estimation, delivery and keep the flow of visitors. Rituals are performed swiftly by using AI technologies, with special focus on how the behaviours of people are toward different segments of the journey and the visits embarked, future planning and management (Yamin, M. 2019)

These artificial intelligence technologies predict the behaviours based on past data, historical experiences and make the journey of religious pilgrims much smoother. Full maximization efforts are needed to be made, yet to yield more benefits out of these technologies for religious tourism where masses are involved (Asadi,et al 2016).

Technology and Religious Tourism Aspects in Turkey

Turkey holds a dynamic position in the religious tourism sector. Having religious tourists' sites from all major religions draws great numbers of devotees from all religions. Turkey has been ranked as the world`s third-best tourist destination for halal tourism in the year 2019 by Global Muslim Travel Index GMTI (Khaliq, 2019). The country has high revenue collection from religious tourism. Turkey attracted approximately 46 million international tourists in 2018. (OECD, 2020).

Turkish ministry of culture is responsible for formulating policies planning about tourism. They collaborate with association of travel agents, hotels, investors and other chambers of commerce and related unions. The operations are looked over by the precedency. In the year 2019 to promote tourism, a promotional and developmental agency was established.

Ministry of culture Turkey, is responsible for managing the tourist sites, formulate plans and implement them. They work with travel agencies locally and internationally as well. The agency for promoting tourism activates was established in 2019.

Figure 2. Turkish tourism authorities structure
Source: OECD, adapted from the Ministry of Culture and Tourism, 2020

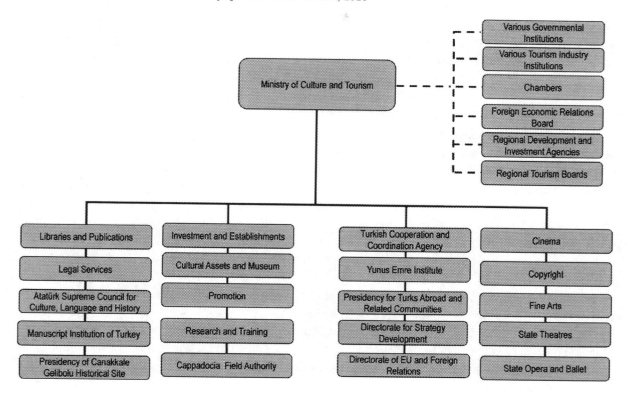

Turkey is taking measures to use technology in its religious tourism sectors. The cultural and tourism ministry aims to utilize technology in its religious tourism portfolio. Ministry offers a 360 degrees view of the religious touristic sites, museums and historical places. The ministry also have some useful portal in the website, https://www.ktb.gov.tr/, and a modern website for more familiarity and opportunities in Turkey, GoTurkey.com. Data in numbers about the tourists, future policies and the governmental structure is mentioned as well. The websites are depicting important statistics, rules and regulations, important documents needed, permissions and future aims. The latter provides blogs and shares experiences in Turkey, the dynamic capacity of Tukey in various tourism aspects and events. Websites offer blogs about different aspects of Turkey and the variety it offers in terms of Tourism.

Turkey is opening gradually for the smart city tourism for its religious sites by using public private partnership, I this regard, renowned think tank Novusens Smart City Institute, in collaboration with the local authorities are making efforts to promote medium and small cities, shifting them to a new city transformation model what they call City Transformation Model – "CITI-Zen", to make cities more liveable, sustainable and competitive (The Smart City Journal, 2020).

Turkey plans a rigorous program at the governmental level with state of the art technology implements aspirations in the coming year, aimed the pandemic hit religious tourism industry. The country aims a V shape recovery specially in this sector and expects over $23 Billion in revenues from this industry. The Culture and Tourism Ministry, the TGA, aims to further develop the ''Go Turkiye'' platform to inculcate more modern facilities, developing major provinces with religious sites using modern communication channels and using the public private partnerships at core. The country hosted over 1,000 YouTubers, bloggers and influencers in 2020 and plans to host over 2,000 in 2021. (Aslan, 2021)

Although the government's machinery is aiming at inculcating technology into religious tourism, there are still areas for further considerations. There need to be more segmented and concentrated policies and implementation of technological resources accordingly, keeping in view the demographics of the segmented market. In a similar vein, measuring the potential ÇAKMAK, & DİLEK, S. (2019) present two models depicting the benchmark effect on religious travel in Turkey. It shows that the one-unit travel by Muslim devotees, increases tourism revenue by 0.83 units, and other religious devotees increase it by 1.02 units. They also present their research in terms of nationalities as well, showing that a 1% increase in the visit to Turkey by a visitor from Arab countries will increase 1.19% of tourism income in Turkey, whereas others will increase it to 0.52%., therefore the contribution of tourists from Arab countries is higher than the other regional countries. They urge to have more customized approaches towards those nationals, launching separate portals and blogs, ease of access to historical information, and more local language guided support. Turkey needs to develop better technological infrastructure, upgrading the travel agent approach and develop the standards according to the EU or major bodies, build better technological infrastructure for people with special needs, more ease in bookings and less reliance on agent services, better branding and portrayal as well (Pırnar and Miral, 2000).

Some points have also been highlighted by industry players. Quoting Ramazan Becer, owner of a tourism company in Turkey Maudlin, (2019) mentions that Turkey can collect revenue of $100 Billion by the year 2023 in this industry. The author also highlights the need for more use of technology in this regard. Tourism companies in big numbers do not have social media presence, they are not keeping the travelers informed about important information during their sacred visits for religious purposes, the digital presence of travel companies is also minimal, resulting in lesser yield in revenues per tourist and also not at par with other famous religious touristic destinations globally. The use of the latest technologies like augmented reality, holograms, artificial intelligence in tourism applications, and virtual reality can further boost the industry. The country though targets higher numbers of tourists by 2023.

CONCLUSION

The religious tourism market is growing exponentially and Turkey is a big market for that. Although the country has ambitious targets for the future, it needs to address some paucity especially in the application of modern technological resources that can further enhance the position and help the tourists have a more comprehensive travel experience. Turkey can also use the technology and project the country more to the potential tourists, by using the latest information and communication technology. Future research can consider seeing the number of tourists coming from different means, and seeing how they rate the technological advancement and facilities in Turkey as compared to other religious touristic destinations. Turkey needs to engage the audience more by using a two-way strategy,

First for the imagery projection, using the eWom more, to spread the word, creating the brand image of the country, make visitors share experiences, engage bloggers and influencers to share the positive word, create buzz and make the unexplored areas a talked about topic, in that way revisits and new visits can be vast.

Secondly, making the experience better by using the Ai, Augmented Reality, Virtual Reality, digital maps to enhance the ease in experience to make the visits, especially the international, more familiar with the religious sites they visit and make the stay informative and comfortable. The government needs to involve marketing and IT organizations to yield much more results in the religious tourism sector in Turkey which is still untapped.

REFERENCES

Abbate, C. S., & Di Nuovo, S. (2013). Motivation and personality traits for choosing religious tourism. Research on the case of Medjugorje. *Current Issues in Tourism*, *16*(5), 501–506. doi:10.1080/13683500.2012.749844

Al-Thoblany, M. S., & Alyuosef, M. I. (2021). The role of digital management in improving the performance of tourism sectors in the Kingdom of Saudi Arabia in the light of the 2030 vision. *Journal of Sustainable Finance & Investment*, 1-15.

Álvarez-García, J., del Río Rama, M. D. L., & Gómez-Ullate, M. (Eds.). (2018). *Handbook of research on socio-economic impacts of religious tourism and pilgrimage*. IGI Global.

Asadi, M. M., Heidari, M., & Asadian, F. (2016). Forecasting religious tourism demand using an artificial intelligence case study: Mashhad city. *International Journal of Humanities and Cultural Studies*, 1597-1617.

AslanD. (2021). Retrieved from www.dailysabah.com: https://www.dailysabah.com/business/tourism/turkey-develops-new-promotion-platform-strategy-to-enhance-tourism-minister-ersoy-says

Barber, R. (1991). *Pilgrimages*. Boydell & Brewer Ltd.

Breazeale, M. (2009). Word of mouse-An assessment of electronic word-of-mouth research. *International Journal of Market Research*, *51*(3), 1–19. doi:10.1177/147078530905100307

Brown, B., & Chalmers, M. (2003). Tourism and mobile technology. In *ECSCW 2003* (pp. 335–354). Springer. doi:10.1007/978-94-010-0068-0_18

Buzinde, C. N., Kalavar, J. M., Kohli, N., & Manuel-Navarrete, D. (2014). Emic understandings of Kumbh Mela pilgrimage experiences. *Annals of Tourism Research*, *49*, 1–18. doi:10.1016/j.annals.2014.08.001

Çakmak, F., & Dilek, S. (2019). Religion and Tourism in Turkey: An Economically Empirical Study. *Uluslararası İktisadi ve İdari İncelemeler Dergisi*, (22), 209–224.

Cerutti, S., & Piva, E. (2016). The role of tourists' feedback in the enhancement of religious tourism destinations. *International Journal of Religious Tourism and Pilgrimage*, *4*(3), 6-16.

Chayes, S. (2015). *Thieves of state: Why corruption threatens global security*. WW Norton & Company.

Chou, C. H., Chang, N. W., Shrestha, S., Hsu, S. D., Lin, Y. L., Lee, W. H., & Huang, H. D. (2016). miRTarBase 2016: Updates to the experimentally validated miRNA-target interactions database. *Nucleic Acids Research*, *44*(D1), D239–D247. doi:10.1093/nar/gkv1258 PMID:26590260

Cohen, E. (1984). The sociology of tourism: Approaches, issues, and findings. *Annual Review of Sociology*, *10*(1), 373–392. doi:10.1146/annurev.so.10.080184.002105

De Ascaniis, S., & Cantoni, L. (2016). Information and communication technologies in religious tourism and pilgrimage. *International Journal of Religious Tourism and Pilgrimage, 4*(3).

De Ascaniis, S., & Cantoni, L. (2016). Information and communication technologies in religious tourism and pilgrimage. *International Journal of Religious Tourism and Pilgrimage, 4*(3).

Graburn, N. H. (1983). The anthropology of tourism. *Annals of Tourism Research, 10*(1), 9–33. doi:10.1016/0160-7383(83)90113-5

Henderson, J. C. (2011). Religious tourism and its management: The hajj in Saudi Arabia. *International Journal of Tourism Research, 13*(6), 541–552. doi:10.1002/jtr.825

Husain, W., & Dih, L. Y. (2012). A framework of a personalized location-based traveler recommendation system in mobile application. *International Journal of Multimedia and Ubiquitous Engineering, 7*(3), 11–18.

Iriobe, O., & Abiola-Oke, E. (2019). Moderating effect of the use of eWOM on subjective norms, behavioural control and religious tourist revisit intention. *International Journal of Religious Tourism and Pilgrimage, 7*(3).

Ivanov, S., & Webster, C. (2019). Conceptual framework of the use of robots, artificial intelligence and service automation in travel, tourism, and hospitality companies. In *Robots, artificial intelligence, and service automation in travel, tourism and hospitality*. Emerald Publishing Limited. doi:10.1108/978-1-78756-687-320191002

Jalilvand, M. R., Ebrahimi, A., & Samiei, N. (2013). Electronic word of mouth effects on tourists' attitudes toward Islamic destinations and travel intention: An empirical study in Iran. *Procedia: Social and Behavioral Sciences, 81*, 484–489. doi:10.1016/j.sbspro.2013.06.465

Jung, T. H., & Han, D. I. (2014). Augmented Reality (AR) in Urban Heritage Tourism. *e-Review of Tourism Research, 5*.

Kenteris, M., Gavalas, D., & Economou, D. (2009). An innovative mobile electronic tourist guide application. *Personal and Ubiquitous Computing, 13*(2), 103–118. doi:10.100700779-007-0191-y

Khaliq, R. u. (2019). *Turkey ranks 3rd 'halal tourist' destination: Report*. Retrieved from https://www.aa.com.tr/en/turkey/turkey-ranks-3rd-halal-tourist-destination-report/1449385

Kim, B., & Kim, S. S. (2018). Hierarchical value map of religious tourists visiting the Vatican City/Rome. *Tourism Geographies*.

Küçük, M. A. (2013). *İnanç turizmi açısından Türkiye'de dinî mekânlar:(Yahudilik-Hıristiyanlık örneği)*. Berikan Yayınevi.

Maudlin, L. (2019). *Weekly Travel News*. Retrieved from www.tourism-review.com: https://www.tourism-review.com/turkey-could-increase-its-tourism-revenues-news11070

Moaven, Z., Khajenoori, B., Forooghan Geransaieh, Z., & Rayanpour, R. (2017). Globalization of Culture and Religious Tourism. *European Online Journal of Natural and Social Sciences: Proceedings, 6*(1), 1.

Ndivo, R. M., & Cantoni, L. (2016). Rethinking local community involvement in tourism development. *Annals of Tourism Research, 57*, 275–278. doi:10.1016/j.annals.2015.11.014

Nolan, M. L., & Nolan, S. (1992). Religious sites as tourism attractions in Europe. *Annals of Tourism Research, 19*(1), 68–78. doi:10.1016/0160-7383(92)90107-Z

OECD. (2020). *OECD Tourism Trends and Policies 2020*. Retrieved from https://www.oecd-ilibrary.org/sites/f3b16239-en/index.html?itemId=/content/component/f3b16239-en

Okuyucu, A., & Somuncu, M. (2013, May). Türkiye'de inanç turizmi: bugünkü durum, sorunlar ve gelecek. In *International Conference on Religious Tourism and Tolerance* (pp. 9-12). Academic Press.

Pfaffenberger, B. (1983). Serious pilgrims and frivolous tourists the chimera of tourism in the pilgrimages of Sri Lanka. *Annals of Tourism Research, 10*(1), 57–74. doi:10.1016/0160-7383(83)90115-9

Pırnar, İ., & Miral, A. C. (2000). EU tourism policy and Turkey's situation during the adaptation process. *Management, 12*(7), 436.

Qurashi, J., & Sharpley, R. (2018). The impact of Smart Media Technologies on the spiritual experience of Hajj pilgrims. *International Journal of Religious Tourism and Pilgrimage, 6*(3), 37–48.

Raj, R., & Griffin, K. A. (Eds.). (2015). *Religious tourism and pilgrimage management: An international perspective*. Cabi. doi:10.1079/9781780645230.0000

Ramos, C. M., Henriques, C., & Lanquar, R. (2016). Augmented reality for smart tourism in religious heritage itineraries: Tourism experiences in the technological age. In Handbook of Research on Human-Computer Interfaces, Developments, and Applications (pp. 245-272). IGI Global.

Rinschede, G. (1992). Forms of religious tourism. *Annals of Tourism Research, 19*(1), 51–67. doi:10.1016/0160-7383(92)90106-Y

Saayman, A., Saayman, M., & Gyekye, A. (2014). Perspectives on the regional economic value of a pilgrimage. *International Journal of Tourism Research, 16*(4), 407–414. doi:10.1002/jtr.1936

Singh, R. P. (2006). 15 Pilgrimage in Hinduism. *Tourism, religion and spiritual journeys*, 220.

The Smart City Journal. (2020). *Smart Tourism*. Retrieved from www.thesmartcityjournal.com: https://www.thesmartcityjournal.com/en/articles/smart-cities-and-smart-tourism-a-narrative-on-tourism-in-turkey

Tidbits, T. (2014). *The importance of the Religious Tourism Marke*. Retrieved from /www.travelmole.com

Türker, N. (2016). Religious Tourism in Turkey. In *Alternative Tourism in Turkey* (pp. 151–172). Springer. doi:10.1007/978-3-319-47537-0_10

Turkish Statistical Institute (TurkStat). (2012). *Tourism statistics*. http://www.turkstat.gov.tr/Start.do;jsessionid=0TgbWtyF6hxbQF2MhVZ9L4b60H8SWBrFr3dj7HrpfLwfyJMSTLTc!- 982956404

Vukonic, B. (1997). Targeted tourism destinations. *Tourism, development and growth. Challenges in Sustainability*, 86.

Vukonic, B. (2002). Religion, tourism and economics: A convenient symbiosis. *Tourism Recreation Research, 27*(2), 59–64. doi:10.1080/02508281.2002.11081221

Wahyono, I. D., Asfani, K., Mohamad, M. M., Aripriharta, A., Wibawa, A. P., & Wibisono, W. (2020, August). New smart map for tourism using artificial intelligence. In *2020 10th Electrical Power, Electronics, Communications, Controls and Informatics Seminar (EECCIS)* (pp. 213-216). IEEE.

Weking, A. N., & Ndala, S. (2018, November). Analysis Of Mobile Application Smart Religious Tourism. In *2018 3rd International Conference on Information Technology, Information System and Electrical Engineering (ICITISEE)* (pp. 69-73). IEEE. 10.1109/ICITISEE.2018.8720958

World Tourism Organization (UNWTO). (2014). *Tourism highlights 2013*. UNWTO.

Yamin, M. (2019). Managing crowds with technology: cases of Hajj and Kumbh Mela. *International Journal of Information Technology, 11*(2), 229-237.

Chapter 6
ICT and PB Learning Combined for the Advancement of Intercultural Education:
The Case of the MIEC Virtual Exhibition

Sara Cerqueira Pascoal
ISCAP, Polytechnic Institute of Porto, Portugal

Laura Tallone
https://orcid.org/0000-0002-2394-3023
ISCAP, Polytechnic Institute of Porto, Portugal

Marco Furtado
https://orcid.org/0000-0002-5297-1146
ISCAP, Polytechnic Institute of Porto, Portugal

ABSTRACT

This chapter intends to describe the case of the MIEC virtual exhibition as well as reflect upon the relevance of ICT, namely Google Arts and Culture, for the promotion of cultural heritage tourism. In this vein, the authors will first approach the issues of cultural tourism and ICT, exploring how virtual exhibitions and digitization have become an important tool to empower institutions and audiences. Secondly, the authors will present, discuss, and assess the project-based learning (PBL) activities, starting with the presentation of the platform, its advantages and disadvantages for learning and teaching. Then, the authors will analyze some of the results obtained from a pedagogical perspective by scrutinizing students' surveys and opinions. These results will also report on the research outcomes of the project, and an accountability of its marketing purposes will be proposed. The chapter will finally put forward the limitations of this ongoing project and intended future research, suggesting how similar projects can be implemented, managed, and assessed.

DOI: 10.4018/978-1-7998-8165-0.ch006

INTRODUCTION

In the academic year of 2017/2018, the Porto Accounting and Business School (ISCAP), belonging to the Polytechnic Institute of Porto (P.Porto), one of Portugal's largest and most prestigious state-run Polytechnic Institutes, opened a pioneer study program in Portugal, the MA in Intercultural Studies for Business – MaISB. This new program offers in-depth training focused on the business world, in order to develop practical, analytical and critical skills for effective communication between cultures, as well as the profitability of knowledge and entrepreneurship in the field of culture. The program presents an innovative approach to the Humanities, based on interdisciplinary methodologies and the application of ICT. It trains professionals capable of autonomous, efficient and integrated performance in intercultural contexts, able to introduce initiatives for the understanding between cultures into business practice, in line with the new epicenters of economic flows and their agents. The objectives of and competencies fostered by MaISB address the need to design highly specialized output profiles, able to respond to the demands of the global market, and to be incorporated in multinationals, expanding domestic and foreign companies, as well as creative and cultural industries, NGOs, local and national public services, international organizations, e-business and ecommerce, educational institutions, tourism enterprises and international marketing, with a focus on self-employment, by providing consulting, mediation, coaching and training services.

MaISB benefits from the activities of the Centre for Intercultural Studies (CEI)[1], which develops basic and applied research on interculturalism and multiculturalism, with a renewed focus on business studies. CEI is a research associate of Lisbon's Universidade Nova[2] and has collaboration partnerships with numerous universities in Europe, Asia, Africa and the Americas, as well as with companies, networks and international entities based in Portugal. Finally, MaISB provides cultural training focused on the new routes of global economic expansion, granting equal importance to the centers from which cultural matrixes once emanated and to the contemporary postcolonial peripheries (or new centers), aware that center and periphery are now interchangeable concepts, in constant renegotiation. In order for graduates to have high potential for employment in the country and abroad, and also be able to create their own employment, MaISB understands the knowledge of culture as a profitable commodity, as added value to any company with global aspirations, as a tool and subject for business and economic growth.

In this vein, the course units of French, German and Spanish Culture for Business III, and of Intercultural Communication Technologies of MaISB, engage their students in a project-based learning activity, spanning the entire first term of their second year. With the purpose of encouraging reflection on both cultural heritage and the transformation of cultural assets into marketable cultural tourism products, in the academic years of 2017/2018 and of 2018/2019, MaISB students and respective teachers actively participated in the design and curation of a virtual exhibition hosted in the Google Arts & Culture platform, in partnership with the International Museum of Contemporary Art of Santo Tirso (MIEC).

This chapter intends to describe this project as a PBL assignment, while reflecting upon the relevance of ICT, namely a platform like Google Arts & Culture, for the promotion of cultural heritage tourism. In this vein, the issues of Cultural Tourism and New Technologies are approached, exploring how virtual exhibitions and digitization have become an important tool to empower institutions and audiences. In fact, the new pandemic context of COVID-19 has paved the way to the multiplication of virtual tours and the growing use of social media and hashtags to share and classify contents, giving audiences the opportunity to truly engage with the collections contained in museums and other cultural institutions. Secondly, the authors will present, discuss and assess these PBL activities, starting with the presentation of the Google Arts & Culture platform, its advantages and disadvantages for learning and teaching, as well as its efficient management. This discussion will be followed by the presentation of some results, viewed from a pedagogical perspective, as well as of students' opinions and answers to surveys. These results will also report on the research outcomes of the project and, finally, an accountability of its marketing purposes will be proposed, by examining data obtained from the online visit to the virtual exhibition curated by the students. The chapter will finally put forward the limitations of this ongoing project and intended future research, suggesting how similar projects can be implemented, managed and assessed.

CULTURAL HERITAGE TOURISM AND ICT

Given the fundamental role of culture to identify and acknowledge common values, heritage, as an element for the preservation of peoples' cultural bases, contributes to build collective identity, cohesion and a sense of belonging, i.e., "elements that strengthen the social capital indispensable for any sustainable development process" (Cuenin, 2011, p. 1).

This vision of culture, not only as commodity, but as a tool for development, is reflected in the Treaty on the Functioning of the European Union, whose article 167 stresses the importance of cultural heritage and cooperation between member states to encourage artistic creation, heritage conservation and the dissemination of national cultures (TFEU, 2011). On the other hand, the European Commission points out that:

Culture is at the heart of Europe's rich heritage and history and plays an important role in increasing the attractiveness of places and in reinforcing the unique identity of specific spaces. Culture and creativity can be important drivers and drivers of innovation, as well as a significant source for entrepreneurship. Culture is an important driver for increasing tourism revenue, at a time when cultural tourism is one of the fastest growing and fastest growing segments of the world. Culture also has an important role to play in promoting social inclusion (EU, n.d.).

The evidence of the role of culture and heritage in socio-economic development, through the impetus given to entrepreneurship, economic activity related to tourism and job creation, has led to public policies with greater incidence in the cultural sector (Cuenin, 2011, p. 28). Particularly since the 1990s, there has been an increasing amount of investment in the construction, recovery or rehabilitation of equipment, projects for the requalification of cities' historic centers and incentives for community cultural activity.

Museums take on a special role among these initiatives. On the one hand, the monumentality of the constructed space itself may rise as an element of new centrality within the urban context. In fact, museums have been the subject of extraordinary architectural initiatives, as they are among the main attractions for cultural tourism, drivers of the emerging urban destination (Gravari-Barbas, 2017, p. 107). On the other hand, the appeal of museums has been consolidated through new features and functions – to their educational and artistic use one must add their undeniable incorporation into the leisure circuit, whereby "the visit recovers its autotelic value, it is an end in itself, as part of a particular lifestyle associated with hedonistic and touristic behavior" (Mendoza, s / d, p. 437).

In this vein, the use of culture and heritage as an instrumental variable to achieve objectives related to economic development or urban revitalization, namely by locating business projects and encouraging activities related to tourism and the tertiary sector in general, but also as a tool for image projection.

For this purpose, technology plays an essential role – augmented or virtual reality, artificial intelligence and bots are trending in the tourism sector, and particularly relevant for cultural and heritage tourism. However, as cultural institutions rarely have clearly defined business processes, the interaction between museums as customers and IT developers is far from easy. Furthermore, small museums have insufficient human and financial resources to develop a coherent digitization strategy. The introduction of technologies like Google Arts & Culture is dramatically expanding the audience of the cultural sphere, and in tourism it will provide big opportunities for individualizing user experience, leading to larger audiences and wider geographic scope.

Technological development and the spread of smartphones and tablets have contributed to the growth of virtual exhibitions, making it possible to overcome the limitations imposed by physical expositions and to increase users' interactivity, as it is a very efficient solution from an economic point of view.

A virtual exhibition (VE) is a Web-based hypermedia collection of captured or rendered multidimensional information objects, possibly stored in distributed networks, designed around a specific theme, topic concept or idea, and harnessed with state-of-art technology and architecture to deliver the user-centered and engaging experience of discovery, learning, contributing and being entertained through its nature of its dynamic product and service offerings (Foo, 2008, p. 23).

If virtual exhibitions have in the past been criticized for their lack of "real experience", today technological development allows for immersion and interactivity solutions that should not be neglected. The potential for the virtualization of national and international heritage and treasures has been already highlighted (Lester, 2006), since museums and archive collections are thus not limited by temporal, spatial, or geographical constraints. Anyone, at any time, can access the contents on display, making the most of the artefacts shown to a growing number of audiences.

Virtual exhibitions have the advantage of providing free access to collections that would otherwise remain unknown or hidden from view. Several museums and institutions have therefore created digital collections and virtual visits to their estates, combining these visits with educational strategies in order to promote the institutions. These strategies often work as encouragement for the actual visit, as reminders of previous physical visits (which may thus be completed through digitized information), or, during lockdown periods since March 2020, as a way of providing access even though the venue is closed. In fact, the mission of museums has changed dramatically over the past few years. Formerly, the main mission of museums was the preservation and safekeeping of precious works of art, heritage or cultural heritage, whereas nowadays, as already pointed out, museums have taken on educational and recreational roles (Gombault, 2003).

To this end, institutions must focus on strengthening their image and branding through promotional and marketing campaigns, which must necessarily use not only traditional means, such as publications, lectures and symposia, but also through the strategic organization of properly planned and executed virtual exhibitions. Such an approach may also contribute to highlighting the institutional relevance and the social value of the organization, therefore creating a strong public profile. In turn, increasing the visibility and brand of the institution can be used to help ensure adequate funding and other resources, vital for their sustainability and future growth.

Based on these premises, MaISB students were challenged to become curators of a virtual exhibition of the collection of the Santo Tirso's Museum of Contemporary Sculpture hosted at Google Arts &

ICT and PB Learning Combined for the Advancement of Intercultural Education

Culture platform for the MIEC, using PBL as a strategy to combine ICT with cultural tourism marketing strategies.

PBL, GOOGLE AND MIEC

Santo Tirso is a small city located in the Porto Metropolitan area, surrounded by valleys and mountains and deeply connected to the river Ave. The richness of the region's natural resources is complemented with a very important historical and cultural legacy, made up of archaeological wealth, religious and secular traditions, monuments and sites and a fine regional cuisine of characteristic flavors. Its industry-centered economy, based on textiles and plastics, has been trying to diversify itself, spreading to areas like tourism, making the most of the strategic location of the city and of the importance of its cultural heritage, like the Santo Tirso's S. Bento Monastery, founded in the tenth century, but also on new tourist attractions, like the International Museum of Contemporary Sculpture, MIEC, whose visitor's center, opened in 2016, was designed by Pritzker winners Eduardo Souto de Moura and Álvaro Siza Vieira.

Featuring artists from all over the globe, from China to Argentina, 57 artworks are distributed all over Santo Tirso, turning the entire town into a true open-air museum. Within an area roughly covering 20 sq. km., artists of more than twenty different nationalities from four continents are represented, bringing to Santo Tirso a wide variety of discourses and providing "samples" of the most significant contemporary art trends and schools. This diversity allowed the students involved in the virtual exhibition project to select a corpus directly related to the country or region under study, and to focus on the relationship between cultural assets and the economic and social advancement of a particular geographical area.

In order to fully develop its potential, MIEC has already held a considerable number of cultural events since the day of its opening. Contrary to several examples found in Portugal, in which the initial investment in infrastructure is not followed by a consistent program of activities, MIEC has succeeded in presenting a series of initiatives, such as temporary exhibitions, educational programs, lectures, performances, etc., the quality of which shows the commitment to turning the town into a cultural reference of more than local scope. This fact partly explains the warm enthusiasm with which MIEC has welcomed and embraced the Google Arts & Culture project, a very relevant aspect in what concerns MaISB and its students, as the institutional support provided by MIEC included unrestricted access to the museum's documentary material. In return, MaISB students were able to curate a virtual exhibition of MIEC's collection for the Google Arts & Culture platform, collaborating in a strategic plan to promote Santo Tirso, thus helping a small city Museum to participate in a project that intends to promote cultural tourism and to make the Museum's collection accessible to the widest possible audience.

The Google Arts and Culture Platform

In the new millennium, the introduction to digitization and the Internet has brought about an enormous availability of archives of images and multimedia documents, which have paved the way to several experimental projects aimed at attracting the general public's attention to cultural heritage. Google Arts & Culture's mission is to help museums by making new technologies available to partner institutions.

The Google Cultural Institute was created in 2011[3], following the launch of the Google Arts & Culture, formerly known as Google Art Project. It aims at disseminating cultural material and making cultural heritage digitally available and accessible to anyone with an Internet connection. As explained by Sood (2011), Head of the former "Google Art Project", the platform

[…] started when a small group of us who were passionate about art got together to think about how we might use our technology to help museums make their art more accessible—not just to regular museum-goers or those fortunate to have great galleries on their doorsteps, but to a whole new set of people who might otherwise never get to see the real thing up close.

Parented by Google, the Google Arts & Culture has partnered with several museums around the world. By using street view technology, the platform provides free virtual visits to some of the world's most important art collections. While "rambling" through the galleries, visitors may also see high-resolution images of selected artworks from each museum. According to Google, its relationship with the institutions is not ruled by any curatorial imposition, and each museum may choose the number of galleries, artworks and information to be made available.

As for the Portuguese cultural heritage, it was only at the end of 2017 that the Portuguese government acknowledged the importance of the Google Arts & Culture platform regarding the potential visibility of the Portuguese cultural heritage. The partnership between the Ministry of Culture, through Direção-Geral do Património Cultural (DGPC), with Google Arts & Culture, was initially planned to make the collections of seven national museums available online, namely Museu de Arqueologia, Museu de Arte Antiga, Museu de Arte Contemporânea-Museu do Chiado, Museu Nacional do Traje, Museu do Teatro e da Dança, Museu do Azulejo and Museu dos Coches, all of them in Lisbon.

"Portugal: Art & Heritage"[4] by Google Arts & Culture is a project launched in 2017 by the Ministry of Culture and the DGPCP. Twenty-two national institutions made their collections available, and more than 3,000 artworks were captured by Google's Art Camera, a technology capable of super high-resolution digitization, thus allowing viewers to see details on the Web that might otherwise not be made out. "The Great Panorama of Lisbon" is one of the examples, a huge panel contained in the Tile Museum that can virtually be seen to the minutest detail on Google's website. In addition to 60 purposely created exhibitions, there are also 20 new virtual reality tours, thus acknowledging the rising importance of cultural digitalization for the promotion of Portuguese cultural heritage.

As the Google Cultural Institute (2018) points out, "magic happens when technology meets culture". In fact, the creation of Google Arts & Culture platform and its consequent innovative technology previously mentioned, lets users, from all around the globe, "discover artworks, collections and stories… like never before" (*idem*). Ultimately, the platform encourages users and cultural institutions to curate and share with the world their own collections of art, landmarks and historical events.

A similar project to the one described in this chapter had already been put in place at the Faculty of Arts and Humanities of the University of Porto (FLUP), under the MA in History of Portuguese Art at FLUP, bringing together teachers and students from two mandatory course units: Project Seminar I and Project Seminar II (Botelho, Rosas, & Barreira, 2017). In 2015, FLUP launched its first exhibition, entitled "Porto Património Mundial" (*idem*), whereas its second exhibition, "Sabrosa: Território e Património", was launched a year later, in September of 2016. Both exhibitions disseminated their results in bilingual format (Portuguese and English) and presented two sites inscribed on UNESCO's World Heritage List (*idem*). Since then, FLUP has added 4 more exhibitions and a great deal of digital material to its virtual catalogue.

ICT and PB Learning Combined for the Advancement of Intercultural Education

In spite of the variety and richness of its collection, MIEC is undeniably a small-town institution, subject to the constraints of limited human and material resources. On the other hand, MaISB teachers and students alike saw in MIEC a unique opportunity to carry out a cooperation project, in which both parties profited from the other's skills and means. That was the beginning of an ongoing initiative which, in addition to giving further visibility to Santo Tirso, led to a project-based learning activity spanning two years and branching into several pedagogic outcomes, the most relevant being the virtual exhibition of MIEC's collection at Google Arts & Culture platform (See Figure 1).

Figure 1. Entry page to MIEC's virtual exhibition at the Google Arts & Culture platform

When choosing a PBL strategy, we in fact attempted to meet one of the general objectives of the MaISB, namely the development of entrepreneurship skills linked to the creative industries, in which culture is seen as a profitable commodity that may be used for socioeconomic development. PBL, as has been shown in the literature (Almula, 2020), is an effective teaching-learning, student-centered strategy to promote active and in-depth learning by engaging students in real research and a collaborative environment. As argued by Bell (2010, p. 39):

Project-Based Learning (PBL) is an innovative approach to learning that teaches the multitude of critical strategies for success in the twenty-first century. Students drive their own learning through inquiry, as well as work collaboratively to research and create projects that reflect their knowledge. From gleaning new, viable technology skills, to becoming proficient communicators and advanced problem solvers, students benefit from this approach to instruction.

The adoption of a PBL methodology involving the curation of a virtual exhibition of the MIEC collection in the Google Arts & Culture platform fulfills the following objectives: (1) to involve its members – MaISB students and teachers – in an in-depth and collaborative research project; (2) to provide an opportunity to explore multiple perspectives of a certain topic; (3) to inform about the purpose and general guidelines of the International Museum of Contemporary Sculpture of Santo Tirso and its collection; and (4) to cooperate with others to foster communication and sharing of information and experiences, namely teachers, museum professionals, artists, etc. (Dumitrescu et al., 2014, p. 103). The results and assessment of this project are presented in the next section.

RESULTS AND LIMITATIONS

Pedagogical Results

Methods

The assessment of the PBL activity employed an approach combining the collection and analysis of quantitative and qualitative data (Creswell, 2009).

In order to analyze the project from a pedagogical point of view, a questionnaire comprising 13 questions assessed the quality of PBL implementation from the students' perspective. The respondents were recent MaISB graduates, who completed the survey in May 2020, i.e., 6 to 18 months after graduation.

Throughout the project and at the end of the semester, teachers also recorded students' opinions, criticism and self- and peer assessment. The aim was to examine students' perceptions and insights about project implementation and outcomes, to grasp which skills they had developed, what views they had about the project, as well as find out and compare their expectations at the beginning and the results at the end. It also aimed at briefly examining how students' perspectives of the PBL outcomes relate with and respond to the objectives previously outlined.

The questionnaire, developed using Google Forms, was distributed by e-mail to all the students involved in the PBL assignment (see Appendix 1). It consisted of 11 closed-ended questions using a five Likert scale (Strongly disagree, Disagree, Neither agree nor disagree, Agree, Strongly agree) and two open questions, asking for a description of the project in 3 to 6 keywords and an overall assessment of the PBL. Out of 26 students, a total of 13 (50%) responded to the survey and the relatively small size of the sample is one of the limitations of this study. The other is the recent nature of this PBL which provides a still limited amount of experiences and data for analysis.

Data Analysis

Overall, the answers to the survey clearly show that students found the project very interesting and useful (Figure 2).

From the opinions collected, two major arguments seem to explain the students' interest in and positive perception of the project's relevance. On the one hand, students expressed their enthusiasm for pursuing a real project, with a platform of great visibility such as Google:

From the start I felt involved with this project. I found that to produce something that can be accessed, in 'real life', was so interesting and that it could serve as a great experiment and experience (Student 1).

On the other hand, the possibility of making their work known to a wider audience also seems to have been a strong motivation:

Overall, I considered the 'MIEC for Google Arts & Cultures' project quite interesting, since I was not very familiar with this particular product of Google, and it sure made me more aware of all the potential it has. It was also a matter of pride, I guess, because not every day we are presented with the possibility to share something that comes from Portugal with the whole wide world. (Student 2).

ICT and PB Learning Combined for the Advancement of Intercultural Education

Figure 2. Interest of the PBL

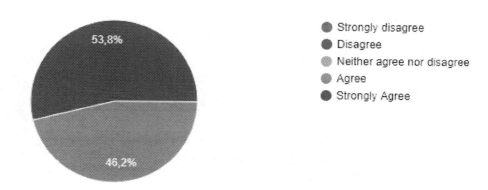

A large majority of the students (76.9%) believed that the project helped them develop creative thinking (Figure 3), which, in fact, was one of the goals outlined, and is aligned with MaISB objectives. Indeed, one of the purposes of the use of a PBL strategy was to provide an opportunity to explore multiple perspectives of a certain topic, thus developing creativity and innovation skills.

Figure 3. Promotion of creative thinking by the PBL

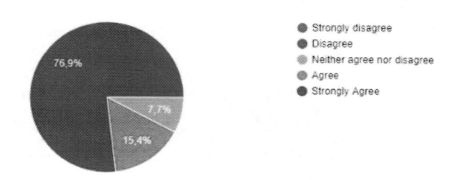

Even if it was initially felt as confusing by students, given the interdisciplinary nature of the tasks (Figure 4), their involvement in a PBL strategy was overall rewarding, as pointed out by one of the students:

Regarding the process and dynamics of the project, I believe that receiving feedback from some of my colleagues and giving feedback was of the uttermost importance since I could have an idea on how to follow a common pattern. (Student 3).

Figure 4. Interdisciplinary nature of the PBL

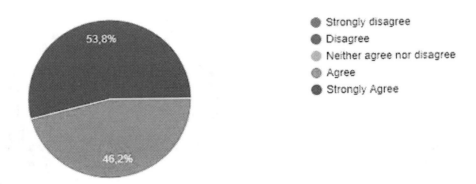

The interdisciplinary nature of this PBL was also described with mixed feelings by some students, as they found it confusing and time-consuming, although they also felt that they were expanding their understanding and achievement among disciplines.

Figure 5. Technology skills required by the PBL

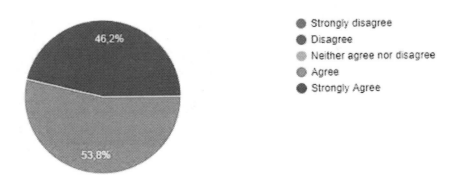

One of the main objectives of the PBL activity was, as mentioned above, to integrate new technologies into the development of cultural tourism and the promotion of MIEC and the town of Santo Tirso. Working with a platform like Google Arts & Culture involves working with Google technology, like Google Street View and high-resolution images, experiencing it up close, as the Google art project allows you to see the stunning details in a quite unique way (Figure 5).

Certainly, creating a virtual exhibition for Google also involves using image and video editing software. In order to help develop student's skills, three masterclasses were conducted, dealing with Adobe Premiere, Adobe Photoshop and Creative Writing. In addition to these masterclasses, digital storytelling was one of the main subjects of the curriculum. As shown in Figure 6, a large majority of the surveyed students acknowledged having developed technology skills. 23.1% neither agreed nor disagreed with the statement on Question 10, and 7.7% (one student) even felt it did not help at all. This was a particular case of a student who already had vast experience with the use of ICT.

Figure 6. Development of technology skills

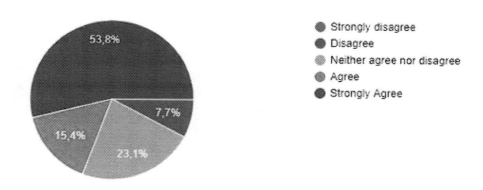

Overall, the final assessment of the project appears to have been clearly positive, as one of the students involved remarked:

Overall, I must say that my expectations didn't fall short from the reality. I admit that in the beginning of this project I felt a little bit lost, not knowing what path to follow or what direction this assignment would take, but soon it all changed, when we received the material from the museum, as I had plenty of information to rely on, and some general guidelines from the professors involved. A huge factor that played an important role on the making of this project was the visit we took to the museum. In my opinion, it was the tipping point where we students, as a whole, could figure out what we were headed for. Seeing the sculptures live and hearing the explanation of the museum's guide really made me more comfortable and motivated to work on this assignment. Nonetheless, the communication between the professors and students could not have been more balanced, as all of us, in my opinion, had the time to express their vision and outlook on certain aspects and receive feedback, both from the professors and the students. Also, the professors were very appreciative of the ideas and feedback students had to offer. Generally, the outcome of this project was exceptionally positive. I will certainly be glad to be part of this project in a near future, as I feel that I want to accomplish and see, in fact, the information being uploaded to the Google Arts & Culture, with the input that I've developed. (Student 4)

When asked to summarize in 3 keywords what they thought about the project, students also seemed very much aware not only of the potential of the Google Arts & Culture Platform to promote a small city like Santo Tirso, but also to encourage cultural tourism and to generate visits, either virtual or physical, to MIEC's exceptional collection (see Figure 7).

Figure 7. Keywords of the PBL according to students

12. Describe in 3 to 6 keywords the best of the project

10 respostas

Cultural, Promotion, Discovery, Requalifying

The research part, learning creative writing and being able to be creative

Cultural, good for storytelling skills development

Know more about a cultural project loke google arts & culture.

Culture, dissemination of knowledge, technology

Work With Art

Making art otherwise unknown/undiscovered available worldwide

Learning about Santo Tirso and the sculptures.

visibility; accessibility; promoting local cultural attractions;

It is worth pointing out that the students' involvement in the experience has materialized in a considerable number of already published academic papers (Pascoal, Tallone, Furtado & Ribeiro, 2018, 2019, 2020, 2021). In addition, two master's theses related to the MIEC exhibit deal with the technological

ICT and PB Learning Combined for the Advancement of Intercultural Education

aspects of the design of virtual exhibitions (Costa, 2018), as well as with creative writing and storytelling strategies for the construction of compelling narratives (Marques, 2020).

Virtual Exhibition Assessment: Improved Visibility of MEIC's and Santo Tirso

MIEC's virtual exhibition hosted at Google Arts & Culture is intended to offer suitable conditions for what has become known as "tourist experience", which, following the definition provided by Pine and Gilmore (1999), includes a "set of activities in which individuals engage on personal terms". In fact, the visit made by MaISB students in October 2017 proved that both the museum and its surroundings were capable of catering for a wide variety of interests and expectations - from direct contact with and deeper understanding of contemporary art to a casual stroll through the streets and parks of Santo Tirso. In addition, this exhibition will hopefully draw attention to Santo Tirso and include this small and dynamic Portuguese town in a possible tourist route devoted to contemporary art and particularly to public sculpture.

First introduced during the 1990s, place branding and marketing is a very important strategy used by big cities, aimed at developing their competitiveness and success. According to Baker (2007, p. 19), "the level of esteem that a city's name evokes has a direct impact on the health of its tourism, economic development, prestige and respect". Therefore, a city's name and reputation should be recognized, appreciated and managed. This applies to cities of all sizes, but is even more relevant in the case of smaller ones, driven by the changing paradigms in economy and tourism, in which new emerging styles of consumption seem to shift from standardization to different, authentic and unique experiences. The cultural turn in economy and tourism, followed by a creative turn (Richards, 2011), indeed related to globalization and commodification, has led to the development of economic strategies in which culture and creativity play a relevant role in the branding of cities in constant competition in order to promote growth by using innovation and technology.

According to "Portugal's City Brand Ranking" (Bloom Consulting, 2019), Santo Tirso is ranked number 48 out of the 308 Portuguese municipalities. In just five years, from 2013 to 2018, Santo Tirso rose 12 positions at the national level. At a regional context, Santo Tirso is now number 16 out of the 86 northern municipalities. The primary objective of this ranking is to measure the national and international impact borne by perceptions and reputation over time in each country or place brand, taking three different categories into consideration – business, talent and tourism. These results seem to confirm the enormous economic and tourist potential of this small city, enhanced by a powerful promotion strategy, which is emphasized by the city's former mayor, Joaquim Couto: "we have developed a set of policies around the well-being of the people of Santo Tirso and of those who visit us, and this is further evidence that we are on the right track" (CMST, 2017). Santo Tirso has risen to prominent positions in all the indicators analyzed, due to low unemployment and crime rates as well as to growing purchasing power, hotel occupancy rate and rising investment. "Tourism, investment and commitment to quality of life allow us to promote the Municipality and attract businesses and visitors," explains Joaquim Couto, adding that "the Santo Tirso brand is increasingly recognized across borders, as a result of large-scale initiatives like the Easter Market, or cultural initiatives like the International Museum of Contemporary Sculpture" (*idem*).

Of course, the Google Arts & Culture platform also has some limitations. Udell (2019) has conducted a study, in which she analyses Google Arts & Culture within the context of larger museum trends in virtuality, and interviewed museum professionals responsible for their institutions' virtual presence, with the purpose of giving museums more insight into what the platform can reasonably accomplish within their specific institutions. As Udell (2019, pp. 32-33) points out:

Some museums—smaller institutions in particular—have found the uploading process troublesome and, as such, have far fewer objects in their collections. Some of these issues are workflow related, as in the case of one curator of a historical archive. (…) Other museums have had trouble integrating their collections into the platform because of their content or format. (…) Others use the platform as a stopgap in order to give their visitors access to collections while updating or developing their own museum websites and collections portals. (…) Other museums use the exhibits similarly to how they share collections on the platform, to showcase items and information that cannot be physically viewed at the museum.

Overall, Udell concludes that smaller institutions do not report as much satisfaction with Google Arts & Culture and cannot sustain the partnership for extended periods of time because of the strain on museum resources. As shown by the statistical data provided by the platform itself, the PBL project seems to overcome some of these constraints while it capacitates students with entrepreneurship, creativity and technology skills.

Data Regarding Online Visits to MIEC's Virtual Exhibition

This section deals with some data regarding visits to the virtual exhibition, considering numbers and figures retrieved from the Google Arts & Culture platform for the period from the launch of the exhibit, in mid-October 2019, to April 2021. The following analysis is mainly focused on the total number of page views and viewers[6], bearing as well in mind lockdown and non-lockdown periods due to the current COVID-19 pandemic – represented respectively by red and blue columns or lines in the figures below (the period before the pandemic is represented in light green). Even though lockdown measures have been defined differently and individually by each country's government and healthcare administrations, the analysis will include the months of March, April, October, November, December 2020, and January and February 2021 as a general lockdown period, while the rest of the months will be regarded as those in which restrictions may have been lifted or loosened (Figures 8 and 9).

During the first two weeks after the launch of the online exhibition (mid-October 19), over 200 viewers visited more than 300 of its items on the Google Arts & Culture platform. As also shown in Figures 8 and 9, an almost tenfold increase in the number of page views and viewers was recorded during the following month, having these numbers reached their highest peak during the period under analysis. The fairly high number of page views and viewers recorded in the first two months of the virtual exhibit may be related to its novelty, which might have aroused the curiosity and interest of regular visitors to the Google Arts & Culture platform. It might as well have been the result of direct and indirect dissemination carried out by partner institutions and stakeholders taking part in the project[7].

After having generally plummeted in the following three months (December 2019 and January and February 2020), numbers of both page views and viewers started to rise again in March and April 2020. This substantial increase coincided with a first mandatory lockdown period of the population worldwide, to contain the spread of the COVID-19 outbreak. The compulsory closure of public and private institutions, including museums and art galleries, turned online exhibitions into practically the only way of accessing artworks on public display.

Figure 8. Number of page views

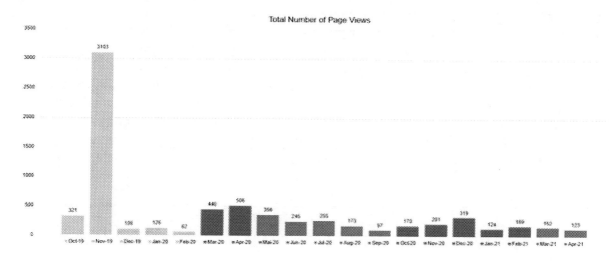

Figure 9. Number of viewers

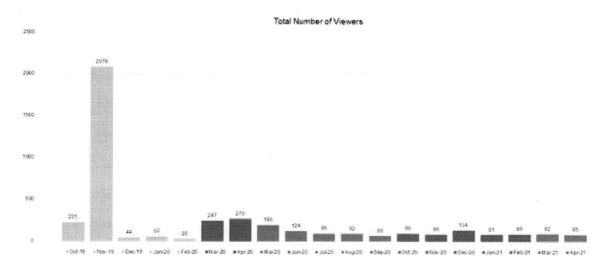

As seen in both charts above (Figures 8 and 9), the number of page views and viewers started to decrease in the late Spring and Summer months in 2020, i.e. between May and September. This may be linked to the fact that from May 2020 onwards, many countries (including Portugal) began to lift lockdown rules. As MIEC hosts a permanent physical open-air exhibition, visitors to the exhibition would not be exclusively limited to a virtual platform to have access to the museum's collection but could have chosen to visit the exhibition on site.

It should also be pointed out that during the following Autumn and Winter months, the numbers start to rise again, especially those related to page views. A possible reason for this pattern may be found in the colder weather, which discourages physical visits to open-air venues – both domestic and international tourists may have preferred to visit the exhibit on the Google Arts & Culture platform, particularly in December 2020, when 134 viewers visited more than 300 items of the MIEC virtual exhibit. It may, however, be related to another confinement period adopted by many countries, since numbers of confirmed COVID-19 cases with new variants of the SARS-CoV-2 virus began to rise significantly. Although the number of viewers are somehow stable when comparing the last two months of the lockdown period (January and February 2021) with the following months, when restrictions started to be gradually lifted again (March and April 2021), the number of page views start to fall once more: fewer viewers were recorded in April 2021, probably due to the fact that cultural institutions and venues started reopening their doors, and physical exhibitions during the second half of that month became accessible again.

Figure 10. Number of viewers (lockdown and non-lockdown periods)

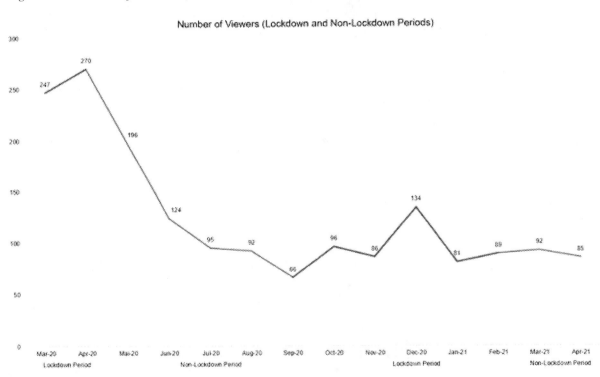

As shown in Figure 10, the numbers of viewers to MIEC's virtual exhibit on the Google Arts & Culture platform is generally higher during a lockdown period than during a period in which no restrictions have been imposed. It is also visible that there is a tendency for the numbers of viewers to rise during lockdown periods, whereas numbers during lighter restrictions generally decrease or stay stable. The comparison of the total numbers of visitors to the virtual exhibit in both lockdown and non-lockdown periods clearly shows more viewers accessing MIEC's exhibition on the Google Arts & Culture platform during lockdown periods, as shown in Figure 11:

Figure 11. Total number of viewers (14-month period)

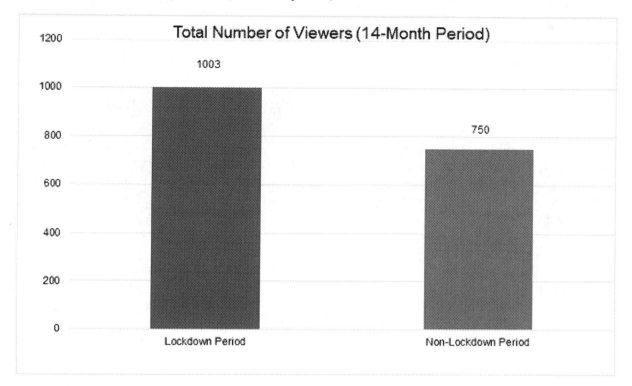

CONCLUSION

The implementation of an interdisciplinary PBL approach, involving students, teachers and external institutions, such as MIEC, in the design of a virtual exhibition on the Google Arts & Culture platform, meets training requirements that respond to the demands of the market, by engaging students in the creation and management of a project combining technology, cultural entrepreneurship and creative industries. Taking as a starting point MIEC's exceptional collection, students were challenged to investigate the concept of public art in more depth, as well as its connection with the surrounding space and the target audience. They also had to create a narrative that would support the presentation and curation of a virtual exhibition, with the purpose of promoting and providing access to the collection of this Museum to a wider audience. Then, they had to understand and make use of technology to market and create a digital story, involving the know-how behind the Google Art & Culture platform works, and using Adobe Photoshop and Premiere to create a digital story. At the end of the PBL assignment, they experienced the sense of accomplishment provided by participating in a genuine project and carrying out a real task with measurable effects in publicizing the Museum and learning about culture, arts and technology. In addition, the Google Arts & Culture platform has the advantage of providing gigapixel images, allowing for the creation of virtual exhibitions that are not limited to recreating the physical museum but work as an extension of the cultural and tourist experience.

Among the thirteen advantages of virtual exhibitions listed by INDICATE (2012), it is worth pointing out those which further complement the study previously conducted, such as the promotion of the cultural heritage contained in the institution, the access to more material than that which is actually on public display, the possibility of more detailed observation of the pieces, their low cost, the access to people from all over the world, and the absence of physical or time constraints[8]. Throughout the PBL project, students had the opportunity to confirm these advantages hand, thus making the sometimes difficult connection between theory and practice.

By partnering with Google, all stakeholders involved, including students, teachers and institutions, expect to pursue research and contribute to develop new stories about Northern Portugal's cultural heritage, promoting cultural tourism initiatives and empowering local communities, by fostering employment and sustainability. As Google Arts & Culture continues to provide ready-to-use and constantly updated technology to cultural institutions, these may now increasingly make use of the next focus of the platform, after the development of Augmented and Virtual reality technologies (AR and VR). The PBL project initiated in 2017 may thus find its logical continuity, by incorporating these features, thus providing students with the opportunity of experiencing the latest tools for the design of virtual exhibitions, as well as offering smaller institutions like MIEC the most appropriate "window" to show its unique collection.

REFERENCES

Almula, M. A. (2020). The Effectiveness of the Project-Based Learning (PBL) Approach as a Way to Engage Students in Learning. *SAGE Open*, 1–15. https://journals.sagepub.com/doi/full/10.1177/2158244020938702

Baker, B. (2007). *Destination Branding for small cities: the essentials for successful place branding*. Creative Leap Books.

Bell, S. (2010). Project-based learning for the 21st century: Skills for the future. *The Clearing House: A Journal of Educational Strategies, Issues and Ideas, 83*(2), 39–43. doi:10.1080/00098650903505415

Bloom Consulting. (2019). *Portugal City Brand Ranking*. Available at https://www.bloomconsulting.com/pt/pdf/rankings/Bloom_Consulting_City_Brand_Ranking_Portugal.pdf

Botelho, M. L., Rosas, L., & Barreira, H. (2017). Designing exhibitions at Google Cultural Institute: between pedagogical experiences and the creation of heritage diffusion products. *Libro de Actas V Congresso Internacional Cidades Criativas, CITCEM / Icono14*, 128-138.

CMST – Câmara Municipal de Santo Tirso. (2017). *MIEC já é uma referência nacional e internacional*. Available at: https://www.cm-stirso.pt/noticia/miec-e-ja-uma-referencia-nacional-e-internacional

Costa, H. (2018). *Designing a Virtual Exhibitions for Google Arts & Culture: Public Art, Tecnhology and Intercultural Communication* (Master's thesis). Available at https://recipp.ipp.pt/bitstream/10400.22/12646/1/Hugo_Costa_MISB_2018.pdf

Creswell, J. W. (2009). *Research design: Qualitative, quantitative, and mixed methods approaches* (3rd ed.). Sage Publications, Inc.

Cuenin, F. (2011). *Patrimonio cultural y desarrollo socioeconómico: la recuperación de áreas centrales históricas*. BID – Banco Interamericano de Desarrollo. Available at: https://publications.iadb.org/es/publicacion/13208/patrimonio-cultural-y-desarrollo-socioeconomico-la-recuperacion-de-areas

Dumitrescu, G., Lepadatu, C., & Ciuera, C. (2014). Creating virtual Exhibitions for Educational and Cultural Development. *Informações Econômicas*, *18*(1/2014), 102–110. doi:10.12948/issn14531305/18.1.2014.09

EU – European Commission. (n.d.). *Culture*. Available at: https://ec.europa.eu/regional_policy/en/policy/themes/culture/

Foo, S. (2008). Online virtual exhibitions: Concepts and design considerations. *Bulletin of Information Technology*, *28*(4), 22–34.

Gombault, A. (2003). La nouvelle identité organisationnelle des musées. Le cas du Louvre. *Revue française de gestion*, *142*, 189-203. Available at https://www.cairn.info/revue-francaise-de-gestion-2003-1.html

Google. (2018). *Partners*. Available at Google Cultural Institute: https://www.google.com/culturalinstitute/about/partners/

Gravari-Barbas, M. (2018). Arquitectura, museos, turismo: la guerra de las marcas (A. Ávila-Gómez & D.C. Ruiz-Robayo, Trans.). *Revista de Arquitectura*, *20*(1), 102-114. Available at: https://www.researchgate.net/publication/325978618_Arquitectura_museos_turismo_la_guerra_de_las_marcas

INDICATE. (2012, August). *Handbook on virtual exhibitions and virtual performances*. Available at: www.indicate-project.eu/getFile.php?id=412

Marques, A. (2020). *Using Storytelling and Creative writing for the virtual promotion of Arts & Culture* (Master's thesis). Available at: https://recipp.ipp.pt/handle/10400.22/17528

Mendoza, M. L. (n.d.). *Museo y Ocio. Nuevos paradigmas para el museo del siglo XXI*. Biblioteca Digital da Faculdade de Letras da Universidade do Porto. Available at: https://ler.letras.up.pt/uploads/ficheiros/10372.pdf

Pascoal, S., Tallone, L., & Furtado, M. (2020). Cultural Tourism: using Google Arts & Culture platform to promote a small city in the North of Portugal. In *Advances in Tourism, Technology and Smart Systems, Smart Innovations, Systems and Technology 171* (pp. 47–56). Springer Nature Singapore. doi:10.1007/978-981-15-2024-2_5

Pascoal, S., Tallone, L., & Furtado, M. (2021). The Impact of COVID-19 on Cultural Tourism: Virtual Exhibitions, Technology and Innovation. In *Advances in Tourism, Technology and Smart Systems - Proceedings of ICOTTS'20* (vol. 2). Singapore: Springer.

Pascoal, S., Tallone, L., Furtado, M., & Ribeiro, S. (2018). Marketing public Art: using project based learning to teach creativity and entrepreneurship. In *Polissema 18 Revista de Letras do ISCAP, S. Mamede Infesta*. Instituto Superior de Contabilidade e Administração do Porto. Available at: https://parc.ipp.pt/index.php/Polissema/article/view/3203

Pascoal, S., Tallone, L., Furtado, M., & Ribeiro, S. (2019), Promover o património cultural através do empreendedorismo e da criatividade: o projeto Google Arts & Culture. In *Sensos-E, Revista Multimédia de Investigação em Educação*. InED - Centro de Investigação e Inovação em Educação, da Escola Superior de Educação do Instituto Politécnico do Porto. Available at: https://parc.ipp.pt/index.php/sensos/article/view/3038/1497

Pine, B. J., & Gilmore, J. H. (1999). *The experience economy: work is theatre & every business a stage*. Harvard Business School.

Richards, G. (2011). Creativity and tourism: The state of the art. *Annals of Tourism Research*, 38(4), 1225–1253. doi:10.1016/j.annals.2011.07.008

Sood, A. (2011, February 1). *Explore museums and great works of art in the Google Art Project*. Available at: https://googleblog.blogspot.com/2011/02/explore-museums-and-great-works-of-art

TFEU - Treaty on the Functioning of the European Union. (2011). Available at: https://eur-lex.europa.eu/legal-content/EN/TXT/HTML/?uri=CELEX:12012E/TXT&from=EN

Udell, M. K. (2019). *The Museum of the Infinite Scroll: Assessing the Effectiveness of Google Arts and Culture as a Virtual Tool for Museum Accessibility* (Master's thesis). University of San Francisco. Available at: https://repository.usfca.edu/capstone/979

Zucconi, F. (2018). Heritage and Digital Technology: Google Arts & Culture. Cartaditalia, Rivista di cultura italiana contemporanea, 9(2), 350-361.

KEY TERMS AND DEFINITIONS

Culture Commoditization: Process of transforming cultural assets in a commodity, for commercial purposes.

Google Arts and Culture: An online platform of high-resolution images and videos of artworks and cultural artifacts from partner cultural organizations throughout the world.

Interculturalism: Involves moving beyond mere passive acceptance of a multicultural fact of multiple cultures effectively existing in a society and additionally promotes dialogue and interaction between cultures.

MIEC: The International Museum of Contemporary Art of Santo Tirso, conceived as a forum for dialogue between different contemporary art trends, as well as for debating and disseminating public sculpture. MIEC comprises 57 sculptures distributed across the town of Sato Tirso, created by 53 distinct artists, from more than 20 nationalities giving shape to an authentic open space museum.

Multiculturalism: The co-existence of diverse cultures, where culture includes racial, religious, or cultural groups and is manifested in customary behaviors, cultural assumptions and values, thinking patterns, and communicative styles.

PBL: A teaching and learning methodology in which students learn and develop skills by engaging and responding to real-life, authentic complex questions, problems, or challenges.

Virtual Exhibition: A Web-based hypermedia collection of captured or rendered multidimensional information objects, designed around a specific theme, topic concept or idea.

ENDNOTES

[1] https://www.iscap.pt/cei/
[2] https://ielt.fcsh.unl.pt/comissao-executiva/

ICT and PB Learning Combined for the Advancement of Intercultural Education

3   Initially with only 17 museums as partners, when the second phase of the project was launched in April 2012, the number of digitized collections had grown to 151.

4   https://artsandculture.google.com/project/portugal-art-and-heritage

5   Virtual exhibition available at: https://artsandculture.google.com/exhibit/museu-internacional-de-escultura-contempor%C3%A2nea/xAISBGFGJpdILg

6   A unique viewer may have, during one visit, several page views on the platform.

7   For the involvement of stakeholders, see: Google Arts&Culture lança online a página do ISCAP e a primeira exposição virtual — ISCAP | P.PORTO (ipp.pt), Google Arts&Culture lança exposição virtual do ISCAP — P.PORTO | Ensino Superior Público (ipp.pt), CEI cria parceria com o Google Cultural Institute — ISCAP | P.PORTO (ipp.pt)

8   For a full list of the advantages of virtual exhibitions, see INDICATE, 2012, p. 19.

APPENDIX

Google Arts & Culture and MIEC PBL Assessment Survey:

1 - I found the Google Arts & Project very interesting
    Strongly disagree
    Disagree
    Neither agree nor disagree
    Agree
    Strongly agree

2 - I think the project was very useful
    Strongly disagree
    Disagree
    Neither agree nor disagree
    Agree
    Strongly agree

3 - The project promotes creative thinking
    Strongly disagree
    Disagree
    Neither agree nor disagree
    Agree
    Strongly agree

4 - The project promotes entrepreneurship
    Strongly disagree
    Disagree
    Neither agree nor disagree
    Agree
    Strongly agree

5- The project requires the use of multiple interdisciplinary skills
    Strongly disagree
    Disagree

Neither agree nor disagree
   Agree
   Strongly agree
6 - The project requires research skills
   Strongly disagree
   Disagree
   Neither agree nor disagree
   Agree
   Strongly agree
7 - The project requires creative writing skills
   Strongly disagree
   Disagree
   Neither agree nor disagree
   Agree
   Strongly agree
8 - The project requires teamwork and collaborative spirit
   Strongly disagree
   Disagree
   Neither agree nor disagree
   Agree
   Strongly agree
9 - The project requires technology skills
   Strongly disagree
   Disagree
   Neither agree nor disagree
   Agree
   Strongly agree
10 - The project helped me develop technology skills
   Strongly disagree
   Disagree
   Neither agree nor disagree
   Agree
   Strongly agree
11 - I would recommend the project to other colleagues
   Strongly disagree
   Disagree
   Neither agree nor disagree
   Agree
   Strongly agree
12 - Describe the project in 3 to 6 keywords
_____

13 - What was your general opinion about the project?
_____

Section 2
Technology and Tourism

Chapter 7
Technology Use and Innovation Strategies in Event Tourism

Tuba Türkmendağ
Atatürk University, Turkey

Zafer Türkmendağ
https://orcid.org/0000-0002-7712-1500
Atatürk University, Turkey

ABSTRACT

Event tourism has undergone a serious change in the world with developing technology and innovations. In this respect, this chapter examines the direct, marketing, and management effects of technology on event tourism with a literature review. Studies in this field in the literature show that technologies such as artificial intelligence, big data, robots, decision support systems, internet of things, 5G cause behavioral changes in tourists; thus, event organizers use these technologies effectively to keep up with this change. In this context, academic studies in the field, new technologies, and methods used, innovation strategies are explained in detail in the book section, and a framework has been developed and presented to examine smart event tourism in detail. The results of the research are thought to contribute to the literature and offer managerial solutions.

INTRODUCTION

Technology is an emerging concept in event management (Park and Park, 2017). Thus, events should also be included in studies for a better understanding of the field and make developments for its effectiveness. Events generally have important processes like timing, information sharing, and communicating. Moreover, attendants may have particular characteristics and needs which make technological advancements important for managers to collect information required for their development strategies. This study, thus, aims to examine studies in the literature on how technology can improve the effectiveness of event management and what are the new technologies and developed methods. It also aims to

DOI: 10.4018/978-1-7998-8165-0.ch007

find out how event organizers handle the processes, collaborate, communicate, and benefit by using the information technologies.

The technological aspect of events focuses on the knowledge and use of events considering them as a cultural phenomenon while the image aspect is related to the public opinion and popularity of events at a destination (Ziyadin *et al.*, 2019). The technological aspect is related to digitalization and transformation of intangible assets into knowledge to manage events productively. Thus, knowledge of event tourism and its management became one of the most important concepts from a theoretical point of view. They can also be used to better develop innovations for both management and marketing. Boosting productivity and competition in the market requires an understanding of customer needs and make innovations coming into existence in online environments (Ungerman, Dedkova and Gurinova, 2018) and integrating them into the production or service processes. Hence, managers may use social media, Bluetooth, RFID, WI-FI, Mobile roaming, web search, online booking data to generate big data that provide particular information for the long-term success of the firm (Li *et al.*, 2018). Further, events are special memorable experiences that are affected by inter-activity, personalization, and informativeness. Many smart tourism technologies provide information to tourists about events within the destination and enable them to share their unique experiences (Jeong and Shin, 2020).

As e-tourism brings together the producer and the consumer in a virtual environment, it enables the destinations and products to be redesigned together (Buhalis and O'Connor, 2005). Considering the discussion, some important themes were pointed out which make technology more useful and efficient in events. The results provide important outcomes for the academicians and managers within the tourism industry.

BACKGROUND

Technology Use and Innovation in Event Tourism

Tourism technologies also have transformative power over destination resources and actors. As they move into the smart tourism ecosystem, actors and visitors can co-create or destroy tourism values. For this reason, handling the paradigms in this area with a multidisciplinary approach can offer different perspectives and positivist approaches for the participation of visitors in the activities (Tussyadiah, 2017; Sigala, 2018). In tourism, brands can provide real-time services to their consumers with whom they have connected via social media thanks to technology and they can co-create new products or innovations together using the feedback they receive from consumers (Buhalis and Sinarta, 2019). Visitors become more creative in participating in events, especially with the opportunities offered by mobile technologies, such as taking photos and videos. Moreover, this consumer-generated content triggers other visitors, creating great changes in the visit experience. Naturally, this creative visitor class seeks new experiences and pays attention to the presence of technology and innovative products in their experiences (Gretzel and Jamal, 2009). For example, with the *Playtown* event organized in Portugal, innovation was attempted by creating works that enable people to interact with the use of technology in different parts of a city. This project was created in 3 stages and by applying different co-creation processes, very useful innovation ideas have emerged in the city (Marques and Borba, 2017). While these new technologies enable actors to share information in the new ecosystem, they also provide a resource-based view to co-creating and liability and allow the correct distribution of resources such as using online check-in in advance to prevent queuing at the door (Barile *et al.*, 2017). The visibility of events in tourism has expanded with the advancements in technology and imaging. With the use of technology, the modern tourist increases the value of entertainment and interaction in their spare time by communicating with other tourists or local people. From a technological perspective, it can be said that event tourism comprises many parts of cultural tourism. The image point of view indicates the picture that gives information about how interesting the activities can be and their features. These two perspectives can create opportunities for managers and planners in event-based tourism, such as increasing the number of participants, creating a tourist attachment to event and increasing revenues (Ziyadin *et al.*, 2019).

Visitors become addicted by constantly using new technologies such as mobile and wearable technology. This naturally differentiates the experience and perceived value for the visitor. Therefore, businesses invest in smart tourism applications, including artificial intelligence and big data, in order not to remain unaware of technologies such as Uber and Airbnb which change the rules of play in the industry (Gretzel *et al.*, 2015). Consumers can search for the information they want, wherever and whenever they want, without relying on conventional desktop computers. Mobile phones enable businesses to reach their consumers more frequently through notifications. In the era of mobile phones, the old host-visitor approach and relationships began to be replaced by an information-based and personalized experience (Anne Coussement and J. Teague, 2013). However, determining the use of technology according to a single type of user may not be a correct method, because it may vary according to demographic characteristics. Pesonen et al. (2015), in their research, it was determined that older users have different uses compared to young people, older users mostly prefer websites, they do not seek special marketing in their website design, and they seek help from young people while using them. As mobile phone usage can provide more data about events and touristic activities, it is very beneficial for consumers to offer innovative experiences. In addition, mobile technologies are used to effectively communicate businesses with consumers by providing instant information exchange for mapping and smart city systems (Kim and Kim, 2017).

Cai, Richter, and McKenna (2019) examined the studies conducted in the field of "technology usage" across three categories: operational, organizational use, and users. In the operational type, information technologies can provide interaction, online connection, real-time service by collecting information and processing data. Organizational use of information technologies provides competitive and strategic information by supporting corporate governance. In terms of users, the use of information technologies determines individual characteristics, expectations are discovered, supports the user, and creates changes in the behavior of the end-user. According to the smart tourism event experience model put forward by Bustard et al. (2019), the digital event experience consists of interrelated 4P (people, processes, personalization, and places) and 7R (rituals, realms, realities, renewal, review, relational, and resourcing) elements. *Personalization* is when smart tourism makes people's experiences personal. *People* are a part of this system as users or consumers. *Processes* are elements that create integration and value in the smart tourism ecosystem. *Places* are smart places where people come together for events and are important for centralized competition. The connections between these four elements, which are important in creating the value of digital activity experience together, make up seven elements. The elements in the model and their connections are summarized in Figure 1.

Event managers and planners need to consider the habits of generations while identifying technological developments. While the baby boomer generation considers factors such as idealism, image, nostalgia, teamwork, health; Generation X seek global awareness, choice, change, individualism; Generation Y, on the other hand, seeks values for high self-confidence, difference, connectedness, following technology, and global citizenship. Baby boomers may prefer traditional face-to-face meetings; Generation X prefer well-designed virtual meetings; while Generation Y prefers live events that include gamified virtual experiences, of which the meeting time and place are added to their calendar via e-mail, their faces and voices are recognized, and the speakers can be seen with high resolutions (Sox *et al.*, 2016). Further developments in technologies such as artificial intelligence and robotics offer opportunities to improve the visitor experience at events as well as provide better service. Digital assistant, chatbot, consultant robot, waiter robot, carrier robot, etc. used in the event industry. Artificial intelligence-based applications create added value while reducing costs in events (Ergen, 2021). Likewise, virtual reality can digitize many experiences related to events and also creates important opportunities for event planning and management (Thomson *et al.*, 2021).

Figure 1. Categories of co-creation of the digital event (Bustard et al., 2019, p. 119)

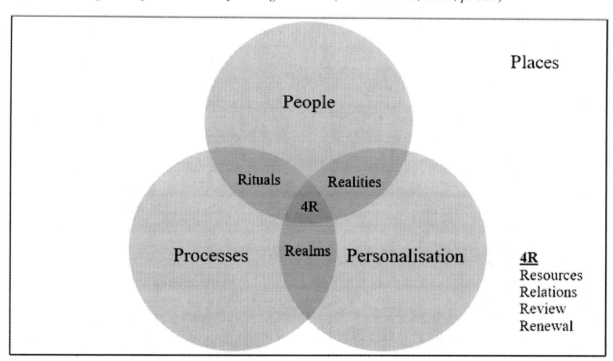

Innovation and ICT in Event Tourism Marketing

The continuous growth of the tourism sector and the increasing diversity has brought destination competitiveness to an important position for many tourism regions (Bustard *et al.*, 2019). Its implications for tourism arise with its contribution to regional economic development. For this reason, policymakers consider effectiveness as a valuable tool that can strengthen the growing local economy through increasing the tourist attraction, improving the image of the destination, and increasing its visibility (Mainolfi and Marino, 2020). In this context, event tourism is a rapidly growing sector with very strong economic returns, where big shows and events are regularly held (Rajesh, 2014). Events affect the development of many destinations and are prominently included in marketing plans. The roles and effects of planned activities in tourism are explained well, increasing the competitiveness of the destination (Getz, 2008; Ziyadin et al., 2019) and creating a strong destination image (Kim and Chalip, 2004; Getz, 2008; Quinn, 2009; Wong, 2011). Therefore, it is predicted that the activities that can be used to expand alternative tourism products, the number of participants, and the budget allocated to the event will increase (Harb et al., 2019). When event tourism is analyzed from the demand and supply side, the demand perspective requires determining who and why travels for events, who attends the events during the travel and how much the participants in event tourism spend (Getz, 2008). Very different tangible or intangible factors such as theme, physical design, performance shows used in events determine visitor experiences (Yang and Tan, 2017). The destination management should work with the event organizers to include the event in the marketing communication of the destination and to advertise and promote the destination to offer better experience to visitors. To ensure that the destination matches the event adequately, the name or symbols of the destination should be placed on the event logo (Chalip and Costa, 2005).

It will not take much to forget an event that has not turned into an experience because events are temporary while experiences are valuable for life (Crowther, 2011). There are basic elements that businesses must demand to market the event. In business, a strategic approach based on the analysis of the customer's purchasing process and periodic sales can help meet the customer's expectations. When events, such as contests, congresses (or meetings), events, festivals, media events, parties, sports, are combined with appropriate marketing programs, they play a key role in achieving sales targets at any given time, and event marketing enables them to become a marketing innovation leader (Chu and Tseng, 2013). In events, marketing and management departments engage in risk management by finding effective solutions to different problems. Creative solutions create new and unique experiences, improving customer loyalty and team spirit (Daniel, Bogdan and Daniel, 2012). A modern and forward-thinking event marketer must continually develop and use their skills to uncover the mysteries of event marketing that may occur over the next few decades. The event marketer can anticipate future needs and meet them with activities essential to human productivity and well-being. The experienced and professional event marketer will constantly monitor trends and build the marketing plan and product to meet future needs (Willett et al., 1995). Since effective management is important for event marketing, to define and design the future in organizations, there is a need for a constructive event marketing strategy that can respond to new circumstances. Event marketing can make a strong impression to grab customers' attention. Well-planned event marketing can not only have a successful impact on customers but can also generate higher business revenue (Chu and Tseng, 2013). When determining market trends, the experienced event marketer considers bad developments such as demographics, income, technological development, media, search words, communication in different languages, or terrorism. Technological applications such as video conferencing over the internet are recorded in real-time and motivate the participants to participate in the event (Willett et al., 1995).

Putting the use of ICT at the center of innovation mechanisms concerns to meet the increasing challenges of global competition, sustainability, and resource optimization is an important condition for achieving excellence in innovation. The marketing research process, which includes revealing customer and market needs and expectations as well as innovative work, corporate sustainable innovation; gains concrete accountability for strategic decisions to be a bridge between customers and market needs and expectations and to gain competitive advantage (FleacĂ, FleacĂ and Maiduc, 2016). Koo et al. (2016) express the importance of events in the competition of smart tourism destinations. Consumers' desire to have more original experiences in their spare time pushes them to seek participation in events and

Technology Use and Innovation Strategies in Event Tourism

festivals (Getz and Page, 2014). Such events play a critical role in creating a destination image and achieving the success of marketing efforts, providing a competitive advantage by offering visitors extraordinary experiences (Getz, 2008) through using intelligent systems that include many methods such as decision support systems, autonomous agents that search and Web resources, environment intelligence, and systems that create augmented realities. In smart tourism destinations, there is a need for stakeholders to be dynamically connected through a technological platform where information about tourism activities can be shared instantly. These technologies provide useful information to consumers and businesses to make better decisions in co-creating an enjoyable tourism experience (Buhalis and Amaranggana, 2013; Gretzel et al., 2015). The fact that tourism and hospitality businesses add unique activities to their existing product profile and deliberately incorporate various activities into their businesses to create new customer experiences constitutes an example of innovation practice (Yang and Tan, 2017). By designing unique experiences and unforgettable digital encounters with the Internet of Things (IoT), Near Field communication (NFC), and Artificial Intelligence (AI) through mobile or wearable technologies, opportunities are created to create events and offer smart experiences in the context of smart tourism (Tussyadiah, 2017).

Users can easily create and share information in online environments as Web 2.0 and virtual social places emerged (Cheung and Lee, 2009). Therefore, the adaptation of people has led event marketers to realize the importance of social media as a marketing tool. Virtual worlds have turned into a marketing channel that enables marketers to communicate with their customers, advertise, sell products and conduct marketing research (Kaplan and Haenlein, 2010), and customers use to exchange experiences and information (Gretzel, 2006). Thanks to social network sites, it is possible to announce an event to the target audience, provide information, and interact with the consumer/customer (Harb et al., 2019). Social media provides an opportunity to manage these relationships efficiently and at a low cost (Donath and Boyd, 2004). The large amount of data received from GPS-based applications such as Foursquare, Gowalla, and Facebook, and the use of this data to analyze user behavior in social networks is seen as an important issue for event marketing (Chernova et al., 2020). Social media; can be used as a Web 2.0-based application that contains various online information resources and carries the content created by the consumers to share information for education about products, brands, services, and problems (Lee and Lee, 2014). Another technology usage area in the tourism industry is travel blogs. Popular blogging platforms include TripAdvisor and Travelocity. These blogs contain consumer reviews of tourism products, positive or negative perceptions about the product. These posts affect the value of a tourism brand in the market and emphasize the importance of managing online communication (Hede and Kellett, 2012). At the same time blogs and social media platforms and information about events in popular tourist destinations in the sharing, users can provide both information you can learn both, in the promotion of the event, share photos and videos related to the event, it is possible to share the impression after the event. The presence of real information and data by those who experienced the event is more attractive to the followers, thus increasing interest in the event and positive word-of-mouth marketing can be realized. For example, *TripAdvisor* and *Travelocity* such as blogs environment for the information to seek to focus on Facebook used widely for tourism organizations, YouTube, Myspace, Flickr, and Twitter social media platforms such as the one between members of the brand community dialogue created refers to clicks (Noone, McGuire and Rohlfs, 2011). Another technology in the context of event tourism is virtual tours. Using this technology, the exhibitor can experience it virtually even if it is not physically located in a specific destination. Virtual tours can be an alternative to physical travel, albeit partially, due to the lack of financial means, insufficient time and epidemic diseases restricting travel. In addition, virtual tours can be a good promotional tool for pre-visit marketing in event tourism. For example, within the context of the *secondlife.com* web-based internet application project, destinations have been created in a virtual environment and users can interact with each other by creating new products or services. In the tourism sector, many accommodation businesses have created virtual offices to make their own advertisements and promotions using this web application (Lee and Wicks, 2010).

With the increasing use of mobile computing in the event industry, there has been a significant technological innovation. Thanks to this mobile technology, consumers can buy their tickets instantly and use their e-tickets in the event area. In addition, it eliminated the problems such as waiting in line, losing or forgetting the ticket. In addition, the event organizer can communicate quickly with the participants through social networks. Thus, participants can learn about the events and program changes instantly. In addition, participants can provide feedback for planners by sharing their experiences and media information through these networks (Ziyadin *et al.*, 2019). Consumers are in communication with others through the mobile devices, which in background produce and exchange data with other devices, during or after the event. These data and the traces can be kept in a database and big data can be obtained and used for consumer analysis or product innovation (Buhalis and Amaranggana, 2013). It is also used by event organizations to create online brand communities through Web 2.0 platforms, social networking events. For example, the Organizing Committee of the 2012 London Olympic Games has been using social media (Hede and Kellett, 2012) which have become a significant source of information for customers in the tourism industry (Xiang and Gretzel, 2010).

Innovation Strategies and Technological Advancements in Event Management

The fact that technology allows the visitor experience to seek more information, to be informed with notifications, to make evaluations, to receive suggestions, and to provide virtual experiences has been a driving force for event managers to develop themselves and adopt differentiation strategies in the field of technology (Robertson *et al.*, 2015; Backman, 2018). Due to the developments in information technologies, tourism enterprises change their value chains by making large investments in the re-engineering of information technologies. Technology creates opportunities for experience-centered tourism strategies as concrete assets are presented as information in abstraction. The data obtained from the interactions with the participants can be converted into intelligence and used for competition (Stamboulis and Skayannis, 2003). Deficiently, only 1% of mobile technology research in the field of tourism and hospitality has been done on conventions and events. This little research has led to a lack of knowledge about the importance of mobile computing in activities (Law, Chan and Wang, 2018), whereas they are mostly used by participants of events. For example, thanks to the *MyCrowd* mobile application developed in Malaysia, local people and tourists shared their knowledge and experience in participating in the event. Event planners have become more recognized by promoting their activities through this application. This application also provided attendees with up-to-date information about event timings and plans, location, prices and promotions, and live streams before and after the event (Arharmid *et al.*, 2017).

Besides, the activities where technology is used the most in events are projector viewing, card payment, communication with multi-purpose mobile applications, live display, event diagramming, crowd management. Technology provides efficiency by saving time in event planning, reducing costs, providing better communication and network, creating brand awareness and added value, making the event more accessible, and providing a better planning experience. Nevertheless, the use of technology in the organization of events also has negative effects such as time-consuming data, technological infrastructure is costly, difficult to learn, not being used sufficiently, and employees taking their jobs. Event technologies offer options for creating the desired effect beyond simple communication or making things easier (Mehrotra and Lobo, 2020). As the beneficiary elements have an important place in the use of technology, event organizers can provide training to the users, explaining the important features and benefits that can be obtained from the use. In addition, the use of technology should be supported by increasing the impact of individual innovation on expected performance and effort (Ozturk et al., 2021). Planners should pay attention to these factors when integrating technology in their activities, as perceived utility and pleasure affect efficiency satisfaction due to its attitude towards use. For this, for example, they can make the use of mobile applications more enjoyable by creating gamified activities which make them participate in taking event photos and adding features of translation, and enabling them to view the presentations on a mobile screen (Talantis, Shin and Severt, 2020).

One of the most important issues in events is that managers and employees can fulfill their responsibilities on time. Event managers need to be able to offer their customers planned work on the dates and times they promise. In addition to coordination among employees, time management also affects job-related performance (Ahmad et al., 2012). Therefore, taking advantage of technology in terms of both time and performance provides great benefits in events. Moreover, it is inevitable for the managers to produce innovative solutions and to take measures to remove the obstacles to innovation. Their good innovation skills provide competencies such as designing impressive services at their events, exchanging ideas or collaborating with other event organizers and providing efficiency in logistics (Ahmad and Daud, 2016). Event planners see the internet as a communication and marketing tool. Congress centers still invest a very small amount of their budgets (5%) on their websites due to technological infrastructure costs, lack of information, and administrative problems. However, the use of technology offers opportunities for event managers and marketers in terms of coordination and promotion. In the information age, congress offices need to integrate technologies into business processes like all event companies (Casanova, Kim and Morrison, 2006; Kim, Jang and Morrison, 2011). The clusters created by the network structures for event managers can make their strategies functional (Stokes, 2006). With the help of technology, these networks have been expanded multidimensionally and offer managers opportunities for collaboration and awareness. Besides, through Information and Communication Technologies (ICTs), also tourism stakeholders can have the opportunity to work together (Buhalis and Amaranggana, 2013). It is important for organizations and event management companies in the event sector to understand the specific needs of different event venues, as they provide the opportunity to maximize the potential of creating unforgettable events. In the event sector, it is extremely important to ensure that customer requests and needs are effectively met with new product development or innovation which bring businesses to success in sustainable competition (Hassanien and Dale, 2012).

Users must believe that the usage of technology will fulfill the tasks they want, although it varies from context to context. Since hedonic factors related to technology affect the use of tourism-related applications, where entertainment is a part of the experience, event managers make their technology designs in a way that increases the experience gained from the event (Van Winkle et al., 2019). Digital experience can be dealt with operationally with the topology of sensing, linking, organizing, and performing. This topology also gives practitioners the chance to see opportunities to innovate in digital experiences in activities (M. Van Winkle et al., 2016). Scenario-based design can be used to create a technology-enhanced service, collaborate between stakeholders and create a common vision. This approach provides efficient outputs in technology-based initiatives, increasing the usability for successful applications (McCabe, Sharples and Foster, 2012). Further, conducting pre-event training in a specific format, understandable and simulated increases the competence and performance of employees, while ensuring development and effective coordination in business processes (Landey and Silvers, 2005). In addition to planning, organizing, marketing, and financial, technological skills such as computer use are also highly sought after in recruiting event managers (Arcodia and Barker, 2002).

Since security is one of the most important issues for consumers, functions such as positioning and sharing personal information can negatively affect the attitude towards using technology (Gretzel et al., 2015). Blockchain technology, which has been heard a lot with bitcoin recently, provides safe use in the tourism sector, causing users to participate more in tourism activities (Calvaresi et al., 2019). Consequently, perceived security positively affects the use of technology. Therefore, event planners evaluate encrypted data storage options by choosing platforms that make users feel safe for their personal information (Ozturk et al., 2021). As a result of these facts, many event organizers adopt security information and event management system to their technological systems which is a sub-branch of computer security that analyzes daily information on services and products, real-time alerts. Thanks to this, experts on the system take measures by examining security vulnerabilities and threats and respond by determining them. For example, security information and event management have been used to protect the Olympic Games system from undesirable phenomena. Since the Olympic games are huge games in which participants compete and participate around the world, there are huge flows of information. For example, in London 2012, in 79-day races, in 26 sports, in 94 fields, 17,000 athletes, 20000 journalists, 70000 volunteers, 4000 information technology employees, 900 servers, 10000 computers, and 1000 network and security vehicles were used. Since what is expected of this massive system is to provide real-time information to viewers, broadcasters, and commentators around the world, 11 million transactions are processed daily. Since the greatest threat to this complex and difficult-to-control system is being prepared for threats and being able to respond immediately, applications such as security information and event management are of great importance in the realization of the event (Rieke et al., 2012).

The damages events cause on the environment, which is one of the negative effects of such activities, can be repaired with approaches such as sustainable practices and green efficiency. Event managers must pay attention to environmentally protective practices such as energy efficiency, waste reduction, water-saving, eco production, proper communication, and sustainable development to create green events (Ahmad et al., 2013). While information technologies enhance innovation by giving them the ability to monitor and evaluate the products, they also give chances to event managers to do the same things for the waste, energy, and communication (Ali and Frew, 2014). The use of green communication and information technologies in event management provides long-term benefits for stakeholders, providing successful sustainable outcomes and increasing the experience quality of event participants. In addition, the use of technology has reduced paper consumption, facilitated vendor selection, and improved consumer feedback procedures (Slocum and Lee, 2014).

SOLUTIONS AND RECOMMENDATIONS

Event tourism is largely transferred to the virtual environment with the effect of digitalization. The services offered by the virtual world support the realization of events more efficiently and without errors. To achieve this, it is important for event organizers to follow new developments in the field of technology as well as to develop their technologies and innovative products. According to the results of the literature review, the use of technologies such as web-based services, artificial intelligence, big data collection and analysis, augmented reality, virtual reality, hologram presentation, drones, robots for events has become more of an obligation than a necessity. Therefore, event companies should attach importance to this area, in other words, increase their investments in technological infrastructure and superstructure, procure software solutions professionally, digitize the processes in the organization, search as criteria for personnel recruitment, provide training and be open to change.

In addition, technology has created its Z generation while creating great changes in the habits of the X and Y generations as well. The very different habits and perspectives of this new generation than the previous ones are driving businesses to changes in the field of marketing. According to the literature, this change is two-way: *for the consumer*, technology has begun to provide convenience, variety, and personalization in doing or choosing their business; To become more attractive to consumers *in terms of business*, it has started to get to know the consumer better with the analysis of the big data generated by the technology invested in. In this regard, businesses should turn to high-use applications where they can obtain more data about their consumers and create user-friendly interface designs. Since the events are very prone to digitalization due to their abstract and information-based structure, it can be said that the enterprises operating in this sector are under the pressure of technological developments. So much so that the obtained big data is necessary for artificial intelligence models to reach saturation and consequently to make the right decisions. Decision support systems can also provide more accurate results by obtaining information about tourists/consumers or processes. On the other hand, artificial intelligence models, especially used in mobile computing, and their ability to develop suggestions for consumers can be integrated into applications of event tourism. In addition, these suggestions can be made not only via mobile devices but also with human form robots or voice guidance devices.

As a result of the literature review on smart event tourism, it has been determined that this phenomenon comprises different elements. Considering the technological, digital marketing, and management information systems perspective, a framework has been proposed for smart event tourism as indicated in Figure 2. The dimensions in this framework are interrelated and when they work in harmony, they can create effective smart event tourism: In *process management*, the processes followed to realize the event can be realized autonomously with technology. *Time management* is provided in terms of technology improving speed and planning in events. *Technological infrastructure* (hardware) specifies the hardware elements required for the use of applications or communication at events. *Services* (applications) include algorithms developed for the use of technology before, during, or after the event. *Communication* (network) is the exchange of data between technological devices used during events so that information can be shared. *Security* is an issue that should be handled with care in event planning and is an element that concerns all stages of the event and measures must be taken in all other dimensions to hold events. Security for events includes taking necessary precautions by foreseeing the possible elements that may prevent the activity to be carried out as planned, attacks on the ICT infrastructure, the ways of penetrating the information technology systems, the elements that may prevent the operation of the activity 24/7. Using this framework, researchers and industry professionals can carry out their work and planning. Since the proposed framework determines the sub-areas that arise when technology is integrated into the activities, it can be a guide for planners.

Smart activities can be carried out in three ways depending on the technology density they have: (1) *Technology-supported events,* include technology use only as a piece of equipment, and support the physical realization of the event. Technologies used for communication, program preparation, information distribution, kiosk use, and presentation mirroring are included in these activities. The main thing in this event type, which also constitutes event tourism, is that people come together in a physical environment and become influenced. (2) *Virtual events* are performed in decentralized virtual environments rather than in one physical place. These events can be done through meeting and video conferencing applications. In such events, participants can connect from their places and interact within the limitations given by the conferencing applications. (3) *Hybrid events,* are carried out simultaneously in physical and virtual environments. Participants choose to be present at such events either physically or virtually. The physical event is broadcasted on the web with video conferencing applications in the virtual environment to the participants at distant locations and present them in the physical environment with various technologies. Especially after the pandemic, it is thought that such events will become widespread.

Figure 2. Smart Event Tourism Framework

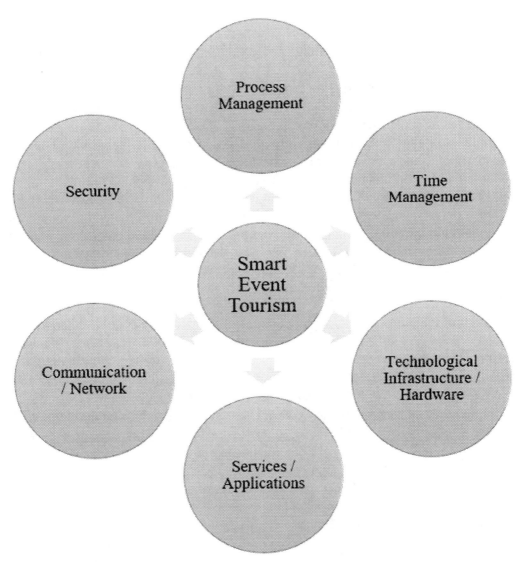

Finally, innovative solutions can be produced with the use of technological devices for carrying capacity and negative environmental effects, which is one of the most important issues in event tourism. By integrating the guest management system into the event reservation system, it is possible to reduce the demand with marketing tactics such as demarketing, as well as planning sustainable development by using the positioning services available on mobile devices. Approaches such as a green event, which has attracted considerable attention in recent years, can be used in environmentally friendly practices such as energy efficiency, water efficiency, carbon footprint, and reduction of environmental wastes with technological innovations, and can attract the attention of environmentally sensitive tourists and minimize negative damages.

FUTURE RESEARCH DIRECTIONS

Since technological developments and their use in event tourism are rarely discussed in the literature, researchers may turn to conceptual studies involving new generation activities. Since technology addresses a wide range of fields, research can be handled from a wide variety of angles. The use of new technologies such as 5G, artificial intelligence, big data, internet of things in event tourism and their effects on tourist behavior can be examined qualitatively or quantitatively. In addition, smart event tourism can be examined in depth by using it as a guide for future researches proposed in this study. Finally, future studies can be made on the planning behavior of tourists before the events, determining the relationships between the data obtained from the mobile devices used by the tourists during the event and their behavior patterns, modeling decision support systems that provide efficiency in event tourism with big data, and the use of robots in events. In this context, it has been observed that there are many gaps in the literature on the subject and it offers researchers important study opportunities.

CONCLUSION

Technology has caused changes in behavior and business processes in tourism and event tourism as it affects all areas of life. Tourists do not travel without a mobile phone, nor do event managers organize events without a computer. Therefore, discussing the effects of technological developments in event marketing and management contributes to the field. To benefit from applications and innovation in branding and promotion of events, it is necessary to look customer experience-oriented and to carry out a kind of co-creation process with the customer by receiving feedback. Information technologies have changed consumption habits and added different virtual dimensions to the activities. Participants no longer want to participate in a simple event, but want to be in a more interactive structure that provides different experiences with technological innovations. For this, managers must follow the most up-to-date technological developments and integrate them into their marketing strategies.

During the events, the participants may need information about both the events and the place they took place. These can be done instantly and with fewer costs thanks to the mobile applications created. The possibilities offered by mobile computing, wearable technologies, object recognition algorithms can produce data that can be used to obtain very different results about the event, such as the number of participants, activities, demographic characteristics, the interest in which activities, and their thoughts about the activities. These data allow managers to create strategic information to help manage their activities more efficiently and intelligently. In the light of the results obtained through data mining or analysis, they can improve business processes or recognize their participants and develop automated suggestions for them using artificial intelligence models.

REFERENCES

Ahmad, J., & Daud, N. (2016). Determining Innovative Tourism Event Professional Competency for Conventions and Exhibitions Industry: A Preliminary Study. *Procedia: Social and Behavioral Sciences*, *219*, 69–75. doi:10.1016/j.sbspro.2016.04.041

Ahmad, N. L., Mohd. Yusuf, A. N., Mohamed Shobri, N. D., & Wahab, S. (2012). The Relationship between Time Management and Job Performance in Event Management. *Procedia: Social and Behavioral Sciences*, *65*, 937–941. doi:10.1016/j.sbspro.2012.11.223

Ahmad, N. L., Rashid, W. E. W., Razak, N. A., Yusof, A. N. M., & Shah, N. S. M. (2013). Green Event Management and Initiatives for Sustainable Business Growt. *International Journal of Trade, Economics and Finance*. doi:10.7763/IJTEF.2013.V4.311

Ali, A., & Frew, A. J. (2014). ICT and sustainable tourism development: An innovative perspective. *Journal of Hospitality and Tourism Technology*, *5*(1), 2–16. doi:10.1108/JHTT-12-2012-0034

Anne Coussement, M., & Teague, T. (2013). The new customer-facing technology: Mobile and the constantly-connected consumer. *Journal of Hospitality and Tourism Technology*, *4*(2), 177–187. doi:10.1108/JHTT-12-2011-0035

Arcodia, C., & Barker, T. (2002). A review of web-based job advertisements for australian event management positions. *Journal of Human Resources in Hospitality & Tourism*, *1*(4), 1–18. doi:10.1300/J171v01n04_01

Arharmid, A., Anuar, K., Fauzi, I., & Wee, H. (2017). Mycrowd: Mobile Application For Event Tourism. In Creative Innovation without Boundaries (pp. 146–150). MNNF Publisher.

Backman, K. F. (2018). Event management research: The focus today and in the future. *Tourism Management Perspectives*, *25*, 169–171. doi:10.1016/j.tmp.2017.12.004

Barile, S., Ciasullo, M. V., Troisi, O., & Sarno, D. (2017). The role of technology and institutions in tourism service ecosystems: Findings from a case study. *The TQM Journal*, *29*(6), 811–833. doi:10.1108/TQM-06-2017-0068

Buhalis, D., & Amaranggana, A. (2013). Smart Tourism Destinations. In Information and Communication Technologies in Tourism 2014 (pp. 553–564). doi:10.1007/978-3-319-03973-2_40

Buhalis, D., & O'Connor, P. (2005). Information communication technology revolutionizing tourism. *Tourism Recreation Research*, *30*(3), 7–16. Advance online publication. doi:10.1080/02508281.2005.11081482

Buhalis, D., & Sinarta, Y. (2019). Real-time co-creation and nowness service: Lessons from tourism and hospitality. *Journal of Travel & Tourism Marketing*, *36*(5), 563–582. doi:10.1080/10548408.2019.1592059

Bustard, J. R. T., Bolan, P., Devine, A., & Hutchinson, K. (2019). The emerging smart event experience: An interpretative phenomenological analysis. *Tourism Review*, *74*(1), 116–128. doi:10.1108/TR-10-2017-0156

Cai, W., Richter, S., & McKenna, B. (2019). Progress on technology use in tourism. In Journal of Hospitality and Tourism Technology (Vol. 10, Issue 4, pp. 651–672). doi:10.1108/JHTT-07-2018-0068

Calvaresi, D., Leis, M., Dubovitskaya, A., Schegg, R., & Schumacher, M. (2019). Trust in Tourism via Blockchain Technology: Results from a Systematic Review. In *Information and Communication Technologies in Tourism 2019* (pp. 304–317). Springer International Publishing., doi:10.1007/978-3-030-05940-8_24

Casanova, M. B., Kim, D. Y., & Morrison, A. M. (2006). The relationships of meeting planners' profiles with usage and attitudes toward the use of technology. In Journal of Convention and Event Tourism (Vol. 7, Issues 3–4, pp. 19–43). doi:10.1300/J452v07n03_02

Chalip, L., & Costa, C. A. (2005). Sport event tourism and the destination brand: Towards a general theory. Sport in Society. doi:10.1080/17430430500108579

Chernova, D. V., Sharafutdinova, N. S., Novikova, E. N., Nasretdinov, I. T., Xametova, N. G., & Valeeva, Y. S. (2020). Evaluation of Event Marketing in IT Companies. In Lecture Notes in Networks and Systems (Vol. 84, pp. 487–493). doi:10.1007/978-3-030-27015-5_59

Cheung, C. M. K., & Lee, M. K. O. (2009). Understanding the sustainability of a virtual community: Model development and empirical test. *Journal of Information Science*, *35*(3), 279–298. doi:10.1177/0165551508099088

Chu, K., & Tseng, C. (2013). Research of Service Innovation on Event Marketing Performance. *International Journal on Advances in Information Sciences and Service Sciences*, *5*(12), 97–104. doi:10.4156/aiss.vol5.issue12.11

Crowther, P. (2011). Marketing event outcomes: From tactical to strategic. *International Journal of Event and Festival Management*, *2*(1), 68–82. doi:10.1108/17582951111116623

Daniel, M., Bogdan, G., & Daniel, Z. (2012). The Use of Event Marketing Management Strategies. *Procedia: Social and Behavioral Sciences*, *46*, 5409–5413. doi:10.1016/j.sbspro.2012.06.448

Donath, J., & Boyd, D. (2004). Public displays of connection. *BT Technology Journal*, *22*(4), 71–82. doi:10.1023/B:BTTJ.0000047585.06264.cc

Ergen, F. D. (2021). Artificial Intelligence Applications for Event Management and Marketing. In *Impact of ICTs on Event Management and Marketing* (pp. 199–215). IGI Global. doi:10.4018/978-1-7998-4954-4.ch012

Fleacă, E., Fleacă, B., & Maiduc, S. (2016). Fostering Organizational Innovation based on modeling the Marketing Research Process through Event-driven Process Chain (EPC). *TEM Journal*, *5*(4), 460–466.

Getz, D. (2008). Event tourism: Definition, evolution, and research. *Tourism Management*, *29*(3), 403–428. doi:10.1016/j.tourman.2007.07.017

Getz, D., & Page, S. J. (2014). Progress and prospects for event tourism research. *Tourism Management*, *52*, 593–631. doi:10.1016/j.tourman.2015.03.007

Gretzel, U. (2006). Consumer Generated Content -Trends and Implications for Branding. *Ereview of Tourism Research*.

Gretzel, U., & Jamal, T. (2009). Conceptualizing the Creative Tourist Class: Technology, Mobility, and Tourism Experiences. *Tourism Analysis*, *14*(4), 471–481. doi:10.3727/108354209X12596287114219

Gretzel, U., Sigala, M., Xiang, Z., & Koo, C. (2015). Smart tourism: Foundations and developments. *Electronic Markets*, *25*(3), 179–188. doi:10.100712525-015-0196-8

Harb, A. A., Fowler, D., Chang, H. J., Blum, S. C., & Alakaleek, W. (2019). Social media as a marketing tool for events. *Journal of Hospitality and Tourism Technology*, *10*(1), 28–44. doi:10.1108/JHTT-03-2017-0027

Hassanien, A., & Dale, C. (2012). Drivers and barriers of new product development and innovation in event venues: A multiple case study. *Journal of Facilities Management*, *10*(1), 75–92. doi:10.1108/14725961211200414

Hede, A. M., & Kellett, P. (2012). Building online brand communities: Exploring the benefits, challenges and risks in the Australian event sector. *Journal of Vacation Marketing*, *18*(3), 239–250. doi:10.1177/1356766712449370

Jeong, M., & Shin, H. H. (2020). Tourists' Experiences with Smart Tourism Technology at Smart Destinations and Their Behavior Intentions. *Journal of Travel Research*, *59*(8), 1464–1477. doi:10.1177/0047287519883034

Kaplan, A. M., & Haenlein, M. (2010). Users of the world, unite! The challenges and opportunities of Social Media. *Business Horizons*, *53*(1), 59–68. doi:10.1016/j.bushor.2009.09.003

Kim, D., & Kim, S. (2017). The Role of Mobile Technology in Tourism: Patents, Articles, News, and Mobile Tour App Reviews. *Sustainability*, *9*(11), 2082. doi:10.3390u9112082

Kim, D. Y., Jang, S., & Morrison, A. M. (2011). Factors affecting organizational information technology acceptance: A comparison of convention and visitor bureaus and meeting planners in the United States. *Journal of Convention & Event Tourism*, *12*(1), 1–24. doi:10.1080/15470148.2010.551291

Kim, N. S., & Chalip, L. (2004). Why travel to the FIFA World Cup? Effects of motives, background, interest, and constraints. *Tourism Management*, *25*(6), 695–707. doi:10.1016/j.tourman.2003.08.011

Koo, C., Shin, S., Gretzel, U., Hunter, W. C., & Chung, N. (2016). Conceptualization of Smart Tourism Destination Competitiveness. *Asia Pacific Journal of Information Systems*, *26*(4), 561–576. doi:10.14329/apjis.2016.26.4.561

Landey, J., & Silvers, J. R. (2005). The miracle of training in event management. *Journal of Convention & Event Tourism*. Advance online publication. doi:10.1300/J452v06n03_03

Law, R., Chan, I. C. C., & Wang, L. (2018). A comprehensive review of mobile technology use in hospitality and tourism. *Journal of Hospitality Marketing & Management*, *27*(6), 626–648. doi:10.1080/19368623.2018.1423251

Lee, B. C., & Wicks, B. (2010). Tourism technology training for destination marketing organisations (DMOs): Need-based content development. *Journal of Hospitality, Leisure, Sport and Tourism Education*, *9*(1), 39–52. doi:10.3794/johlste.91.241

Lee, S. S., & Lee, C. H. (2014). An Exploratory Study of Convention Specific Social Media Usage by Attendees: Motivations and Effect of Generations on Choice of Convention Information Source and Intention to Use Mobile Application. *Journal of Convention & Event Tourism*, *15*(2), 135–149. doi:10.1080/15470148.2013.862514

Li, J., Xu, L., Tang, L., Wang, S., & Li, L. (2018). Big data in tourism research: A literature review. *Tourism Management*, *68*, 301–323. doi:10.1016/j.tourman.2018.03.009

Mainolfi, G., & Marino, V. (2020). Destination beliefs, event satisfaction and post-visit product receptivity in event marketing. Results from a tourism experience. *Journal of Business Research*, *116*, 699–710. doi:10.1016/j.jbusres.2018.03.001

Marques, L., & Borba, C. (2017). Co-creating the city: Digital technology and creative tourism. *Tourism Management Perspectives*, *24*, 86–93. doi:10.1016/j.tmp.2017.07.007

McCabe, S., Sharples, M., & Foster, C. (2012). Stakeholder engagement in the design of scenarios of technology-enhanced tourism services. *Tourism Management Perspectives*, *4*, 36–44. doi:10.1016/j.tmp.2012.04.007

Mehrotra, A., & Lobo, J. (2020). Technology Driving Event Management Industry to the Next Level. *ICRITO 2020 - IEEE 8th International Conference on Reliability, Infocom Technologies and Optimization (Trends and Future Directions)*, 436–441. 10.1109/ICRITO48877.2020.9198025

Noone, B. M., McGuire, K. A., & Rohlfs, K. V. (2011). Social media meets hotel revenue management: Opportunities, issues and unanswered questions. *Journal of Revenue and Pricing Management*, *10*(4), 293–305. doi:10.1057/rpm.2011.12

Ozturk, A. B., Wei, W., Hua, N., & Qi, R. (2021). Factors affecting attendees continued use of mobile event applications. *Journal of Hospitality and Tourism Technology*. doi:10.1108/JHTT-03-2020-0058

Park, S. B., & Park, K. (2017). Thematic trends in event management research. In International Journal of Contemporary Hospitality Management (Vol. 29, Issue 3, pp. 848–861). doi:10.1108/IJCHM-09-2015-0521

Pesonen, J., Komppula, R., & Riihinen, A. (2015). Typology of senior travellers as users of tourism information technology. *Information Technology & Tourism*, *15*(3), 233–252. doi:10.100740558-015-0032-1

Quinn, B. (2009). Festivals, events, and tourism. In The SAGE Handbook of Tourism Studies (pp. 483–503). doi:10.4135/9780857021076.n27

Rajesh, R. (2014). Issues and Trends of Event Tourism Promotion in Destinations: Puducherry, an empirical Study. *IJSSTH*, *1*(6), 25–41.

Rieke, R., Coppolino, L., Hutchison, A., Prieto, E., & Gaber, C. (2012). Security and reliability requirements for advanced security event management. Lecture Notes in Computer Science (Including Subseries Lecture Notes in Artificial Intelligence and Lecture Notes in Bioinformatics), 7531 LNCS, 171–180. doi:10.1007/978-3-642-33704-8_15

Robertson, M., Yeoman, I., Smith, K. A., & Mcmahon-Beattie, U. (2015). Technology, society, and visioning the future of music festivals. *Event Management*, *19*(4), 567–587. doi:10.3727/152599515X14465748774001

Sigala, M. (2018). New technologies in tourism: From multi-disciplinary to anti-disciplinary advances and trajectories. *Tourism Management Perspectives*, *25*, 151–155. doi:10.1016/j.tmp.2017.12.003

Slocum, S. L., & Lee, S. (2014). Green ICT practices in event management: Case study approach to examine motivation, management and fiscal return on investment. *Information Technology & Tourism*, *14*(4), 347–362. doi:10.100740558-014-0019-3

Sox, C. B., Campbell, J. M., Kline, S. F., Strick, S. K., & Crews, T. B. (2016). Technology use within meetings: A generational perspective. *Journal of Hospitality and Tourism Technology*, *7*(2), 158–181. doi:10.1108/JHTT-09-2015-0035

Stamboulis, Y., & Skayannis, P. (2003). Innovation strategies and technology for experience-based tourism. *Tourism Management*, *24*(1), 35–43. Advance online publication. doi:10.1016/S0261-5177(02)00047-X

Stokes, R. (2006). Network-based strategy making for events tourism. *European Journal of Marketing*, *40*(5–6), 682–695. doi:10.1108/03090560610657895

Talantis, S., Shin, Y. H., & Severt, K. (2020). Conference mobile application: Participant acceptance and the correlation with overall event satisfaction utilizing the technology acceptance model (TAM). *Journal of Convention & Event Tourism*, *21*(2), 100–122. doi:10.1080/15470148.2020.1719949

Thomson, A., Proud, I., Goldston, A. L. J., & Dodds-Gorman, R. (2021). Virtual Reality for Better Event Planning and Management. In *Impact of ICTs on Event Management and Marketing* (pp. 177–198). IGI Global. doi:10.4018/978-1-7998-4954-4.ch011

Tussyadiah, I. P. (2017). Technology and Behavioral Design in Tourism. In *Design science in tourism* (pp. 173–191). Springer. doi:10.1007/978-3-319-42773-7_12

Ungerman, O., Dedkova, J., & Gurinova, K. (2018). the Impact of Marketing Innovation on the Competitiveness of Enterprises in the Context of Industry 4.0. *Journal of Competitiveness*, *10*(2), 132–148. doi:10.7441/joc.2018.02.09

Van Winkle, C., Cairns, A., MacKay, K., & Halpenny, E. (2016). Mobile device use at festivals: Opportunities for value creation. *International Journal of Event and Festival Management*, *7*(3), 201–218. doi:10.1108/IJEFM-04-2016-0025

Van Winkle, C. M., Bueddefeld, J. N. H., Halpenny, E. A., & MacKay, K. J. (2019). The unified theory of acceptance and use of technology 2: Understanding mobile device use at festivals. *Leisure Studies*, *38*(5), 634–650. doi:10.1080/02614367.2019.1618895

Willett, W. C., Sacks, F., Trichopoulou, A., Drescher, G., Ferro-Luzzi, A., Helsing, E., & Trichopoulos, D. (1995). Mediterranean diet pyramid: A cultural model for healthy eating. *The American Journal of Clinical Nutrition*, *61*(6), 1402S–1406S. doi:10.1093/ajcn/61.6.1402S PMID:7754995

Wong, I. K. A. (2011). Using Destination Attributes to Promote Event Travel: The Case of Macau. *Journal of Convention & Event Tourism*, *12*(4), 241–252. doi:10.1080/15470148.2011.619884

Xiang, Z., & Gretzel, U. (2010). Role of social media in online travel information search. *Tourism Management*, *31*(2), 179–188. Advance online publication. doi:10.1016/j.tourman.2009.02.016

Yang, F. X., & Tan, S. X. (2017). Event innovation induced corporate branding. *International Journal of Contemporary Hospitality Management*, *29*(3), 862–882. doi:10.1108/IJCHM-09-2015-0512

Ziyadin, S., Koryagina, E., Grigoryan, T., Tovma, N., & Ismail, G. Z. (2019). Specificity of using information technologies in the digital transformation of event tourism. *International Journal of Civil Engineering and Technology*, *10*(1), 998–1010.

KEY TERMS AND DEFINITIONS

Artificial Intelligence: Intelligence demonstrated by machines through big data instead of humans.

Blockchain: It is a distributed and immutable ledger that provides tracking of assets or information in a network.

Green Communication: Communication systems and networks which are basically developed for energy-efficiency.

Innovation Leader: Who is best innovator or first to realize innovations in the market.

Real-Time Service: Applications that contain processes or activities that meet the information needs of customers interactively.

Virtual Social Places: Applications that provide digital channels where people can share words, ideas or media, consume or sell through network connections over the internet.

Virtual Tours: The digital presentation of recorded cultural assets, texts, historical, cultural and natural places through VR or AR technologies.

Chapter 8
Virtual Tourism and Challenges in a Post-Pandemic Context

Carla Sousa Martins
https://orcid.org/0000-0003-2714-9676
Polytechnic Institute of Cávado and Ave, Portugal

Ana Carvalho Ferreira
Polytechnic Institute of Cávado and Ave, Portugal

Catarina Silva Pereira
Polytechnic Institute of Cávado and Ave, Portugal

Bruno Barbosa Sousa
https://orcid.org/0000-0002-8588-2422
Polytechnic Institute of Cávado and Ave, Portugal & CiTUR, Portugal

ABSTRACT

The role played by technologies of information and communication, ICT, has become increasingly important in the way of life of societies. As well as technologies to revolutionize or everyone's way of life, it also brings a sense of alertness to match. This chapter aims to present a reflection on the importance of virtual tourism in the pandemic scenario (new coronavirus) and the main challenges in the post-pandemic period. The tourist sector must continue to communicate with clients in order to retain them. In this way, several companies choose to enter into a partnership with digital influencers, seeing that they are presented as a link between the company and the customers. From an interdisciplinary perspective, the chapter presents contributions to marketing, (virtual) tourism, and pandemic management.

1. INTRODUCTION

Technologies are increasingly present, as a part of the society in which we are inserted which, in addition to revolutionizing the way of life of all of us, has also caused great changes in the tourism context, with the emergence of new market niches. The internet has become one of the main media, facilitating

DOI: 10.4018/978-1-7998-8165-0.ch008

travelling to any part of the world in just one click. The recent global pandemic, caused by the Covid-19, has changed not only the way we currently travel, but it has also highlighted the important role played by Virtual Tourism and Gamified Virtual Experiences. Faced with this scenario, several companies in the tourism sector had to reinvent themselves, using virtual environments and digital tools, as an opportunity to maintain and expand their business (López García et al., 2019). The need to invest in marketing and communication strategies was also highlighted, in order to adapt to the new consumer's behavior, which arose during the pandemic crisis and that will possibly endure. We live in the Age of Influence, in which the majority of the world's population is connected to the web. New segments and market niches are generated by the use of ICT, meeting and adapting to the needs of new generations, leading to the burst of new business models. So, technology, covid-19 and new consumer behavior have brought to light a new type of tourism – Virtual Tourism.

Tourism, assumes itself as a multifaceted and geographically complex activity that increasingly generates new (and different) market segments with different individual interests (Sousa, Magalhães & Soares, 2021). The term niche, in a marketing perspective, refers to two key interrelated ideas: that there is a place in the market for the product, and that there is an audience for that same product. This refers to a specific product capable of keeping up with the needs of a specific market segment (Santos et al., 2021). In this chapter, we propose to study this tourism segment and its role, to mitigate the impact of Covid 19, both in tourism enterprises and tourist consumption. The main objectives of this work are: Conceptualize Virtual Tourism; Understand the impact that new technologies have on the design of new products and services in Tourism; Study the analogy between Tourism Marketing and Virtual Tourism; Analyze the impact of Virtual Tourism and Gamified Virtual Experiences in Pandemic time; Understand the potentialities and limitations of this tourism segment.

This Study is divided into different themes that are related to others, namely, Tourism and ICT; Marketing, Internet and Tourism and Virtual Tourism., We start by realizing the Impact of virtual tourism in pandemic time and In the end, we describe the final considerations about the limitations of the study and present what future studies can be carried out, based on this study.

THEORETICAL FRAMEWORK

Tourism and ICT

Over the years there has been an increase in competition among tourism destinations (Ferreira & Sousa, 2020), leading to the need for a deeper understanding about the tourism realm, impact and management. Tourism, as an area of study, has expanded its scope, reflecting an increasing recognition in the academic community paralleled by the application of interdisciplinary concepts and methods (Jafari & Aaser 1988). Areas in tourism research entail, for example, planning of tourism destinations, local development, environmental impact, territorial brand management and tourist loyalty (Sousa & Rodrigues, 2019; Alves et al., 2020). The field of tourism marketing, in particular, has faced increasing challenges in capturing market dynamics, such as, market fragmentation and diversity. New habits, needs and trends in the global tourism arena create more sophisticated consumers who systematically look for different and specific experiences. Such context calls for new market approaches (Sousa & Silva, 2019).

Increasingly, ICT (Information and Communication Technologies) play an important role in the tourism sector, such as Internet Marketing, from websites to social networks, as well as platforms, to promote the interest of those who understand tourism is a sector of social transformation and territorial development and seeks to achieve sustainable development. (Rodriguez & Rodriguez, 2018; Gössling, 2021) However, due to the flow of tourists, tourism may have negative effects, in terms of natural and cultural resources, affecting the tourism heritage, namely: the emergence of economic opportunities, which attract countless people, overcrowding the area; the creation of a low-quality image of the destination, derived from the commitment of the tourist experience; and the fact that social conflicts arise, which deteriorate cohesion and roots, thus creating a circle of destruction that may lead not only to the impoverishment of communities, but also to the destruction of natural and cultural heritage (Moreno, 2007; Perdomo, 2007; Yunis, 2006 cited by Rodriguez & Rodriguez, 2018).

The Internet is the ICT most powerful tool, having become a necessity today. Something positive that the Covid-19 pandemic caused, was the fact that the world had to readjust to a new reality, which for many was not new, but for others, it is a new area to be discovered. (Rodriguez & Rodriguez, 2018).

Globalization has always acted positively when it comes to ICT, changing the face of business competition, establishing a new paradigm, this being the basis of the so-called "third industrial revolution". It may be possible to say that this year, the world has gone through a new globalization, for everything that has happened, namely with ICT as already mentioned (Rodriguez & Rodriguez, 2018).

This new paradigm considers the change of the "Information Society", leading to new consumption habits that modify the structure of the-tourism market, with a readaptation of companies and destinations to ICT. This can originate some changes, namely the emergence of new forms of production and provision of services; formation of a diversified offer of tourist destinations; the emergence of an internationalized approach to tourism; increased travel due to low-cost packages; the level of customization of the superior tourist offer; clarity in increased social responsibility; and the increase in tourism in geographic areas far from the coast (Rodriguez & Rodriguez, 2018).

According to Vilaseca et al. (2007, p. 219) "the more mature a service is, the greater the capacity for innovation it has", that is, tourism growth increases its capacity to rethink new strategies. The use of ICTs allows destinations to improve their competitiveness and thereby increase their visibility. According to Rodriguez & Rodriguez (2018), the high growth of tourism in the world, is, among others, aided by using ICTs, which enable the displacement of people who would not be able to do it by traditional means, such as booking travel online.

As the tourism sector is active about information, ICT has not only transformed how companies relate to customers, thus creating an improvement in the productive and competitive capacity of those who adhere to new technologies, but also the loss of customers who do not fit into new technologies (Rodriguez & Rodriguez, 2018). According to UNCTAD (Goldbaum, 2006) a large proportion of tourism revenue is originated by developing countries, and goes to large multinationals in the sector. However, "the Internet offers an opportunity to change this pattern, as tourism providers (...) can directly access customers".

Tourism E-Commerce

Tourism is characterized by the sale of services, from the sale of airline tickets, to accommodation and experiences among others. Web 2.0 and new technologies have transformed the commercialization of these services and have caused impacts, such as the globalization of competition, an increase in the number of suppliers, a decrease in the number of sales intermediaries, as well as a greater speed in the dissemination of information about products and services (Ramos, 2011). E-commerce "is a system of transactions or realizations of commercial activities and business communications through computer networks, specifically related to the purchase and sale of products and services, and the transfer of funds through digital communications" (Fiore, 2001).

According to Veloutsou and Guzmán (2017) virtual environments provide many opportunities and various contexts for individual and group brand-centric relationships to evolve. Due to brands almost ubiquitous online presence, consumers clearly form relationships with online brands (Veloutsou & Mafe, 2019). Online brand-enabled relationships can flourish in many platforms, including social media, primarily Facebook (where most online brand–enabled relationship research is conducted), but also on Twitter, Pinterest, and Google+, travel sites as TripAdvisor, trading platforms, such as eBay, general company web pages, dedicated brand-community websites and online forums (Sousa et al., 2021).

In a scenario of technological development, and change in the way people relate to brands, it is essential to adjust the communication strategies of companies that are required to be present in the most varied communication formats to reach the intended targets. Social networks have already been perceived by companies as a great mechanism to help them reach their marketing goals and goals, especially in aspects such as customer engagement, customer relationship management and communication. In different contexts, companies look for ways to introduce social networks into the most diverse aspects of communicating with their customers, whether through interactivity, promotion, facilitating access to information, and even improving customer buying behaviour (Sousa et al., 2021).

The use of the Internet in companies in the tourism sector may be a positive factor, such as the case of e-commerce, which helps in the sale of services by companies, but like everything, it has a negative side, such as the fact that the customer buys directly from a specific supplier without being in touch with intermediaries, such as travel agencies (Marsilio & Vianna, 2015, p. 453).

The development of a strategy to understand the impact of e-commerce in the economy, overcomes a simple electronic transaction of goods and services. it is necessary to have a good understanding of the company's business, the market segment where the company intends to operate, the digital tools available for use, the knowledge of the most used forms of communication and the resources available for this investment. That said, using digital marketing tools, new dimensions are offered to digital communication and the relationship with the market, such as interactivity through email marketing; personalization through excellent service at a low cost; globalization, where the company publishes its website on the internet; the integration of several points, how to integrate partners and suppliers online; the approach to technology, allowing the dissemination of products in different ways; convergence; and the democratization of information (Kendzerski, 2005). With this, knowing the target audience is an asset to have the information and data necessary for all departments, thus managing to analyze and transform this general information into useful information (Kendzerski, 2005).

It is increasingly noticeable that the internet has changed the way people work, due to the excitement with technology, dominating strategic objectives through these tools as adepts of communication, sales, service and gaining customer loyalty, more and more, it is essential that companies have this business vision (Kendzerski, 2005).

Currently, tourism is going through a complicated moment, mainly in the economic-financial context. The heavy measures implemented by the government, affect the entire economy, all companies, put jobs at risk, and affect the standard of living and consumption of the population. Although many sectors can find alternatives, for example, restaurants can opt for the takeaway service or home delivery, activities and companies directly linked to tourism are more fragile. Despite this, the current client is increasingly individualistic, informed, demanding, and sophisticated and looks for increasingly personalized experiences. The internet is the most used channel to search for information about travel and destinations, since it is the medium that brings together a huge number of information sources, not only on the websites of agencies and other platforms related to tourism, such as TripAdvisor, but also for general information about airfares, jettisoning, culture, among others (Da Cruz Vareiro & De Sousa Pinheiro, 2017).

Companies must be aware of this information, such as choosing a vacation destination, which can also lead to preparing the trip individually. That said, "the proliferation of internet-only airfares, vacation packages sold online, as well as the penetration of low-cost airlines, make the travel sector one of the biggest revenue generators for e-commerce (Da Cruz Vareiro & De Sousa Pinheiro, 2017, p. 237).

Marketing, Internet, and Tourism

The world of Internet Marketing is constantly evolving, in a very demanding virtual world, in which the consumer seeks to get all possible information about the product or service before purchasing. It is essential to segment the market and consumers as well, to keep up with all trends and consumer preferences, as these same trends are highly changeable. Since Marketing is the task of "creating and executing a strategy that delivers the right message to the right people" to achieve the sale, the Internet presents an increase in the options available to achieve this goal". Thus, the concept of E-Marketing or Digital Marketing emerges, irrefutable reality of the day (Moita, 2017, pp. 160-171). In this context, and according to Ferreira and Sousa (2020), facebook is the most widely used social networking site in the world, allowing businesses to reach many more people and more occurrences than companies using other means such as calls, emails or through meetings / meetings. The Facebook is considered an attractive social network for digital marketing specialists and for online ads. These ads use social networks to connect customers to businesses, thereby creating new opportunities for customers to get to know their brands and products.

In Tourism, ICT has generated new business models and has changed the structure of promotion and distribution of the tourist product. Moita, 2017 states that "factors such as diversification of tourism supply and change in demand (quantitatively and qualitatively), constitute great challenges to the performance of different tourism players. (...) for those who can meet new trends and the new global market, a range of new business opportunities, new distribution channels, and new market niches are emerging." As a Service Industry, the various tourism companies depend, on the marketing activity to better position themselves and face an increasingly competitive market.

Following the trend of a world reality and a profile of the most technological tourist, Portugal realized the importance of increasing its online presence, through digital strategies that give greater representation to the Destination. Since 2013, Turismo de Portugal has begun to review strategies, increasing to five million euros the budget for Internet campaigns. This promotion was reflected in the increase in the number of tourists and the achievement of several awards and distinctions around tourism. In the Tourism Strategy 2027, there is a patent expansion of social networks, the redefinition of the business model according to the growing impact of the Millennium generation, and the definition of ICT as the engine of the economy. This strategic vision aims to affirm Portugal as Smart Destination, with several digital measures of national and regional scope (Silva, 2018).

Digital Marketing, Practices, and Trends

Year after year digital marketing has been consolidating itself as one of the most efficient tools to attract consumers and expand the reach of the brand. The tools and practices possible for this function are very diverse and every day new trends that elevate Marketing to new practices arise.

In the tourism industry, Digital Marketing has changed the way companies approach their customers. Digital Marketing requires a greater ability to track user behavior and campaign performance in real-time. This new form of marketing and new technologies evolved so fast, that they have changed the way tourists travel, plan, and experience their holidays. Generations such as Millennials present themselves as the prototype of the tourist of the future and their preferences and consumer trends, are the subject of analysis by tourist organizations. Based on this generation, it is likely that the new tourist is the one who is connected to a mobile device, with access to a variety of sources of information, interacting in a social network where it supports the eyes of other tourists through augmented reality that facilitates interaction with the scenario in different new ways (Magano & Cunha, 2020).

The Role of Social Networks in Promoting a Tourist Product

The Internet has made it possible for people to join others in sharing interests, researching new sources of information, and publishing content and opinions. The so-called "social web" provides resources that allow those who have access to technology, the possibility of having a voice. The use of social networks is one of the most popular activities and it is undeniable the impact that social media have had on society, a little all over the world (Silva, 2018).

Since social networks are translated into online communities, where millions of users interact, these are now extremely important for the success of the activity of companies and tourism organizations.

Social Media Marketing is used in all sectors and refers to the use of different technologies, channels, and software, to create, communicate, deliver and exchange offers that have their value to different stakeholders (Jacobson, Gruzd, & Hernández-García, 2020).

For companies, social networks are used as a communication tool to promote and sell products, while for the public, they are commonly used as a place of information sharing and interacting with other users. In this way, Marketers use the information generated by social networks, with three main objectives: evaluation of the customers' opinion, through the collection and processing of data; develop a personalized offer and enhance the relationship with the customer, since, through the generation of content per user, they can reach new customers, engage customers in a relationship with the brand and retain them through interaction with them and other users (Jacobson, Gruzd, & Hernández-García, 2020).

Social Media revolutionized Marketing, leading to profound changes in market analysis, although still important, traditional promotion channels have lost some strength, which translates into the need to combine integrated strategies on both fronts of Marketing, thus extending the sphere of influence of companies.

About tourism and social networks or Social Media, they changed the way they think and make decisions and took the experience of planning and making a trip, to a new level. It has enabled a more democratic choice of destinations, bringing to the tourist map, less-known destinations. Social Media is the new place where tourists collect information about destinations and choose the destination through suggestions from other users. A new consumer-traveler was born, more participatory in the act of consumption, to which tourism organizations should be attentive when planning their business model.

Many authors claim in recent years that the presence of companies and destinations in social networks provides the attraction of new tourists and maintains existing ones, social media, allow a greater reach and interaction.

Today, the reality of social media marketing presents new nuances, since consumer behavior is influenced by different factors, particularly about the influence of opinion leaders. For this reason, Marketers begin to develop more detailed strategies in the field of Influence Marketing, where an association relationship is established between the Brand and a certain influencer, to reach a greater number of potential consumers (Ferreira, 2018). Also, the Destiny Management Organizations (DMO), have adopted new strategies, like using the digital influencers to promote their tourism resources and attract new tourists, like Madeira Island and Alentejo, that bet in Digital Marketing, associated with public figures, like actors, models, bloggers, and others, using the influence they have on their followers, (Barreiro, Breda & Dinis, 2019).

Digital Influencers, a New Reality

We find ourselves in the Age of Influence, where purchasing decisions are greatly influenced by family, friends, brand communication, and a diversity of people we follow on social networks. With the appearance of social media, the Internet becomes a participatory platform which allows people to collaborate and share information,, turning normal people into world known influencers, which attracts the brands, and become, a lucrative activity both to companies and influencers. (Leung, Law, van Hoof & Buhalis, 2013; Simas & Júnior 2018).

In this matter, influencers are individuals who can stand out on social networks due to their opinion or behavior in each context. (SanMiguel, 2020) They are virtual opinion-makers, who exercise massive power since they hold a lot of creativity with their followers. The use of social networks stimulates the idea of belonging to a group, and the amount of information to which the new consumer is exposed daily, makes him rely only on the F Factor (family, friends, Facebook friends, and followers) and this favors the role of digital influencers (Ramalho, 2019).

According to the different existing social platforms, several authors have presented different typologies of digital influencers over the last few years. Following technological evolution, typologies of influencers, such as Avatars and others who use cutting-edge technology such as Augmented Reality and 4D have appeared, producing innovative content that captures more and more adherents and transforming the consumer process of the new generations.

In tourism, influencers have become the new travel guides, either by reporting their first-person experience creating a greater proximity, credibility, and authenticity that travel brochures do not have, or because visitors today seek a more personal and creative approach that conveys emotions to them. The individual is subjected to social influence before the trip when he receives feedback through comments or other content about travel, on social media and creates expectations about it (Ferreira, 2018).

"Digital influencers, when making use of their profiles on social networks, not only advertise products, brands, and services, but also tourist destinations, through photo posts and videos, due to the trips made (...) The image, therefore, acts as a motivating element of the tourist's desire to want to know a destination. (Perinotto, Mota, & Ferreira, 2018).

According to this, the information that opinion leaders provide, directly affects consumer's purchasing decisions, and drives the consumption of tourism products/services. Observing the new practices, it is possible to foresee a transformation in tourism supply and demand.

Virtual Tourism

Over the years, society has come to recognize the important role played by ICT in their daily lives. ICT has been developing over the years, and there is a daily relationship with the world of technologies, so it becomes essential, to accompany this technological growth and adapt to it.

According to Fernandes (2015) today, virtual reality has been causing some changes in various sectors of the economy, revealing itself as a new tool for the communication and dissemination of experiences. One of the sectors that has been following this technological evolution, is the tourism sector. This sector has undergone intense changes, not only due to technological developments but also because of the increase in content produced online, which influences consumer behavior. As we know, tourism is one of the economic activities that most contributes to the development of the economy, thus, virtual reality was adopted, as being a new innovative marketing strategy for the advertising of products and services, increasing competitiveness in the market (Oliveira & Correa, 2017).

In the field of tourism, virtual reality is described as: "a sensory experience mediated by a computer that facilitates access to the visual and auditory dimensions of a tourist destination" (Sambhanthan & Good, 2013). The authors Oliveira and Correa (2017) state that technology enables the sharing of communication and interaction by consumers and organizations and develops basic business functions such as e-Commerce or e-Marketing, and finally, e-Management or electronic management.

In the Guttentag's opinion (2010), virtual tourism is much more than technology applied to tourism, it is the combination of several concepts and factors that together make a successful product. As an example, we have restaurants that have an application that serves to call the waiter, see the menu, and even ask for the bill; the theme parks that allow children to learn more about their childhood heroes and even the museums, which link fun with technology, allowing the little ones to learn more, interactively. It is considered that virtual tourism represents much more than seeing a certain destination through a mobile device, such as a computer, tablet, or smartphone. It is the ability to provoke desires and needs to look for more and to know more.

According to Magalhães (2017), the main objectives of this type of tourism are based on complementing physical travel, particularly as an aid element in the consumer's purchase decision and the planning of tourist trips. However, there are situations in which virtual tourism is chosen, as a substitute for physical travel, mainly because it manages to break the spatial, temporal, and other barriers related to the conditions of the place, and enables the experience of travelling to disabled individuals, who otherwise, were unable to do so.

In short, virtual tourism has become essential these days, since it allows everyone, regardless of their social class, to travel without leaving home, offering the opportunity to learn more about a particular place, as well as experiencing unique experiences (Magalhães 2017).

As mentioned in Sussamann and Vanhegan (2000) technological evolution allows to relate several fields, namely the area of tourism in which virtual reality can be practiced, namely in the areas of tourism policy and planning, which are related to sales, promotion, interest, among others. In this way, these authors identify the main potentialities of the implementation of virtual reality in the tourism sector, as a complementary component to traditional tourism, being these:

- Virtual tourist experiences appear to be easy to perform and have low costs. (Caproni, 1992, as referred to in Sussamann & Vanhegan 2000).
- As mentioned in Santos (2014), one of the impossibilities of being able to travel is the lack of time available. Contrary to this factor, virtual tourism allows tourists to travel without having to leave home, reconciling the factors of time and availability of the tourist.

According to Bauer and Jackson (1994, as mentioned in Sussmann & Vanhegan, 2000), there are developing countries that do not have self-promotion skills, however, virtual reality presents itself as a support to these same countries, enabling them use others, which are more accessible marketing techniques.

- Following Leston (1996, as mentioned in Sussmann & Vanhegan, 2000) one of the sectors where virtual reality can be applied, is in travel agencies, as being a travel planning tool for their clients, as the client can explore the place before the purchase, getting more informed about it, thus avoiding disappointments during the visit.

Virtual reality can be understood not only as a strategy in the promotion of tourism, but also as a complement to traditional tourism. This relationship influences the tourism sector, revealing itself as an asset for it. According to the characteristics that virtual tourism has, the same in some pertinent examples may replace physical travel. (Ghisi & Macedo, 2006; Gomes & Araújo, 2012; Guttentag, 2010; Haz López, Cruz Yagual et al., 2016; Prideaux, 2005, as mentioned in Sussmann & Vanhegan, 2000). Then, examples are presented that justify the situation exposed above.

- Authors Rafael and Almeida (2014) consider that tourists can learn more about a specific place, through for example, the online zooming platform.
- According to the author Pereira (2016), virtual tourism allows tourists to travel in time, and to learn more about times and places that currently do not exist, taking as an example, the Tower of London in the year 1255. The use of a smartphone and virtual reality equipment is essential for you to enjoy this trip to the past.[1]
- Caneday (1992, as mentioned in Sussmann & Vanhegan, 2000) defends virtual tourism as an asset for tourists who have some type of disability, whether physical or psychological since it allows them to know and visit a tourist destination. To complete this idea, Renfrew (1996, as mentioned in Sussmann & Vanhegan, 2000) considered that the same happens with inaccessible places, because they are protected/preserved natural places, or even because they are dangerous and unsafe places.

Virtual tourism presents itself, currently as the future of tourism. Derived from the outbreak caused by Covid-19, this type of tourism has become a kind of escape from the pandemic. However, despite the numerous advantages in the implementation of virtual reality, there are some obstacles for some areas of tourism, namely travel agencies and for the consumer/tourist himself. Therefore, some barriers to virtual tourism will be presented (Magalhães 2017).

- The human being is considered a sociable being, and thus, when opting for virtual tourism, the tourist may miss the real experience he has when he physically moves to a certain place, especially the social experience. However, the authors Sussamannv & Vanhegan (2000) argue that this

barrier can be interpreted as a positive point since some tourists find it difficult to interact with local cultures, and by not enjoying the social experience, it will contribute to the nonexistence of cultural constraints.
- The consumer/tourist may come to overconsume this type of tourism and this can cause addiction, therefore, in these cases, there may be social consequences, making the consumer/tourist unwilling to communicate with other people (Sussamann & Vanhegan 2000).
- Since virtual tourism is carried out online, experiences and memories fall far short when compared to physical visits (Sussamann & Vanhegan 2000).
- Since virtual tourism does not fit into the concept of traditional tourism, this ends up losing its essence and becomes artificial and as advocated by Sussmann and Vanhegan (2000), it comes to be an artificial distraction.

It is now necessary to make a distinction between the concepts of augmented reality and virtual reality. Although these concepts are identical, both realities have different characteristics and objectives.

For Pedrosa and Zappa-la Guimarães (2019), augmented reality is defined as a system that makes it possible to expand the relationship between the subject, the real and the virtual world, elaborating scenarios and realities that are common between the two worlds. To complement this idea, Azuma, et al. (2001), emphasizes that augmented reality integrates real and virtual elements and transforms them into real scenarios, being able to easily distinguish the real from the virtual. This concerns an immersion environment created through technological resources, in which the user practices a certain function. The same authors argue that in augmented reality other senses are included in addition to sight, such as smell, hearing, and touch, based on visual display or not, managing to enrich the user's experience.

To complete this idea, the brands Nintendo, Niantic Labs, and The Pokémon Company released in 2016, the viral game Pokémon GO for smartphones, whose purpose was to capture Pokémon's through a real map of the territory, in several countries are an example of how the contents of augmented reality can have good results around entertainment (Rodrigues, 2018).

In this line, Gamification has brought more interaction between tourism destiny experiences and their consumers. Due to the increased use of mobile phones, gamification is seen by tourism companies and organizations as a major trend to attract and entertain visitors. It can be used in tourism as a strategy to engage tourists, with, for example, city games, interactive museum games, or treasure hunts. It also contributes to tourists' visit satisfaction, promoting their loyalty, and it can be by itself a marketing strategy to promote the destiny with a system of points each time the consumer uses a touristic product or service like frequently fly programs on-air companies or Foursquare that give gifts in local restaurants, according to visitors achievements, or when they comment on digital platforms or social media, like in google local guides, TripAdvisor, and others, (Xu, Weber, & Buhalis, 2013).

On the other hand, virtual reality presents itself as a three-dimensional environment created by the computer, most of the time with immersive and interactive resources, where there is a clear dependence on the use of equipment in closed environments, for example, helmets, headphones, and projectors connected to glasses and smartphones Kriner (2001, as mentioned Quinquiolo, Santos, & Souza, 2020).

Authors Sherman and Craig (2003, as mentioned in Pedrosa & Zappa-la Guimarães 2019) consider that virtual reality incorporates four indispensable components for experimentation, namely, the virtual world; immersion; sensory feedback, and interactivity. They define virtual reality as a resource formed by computer simulations that identify the participant's position and actions and replace or increase the return of one or more senses, causing the sensation of being mentally immersed or present in the simulation, like a virtual world. In addition to having the ability to reproduce real-life, virtual reality makes it possible to transport users to another world. With virtual reality, the user is transported to a simulated environment, disconnecting him from everything around him.

For all those wishing to experience a new experience through virtual reality, they can opt for the Baths of Caracalla, located in Rome, Italy, where virtual reality technology is applied, to call tourists' attention. This advanced technology enables tourists to travel, in real-time, to the past, thus managing to compare it with the present (Taufer & Ferreira, 2019). Another example of the virtual experience in Tourism is in Manhattan, New York. The tourist is offered the opportunity to learn more about it, before arriving at the place. By using 3D glasses, tourists can immerse themselves inside the hotel, to get to know the space, and define their room. The Renaissance New York Midtown Hotel was one of the first to apply this type of technology. In Brazil, the Itaipu Binacional Hydroelectric Plant uses 3D glasses and a video consisting of 360-degree images and computer graphics, to transport tourists into the factory, being virtually accompanied by two guides (Taufer & Ferreira, 2019).

Currently, there are also several amusement parks using this type of technology, namely the VR Time Machine Dinosaur Park and the Jurassic VR- Google Cardboard, and finally, the Safari tours adventures VR 4D, which provides the experience of a safari, in a park designed by computer graphics (Taufer & Ferreira, 2019). Leite (2020) draws an analogy between augmented reality and virtual reality. The same refers that virtual reality tries to transport the users to the virtual environment using equipment in closed environments, while the augmented reality does not have any type of restrictions about the environment. In the virtual environment coming from augmented reality, it is taken to the physical environment so that there is a more natural interaction among the users.

Contribution of Virtual Tourism to Mitigate the Negative Impact of Covid-19 On the Sector

The rapid development of technologies has resulted in the emergence of innovative digital media and methods that give new life to tourism products. Digital technologies such as Laser Scan help create and recreate two- or three-dimensional environments and objects, offering a digital or physical experience. Replicas can be presented through virtual reality, augmented reality, or mixed reality (Bec, Moyle, Schaffer, & Timms, 2021).

During mandatory confinement, due to Covid 19 and borders closed in almost every country in the world during March and April, museum platforms and websites emerged, and destinations that allowed people to travel without leaving home, which helped combat anxiety, because of isolation, uncertainty, and loneliness. AirPano, Google Arts & Culture, Era Virtual, Go tours, You visit, British museum and Oceanarium of Lisbon, are just some of the many examples of sites that transport us to the virtual trip. It is even possible to book a trip on schedule, with a tour guide, for a symbolic value, and on the day and time scheduled, through video conference, you will be accompanied on a visit entitled to know all the history and all curiosities about the chosen destination, as if it were a conventional tour.

Digital technologies bring potential to tourism, such as enhancing the preservation of historical sites and educating its visitors to this end. The virtual experience can also generate revenue for destinations, reducing the impacts of seasonality and promoting its economic sustainability, since it will be available for purchase online. This experience will stimulate the desire to visit the destination, functioning as a marketing tool (Bec, Moyle, Schaffer, & Timms, 2021).

Figure 1. Virtual Technology for Second Chance Tourism Model
Font: *(Bec, Moyle, Schaffer, & Timms, 2021)*

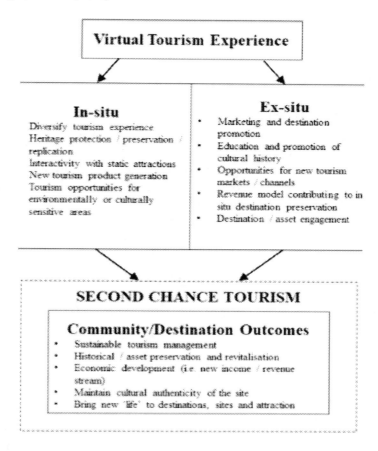

Whether virtual tourism will be the way to travel in the future, it is not yet known, and studies emerge on its possible impacts, to understand, whether conventional tourist demand will suffer a decrease or increase, attracting tourists for certain trips. The dynamics of this society directly affect tourist activity, which has become one of the most important economic and social activities of the century. The tourist is becoming increasingly demanding, looking for more knowledge, and authentic experiences, which leads him to look for new services, products, and markets.

CONCLUSION

It is possible to conclude that new technologies have led to the appearance of new forms of Tourism Marketing, revolutionizing in a certain way, the physiognomy of how to travel. Tourists are increasingly demanding and technological, designing new products and niches. In this sense and responding to the needs of new generations, namely millennials and generation z, who are increasingly technological experts and concerned with the sustainability of destinations, Virtual Tourism has emerged. The COVID-19 pandemic positively provided an opportunity for Virtual Tourism, since, due to confinement, borders were closed and for health reasons, tourists were afraid to travel. Motivated by the lack of jobs and income, workers and tourist companies created online solutions and took advantage of existing solutions to overcome the crisis in the sector, such as visits to museums, visits to cities, online tourist guides, among others.

Today, Virtual Tourism is presented, and boosted by the pandemic, as a cohesive tourism product that will allow an alternative source of revenue for destinations and will promote preservation and sustainability initiatives, regarding its history, environment, and economy. Virtual tourism is gaining more and more notoriety in the market, as it allows an individual, without moving, to experience unique sensations. According to information from the literature, it is understood that virtual tourism currently consists of immersive environments and experiences of various types, which include digital and face-to-face tools, namely, virtual games that are already part of young people's routine, who use digital technologies to create unique sensory experiences such as virtual tours created using 3D glasses, among others. Although there are still many questions regarding the evolution of the tourism sector, it is possible to identify positive aspects for the adoption of this new segment, in the most diverse aspects. Even the concept of Second Chance Tourism came up (Bec, Moyle, Schaffer, & Timms, 2021). The elaboration of this chapter was enriching and allowed me to conceptualize Virtual Tourism, opening the spectrum to its potentialities and limitations. In the future, there will still be much to explore about this segment, namely about the new products and services that may arise from it, outline the profile of its consumer, and quantify what economic impacts it will have on destinations.

REFERENCES

Alves, G. M., Sousa, B. M., & Machado, A. (2020). The Role of Digital Marketing and Online Relationship Quality in Social Tourism: A Tourism for All Case Study. In J. Santos & O. Silva (Eds.), Digital Marketing Strategies for Tourism, Hospitality, and Airline Industries (pp. 49–70). IGI Global. doi:10.4018/978-1-5225-9783-4.ch003

Azuma, R., Baillot, Y., Behringer, R., Feiner, S., Julier, S., & MacIntrye, B. (2001, Nov.). Article. Recent Advances in Augmented Reality, 34-47.

Barreiro, T., Breda, Z., & Dinis, G. (2019). Marketing de Influência e Influenciadores Digitais: aplicação do conceito pelas DMO em Portugal. *Marketing & Tourism Review, 4*(1).

Bec, V., Moyle, B., Schaffer, V., & Timms, K. (2021). Virtual reality and mixed reality for second chance tourism. *Tourism Management, 83,* 104256. doi:10.1016/j.tourman.2020.104256

Da Cruz Vareiro, L. M., & De Sousa Pinheiro, T. C. (2017). A Influência Da Crise Na Escolha Pelo Consumidor Entre Agências De Viagens Ou Operadores On-Line. *Turismo - Visão e Ação, 19*(2), 220.

De Oliveira Magalhães, M. (2017). *Estudo da utilização de vídeos 360º na experiência turística.* Academic Press.

De Oliveira, R. K., & Correa, C. (2017). Virtual Reality como estratégia para o marketing turístico. *Virtual Reality, 10*(23).

Fernandes, F. A. R. (2015). A indústria hoteleira e as reclamações online: o caso TripAdvisor (Master). FEP, Porto.

Ferreira, J., & Sousa, B. (2020) Experiential Marketing as Leverage for Growth of Creative Tourism: A Co-creative Process. In Advances in Tourism, Technology and Smart Systems. Smart Innovation, Systems and Technologies (vol 171. pp 567-577). Springer. doi:10.1007/978-981-15-2024-2_49

Ferreira, A. (2018). *A Influência dos Social Media e dos Digital Influencers na intenção de visita e na imagem do destino.* Vila Nova de Famalicão: Universidade Lusíada.

Fiore, F. (2001). *E-marketing Estratégico.* Academic Press.

Goldbaum, S. (2006). World investment report 2005: transnational corporations and the internalization of R&D. *Revista de Economia Política, 26*(3). doi:10.1590/s0101-31572006000300009

Gössling, S. (2021). Tourism, technology and ICT: A critical review of affordances and concessions. *Journal of Sustainable Tourism, 29*(5), 733–750. doi:10.1080/09669582.2021.1873353

Guttentag, D. A. (2010). Virtual reality: Applications and implications for tourism. *Tourism (Zagreb).*

Jacobson, J., Gruzd, A., & Hernández-García, Á. (2020). Social media marketing: Who is watching the watchers? Journal of Retailing and Consumer Services.

Jafari, J., & Aaser, D. (1988). Tourism as the subject of doctoral dissertations. *Annals of Tourism Research, 15*(3), 407–429. doi:10.1016/0160-7383(88)90030-8

Kendzerski, P. (2005). *Web Marketing E Comunicação Digital.* Academic Press.

Leite, B. S. (2020). Aplicativos de realidade virtual e realidade aumentada para o ensino de Química. *Revista de Estudos e Pesquisas sobre Ensino Tecnológico, 6.*

López García, J. J., Lizcano, D., Ramos, C. M., & Matos, N. (2019). Digital marketing actions that achieve a better attraction and loyalty of users: An analytical study. *Future Internet, 11*(6), 130. doi:10.3390/fi11060130

Magano, J., & Cunha, M. (2020). Digital marketing impact on tourism in Portugal: A quantitative study. *African Journal of Hospitality, Tourism and Leisure, 9.*

Marsilio, M., & Vianna, S. L. G. (2015). Agências de Viagens e Turismo e o Impacto da Internet: um Estudo Bibliométrico. *Turismo - Visão e Ação, 16*(2), 450–476.

Moita, P. (2017). e-Business em Turismo. In F. Silva & J. Umbelino (Eds.), Planeamento e Desenvolvimento Turístico (pp. 159-171). Lisboa: Lidel.

Pedrosa, S. M., & Zappala-Guimarães, M. A. (2019). *Realidade Virtual e Realidade Aumentada: refletindo sobre usos e benefícios na educação.* Academic Press.

Pereira, N. (2016). *Fazer turismo no passado, com uma aplicação de realidade virtual.* Euronews.

Perinotto, A., Mota, D., & Ferreira, H. (2018). *As Mídias Sociais e os Influenciadores Digitais na Promoção de Destinos Turísticos.* Anais Brasileiros de Estudos Turísticos.

Quinquiolo, N. C., Santos, C. A., & Souza, M. A. (2020). Uso dos softwares de Realidade Aumentada como Ferramenta Pedagógica: Apresentação do Aplicativo Virtual TEE. Academic Press.

Rafael, C., & Almeida, A. (2017). Impacto da informação online na formação da imagem de destino virtual. *Dos Algarves: A Multidisciplinary E-Journal*, (23), 27-50.

Ramalho, B. (2019). *O Papel dos Influenciadores Digitais Portugueses na Promoção de um Destino Turístico*. Vila do Conde: Politécnico do Porto.

Rodrigues, R. A. C. S. (2018). *Realidade virtual e realidade aumentada: o papel das tecnologias nas estratégias de marketing em Portugal* (Doctoral dissertation).

Rodriguez, A., & Rodriguez, S. (2018). Impacto de las tic en el turismo: Caso colombiano. *Cuadernos de Turismo*, *41*, 399–418.

SanMiguel, P. (2020). *Influencer Marketing*. Editorial Almazura.

Santos, V., Ramos, P., Sousa, B., & Valeri, M. (2021). Towards a Framework for the Global Wine Tourism System. *Journal of Organizational Change Management*. Advance online publication. doi:10.1108/JOCM-11-2020-0362

Santos, A. (2014). *Visitas imersivas em contexto turístico* (Doctoral dissertation). Instituto Politécnico do Porto. Instituto Superior de Engenharia do Porto.

Sambhanthan, A., & Good, A. (2013). *A virtual world model to enhance tourism destination accessibility in developing countries*. Cornell University.

Silva, J. (2018). *Marketing digital e Redes Sociais no Turismo: O caso do Municipio de Ovar*. Universidade de Aveiro.

Simas, D., & Júnior, A. (2018). Sociedade em Rede: Os Influencers Digitais e a Publicidade Oculta nas Redes Sociais. *Revista de Direito. Governança e Novas Tecnologias*, *4*(1), 17–32. doi:10.26668/IndexLawJournals/2526-0049/2018.v4i1.4149

Sousa, B. B., Magalhães, F. C., & Soares, D. B. (2021). The Role of Relational Marketing in Specific Contexts of Tourism: A Luxury Hotel Management Perspective. In Building Consumer-Brand Relationship in Luxury Brand Management (pp. 223-243). IGI Global. doi:10.4018/978-1-7998-4369-6.ch011

Sousa, B., & Rodrigues, S. (2019). The role of personal brand on consumer behaviour in tourism contexts: The case of madeira. *Enlightening Tourism. A Pathmaking Journal*, *9*(1), 38-62. doi:10.33776/et.v9i1.3597

Sousa, B., & Silva, M. (2019). Creative tourism and destination marketing as a safeguard of the cultural heritage of regions: The case of sabugueiro village. *Revista Brasileira de Gestão e Desenvolvimento Regional*, *15*(5), 78–92.

Sussamann, S., & Vanhegan, H. J. (2000). Virtual Reality and the Tourism Product: Substitution or Complement? Realidade Virtual no Turismo: Entretenimento ou Mudança de Paradigma? *Rosa dos Ventos, 11*(4), 908-921.

Veloutsou, C., & Guzmán, F. (2017). The evolution of brand management thinking over the last 25 years as recorded in the Journal of Product & Brand Management. *Journal of Product and Brand Management, 26*(1), 2–12. doi:10.1108/JPBM-01-2017-1398

Veloutsou, C., & Mafe, C. R. (2019). Brands as relationship builders in the virtual world: A bibliometric analysis. *Electronic Commerce Research and Applications, 39*, 100901. Advance online publication. doi:10.1016/j.elerap.2019.100901

Vilaseca i Requena, J., Lladós i Masllorens, J., Garay Tamajon, L., & Torrent i Sellens, J. (2007). Tecnologías de la Información y Comunicación, innovación y actividad turística: Hacia la empresa en red. *Cuadernos de Turismo, 19*, 217–240.

Xu, F., Weber, J., & Buhalis, D. (2013). Gamification in Tourism. *Information and Communication Technologies in Tourism 2014: Proceedings of the International Conference.*

KEY TERMS AND DEFINITIONS

Consumer Behavior Online: The study of individuals, groups, or organizations and all the activities associated with the purchase, use and disposal of goods and services, including the consumer's emotional, mental and behavioral responses that precede or follow these activities in the online environment.

Digital Marketing: Is the marketing of products or services using digital technologies, mainly on the Internet, but also including mobile phones, display advertising, and any other digital medium.

E-Satisfaction: The contentment of a consumer with respect to his or her prior purchasing experiences with a given retail-oriented website.

E-WOM: Is any positive or negative statement made by potential, actual or a former customer which is available to a multitude of people via the internet.

Online Relationship: Is an integrative and multidimensional concept, such as relationship quality in an offline context.

Social Media: Social media are interactive computer-mediated technologies that facilitate the creation and sharing of information, ideas, career interests and other forms of expression via virtual communities and networks.

Social Networks: Is a social structure composed of persons or organizations, connected by one or several types of relationships, which share common values and goals.

Virtual Tourism: Is a simulation of an existing location, usually composed of a sequence of videos or still images. It may also use other multimedia elements such as sound effects, music, narration, and text. Virtual tourism is essentially a hybrid concept- it combines both the notions of virtual reality and tourism. In essence, virtual tourism facilitates a tourism experience, without actually having to travel anywhere. Virtual tourism takes many different forms and comes in vary degrees of technological capability.

ENDNOTE

[1] Available in: https://pt.euronews.com/ accessed on December 10, 2020

Chapter 9
Relationship Between ICT and Tourism:
The Case of Mediterranean Countries

Selman Bayrakcı
Necmettin Erbakan University, Turkey

Ceyhun Can Özcan
Necmettin Erbakan University, Turkey

ABSTRACT

The relationship between tourism and information and communication technology (ICT) is called electronic tourism or e-tourism. The use of ICT makes markets from local to global and has a positive effect in increasing the market share of firms. Managing, planning, developing, and marketing tourism data through ICT increase the development and economic potential of tourism. ICT has provided the strategic management of all tourism-oriented companies and revolutionized the operations within the tourism distribution channel, causing tourism-related stakeholders to reassess their actions and positions. The purpose of this chapter is to reveal the relationship between ICT and tourism in the case of 14 Mediterranean countries from approximately 1995–2019. Dumitrescu and Hurlin Panel causality test was used for this analysis. The main findings indicate that ICT stimulates tourism that, in turn, boosts ICT even further in some countries (Algeria, Egypt, Morocco, Tunisia, and Turkey).

INTRODUCTION

International tourism continues to be the world's largest and fastest-growing sector, accounting for more than a third of the value of the global service trade. According to the International Tourism Highlights published by the United Nations World Tourism Organization (UNWTO) in 2020, 2019 was another year of strong growth, through international arrivals grew below the exceptional rates seen in 2017 (+7%) and 2018 (+6%). Reaching two years before UNWTO's estimate, the tourism industry reached 1,460 million international tourist arrivals and 1,481 billion dollars international tourism receipts in 2019.

DOI: 10.4018/978-1-7998-8165-0.ch009

For seven years in a row, tourism exports have grown faster than goods exports. It is forecasted that this growth will continue to shape the tourism sector along with digitalization, innovation, accessibility, and social changes (UNWTO, 2020).

Recently, a radical change has been experienced in the structure and organization of the tourism sector with the ICT applications applied around the world (Aramendia-Muneta & Ollo-Lopez, 2013; Buhalis, 1998; Januszewska et al., 2015; Minghetti & Buhalis, 2010). The convergence between internet-informatics and communication-multimedia has provided new channels for both tourists and destinations to strengthen their communication processes while reducing search and distribution costs (Buhalis & Law, 2008). All tourism-oriented companies, such as tour operators, travel agencies, rental agencies, cruiser, and hotels, are widely experiencing the increasing impact of information and communication technology. Therefore, the tourist-buying process is based on information collected from many different channels. ICT is focused on designing the new scientific paradigm (through innovation, collaboration, collaboration with customers) of tourism development based on modern e-technologies. ICT application in the tourism economy supports the effective functioning of businesses because it speeds up management procedures and increases both the efficiency and quality of economic transactions performed in a business. Using modern information technologies enables a tourism business to use its resources in the fastest way possible (Januszewska et al., 2015).

ICT can provide the necessary tools and applications to perform tourism management more effectively. Thus, ICT can become an important determinant of organizational competitiveness and efficiency by enabling the tourism sector to increase its market share and expand its capacity to initiate innovations (Aramendia-Muneta & Ollo-Lopez, 2013). The chapter aims to reveal the relationship between ICT and tourism. Accordingly, a demand model was created for 14 Mediterranean countries between 1995 and 2019. Dumitrescu and Hurlin (2012) panel causality tests were applied to the model.

In this chapter, first, the relevant Conceptual Framework and Literature Review have been made and the issue has been discussed by integrating it with the literature. In the continuation of the chapter, there is the Methodology and Conclusion section. Under the title of conclusion, the results obtained from the literature and the results of this study are discussed and interpreted.

CONCEPTUAL FRAMEWORK

ICT (Information and Communication Technology)

Technological developments took place in four different stages in the form of obtaining, storing, processing, and transmitting information throughout human history. From the first stage to the last stage, the limitations on speed, distance, quantity, and reliability of the information obtained were gradually reduced (Vural, 2005). This age we live in today is known as the "Information Age". We are in the middle of this "Information Age". In the last decade, the rapid convergence of information and communication technologies has pushed people to use these two concepts together. All over the world, ICT has become increasingly important in every aspect of our daily life and work. ICT refers to technologies that provide access to information through telecommunications. Similar to Information Technology (IT), but primarily focuses on communication technologies (Kaya, 2020).

ICT is revolutionizing people's lives and the operations of businesses. Business organizations use ICT to process, store, disseminate and promote their products and services globally. With the use of the

Internet, people can access information from anywhere at any time. Therefore, living without the help of ICT becomes inevitable (Wagaw & Mulugeta, 2018). ICT is a general term used to describe various technologies that facilitate information by creating, acquiring, processing, and transmitting it. This process covers the internet, telecommunications, broadcasting, and microelectronics. Some common ICTs found in many developing economies are radio, television, and media. Adeyemi & Olaleye (2010) expanded these further and defined projectors, printers, radio tapes, televisions, computer hardware and software, dish antennas, photocopiers as ICT tools. Today, modern ICTs such as the internet, fax, e-mail, and mobile phone are available in many countries around the world. ICTs provide an effective tool for communicating knowledge and information. Mobile phone use is the fastest growing tool of ICT (Nyandro, 2016).

With the emergence and development of ICT, the removal of country borders also called globalization, and their cultural convergence have accelerated. These developments have been integrated into production systems and have become one of the important policy tools of companies in the world where competition is increasing. (Aytun et al., 2018). Information and communication theories have become an important driving force in the economic development of countries in a global world. The knowledge component plays a key role in creating the competitive potential of countries and improving international relations. (Petkova et al., 2019). ICT refers to various technological tools and resources used to collect, process, store, or exchange information in digital format. Their rapid development in recent years has made them important for companies, organizations and even countries in terms of economic growth and increasing competitiveness. (Tarutė & Gatautis, 2014). The rapid development of ICT worldwide over the past three decades has attracted increasing attention from many economists and researchers who focus on examining the business impact of ICT diffusion. (Bahrini & Qaffas, 2019).

While information technology in this term refers to advanced techniques and production methods in which information is the main source in the production of goods and services, the purpose of this technique and production is to create and develop the information needed. Therefore, as a concept of information technologies; It also includes computing and communication technologies based on microelectronics, while defining technologies that enable effective and efficient structuring of processes such as recording, storing, producing information by passing it through a certain processing process, accessing, storing, and transferring this information. Communication technology, on the other hand, is the techniques and applications that bring functionality to electronic intermediaries and audio and visual transmission functions, and these techniques and applications mainly serve the purpose of producing information and spreading the information flow quickly and effectively (Oğrak, 2010). In this sense, it is possible to say that the term information and communication technology means any tool, system, application, and technique that enables to create, transform, store and disseminate any information or data. Communication technologies also provide access to electronic information, which is the most powerful source of information technologies, without limitation of time and space (Odabaş & Akkaya, 2017).

Relationship between ICT and Tourism

Tourism is a sector that creates significant wealth at both global and local levels. Appropriate dissemination of ICT in this sector can increase the social and economic impacts that many citizens and organizations in developed and developing countries can benefit from. With the development of information technologies, it did not take long for ICT to become an indispensable part of modern life. In this context, information technologies cannot be ignored in any sector. Information technologies both reduce costs and increase efficiency. In addition, it raises the service quality to higher levels (Alford & Clarke, 2009). According to Sarı ve Kozak (2005), information technologies have led to the emergence of different channels in the tourism sector.

Since tourism is one of the most important sectors in today's world, many countries are competing to attract tourists with all means of communication and this communication has become the main driving force of tourism sectors all over the world. The role of communication is to inform potential tourists and influence their choices about tourist destinations and the types of tourist products they purchase (Wagaw & Mulugeta, 2018). Therefore, the widespread use of ICT in the tourism industry has created a more competitive environment and has become an indispensable element of business development (Berné et al., 2015).

As expressed by Spencer (2014), for developing countries interested in maintaining their tourism product, there is a critical need to explore their readiness, willingness, and ability to adopt new technology into their marketing, sales, and general interaction with an ever-evolving tourism market. Not only have ICTs made it easier for developing countries to market and distribute their products and increase their customer base, but they have also made it easier for investors to access market and management data, to share information, and to build trading partnerships. Moving into the e-business arena has provided opportunities for tourism stakeholders to offer fully developed web portals as comprehensive Destination Management Systems (DMS) that include booking and transaction facilities—thus promoting the opportunity to increase sales and to generate more revenue for the local economy. The Caribbean is competing with developed nations, which have largely integrated ICT in every aspect of the service industry (A. Spencer, 2019). According to Chevers (2015), American and European hotels have adopted ICT and successfully integrated systems like computer reservation system (CRS), customer relation management (CRM), enterprise resource planning (ERP), supply chain management (SCM), project management system (PMS), knowledge management system (KMS), and office automation system (OAS) and can realize the intended benefits (A. Spencer, 2019).

Adopting information and communication technologies such as computers and smartphones can facilitate tourism participation. Adoption of ICT allows people to browse tourism information widely through "apps" such as TripAdvisor, Booking.com, Agoda.com and Travelzoo, and their transaction costs (for example, information search costs and bargaining costs for cheapest accommodation) and their associated helps to reduce uncertainty (Zhu et al., 2021). One of the most effective tools of ICT is seen as the internet. Therefore, the subject of the internet will be explained separately. One of the most effective tools of ICT is seen as the internet. Therefore, the subject of the internet will be explained separately. The term internet used here is not merely to receive or send information from the internet. This term also includes concepts such as e-commerce, reservation, and social media, etc.

The travel and tourism sector was one of the first to be affected by the Internet with airlines offering tickets directly to consumers via the web and new travel intermediaries springing up and becoming major forces in the industry (Standing et al., 2014). A significant amount of destination marketing has also shifted to the web and in recent years Web 2.0 approaches have spawned large amounts of user-generated content in the form of travel blogs and reviews (Huang et al., 2010) and this often appears highly ranked in search engines when consumers enter keywords (Xiang & Gretzel, 2010).

The development and use of networked technologies such as the Internet leaves no industry unaffected, but perhaps affects the tourism industry more than any other. Tourism and technology, two of the largest, fastest-growing, and most dynamic industries have become inextricably linked and together they are changing the way society works (Sheldon, 1997).

The travel and tourism industries are information-driven and therefore highly receptive to the benefits of using the internet (Andreu et al., 2010). Internet use is gaining increasing acceptance among major stakeholders in the industry, including travel agencies (Abou-Shouk et al., 2013). In addition, more and more tourists are using websites to make reservations and/or get useful information (Bhat & Shah, 2014).

LITERATURE REVIEW

Tourism is a sector that creates significant wealth at both global and local levels. Appropriate dissemination of ICT in this sector can increase the social and economic impacts that many citizens and organizations in developed and developing countries can benefit from. Differences in owning, controlling, processing, communicating, and distributing knowledge have a greater impact on tourism production and consumption than in other economic sectors. These differences are determined by both the technological tools available to widely provide and distribute accurate information and the ability to use these tools effectively. The development of the Internet has changed the entire value chain of tourism creation, marketing, distribution, and consumption. For example, Buhalis and Kaldis (2008) showed that SMEs operating in the tourism sector in Athens will provide potential benefits with the increase in Internet usage (technology-based distribution channels). The authors argued that the adoption of electronic distribution channels and the internet as a marketing tool contributed to the development of e-tourism. Therefore, the internet makes searching destinations, tourism providers and services easier, and richer than traditional channels. Additionally, ICT increases the opportunities for direct relationships between consumers and suppliers and bypassing offline and online intermediaries. Using ICT also allows users to evaluate alternatives in terms of product features and price and to create personalized routes (Buhalis & Kaldis, 2008; Minghetti & Buhalis, 2010). According to Kumar et al. (2019), consumers are affected using and consuming ICT products aimed at changing consumer behavior and new growth opportunities. Alternatively, ICT can reduce market errors caused by information asymmetry by generating, storing, and transmitting data. The direct effects of ICT are related to the production of ICT products that can be differentiated in software and hardware production. Indirect effects are related to the growth effects caused by the application of ICT products. The implementation of ICT can directly reduce communication costs and raid production costs by developing new opportunities to improve production processes.

The importance of ICT is known by many countries. For example, Russia has planned five major objectives for developing tourism, one of which is related to the development of ICT infrastructure. Since digitalization and tourism are inseparable, projects have been initiated for its development. Some of those (Sheresheva, 2018):

- development of a unified information system "Electronic tour";
- creation of an information system that provides, on a reciprocal basis, visa-free group tours;
- creation of a pan-Russian database of tourist facilities, tourism industry organizations and tourism specialists; and
- creation of a database of activities related to the use of foreign tourist vessels.

This subject has been examined in the literature and some studies have been included. Kumar and Kumar (2012) analyzed the relationship between ICT, tourism, and Fiji's economic growth between 1980 and 2008 through the Boundary Test and the Granger Causality Test. Using the Boundary Test, they predicted an economic growth equation and found that tourism contributed 0.19% to the economy in the short term and about 0.23% in the long term; they stated that the contribution of ICT to the economy was 0.89% in the short term and 1.07% in the long term. Granger Causality Test results reveal that there is a one-way causality from capital stock to ICT from ICT to tourism and from GDP per capita to tourism. For this reason, they stated that ICT investments and the development of the tourism market are critical for the growth and development of Fiji. Studying the impact of ICT on tourism demand with a larger sample, Kumar and Kumar (2020) used mobile and broadband subscriptions to proxy for ICT. Additionally, they include the price and income of the source country and target destination in the model. Researchers used the pooled mean group approach for nine countries and the period 1995–2017 and 2002–2017. The causality analysis results show that ICT positively affects tourism demand and affects technology-based growth in major tourist destinations. In another study, Kumar and Sharma (2017) investigated the growth hypothesis based on ICT and tourism in India's case and Thailand using the data of 1995 and 2014 using cointegration, error correction models, and Granger causality tests. The study tests the existence of the long-term equilibrium relationship between international tourism, ICT, and economic growth. The researchers concluded that tourism and ICT have a significant impact on economic growth in Thailand. Alternatively, it has been concluded that tourism affects economic growth in the Indian economy and the use of ICT has not reached the expected level.

Adeola and Evans (2019) investigated the linear and non-linear effects of mobile phones and the Internet on tourism in Africa between 1996 and 2017, using the system general method of moments, which explains the cross-sectional dependence. Research results show that mobile penetration and internet use have significant negative effects on tourism, and quadratic mobile penetration and square of internet usage have significant positive effects. In their next study, Adeola and Evans (2020) examined the relationship between ICT, infrastructure, and tourism development between 1996 and 2016 in 40 countries in Africa using Dynamic Panel Gravity Model. Researchers claim that ICT and infrastructure have a statistically positive effect on the development of tourism, and the number of inbound tourists will increase as investments in ICT and infrastructure increase. Kumar et al. (2019) analyzed the relationship between ICT and tourism in Israel between 1960 and 2016, using the ARDL Boundary Test and the Granger Causality Test. Researchers have revealed that ICT has a positive effect in the short and long term, but the number of tourists visiting has a positive effect only in the long term. Additionally, they pointed out that ICT is the driving force in Israel's economic growth. In another sample, Lebbe and Aslam (2020) used an exploratory data analysis technique, the unit root test, and bivariate cointegration technique as analytical tools to test the long-term relationship between ICT and tourism demand in Sri Lanka during the period 1990–2018. The analysis results of the researchers indicate a positive relationship between ICT and tourism demand in Sri Lanka, and according to the result of the bivariate co-integration test, ICT in Sri Lanka has a long-term relationship with tourism demand. Likewise, Castro et al. (2020), who investigated the relationship between ICT and tourism economically, used a composed index of internet users, fixed broadband and mobile cellular subscriptions variables for ICT. The study results show that ICT is effective in the economic growth of tourism. The results also reveal that an increase in the burden caused by non-working people on a nation's working-age population has adverse effects on economic growth, while urbanization and inflation are insignificant. Promoting technology advancements, ICT diffusion and tourism expansion can foster economic growth.

Evaluating the negative aspects of ICT, Tsokota et al. (2019) in their work indicate that a combination of ICT, especially the internet, government policies deemed retrogressive and economic refugees emigrating from tourist-seeking countries have contributed to the soiling of the image, reputation and identity of Zimbabwe as an attractive tourism destination on a global scale. This has had an adverse effect on the growth of the tourism sector in the country.

Additionally, the researchers point out that according to the test result of the Granger causality test, there is a one-way Granger causal relationship from ICT to tourism demand.

When the studies in the literature are reviewed, we can list the relationship between ICT and tourism as follows (Ronald R. Kumar & Kumar, 2012; Mandić & Garbin Praničević, 2019; Minghetti & Buhalis, 2010; Zaidan, 2016):

- ICT improves and facilitates the interaction between the tourism sector distribution channels.
- ICT contributes to the increase in productivity by facilitating the information exchange between tourism employees.
- The tourism sector can reach its consumers faster and more easily through ICT.
- ICT offers effective, fast, and cheap opportunities to tourism businesses in marketing.
- Businesses can create an advantage over their competitors by creating databases about their consumers (target audiences).
- As ICT provides information infrastructure required by the tourism sector, it contributes to better usage of resources in the tourism sector.
- ICT increases the interaction of tourism businesses in the supply chain and between departments.
- The increase in the use of ICT also enables an increase in the demand for tourism.
- For tourists, ICT facilitates access to information such as easy access to information, price comparison, access to information and comments about the destination to be visited, ease of choosing between accommodation and food and beverage businesses.
- Additionally, telecommunication products increase the vacation experience of tourists by providing rapid access to information during their active travels.

METHODOLOGY

Data and Variables

To undertake the statistical analysis, data are assembled from WDI (World Development Indicators) databases. For the purposes of estimation, Internet User and International tourist arrivals are used.

This study uses the sample selected 14 Mediterranean Countries: Algeria, Croatia, Cyprus, Egypt, Arab Rep., France, Greece, Israel, Italy, Malta, Morocco, Slovenia, Spain, Tunisia, Turkey. The study uses the sample period 1995 to 2019, a period for which all relevant data are available. In the literature, there are several models to estimate the relationships between these variables. This study is based on the model for panel data:

Table 1. Data description

Variables	Code	Unit	Source	Period
International tourism	*lnta*	Number of arrivals	WDI	1995–2019
Individuals using the Internet	*lniu*	% of the population	WDI	1995–2019

$$lnta_{it} = a_0 + \beta_1 lniu_{it} + \varepsilon_{it} \tag{1}$$

where at cross-section *i* and period *t*, **lnta** is the natural log of tourists arriving, **lniu** is the natural log of individuals using the Internet and ε is the error term.

PANEL GRANGER CAUSALITY TEST

Testing causality in a panel framework has attracted interest during the last decade, and different approaches have been developed to examine the direction of causality in a panel data context. One attempt is based on estimating a panel vector autoregressive or vector error correction model by means of a generalized method of moments (GMM) estimator. This approach is, however, not able to consider either cross-sectional dependence or heterogeneity. GMM estimators, furthermore, can produce inconsistent and misleading parameters unless slope coefficients are, in fact, homogeneous (Pesaran et al., 1999).

The second approach proposed by (Kónya, 2006) is sufficient to account for cross-sectional dependency and heterogeneity across cross-sections. This approach employs the seemingly unrelated regressions (SUR) estimation method developed by Zellner (1962) to control for contemporaneous correlations (cross-sectional dependency) and produces bootstrap critical values to make results robust irrespective of unit root and co-integration properties. Although Konya's testing procedure has attracted much interest in empirical applications, this approach includes a drawback for the panel data sets if the number of cross-sections (N) is not reasonably smaller than time periods (T) because the SUR estimator is only feasible for panels with large T and small N (Pesaran et al., 1999).

The third approach proposed by Dumitrescu and Hurlin (2012) is based on averaging standard individual Wald statistics of Granger tests under the assumption of cross-section independency. This approach, thereby, controls for heterogeneity but it is not able to account for cross-sectional dependence (Ozcan et al., 2017).

In this study, a panel causality test developed by Dumitrescu and Hurlin (2012) was used. This test can be used when N is growing, and T is constant. Moreover, it can also be used when T>N and when N>T. The test, which is based on VAR, assumes that there is no cross-sectional dependency. Yet, the Monte Carlo simulations show that even under the conditions of cross-sectional dependency, this test can produce strong results. This test is used for balanced and heterogeneous panels. There are two distributions in this test: asymptotic and semi-asymptotic. Asymptotic distribution is used when T>N, while semi-asymptotic distribution is used when N>T. When there is a cross-sectional dependency, simulated and approximated critical values, obtained from 1.000 replications, are used (Akbas et al., 2013).

Apart from these, individual remainders for each cross-sectional unit are independent. This test is based on the normal distribution and allows for heterogeneity. Also, individual remainders are independently distributed among the groups. In this test, homogenous non-stationary (HNC) hypothesis was used for the analysis of causality relationship and heterogeneous models. For T>N asymptotic and for N>T semi-asymptotic, a distribution was used in the HNC hypothesis. When there is a cross-sectional dependency, simulated and approximated critical values are used (Akbas et al., 2013).

Empirical Results

Descriptive analyzes of variables are included in Table 2. Descriptive statistics provide important information about variables.

Table 2. Descriptive statistics

	lniu	lnta
Mean	1.1905	7.0070
Median	1.5491	6.9164
Maximum	1.9576	8.3304
Minimum	-2.7598	5.7160
Std. Dev.	0.8935	0.6856
Skewness	-2.0022	0.2675
Kurtosis	7.1602	1.8608
Jarque-Bera	486.2541***	23.1008***
Prob.(JB)	0.0000	0.0000
Sum	416.7076	2452.480
Sum Sq. Dev.	278.6293	164.0828
Observations	350	350

*, **, and *** respectively denote statistical significance at 10, 5, and 1 percent.

Table 2 displays the basic statistics of the two variables of our data. Specifically, it contains the skewness, kurtosis, standard deviation and the mean, minimum and maximum values of two variables in this study. The descriptive statistics analysis shows that the Jarque-Bera test statistics for both variables are normally distributed in the series. In empirical studies, having a normal distribution of the variables is very important for the consistency of the analysis. In addition, Table 2 shows that the mean values of lniu and lnta variables are 1.1905 and 7.007, respectively. There are 350 observations in total.

Table 3 shows the unit root test results of the variables. In the causality test, the series must be stationary at the same level. It is concluded that both variables are stationary in their differences. With the stationary of the series, causality analysis can be started. In Tables 4 and 5, Dumitrescu & Hurlin panel causality test findings are summarized. The Dumitrescu & Hurlin panel causality test hypotheses are as follows:

H_0: lnta does not cause lniu
H_1: lnta causes lniu

Table 3. PANIC panel unit root test

	Constant		Constant and Trend	
Levels	**Statistic**	**p-value**	**Statistic**	**p-value**
lnta				
$Z^c_{\hat{e}}$	-1.9712	0.9756	-1.0846	0.8609
$P^c_{\hat{e}}$	13.2489	0.9917	19.8837	0.8687
lniu				
$Z^c_{\hat{e}}$	-2.1240	0.9832	-2.6686	0.9962
$P^c_{\hat{e}}$	12.1051	0.9961	8.0299	0.9999
First difference				
lnta				
$Z^c_{\hat{e}}$	7.1976***	0.0000	6.6709***	0.0000
$P^c_{\hat{e}}$	81.8622***	0.0000	77.9206***	0.0000
lniu				
$Z^c_{\hat{e}}$	2.5971***	0.0047	1.0381***	0.0496
$P^c_{\hat{e}}$	47.4351***	0.0123	35.7682***	0.0486

$P^c_{\hat{e}}$ is a Fisher's type statistic based on *p*-values of the individual ADF tests. $Z^c_{\hat{e}}$ is a standardized Choi's type statistic for large N samples. The maximum number of common factors was taken as 3.

The findings obtained reveal that there is a causality relationship between ICT and Tourism. Firstly, the findings of the causality relationship from tourism to ICT are reported in Table 4. The findings obtained show that tourism in Croatia and Malta is the cause of ICT. It has 1% and 5% significance levels, respectively. For the panel group effect, the Panel $Z_{N,T}$ statistic (for T> N) is insignificant. In other words, it is concluded that tourism is not the cause of ICT.

The hypothesis that ICT is the cause of tourism or not is tested in Table 5. The findings obtained show that ICT is the cause of tourism in Algeria, Egypt, Morocco, Tunisia, and Turkey. Considering the panel group effect, it is concluded that ICT is the cause for tourism at the 10% significance level.

CONCLUSION

In this study, the relationship between ICT and tourism between 1995 and 2019 was examined using the Dumitrescu & Hurlin Panel causality test. The main findings indicate that ICT stimulates tourism, which, in turn, boosts ICT even further in some countries (In Algeria, Egypt, Morocco, Tunisia, and Turkey).

The findings from the study have similar to the Kumar and Kumar (2020) study in the literature. Additionally, the causality relationship supports the finding that ICT stimulates tourism, as in the Adeola and Evans (2019) study.

When both causality results are evaluated together, it is concluded that the causality relationship from tourism to ICT is weak, while the causality relationship from ICT to tourism is strong. The findings are instructive for researchers and policymakers. It is possible to offer some suggestions to policymakers

Table 4. Dumitrescu & Hurlin panel causality between ICT and tourism (lnta ≠> lniu)

	Ho: lnta does not cause lniu		
Countries	Lag	Wald	p-val
Algeria	1	0.003	0.954
Croatia	1	8.664***	0.003
Cyprus	1	0.000	0.986
Egypt, Arab Rep.	1	1.500	0.221
France	1	0.539	0.463
Greece	1	0.030	0.864
Israel	1	2.663	0.103
Italy	1	0.199	0.655
Malta	1	3.629*	0.057
Morocco	1	0.180	0.671
Slovenia	1	0.202	0.653
Spain	1	1.424	0.233
Tunisia	1	0.471	0.492
Turkey	1	0.024	0.876
		Test Stat.	p-val
Panel W_{bar}		1.395	0.465
Panel $Z_{N,T}$		1.045	0.296
Critical Values:	1%	5%	10%
	4.241	2.556	1.911

Notes: ≠> denotes non-Granger causality hypothesis. The optimal lag(s) are selected by Schwarz information criterion by setting maximum lags to 3 in VAR model. The bootstrap critical values are based on 1000 bootstrap replications. *, **, and *** respectively denote statistical significance at 10, 5, and 1 percent.

in the development of the tourism sector in the Mediterranean countries as well as for many countries. Therefore, ICT and capital investments can be supported to encourage technological advances that support the tourism sector. Thus, ICT can help businesses in the tourism sector gain a competitive advantage by providing opportunities such as access to reliable and accurate information, establishing closer relationships with suppliers and customers, maintaining price leadership in the market, differentiating, and developing their products. Additionally, countries, promoting their touristic products through ICT may contribute to the increase in tourism demand. Social sharing such as sharing information about destinations, easy access, evaluation of accommodation facilities for tourists, positively affects the tourism demand of countries. Finally, it is difficult to make definitive judgments about the relationship between ICT and tourism. Because ICT is constantly changing and developing. Therefore, the tourism sector should follow the developments in ICT continuously, in terms of the promotion and development of tourism.

Like many developing countries, it is possible to offer several suggestions that Mediterranean countries should pay attention to in the development of the tourism sector in general:

Table 5. Dumitrescu and Hurlin panel causality between ICT and tourism (lniu ≠> lnta)

	Ho: lniu does not cause lnta		
Countries	**Lag**	**Wald**	**p-val**
Algeria	1	3.555*	0.059
Croatia	1	0.212	0.645
Cyprus	1	0.592	0.442
Egypt, Arab Rep.	1	4.362**	0.037
France	1	1.504	0.220
Greece	1	0.45	0.502
Israel	1	1.483	0.223
Italy	1	0.013	0.910
Malta	1	0.105	0.746
Morocco	1	2.719**	0.099
Slovenia	1	0.422	0.516
Spain	1	0.072	0.789
Tunisia	1	3.379**	0.066
Turkey	1	4.376**	0.036
		Test Stat.	**p-val**
Panel W$_{bar}$		1.66	0.264
Panel Z$_{N,T}$		1.747**	0.081
Critical Values	**1%**	**5%**	**10%**
	4.105	2.529	1.888

Notes: ≠> denotes non-Granger causality hypothesis. The optimal lag(s) are selected by Schwarz information criterion by setting maximum lags to 3 in VAR model. The bootstrap critical values are based on 1000 bootstrap replications. *, **, and *** respectively denote statistical significance at 10, 5, and 1 percent.

- ICT and capital investments can be encouraged to ensure that technological advances that support the tourism sector are promoted.
- ICT policy and regulation need to be strengthened to support a smooth liberalization process. In addition, facilitating travel in the tourism sector will help promote international travel.
- To ensure economic growth, ICT education at all levels needs to be improved. There needs to be a long-term policy strategy for recruiting ICT talent and for ICT to flow into various sectors, including tourism.
- Making e-tourism a priority will create greater awareness of the importance of ICT in tourism.
- Effective marketing and promotion, where international tourists can communicate and receive real-time advice on their travels via the internet and mobile phones, is important in terms of building and maintaining the trust of tourists.

REFERENCES

Abou-Shouk, M., Lim, W. M., & Megicks, P. (2013). Internet Adoption by Travel Agents: A Case of Egypt. *International Journal of Tourism Research*, *15*(3), 298–312. doi:10.1002/jtr.1876

Adeola, O., & Evans, O. (2019). Digital tourism: Mobile phones, internet and tourism in Africa. *Tourism Recreation Research*, *44*(2), 190–202. doi:10.1080/02508281.2018.1562662

Adeola, O., & Evans, O. (2020). ICT, infrastructure, and tourism development in Africa. *Tourism Economics*, *26*(1), 97–114. doi:10.1177/1354816619827712

Adeyemi, T. O., & Olaleye, F. O. (2010). Information Communication and Technology (ICT) for the Effective Management of Secondary Schools for Sustainable Development in Ekiti State, Nigeria. *American-Eurasian Journal of Scientific Research*, *5*(2), 106–113.

Akbas, Y. E., Senturk, M., & Sancar, C. (2013). Testing for causality between the foreign direct investment, current account deficit, GDP and total credit: Evidence from G7. *Panoeconomicus*, *60*(6), 791–812. doi:10.2298/PAN1306791A

Alford, P., & Clarke, S. (2009). Information technology and tourism a theoretical critique. *Technovation*, *29*(9), 580–587. doi:10.1016/j.technovation.2009.05.006

Andreu, L., Aldás, J., Bigné, J. E., & Mattila, A. S. (2010). An analysis of e-business adoption and its impact on relational quality in travel agency–supplier relationships. *Tourism Management*, *31*(6), 777–787. doi:10.1016/j.tourman.2009.08.004

Aramendia-Muneta, M. E., & Ollo-Lopez, A. (2013). ICT Impact on tourism industry. *International Journal of Management Cases*, *15*(2), 87–98.

Aytun, C., Akın, C. S., & Akın, S. (2018). Turizm ve Bilgi İletişim Teknolojileri İlişkisi. *İzmir International Congress on Economics and Administrative Sciences*, 2633–2643.

Bahrini, R., & Qaffas, A. A. (2019). Impact of Information and Communication Technology on Economic Growth: Evidence from Developing Countries. *Economies 2019*, *7*(1), 21. doi:10.3390/economies7010021

Berné, C., García-González, M., García-Uceda, M. E., & Múgica, J. M. (2015). The effect of ICT on relationship enhancement and performance in tourism channels. *Tourism Management*, *48*, 188–198. doi:10.1016/j.tourman.2014.04.012

Bhat, S. A., & Shah, M. A. (2014). *Diffusion of Internet Technology in the Tourism Sector: An Empirical Study*. doi:10.1080/15475778.2014.904674

Buhalis, D. (1998). Strategic use of information technologies in the tourism industry. *Tourism Management*, *19*(5), 409–421. doi:10.1016/S0261-5177(98)00038-7

Buhalis, D., & Kaldis, K. (2008). eEnabled Internet Distribution for Small and Medium Sized Hotels: The Case of Athens. *Tourism Recreation Research*, *33*(1), 67–81. doi:10.1080/02508281.2008.11081291

Buhalis, D., & Law, R. (2008). Progress in information technology and tourism management: 20 years on and 10 years after the Internet-The state of eTourism research. *Tourism Management, 29*(4), 609–623. doi:10.1016/j.tourman.2008.01.005

Castro, C., Ferreira, F. A., & Nunes, P. (2020). Digital Technologies and Tourism as Drivers of Economic Growth in Europe and Central Asia. *Smart Innovation. Systems and Technologies, 209*, 341–350. doi:10.1007/978-981-33-4260-6_30

Chevers, D. A. (2015). Evaluating the Impact of ICT Usage on the Performance of Jamaican Hotels: A Conceptual Perspective. *Journal of Tourism and Hospitality Management, 3*(1–2), 22–31.

Dumitrescu, E. I., & Hurlin, C. (2012). Testing for Granger non-causality in heterogeneous panels. *Economic Modelling, 29*(4), 1450–1460. doi:10.1016/j.econmod.2012.02.014

Huang, C. Y., Chou, C. J., & Lin, P. C. (2010). Involvement theory in constructing bloggers' intention to purchase travel products. *Tourism Management, 31*(4), 513–526. doi:10.1016/j.tourman.2009.06.003

Januszewska, M., Jaremen, D. E., & Nawrocka, E. (2015). The effects of the use of ICT by tourism enterprises. *The Effects of the Use of ICT by Tourism Enterprises, 16*(2), 65–73. doi:10.18276mt.2015.16-07

Kaya, T. (2020). *Tarımsal alanda bilgi ve iletişim teknolojilerinin kullanımı: Adana ili örneği*. Çukurova Üniversitesi.

Kónya, L. (2006). *Exports and growth: Granger causality analysis on OECD countries with a panel data approach.* doi:10.1016/j.econmod.2006.04.008

Kumar, N., & Kumar, R. R. (2020). Relationship between ICT and international tourism demand: A study of major tourist destinations. *Tourism Economics, 26*(6), 908–925. doi:10.1177/1354816619858004

Kumar, R. R., & Kumar, R. (2012). Exploring the nexus between information and communications technology, tourism and growth in Fiji. *Tourism Economics, 18*(2), 359–371. doi:10.5367/te.2012.0117

Kumar, R. R., Stauvermann, P. J., Kumar, N., & Shahzad, S. J. H. (2019). Exploring the effect of ICT and tourism on economic growth: A study of Israel. *Economic Change and Restructuring, 52*(3), 221–254. doi:10.100710644-018-9227-8

Kumar, S., & Sharma, D. (2017). Study of ICT and tourism led growth in India and Thailand. *Social Science Asia, 3*(3), 24–31. https://socialscienceasia.nrct.go.th/index.php/SSAsia/article/view/17

Lebbe, A., & Aslam, M. (2020). Long-run relationship between ICT and Tourism Demand in Sri Lanka. *Journal of Information Systems & Information Technology, 5*(1), 68–74. http://ir.lib.seu.ac.lk/handle/123456789/5435

Mandić, A., & Garbin Praničević, D. (2019). Progress on the role of ICTs in establishing destination appeal: Implications for smart tourism destination development. *Journal of Hospitality and Tourism Technology, 10*(4), 791–813. doi:10.1108/JHTT-06-2018-0047

Minghetti, V., & Buhalis, D. (2010). Digital divide in tourism. *Journal of Travel Research, 49*(3), 267–281. doi:10.1177/0047287509346843

Nyandro, C. K. (2016). *Factors Influencing Information Communication Technology (ICT) Acceptance and Use in Small and Medium Enterprise (SMEs) in Kenya*. Capella University.

Odabaş, H., & Akkaya, M. A. (2017). *Bilişim Teknolojilerinin Bilgi Merkezlerine ve Hizmetlerine Etkileri*. Hiperlink Publisher.

Oğrak, A. (2010). *Bilgi Teknolojilerinin Kobi'lerin Rekabet Gücü Üzerindeki Etkileri: İnegöl Mobilya İşletmelerinde Bir Uygulama*. Selçuk University.

Ozcan, C. C., Aslan, M., & Nazlioglu, S. (2017). Economic freedom, economic growth and international tourism for post-communist (transition) countries: A panel causality analysis. *Theoretical & Applied Economics, 24*(2).

Pesaran, M. H., Pesaran, M. H., Shin, Y., & Smith, R. P. (1999). Pooled Mean Group Estimation of Dynamic Heterogeneous Panels. *Journal of the American Statistical Association, 94*(446), 621–634. doi:10.1080/01621459.1999.10474156

Petkova, L., Ryabokon, M., & Vdovychenko, Y. (2019). Modern systems for assessing the informatization of countries in the context of global sustainable development. *Baltic Journal of Economic Studies, 5*(2), 158–170. doi:10.30525/2256-0742/2019-5-2-158-170

Sarı, Y., & Kozak, M. (2005). Turizm Pazarlamasına İnternetin Etkisi: Destinasyon Web Siteleri İçin Bir Model Önerisi. *Akdeniz İİBF Dergisi, 5*(9), 248–271. http://acikerisim.mu.edu.tr/xmlui/handle/20.500.12809/8606

Sheldon, P. (1997). *Tourism information technology*. CAB International.

Sheresheva, M. Y. (2018). The Russian tourism and hospitality market: new challenges and destinations. In Worldwide Hospitality and Tourism Themes (Vol. 10, Issue 4, pp. 400–411). Emerald Group Publishing Ltd. doi:10.1108/WHATT-04-2018-0027

Spencer, A. (2019). ICT and Caribbean Tourism. In *In: Travel and Tourism in the Caribbean*. Palgrave Macmillan.

Spencer, A. J. (2014). Tourism and technology in the global economy: Challenges for small island states. *Worldwide Hospitality and Tourism Themes, 6*(2), 152–165. doi:10.1108/WHATT-12-2013-0047

Standing, C., Tang-Taye, J.-P., & Boyer, M. (2014). *The Impact of the Internet in Travel and Tourism: A Research Review 2001–2010*. doi:10.1080/10548408.2014.861724

Tarutė, A., & Gatautis, R. (2014). ICT Impact on SMEs Performance. *Procedia: Social and Behavioral Sciences, 110*, 1218–1225. doi:10.1016/j.sbspro.2013.12.968

Tsokota, T., Solms, R., & Greunen, D. (2019). The reticent effect of ICT on tourism: A case study of Zimbabwe. *African Journal of Hospitality, Tourism and Leisure, 8*(3).

UNWTO. (2020). *International Tourism Highlights, 2020 Edition*. UNWTO.

Vural, Z. B. A. (2005). Enformasyon iletişim teknolojileri: Gelişimi, doğası ve ahlaki konular. *Yeni Düşünceler, 1*(1), 125–136.

Wagaw, M., & Mulugeta, F. (2018). Integration of ICT and tourism for improved promotion of tourist attractions in Ethiopia. *Applied Informatics 2018, 5*(1), 1–12. doi:10.1186/s40535-018-0053-x

Xiang, Z., & Gretzel, U. (2010). Role of social media in online travel information search. *Tourism Management, 31*(2), 179–188. doi:10.1016/j.tourman.2009.02.016

Zaidan, E. (2016). *Analysis of ICT usage patterns, benefits and barriers in tourism SMEs in the Middle Eastern countries: The case of Dubai in UAE.* doi:10.1177/1356766716654515

Zellner, A. (1962). An Efficient Method of Estimating Seemingly Unrelated Regressions and Tests for Aggregation Bias. *Journal of the American Statistical Association, 57*(298), 348–368. doi:10.1080/01621459.1962.10480664

Zhu, Z., Ma, W., & Leng, C. (2021). *ICT adoption and tourism consumption among rural residents in China.* doi:10.1177/13548166211000478

ADDITIONAL READING

Adeola, O., & Evans, O. (2019). Digital tourism: Mobile phones, internet and tourism in Africa. *Tourism Recreation Research, 44*(2), 190–202. doi:10.1080/02508281.2018.1562662

Adeola, O., & Evans, O. (2020). ICT, infrastructure, and tourism development in Africa. *Tourism Economics, 26*(1), 97–114. doi:10.1177/1354816619827712

Buhalis, D., & Kaldis, K. (2008). eEnabled Internet Distribution for Small and Medium Sized Hotels: The Case of Athens. *Tourism Recreation Research, 33*(1), 67–81. doi:10.1080/02508281.2008.11081291

Buhalis, D., & Law, R. (2008). Progress in information technology and tourism management: 20 years on and 10 years after the Internet-The state of eTourism research. *Tourism Management, 29*(4), 609–623. doi:10.1016/j.tourman.2008.01.005

Kumar, N., & Kumar, R. R. (2020). Relationship between ICT and international tourism demand: A study of major tourist destinations. *Tourism Economics, 26*(6), 908–925. doi:10.1177/1354816619858004

Kumar, R. R., Stauvermann, P. J., Kumar, N., & Shahzad, S. J. H. (2019). Exploring the effect of ICT and tourism on economic growth: A study of Israel. *Economic Change and Restructuring, 52*(3), 221–254. doi:10.100710644-018-9227-8

Neidhardt, J., & Wörndl, W. (2020). Information and Communication Technologies in Tourism 2020. In J. Neidhardt & W. Wörndl (Eds.), *Information and Communication Technologies in Tourism 2020.* Springer International Publishing., doi:10.1007/978-3-030-36737-4

Ramos, C. M. Q., & Rodrigues, P. M. M. (2013). The importance of ICT for tourism demand: A dynamic panel data analysis. In Quantitative Methods in Tourism Economics (pp. 97–111). Physica-Verlag. doi:10.1007/978-3-7908-2879-5_6

KEY TERMS AND DEFINITIONS

Individuals Using the Internet (% of Population): Computer, mobile phone, personal digital assistant, game machine, digital TV, etc. usage statistics of vehicles, indicator.

International Tourism: Participation of citizens of the country in touristic travel between each other.

Panel Data: Gathering cross-sectional observations of units such as individuals, countries, firms, and households over a period.

Tourism Demand: The tourist trend from a tourist sending center to a tourist attraction center.

Tourism Sector: The department that operates in the field of tourism, which includes many businesses such as accommodation, food and beverage and transportation, etc.

WDI (World Development Indicators): Compilation, indicator of the World Bank's international statistics on global development.

Chapter 10
Digital Detox, Trends, and Segmentation in Tourism

Beatriz Juncal
Polytechinc Institute of Cávado and Ave, Portugal

Gabriela Vides
Polytechinc Institute of Cávado and Ave, Portugal

Pedro Matos
Polytechinc Institute of Cávado and Ave, Portugal

Bruno Barbosa Sousa
https://orcid.org/0000-0002-8588-2422
Polytechnic Institute of Cávado and Ave, Portugal & CiTUR, Portugal

ABSTRACT

The chapter aims to demonstrate the growing importance of the concept of 'digital detox' as a segment of the tourism market to indicate the reasons and factors that encourage its demand, the diversity of establishments, the strategies employed by them, the limits, facilitating the adaptation to market conditions, and assisting in the development of marketing strategies that respond to customer needs. Through a content analysis of some research papers from the last 10 years and websites, as well as an interview with the founder from one of the establishments specialized in "disconnection with technologies" experiences, the "Offline House," this study presents inputs on marketing (digital), tourism (niches), and consumer behavior.

INTRODUCTION

Technological evolution has introduced a new communication paradigm, as well as changing the way people relate to each other (Saprikis, 2018). The implementation of New Information and Communication Technologies (ICT) is a given in today's society, with a constant connection to them. While digital technologies and digital devices have made our lives more convenient and efficient, they are associ-

DOI: 10.4018/978-1-7998-8165-0.ch010

ated with physical, mental, and social problems. In response to this, people desire to temporarily ditch their digital devices and refrain from the always-wired world when holidaying (Jiang & Balaji, 2021). Contact with a smartphone or a computer is uninterrupted, as they are crucial tools for the development of any work activity, as well as means of communication present in the personal and daily lives of users. However, this inseparability may be of little benefit. Given this new scenario, the concept of Digital Detox emerges, which aims to provide tools that help control the consumption of technological and communication means. This is directed, primarily, to people who show any trace of addiction, concerning their mobile devices. Knowing market trends and being aware of changes in consumer needs is of fundamental importance for the creation and development of products and packages related to disconnected tourism (Pawłowska-Legwand & Matoga, 2020). We intend to demonstrate the growing importance of this new concept, indicate the reasons and factors that encourage its demand, the diversity of establishments, the strategies employed by it, the limits, facilitate adaptation to market conditions, and assist in the development of marketing strategies that respond to customer needs. This knowledge and awareness can facilitate flexible adaptation to market conditions and can help to design marketing strategies that respond to customer needs, based on available resources or service sets, and within the new context (Pawłowska-Legwand & Matoga, 2020).

THEORETICAL BACKGROUND

Digital Detox: its Importance in Contemporary Society

The term Digital Detox is relatively recent, first appearing in 2010 on some websites. It was formally defined in 2014 by Oxford Dictionaries as a period in which an individual disconnects from all electronic equipment, such as cell phones or computers, which presents itself as an opportunity to reduce stress or focus on social interactions, in the physical world. The concept arises from the need to intervene in the new behaviours acquired by users, who according to Konok (2016) and Bivin et al. (2013), began to show signs of anxiety and stress when separating the mobile device, having an impact on physical health and mental. Mobile phones present themselves as the most addictive, and therefore more stressful, device, and teenagers are the age group that has the highest dependency rate (Miksch & Schulz, 2018). Then there are young adults who, according with same authors, despite having a risky behaviour, are more aware of their relationship with new technologies, and the negative effects that result from them. They admit to experiencing a feeling of nervousness and anxiety when offline and recognize that there is a greater interaction with devices than that initially planned (Miksch & Schulz, 2018).

The benefits of technology make us dependent on it and the negative effects of this dependence are reflected in professional, social, and private lives of users (Miksch & Schulz, 2018). Overuse causes loss of productivity, distraction from tasks, addictive behaviour, increased levels of stress and lack of concentration. The negative effects have a professional and academic repercussion, consisting of a decrease in performance in both environments, and affect the general well-being of the user, impacting their health (especially regarding psychological disorders) (Miksch & Schulz, 2018). The overuse of communication technologies has physical and mental consequences, and a dependent user may have higher levels of stress, and signs of anxiety and depression (Miksch et. al, 2018; Syvertsen, & Enli, 2020). In this way, the exacerbated and permanent connection leads to the worsening of the feeling of loneliness and less satisfaction with life. Syvertsen et al. (2020) also warn of the loss of sense of space and the disturbance of the perception of time. The online connection, more specifically the connection to the social networks, can also lead to the distortion of the image itself in a negative way, a consequence of the constant comparison with others, and then, excessive use is also associated with problems of users' self-esteem (Purohit, Barclay & Holzer, 2020). Furthermore, the continued use of social networks contributes to the phenomenon of FOMO (Fear of Missing Out), which consists of the constant concern of not being present, while others are experiencing rewarding and pleasant experiences, shared online (Formica, 2015).

The consequences of this unhealthy consumption habits imply the degradation of physical health, as they lead to a more sedentary life, combined with the practice of a less healthy and balanced diet (Syvertsen & Enli, 2020; Jiang & Balaji, 2021). The consequences are also seen in the users' personal lives, influencing interpersonal relationships (Miksch & Schulz, 2018). The feeling of loneliness caused, comes from the progressive removal of the user from his personal relationships, caused by the reduction in the quality of communications between family and friends, which ultimately leads to social isolation (Miksch et. al, 2018; Syvertsen & Enli, 2020). In this way, there is a devaluation of encounters in real life and face-to-face meetings, potentiating their end, presenting themselves as a danger to offline relationships.

Given all the negative effects mentioned above, inevitably there is the development of literature that aims to present preventive measures to combat the excessive use of digital devices. Therefore, these measures provide the basis for several Digital Detox programs. Due to greater awareness on the part of the user, this being the maximum goal of the measures and programs implemented so that it is possible to reduce the use of technologies, the creation of barriers and a structure through rules is encouraged, with a view to awareness and encourage offline activities. The purpose will be the creation of strategies that limit the time of use of the devices, and the implementation of routines without technology. However, within these new practices, personal rules are presented as a more conscious and effective decision, than established behavioural rules (Miksch & Schulz, 2018). Although there is no consensus in the terminology, as the term is presented both as a period and as a gradual process, in neither case is abstention and permanent disconnection advised. That said, it is natural that digital detox programs focus, as already mentioned, on promoting and encouraging temporary abstinence and personal awareness of users.

Tourist Profile: Factors

For the purposes of this work, it is necessary to understand and distinguish the concepts of "digital natives" and "digital immigrants". As stated by Guo, Dobson & Petrina (2008), digital natives - also called 'net-generation' - are those who have grown up with digital devices and have been involved with ICT (information and communication technologies) since a young age. In contemporary society, digital natives are those who were born after 1980. On the contrary, digital immigrants are those who were born before 1980 and therefore did not grow up in the digital world but adopted the new technology at some point later in life (Bennett, Maton, & Kervin, 2008; Margaryan & Littlejohn, 2008; Prensky, 2001).

Digital natives are usually the group related to passive resistance when disconnected from digital media. Passive resistance refers to a forced disconnection and therefore, users often experience anxiety tensions when disconnected. However, digital immigrants can also be related to passive resistance such as psychological conditions such as cyberphobia (fear of working with any type of technology or digital medium). Rejection, on the other hand, is autonomous and includes the rejection of digital devices due to technological complexity or change costs. This rejection can also be considered. Conscious rejection assumes that a person who has fully embraced digital technology for an indefinite period (private life) or at certain times (related to work), determines through a conscious assessment that the use of digital technology has a negative effect on their and therefore stops or rejects the use of digital technology for a defined or indefinite period. These negative factors mainly include health and sociological factors (Olavarria, 1998).

Thus, the main motivations for digital immigrants to take a vacation in the concept of digital detox can be related to psychological factors (such as cyberphobia), technological factors (due to the technological complexity of the devices), and physical health factors (negative health effects of through use of ICT). On the other hand, the motivations for digital natives to get out of the routine can also be related to psychological factors (anxiety tensions when they are not able to connect). The following subsections will delve further into psychological, sociological, technological, and physical health factors.

Physical Health Factors

Health factors are the physical risks caused by overuse. One of the highest health risks to which digital users, especially computer users, are being exposed are musculoskeletal symptoms (MSS) and disorders (MSD), referring to "joint disease, rheumatoid arthritis and osteoarthritis, spinal disorders, low back pain and severe trauma "(World Health Organization, 2003). The second and the most common health problem that occurs with the use of digital devices is sleep problems. Research has indicated that especially the blue light on smartphone screens emits diodes that influence the circadian system, the body's time control system that regulates sleep needs (Donnelly, 2012; Lin, et al., 2014; Paris, et al., 2015; World Health Organization, 2014). According to Thomee (2012), the Swedish National Public Health Survey in 2010 reported that the intensive use of computers and mobile phones (intensive: more than 2 hours without breaks) has been prospectively associated with sleep disorders among both men and women. Another health issue that can be addressed is obesity.

As stated by the World Health Organization, obesity is expected to increase dramatically in the distant future (World Health Organization, n.d.). Several studies have shown that the reason for this can be explained by analysing the lifestyle of the population, such as eating habits, as well as the use of digital devices (television and computers), reducing the extent of physical activities and leisure alternatives. The last health issue that may be related to the use of digital technology is the Computer Vision Syndrome, also referred to as Digital Eye Tension. According to investigations by the American Optometry Association, people who spend more than two hours at the computer are at risk for digital eye strain and other problems related to vision and eyes.

Psychological Factors

Psychological factors in relation to digital devices are often related to addiction. One of the most common forms of digital addiction in contemporary society is Internet addiction. According to the World Health Organization, there are two typical psychological factors, including so-called "withdrawal", referring to "feelings of anger, tension, anxiety and / or depression when the Internet / computers are inaccessible" (World Health Organization) Saúde, p. 13), and "negative repercussions" or "conflict", indicating "self-imposed social isolation and disintegration, lying, discussion, poor academic and professional performance and fatigue" (World Health Organization, 2014, p. 14).

As noted in the studies by Pearce & Gretzel (2012) and Paris et al. (2012), the tensions that can occur due to inaccessibility of digital devices are social communication tensions, work communication tensions, safety leakage tensions, and immediate connection tensions. However, inaccessibility to ICT can even lead to suicidal ideation. Kim et al. (2006) examined the relationship between Internet addiction, depression, and suicidal ideation in adolescents. The study concluded that the high dependence on the Internet among Internet addicts was more related to suicidal ideation than to depression.

Sociological Factors

As sociological factors, we can understand as factors that affect the human mind of thinking and behaving in social situations. According to the current literature, a very common sociological issue resulting from digital addiction concerns problems in relationships. Research in the UK indicated that people with digital addiction often face difficulties in their relationships (Donnelly, 2012). Young (1998) determined that 53% of users addicted to digital technologies ended up with marital discord, separation, and divorce. Another common problem related to digital addiction that can be mentioned is work-related problems. While, in one hand, employees benefit from digital devices in the workplace as they facilitate the flow of communication, there is concern that, on the other hand, it is also a distraction among employees (Young, 2004). Also, in social terms, employees more often lack quality time with their family after work hours since they are 24/7 connected to ICT and are contactable by their employer. According to Neuhofer & Ladkin (2017, p. 350), a "healthy" work-life balance is an amalgamation of health, good personal relationships, mental well-being, and productivity and satisfaction in life and work. Because of this, several European political parties are calling for a legislative proposal that workers no longer must be accessible after hours (Asscher, 2017). The last sociological factor that can be named is loneliness. According to research by Karapetsas et al. (2015), there is a highly positive correlation between dependence on digital devices and feelings of loneliness. Furthermore, other studies have shown that a student with poor communication skills is more prone to digital addiction than those with better interpersonal skills. With its negative impacts on work or relationships, it is expected to further isolate from healthy social activities therefore leading to more loneliness (Ceyhan & Ceyhan, 2008; Coget, Yamauchi, & Suman, 2002; Junghun, LaRose, & Peng, 2009).

Technological Factors

In Europe, ICT innovation is well established. Many countries in Europe today are creating government interventions to further accelerate ICT innovation within and across national borders (King et al., 1994; Schaffers, 2011). One example of this was the effort to reduce telecommunication charges for customers traveling abroad. Since early 2007, roaming prices have been reduced by 90% and as of June 2017, roaming costs have ended for individuals who travel periodically within the European Union (European Commission, 2016).

However, this has also led to digital fatigue or so-called "technology fatigue," the fatigue of constant use of digital devices. It is claimed that technology fatigue especially affects older people (Griffiths, 2007). Although, taking all ages into consideration, digital fatigue has recently become noticeable in the e-book world where sales have lately declined precipitously. According to Kozlowski (2016), the decline in e-books is a cause of customers' realization to have a lack of concentration and conceptual comprehension while reading from an e-reader device (Kjee, 2016).

In the last decade, in response to different studies emphasizing the negative effects of ICT on people's lives, several companies have begun instituting changes in the way employees use it at work and outside of work. As mentioned earlier, not only are European political parties demanding a legislative proposal that employees no longer must be contactable after hours, but many employers in France have already begun to prohibit employees from responding to emails outside of business hours. In addition, companies like Facebook, Apple, Square, Twitter, Google, and Airbnb have gone even further and sent employees to technology-free retreats for their sociological and physical well-being (Michaels, 2016).

TOURIST PROFILE: MOTIVATIONS

Technology has been changing many daily routines, as cell phones, computers, and other digital technologies now often replace time with friends and family (Stone, 2009). These digital technologies have become an important part of everyday life and affect communication (Belk & Llamas, 2013; Savci & Aysan, 2017). Thus, by 2017, over 50% of the world's population is using the internet daily, 37% actively use social media, and 66% own a smartphone (Kemp, 2017). Although digital technologies have brought various benefits to professional, private, and social life (Inauen et al. 2017; Rich, 2004; Walsh, White & Young, 2009), it has been recognized that with the overuse of digital technologies in today's hyper-connected society, various problems are emerging (Montag & Walla, 2016). Ofcom (2016) explored people's perceptions of their internet use, their attitudes towards connectivity and whether people have a desire to reduce interaction with their devices. Previous research into problematic technology use has found it important to moderate the use of the internet and digital devices and to monitor the uses to which they are put (Kraut et al. 1998; Powers, 2010).

The problem that arises reflects the contradiction between increasing digitalization in the professional, private, and social environment and the greater possibilities that technology has brought to these areas, on the one hand, and increasing awareness and attempts to reduce digital interaction among young adults, on the other. Thus, it is unknown what young adults do to reduce interaction with digital technology and what drives them to put motivations into action. Therefore, investigating actions and motivations in professional, private, and social settings seems to be a suitable and appropriate context to reflect the life circumstances of a young adult and to further capture efforts to actively reduce the use of digital technologies. (environments that are most affected by technology use). This problem was studied by Linda Miksch and Charlotte Schulz in their May 2018 article "Disconnect to Reconnect: The Phenomenon of Digital Detox as a Reaction to Technology Overload."

At the professional level, previous literature in the field of negative impacts of digital technology has revealed that an overuse of technology causes loss of productivity and distraction from a task (Duke & Montag, 2017; Montag & Walla, 2016), addictive behaviour (Duke & Montag, 2017), increased stress levels, and poor concentration in the workplace (Tarafdar et al. 2017). Moreover, in the study environment, an abuse of digital technologies while studying has negative effects on academic performance (Aljomaa et al, 2016; Carrier et al. 2015; Lepp, Barkley & Karpinski, 2014, van der Schuur et al. 2015; Samaha & Hawi, 2016). Loss of concentration and the ability to remember has also been discussed within the study environment (Chen & Yan, 2016, Kraushaar & Novak, 2010; Kuznekoff & Titsworth, 2013).

With respect to negative impacts on the private environment, the existing literature has found negative consequences of excessive digital use on well-being. In particular, it causes loneliness (Bonebrake, 2002; Huang, 2010; Kim, 2018; Stepanikova, Ni & He, 2010; Yao & Zhong, 2014), stress (Hampton, Lu & Shin, 2016; Kraut et al. 2002), depression (Bonebrake, 2002; Campbell, Cumming & Hughes, 2006; Fortson, Scotti & Chen, 2007; Huang, 2010), less life satisfaction (Carden, 2006; Huang, 2010) which in turn encourages addictive behaviour with digital technologies (Elhai et al. 2016; Haug et al. 2015; Lei et al. 2017; Pérez, Monje & Ruiz, 2012).

Within the stream of negative impacts on social interactions, existing literature has found that an overuse of digital technology reduces the quality and depth of communications with friends and family (Bucher, Fieseler, & Suphan, 2013; Rotondi, Stanca, & Tomasuolo, 2017). It also reduces face-to-face relationships, social support, and communication skills (Kim, 2017; Kraut et al. 1998; Lee & Robbins, 1998; Savci & Aysan, 2017). The literature has also discussed impacts on relationship formation, increasing isolation and loneliness (Amichai-Hamburger, Wainapfel, & Fox, 2002; Yao & Zhong, 2014).

In a professional environment, where one must perform tasks and usually meet certain deadlines, self-control over concentrating on one's tasks is an essential characteristic. Many of the respondents mentioned the importance of maintaining self-control over the use of digital technologies as one of their main motivations for reducing interaction with digital technologies. Furthermore, participants particularly express the desire to increase their self-control by being able to mediate digital use.

Not only in professional life, but also in young adults' private lives, maintaining self-control was a very stressful motivation for reducing digital technology use. In addition to the motivations to regain and maintain control, the acknowledged feeling of loss of control was frequently mentioned, particularly in the case of the smartphone. Also, in the private environment, self-control has been related to the frequent fear of missing out. Participants state that they always felt the need to check their smartphone for messages or social media through the computer. This urge encouraged the development of a higher level of perceived stress and the feeling of loneliness in case there were no new messages. To prevent these feelings and thus to maintain control, these negative feelings motivated them to reduce the use of digital technology in their private lives. As the smartphone seemed to be the most frequently used digital technology and the one that young adults were most concerned about, the attribution of human capabilities to this device shows that smartphones are an integral part of young adults' lives.

The observations mentioned in terms of self-control are related to the frequently expressed problem of being distracted by the computer, smartphone, social media, or other digital technologies. Distraction reduces the participants' sense of self-control, which was discovered in both professional and private settings. Thus, the research revealed that young adults show a strong motivation to only have control over their individual wants and needs when it comes to how and when they use digital technologies.

To increase the performance in their professional and private environments, participants are motivated to mediate interaction with digital technologies. Here, participants stated that spending time with various technologies such as the computer, smartphone, tablet, and television consume too much time. The research clearly revealed that young adults highly value their private time, which for them takes place offline, i.e., without any access to the Internet. Rather, they want to spend their private lives with something that is considered more valuable, such as nature or hobbies.

When it comes to the professional environment of young adults, motivation to increase performance also plays a crucial role in reducing or replacing digital technologies while working or studying. Maintaining focus on a task while studying or working is related to the issues of increasing concentration, as well as eliminating potential distractions and disturbances that can result from interacting with digital technologies at the same time. Thus, the themes of concentration, distraction, and disruption that emerged throughout many interviews represent the desire to maintain focus while studying or working on a task. In this regard, many participants state that they find their study and work more productive, more efficient, and faster, as well as with a better quality of result when digital devices are not fully engaged.

It has thus become evident that the "performance enhancing" motivation is observable in both the private and professional environments of young adults. This is since the former leads young adults to a complete elimination of digital devices, while the latter involves actions that follow a reduction and replacement behaviour.

One theme that has emerged is the motivation to improve well-being, within the professional environment, this refers to a satisfaction with work. In this regard, reduced interaction with technology in their work life makes them feel satisfied. For example, it was often mentioned that they feel freer, less stressed, or even happier when they work and study without having technology involved. Thus, to avoid the negative feelings that are perceived to be related to digital technologies, and thus improve their well-being, young adults reduce and replace those in their work and study environment. Particularly in the case of social media, these negative feelings were also noted beyond their professional lives. Young adults reduce their interaction with social media, with the smartphone, also in their private environment, as it was said to be the most used feature on the device. To improve their inner emotional state, but also to avoid these negative feelings in the first place, they were motivated to reduce the use of digital technologies also in their private life. This mainly refers to the use of the smartphone, as this was the medium to which social networks are most accessible. In addition to the intensely discussed emotions, participants frequently mentioned the perception of negative impacts on their mental health, which motivates them to reduce their use of digital technology. In this context, it was frequently stated that they consider their interaction with technology, particularly with the smartphone, as addictive. The concern about negative impacts on mental health was raised by many participants, as they stated that they sometimes even have panic attacks caused by the fear of failure in case they are not connected to the Internet, social networks or in contact with their smartphone. Thus, having reduced interaction with digital technologies, participants collectively experienced greater satisfaction with work in terms of reduced stress, happiness, rewarding feelings, and decreased disappointment and guilt. Furthermore, in private life, improving emotional state, the recognized mental health impacts collectively motivated to reduce digital technology use.

"Being in the moment" seems to be one of the main initiators for initiating reduction. This importance is emphasized when spending time with friends and family, as well as when spending time with oneself. This motivation therefore occurred in both the social and private settings of the young adults as an impetus to reduce digital technology interaction. Many of the respondents mentioned that time to "be in the moment," being disconnected from digital technologies and spending time with family and friends in real life, is seen as very valuable. Additionally, the importance of "being in the moment" was stressed, especially during special events and occasions. Thus, it becomes observable that here, "in the moment" implies being present for someone who deserves more attention at that moment, such as a wedding or a birthday celebration. The motivation to "observe details," was also pointed out as observing the situation through one's eyes rather than through a camera or as simple everyday observations of nature. All the motivations mentioned, adding the feeling of freedom, joy, or focus, determine the relevance of taking a break from digital technologies to be able to "be in the moment."

The last of the five findings of the research study on the motivations that lead young adults to reduce interactions with digital devices, is embedded in social life. Thus, the factor of "maintaining relationships" was very frequently emphasized by the respondents, implying increased social engagement on the one hand, as well as the avoidance of negative influences on real-life relationships on the other. First, regarding social engagement, many of the participants mentioned that the quality of face-to-face conversations is increasing when there is no digital technology in between. Moreover, formulations such as "deeper conversations" and "taking conversations to a whole new level" seem to imply that offline conversations are not shallow, but rather in-depth. Furthermore, the participants stressed not only the depth and quality of the conversation, but also the connection and relationship with the other person as such. Thus, it became evident that without having a digital technology involved, a stronger connection develops. Their need for verbal interaction and dialogue during a face-to-face conversation, rather than a monologue, was also mentioned. It is also of central importance to influence others in your social environment towards more offline living and to function as a good example.

Second, referring to the issue of preventing negative influence on real-life relationships, the motivation for reducing interaction with digital technology when being with other people comes from negative feelings that participants experienced. These range from frustration and stress over disrespect and appreciation to wasting time. Themes such as disrespect and discourtesy emerged from the interviews conducted with young adults. In more detail, participants perceive passive behaviour of their conversation partners, which means not actively listening due to smartphone interactions, as impolite, rude, and less trustworthy. During the interviews, the importance of giving and receiving appreciation during face-to-face interactions emerged as an essential motivation for leaving out digital devices during social interactions to avoid creating a barrier between the individual and the other person.

In conclusion, it can be argued that engaging digital technologies during real face-to-face interactions diminishes personal relationships. This sometimes even results in not meeting a certain person again.

For the purposes of this work, it is necessary to understand and distinguish the concepts of "digital natives" and "digital immigrants". As stated by Guo, Dobson & Petrina (2008), digital natives - also called 'net-generation' - are those who have grown up with digital devices and have been involved with ICT (information and communication technologies) since a young age. In contemporary society, digital natives are those who were born after 1980. On the contrary, digital immigrants are those who were born before 1980 and therefore did not grow up in the digital world, but adopted the new technology at some point later in life. (Bennett, Maton, & Kervin, 2008; Margaryan & Littlejohn, 2008; Prensky, 2001).

Digital natives are usually the group related to passive resistance when disconnected from digital media. Passive resistance refers to a forced disconnection and therefore, users often experience anxiety tensions when disconnected. However, digital immigrants can also be related to passive resistance such as psychological conditions such as cyberphobia (fear of working with any type of technology or digital medium). Rejection, on the other hand, is autonomous and includes the rejection of digital devices due to technological complexity or change costs. This rejection can also be considered. Conscious rejection assumes that a person who has fully embraced digital technology for an indefinite period (private life) or at certain times (related to work), determines through a conscious assessment that the use of digital technology has a negative effect on their and therefore stops or rejects the use of digital technology for a defined or indefinite period. These negative factors mainly include health and sociological factors (Olavarria, 1998).

Thus, the main motivations for digital immigrants to take a vacation in the concept of digital detox can be related to psychological factors (such as cyberphobia), technological factors (due to the technological complexity of the devices), and physical health factors (negative health effects of through use of ICT). On the other hand, the motivations for digital natives to get out of the routine can also be related to psychological factors (anxiety tensions when they are not able to connect). The following subsections will delve further into psychological, sociological, technological and physical health factors.

DIGITAL DETOX IN A TOURIST CONTEXT

The trend of disconnected tourism creates possibilities for the development of business and other institutions related to hospitality. In response to the increasing number of needs dependent on digital devices or the Internet, several hotels around the world are developing offers and programs to attract the market for "digital escapers", where guests are made available not to use their technological devices. Thus, for this type of tourism, the importance of 'dead zones' is revealed, areas where technological communication is limited or unavailable (Pearce & Gretzel, 2012), to pass a root of escape from everyday life, tranquillity and reconnection with nature, providing a distinctive tourist experience because of these limits between daily life and space for tourism. These limitations can be involuntary, when the location is usually in rural areas, far from urban centers, or intentional, when there is a purposeful block of access to technologies.

Regarding the evolution of this market, according to the analysis of Li, Pearce, and Low of 2018 (Pawłowska-Legwand & Matoga, 2020), it was possible to identify 3 stages of development between 2009 and 2017: the introduction, where the concept was indicated as an example of a change in hosting services and as a superior product provided by resorts and hotels in the United States and Europe. Then, in destination management, some regions began to be promoted as favorable and suitable places for this type of experience. In the second stage of growth, specialized companies with no segment have already appeared on the market. Finally, in its development, it has been possible to observe a rapid growth of companies and institutions, which supply various products of this niche, based mainly on the natural environment and cultural heritage. According to Li et al., a diversification of free digital holiday products created by various tourism associations started in 2016, both by companies and by destination management. Some countries are determined to take steps to ensure that customers deliver their mobile devices and/or other technologies, and hotel establishments are the first to implement programs and services that help visitors enjoy the experience to the fullest, regardless of the purpose of each traveler. That is why these types of hotels are already operational.

Hotels with digital detox packages offer completely different points of sale for a technological breakdown. On the one hand, some motivated by the concern with the strong impact of technology on their customers, try to prevent them from going online and losing their experiences, and on the other hand, others take advantage of the concept to increase sales, promoting their spa, introducing new relaxation concepts and offer 'digital detox' products for the well-being of the body.

As international examples of the offer of digital detox packages we find the Hotel Westin Dublin, in Ireland, where guests are encouraged to keep electronic devices in a safe for the duration of the stay, receive a kit to plant a tree, a daily newspaper, a map from the city, board games and a special type of relaxing bed in the room; the Hotel Monaco Chicago, in the USA, with a similar mechanism, but adding the "Comfortable Suite", where visitors can have access to facilities that make their stay more pleasant and comfortable, such as relaxing music, heating towels, massage tools, among others, (Hinojosa, 2014; Carrington, 2012, Vargas La Rosa, 2019); Lake Placid Lodge in New York, which offers a two-night package, called "Check in to Check out", where participants deliver their digital devices to the reception and participate in cooking classes, snowshoe expeditions, yoga and other activities without technology; the 'Digital Detox of San Francisco' movement, which organizes three- and four-day retreats in various locations in northern California, where tourists participate in a variety of Zen activities, including yoga, hiking and quiet meals; Vincci Hotels, in Spain, where guests are invited to participate in a body massage session, access to the swimming pool, heated swimming pool, among others; and, also in Spain,

Digital Detox, Trends, and Segmentation in Tourism

the VIVOOD Landscape Hotels, which have completely transformed their local environment into a community, offering many options such as suites with or without a pool, premium villas with a pool and spa.

Several establishments offer this escape from technology, and the opportunity to relax and reconnect with nature as is the case with farms, which offer agritourism, healthy food, tasting dishes and wines, preparation of typical local dishes, horseback riding, others, and from monasteries, Christian or Buddhist convents and Hindu monasteries, which offer thematic workshops, participation in the daily life of monks/nuns, performing similar functions, spiritual guidance and religious practices, such as praying, silence, contemplation, pilgrimage, and fasting. In terms of experiences and activities, we often find local walks and excursions, as a way to visit the sights of a place; spa and wellness, offering body treatments and recreational facilities; yoga; gymnasium; surf; cycling; camping, rural tourism, and ecotourism; nautical activities; survival and radical sports; team games; spiritual retreats and addiction treatment clinics, which also include medical tourism, which offers medical care and therapy; individual consultations with therapy and group therapy.

In Portugal, there are already some accommodations focused on turning off technologies, which promote contact with nature, skills development, relaxation activities, and reconnection with our interior. Some do not have a purposeful connection with technologies and others are located in such dead zones where the "wi-fi" does not even reach. In the North, we have Quinta do Convento da Franqueira (Barcelos), which has rooms with a relaxing atmosphere, a swimming pool with spring water, an isolated and quiet indoor and outdoor space, and an open space where you can enjoy a walk. which extends over the farm's 14 hectares. To have access to the internet, guests need to go to the main house of the Quinta. Then we have the Moinhos de Oval (Gove, Porto), in a remote location, near a stream, which invites guests to reconnect with nature and do not have WiFi on purpose. In Coimbra, we have the Xisto villages, where the internet just arrives at the village cafe and the mobile network is also rare. In addition to contact with nature, guests can enjoy the art of the restored houses and meet artists. The Óbidos Lagoon Wellness Retreat (Leiria coast), offers a "digital detox" program, with several modalities, such as unlimited access to the spa, where you can enjoy massages, sauna, outdoor jacuzzi, and saltwater pool, to renew the body and the mind. In Castelo Branco, we have the Moinho do Maneio (Penacamor), which offers a unique experience to sleep among nature and under the stars, in an inflatable bubble, drawing the idea of a return to the past, childhood memories around the campfire with the family. It also offers reiki, massages, canoeing and trampolining, or walking, quad biking, horseback, or mountain biking. On the Vincentian coast, we have the Offline House (Arrifana, Aljezur), which in addition to not having WiFi, on arrival the smartphone is "confiscated" and kept in a locker. Here, various offline experiences and socializing among guests are promoted, without technological intervention. In Alentejo, on the lake of Alqueva, the Amieira Marina houseboats, which are not equipped with internet, have only the master at the helm and endless water punctuated by practically deserted and paradisiacal islands. At night, you can count on a unique panorama of the starry sky, due to the low light pollution. And finally, in the South, Conscious Earth (Algarve) challenges the guest to reconnect to himself in a kind of retreat, of at least 3 nights, with various activities of yoga, meditation, art, fasting practices, among others.

'Offline Portugal' is a community movement with the mission of bringing our power back to us, in the face of technological dependence. Under the motto "disconnect to reconnect" he suggests that you leave the "comfort zone" of the web and try alternatives such as surf classes, yoga sessions, and evenings animated by music and board games. Thus, it invites guests to reconnect with themselves, with others, and with nature.

Talking to the founder, Bárbara Miranda, we realized that location plays an important role in participating in the programs they offer because when isolated, close to the beach, with a favorable climate, it transcribes a feeling of tranquillity and escapes from everyday life. According to her, the age group that covers the most ranges from 30 to 40 years of age, and further confirms that, although young people spend more time on mobile phones, parents between 20-30 years of age are the least resistant to the temptation to go. to your phone. In terms of tourist attraction marketing strategies, the movement relies heavily on the development of the website, social networks, and advertisements on the search engine, although they try not to spend a lot of time online, and, to spread the word, which corresponds to 50% of the original dissemination of this product to the guests they have received. They also resort to partnerships with various platforms of the various activities they offer, to feedback and interaction with customers, and have started making videos about the experiences to pass on the website and social networks. In the future, they are thinking of changing locations, reducing costs, transform the space (more peaceful and inspiring), promote more partnerships, balance offline with online, and reach a new audience (high-level entrepreneurs). Concerning tourist attraction strategies, we realize that digital detoxification is mainly added to a marketing offer and communication as a unique selling proposition. As the main strategy, or one that has more impact on the sale of the concept, is the dissemination and importance of the negative consequences of addictions to technologies. Here, establishments encourage the customer to spend more time with family/friends; they introduce associations with childhood and adolescence memories to the experiences they offer; they have programs with the opportunity to develop skills and personal growth; provide the opportunity to learn about local traditions and spend leisure time away from the city; encourage you to relax and enjoy the moment; encourage you to store your mobile devices throughout your stay and use apps that help reduce time spent online. A strong point of attraction in this market is also the location. These establishments usually have calm surroundings and pleasant landscapes of mountains, seaside or near lakes, or just less urbanized areas. Some food and beverage outlets offer customers promotions for leaving their mobile devices with the receptionist for the entire dinner, such as Eva Restaurant in Los Angeles, which has been offering a 5% discount since the summer of 2012 and in Mexico and Costa Rica, yoga retreat houses offer 15% discounts to customers if they give up their iPhone.

FINAL CONSIDERATIONS

It has become evident that a digital detox behavior becomes a trend that intensifies the relevance of considering this phenomenon in business contexts, especially in the field of marketing, and besides, reinforces the need for new research in this field. The setback to going offline and disconnection leads to a change in consumer behavior and strongly influences future marketing and branding strategies. So, to remain relevant for consumers, it is necessary to study the adaptations of existing products and communication measures towards changing customer behavior, new groups of emerging customers, as well as the development of completely new business areas (Miksch & Schulz, 2018).

In this sense, we are faced with the following approaches that organizations may adopt. Marketing managers can take advantage of the pioneer advantage and pay attention to emerging concerns about technology addiction. Digital detox as a new lifestyle: strategies to support the population sensitized to the problem are suggested. As for the dissemination of the trend, they may resort to communication and support from public figures and word of mouth by colleagues/friends/family. To remain relevant to new and existing consumer groups, companies need to adapt their existing product line, with, for example, minor adaptations to facilitate the application of offline functions. Finally, considering digital detox within an organization has the potential to serve as an effective strategy, because the marketing of digital detox measures in the job market can promote the image of a company for existing and future employees, ie, take into account behavior change with digital technology internally, supporting the well-being of its employees. To conclude, the authors it is pertinent that future research addresses the challenge of the pandemic COVID-19, as this could be a "step back" in this type of tourism, and more experiences will be needed on the reaction to digital detox in children of the new generation Alpha, who they deal with technologies from a very young age, to build some theory about the future about the 'digital detox' in tourism.

LIMITATIONS AND FUTURE POSSIBILITIES

The lack of literature presents itself as the main limitation, to understand this concept, relatively recent, which is the Digital Detox. Within the tourism and hotel context, research is in an embryonic phase, as the supply of facilities is still considerably low. In the national scenario, this offer is even more conditioned, considering that we only obtained the testimony of a digital detoxification plan, this being the only one in Portuguese territory.

In this sense, part of the existing literature on the concept states that there is little evidence that proves that the use of smartphones is considered a type of behavioural dependence, therefore, there is a contradiction, regarding the studies carried out, that declares the malignant effects of excessive use of technology (Wilcockson, T. D., et al., (2019). Such statements can invalidate the need for treatment, as would be detoxification. First, a behavioural addiction is defined by the DSM-V as an addiction disorder, which does not involve the ingestion of psychoactive substances (APA, 2013). Kim, Wong and Oh (2016) defend the positive effects of smartphones and social networks on behaviour and social engagement, and according to Wilcockson, T. D., Osborne, A. M. and Ellis, D.A., (2019) the addictive behaviours of users of digital technological devices, do not they are like the symptoms or behaviours that other addicts have.

In addition, a study carried out by the authors mentioned above, in 2019, where the characterization of the user's behaviour when faced with the total separation of the smartphone, during a period of 24 hours, was concluded, concluded that the emotional functioning is not altered with the abstinence from the mobile phone, and that although there is a feeling of anxiety, it does not necessarily reflect a form of addiction. About user engagement in program plans established by hotel organizations or entities, the main limitation is that the demand for these programs must be voluntary and active, with difficulties in convincing people to participate. Other limitations may be due to the price established for the proposed detox activities / programs, the lack of accessibility to the means that promote these activities, and, ultimately, the resistance on the part of the users.

Thus, given the limitations presented, and future limitations that may arise, there is a need to solve some of the problems mentioned, namely the practical approach that can be established, which aims at behavioural change, about the habits of use and consumption of technology. In this way, tour operators and hotel entities can take advantage of the status of pioneers, paying attention to emerging concerns regarding behavioural change, manifested by the excessive use of technology. However, if they want to maintain relevance for the group of new and existing consumers, there is a need to adapt their line of available products, including new programs and activities, namely, to facilitate the application of offline functions on digital devices (Miksch & Schulz, 2018).

REFERENCES

American Psychiatric Association (APA). (2013). *Diagnostic and Statistical Manual of Mental Disorders* (5th ed.). American Psychological Association Press.

Desligar: "detox digital" em 8 alojamentos livres de wi-fi. (2020). Retrieved 10 November 2020, from https://boacamaboamesa.expresso.pt/boa-cama/2019-08-05-Desligar-detox-digital-em-8-alojamentos-livres-de-wi-fi

Dickinson, J. E., Hibbert, J. F., & Filimonau, V. (2016). Mobile technology and the tourist experience:(Dis) connection at the campsite. *Tourism Management*, *57*, 193–201. doi:10.1016/j.tourman.2016.06.005

Egger, I., Lei, S. I., & Wassler, P. (2020). Digital free tourism–An exploratory study of tourist motivations. *Tourism Management*, *79*, 104098. doi:10.1016/j.tourman.2020.104098

Fan, D. X., Buhalis, D., & Lin, B. (2019). A tourist typology of online and face-to-face social contact: Destination immersion and tourism encapsulation/decapsulation. *Annals of Tourism Research*, *78*, 102757. doi:10.1016/j.annals.2019.102757

Formica, S. (2015). *Digital detox: 7 Steps to find your inner balance*. Sandro Formica.

Hoving, K. (2017). *Digital Detox Tourism: Why disconnect? What are the motives of Dutch tourists to undertake a digital detox holiday?* Academic Press.

JB B, M. P., Thulasi, P. C., & Philip, J. (2013). Nomophobia-do we really need to worry about. *Reviews of Progress*, *1*(1), 1–5.

Jiang, Y., & Balaji, M. S. (2021). Getting unwired: What drives travellers to take a digital detox holiday? *Tourism Recreation Research*, ●●●, 1–17.

Kim, Y., Wang, Y., & Oh, J. (2016). Digital media use and social engagement: How social media and smartphone use influence social activities of college students. *Cyberpsychology, Behavior, and Social Networking*, *19*(4), 264–269. doi:10.1089/cyber.2015.0408 PMID:26991638

Konok, V., Gigler, D., Bereczky, B. M., & Miklósi, Á. (2016). Humans' attachment to their mobile phones and its relationship with interpersonal attachment style. *Computers in Human Behavior*, *61*, 537–547. doi:10.1016/j.chb.2016.03.062

Miksch, L., & Schulz, C. (2018). *Disconnect to reconnect: The phenomenon of digital detox as a reaction to technology overload*. Academic Press.

Pawłowska-Legwand, A., & Matoga, Ł. (2020). Disconnect from the Digital World to Reconnect with the Real Life: An Analysis of the Potential for Development of Unplugged Tourism on the Example of Poland. *Tourism Planning & Development*, 1–24. doi:10.1080/21568316.2020.1842487

Purohit, A. K., Barclay, L., & Holzer, A. (2020). Designing for digital detox: Making social media less addictive with digital nudges. In *Extended Abstracts of the 2020 CHI Conference on Human Factors in Computing Systems* (pp. 1-9). ACM.

Saprikis, V., Markos, A., Zarmpou, T., & Vlachopoulou, M. (2018). Mobile shopping consumers' behavior: An exploratory study and review. *Journal of Theoretical and Applied Electronic Commerce Research*, *13*(1), 71–90. doi:10.4067/S0718-18762018000100105

Syvertsen, T., & Enli, G. (2020). Digital detox: Media resistance and the promise of authenticity. *Convergence*, *26*(5-6), 1269–1283. doi:10.1177/1354856519847325

Vargas La Rosa, M. (2019). *Application of digital detox hotels for digital detoxification*. Academic Press.

Wilcockson, T. D., Osborne, A. M., & Ellis, D. A. (2019). Digital detox: The effect of smartphone withdrawal on mood, anxiety, and craving. *Addictive Behaviors*, *99*, 106013. doi:10.1016/j.addbeh.2019.06.002 PMID:31430621

KEY TERMS AND DEFINITIONS

Consumer Behavior Online: The study of individuals, groups, or organizations and all the activities associated with the purchase, use and disposal of goods and services, including the consumer's emotional, mental, and behavioral responses that precede or follow these activities in the online environment.

Digital Marketing: Is the marketing of products or services using digital technologies, mainly on the internet, but also including mobile phones, display advertising, and any other digital medium.

E-Satisfaction: The contentment of a consumer with respect to his or her prior purchasing experiences with a given retail-oriented website.

E-WOM: Is any positive or negative statement made by potential, actual or a former customer which is available to a multitude of people via the internet.

Online Relationship: Is an integrative and multidimensional concept, such as relationship quality in an offline context.

Social Media: Social media are interactive computer-mediated technologies that facilitate the creation and sharing of information, ideas, career interests and other forms of expression via virtual communities and networks.

Social Networks: Is a social structure composed of persons or organizations, connected by one or several types of relationships, which share common values and goals.

Chapter 11
Innovation Dynamics Through the Encouragement of Knowledge Spin-Off From Touristic Destinations

Sofia Vairinho
University of the Algarve, Portugal & Facultad de Derecho, Universidad de Huelva, Spain

ABSTRACT

The present approach aims to explore the innovation dynamic that may lead to knowledge opportunities in a specific regional cluster characterized by a strong touristic positioning. The new technology-based companies, namely the spin-out created from university research, represent a possible and reliable approach to the economy stimulation. This said, it is mandatory to explore the topics that will allow a reflection on the networks associated with innovation processes, developed from the relations between the public universe (including universities and research centers), and the new technology or humanistic based companies. This chapter intends to be a contribution to the discussion of innovation clusters and sets the preliminary issues to discuss and implement an innovation ecosystem. This chapter explores and reflects the importance of regional innovation clusters dynamics, setting and describing the steps and specific strategical procedures in order to implement an innovation ecosystem, using as example a specific touristic territory.

INTRODUCTION

This chapter aims to explore the innovation dynamic that may lead to knowledge opportunities in a specific regional cluster characterized by a strong touristic positioning and gives relevance to the touristic entrepreneurship approach and the impact of academic spin-off companies, by presenting a case study of a regional innovation strategy.

International approaches demonstrate that universities can play an important role as driving levers for new companies by incorporating creativity into the new businesses. It is noted that Education should,

DOI: 10.4018/978-1-7998-8165-0.ch011

at all levels, develop knowledge, stimulate creativity, entrepreneurial and also finance competences (Stefani et al., 2020) and that the creation of new businesses based on university research can become an important driver for the establishment of innovation policies, which is the case in many countries (Wright et al., 2007). However, it should be noted that some universities are successful when involved in the process of setting up and developing new technology-based companies, while others have many difficulties in this path. This differentiation also encompasses the way academics relate with doctoral students and entrepreneurs (Boh et al., 2016). In this context, the characteristics of the university and its surroundings are very important (Rasmussen et al., 2015), especially if we emphasize this approach into a strong touristic region.

The new technology based companies, namely the spin-out created from university research, represent a possible and reliable approach to stimulate the economy.

Is mandatory to explore the topics that will allow a reflection on the networks associated with innovation processes, developed from the relations between the public universe (including Universities and Research Centers), and the new technology or humanistic based companies.

In this scenario there are important services that a region, aligned with a marketing perspective of a well-known and reliable touristic destination and the university strategy have identified as priorities. The definition of an innovation regional strategy has to rely in a diversity of opportunities for the establishment of spin-off or start up companies. This diversity may benefit from the geographical and environmental characteristics of a particular touristic destination, but has to interact with other sectors, namely with the ICT sector, forcing the creation of regional support strategies for the implementations of new products, services and new companies. A specific region that aim to develop an innovative cluster needs to define a strategy and need to create the sources and links that will provide the support to the establishment of new spin-off or start-up companies, providing services such as: the pre-incubation, incubation and acceleration services. Those can be expressions of a reliable partnership between local authorities and, for example, the university in order to stimulate local companies that may grow to international markets.

Also aligned with this perspective are the tangible assets of the companies that are becoming intangible assets as the new digitalization era arrives in a vertiginous velocity. The strategy of identifying good practices that will allow the definition of a reliable legal framework represent opportunities to clarify the new mission of universities and also of the State and stakeholders, in terms of diversifying the economy opportunities.

Through the present approach we aim also to bring highlight to the importance of the intellectual property rights approach, namely through the brand definition, in order to obtain a successful business strategy and projection for spin-off companies. University spin-off companies are usually dealing with the novelty of presenting a new product or new service to the economic society, or the consumer. There are industrial property strategies that need to have a support and a strategic definition in order to properly present the emergent company to the society.

Innovation is usually the scope of the new technology based companies that arise from the knowledge developed within Universities, although some of these new spin-off companies tend to minimize the importance of a well-defined brand and marketing strategy on their business plans. This approach gains presently more importance specifically in the touristic activities sector, considering the post Covid-19 pandemic context and the new tendencies for attracting clients for touristic regions.

The purpose of the present methodology depends on the necessity of elaborating an industrial property pre diagnosis to those emergent companies in order to maximize their knowledge by the time the company needs to get ready for the market. This approach relies on the importance of being aware of the world best practices and legal procedures in order to obtain and to secure a potential essential industrial property right (such as a trademark, a design, or even a patent) for the spin-off. The efforts of globalizing industrial property rights and the necessity of providing to these emergent companies - and for the startup companies in general - new faster and more accessible industrial property rights justified the changes in European institutions, such as the European Union Intellectual Property Office.

In the European Union Intellectual Property Office (for example), you are able to submit and to obtain European rights such as the European Union Trade Mark or the Community Design in very competitive prices.

We can therefore state that in the present global economy the competitiveness and the development of new innovative products and services represent unique opportunities to operate in an international level, if a supportive entrepreneurial an innovative ecosystem is settled. Some of those new products of services might arise from new university spin-off companies that are stimulated to bring knowledge to the society. Those companies require a branding and strong marketing strategy, based on a proper business and legal advice in terms of identify potential markets to protect the main industrial property rights that can also be one of the main assets of the emergent company.

This chapter explores and reflects the importance of regional innovation clusters dynamics, setting and describing the steps and specific strategical procedures in order to implement an innovation ecosystem, using as example a specific touristic territory. It also aims to demonstrate, through the presentation of an empirical exploration in a specific touristic region, the importance of touristic entrepreneurship and the impact of academic spin-offs, presenting a case study of a regional innovation strategy.

This discussion is based on local evidences, using the case of Algarve Region as a case study where a regional innovation strategy is trying to be implemented in order to incentivize more innovative and global spin-off companies. We intend to demonstrate that through university activities it is possible do stimulate emergent research and business clusters, that can lead to the creation of new technology based companies, specifically the ones that are born within the tourism sector, although the emerging question is: will these companies be enough to stimulate the attraction of international technological gurus and multinational enterprises to develop R&D activities in the Algarve Region? To answer this question University of Algarve, local authorities and regional companies are engaged in stimulating an existing touristic cluster through the consolidation of a technological destination, characterized by the support on a specific and emerging technological cluster.

The present chapter is divided into three sections. The first section presents the theoretical background that stresses the role of universities and research as impulse to innovative new businesses, and how can we improve these regions known by its natural touristic destination. The second section relates to the role of universities in supporting spin-off companies. The related subsections to this section develop the challenges, constraints, realities and best practices; the entrepreneurial initiatives: from ideas competitions to incubation support; presenting some case studies; the situation in Portugal; and the particularities of a Portuguese region, known as a strong touristic destination, and the importance of its university: The case of University of Algarve and the Algarve region as a touristic destination for entrepreneurial tourism – structure of the ideas competitions; constitutions of juries and selection criteria; management preparation and results. The third section presents the solutions and recommendations, arising the issue of the Universities participation models, including two subsections related with the incubation of spin-off companies: incubation regulations and emerging spin-offs companies pursuing a legal status in an entrepreneurial touristic context; and the support to university 'spin-off': The different kinds of support in various stages of incubation. The chapter ends with the presentation of the future research directions and the conclusions.

BACKGROUND

International approaches demonstrate that universities can play an important role as driving levers for new companies by incorporating creativity into the new businesses. Aligned with this statement it is important to set the proper literature background in order to limit the present approach. For this reason, the basis of the present work relies on innovation as the engine of economic growth and social change (Nelson and Winter (1982); Schumpeter (1911, 1942); Freeman and Louçã (2001)).

Indeed, it is noted that Education should, at all levels, develop knowledge, stimulate creativity, entrepreneurial and also finance competences (Stefani et al., 2020) and that the creation of new businesses based on university research can become an important driver for the establishment of innovation policies, which is the case in many countries (Wright et al., 2007). However, it should be noted that some universities are successful when involved in the process of setting up and developing new technology-based companies, while others have many difficulties in this path. This differentiation also encompasses the way academics relate with doctoral students and entrepreneurs (Boh et al., 2016). In this context, the characteristics of the university and its surroundings are very important (Rasmussen et al., 2015), especially if we emphasize this approach into a strong touristic region.

In a context of clear commitment to innovation at the regional level that comprises the implementation of concepts and procedures to attract heterogeneous companies, it is urgent to discuss and reflect on innovation network models as an essential element to reinforce the characteristics and scope of innovation business (Laperche *et al.*, 2010). This said it is required to understand the complex system of networks as an ecosystem of innovation, where the intersection of relationships between companies, universities, institutions and communities allows us to structure a conglomerate that will surpass the traditional and virtuous triple helix model (Etzkowitz and Leydesdorff, 2001).

This reflection focuses on specific action measures developed within the university context in order to stimulate the implementation of informal innovation clusters, aligned or apart of the touristic sector.

In this context, and in particular as case study, there are cases of companies that by integrating the regional ecosystem in the Algarve Region (south region in Portugal), assumed a clearly innovative position in a regional, national and international context, assuming particular relevance if we consider the Algarve as a touristic destination, *tout court*.

Regarding the support to new companies in a regional university context we highlight the University of Algarve's role, the only public higher education institution in region of Algarve, that through its Entrepreneurship and Technology Transfer Division has assumed a strategic relevance, promoting and leveraging new business, namely through the establishment of competitive business ideas contests, that aim to help the modification of new project and services offered by the Region, taking as an advantage the positioning of the region as a touristic destination in order to attract also entrepreneurial tourism.

The encouragement and commitment to entrepreneurship promotion strategies bring together relevant international good practices and provide an important stimulus for the emergence of new business ideas.

Public incentive has a direct or indirect correlation in the creation of technology-based companies, and knowledge production infrastructures represent a crucial force for the evolution of a knowledge-based economy (Rutten and Boekema, 2009).

Based on these assumptions, this article aims, through the analysis of a set of companies' case studies, which resulted from the entrepreneurial dynamics of the University of Algarve, to evaluate, simultaneously, the conditions of creation and affirmation, or establishment, of these companies. Particular and detailed attention will be focused on the benefits provided by the regional ecosystem, recognizing that the level of development of the regions constrains those benefits (Fernández-Serrano et al, 2019). The density of networks that have been being developed taking advantage of the touristic positioning of the region, are useful for contacts of all kinds, which is made available for start-ups in the university context, stimulating innovation axes that guarantee their affirmation in the national and international spaces.

This article aims to identify and characterize the relationships that underlie innovation, provided by the university environment. This reflection will focus on the in-depth analysis of several companies, with a course, or life circle, of about 10 years each, addressing not only the conditions of their creation (in relation with the University's R&D areas), but also their evolution, in the areas of research, production, installed capacity, human resources, design, regional strengthening contexts and various market levels. The commitments, difficulties, challenges, successes, strategies, growth model or challenges that have been put to the management board along the way will be presented and discussed (Lee and Kelly, 2008).

The main companies are linked to different activity sectors (marine sciences, applied physics and information and communication technologies). The intended evaluation will address issues such as the impact on their distinct social and activity objects, the various aspects related to the products or services identification to be displayed to the market, the difficulties and / or advantages in protecting their innovations through intellectual property rights, the model of participation strategies in the diverse markets they attend and also their future options in terms of business expansion and internationalization.

THE ROLE OF UNIVERSITIES IN SUPPORTING SPIN-OFFS.

Challenges, Constraints, Realities and Best Practices

Entrepreneurship, in recent times, has been a flag widely held not only at the initiative of governments, but also by the various agents inserted in the university and business sectors. The logic of each of these promoters is based on different assumptions, sometimes coincident, but sometimes revealing even contradictory goals. The differentiation that exists also results, in addition to their objectives, from different contexts that influence the dynamics and policies to foster entrepreneurship. We are dealing with a diversity of strategies that, in a different way, can drive the establishment of small businesses or, in another plan, the creation of units of high technological intensity, aligned to certain sector, such as the touristic sector. Whereas they try to alleviate high unemployment rates or, in another challenge, to empower independent units that are derived from medium and large enterprises, specially identified in enterprises crises context, such as the COVID-19 pandemic side effect namely in the touristic sector. Diversity is high and there is currently no community that does not want to define its entrepreneurship promotion policy.

In recent years, and in order to reflect the innovation strategies that need to be considered, we have found a high level of dual-focused entrepreneurship. It has expression simultaneously in developing societies with low income (Bosma and Donna, 2018) or also in developed societies with high income. In the first case, the predominance of entrepreneurship is concentrated in low value added activities related to agricultural production, handicrafts and retail trade. In the case of developed societies, the focus of entrepreneurship is distributed between activities that alleviate unemployment or stimulate technology-based and knowledge-intensive projects.

The behavior of entrepreneurs is equally diverse and depends on many factors (Stam, 2015). Talent, leadership and knowledge are components that characterize the entrepreneur's profile. These are necessary aspects for the success of their initiatives. In addition to these components, the success of their projects is also conditioned by external characteristics that directly influence the dynamics of entrepreneurs: logistic support services, financial services and network access.

To these components, Stam (2015) adds another type of aspects that condition the performance of entrepreneurs. Among these aspects are the context characteristics that can facilitate or hinder the development of entrepreneurial initiatives. We can identify some of those aspects that set the context:

- Physical infrastructures;
- Formal institutional structures;
- Market;
- Corporate culture;
- Informal structures for local (or regional) regulation.

Physical components depend, in a large extent, on public investment that contributes to the creation of supportive entrepreneurship initiatives. The promotion of incubation services, co-working or logistic support spaces are among the initiatives that the public authorities have secured. Other solutions have also been mobilized, university wide or integrated into associative solutions, in which case they reflect the maturity of the social and business environment in terms of business creation support and the enhancement of resources.

The formal institutional structures cover the administrative mechanisms that affect the recognition, installation and operation of entrepreneurial initiatives. Much progress has been done in this area, simplifying procedures and ensuring access to full activity through standard regulation and procedures, sometimes limited on time, but which meet the needs of proto-enterprises at an early stage. The openness of the administrative authorities that dominate the licensing permits and the installation of new business ideas has been fundamental and has contributed to fostering and expanding entrepreneurship.

The market, especially the expression that demands for goods and services, as in identifying and selecting the best entrepreneurial initiatives, has been decisive. The failure of many of the initiatives is often due to the weak training and experience of entrepreneurial teams. However, the lack of convergence with the needs of the market, including in this concept emerging aspects that characterize it, will cause many of the entrepreneurial initiatives to fail.

Entrepreneurial culture enables the generation of a local (or regional) environment that can be crucial for the implementation of new business initiatives, regardless of their size and scope. A closed business environment, exclusively oriented towards its performance and avoiding partnerships of all kinds with other entities (business or not) is doomed to failure in our open society, once the relevance of regional, national and international partnerships may not be neglected in a context of innovation promotion, benefiting from a touristic privileged location. By contrast, a business environment welcoming and supporting new initiatives creates a win-win, dragging mutual benefits and moving forward. Often, traditional entrepreneurs assume the role of mentoring and funding new initiatives, regardless of the specific productive areas of mutual interest.

Finally, the informal structures of social regulation, with local or regional scope, correspond to Community cultures that accumulate know-how (or tacit knowledge), that adopt cultural conventions or build interpersonal ways of relationships that facilitate (or not) the entrepreneurial projects (Scott, 1998). The regional and local cultural environment often provides a multifaceted support to the development of processes and growth in an innovative perspective. Moreover, in many cases, local networks of global relationships facilitate the internationalization of projects, which represents an added value that is not always considered.

This framework of regional multifaceted commitment to innovation will make possible to clarify and better explain the guiding principles of entrepreneurship, its roots, the contextual constraints, the expected outcomes and also the impact on the institutions that promote them. The literature referenced "black box effect" is beginning to be overcome with the multiplication of studies focused on different experiences, what allows a better understanding of the dynamics, of the constraints imposed by the contexts, of the methodologies that bring out the talents (even latent ones) or of the strategies of the different teams. The holistic characterization and enhancement of this complex is translated into what is called an entrepreneurial ecosystem.

The influence of certain circumstances and opportunities generated within the most diverse geographical contexts can act as levers for entrepreneurial activity, which may lead to the realization of innovative ecosystems capable of propelling new technology or humanistic companies. For this reason, it can be considered to emphasize some questions, such as: Who makes the decision? Who supports the decision making process? Who limits the meaning of the decision? How wide is the decision?

In this alignment it is stated the prominent role played by universities in the development of the entrepreneurial complex and innovation clusters, with particular emphasis on the promotion of technology-based initiatives or aligned with the touristic sector in a touristic region challenged to innovate. The relations of the R&D units with the proto-companies, as well as the role of the various agents of the academic community in the animation of this complex are interesting aspects, which the example of the University of Algarve (Portugal) allows to illustrate in a context of regional innovation strategy.

Entrepreneurial initiatives: From Ideas Competitions to Incubation Support

The initiatives that have been triggered in the university context represent an instrumental lever in the creation of new companies.

The role of universities in promoting initiatives that stimulate entrepreneurial activity contains an additional stimulus in the creative drive that can be attributed to researchers, faculty and students, in the offspring of sedimentation or practical realization of applied research.

In this regard, the positioning of certain universities within the dynamics that contribute to the emergence of entrepreneurial ecosystems needs to be taken into account (Spigel, 2015).

The promotion of new spin-off companies, namely on the ICT and tourism sector within a touristic region can be stimulated by the education process strategically stimulated in certain areas by universities. The literature indicates that the increase in the number of spin-offs created (Clarysse et al., 2005) is influenced by the implementation of policies for the creation of new university-based companies (Grimaldi et al., 2011). In this sense, and in ecosystems strongly successively influenced by entrepreneurial policies, it is found that universities compete with each other in the context of patenting, licensing and on the creation of start-up companies (Siegel and Wright, 2015). Vicentt (2010) considered that while policies promoting entrepreneurial initiatives are quite costly, university-based spin-offs have a positive impact on the economy and contribute to local economic dynamics. It can be argued that the cost of those policies generates a highly rewarding outcome.

Schaeffer and Matt (2016) characterize the role of university and its TTO (Technology Transfer Office) in the sustainable development of an entrepreneurial ecosystem in alignment with Youtie and Shapira (2008) on the demonstration how a university in a 'non mature' context contributes to the creation of local entrepreneurial dynamics, becoming a HUB organization, appeasing the boundaries between the various actors involved in the dynamics of local entrepreneurial ecosystems.

For Schaeffer and Matt (2016), there are universities that are progressively contributing to the transformation of an 'unripe' entrepreneurial ecosystem into a more sustainable model through the university model as a hub, whereas a TTO in a hub university develops mediation functions with institutional and local entrepreneurs partners that allow leveraging and settling entrepreneurial projects and stimulate entrepreneurial activity.

In the wake of what it is being said, it is possible to note the initiatives taken by universities with regard to the identification of entrepreneurial ideas during ideas contests.

In this regard, Russell *et al.* (2008) show an overview of the objectives and nature of the business plans competitions, emphasizing the importance and how the ideas contests contribute to an appreciation of the skills of the participants and favor or benefit the organizing institutions, especially the higher education institution.

Russell *et al.* (2008) present an analytical study of former contestants and organizers of ideas competitions within a specific geographic context (Australia).

The same authors reinforce the importance of ideas (or business plans) contests, particularly in higher education institutions, and they present as evidence the development of entrepreneurial characteristics and skills developed by students and which tend to be improved. Thus, it is possible to encourage the creation and emergence of ideas and the technologies that can turn into successful businesses.

The key aspects on the development of a business plan are embodied in an educational context, notably in terms of participant learning and of evaluation by the contest juris. The challenges faced by the institutions in implementing these competitions are diverse. However, there are fundamental aspects oriented to a conductive environment to innovation and to the creation of new ideas (Russell *et al.*, 2008).

The creation of an environment that stimulates creativity and innovative ideas is only possible if the structural characteristics of entrepreneurship are settled and if several factors that can justify the creation of new businesses are gathered together.

In this regard, Landström *et al.* (2013) defend the importance of defining the concept of innovation and entrepreneurship, based on knowledge. These authors argue that it needs to be considered two research fields that should be seen as separately. Also according to the defended by Schumpeter (1934), there are interrelated works, especially when taking into account the evolutionists approach, the geographical differences in innovation and entrepreneurship, and also in the field of innovation management (corporate entrepreneurship) and new technology-based companies.

In this context, ideas competitions assume relevance, namely if we consider that they naturally create conditions that meet those that define an environment that favors learning, and the benefits that this type of initiative brings to the participants and to the institutions are undeniable (Russell et al., 2008).

Russell et al. (2008) propose a reflection on how we should generally use the incentive to the learning of entrepreneurial techniques, calling on government entities and higher education institutions to create and promote competitions of this kind.

The ideas context are also a way of engaging communities and stimulation innovation. A touristic region can benefit from the involvement of public partners in this process, such as universities and local government, and also has the possibility to integrate foreign stakeholders in the process.

Some Case Studies

The role of universities in the encouragement of knowledge spin-off from touristic destinations can drive the innovation process towards a touristic entrepreneurship approach, where the impact of academic spin-off represents a strategy for a specific regional innovation strategy.

Goldfarb and Henrekson (2002) present a reputable study that encompasses two systems, the Swedish and the United States of America (USA). According to these authors, the system adopted by the USA is more focused on creating economic incentives for universities to commercialize their research results, while Sweden, similar to most countries in the European Union, do not stand out great relationship concerns that can link the academia with the market. These countries have implemented mechanisms by their governments to try to facilitate market access.

Those authors consider that due to the competitive USA environment between universities, the involvement of academic inventors in the transfer of ideas to the private sector is facilitated or even encouraged.

Aligned with this perspective but in a European context, it can be considered the example of the small entrepreneur that identifies new resources, on knowledge, financial and social new products and services (Boutillier, 2019), and that contributes for a unique new eco-innovation system.

The innovation systems may grow in response to regional development challenges, but there is a work of stimulation that needs to be previously carried out.

Goldfarb and Henrekson (2002) consider that regarding the commercialization support of the academic research results, generally, the ideas that come to technology licensing offices come in a primitive state. Only a very small percentage is ready to be licensed and marketed. The Universities infrastructures and the support provided to researchers are the factors that influence the successful commercialization of certain technology, in general terms, because purely academic research is so distant from applied research or commercial promotion, it is difficult to build relationships between sponsors and high profile academics. While commercial research also aims to enhance the reputation of the academic and make his work useful to others, many academics still prefer to move away from commercialization because it diverts research's attention from its fundamentals.

Fortunately, there are mechanisms that encourage academics to enter in projects for commercial purposes, and it is increasingly common for academics to also be entitled to financial compensation while they are conducting their research. However, for Goldfarb and Henrekson (2002), this type of incentive is ineffective, so perhaps a new approach should be considered in which academics are paid according to their performance in producing the most results.

For these authors the American system is characterized by a bottom-up approach that allows technology to be marketed and commercialized through small businesses and gives the private sector more freedom to exploit it, although the exploitation of intellectual property mechanisms by universities may seem adverse to the academic.

Goldfarb and Henrekson (2002) state that state, that IP allows academics to continue their research and development without having to worry about business aspects. It also reduces tremendously the cost of research because most are handled by the university in exchange for rights on the developed technology and it is considered that the technology transfer offices are also useful in the sense that after the invention is presented, help is provided to the inventor with some support mechanisms and also with some assistance with the negotiation techniques throughout the entire process.

The authors realize that, unlike in Europe generally, US institutions / universities are highly competitive and independent and compete in many ways, for example; there are competitions for students, competition between students, competition for teachers, and teacher competition to support the research that is developed. Because of this competitive spirit, USA universities are more prone to an economic perspective associated with research.

University professors are normally very focused on their research, so choose to teach one level closer to the scientific frontier making students engaged in assisting the advance of that frontier. Teachers are also paid according to their economic value, which is a great incentive and perhaps a big reason why universities are more economically inclined.

Goldfarb and Henrekson (2002) conclude that in many European Union countries, research and teaching were very separate, which has unique benefits, given the recognized great scientific production of Swedish excellence, but there is little incentive for academics to pursue marketing and commercialization of their technologies.

For the authors, the emergence in the USA of flexibility to take advantage of research with commercial value comes from the lack of established legislation proper of a common law state, as well as intensive competition for monetary funds for research. Following the reflection developed by these authors, the following aspects can be identified:

- The strategic definition of policies involving universities in the commercialization processes should benefit the investment in applied research of these institutions, namely in the protection of their intangible assets.
- Facilitating the involvement in commercial activities of the inventors or researchers does not require great incentives to commercialize its technology, but also those agents should not bear any consequences that hinder their research on its university environment.
- Granting intellectual property rights to universities works best in the USA because universities are autonomous and competitive institutions.
- The universities owned by the state in the European Union are forced to follow all laws and rules imposed by it. It is not known if implementing similar policies to the USA would provide sufficient incentives to universities rectors and administrators to commercialize research or if the benefits would be sufficient to cover the costs of sacrificing academic standards and rules.

Another interesting approach comes from Norway: Cico (2019) identifies the strong impact that IT (Information Tecnologies) bootcamp on student learning can have on the conceptualization and integration of students on the spin-off or start up creation process, through the formation and training based on university course external activities such as Hackathon and bootcamp.

Raedersdorf Bollinger (2019) gives relevance to the smooth implementation of innovation processes and gives relevance to innovative tools. This earlier interaction of students with reality problems through the participation in hackathon and bootcamps sets an important step for the development of new products and services using as a common denominator the ICT sector.

In this context it can be useful to have, in an innovation regional perspective, a reliable transversal ICT innovative structure, based on University spin-off, that can act diversely in different sectors, such as supporting other areas, as health, sea industry, renewable energies and the new touristic spin-off companies, with the development of new products or specialized services, based, for instance, on Virtual Reality, Artificial Intelligence, Block chain, IoT (internet of things), among others.

Also with relevance for the implementation of an innovative cluster is the financial support within the innovative region, and in this particular the ICT sector might have an important role in helping researchers and entrepreneurs on the crowdfunding process, advising and motivating the process, in order to stimulate new spin-offs (St. John, 2021).

Situation in Portugal

The impact of academic spin-off represents a strategy for a specific regional innovation strategy, but to incentivize and maximize the development of new products or services there are strategies that benefit from the knowledge and entrepreneurial ideas of university students and teacher, and in some contexts, of the entire country.

In Portugal, the idea contest model is widespread and several institutions, including universities, organize their editions. Some of these contests assume a national strategic importance and can be considered a way for big business to approach and to exploit the knowledge developed within universities.

The Portuguese universities are assuming a role on the approximation with the business or enterprises sector and with the local dynamics that stimulates and stirs students, teachers and researchers for entrepreneurial initiatives.

In this regard we may refer, for illustrative purposes only, the ideas contests promoted by a large Portuguese electricity distribution company. The contest, known as EDP University Challenge, takes place annually in Portugal since 2010, and has featured more and 1090 teams with more than 3974 participants. It should be noted that, according to the promotion strategy of the company, this competition has already taken on a global dimension and is launched annually in seven different countries (Portugal, Brazil, Spain, Italy, United Kingdom and France), in which three local finalists are selected to compete in the Global Final. This initiative of a large company aims to encourage college students to apply their academic knowledge in the development of a project focused on an electricity related theme and is directed to a sense of internationalization of the contest, allowing to put face to face projects from different countries, translating different realities and dynamics.

This example is designed to attract students from many areas related to entrepreneurship, through a minimum stimulus able to attract creativity and innovation to the corporate environment.

In relation to the prizes awarded, there is a financial component associated with the initiative, because there is a competition triggered by a business entity.

Briefly, in terms of compensation associated with the award of prizes, it should be noted that the amounts of the prizes awarded match roughly the figures presented by Russel *et al* (2008).

In the first editions of the competition, the prize was given only to the 1st place, which was divided by all team members. In more recent editions, the value of the first prize has been reduced, but they have started to award the second and third prizes. They also changed the distribution of the prize amount: instead of being evenly distributed by the team, 25% is given to the team coordinator teacher and the rest is divided by the students.

In the several editions of the EDP (Electricity of Portugal) University Challenge competition, it was observed that the jury team consisted of members from three different companies, with two of them outside the sponsoring company's perimeter. Seth forth as example and according to Russell *et al* (2004), there is a distinction between categories of experts in the constitution of jurors. These represent companies whose activity and technology are predominantly present in many of the applications submitted (information and communication technologies, management consulting, etc.).

As this company many others are gaining interest in Innovation and Creativity in young people and in education, although as we can see from the above mentioned data, it is possible to compare them with data from 2008, showing that Portugal is extremely delayed compared to other countries.

Another interesting example that demonstrates the interest that the competitions have shown is the case of the "Poliempreende Program". It corresponds to a Program organized in Portugal by the national network of Polytechnic Higher Institutes and Polytechnic Schools not integrated in the Institutes. The program management is rotary and each year there is a different institution that organizes the national competition.

The contest has two distinct stages. A first stage corresponds to a regional presentation and selection, organized within each of the institutions committed to the competition and with distribution of prizes covering the top three. For the second stage, at which to the winners of the various regional competitions are presented, three awards are also distributed.

The jury of regional and national competitions is made up of company-related personalities who validate and select proposals for business ideas.

Prizes are delivered in a fragmented manner. A first installment of the monetary value is distributed at the award ceremony. A second installment is granted only after the official legal company's commencement of business or after a presentation of the technology transfer agreement to the company. This methodology makes it possible to encourage the start of the activity and to prevent the process from being confined to the award for any reason, without guaranteeing that the project will be implemented.

The Case of University of Algarve and the Algarve Region as a Touristic Destination for Entrepreneurial Tourism – Structure of the Ideas Competitions; Constitutions of Juries and Selection Criteria; Management Preparation and Results

Given the landscape that has characterized the new dynamics in universities, the development of strategies under its third mission has been multiplied. The University of Algarve, although a small institution located in a peripheral region, has also endowed it with this strategy, combining it with regional needs in order to encourage knowledge spin-off in strategic areas for the university, such as tourism and ICT. The University's areas of expertise have been responsible for promoting and creating spin-offs and supporting start-ups. These areas of expertise naturally concentrate the highest scientific research competencies and the intensity of knowledge transfer is crucial for the creation of proto-enterprises and micro-enterprises.

These areas of expertise are particularly important in terms of internationalization. Research projects with results that can be in transferred to the business environment and simultaneously with international components accelerate the affirmation of the companies that are being created benefiting from the results of these projects.

The support and incentive programs for the creation of new companies at the University of Algarve were developed in accordance with norms that, in one hand, encourage the emergence of the best ideas and the exploitation of the research projects results and, on the other hand, ensures that material and immaterial support leads to a high success rate.

Several characteristics can be valued:

1. Competition covering the various areas of knowledge, but with greater focus on the areas of specialization of the University;
2. Early definition of the benefits that the first classified may obtain, usually translated into services and facilities;
3. The projects are presented and defended publicly pear a mixed panel (business and academic);
4. Organization, after an initial screening, of curt duration courses, oriented for business management training, compulsory for the competing teams, as a procedure that allows to make a first selection of candidates who manage to reconcile technical scientific valences with management skills;
5. Benefits will include real or virtual incubation facilities, identification of mentors for the company follow-up, contacts with funding entities, insertion into thematic networks (local, national and international);
6. A major effort is made to establish (or maintain) contacts between start-ups and University research centers with the goal to generate possible new products or services;
7. Possibility to participate in periodic workshops organized to discuss new realities and strategies, but also to identify new shared projects.

SOLUTIONS AND RECOMMENDATIONS: THE UNIVERSITIES PARTICIPATION MODELS

According with the procedures in force in the Portuguese legal system, we can distinguish within the culture and university policies legal instruments that help universities in its connection with the new technology - based companies, giving a complement to the definition of regional innovation dynamics.

In this sense, we can address the context of public universities in which we have been witnessing the establishment of Internal Regulations to legitimize the existence of new spin-off companies and their link with the developed research, which, in this particular, dictates the existence of the emerging company. It should be also noted that these institutions admit a distinction between the concept of 'spin-off' and 'start-up', in the sense that it is considered a 'start-up' business the new companies that are created and formed by alumni, former students, former researchers and former teachers. Start-up companies should maintain a relationship with the mater public institution, set forth as example of cooperation the recruitment of new elements, namely students of the public university, for the development of research and development projects, for example.

Given the above, it is urgent to analyze some of the regulations that have been applied in the most diverse University contexts. In Portugal, in general and abstract terms we can note that Universities, due to the absence of normative provisions, chose to regulate internally the activity related to the creation of new university technology base companies. To incentivize and promote a touristic entrepreneurial and innovative region it is important to have well defined and established regulations and procedures.

In this regard, it should be noted that some regulations embody, for example, the concept of spin-off. A new company is considered a true university spin-off if it meets certain requirements. The enumeration may be considered as an alternative, non-cumulative identification, as the new company may meet one or all of the following elements:

- In order to enhance the binding to the university at least one of entrepreneurs should be part, has a legal bond or any another connection to the University, highlighting in this particular that the said connection passes through being a student, researcher, teacher or other;
- The University effectively supports the creation of the company (through training, providing business development, networking, incubation, etc.);
- The company aims to exploit, - as is the case in the majority of educational and research institutions -, the (applied) knowledge of the University, formalized through a know-how or patent license;
- The university authorizes the use of a logo or trademark associated with the activity related to supporting university spin-offs;
- The access to specialized services is provided by the University, including the pre-incubation services, incubation and acceleration of companies.

In this sense, we can identify diverse attribution processes or ways for granting the 'spin-off status'. However, the attribution criteria for the award of spin-off status may differ according to the different scope of the public education and research institutions.

It should also be noted that the regulations associated with the creation of new university companies are linked to the intellectual property regulations in force in universities, and, by extensive interpretation, to the provisions of the Portuguese Copyright and Related Rights Code and the Portuguese Industrial Property.

In this regard, it should be noted that Portuguese Universities are the holders of the intellectual property rights developed in them, considering the application of article 58 of the mentioned Industrial Property Code which describes that " if the invention is made during the execution of an employment contract where the inventive activity is foreseen, the right to the patent belongs to the respective company '. And most of all, the University, or the Institution, can benefit, under the terms of article 58 (8) of the Industrial Property Code industrial, because

"Unless otherwise specified, the preceding provisions shall apply to the Public Administration and, also, to its employees for any reason, without prejudice to the following article. ", which provides the direct involvement of Public Universities in the process of protection and commercialization of industrial property rights. "Article 59 - Research and development activities; 1 - It belongs to the public legal person whose statutory scope includes research and development activities, the inventions made by their workers or collaborators as a result of their research activities."

There is therefore evidence that within the European area the legal and administrative framework is starting to take the first steps towards simplifying the participation of teachers and researchers in the commercialization of intangible rights or assets what can improve the relation between academia and industry, in order to encouraged the knowledge spin-off, especially the ones from a touristic region.

Incubating Spin-Off Companies: Incubation Regulations and Emerging Spin-Offs Companies Pursuing a Legal Status in an Entrepreneurial Touristic Context

In order to create an innovation cluster where dynamic entrepreneurial initiatives take form the assumption of a legal framework represents a highlighted role in an entrepreneurial touristic context, where a touristic region needs also to be attractive to companies, spin-off, start-up or multinational companies. As it is mentioned, among universities and research centers oriented by the public penchant we assist to an assignment of the spin-off company status that is guided by a 'case by case' definition assumed by each different entity on its internal regulations.

Legal elements are created to support the implementation of the applicability of the of the 'spin-off' concept, regarding the non-mandatory regulation that each institution performs, assuming and incorporating such nomenclature within their specific internal regulations.

Usually, and given the various regulations adopted by the different institutions, it is possible to note an impact on various elements and at different times, as above mentioned. There is a recognition and institutional commitment to promote an entrepreneurial culture, identifying and selecting physical spaces that can respond to the various incubation needs of the emerging companies. This is accompanied by the establishment of business spaces, pre-laboratory, laboratory, accelerating or maturing business ideas, resources and support services, among other elements.

It should be noted that these elements are mirrored in the internal regulations of each institution, either in the form of regulations for the creation of spin-off companies, or through the implementation of incubation regulations or guidelines in their own spaces that affect higher education institutions.

In the light of the university spin-off company's regulations, it is possible, in the course of the analysis of the various regulations applicable in Portugal, to recognize different elements that allow a public institution to consider a given start-up company as a capable entity of integrating the concept of a new university spin-off company. As it has been already stated, this happens in a fragmented way, as there is no national standard applicable law applicable to all higher education institutions. These institutions have the autonomy to create their own strategies.

In this sense and as predominant elements in the internal policies of each public institution, we identified the following elements:

1. Need for identification, presentation and selection of innovative ideas, or business ideas ready to be presented as future companies (pre-selection phase of the new business ideas based on knowledge characterized by innovative features within the higher education or research institution);
2. Evaluation of the innovative capacity of the emerging company in terms of innovative scientific knowledge and market;
3. Evaluation of the promoting entrepreneurs profile taking into account the business idea, its implementation and viability in the market, in order to verify if this profile is in harmony with the objectives of the new company.
4. Identification of a license agreement, whereas there is use of intellectual property rights or other know-how of the University or of the related institution.

It should be noted that under the Portuguese legal approach, and considering the existing regulations, we are witnessing an (apparent or possible real) overlap of contents with regard to the national regulations for the creation of new spin-off companies and in relation to the business incubation regulations.

Supporting University 'Spin-Off': The Different Kinds of Support in Various Stages of Incubation

In this regard and considering the innovation dynamics and the regional strategies for supporting university spin-off companies, it should be noted that university incubation regulations are prominent, firstly because of their role as a driving force behind business dynamics within university *campi*.

If we focus on the new mission that is being committed to universities, there is an effort to support young university students and their initiatives to enter the labor market, which involves the realization of various projects.

In this context, higher education institutions, universities and public research centers began by defining their own regulations to ensure that students, faculty and researchers have access to public university spaces, including the use of equipment, laboratories and other related facilities. These measures provide spin-off promoters a broad range of support services including access to business plan development, specialized funding sources, and support for corporate or industrial licensing processes, strategy and pre –financing, diagnostics and company studies on Intellectual Property, training in business management, business presentations support such as in preparing a "pitch" and " networking" with potential investors (public and private).

In the light of what has been presented, and bearing in mind that in the Portuguese context we are witnessing a regulatory approach that is currently promoting and looking for a conceptual definition of a 'spin-off' company under the incubation regulations defined by higher education institutions. We point out that according to the analysis of various Regulations in force, we identified the existence of several phases that support and help on the follow up of the state of development of a given company.

We can therefore identify in the incubation regulations, (and similar to the national strategy defined in the opening of calls for specific funding) the identification of three distinct phases.

Nevertheless, as it has been said, some public higher education institutions and research centers hosting business incubation projects tend to include in their regulations, taking advantage of this normative instrument, the definition of the concept of a new 'spin-off' company.

Given the above mentioned, we can identify three essential moments regarding the support that can be performed by each incubating institution, focused on the University incubation support services:

- The pre-incubation phase: An initial moment in which is privileged the access to core services offered by the University and when is provided and promoted the proper support for the validation of technology and business model. At this level, the University can help on the establishment of the new company, with all the necessary elements to make the product marketable and add value to the creation of a new company. At this moment we cannot talk about a real company, since the 'spin-off' still remains as a project status.

- The incubation phase: This phase stands out for assuming the legal constitution of the company by the promoters of the new spin-off company. At this moment, the host entity selects companies whose main activity is the development and market valuation of the technology (product or service), and it is essential that in a previous moment or at this moment the company has already tests on the effectiveness of the new product or service, proven for proof of concept. It is understood that at this stage the new spin-off company takes over and evolves into a business that is actually outsourced to the host institution, and should therefore be considered as a university spin-out.

- The post incubation or business acceleration phase: is a moment characterized by the total sufficiency and independence of the new company. At this stage the emerging company is characterized by its ability to develop its business in view of its ability to respond to market needs, considering the response that the company can achieve in terms of production, sales, marketing and management. This phase is characterized by the existence of the maturity and self-sufficiency of the company that, according to some authors, can now be dubbed 'start-up', if we consider and make a parallelism with the previous evolution. In this case, if the company already has the means and resources for its consolidated growth, and, as a result of the analysis of the sample's incubation regulations, it is clear that there is an ability of articulation with the University, as it may continue to encourage privileged relations between the public institution and the start-up company.

This approach builds on an understanding that derives from the analysis of the different incubation regulations that have been explored and considered. They contain the necessary elements for the understanding and for the approach presently carried out into the legal understanding of new spin-off technology-based companies and to the support in answering the needs of the university emerging companies.

FUTURE RESEARCH DIRECTIONS AND CONCLUSION

The impact of innovative initiatives sets the framework for a study on the impact of touristic entrepreneurship and how can a region, characterized as a touristic destination, be also attractive for the encouragement of knowledge spin-off, for start-up and also for international companies. This will be only possible if certais structures and contions will be in place.

As case study, the University of Algarve, like almost all Portuguese universities, has created in its internal structure an organization, a technology transfer office, that has ensured the interface between research centers and companies, stimulation innovation dynamics. In addition, this organism is responsible for the encouragement of spin-offs contests, for the management of a University Incubator, for the management strategy mechanisms of intellectual property rights and, very often, by the spread, in the various degrees of higher education, of entrepreneurship training. Also, the collaboration with secondary education and regional high schools, has enabled the awareness of young pre-university students about entrepreneurship.

A large number of spin-off companies in the marine science, information and communication technology, radiological physics or precision agriculture sectors have come out of ideas competitions, of research center projects or of doctoral groups made themselves autonomous and converted into business activities. The survey which was carried out under this article proves the impact of the University of Algarve on the creation of academic spin-off and Start-up companies.

The conditions assumed by the University of Algarve allow confirming that the bet on entrepreneurship has significant effects on the business dynamics of the Region. In this regard, it should be noted that from the companies surveyed, they were either derived directly from research generated at UAlg or were created by students. All of the interviewed companies unanimously confirmed that they had received significant support from the University TTO. This was an important factor in their evolutionary and corporate sedimentation process, once University, namely through its TTO, in the early years of activity of a university company 'spin-off'. The Technology Transfer Office provides a wide range of several services, including the support in business incubation, the definition of business strategy, aid in the preparation of business plan, intellectual property and knowledge transfer, including support in identifying national and international strategic partners and engaging emerging companies in networks and consortium projects. It is this complex that requires new dynamics from the University (and its researchers), but also generates a significant impact on the region's productive sector.

The experience of the University of Algarve TTO reveals the need of identifying and making available to Academia a specialized range of expertise on technical and administrative skills in order to accompany and develop the so-called entrepreneurial ecosystem. Firstly, Universities may have to abandon its ivory tower and open themselves, broadly, to society. In this domain, it will be worth stressing that the leadership of science production lies with the research centers. They may respond to societal needs, challenging companies to explore technological (and other) areas of social interest, and structure partnerships with diverse entities (business, management, local authorities, etc.) to add knowledge and technology to the social acquis of innovation.

A second concern reveals that these tasks are eminently professional. The management of science, the identification of opportunities, the validation of knowledge and technology with market interest, the domain of intellectual property mechanisms (including the negotiation details of technology transfer contracts), as well as related aspects on the commercialization process require professional skills and active networks. In alignment with this concern the work of Raedersdorf Bollinger (2019) has particular importance because it considers whether some management tools facilitate the smooth implementation of an innovation process considering that the relevance of these tools are depending on many factors including the type of innovation expected in a certain context. For this reason it is important to have a reliable transversal ICT innovative structure, based on University spin-off, that can act diversely in different sectors, such as supporting the new touristic spin-off companies, with the development of new products or specialized services, based, for instance on virtual reality, artificial intelligence, block chain, IoT (internet of things), among others.

A third line of activity encompasses the creation of living, dynamic and strategic objective networks. The various activities of this entrepreneur ecosystem require an intense interplay and a prospective positioning, able to anticipate needs and to generate a mutually winning environment.

A fourth concern takes up the necessary simplification of administrative procedures for the university 'spin-off' creation, and maintenance of companies, with a studied financing viability for the first years of operation and, in addition, the flexibility of the participation of teachers and researchers of higher education in business projects that are committed to the level of scientific research and production of knowledge, Internationalization closes this set of concerns, which should be present and also reflected in ideas competitions, incubators animation, technology transfer contracts, financing strategies, building partnerships and networks and looking for markets.

In conclusion this chapter explores and reflects the importance of regional innovation clusters dynamics, setting and describing the steps and procedures in order to implement an innovation ecosystem, using as example a specific touristic territory. This chapter demonstrates through the presentation of an empirical exploration in a specific touristic region the importance of touristic entrepreneurship and the impact of academic spin-offs, presenting a case study of a regional innovation strategy, based in an intellectual property strategy, aligned with the implementation of regional technology transfer offices that promote and incentivize the necessary regional, national and international links that allow a touristic region to interact with different governmental and entrepreneurial actors in order to stimulate the creation of valuable new spin-off companies and profitable startups, able to diversify their products through a direct contact with a regional university able to provide research and knowledge in many transversal sectors and support areas, such as ICT, tourism, sea sector, health, biotech and renewable energies.

A "Region" can be attractive as a touristic destination by its natural benefits, but in can also be in many other, direct or indirect, ways as a touristic entrepreneurial and innovative region capable of attracting multinational entrepreneurial players. Exploiting a touristic destination that offers you an innovative ecosystem to invest may be the ignition point to optimize a specific Touristic Region as it was initially known towards an innovative cluster.

ACKNOWLEDGMENT

Direct acknowledgment to fellow researcher and contributor to these results both in practical and theoretical perspective are to Doctor João Guerreiro, former Rector of University of Algarve.

Statement: This research received no specific grant from any funding agency in the public, commercial, or not-for-profit sectors.

REFERENCES

Boh, W., De-Haan, U., & Strom, R. (2016). University technology transfer through entrepreneurship: Faculty and student spinoffs. *The Journal of Technology Transfer*, *41*(4), 661–669. doi:10.100710961-015-9399-6

Bosma, N. D., & Onna, K. (2018). Global Entrepreneurship Monitor, Global Report 2018/2019. *GEM: International Journal on Geomathematics*.

Boutillier, S. (2019). Small Entrepreneurship, Knowledge and Social Resources in a Heavy Industrial Territory. The Case of Eco-Innovations in Dunkirk, North of France. *Journal of the Knowledge Economy*, *10*(3), 997–1018. Advance online publication. doi:10.100713132-017-0511-z

Cico, O. (2019). The Impact of IT Bootcamp on Student Learning - Experience from ICT Enabled Experiential-Based Course. Software Business, 430-435. doi:10.1007/978-3-030-33742-1_37

Clarysse, B., Wright, M., Lockett, A., Van de Velde, E., & Vohora, A. (2005). Spinning out new ventures: A typology of incubation strategy from European research institutions. *Journal of Business Venturing*, *20*(2), 183–216. doi:10.1016/j.jbusvent.2003.12.004

Etzkowitz, H., & Leydesdorff, L. (2001). Universities and the Global Knowledge Economy. *Continuum*.

Fernandez-Serrano, J., Martinez-Román, J., & Romero, I. (2019). The entrepreneur in regional innovation system. The comparative study for high- and low income regions. *Entrepreneurship and Regional Development*, *31*(5-6), 5–6, 337–356. doi:10.1080/08985626.2018.1513079

Freeman, C., & Louçã, F. (2001). *As time goes by. From the industrial revolutions to the information revolution*. Oxford University Press.

Goldfarb, B., & Henrekson, M. (2002). *Bottom-up versus top-down policies towards the commercialization of university intellectual property*. Elsevier Science BV.

Grimaldi, Kenney, Siegel, & Wright. (2011). 30 years after Bayh-Dole: reassessing academic entrepreneurship. *Research Policy, 40*, 1045-1057.

Landström, H., Aström, F., & Harirchi, G. (2013). *Innovation and Entrepreneurship Studies: One or Two Fields of Research?* Springer + Business Media.

Laperche, B., Sommers, P., & Uzunidiols, D. (Eds.). (2010). Innovation and Cluster Networks. In The Knowledge Backbone. Peter Lang.

Lee, H., & Kelley, D. (2008). Building dynamic capabilities for innovation: An exploratory study of Key Management Practices. *R & D Management, 38*(2), 155–168. doi:10.1111/j.1467-9310.2008.00506.x

Nelson, R. R., & Winter, S. G. (1982). *An Evolutionary theory of Economic Change.* The Belknap Press of Harvard University Press.

Raedersdorf Bollinger, S. (2019). Creativity and forms of managerial control in innovation processes: Tools, viewpoints and practices. *European Journal of Innovation Management, 32*(2), 214–229. doi:10.1108/EJIM-07-2018-0153

Rasmussen, E., & Wright, M. (2015). *How can universities facilitate academic spin-offs? An entrepreneurial competency perspective.* Springer Science, Business Media New York. doi:10.100710961-014-9386-3

Russell, R., Atchinson, M., & Brooks, R. (2008). Business plan competition in tertiary institutions: Encouraging entrepreneurship education. *Journal of Higher Education Policy and Management, 30*(2), 123–138. doi:10.1080/13600800801938739

Rutten, R., & Boekema, F. (2009). Universities and Regional Development. Regional Studies, 43(5), 771-775.

Schaeffer & Mirelle. (2016). Development of an academic entrepreneurship in the non-mature context: the role of the University of the hub organisation. *Entrepreneurship & Regional Development, 28*(9-10), 724-745.

Schumpeter, J. A. (2008). *The theory of economic development.* Transaction Publishers. (Original work published 1911)

Schumpeter, J. A. (2008). *Capitalism, socialism and democracy.* Harper Perennial. (Original work published 1942)

Scott, A. (1998). *Regions and the World Economy.* Oxford University Press.

Siegel, D. S., & Wright, M. (2015). Academic entrepreneurship: Time for a rethink? *British Journal of Management, 26*(4), 582–595. doi:10.1111/1467-8551.12116

Spigel, B. (2015). The relational organization of entrepreneurial ecosystems. *Entrepreneurship Theory and Practice, 12*, 1-24.

St. John, J., St. John, K., & Han, B. (2021). Entrepreneurial crowdfunding backer motivations: A latent Dirichlet allocation approach. *European Journal of Innovation Management.* Advance online publication. doi:10.1108/EJIM-05-2021-0248

Stefani, U., Schiavone, F., Laperche, B., & Burger-Helmchen, T. (2020). New tools and practices for financing novelty: A research agenda. *European Journal of Innovation Management*, *23*(2), 314–328. doi:10.1108/EJIM-08-2019-0228

Tam, S. (2015). Entrepreneurial Ecosystems and Regional Policy: Sympathetic A Critique. *European Planning Studies*, *23*(9), 1759–1769. doi:10.1080/09654313.2015.1061484

Vicentt, P. S. (2010). The economic impacts of academic spin-off companies and their implications for public policy. *Research Policy*, *39*(6), 736–747. doi:10.1016/j.respol.2010.02.001

Wright, M., Clarysse, B., Mustar, P., & Lockett, A. (Eds.). (2007). Academic entrepreneurship in Europe. Edward Elgar.

Youtie, J., & Shapira, P. (2008). Building an Innovation Hub: A Case Study of the Transformation of University Roles in Regional Technological and Economic Development. *Research Policy*, *37*(8), 1188–1204. doi:10.1016/j.respol.2008.04.012

KEY TERMS AND DEFINITIONS

Entrepreneurship: Refers to the enthusiasm to start a new business and to the incentive for value creation among new project ideas in order to get them into the market.

Innovation Networks: A network of contacts and relations that may involve different actors (companies, universities, R&D entities, enterprises) that increment and foster new business and innovative ideas.

Intellectual Property: Intellectual property refers to creations of the mind, such as inventions, linked to patent protections under the industrial property rights; commerce distinctive names and images, such as trademarks, under industrial property rights protection; literary and artistic works; designs.

Technology Transfer and Commercialization: The process of converting innovative research results into marketable products, that may include, among others, licensing processes or spin-off creation.

Touristic Destinations: Geographic area often visited by tourists with point(s) of interests.

University Spin-Off: Companies that result from the research results or inventions developed within universities.

Section 3
Social Media and Tourism

Chapter 12
Tourist Social Media Engagement:
Conceptualization and Indicators

Rayane Ruas
University of Aveiro, Portugal

Belem Barbosa
https://orcid.org/0000-0002-4057-360X
University of Porto, Portugal

ABSTRACT

Social media are transforming relationships with customers for all sectors, including tourism. Since the search for information is a critical aspect of tourist purchase decision process, the importance of social media for tourism is evident. However, the presence of tourism brands in social media is not enough to have an impact on tourist purchase decisions: it is necessary to generate engagement. This chapter aims to conceptualize tourist engagement on social media and identify tourist engagement indicators. Tourist engagement was conceptualized through a literature review that identified four dimensions of engagement: popularity, commitment, virality, and post engagement. A set of indicators is proposed to measure tourist engagement in each of these dimensions. The proposed TSM engagement framework was validated through a mixed-method approach, using secondary data and interviews carried out with Brazilian tourist destinations.

INTRODUCTION

In the hospitality and tourism industry, social media (SM) are profoundly changing traveler behaviors, mostly in the travels' information searching, planning, and post-experience sharing stages. The globally increasing penetration rates and the popularity of SM in travel decisions transformed these platforms into an essential component of marketing strategies of hospitality and tourism companies. Additionally, SM

DOI: 10.4018/978-1-7998-8165-0.ch012

Tourist Social Media Engagement

has become a prevalent source of marketing intelligence of tourism companies (Albayrak et al., 2020), thus making them indispensable tools for destination managers and hospitality companies, among others.

Social media, which broadly refers to online tools based on social interactions and user-generated content, is characterized by three main features that distinguish these technologies from other web-based tools: real-time communication, many-to-many interactions, and user-generated content. Indeed, social media users can interact in real-time with peers in many-to-many networks by posting their comments, photos, or videos in real-time. These features have boosted social media diffusion worldwide at both individual and organizational levels (Peters et al., 2013).

Overall, social media are transforming the tourism industry from its traditional and information. Since the search for information is a critical aspect of tourists' purchase-decision process, the importance of social media for the tourism industry is evident. Social media have radically changed how tourists interact with tourism brands and make purchasing decisions. Before deciding to travel, most tourists look for online information and reviews provided by managers and other tourists on social media. Indeed, the literature demonstrates that travel decisions are influenced by social media, and tourists' online behavior could predict the demand for destinations (Villamediana et al., 2019).

One essential aspect to analyze in this regard is customer engagement (CE). In today's highly dynamic and interactive business environment, the role of customer engagement in co-creating customer experience and value is receiving increasing attention from business practitioners and academics alike. It is suggested that within interactive, dynamic business environments, CE represents a strategic imperative for generating enhanced corporate performance, including sales growth, superior competitive advantage, and profitability (Brodie et al., 2013).

It should be stressed that the mere presence of a destination or a DMO in a virtual environment is not enough to promote the image of the destination and to heighten intentions to visit. In fact, social media should be viewed as a strategic resource to increase tourism and for obtaining a holistic understanding of the tourist experience (Galvez-Rodriguez et al., 2020), as the presence of tourism brands in social media is not enough to have an impact on tourists' purchase decisions; it is necessary to generate engagement (Villamediana et al., 2019).

The level of engagement obtained will depend on the user's involvement in and interaction with the information provided on social media about the destination, considering both the amount of time and the degree of attention dedicated to its evaluation (Rodríguez et al, 2020).

The focus of this chapter is tourists' engagement in social media. The study of engagement is a complex issue, not only because it has recently been of interest in the marketing field (Brodie et al., 2013), but also because the literature does not provide a single and consistent definition of engagement (Brodie *et al.*, 2011; Kim, 2020). Moreover, research on engagement still has aspects that have seldom been studied, and there are no consistent or conclusive results in many areas (Villamediana et al., 2019). With the widespread adoption of these social technologies, practitioners and academics have recognized the need to quantify the contribution of social media activities used for business purposes, both concerning financial contribution and value generated by social media data from users' conversations. Hence, there is a gap in the literature, as the contributions on measuring tourist engagement are particularly scattered and contradictory; although the literature recognizes social media engagement is a multidimensional construct, several studies approach it in a simplistic way, considering only a few indicators (e.g., number of likes, number of shares) to evaluate it. As it will be demonstrated in this chapter, such simplistic approaches, although simple to execute, do not provide the depth and detail managers need to guide their social media strategies. For that reason, this chapter systematizes the contributions scattered in the literature, and proposes a holistic analysis of social media engagement, comprising three macro dimensions of destinations' social media (popularity, commitment, and virality) and also the consideration of post engagement. Additionally, this chapter also proposes the consideration of advertising, due to its power to increase the reach of publications, and arguably affect the engagement potential.

In this context, the research problem outlined for this chapter is: how to measure tourist engagement? The research objectives defined for this chapter are (i) to conceptualize tourist engagement on social media, (ii) to identify tourist engagement indicators that are mostly suggested by the literature for tourist engagement, and (iii) to propose a model to measure engagement that can be effectively adopted by destination and DMO's managers to assess social media engagement.

To achieve the defined objectives, a literature review on the subject was performed. Additionally, a study adpting mixed-method approach was conducted. Quantitative secondary data from eight Brazilian destinations was analysed, and qualitative interviews were carried out with six destinations' social media managers to further identify the challenges and discuss solutions for measuring engagement. A measurement framework is proposed in these pages, which was tested and validated with the study.

This chapter makes several contributions. Firstly, it systematizes concepts and contributions scattered in the literature regarding tourists' engagement in social media. Furthermore, it analyses engagement assessment indicators adopted by the literature. The indicators pointed out by the literature proved to be straggling, so this chapter proposes the TSM Engagement Framework for evaluating engagement with tourism destinations on social media. The proposed framework has practical application for academics, public and private tourism managers, digital marketing professionals, and social network managers.

The remainder of the chapter is organized as follows. Next section contains the literature literature review, focusing on the concepts and measures of engagement in social media. Then, the methodology used for the development of the study is presented. The following sections present the quantitative results obtained from secondary data, and the results of the interviews. Finally, the Tourism Social Media Framework was proposed based on the information collected. The chapter includes also final considerations, with solutions, recommendations, and suggestions for future research.

BACKGROUND

In order to identify how to measure tourist engagement, this study started with a literature review on this topic, considering articles indexed by the SCOPUS database, and using a combination of keywords: "engagement", "user engagement", "tourist*", "measure", "indicator*", and "framework". As a result, forty-nine articles were found, of which twelve stood out as especially relevant for the topic and objectives of this chapter. Their contributions are analyzed in the following sections, including in Table 1.

Conceptualization of Tourist Engagement

More than three decades ago, Kahn (1990) defined engagement as "task behaviors that promote connections to work and others". Customer engagement can also be defined as customers' connection to a brand which is manifested in cognitive, affective, and behavioral actions beyond the purchase situation. Examples of behavioral manifestation include participation in activities such as customer-to-customer interactions, blogging, writing reviews, as well as other similar activities that are centered on the brand (So et al., 2014).

In the marketing field, engagement is considered a key aspect in consumers' relationships with brands. In this sense, engagement is considered as a predictor of variables related to purchase intention and behavior, brand loyalty, consumer satisfaction, value, trust, affective commitment, among other variables (Villamediana et al., 2019). Engagement has also been discussed in the advertising literature where it is suggested that it may be used as a proxy measure of the strength of a company's customer relationships, based on the extent to which customers have formed both emotional and rational bonds with a brand. Engagement is therefore argued to include feelings of confidence, integrity, pride, and passion of a brand (McEwen, 2004).

The literature provides several important contributions to further understand engagement. Agostino and Sidorova (2016) contributed to its conceptualization by stressing that engagement shows the ability of a company to establish dialogue with customers on social media, and enables the quantification of this dialogue, namely with tne number of responses generated by posts. Brodie et al. (2013) stressed that the term engagement has been used in a variety of academic disciplines including sociology, political science, psychology, and organizational behavior.

Within the academic marketing and service literature, very few academic articles used the term consumer engagement, customer engagement, or brand engagement before 2005. Since then, the number of mentions to those terms is increasing. Brodie et al. (2013) suggest that the conceptual roots of customer engagement may be explained by drawing on theory addressing interactive experience and value cocreation within marketing relationships. From a customer's point of view, the concept of engagement presents some very important characteristics as interaction and co-creative experiences related to a focal service or a brand. Also stressed is the relationship with engagement, involvement, and loyalty, which could be antecedents and/or consequences from engagement.

Bringing the discussion into the online environment, Galvez-Rodriguez et al. (2020) explained that the term engagement refers to the process of interactions within and among groups. These authors explain that, by achieving tourists' online engagement, DMOs can achieve a continuous feedback process, thus supporting the dynamic development and evolution of the destination's brand and image. In line with these contributions, Lehmann et al. (2012) argue that user engagement is the quality of the user experience that emphasizes the positive aspects of the interaction, and in particular, the phenomena associated with being captivated by a web application, and so being motivated to use it.

But the attributes of engagement are highly intertwined, a complex interplay of user-system interaction variables (O'Brien & Toms, 2010). Villamediana-Pedrosa et al. (2019) also point out that engagement can be positive or negative, according to the user's behavior and the connections created with the brand on social media.

According to Bowden (2009), the process of engagement traces the temporal development of loyalty by mapping the relationships between the constructs of calculative commitment, affective commitment, involvement, and trust, as customers progress from being new to a service brand. Bowden (2009) considers that after consumption, the customer goes through a process of satisfaction that leads to a calculative commitment, which can be positive or negative. If calculative commitment is positive this leads the him to consume again. Since he is already a consumer and is repeating the experience, satisfaction is already assumed and leads to trust and involvement, which generates an affective commitment in the form of loyalty. It should be noted that this proposal was not developed specifically to comprise the particularities of the digital and social media environment. However, it is useful for understanding the process of engagement and measure engagement on social media, assuming that the reasons that generate engagement with a brand, whether in the physical or digital world, may be the same.

Harrigan et al. (2017) have considered the context of social media and proposed a conceptualization of tourists' engagement. Based on the concepts of customer engagement with tourism brands by So et al. (2014) and consumer brand engagement by Dwivedi (2015) and (Hollebeek et al., 2014), Harrigan et al. (2017) concluded that customer engagement is a multi-dimensional construct consisting of three dimensions: cognitive (customer focus and interest in a particular brand), emotional (feelings of inspiration or pride caused by a particular brand), and behavioral (customer effort and energy necessary for interaction with a particular brand). Hence, Harrigan et al. (2017) proposed a conceptualization of tourist engagement comprising three dimensions: Behavioral, Emotional and Cognitive. The behavioral dimension considers the interaction, the vigor (level of energy and resilience in the interactions) and the activation (level of energy, effort and time spent on a brand) of engagement. The emotional dimension refers to the identification, i.e., the degree of brand belonging. The cognitive dimension is the most complex, and considers absorption, dedication, affection, enthusiasm, attention, and cognitive processing.

Overall, the literature on customer engagement is vast, however, a solid concept of customer engagement has not been identified, especially when referring to the tourism sector. Based on the literature review carried out, tourist engagement in social media will be understood in this chapter as a subjective and multidimensional tourist involvement with a destination, which involves the value, the activity, and commitment that the tourist has with the destination and can be expressed by boosting popularity and virality in the destination's social media presence.

Tourist Engagement Metrics

Metrics are needed to measure user engagement, not only in social media but also in a business, with a brand, or website. That also applies to tourists, in the case of destinations and DMO. This section of the chapter reviews the contributions in the literature regarding engagement metrics.

Table 1 presents a summary of the indicators identified in the literature to measure tourists' engagement in social media, particularly in social networking sites. It is noteworthy that the division into three dimensions (i.e., popularity, commitment, and virality) was only performed by Bonson and Ratkai (2013) and by Villamediana-Pedrosa et al. (2019), The contributions and considerations of other other authors identified in the table were codified and organized accordingly.

Some contributions in the literature propose simple indicators for engagement on social media, considering the basic activities performed by users, such as liking and sharing. Alternatively, the multidimensionality of engagement was considered by other authors (e.g., Bonson & Ratkai, 2013; Villamediana-Pedrosa et al., 2019), resulting in more complex sets of engagement measures. It is also worth mentioning that several the authors, such as Grave (2019), Barger and Labrecque (2013), and Peters et al. (2013), also present economic indicators in addition to engagement indicators, such as sales volume, return on investment, lead generation, among others. These type of indicators are beyond the focus of this chapter.

Tourist Social Media Engagement

Table 1. Metrics per dimension of social media engagement proposed by extant literature

Dimension	Indicators	Authors
Popularity	Numbers of Followers	Agostino and Sidorova (2016), Grave (2019), Hoffman and Fodor (2010), Lehmann et al. (2012), Perreault and Mosconi (2018), Peters et al. (2013), Töllinen and Karjaluoto (2011)
	Numbers of new Followers	Barger and Labrecque (2013), Peters et al. (2013)
	Numbers of Interactions	Grave (2019), Hoffman and Fodor (2010), Lehmann et al. (2012), Perreault and Mosconi (2018), Peters et al. (2013), Töllinen and Karjaluoto (2011)
	Numbers of Interactions in the page /followers	Barger and Labrecque (2013), Bonson and Ratkai (2013), Hoffman and Fodor (2010), Peters et al. (2013), Töllinen and Karjaluoto (2011)
	Numbers of Reactions in posts / total of posts	Barger and Labrecque (2013), Bonson and Ratkai (2013), Hoffman and Fodor (2010), Peters et al. (2013), Villamediana-Pedrosa et al. (2019)
	Total interactions/total posts	Barger and Labrecque (2013), Bonson and Ratkai (2013)
	Public dispersion	Töllinen and Karjaluoto (2011)
Commitment	Interaction / Reach	Grave (2019)
	Number of Comments	Agostino and Sidorova (2016), Barger and Labrecque (2013), Hoffman and Fodor (2010), Perreault and Mosconi (2018), Töllinen and Karjaluoto (2011), Villamediana-Pedrosa et al. (2019)
	Number of posts with comments / total posts	Barger and Labrecque (2013), Bonson and Ratkai (2013)
	Total comments/total posts	Barger and Labrecque (2013), Bonson and Ratkai (2013), Peters et al. (2013)
	Number of user-generated items	Barger and Labrecque (2013), Hoffman and Fodor (2010), Perreault and Mosconi (2018), Peters et al. (2013), Töllinen and Karjaluoto (2011)
	Number of user-generated items/ followers	Barger and Labrecque (2013), Peters et al. (2013)
	Recommendations	Töllinen and Karjaluoto (2011)
Virality	Page reach	Grave (2019), Perreault and Mosconi (2018), Peters et al. (2013), Villamediana-Pedrosa et al. (2019)
	Post Advertising	Grave (2019)
	Numbers of shares	Agostino and Sidorova (2016), Kesgin and Murthy (2019), Perreault and Mosconi (2018), Töllinen and Karjaluoto (2011), Villamediana-Pedrosa et al. (2019)
	Number of posts with shares/total posts	Barger and Labrecque (2013), Bonson and Ratkai (2013)
	Total shares/total posts	Barger and Labrecque (2013), Bonson and Ratkai (2013), Peters et al. (2013)
	(Shares/posts)/followers	Barger and Labrecque (2013), Bonson and Ratkai (2013), Peters et al. (2013)

EXTENDING THE SET OF ENGAGEMENT INDICATORS: THE TSM ENGAGEMENT FRAMEWORK

Based on the literature review, and acknowledging the challenges faced by DMOs social media managers in managing and monitoring social media engagement, this chapter proposes, tests, and validates a set of indicators of tourist engagement on social media: the Tourist Social Media (TSM) Engagement Framework, presented in detail in Table 2. It is important to note that this is the version validated in the study, as demonstrated in the following sections, hence the justification of the framework combines contributions from both extant literature and managers participating in this study.

Two main innovations stand out in this proposal. Firstly, and in line with Barger and Labrecque (2013), Peters et al. (2013) and Rahman et al. (2016), this framework proposes to assess engagement not only at a page or profile, but also at the post level, originating a fourth dimension of social media engagement. Secondly, this proposal includes additional metrics, particularly hashtags and advertising.

So, the proposed model maintains the three dimensions pointed out by Bonson and Ratkai (2013) and Villamediana-Pedrosa et al. (2019) - popularity, commitment and virality -, which analyze tourist engagement from a macro point of view. However, the framework includes also an individualized approach to the posts, as suggested by Barger and Labrecque (2013), Peters et al. (2013), and Rahman et al. (2016), and consequently has a fourth dimension: post engagement.

The popularity dimension is related not only to the dissemination of the message but also to the levels of general interactions with the content. Thus, for the analysis of popularity, the audience and its growth in the analyzed period increased - measured by the number of followers -, the number of interactions on the page related to the number of followers, and the number of posts made. The geographical dispersion of the public was also included, as suggest by Töllinen and Karjaluoto (2011). It can be analyzed by the volume of followers who are residents of the destination in question, and which is the public.

The commitment dimension is related not only to the interaction on the page but also to the quality of this interaction. Therefore, analyze interactions, comments, posts, and the model also included user-generated content, as suggested by Barger and Labrecque (2013), Hoffman and Fodor (2010), Perreault and Mosconi (2018), Peters et al. (2013), and Töllinen and Karjaluoto (2011), which can be measured by spontaneous publications made by users who tag the profile, and by content that includes hashtags created by the destination for tourism promotion. It is worth noting that the literature review did not explicitly mentioned the use of hashtags, however, this is a recent behavior in social media, and was included from the contributions made by the managers during the interviews.

The viral dimension measures the reach of the page and its content, so the metrics usually analyzed are the shares. However, the proposed framework includes some complementary variables, such as reach, in line with Grave (2019), Perreault and Mosconi (2018), Peters et al. (2013), and (Villamediana-Pedrosa et al., 2019). Reach is a relatively recent metric used by social networking sites that refers to the number of people who were impacted by the page. This framework also considers advertising effort that was carried out on the page and its posts, considering its possible impact on reach. One should note that Grave (2019) considered advertising in the lack of other indicators. Alternatively, this framework includes not only the advertising but also page boost to rigorously consider all factors affecting engagement. As seen in the analysis of secondary data, this resource can significantly impact the engagement analysis on other dimensions.

Finally, for the analysis of post engagement, the framework replicate the same structure, i.e., the dimensions of the model, at the post (micro) level. Therefore, managers could analyze posts individually to understand which ones got the best performance in terms of engagement and generate inputs to identify the reasons for this performance and possibilities to replicate the performance. To achieve better results, the suggestion is to analyze and compare posts that were created to one particular objective, so that managers can identify which approach presented the the best performance.

As it will be demonstrated in the next sections that present the quantitative and qualitative results, this study demonstrates that currently, the social media platforms offer a lot of information about the audience and their interactions with the content and with the pages. Given these possibilities, the TSM

Tourist Social Media Engagement

Table 2. Metrics per dimension of social media engagement suggested by this chapter: TSM Engagement Framework

Dimension	Metrics	Formula	Measures
Popularity	Number of Followers	Number of followers	Audience
	Number of new Followers	New followers / last month followers	Audience Grow
	Interactions in the page and Number of followers	Number Interactions in page /followers	Interactions in page by followers
	Likes in posts and Number of posts	Number of posts with likes/total of posts	% of the posts that have likes
	Interactions in posts and Number of followers	Total interactions/total posts	Interactions by posts
	Interactions posts and Number of followers	(Interactions/posts)/ followers	% of followers that interactions by post
	Public Location	% local public	Public dispersion
Commitment	Interactions	Interaction / Reach	% of interactions by reach
	Number of Comments	Number of posts with comments / total posts	% of total posts that have been commented
		Total comments/total posts	Numbers of comments per post
	Comments and Number of followers	(comments/posts)/ followers	comments per post by followers
	User-generated items	Number of user-generated items	Total User-generate Content
	User-generated items and Number of followers	Number of user-generated items/ followers	Content generates by followers
	Hashtag mentions	Number of publications in hashtag	Total User-generated content under the hashtag
		Number of publications under the hashtag - Number of publications under hashtag at last month	User-generated content under the hashtag last month
Virality	Reach	Reach of page	Reach of page
	Advertising	Page Boost	Advertising days
		Post Advertising	% Posts advertising
	Shares	Number of posts with shares/total posts	The average number of shares per posts
		Total shares/total posts	% of the total posts that have been shared
	Shares and Number of followers	(Shares/posts)/followers	% of followers that share by post
Post Engagement	Popularity	Post Reach	Post Reach
		Reach / Interaction	Interactions by reach
	Content value	Post Interactions	Post Interactions
		Type of post	Type of post
		Number of Interactions/ followers	% of interactions by followers
		Comments/followers	% of comments by followers
	Content virality	Shares/followers	% of shares by followers

Engagement Framework aims to enrich the engagement analysis and measurement page. Additionally, if this framework is applied in repeatedly as a routine (e.g., bi-weekly, monthly, bi-monthly) and assess the indicators' evolution, the framework will enable to to better understand and identify the best strategies to improve engagement.

METHOD

This chapter uses mixed methods research, i.e., combines quantitative and qualitative methods. According to Bryman (2016) this approach is particularly suitable for a more detailed evaluation and validation of results, and enables to overcome some of the limitations of both qualitative and quantitative methods. In the case of this chapter, the first stage of the research comprised a quantitative analysis of secondary data, which was followed by a series of interviews that further validated the findings. The joint use of qualitative and quantitative research allowed to gather more information than could be achieved by one sole method, and offered validation benefits (Bryman, 2016) that are of particular importance considering that this chapter proposes a framewok for measuring tourists' engagement that aimed to be relevant and useful for managers.

Regarding the quantitative stage, secondary data was collected from Brazilian tourist destinations, comprising reports and statistics provided by their pages on social networking sites. Participants were identified through the snowball technique, in which personal contacts were asked to identify DMO social media managers that could be invited to this study. In total, 18 managers of various Brazilian destinations were contacted and eight promptly agreed to participate in the study. Participants in this study are presented in Table 3. Participants include cities, region, and states that are prominent tourist destinations in Brazil.

Table 3. Sample characteristics

Destination	Territory	Manager	Instagram	Followers (thousands)	Monitoring Frequency
Belo Horizonte	City	Public	@belohorizonte.mg	31.7	Weekly
Brasília	City	Private	@visitebrasilia	50.1	Weekly
Circuito das Águas	Region	Public	@circuitodasaguas_mg	3.1	Occasional
Goiás	State	Public	@goiasturismo	40.8	Occasional
Mato Grosso do Sul	State	Public	@visitmsoficial	5.4	Monthly
Minas Gerais	State	Public	@visiteminasgerais	119.2	Biweekly
Rio Grande do Norte	State	Public	@visiteriograndedonorte	18.8	Weekly
São Luiz	City	Public	@turismo.saoluiz	7.2	Monthly

Data was collected between April 18 and May 9, 2021. Subsequently, the data were organized in a spreadsheet to allow better visualization, data processing, and calculation of indicators.

Furthermore, interviews were conducted with destinations' social media managers to further explore the challenges associated with the evaluation of tourists' engagement in social media, and to assess the effectiveness of the framework developed during this study and presented in the following sections. The qualitative analysis aimed at interpreting phenomena and attributing meanings to the participants. Indeed, qualitative methodology can be characterized as the attempt to understand and describe in detail the meanings and characteristics of the object under study, allowing an analysis that will be expressed through narrative (Bryman, 2016). From the eight participants in the quantitative stage, six managers also accepted to participate in the interview.

The interviews were conducted using online videoconferencing channels and were scheduled between May 10th and 11th, according to the availability of the managers, with a duration of 30-45 minutes. The interview outline was prepared by the researchers and comprised questions about how the managers usually monitored engagement level on social media, the relevance and difficulties on engagement monitoring. Afterwards, a framework for measuring tourists' engagement os social media that resulted from the literature review and the quantitative stage of the research was presented to the participants, who were asked their opinion and improvement recommendations on the proposal. Finally, participants were asked to analyse the feasibility and relevance of the proposed framework for their engagement monitoring. The interviews were audio recorded, transcribed, and subject to thematic content analysis (Bryman, 2016).

The Set of Engagement Indicators in Practice

Initially, general analytics from participants' Facebook and Instagram pages was requested. Considering that for all participants the main social networking site was Instagram, data analysis and model testing was performed based on Instagram data. However, it should be noted that the model can be applied and used for other social networking sites, such as Facebook, Twitter, and YouTube.

Next sections present the analysis for each of the dimensions found on the literature: popularity, commitment, virality and post engagement. Regarding post engagement, the three posts with greater reach for each destination were chosen. This is because the volume of content per page was very different and it was necessary to standardize the volume to be analyzed. It is important to mention that each page has its own dynamics, volume of publications, objectives and different audiences. The purpose of the work is not to compare the results of one with the other, but to observe the behavior, features and structuring of the framework in different scenarios.

Popularity Analysis

As mentioned in the literature review, the popularity dimension is related not only to the dissemination of the message but also to the levels of general interactions with the generated content (e.g., Grave, 2019; Hoffman & Fodor, 2010; Lehmann et al., 2012; Perreault & Mosconi, 2018; Peters et al., 2013; Töllinen & Karjaluoto, 2011). The results of secondary data collection are presented in Table 4.

As shown in Table 4, the growth of the audience is quite varied. For pages with a greater number of followers, the growth rate tends to be lower. In interactions by followers, it is interesting to note that destination 1 reaches 1.3 interactions per follower, which is a very relevant value, and compared to destination 8, which has an approximate value of audience, it presents 0.4 interactions per follower.

The percentage of posts with likes proved to be an irrelevant indicator, as it does not quantify the volume of likes in the post, but if among the posts made, all of them received at least 1 like. As shown in Table 4, there was no variation in the indicator for the eight quite different scenarios analyzed.

Table 4. Popularity Analysis

Measures	Destination 1	Destination 2	Destination 3	Destination 4	Destination 5	Destination 6	Destination 7	Destination 8
Audience	50,100	31,700	7,218	5,462	18,852	119,200	3,117	40,886
Audience Growth	2.67%	1.02%	16.65%	3.43%	3.01%	2.57%	0.03%	3.93%
Followers' interaction with page	1.357	0.297	0.002	0.197	0.085	0.701	0.325	0.401
% of the posts that have likes	100%	100%	100%	100%	100%	100%	100%	100%
Interactions by post	503.70	348.19	0.49	63.35	320.60	1817.39	72.29	546.73
% of followers that interact by post	1.01%	1.10%	0.01%	1.16%	1.70%	1.52%	2.32%	1.34%
Public dispersion	44.60%	57.50%	59.60%	n.a.	26.00%	20.00%	6.40%	33.00%

The number of interactions per post proved to be a very interesting indicator (Barger & Labrecque, 2013; Bonson & Ratkai, 2013), and in the interviews, it was received with great surprise by managers, since it is possible to have a macro view of the interaction by publication carried out. For this indicator, destination 6 stood out during the analyzed period, as it had an average of 1,817 interactions per post. The percentage of interactions per post per follower proved to be quite low.

Finally, the dispersion of the public was another information that proved to be very interesting (Töllinen & Karjaluoto, 2011), and brought a more qualitative analysis to the popularity of the page, in which audiences are observed from their geographical location. As the objects for this study were pages for tourism promotion, an audience from other locations is particularly relevant. Thus, destination 7 was the one with the best dispersion of the public, with only 6.7% local residents, which means that more than 93% of the followers are from another locations, that is, tourists.

Commitment Analysis

The commitment dimension is related not only to the interaction on the page but also to the quality of this interaction. Therefore, it considers interactions, comments, posts, user-generated content, as noted by extant literature (Barger & Labrecque, 2013; Hoffman & Fodor, 2010; Perreault & Mosconi, 2018; Peters et al., 2013; Töllinen & Karjaluoto, 2011). Details on commitment analysis are presented in Table 5.

In commitment, the first measurement analyzed is the percenteage of interaction by reach. Considering that greater interaction is better, destinations 1 and 7 have better values for this indicator with 61.23% and 57.01%, respectively. Next, the number of posts with comments is analyzed, and again it is identified that the indicator, which needs to be extracted manually, does not show variability in the sample. However, it may be an interesting metric for pages recently launched.

The number of comments per post is pointed out as another interesting indicator to assess commitment. Destination 6 presented an average of 35.48 comments per post, which demonstrates that evaluating only the interaction per post is not enough to assess commitment. Since destination 6 did not have one of the best levels of interactions, however, it has a higher volume of comments per post, which presents a page with fewer interactions and higher quality.

Table 5. Commitment Analysis

Measures	Destination 1	Destination 2	Destination 3	Destination 4	Destination 5	Destination 6	Destination 7	Destination 8
% of interactions by reach	61.23%	23.44%	25.00%	0.05%	10.80%	35.16%	57.01%	24.98%
% of total posts that have been commented	100%	100%	100%	100%	100%	100%	100%	100%
Numbers of comments per post	12.76	6.44	17.06	3.18	8.00	35.48	1.29	13.17
comments per post per number of followers	0.025%	0.002%	0.236%	0.058%	0.042%	0.030%	0.041%	0.032%
Total user-generate content	x	134	x	x	x	x	x	x
Content generate by followers	x	0.04%	x	x	x	x	x	x
Total user-generated content in the last month	137,280	641,706	1,165	1,035	2,017	460,555	2,592	39,591
User-generated content in the last month	x	x	x	x	x	x	x	x

Similar to popularity, the percentage of followers who commented per post proved to be quite low. Still, in the long run it can show the evolution of the page's commitment, and thus be particularly relevant to managers.

The metric user-generated content proved to be quite difficult to extract and only one of the participants provided the data. This is because the reports provided by social networking sites do not present this indicator to managers. Thus, the measurement method must be manual and continuous, considering the notifications received each time the profile is tagged in a post. Despite the difficulty of measuring the indicator, it is relevant to identify the spontaneous content generated by the audience, as presented by de literature review.

Finally, the measurement of hashtag proved to be an easier way to measure the content generated by users, which is coded by social networking sites and allows easier monitoring, especially on Instagram and Twitter. However, it also has its limitations since the profiles themselves use it to categorize their content and strengthen it. It is important to note that the inclusion of the indicator occurred after data collection, so it was not possible to measure growth over a period analysis. Still, for those who adopt the model, it is possible to calculate this indicator periodically and analyse its dinamics.

Virality Analysis

The viral dimension measures page and content reach, and the metric most frequently analyzed is the number of shares (e.g., Agostino & Sidorova, 2016; Kesgin & Murthy, 2019; Perreault & Mosconi, 2018; Töllinen & Karjaluoto, 2011; Villamediana-Pedrosa et al., 2019). Table 6 presents the data collected regarding virality.

Table 6. Virality Analysis

Measures	Destination 1	Destination 2	Destination 3	Destination 4	Destination 5	Destination 6	Destination 7	Destination 8
Reach of page	111,057	40,100	63,200	210,000	14,842	237,800	1,775	65,656
Advertising days	None	None	None	30	None	None	None	None
% Posts advertising	None	None	None	100%	None	None	None	None
% of the total posts that have been shared	x	85%	x	x	100%	x	43%	90%
The average number of shares per posts	22.26	10.89	20.72	12.35	12.20	70.13	1.29	22.77
% of followers that share by post	0.044%	0.003%	0.287%	0.226%	0.065%	0.059%	0.041%	0.056%

Reach is an interesting metric for evaluating virality (Grave, 2019; Perreault & Mosconi, 2018; Peters et al., 2013; Villamediana-Pedrosa et al., 2019). Destinations 6 and 4 were the ones that achieved the best reach, however, the audience for destination 6 is considerably higher than the others, and destination 4 is the only one that works with advertising.

The advertising means that, through payment, the content is presented to a larger number of people. Let's analyze the impacts on the engagement of destination 4, since it was the only one that uses this resource. Due to the boost, the destination has the best reach, even without having a large audience. However, regarding commitment, it was the one that obtained the worst relationship between interactions by reach, one of the lowest number of comments per post, and the lowest user-generated content. This shows that the boost can be carried out for different purposes, and possibly the applied objective was reached. Indeed, this strategy must be associated with management objectives. Referring to page engagement, it is evident that it can compromise some metrics and it is necessary to consider these aspects when analyzing the model.

Considerin share behavior, destinations 5, 8 and 2 were the only ones that presented these metrics. Arguably, this could mean that it can be considered more difficult to measure, even if the platforms present this indicator. During the analyzed period, destination 5 obtained at least one share in all posts, which demonstrates not only the virality but also the commitment of the audience and the connection between the content posted and the audience. The average share per post was confirmed as an interesting metric.

Tourist Social Media Engagement

Post Engagement' Analysis

Table 7. Post Engagement' Analysis

	Destination 1			Destination 2			Destination 3		
Post Reach	39,755	25,077	21,889	755	944	623	25,105	13,175	8,664
Post Interactions	3,024	1,928	2,049	16	29	18	1706	692	624
Interactions by reach	12.61	12.52	0.10	0.05	0.08	17.94	14.17	18.61	0.08
Type of post	Photo	Photo	Photo	Photo	Photo	Carousel / Photos	Photo	Photo	Carrosel
% of interactions by followers	6.29%	4.00%	43.69%	4.75%	3.66%	0.20%	24.55%	9.81%	120.03%
% of comments by followers	0.257%	0.150%	0.070%	0.004%	0.003%	0.015%	0.914%	0.222%	0.804%
% of shares by followers	0.000%	0.000%	0.000%	4.659%	3.578%	3.190%	0.000%	0.000%	0.000%
	Destination 4			Destination 5			Destination 6		
Post Reach	1,510	1,218	1,054	5,541	4,365	2,943	71,666	62,229	54,025
Post Interactions	96	106	98	379	315	209	6723	4284	2969
Interactions by reach	15.57	11.38	0.09	13.13	12.37	0.08	10.29	13.95	16.49
Type of post	Photo	Photo	Photo	Photo	Photo	Photo	Carousel / Photos	Carousel / Photos	Photo
% of interactions by followers	1.78%	1.96%	19.30%	2.24%	1.87%	15.61%	5.84%	3.74%	2.75%
% of comments by followers	0.018%	0.018%	0.018%	0.048%	0.085%	0.037%	0.107%	0.076%	0.107%
% of shares by followers	0.000%	0.000%	0.000%	0.122%	0.085%	0.122%	0.000%	0.000%	0.000%
	Destination 7			Destination 8					
Post Reach	881	820	390	24.851	16.047	14.620			
Post Interactions	190	123	69	1,647	1,421	758			
Interactions by reach	4.38	6.56	5.49	13.45	10.59	18.09			
Type of post	Photo	Photo	Photo	Photo	Photo	Photo			
% of interactions by followers	6.45%	4.01%	2.28%	4.52%	3.71%	1.98%			
% of comments by followers	0.160%	0.000%	0.064%	0.086%	0.022%	0.034%			
% of shares by followers	0.000%	0.000%	0.000%	0.120%	0.068%	0.046%			

For the analysis of post engagement, the dimensions of the framework were applied at the post level. In this study, the three posts with the highest reach were considered. Details are presented in Table 7.

As shown in Table 7, a single indicator is not enough to assess the success of a post. For this reason, the model proposed by this chapter explores in more detail the engagement with posts, as proposed by Barger & Labrecque (2013), Peters et al (2013), Rahman et al (2016). It is worth mentioning that the success of a post can vary according to the objectives and strategies of social media managers. As confirmed during the interviews, there are those who seek reach, others who seek engagement, others who try to reach a specific audience. In addition, the same profile can adopt different strategies for each post.

Therefore, the framework proposed by this chapter suggests the evaluation of posts individually. During the interviews, it was confirmed that this is an interesting strategy and that the framework includes relevant variables to evaluate each post. Hence, although reach and interactions are related, they are independent. The analysis of interactions by posts, a relevant indicator to measure the engagement of the post, showed that in some cases posts with less reach had a higher percentage of interaction. So, the suggestion is to compare posts that were created with the same objective in order to identify which better approached the expected result.

Final notes

The practical application demonstrated that the model is viable from the data point of view and the indicators are capable of being calculated and contribute to the evaluation of social media engagement. It also contributed to improving the model generated from the literature review, since during its composition and analysis other indicators were identified and added. As such, the practical application confirmed the relevance of the dimensions and their characteristics, in order to achieve better organization of the indicators and to understand what was being measured. Overall, this allows for the best applicability of the model. Still, it demonstrated the complementarity of the dimensions and the strong relationship that one has with the other.

In the next session, managers' views of how engagement is usually measured and perceptions of the proposed model are presented.

Managers' Views on the Measurement of Social Media Engagement

The main objective of the interviews was to assess, validate, and collect improvement recommendations for the TSM Engagement Framework. Additionally, the interviews also aimed to better understand the monitoring practices of the participants.

Most of the participants stressed that they monitor engagement on social media regularly, for instance by considering the "monthly social media report" (Destination 6), and tools like Facebook for Business (e.g., Destinations 1 and 3). The frequency of this analysis varied amongst interviewees from weekly to sporadic. Moreover, some participants said that they "evaluate intuitively, not considering specific metrics, but [are] interested in improving that" (Destination 7). The interest for an effective instrument to measure social media success was acknowledged by all participants in this study.

Reach was amongst the indicators that they considered most relevant, along with the number of followers, and interaction. Some participants stressed that analyzing engagement is determinant for identifying the more popular themes and the types of content that should be produced (e.g., Destinations 6 and 2). It was unanimous that measuring audience engagement is essential to develop their social media strategy. According to the participants, knowing what to post to please the audience and meet their expectations (Destination 7) is one of the main challenges of social media management.

Overall, the participants considered the proposed framework interesting and valuable for their professional activity (Destination 8), and a tool to understand the social networking site better (Destinations 1 and 7). They also considered it user-friendly and easy to understand (Destination 4). All the indicators proposed were considered essential, hence no redundancies were detected by the participants. Some of the indicators proposed were so far disregarded by some participants, but triggered all participants' interest and were considered relevant.

Participants did not spontaneously suggest the inclusion of any additional metrics. Still, they considered that could provide relevant insights to guide their strategies (e.g., Destination 1). The participants agreed that any indicator that demanded manually extract information that is not automatically provided by the social media platform needs to be carefully evaluated. Collecting such data would be time-consuming and consequently no viable for some managers (Destination 6), or being considered optional information (Destination 4). As one of the participants summarized, "the automatic indicators already offer a lot of information. Manually collected data could be seldom used to tackle a particular doubt" (Destination 4).

Hence, the participants concluded that the TSM Engagement Framework provided "complete information" (Destination 5) and presents "new indicators and points out other paths besides the traditional ones" (Destination 1), and "it makes sense to perform it to understand my network" (Destination 7). In fact, the participants considered measuring this set of indicators regularly, as they were considered "fundamental for page growth" (Destination 8), "enabling a more detailed analysis" (Destination 3), to "replicate the success and avoid post failures" (Destination 6).

Based on these findings, the TSM Engagement Framework proposed by this chapter was validated by the participants in this study.

SOLUTIONS AND RECOMMENDATIONS

As demonstrated in the previous sections, the TSM Engagement Framework offers a comprehensive set of indicators for monitoring social media activities. With the proposed framework, tourist destination managers, destination marketing managers and even tourism entrepreneurs can evaluate engagement in its several dimensions: popularity, commitment, virality, and post engagement. These four dimensions are complementary and essential for a comprehensive understanding of social media engagement.

In the popularity dimension, engagement is reflected in the volume of followers and their growth, the volume of interactions on the page and its content, as well as the proportion between interactions and followers. The commitment dimension pertains customer focus and interest in a particular brand (Harrigan et al., 2017), and the framework proposes an analysis based on comments and user generated content generated, and the page hashtags. Therefore, this dimension is extremely valuable since the users actively disseminate the brand. Additionally, the framework includes the virality perspective, which considers not only users' sharing behavior, but reflects also on the role of advertising to the dissemination of content. This is because it is currently possible to make a financial investment so that the post is shown more times and to a greater number of users, and managers need to evaluate the return on that investment, including in terms of engagement. Thus, the proposed framework includes advertising actions in order to enable the analysis of its outcomes and performance in terms of engagement generation.

One additional innovation of the model is to consider also post engagement, which highlight the results of the individual posts, in order to extract assertive information for decision-making not related to the content to be generated by the page, but also regarding the interest of the public, which is reflected by the highest levels of engagement.

Hence, it is recommended that this framework is applied by social media managers as part of their monitoring routines. The TSM Engagement Framework contributes to the evaluation of engagement with tourism destinations on social media. The proposed framework has practical application for academics, public and private tourism managers, digital marketing professionals, and social network managers.

As pointed out by some of the participants in this study, these indicators can and should be complemented with a more qualitative analysis of comments and post typologies to further understand what explains social media communication success. Yet, it offers a powerful tool for monitoring engagement and assist social media strategies.

FUTURE RESEARCH DIRECTIONS

Considering practitioners' views on the relevance of the proposed framework to evaluate engagement and guide social media strategy, it is suggested that future research apply the TSM Engagement Framework on various social media platforms. Also, further validation of the model should consider tourism destinations in other countries, where the behavior of the public may be different from that of Brazil.

It is also suggested the adaptation of the TSM Engagement Framework to other publics, within the tourism, hospitality, and leisure sector (e.g., festival goers) and also for different sectors that intensively use social media to communicate and interact with their customers and prospects. Indeed, this framework could be adapted to very different product and service brands, from fashion and cosmetics to food and education institutions. Considering the importance of monitoring and fostering audience engagement through social media, the proposed framework is expected to provide valuable insights to a multitude of social media managers, independently of the type of brand and sector they work with.

Beyond rigorously measuring engagement, managers also need to further understand how social media engagement might affect tourists' choice of destination (Galvez-Rodriguez et al., 2020). Thus, avenues for future research include exploring the relationships between the dimensions of engagement and tourist decision process. Additionally, and as pointed out by extant literature, more research is needed to understand how aspects related to time, and the destination conditions affect tourist engagement (Villamediana et al., 2019).

CONCLUSION

Online engagement can provide valuable feedback on the internal factors that push tourists to select a particular destination. Also, it helps DMOs identify what set of destination attributes pull tourists' desires towards a destination.

Based on the literature review carried out, tourist engagement with destinations' social media is a subjective and multidimensional construct, which involves the value, the activity, and commitment that the tourist has with the destination and can be expressed by boosting popularity and virality of its content.

Compared to the contributions by extant literature, the proposed framework has two additional features. Firstly, it combines both the macro and micro level perspectives, as it considers popularity, commitment, and virality of destinations social media, plus post engagement. Hence, besides considering the overall performance of of destinations' social media in a certain period (e.g., one week, one month), it also analyses the engagement level of the most popular posts or, alternatively, the engagement of posts under a certain marketing objective. Clearly, this feature enables a more comprehensive analysis of tourist engagement, and the comparison of different objectives, strategies, and types of content (e.g., message appeal, informative or entertainment nature, just to name a few), which can more effectively guide managers' decisions on social media strategies and content creation. Secondly, it includes the advertising boosts that were applied to the posts considered in the analysis. Surprisingly, this activity was not reflected in the analyses provided by extant literature, probably because it demands access to information often confidential and only accessible to destinations' social media managers. Clearly, the fact that advertising can substantially increase the reach of the posts, and have strong implications in some of the engagement indicators, particularly reach and interaction, makes it essential to include advertising in engagement measurement.

So, the proposed framework contributes to a better understanding and measurement of the engagement and use of social media by tourists. Moreover, it assists managers to understand tourists engagement and identify strategies to increase this activity since this factor is relevant to the decision to choose the destination. As such, it is expected to provide valuable insights to managers, as acknowledged by the participants in the interviews included in this study.

REFERENCES

Agostino, D., & Sidorova, Y. (2016). A performance measurement system to quantify the contribution of social media: New requirements for metrics and methods. *Measuring Business Excellence*, *20*(2), 38–51. doi:10.1108/MBE-05-2015-0030

Albayrak, T., Caber, M., & Sigala, M. (2020). A quality measurement proposal for corporate social network sites: The case of hotel Facebook page. *Current Issues in Tourism*, 1–16. doi:10.1080/13683500.2020.1854199

Barger, V. A., & Labrecque, L. (2013). An integrated marketing communications perspective on social media metrics. *International Journal of Integrated Marketing Communications*, (Spring), 64–76.

Bonson, E., & Ratkai, M. (2013). A set of metrics to assess stakeholder engagement and social legitimacy on a corporate Facebook page. *Online Information Review*, *37*(5), 787–803. doi:10.1108/OIR-03-2012-0054

Bowden, J. L.-H. (2009). The process of customer engagement: A conceptual framework. *Journal of Marketing Theory and Practice*, *17*(1), 63–74. doi:10.2753/MTP1069-6679170105

Brodie, R. J., Ilic, A., Juric, B., & Hollebeek, L. (2013). Consumer engagement in a virtual brand community: An exploratory analysis. *Journal of Business Research*, *66*(1), 105–114. doi:10.1016/j.jbusres.2011.07.029

Bryman, A. (2016). *Social Research Methods* (5th ed.). Oxford University Press.

Dwivedi, A. (2015). A higher-order model of consumer brand engagement and its impact on loyalty intentions. *Journal of Retailing and Consumer Services*, *24*, 100–109. doi:10.1016/j.jretconser.2015.02.007

Galvez-Rodriguez, M. D., Alonso-Canadas, J., Haro-de-Rosario, A., & Caba-Perez, C. (2020). Exploring best practices for online engagement via Facebook with local destination management organisations (DMOs) in Europe: A longitudinal analysis. *Tourism Management Perspectives*, *34*, 100636. Advance online publication. doi:10.1016/j.tmp.2020.100636

Grave, J. F. (2019). What KPIs are key? Evaluating performance metrics for social media influencers. *Social Media + Society*, *5*(3). Advance online publication. doi:10.1177/2056305119865475

Harrigan, P., Evers, U., Miles, M., & Daly, T. (2017). Customer engagement with tourism social media brands. *Tourism Management*, *59*, 597–609. doi:10.1016/j.tourman.2016.09.015

Hoffman, D. L., & Fodor, M. (2010). Can You Measure the ROI of Your Social Media Marketing? *Mit Sloan Management Review, 52*(1).

Hollebeek, L. D., Glynn, M. S., & Brodie, R. J. (2014). Consumer brand engagement in social media: Conceptualization, scale development and validation. *Journal of Interactive Marketing*, *28*(2), 149–165. doi:10.1016/j.intmar.2013.12.002

Kahn, W. A. (1990). Psychological conditions of personal engagement and disengagement at work. *Academy of Management Journal*, *33*(4), 692–724. doi:10.5465/256287

Kesgin, M., & Murthy, R. S. (2019). Consumer engagement: The role of social currency in online reviews. *Service Industries Journal*, *39*(7-8), 609–636. doi:10.1080/02642069.2018.1553237

Lehmann, J., Lalmas, M., Yom-Tov, E., & Dupret, G. (2012). Models of user engagement. In *International Conference on User Modeling, Adaptation, and Personalization* (Vol. 7379, pp. 164-175). Springer. 10.1007/978-3-642-31454-4_14

McEwen, W. (2004). Why satisfaction isn't satisfying. *Gallup Management Journal Online*, *11*, 1–4.

O'Brien, H. L., & Toms, E. G. (2010). The development and evaluation of a survey to measure user engagement. *Journal of the American Society for Information Science and Technology*, *61*(1), 50–69. doi:10.1002/asi.21229

Perreault, M.-C., & Mosconi, E. (2018). Social media engagement: Content strategy and metrics research opportunities. *Proceedings of the 51st Hawaii International Conference on System Sciences.*

Peters, K., Chen, Y. B., Kaplan, A. M., Ognibeni, B., & Pauwels, K. (2013). Social media metrics: A framework and guidelines for managing social media. *Journal of Interactive Marketing*, *27*(4), 281–298. doi:10.1016/j.intmar.2013.09.007

Rahman, Z., Suberamanian, K., Zanuddin, H., Moghavvemi, S., & Nasir, M. H. N. M. (2016). Social media engagement metric analysis: Study on fan page content. *Journal of Telecommunication Electronic and Computer Engineering*, *8*(8), 71–76.

So, K. K. F., King, C., & Sparks, B. (2014). Customer engagement with tourism brands: Scale development and validation. *Journal of Hospitality & Tourism Research (Washington, D.C.)*, *38*(3), 304–329. doi:10.1177/1096348012451456

Töllinen, A., & Karjaluoto, H. (2011). Marketing communication metrics for social media. *International Journal of Technology Marketing*, *6*(4), 316–330. doi:10.1504/IJTMKT.2011.045911

Villamediana-Pedrosa, J. D., Vila-Lopez, N., & Kuster-Boluda, I. (2019). Secrets to design an effective message on Facebook: An application to a touristic destination based on big data analysis. *Current Issues in Tourism*, *22*(15), 1841–1861. doi:10.1080/13683500.2018.1554625

Villamediana, J., Kuster, I., & Vila, N. (2019). Destination engagement on Facebook: Time and seasonality. *Annals of Tourism Research*, *79*, 102747. Advance online publication. doi:10.1016/j.annals.2019.102747

ADDITIONAL READING

Del Vecchio, P., Ardito, L., Cerchione, R., & Raguseo, E. (2019). Big data in smart tourism: Challenges, issues and opportunities. *Current Issues in Tourism*, *22*(15), 1805–1809. doi:10.1080/13683500.2019.1612860

Ivars-Baidal, J. A., Celdrán-Bernabeu, M. A., Mazón, J. N., & Perles-Ivar, A. S. (2019). Smart destinations and the evolution of ICTs: A new scenario for destination management? *Current Issues in Tourism*, *22*(13), 1581–1600. doi:10.1080/13683500.2017.1388771

Marine-Roig, E. (2017). Measuring Destination Image through Travel Reviews in Search Engines. *Sustainability*, *9*(8), 1425. doi:10.3390u9081425

Munar, A. M. (2012). Social Media Strategies and Destination Management. *Scandinavian Journal of Hospitality and Tourism*, *12*(2), 101–120. doi:10.1080/15022250.2012.679047

Del Vecchio, P., Mele, G., Ndou, V., & Secundo, G. (2018). Creating value from Social Big Data: Implications for Smart Tourism Destinations. *Information Processing & Management*, *54*(5), 847–860. doi:10.1016/j.ipm.2017.10.006

Perreault, M., & Mosconi, E. (2018). Social Media Engagement: Content Strategy and Metrics Research Opportunities. *Proceedings of the 51st Hawaii International Conference on System Sciences*. Retrieved 28 July 2021, from http://hdl.handle.net/10125/50339

Ramos, C. M. Q., Matos, N., Sousa, C. M. R., Correia, M. B., & Cascada, P. (2017). Marketing intelligence and automation: An approach associated with tourism in order to obtain economic benefits for a region. In M. Antona & C. Stephanidis (Eds.), Lecture Notes in Computer Science: Vol. 10277. *Universal Access in Human–Computer Interaction. Design and Development Approaches and Methods. UAHCI 2017*. Springer. doi:10.1007/978-3-319-58706-6_32

Zubiaga, M., Izkara, J. L., Gandini, A., Alonso, I., & Saralegui, U. (2019). Towards smarter management of overtourism in historic centres through visitor-flow monitoring. *Sustainability*, *11*(24), 7254. doi:10.3390u11247254

KEY TERMS AND DEFINITIONS

Followers: Users that opt accompanying a page (e.g., brand, celebrity, company, other individuals), by having that page's posts integrated in the news feed. In some social networking sites followers are can also be called fans.

Impression: Number of times the publication has been viewed by users.

Interactions: Users' actions regarding a post: comments, likes, sharings, clicks, saves, etc.

Reach: Number of people who were exposed to a piece of content (e.g., ad, post).

Social Media Engagement: Level of involvement with the page and its content. This is a particularly important variable to be considered by social media managers, as it is related to loyalty, satisfaction, interest, and behavior, among other behavioural factors.

Social Media Profiles: An account on a social networking site, that belongs and is managed/controlled by individuals, companies, brands, government entities, or influencers, among others.

Social Networking Sites: Online platforms developed to enable many to many communication and interactions among individuals, and that provide several features to facilitate the connection with others based on common interests.

Viral: Publication with a high degree of reach, often shared many times by users on more than one social platform.

Chapter 13
The Role of Social Media Marketing in the Tourism and Hospitality Industry:
A Conceptual Study on Bangladesh

Md Yusuf Hossein Khan
International University of Business, Agriculture, and Technology (IUBAT), Bangladesh

Tanvir Abir
International University of Business, Agriculture, and Technology (IUBAT), Bangladesh

ABSTRACT

Social networking is a series of Web 2.0-based applications that connect, communicate, and exchange ideas, views, perspectives, knowledge, and relationships among internet users worldwide. In the age of social media, businesses' marketing tactics have shifted from bringing products out to encouraging customers to buy things into their stores to foster a more engaging and mutually beneficial relationship. It is a significant player in the online tourism sector since it is a common and influential information source for tourists looking for destination-specific information. This study was conducted qualitatively, and this illustrates and discusses the role of social media marketing and how it works in the tourism and hospitality industries, with an emphasis on Bangladesh in particular, using a range of literature, including academic articles, journals, and books. This study would educate academics, researchers, politicians in tourism industries, and government officials about the importance of social media marketing.

INTRODUCTION

Web development and design of the second generation is described as social media to facilitate connectivity, secure knowledge exchange, interoperability, and global web collaboration (Paris, Lee, & Seery, 2010, p. 531). Today, information on the Internet is changing more rapidly and efficiently with Web 2.0 technologies. It is gradually influencing multiple social and economic influences. Social media is

DOI: 10.4018/978-1-7998-8165-0.ch013

the most developing subject of world history. It has exponentially grown even faster than the Internet. Social networking also offers an immense opportunity for marketing because of its extensive use. Social networking is already an excellent way to meet the prospects and customers of companies of any scale. If you're not talking to your audience directly on social networks such as Facebook, Twitter, Instagram, and Pinterest, your customers already connect with brands through social media. The business will succeed amazingly well, establish loyal brand followers, lead and sell by great social media marketing. Social media plays a very significant role in the travel and hospitality industry. The hotel and tourism sector discusses potential visitors, people on vacation, and people who return from a journey and share experiences.

Social media marketing discussion in tourism and hospitality includes approaches for assessing corporate success on each social media to recognize the best combination that benefits and enhances company strategies (Minazzi, Roberta, 2015). This chapter will describe current social media marketing trends in Bangladesh's tourism and hospitality industry and their effects on demand and supply. It will attempt to clarify what social media marketing is all about. The importance and role of social media marketing in tourism and hospitality are examined, and social media marketing is a digital medium for the modern world and mobile telephony.

BACKGROUND OF THE STUDY

Social Network Marketing has fundamentally altered the way many companies communicate and advertise to their target demographics. The increasing proliferation of the Internet and social media has, in turn, transformed the paradigm of marketing with numerous newly established viewpoints and horizons in the tourism and hospitality industries, and, in this case, Bangladesh is no exception. The social media marketing activity of Bangladesh is rising with the rise of online businesses. The most successful approach is required to find ways of success and expand social media marketing in Bangladesh. As a developing nation, Bangladesh has many more hurdles in its growth.

SIGNIFICANCE OF THE STUDY

Day after day, social media is becoming increasingly important, involving blogs, microblogs, social networking platforms, reviews, interactive sites, etc. In recent years, social media has emerged as a new commercial communication tool. Social media platforms provide better targeting and play an essential part in marketing operations (Chiang, 2019). The spread of social media opens up new opportunities for studying traveler information sharing behavior (Wang, Kirillova, & Lehto, 2016). Today, the world connects via the Internet, and social media networks are accessible globally in millions and billions of lives. Social networking helps you link and improve your brand awareness and maximize the productivity and profitability of your business. With more than three billion people accessing social media every month globally, users and loyalty to main channels continue to grow. Social networking sites such as Facebook, Instagram, Twitter, MySpace, and others have all influenced the buzz of word-of-mouth marketing. Because of the high level of intimacy among users, it is an excellent arena for word-of-mouth (WoM) marketing (Li & Du, 2017).

THE OBJECTIVE OF THE STUDY

This research aims to identify and address current social media marketing operations in Bangladesh and determine whether any changes are necessary. As a result, all future recommendations should be made. Moreover, this study covers the following questions:

1. Explain social media marketing and its global significance.
2. Examine the role of social media marketing in tourism and hospitality promotion.
3. Investigate the advantages and disadvantages of social media marketing
4. Describe how Bangladeshi social media marketing works.
5. Make some key recommendations for strengthening Bangladesh's use of social media marketing.

METHODOLOGY

The qualitative approach, whose authors emphasize secondary studies, will serve as the research's methodological foundation. The authors plan to review and examine a wide range of existing literature such as research papers, articles, and books to highlight and study the significance of social media marketing and how it operates in the tourism and hospitality industry, focusing on Bangladesh.

Literature Review

Tourism is described by the United Nations World Tourism Organization (UNWTO) as "a social, cultural, and economic phenomenon involving the movement of people to countries or places outside their normal environment for personal or business/professional reasons" (UNWTO, 2020). As a tourism branch, hospitality is "a key part of the domestic and international leisure market." Robinson, Lück, and Smith (2013) state that "consistent tourism demand helps the hospitality industry anticipate demand and identify ways to increase consumer spend, resulting in a surge of secondary financial impacts." Since the 1950s, tourism has been a significant economic field and a source of social and environmental change (Twain, 2017). Since the 1970s, it has also been a severe area of study and research in many academic disciplines. Tourism trends are a reflection of the backgrounds and cultures of these regions and countries. Still, tourism is an almost universal phenomenon, a significant income stream for many nations and a high priority for many" (Robinson, Lück, and Smith, 2013). According to Elhadidi and City (2018), social networking websites in recent times give space for individuals to communicate with other people and an excellent opportunity for businesses to contact their target clients through advertising. Companies use social media to develop innovative business models, including a new product marketing platform (Chung & Buhalis, 2008; Ulusu, 2010). As a new marketing channel, online communities allow traders to collect information from their profiles on potential or current users and receive direct responses based on their histories of group use (Sigala, 2003).

Due to the prevalence and use of online communities, most large companies no longer debate whether to create online communities through social media. Cox et al. (2009) are the first to examine the role of social media in travel planning, comparing user-generated content (UGC) sites with other sources of knowledge. According to the study's findings, social media is mainly used after a destination has been selected, particularly for accommodation-related information searches and where to go. Unlike more conventional outlets such as official and governmental tourism websites, Cox et al. (2009) discovered that knowledge collected via social media is not often considered trustworthy and accurate. This means that, rather than being used in place of traditional sources of travel information, social media should be used in combination with them.

According to Muhammedrisaevna, Mubinovna, & U Kizi (2020), the Internet can create tourist enterprise chances by directing advertising to the right target population. One of the primary benefits of the World Wide Web is receiving a rapid response from users of advertising content. This one-of-a-kind feature allows you to change the campaign's entire plan in the middle of it. According to Song and Yoo (2016), social media plays a significant role in the pre-purchase decisions of visitors. Given the intangible nature of travel services and the potential risk during travel decision-making, the effect of social media on consumer behavior in the tourism and travel industry has received considerable attention (Minazzi, 2015). Given the widespread use and importance of social media in various aspects of tourist decision-making, a detailed understanding of social media channels' role in tourist awareness search and decision-making processes is essential (Cox et al., 2009; Zeng and Gerritsen, 2014).

According to Kaplan and Haenlein (2010) and Xiang and Gretzel (2010), social networking is a collection of Web 2.0-based applications that enable Internet users around the world to connect, chat, and exchange ideas and feelings, experiences, knowledge, and relationships. Businesses have changed their engagement tactics from bringing products to encouraging customers to get things into companies to build a genuinely engaging and mutually beneficial partnership in the social media age (Li & Wang, 2011). As a result of social networking, relationships between people and businesses have shifted.

In reality, social factors such as sharing, feelings, and input from friends play an essential role at this stage of consumer behaviour. According to a study conducted on European travelers by PhocusWright (2013), more than half of those surveyed consider reviews from friends and family to be influential or enormously influential in their decision to try a new brand. The majority of researchers agree that social media is becoming more effective in gathering information, comparing alternatives, avoiding undesirable places, and offering suggestions before purchasing (Gretzel 2007; Anderson 2012). Mobile technologies (Buhalis and Law 2008) enable travelers to post photos and videos of their activities on Facebook and communicate with friends in real-time about their experiences through social networks or other mobile apps. Social networking has evolved to the point that it has become a global phenomenon (Yazdanifard and Yee, 2014). As more countries gained Internet access at the turn of the twentieth century, increased Internet use started to impact the economy and social life (Milano, Baggio & Piattelli, 2011). Later, as social networking grew in popularity during the Web 2.0 era, an increasing number of Internet users began to visit social networking websites, causing the social networking structure to change (Milano, et al.,2011; Seth, 2012). Social networking is a type of social media that enables Internet users to connect and exchange information with others (Yazdanifard and Yee, 2014).

As the use of the Internet and information communication technology has increased, social networking sites have changed the way people communicate with one another, especially in the hospitality and tourism industries (Assenov & Khurana, 2012; Clark & Roberts, 2010). These web ads are more trustworthy than ads on traditional media such as tv, radio, newspapers, and magazines since people on social networking sites sponsor them. (Li & Darban, 2012). Furthermore, social networking sites assist in recording customer information so that it can be easily retrieved as needed (Assenov & Khurana, 2012). Furthermore, social networking sites provide social media services that can assist a business in developing brand awareness and a positive image (Bilgihan, et al., 2014). People use social media, especially social networking sites, to keep in contact with friends and family. An individual can see what is going on in the world with just a swipe of the screen or a click of the mouse while sitting comfortably (Yazdanifard and Yee, 2014). The tourism industry should seize the golden opportunity social networking sites offer to attract customers by sharing photos and videos of breathtaking scenery. As loyal customers upload photos of hotels, restaurants, and destinations to their websites (such as Facebook), which directly link to the tourism website, their followers or visitors may read their customers' feedback (Yazdanifard and Yee, 2014).

Furthermore, online reviews, also known as word of mouth (WOM), play an essential in attracting customers (Manap & Adzharudin, 2013). People may be attracted or repelled by online reviews. They also provide information to picture themselves at their destination (Manap & Adzharudin, 2013).

A social networking site serves as a communication tool. The industry has reaped numerous benefits from more accessible access to social networking sites through mobile apps, including the ability to build relationships, increase brand awareness, and maintain customer loyalty (Bredican & Vigar-Ellis, 2014). Consumers can interact with one another, share their experiences, and express themselves, either attracting new customers and retaining existing ones or driving existing customers away.

Many hotels recognize the significance of gaining exposure on social networking sites to increase brand recognition (Assenov & Khurana, 2012). Many in the hospitality and tourism industries that use social networking sites must stay vigilant online to avoid missing out on any updates. As a result, "hotels are working to spend more in terms of employees and time on social media, as it is currently not a very big investment for them" (Assenov & Khurana, 2012, p. 331). These investments in social networking sites in terms of time and resources are considered low-cost, but they result in successful and efficient marketing. Better communication technologies enable suppliers to work more efficiently, communicate more effectively, and be more versatile (Lange-Faria & Elliot, 2012). As social networking sites gain popularity, an increasing number of hotels are joining, which has helped grow their brand and promote their properties (Yazdanifard and Yee, 2014).

From a marketer's perspective, Levinson and Gibson (2010) described social media as "a collection of free or nearly free resources that enable marketers and the community to build content and meaningful dialogue online." "Blogs, photo-sharing sites, video-sharing sites, social networks, audio podcasts, Internet radio, mobile social sharing and communication tools" are some examples of social media (Levinson & Gibson, 2010). Social media can be defined as "that enables anyone to connect with user-created content distributed through easy-to-access online resources" and straightforwardly.

Bangladesh is a wonderfully beautiful country. Bangladesh is a country with a rich and distinguished history, as well as a diverse cultural mix. Bangladesh is an Asian country with a lot of tourism potential (Islam and Islam, 2006). The most rapidly growing market in the world today is the tourism industry. Tourism is going to be the world's biggest economic market. Tourism is a form of the worldwide service industry. The improvement of the service sector would speed up our economic growth. (Sandip, 2014). Tourism is one of Bangladesh's most lucrative industries (Elena et al., 2012). Bangladesh's tourism industry is growing, accounting for 4.4 percent of the country's total GDP in 2018. In FY2019-20, the government has allocated Tk 34 billion to the Civil Aviation (Biman) and Tourism Ministries, which is more than double the previous fiscal year's allocation, indicating that the government of Bangladesh values tourism. From the mid-1990s to the present, Bangladesh's tourism industry has been steadily increasing. The people of Bangladesh participate extensively in social media and affect other visitors by exchanging their impressions, messages, views, and complaints. (Kamal, 2017). In today's marketing model, social media is a huge deal. In terms of efficacy, recent research (Bagaturia & Johnson, 2014) has found that social media is superior to traditional marketing. In January 2020, Bangladesh had 66.44

million internet users. Between 2019 and 2020, the number of internet users in Bangladesh increased by 5.8 million (+9.5%). In January 2020, Bangladesh had 36.00 million social media users. Between April 2019 and January 2020, the number of social media users in Bangladesh increased by 3.0 million (+9.1%). (Reportal, 2020).

People learn about unpopular destinations from such sites and learn more about sites already visited because social media directly impacts the tourism industry (Submitted & Policy, 2020). The efficacy of social networking sites or social media is very apparent in a positive way in increasing the popularity of the country's tourism destinations and mobilizing other businesses built around the tourism spots (Submitted & Policy, 2020). At this time, the majority of companies rely heavily on digital marketing. In recent years, Digital Marketing and Social Media Branding have undergone significant changes all over the world. The primary reason for this is the sector's mobilization. More people are turning to web forums and pages for trustworthy knowledge on various topics (Submitted & Policy, 2020).

DISCUSSION

Advertisements on social media are cheaper than other types of promotion. Creating a profile on the most popular social media site won't cost much money. Social media marketing helps create a company's brand identity and places the company as a business authority (Bansal et al., 2008). User-written feedback, video and photo sharing, blogging, and internet translation are measures of social media's effects on tourism. Travelers use social media to share where they're going, what sights they're going to visit, and where they'll eat for free (Sahoo & B.G, 2017). Using social networking advertising will dramatically increase promotional activities. One of the main benefits of social media marketing is the potential to target large audiences at a low cost (Sahoo & B.G, 2017). One of the benefits of social media, especially beneficial for small businesses, is that it decreases operating costs (Jashi, 2013). Social networking has become an integral part of the trip, leading tourists to precisely what they are looking for, and the tourist destination has grown into a perfect fit. For free, 40% of online travelers use social networking sites to control destination selection (Jashi, 2013). In the 21st century, social networking is an essential part of business marketing and communication (Felix et al., 2017). Social media covers blogs, corporate websites, shared forums, business communities, podcasts, content sharing, and open-source applications (Anderson, 2007). These networks affect consumer understanding, knowledge search, attitudes, decision-making, buying, post-purchase touch, and evaluation (Mangold & Faulds, 2009).

Social networking helps sustain online social structures and connections by encouraging users to upload and post content on Facebook, YouTube, Instagram, and Twitter (Hinterholzer & Joos, 2013). Lange-Faria, Elliot (2012). Users may use social media apps to spread their own opinions, viewpoints, and ideas in social networks through user-generated content and make them accessible to a global audience (Hays et al., 2013). When people like, comment, and share posts on social media, it introduces material to new viewers, including friends and followers. When the word spreads, it steps forward. People share this content with their networks, who share it with their networks, and the content spreads freely across the Internet, resulting in thousands or millions of shares.

Tourism social media sites feature a high degree of interactivity, encouraging users to share their opinions, images, feedback, and discussions via mobile devices. According to eMarketer (2016), social network ad spending accounts for around 20% of digital ad spending worldwide. As social media is now one of the most influential decision-makers in hotel reservations, hoteliers must take advantage of all available opportunities by creating social media-specific sites. Websites and social media provide information on destinations, land, facilities, restaurant experiences, and reviews (Manap KhairulHilmi, 2013). Tourists now have different ways to connect via social media. For destination information and decision-making, most tourists depend on the Internet. The value chain of the tourism industry, beginning with country tourism boards, tourism agents, tour operators, transport and airline firms, hotel and restaurant operators, destination managers, and local tourism managers, uses social media platforms to attract potential clients (Ernestad V., 2010). Social media marketing increases brand awareness, traffic, and search engine rankings, resulting in lower leads and sales (Stelzner, 2011). As a result of social media or web 2.0, the search, discovery, evaluation, confidence, and collaborative information about tourism suppliers and other value chain participants is evolving. As a result, tourists have matured into customers interested in producing tourist goods and selling them. Travelers may become co-producers, co-marketers, and co-consumers by developing user-generated content (UGC) and social media intelligence. Hilmi A. Manap Khairul (2013) describes social media intelligence; travelers may become co-producers, co-marketers, co-consumers.

This user-generated online comment, profile, and photo material, a mix of traveler-shared facts and opinions, is trustworthy for new users. Intelligence sources and their review places to book and purchase travel items such as itineraries and reservations and disseminate experiences after the trip (Sigala M.,Christou E.,Gretzel U.,2012). You can use any Amazon, Facebook, or YouTube comment to generate UGC content. According to Nielsen (2009), the Internet is the popular mass medium for social media marketing. However, social media now rivals conventional marketing methods. The user-generated content value chain is illustrated below. Technological advancements have also influenced consumer behavior in the tourism industry. Marketers can use social media, a low-cost marketing tool, to plan and implement marketing strategies. Marketers' main objective when using social media is to create attention-grabbing content. According to Mahnomen and Runnel (2008), user motives, loyalty, and commitment are crucial to social media success.

Social Media in Decision Making Process

Social networking platforms may promote a high level of consumer engagement and connection with a product or service. The amount of psychophysical energy the consumer spends in the buying process is called the level of customer engagement in the buying process. Increased involvement is associated with greater affective and cognitive decision-making techniques across cultures (Edgett & Cullen, 1993). Highly involved individuals use more criteria when purchasing or consuming, search for more information, consider fewer options, process relevant information in-depth, and shape habits more resistant to change than less involved individuals. As a result, degrees of engagement can impact advertising decisions and responses to information processing. Inadequate management of touchpoints/consumer interactions can lead to attrition among a company's existing consumers. Social media improves consumer relations, loyalty, and satisfaction through customer contact and encounter management, psychological, emotional, visual, auditory, and kinesthetic. Businesses can use social media marketing tools to spread positively, impact consumers, and exchange information. These forums also provide an opportunity to explain any misunderstandings that could hamper consumer purchasing decisions. According to Singh et al. (2008), established societies have formed the habit of creating intelligence, posting it on social media on the Internet, and then making purchasing decisions through the exchange of instant information.

Figure 1. Purchasing process
Source: (Turner and Shah, 2011)

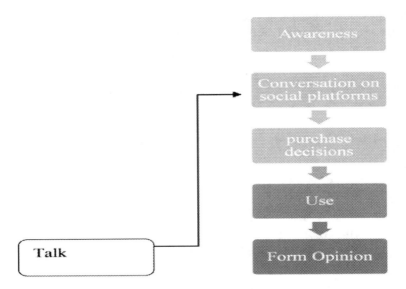

The diagram above clearly shows that when people use a product, they post their experiences on social media platforms, leading others to rethink their purchasing decisions. An organization can use such a platform effectively to connect with customers to help them meet their needs by promptly resolving their problems (Turner and Shah, 2011).

Social media also play an essential role in the launching of products. A wealth of word-of-mouth information on social media brands and products leads to its use as a new platform with a search engine, review site, and price comparison features. It functions as at least two marketing mix elements (location and promotion) and supports the other two Ps (price and product) strategies (Bolotaeva, 2011). Social media, like every other media, poses business challenges. Consumer privacy invasion, aggressive advertising, lack of e-commerce capabilities, lack of brand controls, and certain legal pitfalls can all be severe disruptions to social media. Consumers hate unwanted advertisements and emails, and they are reluctant to share their personal information, which might be compromised online.

According to Eely and Tilley (2009), social media allows people to share their experiences with others even though they have no experience with web creation or coding. Status updates, profiles on social networking websites, links, videos, audio, images, and blog or forum posts can all be used. According to Weber (2009), social media provides many ways for businesses to extend and improve their customer relationships. Companies may use various marketing strategies to advertise a product or service, and conventional advertising and social media marketing both have advantages and drawbacks (Källbäck, 2019). Traditional advertising has the benefit of quickly reaching your local audience through television or radio (Das & Lall, 2016). On the other hand, traditional advertising is challenging to quantify and expensive than social media marketing, which is less costly and easier to track (Das & Lall, 2016). Because of the existence of bots, there is also some controversy with social media ads on Facebook and Instagram. A bot is a computer algorithm programmed to automatically generate content and communicate with people on social media (Ferrara, et al.,2016). Digital marketing has some benefits, according to Das and Lall (2016). These are:

Digital marketing is an immersive method of reaching out to a local and a global audience when necessary. Data is readily available, and outcomes are much easier to assess. Like word of mouth marketing, social media allows you to interact directly with communities and even individual customers. Use social media to build direct relationships with your customers.

As in every other industry, the Big Three Social Media—Facebook, Twitter, and Instagram—were the pioneers in tourism. Although each of these channels has its audience, one of the most popular topics is travel (Digital Travel APAC, 2020). Social networking may be a significant factor affecting the tourism industry. Young people, in particular, may use social media to share their most memorable moments with a large audience (Digital Travel APAC, 2020). Tourism companies should be aware that this is a more profitable way to draw potential customers than traditional advertising and should enable people to share their experiences online (Digital Travel APAC, 2020). Facebook is the most popular website with 1,55 billion monthly users and over 450 million daily users. Millennials make up 89% of Facebook users. With 42 percent of users posting, travel is Facebook's most popular subject. It is considered the king of social media, particularly in tourism (Senouci, 2021). Twitter has around 320 million users, with Millenials representing 32% of the number. According to figures, 37% of Twitter users purchase from a business they follow (Senouci, 2021).

Tourists can be engaged through social media at a cheaper cost and more efficiently than through more traditional contact methods (Kaplan & Haenlein, 2010). A destination must stand out to prosper in the highly competitive global tourism sector (Porter, 1996). A well-developed social media marketing plan may readily clarify the goal. Due to overcrowding and content availability, attracting attention on social media is tricky. Still, some schemes seem to work better than others: innovation, chance to win, celebrity participation, individuality, unexpectedness, competitiveness, consonance, or attractive graphic design (Kiráová & Pavleka, 2015). According to Graham (2005), social networking helps users to participate, generate and share content. Among the social media mentioned are blogs, content forums, social networking sites, virtual gaming environments, and virtual social worlds (2010). Social media contains forums, ratings, comments, social networking sites, microblogging sites, podcasts, and video sharing sites (FPRM, 2009). Social networking functionality in mobile apps has gained prominence in recent years. Smartphones are quickly overtaking desktop computers as the most common social media devices. Social media benefits include increased brand recognition, brand commitment, word of mouth, friends/liking, confidence, and social affirmation (Pergolino et al., 2012; Kiráová, 2014).

The influence and application of social media marketing strategies are critical for meeting global tourist demand. The creation and availability of internet space have significantly altered tourists' incentive to plan and book trips to various destinations. Companies increase their confidence and experience with the social web to access all successful information from travel research on blogs or social networks. Entry to modern information technology is now straightforward, and this has drastically changed the way report is produced and disseminated. As a result, marketers can use social media to stimulate and promote consumer engagement, thereby facilitating tourist awareness throughout the world.

One of the advantages associated, which is especially important for small businesses, is that it reduces operating costs. Social networking has become an essential part of tourists' journey to find what they are searching for, and the tourist destination has become a great match. Social media is being incorporated into the marketing mix for two reasons:

1. Social media directs tourists and consumers to the most relevant travel information;
2. Tourist companies provide personalized messaging and content to specifically interested segments of customers.

Figure 2. The cycle of key steps for successful social media marketing
Source: *Hays et al. (2013)*

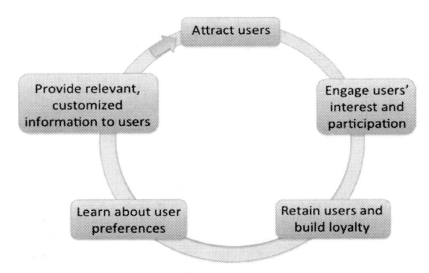

To engage consumers more intimately, the tourism and hospitality industries are turning to social media. About two-thirds of travel companies plan to boost their budgets for social media marketing. Social networking marketing tools are being used for business expansion.

On the other hand, Bangladesh Parjatan Corporation uses only two social media applications: social networking platforms, Facebook site, and Twitter site for microblogging (Alizadeh & Isa, 2015). This was suggested by (Alizadeh & Isa 2014), who observed that Asian countries are less likely than other countries to use social media apps. BPC performs the following roles on Facebook and Twitter: (i) providing information to raise awareness of the destinations among domestic and international tourists, (ii) affecting the decision of tourists to visit destinations; (iii) supporting the promotion of tourism destinations; (iv) transmitting photographs and messages from destinations to prospective visitors; and (v) encouraging a communicative NTO act(Alizadeh & Isa 2014). Bangladesh is one of the world's most beautiful and historically significant countries. It has the opportunity to expand its tourism industry. If resources are effectively used by target-driven market positioning, tourism in Bangladesh can generate more revenue than it does now. BPC has released a report that confirms the country's enormous tourism potential once again. According to the 'Bangladesh Tourism Vision 2020' report, tourist arrivals in Bangladesh are expected to reach 1.30 million by 2020. (Al- Masud, 2015).

RECOMMENDATIONS

Al- Masud (2015) made several recommendations for BPC regarding digital marketing in the tourism and hospitality industries. The following are some of them:

1. It is highly recommended that BPC participate in other social media channels, such as YouTube.
2. BPC will at least contribute to the process of destination marketing because it operates across only two social media applications, providing users with adequate information about destinations and activities and timely responses to their feedback.
3. To ensure integration through its various social media sites, the Facebook page should be mirrored on Twitter. It should also encourage visitors to post on the Facebook page's timeline and mention the community rules to ensure community participation.
4. Developing and integrating creative and exciting content on Facebook, such as interactive apps and edutainment-related resources, will increase their attraction to current and future users.
5. BPC must leverage its various industry suppliers and partners on social media to deliver the tourism product to tourists.

Hossain et al. (2020) make some suggestions for promoting tourism in Bangladesh. To gain the most significant benefits, the industry should develop successful Internet-based advertising programs for disseminating knowledge about its services and facilities. Relevant details should be accompanied by appropriate images and videos, according to the 67 percent sample of tourist respondents. Tourism businesses in Bangladesh should use the Internet to promote themselves because it helps to improve price competition. As a result, the paper suggests performing cost and efficiency comparisons between tourism promotion through the Internet and other promotion methods.

Search Engine Optimization (SEO) must be ensured to provide visitors with basic information on the first page/sight. It is the method of increasing a website's or a web page's popularity in search engines by using "normal" or "unpaid" search results (Glazier, 2011). To maximize traffic, the 'visit Bangladesh' website should consider quality content, (ii) optimization of key backend elements (title tags and meta-tags), (iii) site branding, (iv) fresh destination content, and (v) shareable content. The Internet is an essential tool for visitors to use when making decisions (Govere et al., 2013). Bangladesh should create an informative website to ensure positive tourist experiences. In this regard, a group of marketing, I.T., the ministry, private operators, and tourism experts should take the lead. Users should be able to download information from the Bangladesh tourism industry's website. As a result, they will print information brochures and maps to help them schedule their trips to Bangladesh if necessary. As a result, tourism companies in Bangladesh that use the Internet to promote themselves should make their brochures accessible in PDF (Portable Document File) format online.

A comprehensive understanding of information technology, promotional practices, and tourism marketing is needed for successful internet-based tourism promotion. Firms must provide rigorous training in these fields to their staff to do this. Due to a lack of funds, private tourism companies in Bangladesh cannot engage in large-scale promotional activities. Public sector tourism firms (BTB and BPC) also face a funding shortage in developing required budgets and promoting our tourism.

CONCLUSION

Social media is becoming more popular. It is experiencing a significant effect on a variety of social and economic issues. In the tourism industry, social networking is vital. The tourism industry deals with potential tourists, vacationers, and tourists who wish to share their experiences. According to the report, social media can be used to increase destination awareness, reach out to the masses, encourage travelers to plan their trip, strengthen the destination's image as a favorite destination, target new/specific markets, spread positive word of mouth, increase the number of visitors, create buzz around the goal, and increase the number of Facebook likes. As a result, major destination marketing companies have started to use social media to promote tourist destinations and products. As a result of the studies on social media in the tourism industry, it will be advisable for Bangladesh Tourism to have an excellent social media presence, allowing for direct and effective two-way contact between itself and tourists. Bangladesh Tourism must showcase the most attractive facets of the country's diverse destinations. It would be a failure for any destination in today's corporate world to ignore social media marketing demands since it serves as a means of connecting with consumers and exchanging details about updates, purchases, and giveaways.

REFERENCES

Al-Masud, T. M. M. (2015). Tourism Marketing in Bangladesh: What, Why and How. Asian Business Review, 5(1), 13–19. doi:10.18034/abr.v5i1.47

Alizadeh, A., & Isa, R. M. (2015). The use of social media in destination marketing: An exploratory study. *Tourism (Zagreb)*, *63*(2), 175–192.

Anderson, C. K. (2012). The impact of social media on lodging performance. *Cornell Hosp Rep*, *12*(5), 4–12.

Anderson, P. (2007). What is Web 2.0? Ideas, technologies and implications for education. *JISC Technology and Standards Watch*, 2-64. Retrieved from http://www.jisc.ac.uk/media/documents/techwatch/tsw0701b.pdf

Assenov, I., & Khurana, N. (2012). *Social Media Marketing and the Hospitality Industry: Evidence from Thailand*. Academic Press.

Bagaturi, G., & Johnson, M. (2014). The Impact of Social Media in Marketing Management. *The Journal of Business*, *3*(1), 5.

Bansal, R., Masood, R., & Dadhich, V. (2008). Social Media Marketing-A tool of Innovative Marketing. An International Journal HATAM Publishers J. *Org. Management*, *9*(3), 2014.

Bilgihan, A., Peng, C., & Kandampully, J. (2014). Generation Y's dining information seeking and sharing behavior on social networking sites: An exploratory study. *International Journal of Contemporary Hospitality Management*, *26*(3), 349–366. doi:10.1108/IJCHM-11-2012-0220

Bolotaeva, V. A. (2011). Marketing Opportunities with Social Networks. *Journal of Internet Social Networking and Virtual Communities*.

Bredican, J., & Vigar-Ellis, D. (2014). Smartphone applications-idea sourcing and app development: implications for firms. *South African Journal of Economic and Management Sciences=SuidAfrikaanse Tydskrifvir Ekonomiese en Bestuur swetenskappe, 17*(3), 232-248.

Buhalis, D., & Law, R. (2008). Progress in information technology and tourism management: 20 years on and 10 years after the Internet—the state of eTourism research. *Tourism Management, 29*(4), 609–623. doi:10.1016/j.tourman.2008.01.005

Chiang, I. (2019). Exploring the benefits of social media marketing for brands and communities. *International Journal of Electronic Commerce Studies, 10*(2), 113–140. doi:10.7903/ijecs.1547

Chiang, I. P., Wong, R., & Huang, C. H. (2019). Exploring the benefits of social media marketing for brands and communities. *International Journal of Electronic Commerce Studies, 10*(2), 113–140. doi:10.7903/ijecs.1547

Chung, J. Y., & Buhalis, D. (2008). Information needs in online social networks. *Information Technology & Tourism, 10*(4), 267–281. doi:10.3727/109830508788403123

Clark, L., & Roberts, S. (2010). Employer's use of social networking sites: A socially irresponsible practice. *Journal of Business Ethics, 95*(4), 507–525. doi:10.100710551-010-0436-y

Cox, C., Burgess, S., Sellitto, C., & Buultjens, J. (2009). 'The Role of User-Generated Content in Tourists' Travel Planning Behavior'. *Journal of Hospitality Marketing & Management, 18*(8), 743–764. doi:10.1080/19368620903235753

Das, S., & Lall, G. (2016). Traditional marketing VS digital marketing: An analysis. *International Journal of Commerce and Management Research, 2*(8), 5-11.

Data Reportal. (2020). *Digital 2020: Bangladesh*. Retrieved from: https://datareportal.com/reports/digital-2020-bangaldesh

Digital Travel, A. P. A. C. (2020). *The Role of Social Media in Tourism Marketing*. Retrieved from: https://digitaltravelapac.wbresearch.com/blog/social-media-in-tourism-marketing

Edgett, S. J., & Cullen, C. W. (1993). Service Organization Selection: A Cross-cultural Analysis of the Role of Involvement. *European Journal of Marketing, 27*(2), 33–45. doi:10.1108/03090569310026844

Eley, B., & Tilley, S. (2009). *Online Marketing Inside Out*. Sitepoint Pty. Ltd.

Elhadidi, M. F., & City, Z. (2018). Beyond access to social media: A comparison of gratifications, interactivity, and content usage among Egyptian adults. *Global Media Journal, 16*(30), 108.

eMarketer. (2016). *Worldwide Ad Spending: eMarketer's Updated Estimates and Forecast for 2015–2020*. Author.

Ernestad, V. H. R. (2010). *Social media marketing from a bottom-up perspective - the social media transition*. Retrieved from http:// www.carphonewarehouse.com

Felix, R., Rauschnabel, P. A., & Hinsch, C. (2017). Elements of strategic social media marketing: A holistic framework. *Journal of Business Research, 70*, 118–126. doi:10.1016/j.jbusres.2016.05.001

Ferrara, E., Varol, O., Davis, C., Menczer, F., & Flammini, A. (2016). The rise of social bots. *Communications of the ACM*, *59*(7), 96–104. doi:10.1145/2818717

FPRM. (2009). *Social Media Tools, What You Need to Know.* The Firm of Public Relations and Marketing. Retrieved from: https://www.scribd.com/doc/16536112/Social-Media-for-the-Hospitality-Industr

Glazier, A. (2011). *Searchial Marketing: How Social Media Drives Search Optimization in Web 3.0.* https://www.amazon.com/Searchial-MarketingSocial-Drives-Optimization/dp/1456738925

Graham, P. (2005). *Web 2.0 and Why?* Retrieved from: http//:www.fossbox.org.uk

Gretzel, U. (2007). *Online travel review study: role and impact of online travel reviews. Texas A&M University.* Laboratory for Intelligent Systems in Tourism.

Hays, S., Page, S. J., & Buhalis, D. (2013). Social Media as a destination marketing tool: Its use by national tourism organization. *Current Issues in Tourism*, *16*(3), 211–239. doi:10.1080/13683500.2012.662215

Hinterholzer, T., & Jooss, M. (2013). *Social Media Marketing und Management im Tourismus.* Springer Verlag. doi:10.1007/978-3-642-37952-9

Hossain, A., Suchana, J. J., & Avi, A. R. (2020). Promoting Bangladesh Tourism through the Internet: Theoretical Perspectives and Empirical Evidence. *Canadian Journal of Business and Information Studies*, *2*(5), 87–95. doi:10.34104/cjbis.020.087095

Islam, F., & Islam, N. (2006). *Tourism in Bangladesh: An Analysis of Foreign Tourist arrivals.* http://stad.adu.edu.tr/TURKCE/makaleler/stadbah2004/makale040103.asp

Jashi, C. (2013). Significance of Social Media Marketing in Tourism. *8th Silk Road International Conference "Development of Tourism in Black and Caspian Seas Regions,"* 37–40

Källbäck, J. (2019). *Examines the benefits of social media marketing in contrast to traditional advertising.* Academic Press.

Kamal, S. (2017). Social Media Usage and Impact: A Study on Bangladesh Tourism Industry. *International Journal of Case Studies.* Retrieved from https://www.academia.edu/36958530/Social_media_usage_and_impact_a_study_on_Bangladesh_Tourism_Industry

Kaplan, A. M., & Haenlein, M. (2010). Users of the world, unite! The challenges and opportunities of social media. *Business Horizons*, *53*(1), 59–68. doi:10.1016/j.bushor.2009.09.003

Kiráľová, A., & Pavlíčeka, A. (2015). Development of Social Media Strategies in Tourism Destination. *Procedia: Social and Behavioral Sciences*, *175*, 358–366. doi:10.1016/j.sbspro.2015.01.1211

Lange-Faria, W., & Elliot, S. (2012). Understanding the role of social media in destination marketing. Tourismos. *An International Multidisciplinary Journal of Tourism*, *7*(1), 193–211.

Lange-Faria, W., & Elliot, S. (2012). Understanding the role of social media in destination marketing. Tourismos. *An International Multidisciplinary Journal of Tourism*, *7*(1), 193–211.

Levinson, J., & Gibson, S. (2010). *Guerrilla social media marketing* (1st ed.). Entrepreneur Press.

Li, W., & Darban, A. (2012). *The impact of online social networks on consumers' purchasing decision: The study of food retailers.* Academic Press.

Li, F., & Du, T. C. (2017). The effectiveness of word of mouth in offline and online social networks. *Expert Systems with Applications, 88*, 338–351. doi:10.1016/j.eswa.2017.07.004

Manap, K., & Adzharudin, N. (2013). *The Role of User Generated Content (UGC) in Social Media for Tourism Sector.* Academic Press.

Manap KhairulHilmi, A. A. N. (2013). *The Role of User Generated Content (UGC) in Social Media for Tourism Sector.* Retrieved from http://www.westeastinstitute.com/wp-content/ uploads/2013/07/Khairul-Hilmi-A-Manap.pdf

Mangold, W. G., & Faulds, D. J. (2009). Social media: The new hybrid element of the promotion mix. *Business Horizons, 52*(4), 357–365. doi:10.1016/j.bushor.2009.03.002

Milano, R., Baggio, R., & Piattelli, R. (2011). *The effects of online social media on tourism websites.* Academic Press.

Muhammedrisaevna, T. M., Mubinovna, R. F., & Kizi, M. N. U. (2020). The role of information technology in organization and management in tourism. *Academy, 4*(55).

Muhammedrisaevna, T. M., Mubinovna, R. F., & U Kizi, M. N. (2020). The role of information technology in organization and management in tourism. *Academy, 4*(55).

Öztamur, D., & Karakadılar, İ. S. (2014). Exploring the role of social media for SMEs: As a new marketing strategy tool for the firm performance perspective. *Procedia: Social and Behavioral Sciences, 150*, 511–520. doi:10.1016/j.sbspro.2014.09.067

Paris, C. M., Lee, W., & Seery, P. (2010). The role of social media in promoting special events: Acceptance of Facebook Events. *Information and Communication Technologies In Tourism, 14*, 531–541. doi:10.1007/978-3-211-99407-8_44

Pergolino, M., Rothman, D., Miller, J., & Miller, J. (2012). *The Definitive Guide to Social Marketing. A Marketo Workbook.* Retrieved from: https://www.slideshare.net/ntdlife/definitive-guidetosocialmarketing-32648238

PhoCusWright. (2013a). *Optimizing the mobile travel experience.* Retrieved from https://www.phocuswright.com/free_reports/optimizing-the-mobile-travel-experience

Porter, M. E. (1996). What is strategy? *Harvard Business Review, 74*(6), 61–78. PMID:10158475

Robinson, P., Lück, M., & Smith, S. (2013). *Tourism* (1st ed.). CABI. doi:10.1079/9781780642970.0000

Sahoo, D. S. S., & B.G., M. M. (2017). Role of Social Media in Promoting Tourism Business - A Study on Tourism Promoting in Odisha. *International Journal of Creative Research Thoughts, 23*(9), 272–281.

Sandip, S. (2014). Competitive Marketing Strategies for Tourism Industry in the Light of Bangladesh. *Vision (Basel).*

Senouci, D. (2021). *The importance of social media in tourism: Facebook and Twitter, Amara ingenieria de Marketing*. Retrieved from: https://www.amara-marketing.com/travel-blog/social-media-tourism-facebook-twitter

Seth, G. (2012). *Analyzing the Effects of Social Media on the Hospitality Industry*. Academic Press.

Shao, G. (2009). Understanding the appeal of user-generated media: A uses and gratification perspective. *Internet Research, 19*(1), 7–25. doi:10.1108/10662240910927795

Sigala, M. (2003). Developing and benchmarking Internet marketing strategies in the hotel sector in Greece. *Journal of Hospitality & Tourism Research (Washington, D.C.), 27*(4), 375–401. doi:10.1177/10963480030274001

Singh, S. (2008). *Social Media Marketing for Dummies*. John Wiley and Sons.

Song, S. J., & Yoo, M. (2016). The Role of Social Media during the Pre-purchasing Stage. *Journal of Hospitality and Tourism Technology, 7*(1), 84–99. doi:10.1108/JHTT-11-2014-0067

Stelzner, M. (2011). *2011 Social Media Marketing Industry Report How Marketers Are Using Social Media To Grow Their Businesses*. Retrieved from http://www.socialmediaexaminer.com/SocialMedia-MarketingReport2011.pdf

Submitted, T., & Policy, P. (2020). *Effectiveness of Social Media in Promoting Tourism in Bangladesh By TARANNUM*. Tasnim Effectiveness of Social Media in Promoting Tourism in Bangladesh By.

Turner, J., & Shah, R. (2011). *How to Make Money with Social Media*. F.T. Press.

Twain, M. (2017). *The Traveling Public and Tourism Promoters*. https://www.pearsonhighered.com/assets/samplechapter/0/1/3/4/0134484487.pdf

Ulusu, Y. (2010). Determinant factors of time spent on facebook: Brand community engagement and usage types. *Journal of Yasar University, 18*(5), 2949–2957.

UNWTO. (n.d.). *Glossary of tourism terms*. Retrieved from: https://www.unwto.org/glossary-tourism-terms

Wang, S., Kirillova, K., & Lehto, X. (2016). Travelers' food experience sharing on social network sites. *Journal of Travel & Tourism Marketing, 34*(5), 680–693. doi:10.1080/10548408.2016.1224751

Weber, L. (2009). *Marketing to the Social Web: How Digital Customer Communities Build Your Business*. Wiley Inc. doi:10.1002/9781118258125

Xiang, Z., & Gretzel, U. (2010). Role of Social Media in Online Travel Information Search. *Tourism Management, 31*(2), 179–188. doi:10.1016/j.tourman.2009.02.016

Xiang, Z., & Gretzel, U. (2010). Role of social media in online travel information search. *Tourism Management, 31*(2), 179–188. doi:10.1016/j.tourman.2009.02.016

Yazdanifard, R., & Yee, L.T. (2014). Impact of Social Networking Sites on Hospitality and Tourism Industries. *Global Journal of Human-Social Science: E Economics, 14*(8).

Zeng, B., & Gerritsen, R. (2014). What Do We Know about Social Media in Tourism? A Review. *Tourism Management Perspectives, 10*, 27–36. doi:10.1016/j.tmp.2014.01.001

KEY TERMS AND DEFINITIONS

Bangladesh: Bangladesh is one of the world's most populous countries, with a population of over 164 million; it is the eighth most populous nation on the planet (July 2021 est.). It is 143,998 square kilometers (55,598 square miles) in size and shares a land border with India and Myanmar.

Business: Business is an economic activity that entails the exchange, purchase, sale, or production of goods and services for the purpose of profit and customer satisfaction.

Development: Development is defined as a process that results in growth, progress, positive change, or the addition of physical, economic, environmental, social, and demographic components to an existing system or environment.

Marketing: Marketing is the activity, set of institutions, and processes involved in developing, communicating, delivering, and exchanging offerings that are valuable to customers, clients, partners, and society at large.

Promotion: Promotions encompass the entire set of activities that are used to communicate with the user about a product, brand, or service. The objective is to raise awareness, attract attention, and persuade people to purchase the product in preference to others.

Service Industry: A service industry is a type of economic segment that provides certain intangible activities that are designed to meet a specific requirement.

Social Media: Social media refers to the means by which people interact with one another in virtual communities and networks, in which they create, share, and/or exchange information and ideas with one another.

Tourism and Hospitality: Tourism refers to attractions, activities, and events, whereas hospitality is concerned with providing people with excellent lodging, travel, and other amenities such as restaurants and sports facilities.

Chapter 14
Social Media's Influence on Destination Image:
The Case Study of a World Heritage City

Maria Angeles Garcia-Haro
University of Castilla-La Mancha, Spain

Maria Pilar Martinez-Ruiz
https://orcid.org/0000-0002-5890-5174
University of Castilla-La Mancha, Spain

Ricardo Martinez-Cañas
https://orcid.org/0000-0003-4629-5513
University of Castilla-La Mancha, Spain

Pablo Ruiz-Palomino
University of Castilla-La Mancha, Spain

ABSTRACT

Social media have become key tools for promoting and spreading the image of a tourist destination. In particular, these communication channels are critical for heritage destinations looking to boost awareness and attract a greater number of visitors. However, the tourism marketing literature has devoted limited attention to how these destinations project their image on social media. In order to cover this gap, this chapter focuses on analyzing the image projected by a specific heritage destination—Cuenca, a World Heritage City—on Facebook and Instagram. To this end, the chapter analyzes the posts, comments, and hashtags that have been published on the different tourism pages about Cuenca. The results of the analysis underscore the growing importance of the image projected by destinations on social networks. That said, there is a need to deepen our knowledge about the communication potential of these channels.

DOI: 10.4018/978-1-7998-8165-0.ch014

Social Media's Influence on Destination Image

INTRODUCTION

Today, Spain has one of the most competitive tourism sectors in the world, becoming the second-most visited country since 2017, according to the World Tourism Organization. Without a doubt, tourism is the engine of Spanish economic growth and the sector that contributes the most wealth to the country, accounting for 14.6% of the country's Gross Domestic Product and 2.8 million jobs (UNWTO, 2020).

However, the geographical distribution of tourism in Spain presents important differences between autonomous communities and provinces: the most visited being the so-called "sun and beach" tourism, with the exception of the Community of Madrid, the capital of Spain (Jorrín, 2017). The fact that most travelers choose these destinations means that inland cities face a clear comparative disadvantage with respect to coastal cities. Mainly, Castilla-La Mancha, Extremadura and Castilla y León were the autonomous communities least visited by tourists in 2019 (Jorrín, 2017).

In this regard, the central cities of Spain represent tourist destinations with rich cultural and heritage attractions that have yet to be discovered. In fact, Spain is the third country in the world, behind Italy (53) and China (52), with the highest number of World Heritage sites. Specifically, UNESCO's list includes 46 places, among which are the fifteen World Heritage Cities. Cultural and heritage tourism is an important source of wealth and employment for the Autonomous Community of Castilla-La Mancha, which reached a new record for tourists and overnight stays in 2019 (ElDigitaldeAlbacete, 2019). In terms of natural and cultural heritage, Cuenca is one of the most beautiful and richest provinces in Spain, with its important historical tradition holding particular value. Since its inscription to the World Heritage List in 1996, Cuenca has become one of the main monumental complexes in Spain, according to the official website of the Cuenca Tourist Office. However, the Castilian-La Mancha province has seen both its number of inhabitants and tourists decrease. Since 2011, the province of Cuenca has lost around 20,000 inhabitants and its population density is 12.10 inhabitants per square kilometer, which is below the European Union's 12.5 threshold for a desert zone (CuencaNews, 2018).

Cities in the interior of Spain – and particularly the province of Cuenca – are challenged to stop depopulation and reinforce their competitive position as tourist destinations (CastillaLaManchaMedia, 2018). In order to aid these efforts, scholars need to study and analyze new tourism promotion techniques that will attract more visitors to World Heritage Cities. As Munar and Ooi (2012) indicated, tourist destinations often rely on historical and cultural resources to achieve a competitive advantage in an increasingly complex environment. These new techniques will allow tourism companies to not only innovate, but also contribute to more sustainable tourist destinations, given the close relationship between sustainable development and innovation in tourism (Elmo et al., 2020). As Fayos-Solà and Cooper (2019) indicate, sustainability is crucial for destinations' competitiveness, as it encompasses the protection and conservation of natural resources, socio-cultural heritage and life. Consequently, tourism needs new innovative approaches to ensure its economic, social and environmental sustainability and growth.

In this regard, the health and economic crisis caused by COVID-19 has drastically transformed the paradigm of all economic sectors, and especially tourism. In the last semester, the sector registered its worst data in history, with a 97% drop in visitors and 750,000 jobs at risk (Aranda and Salvatierra, 2020). The coronavirus crisis has changed tourists' travel habits by encouraging them to make more proximal and last-minute trips, as well as follow other clients' opinions when making decisions (Alonso, 2010). In particular, rural tourism shows a certain optimism in the face of the crisis, since the average hotel occupancy this summer has been 54%, 14 points more than the previous year. With their natural environments and lack of crowds, rural destinations have an opportunity to expand their touristic footprint and stem the tide of depopulation (Alonso, 2020). In this sense, social networks can be an important means for tourism companies to inform, advise and entertain consumers as part of the so-called "new normal" (Montes, 2020).

Social media represent an innovative way to balance sustainability with growth (Budeanu, 2013), as they facilitate numerous approaches to the social, environmental and economic aspects of daily activity. For example, social media can help to reduce transport and energy consumption, offer new investment and employment opportunities, according to the OECD (2007), facilitate two-way communication between organizations and local communities, and encourage the exchange of tourist experiences and the promotion of a culture (Budeanu, 2013).

Managing a sustainable tourist destination requires an understanding of how the destination's image factors into tourists' decision-making process (MacKay and Fesenmaier, 2000). Among other things, image management allows one to quickly identify changes in the perceptions of the destination's users (whether positive or negative) (Barich and Kotler, 1991) and then adopt actions that foster positive evaluations (Moutinho, 1987). Because of the development of the Internet – and social media in particular – a destination's image now largely depends on the information generated by other consumers, providers and travelers (Llodrá-Riera et al., 2015). Specifically, social networks have become one of the best tools for promoting a destination to other tourists (Ricou, 2018). By allowing people to evaluate and express their experiences (Munar and Ooi, 2012), social media have changed the ways in which people travel and make tourism decisions (Shen, Sotiriadis and Zhou, 2020), which has ramifications for heritage destinations.

Every day, millions of users around the world use social networks to share photos, videos, comments and suggestions about their trips. These opinions and snapshots are disseminated quickly and in real time, shaping the image of the tourist destination in the minds of other users. Given this enormous reach and diffusion, heritage destinations must be able to effectively manage and promote their tourism image on these web platforms in order to make themselves attractive to travelers. For this reason, and in the face of increasing competition, World Heritage Cities must leverage online media to display the quality and value of their natural and cultural heritage.

Despite the rapid growth of studies on the use of social media in tourism marketing, there is still a need to study the impact of content shared on social networks within the scope of the tourism sector (Dedeoglu, 2018). In particular, scholars need a greater understanding of the role that the image plays in specific destinations, since the dimensions and constituent elements of the image can vary greatly between different places (Chaulagain, Wiitala and Fu, 2019). While the tourism marketing literature has devoted considerable attention to destination image, there are few studies that have analyzed the image that tourists perceive when viewing a heritage destination online. As McNamara and Prideaux (2011) assert, there is a need for more research on visitors' attitudes and behaviors in response to World Heritage Sites, which could generate improved marketing strategies (Remoaldo et al., 2014). From this perspective, González and Herrero (2014) point out that the World Heritage Cities of Spain must be more demanding as tourist destinations in terms of their online positioning in the different electronic word-of-mouth tools. Furthermore, as far as we know, the literature lacks complete and robust investigations into the image of Cuenca as a tourist destination (González-Oñate and Martínez-Bueno, 2012).

The present chapter strives to address this research gap by delving more deeply into the image of a heritage destination: specifically, by analyzing the image that Cuenca's Heritage City projects on social media. Overall, this research proposes to: (1) examine the role of social media, and especially social networks, as sources of tourist information; (2) analyze the importance of the destination image in tourists' decision-making, alongside the role of social media in projecting said image; and (3) conduct a detailed analysis on the image that Cuenca projects on the social networks Facebook and Instagram.

In order to meet these aims, section 2 reviews the literature on the concepts of social media and destination image, as well as the important relationship between them. Section 3 presents the heritage destination under study, Cuenca, and provides a brief description of the city's touristic evolution. Subsequently, section 4 details the methodology applied to this work, while section 5 presents the conclusions and future lines of research.

LITERATURE REVIEW

Social Media as Tourist Information Sources

The term social media has been defined by many authors in the academic literature, but there is no clear, unique and concise definition of the term (Xiang and Gretzel, 2010). One of the most prominent definitions is the one provided by (Carr and Hayes, 2015, p.50], who defined social media as "those Internet-based channels that allow users to interact opportunistically and select their self-presence. This interaction can be in real time or asynchronously towards large audiences, and whose value derives from the content generated by the user and the perception of the interaction with others". As can be seen from this and other definitions provided by relevant authors, these are unique means of communication: Unlike traditional media such as television, radio or written press, social media offer users the opportunity to interact with each other (Kent and Ellis, 2015).

In particular, the social media that have grown the most in popularity are social networks, which are effective at "democratizing information" (Lai and To, 2015, p.139). Since their onset, these platforms have become a vital marketing channel by facilitating interactions between not only people, but also companies, organizations and institutions (Appel et al., 2019). People can use social networks to form groups, collaborate, and increase their own influence within said groups (Kane et al., 2009). According to the latest annual study on social networks, published in 2020 by the consulting firm IAB Spain, 87% of the Spanish population between 16-65 years of age use social networks on a daily basis, which represents more than 25 million people (IABSpain, 2020). Of this percentage, 81% of users use social networks to entertain themselves, 77% to interact and 66% to learn (IABSpain, 2020).

Although the development of social media has permeated all economic sectors, their impact is especially significant in the tourism industry (Litvin, Goldsmith and Pan, 2018). Tourism is an experiential good, meaning that travelers and tourists cannot perceive the quality of the tourism product or service in advance (Luo and Zhong, 2015). Consequently, many tourists rely on the opinions of other people who have previously experienced the tourist destination (Dedeoglu, 2020). Without a doubt, social networks have become one of tourists' most important sources for acquiring and comparing information about the prices, suppliers, availabilities and characteristics of products and processes. Simultaneously, tourists can compare this information with their own opinions and travel experiences, as well as share their evaluations with millions of tourists and companies all over the world (Xiang and Gretzel, 2010; Fotis, Buhalis and Rossides, 2012). Thus, social networks encourage a culture of collaboration and trust that transcends any particular company. If we refer to the IAB Spain study again (IABSpain, 2020), the travel and tourism sector ranks third among the sectors most followed by users on social networks in Spain (39% of users). In response, people have greatly altered their tourism decision-making (Shen et al., 2020). On a daily basis, tourists and travelers use social networks to discover and obtain information about new tourist destinations, share their travel experiences, and express their opinions about hotels, restaurants, airlines, regions and cities in general—all of which potentially impacts the travel decisions of other users (Kazak, 2016). Younger generations are particularly inclined to share travel photographs and comments through these platforms (Lo et al., 2011), which presents new challenges and opportunities for tourist destinations (Sotiriadis, 2017).

The development of mobile technology is only accelerating the enormous popularity of social media in the tourism industry. In fact, new tourists are hyper-connected, digital and multichannel; they use all kinds of social applications to organize their trip, discover a destination, book accommodations, or buy a flight ticket (Bustamante, 2015). This so-called tourist 3.0 or *adprosumer* makes decisions based on the opinions and experiences of other travelers (García, 2016). Thus, they actively participate in online communities, whether via smartphone or computer, as a means of gathering information and planning their activities (TecnoHotelNews, 2018). Because of this process, the image that destinations project is not necessarily the one being articulated and disseminated by travelers and tourists.

The Role of Social Media in the Image of the Destination

The term destination image was coined by Hunt in 1975 in his thesis work "Image: a factor in tourism" (Hunt, 1975). Since then, the concept has been defined, expanded and studied by numerous researchers in the academic literature. In fact, Gallarza, Saura and García (2002: p.68) point out that "there are as many definitions as there are authors interested in their conceptualization". It generally refers to the "set of beliefs and impressions based on the process of information from a variety of sources over time" (Baloglu and McCleary, 1999). This results in a mental construct that represents the attributes or benefits sought in a product or destination (Beerli and Martin, 2004). The image constitutes the identity of a destination and encompasses all of its attributes (Rodríguez and Roget, 2009). In general, the image makes it possible to determine a destination's competitive position and publicize its advantages compared to similar destinations. It is also usually the basis for inspiring loyalty in and personally communicating with tourists, and therefore serves to boost future demand (Bigne, Sánchez and Sánchez, 2001).

Undoubtedly, the image has become an important component of a destination's success and sustainability (Piramanayagam, Rathore and Seal, 2020). It is also fundamental to understanding how tourists select a holiday destination (Smith et al., 2015). It is a direct antecedent of tourists' perceived quality and satisfaction, as well as their intention to visit and recommend the destination (Bigne et al., 2001). In other words, if tourists perceive the destination as positive and favorable, they are more likely to choose that destination (Jeong and Kim, 2019).

Traditionally, the academic literature has highlighted two main agents that influence the image formation process: stimulus factors and personal factors (Baloglu and McCleary, 1999; Beerli and Martin, 2004). Information sources take on a special role as stimulus factors, since they shape what tourists learn about destinations and whether they ultimately decide to visit (Draper, 2016). Indeed, numerous authors have underlined the importance of information sources to a destination's image (Molina, Gómez and Martín-Consuegra, 2010). Tourists who have the desire to travel may actively search for information and turn to different information agents (Baloglu and McCleary, 1999). But the conventional logic has generally been that institutions, tour operators, travel agencies and tourism companies need to invest large amounts of money in order to promote a tourist destination (De Ascaniis, Bischof and Cantoni, 2013).

However, the development of social media has transformed the image formation process. Many tourists now organize their vacations independently from travel agencies and tour operators. Thanks to social media, people can find lower prices, better offers, and easier booking (Jacobsen and Munar, 2012); through social networks and web browsing, they can consult the photographs, videos and reviews of other consumers. Nowadays, anyone with an Internet connection can publish information about a destination that other users can consult, and thereby actively influence a destination's image (Llodrá-Riera et al., 2015). Naturally, all these changes entail a more complex image formation process (Choi, Lehto and Morrison, 2007).

In line with this, the travel literature widely recognizes the role of the Internet and online communities in image formation (Llodrá-Riera, 2012). However, few studies have individually examined the impact of each of these platforms on said image (Choi et al., 2007; Yacout and Hefny, 2015). According to Palacio, Santana and Gil (2012), there is still an important research gap in relation to the factors that influence an image's formation and structure, such as how tourists' perceptions shift in relation to different sources of information (Choi et al., 2007). To date, many studies have focused on examining the post-visit image while ignoring the pre-visit image (Mariussen, Von Ibenfeldt and Vespestad, 2014). However, the pre-trip stage plays a fundamental role in the destination selection process: Destinations with a strong positive image will have a greater probability of being included in tourists' decision-making process, and ultimately chosen (Echtner and Ritchie, 1991).

Given the above, this research examines the image that Cuenca's Heritage City projects online. Specifically, the paper analyzes what is being said about this destination on the social networks with the highest level of users today: Facebook and Instagram.

METHOD

Cuenca, a World Heritage City

As recognized by the Horizon 2020 Spanish Tourism Plan, research on the tourism sector has focused almost exclusively on measuring the volume of tourist flows, which signals a need to delve into other quantitative and qualitative variables. Given that virtual platforms and social networks have become key elements in destination differentiation, it would seem valuable to assess the information and knowledge generated through these means (TourSpain, 2020).

Cuenca is a destination with a wealth of natural and heritage resources. It is located northeast of the autonomous community of Castilla-La Mancha and currently has around 55,000 inhabitants. Undoubtedly, one of the city's most relevant moments was its designation as a World Heritage City by UNESCO in 1996. This title was awarded to it for "exhibiting an exchange of human values within a cultural area of the developing world. of its architecture, technology, arts, urban planning and landscape design and for being an outstanding example of an architectural ensemble that illustrates significant stages in the history of mankind" (La Vanguardia, 2016). Before that declaration, the local and provincial economy of Cuenca did not see tourism as a source of wealth. However, the cultural development and interest aroused by UNESCO's statement caused a notable change in the city's orientation (González-Oñate and Martínez-Bueno, 2012).

Following the declaration, the city created the Cuenca Tourism Foundation and launched the Tourism Dynamization Plan in 1998, representing first attempts at managing the city's tourism and promoting its image as a heritage and cultural destination. The number of travelers that Cuenca received increased until 2007 before beginning to decline: from 388,000 travelers in 2008 to 255,000 in 2014. From 2014 to 2016, the number of travelers and overnight stays began to rise again. Outside of an improvement in 2017, Cuenca's gains have wavered since 2016. This year, for the first time, the average duration of two nights was reached for tourists (CLM24, 2017).

Nowadays, Cuenca is one of the few Spanish cities that is committed to spreading an image of excellence, differentiation and quality, so it does not intend to compete via prices (Abc, 2016). For example, the city has obtained the Starlight certificate, in recognition of the specific qualities that produce starry skies protected from light pollution (Garoz, 2020). More recently, Cuenca received the Smart Tourist Destination badge in recognition of the city capital transitioning into a smart destination (Expreso, 2020). In addition to these initiatives, Cuenca disseminates its image through different online and offline information sources: brochures, maps and tourist guides, the official website of the Cuenca City Council and the Cuenca Provincial Council, the website of the Municipal Tourism Office, tourism portals, digital press, web applications and blogs (both private and promoted).

However, it is still necessary for the city to value its important historical, cultural and monumental legacy (Draper, 2016) in order to become a more attractive destination for travelers. As stated by UNWTO (2020), "tourism is also a fundamental pillar for the conservation of natural and cultural heritage". In this sense, it is also necessary to enhance Cuenca's presence on other online platforms such as social networks, which excel at quickly disseminating and propagating content among users.

Based on these considerations, this research aims to study the image that the city of Cuenca projects as a tourist destination on social networks. In particular, this study analyzes what users say about Cuenca on Facebook and Instagram, which are considered the most popular platforms today. In other words, we seek to understand whether the image that is projected on these web platforms adequately stimulates tourists' desire to visit or if, on the contrary, there is a need to bolster Cuenca's online positioning. This destination lends itself to an original and novel investigation, as there have been few robust efforts to analyze the image of Cuenca as a tourist destination (González-Oñate and Martínez-Bueno, 2012). The first of them analyzed the city's image by interviewing different groups of professionals and entrepreneurs in the community. The second study focused on groups of tourism companies, residents and visitors in Castilla-La Mancha.

Cuenca's image on Facebook

Currently, Facebook has more than almost 2.7 billion users worldwide (Statista, 2020). In Spain, 22 million people use Facebook, according to The Social Media Family (2020) and treat it as the preferred social network (93% of social network users use it for more than one hour a day) (IABSpain, 2020). Today, Facebook is one of users' favorite tools for sharing information related to travel (photos, videos, experiences) (Kim and Fesenmaier, 2017), with some researchers pointing to this platform's increasingly important role in people's pre-trip planning and decision-making (Jadhav et al., 2018).

In order to analyze Cuenca's projected image on Facebook, we first analyzed the Facebook pages containing the keywords "Cuenca Tourism", which produced 104 different result pages. After eliminating those results that belonged to Cuenca (Ecuador), we obtained 96 pages that encompassed shops, bars and restaurants, associations, public bodies and political organizations. To synthesize the results, we prepared a table with the 20 Facebook pages that led the ranking with the highest number of followers (see table 1).

Social Media's Influence on Destination Image

Table 1. Facebook pages related to the search for "Cuenca Turismo"

	Page	Number of Followers	Updated content
1	Turismo Castilla-La Mancha	48.000	Yes
2	Aprende de Turismo	24.000	Yes
3	Vocesdecuenca.es	21.000	Yes
4	Las noticias de Cuenca	17.000	Yes
5	Las cosas de Cuenca	16.000	Yes
6	EstoesCuenca	15.000	Yes
7	CuencaNews	11.000	Yes
8	Ayuntamiento de Cuenca	10.000	Yes
9	Diputación Provincial de Cuenca	10.000	Yes
10	Solera Cuenca	9924	Yes
11	Cuenca es Cultura	7828	No shared content since June, 2020
12	Turismo en Albacete	7103	No profile picture. No shared content since August 28, 2020
13	Cuenca Enamora	5643	Yes
14	Populares de Cuenca	4979	Yes
15	VivoCuenca	4357	Yes
16	Camping Cuenca	3886	No shared content since August 16, 2020
17	Cuenca nos une	3886	No shared content since May 9, 2020
18	TodoBici Cuenca	3752	No shared content since August 22, 2020
19	Turismo San Clemente-Cuenca	3734	Yes
20	Cope Cuenca	3628	Yes

Source: Own elaboration

While most of the pages share updated content and information, there are some that have not published content for a long time. With the exception of #12 all of them have a profile and cover image. Specifically, if we refer to pages that publish content of interest about tourism in Cuenca, we must highlight four pages: "Las Cosas de Cuenca", "Esto es Cuenca", "VivoCuenca", "CuencaEnamora" and specific tourism from one of the towns in the region "Turismo San Clemente-Cuenca". Below we present a detailed analysis of the last 10 posts from these four pages:

"Las Cosas de Cuenca" is the leading page in terms of follower count (17.000). This tourism page deals with relevant news, traditions, gastronomy and festivals in the province. When evaluating users' interactions with the page relative to the number of fans, the page's posts receive relatively few reactions and comments (17 reactions on average).

"Esto es Cuenca": With more than 15,000 followers, this page highlights the most characteristic tourist spots in the province of Cuenca, alongside some curiosities or traditions. On average, each post has more than 730 likes, more than 20 comments, and is shared more than 167 times. User comments generally include statements such as "Cuenca is beautiful", "Cuenca makes you fall in love", "is unique", "beautiful", "beautiful Cuenca", "magical" or "spectacular". Beyond the page's presence on social networks, it one of the most followed travel blogs.

"Vivo Cuenca" informs its followers (more than 4,500) of news related to the hotel industry, tourism and commerce in Cuenca. Despite a smaller number of fans than the previous two pages, this page sees a relatively higher number of reactions. On average, the page's posts have 48 reactions and are shared more than 7 times. As with "Las Cosas de Cuenca", the number of comments is very small.

"Cuenca Enamora" highlights the richness of the province's heritage, art and culture. Unlike the previous pages, it usually publishes content on a weekly (rather than daily) basis. Regarding interactions, each post has an average of 25 likes and 4 shares. This organization's promotion of the hashtag #cuencanenamora is notable, as will be detailed in the following analyses.

Cuenca's image on Instagram

With more than one billion users worldwide (Adame, 2019), Instagram is considered the most influential social network in the tourism industry (Canalis, 2019), including in Spain where it already has 16 million users (TheSocialMediaFamily, 2020). On average, 80 million photographs are shared on the network every day from around the world (Smith, 2016) while more than 150 million users publish Instagram Stories daily (Alcántara, 2017).

In order to analyze Cuenca's image as a tourist destination on Instagram, we performed a search for hashtags containing or related to the word Cuenca. A search using Ingramer platform, the hashtag #cuenca uncovered 2.9 million posts, with about 3,387 posts being made daily, on average.

Of course, many of these posts refer to the city of Cuenca in Ecuador and many others contain geographical connotation. After conducting this search, we uncovered more specific hashtags (see table 2) that align with a greater number of publications about the province of Cuenca:

Table 2. Hashtags related to Cuenca on Instagram

Hashtag (#)	Number of publications
#cuencacity	47.375
#cuencaspain	28.351
#cuencaenamora	24.045
#cuenaesunica	19.204
#cuencaespaña	14.108
#cuencaclub	7.207
#cuencatattoo	3.578
#cuencamágica	3.095
#cuencaesúnica	2.461
#cuencaturismo	2.172

Source: Own elaboration

As can be seen, the hashtags with the highest number of publications were #cuencacity #cuencaspain and #cuencaenamora. There was also a notable use of positive adjectives such as "unique" or "magical". As for other widely used hashtags, the most prominent were #serraniadecuenca, #cuencaturismo, #cuencamagica, #cuencapatrimoniodelahumanidad or #turismocuenca.

Along these lines, Figure 1 represent the most common hashtags featuring the word "Cuenca"

Figure 1. Hashtags similar to #Cuenca
Source: Own elaboration from Tagsfinder webpage

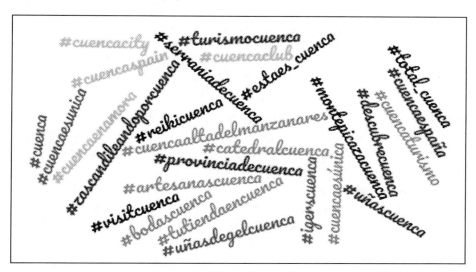

Finally, it is important to examine which keywords (#) related to Cuenca are most used by users in Instagram (see figure 2).

Figure 2. Hashtags related to #Cuenca
Source: Own elaboration from Tagsfinder webpage

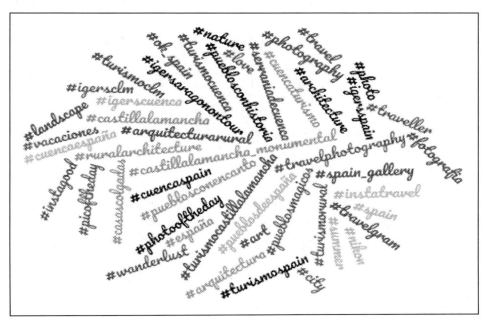

DISCUSSION

Social media and social networks have become important marketing tools for the tourism sector due to their immediacy, influence, capacity for interaction and ease of disseminating information. In the wake of the coronavirus pandemic, these tools have become fundamental channels for companies and tourist destinations looking to promote their image and communicate with travelers, particularly with regard to resolving their doubts and advising them on the different phases of your journey. Now more than ever, users comment on their trips and share their experiences with other tourists. Consequently, social media play an increasingly pivotal role in destination sustainability, especially for smaller locations such as Cuenca.

As is apparent, social networks and mobile technology have fundamentally altered the process of disseminating and promoting a destination's image. Entities responsible for tourism have ceded some control over the image to travelers and tourists who influence others with their opinions, comments and photographs. Consequently, tourism companies and organizations must know how to properly manage the image that they project in these media in order to inspire and motivate users' desire to travel.

Despite the obvious interest in and relevance of social networks, few studies have analyzed the image projected by World Heritage Cities on these platforms. These are destinations with a great wealth of culture and heritage, but their historical legacy is not often known to travelers. In this context, our research contributes to the academic literature on tourism marketing in different ways. First, this study offers an in-depth examination of social networks (as a form of social media) as concrete sources of information in the tourism sector. Second, this research provides a better understanding of the influence of social media on the image of a tourist destination—particularly how they affect users' desire and motivation to visit. We addressed a gap in the existing literature about the role of social networks in the promotion and dissemination of heritage destinations, with a specific focus on the Heritage City of Cuenca. Third, we studied the city's projected image in relation to the two most popular social networks: Facebook and Instagram. In this regard, we analyzed users' comments about Cuenca on these platforms, the most shared pages about Cuenca, and the most used hashtags in the shared publications. This analysis led to the following conclusions.

As a tourist destination, Cuenca's presence on Facebook and Instagram seems scarce and insufficient. In both social networks, there are very few tourism or news pages about the province that exceed 10,000 followers, and some of them have not shared information and updated content of interest for a long time. Moreover, most pages received small numbers of user interactions (i.e., comments, reactions and shares). The analysis highlighted users' difficulty in finding information or publications about Cuenca as a tourist destination in Spain. For instance, a large number of pages and profiles referred to Cuenca as a destination in Ecuador, or have geographical connotation. Consequently, there is a need to focus on hashtags that highlight tourism in the province of Cuenca, such as "cuencaesúnica", "cuencaenamora" or "cuencaspain".

Of course, this research presents several limitations that may open avenues for future studies. First, we focused solely on a single heritage destination; future works should analyze other Heritage Cities and compare the results and conclusions. Second, we only examined the image projected by the destination on popular social networks, but there would be value in assessing other web platforms such as blogs or tourism-specific social networks. Third, this research examined the global image projected by a destination. It would be interesting for future research to examine different dimensions of this global image, such as the cognitive, affective and conative image.

DISCLOSURE STATEMENT

No potential competing interest was reported by the authors. This research received no external funding.

REFERENCES

ABC. (2016). *Cuenca, 20 años como Ciudad Patrimonio de la Humanidad.* ABC. Retrieved from https://www.abc.es/espana/castilla-la-mancha/abci-cuenca-20-anos-como-ciudad-patrimonio-humanidad-201612061402_noticia.html

Adame, M. (2019). *Redes sociales más usadas en el mundo hispano: tips para crecer tu presencia y alcance social.* Hootsuite. Retrieved from https://blog.hootsuite.com/es/redes-sociales-mas-usadas/

Alcántara, B. (2017). *Instagram Stories llega a los 150 millones de usuarios diarios.* Xombit. Retrieved from https://xombit.com/2017/01/instagram-stories-150-millones-usuarios-diarios

Alonso, A. (2020). *El turismo rural se crece frente al coronavirus.* 20 minutos. Retrieved from https://www.20minutos.es/opinion/opinion-turismo-rural-crece-frente-coronavirus-20200927-4396171/

Appel, G., Grewal, L., Hadi, R., & Stephen, A. T. (2019). The future of social media in marketing. *Journal of the Academy of Marketing Science, 48*(1), 79–95. doi:10.100711747-019-00695-1 PMID:32431463

Aranda, J. L., & Salvatierra, J. (2020). *Covid-19 crisis devastates Spain's tourism industry.* El País. Retrieved from https://english.elpais.com/economy_and_business/2020-08-05/covid-19-crisis-devastates-spains-tourism-industry.html

Baloglu, S., & McCleary, K. W. (1999). A model of destination image formation. *Annals of Tourism Research, 26*(4), 868–897. doi:10.1016/S0160-7383(99)00030-4

Barich, H., & Kotler, P. (1991). A framework for marketing image management. *MIT Sloan Management Review, 32*, 94. PMID:10111301

Beerli, A., & Martín, J. D. (2004). Factors influencing destination image. *Annals of Tourism Research, 31*(3), 657–681. doi:10.1016/j.annals.2004.01.010

Bigne, J. E., Sanchez, M. I., & Sanchez, J. (2001). Tourism image, evaluation variables and after purchase behaviour: Inter-relationship. *Tourism Management, 22*(6), 607–616. doi:10.1016/S0261-5177(01)00035-8

Budeanu, A. (2013). Sustainability and Tourism Social Media. In Tourism Social Media: Transformations in Identity, Community and Culture (pp. 87-103). Emerald Group Publishing Limited. doi:10.1108/S1571-5043(2013)0000018008

Bustamante, S. (2015). *Algunas "apps" muy útiles para viajar este verano.* ABC. Retrieved from https://www.abc.es/viajar/top/20150713/abci-apps-diez-viajero-201507072030.html

Canalis, X. (2019). *Marketing en Instagram ¿el nuevo embudo para el turismo?* Hosteltur. Retrieved from https://www.hosteltur.com/127353_marketing-en-instagram-el-nuevo-embudo-para-el-turismo.html

Carr, C. T., & Hayes, R. A. (2015). Social media: Defining, developing, and divining. *Atlantic Journal of Communication, 23*(1), 46–65. doi:10.1080/15456870.2015.972282

Castilla-La Mancha Media. (2018). *Frenar la despoblación: el reto de la provincia de Cuenca.* Castilla-La Mancha Media. Retrieved from https://www.cmmedia.es/noticias/castilla-la-mancha/frenar-la-despoblacion-el-reto-de-la-provincia-de-cuenca/

Chaulagain, S., Wiitala, J., & Fu, X. (2019). The impact of country image and destination image on US tourists' travel intention. *Journal of Destination Marketing & Management, 12*, 1–11. doi:10.1016/j.jdmm.2019.01.005

Choi, S., Lehto, X. Y., & Morrison, A. M. (2007). Destination image representation on the web: Content analysis of Macau travel related websites. *Tourism Management, 28*(1), 118–129. doi:10.1016/j.tourman.2006.03.002

CLM24. (2017). *Las pernoctaciones en Cuenca alcanzan por primera vez las dos noches de duración.* CLM24. Retrieved from https://www.clm24.es/articulo/cuenca/pernoctaciones-cuenca-alcanzan-primera-vez-noches-duracion/20170917193928173394.html

Cuenca News. (2018). *La provincia de Cuenca ha perdido más del 34% de su población desde 1900.* Periódico Digital Cuenca News.es. Retrieved from https://www.cuencanews.es/noticia/57770/provincia/la-provincia-de-cuenca-ha-perdido-mas-del-34--de-su-poblacion-desde-1900.html

De Ascaniis, S., Bischof, N., & Cantoni, L. (2013). Building destination image through online opinionated discourses. the case of swiss mountain destinations. In Information and Communication Technologies in Tourism (pp. 94-106). Academic Press.

Dedeoglu, B. B. (2018). Are information quality and source credibility really important for shared content on socialmedia? The moderating role of gender. *International Journal of Contemporary Hospitality Management, 31*, 513–534. doi:10.1108/IJCHM-10-2017-0691

Draper, J. (2016). An exploratory study of the differences in prior travel experience and tourist information sources. *Tourism and Hospitality Research, 16*(2), 133–143. doi:10.1177/1467358415600216

Echtner, C. M., & Ritchie, J. B. (1991). The meaning and measurement of destination image. *Journal of Tourism Studies, 2*, 2–12.

El Digital de Albacete. (2019). *El turismo sigue batiendo récords en Castilla-La Mancha.* El Digital de Albacete. Retrieved from https://www.eldigitaldealbacete.com/2019/06/18/el-turismo-sigue-batiendo-records-en-castilla-la-mancha/

Elmo, C. G., Arcese, G., Valeri, M., Poponi, S., & Pacchera, F. (2020). Sustainabiliy in tourism as a innovation driver: An analysis of familiy business reality. *Sustainability, 12*(15), 6149. doi:10.3390u12156149

Expreso. (2020). *Cuenca, camino de convertirse en Destino Turístico Inteligente.* Expreso. Retrieved from https://www.expreso.info/noticias/espana/77938_cuenca_camino_de_convertirse_en_destino_turistico_inteligente

Fayos-Solà, E., & Cooper, C. (2019). Conclusion: The future of tourism: innovation and sustainability. *The Future of Tourism,* 325-337.

Fotis, J. N., Buhalis, D., & Rossides, N. (2012). Social media use and impact during the holiday travel planning process. Springer-Verlag. doi:10.1007/978-3-7091-1142-0_2

Gallarza, M. G., Saura, I. G., & García, H. C. (2002). Destination image: Towards a conceptual framework. *Annals of Tourism Research*, *29*(1), 56–78. doi:10.1016/S0160-7383(01)00031-7

García, A. (2016). *Radiografía del perfil del viajero: Del turista tradicional al 3.0*. Hosteltur. Retrieved from https://www.hosteltur.com/comunidad/nota/004536_radiografia-del-perfil-del-viajero-del-turista-tradicional-al-30.html

Garoz, J. (2020). *19 municipios de la Serranía para disfrutar de las próximas lluvias de estrellas*. Voces de Cuenca. Retrieved from https://www.vocesdecuenca.com/provincia/serrania/19-municipios-de-la-serrania-para-disfrutar-de-las-proximas-lluvias-de-estrellas/

González, C. M., & Herrero, J. L. C. (2014). *Aplicaciones de tecnología 3D para el turismo cultural y la difusión del patrimonio: realidad aumentada vs realidad virtual*. Paper presented at the TuriTec 2014, X Congreso Nacional Turismo y Tecnologías de la Información y las Comunicaciones, Universidad de Málaga (UMA).

González-Oñate, C., & Martínez-Bueno, S. (2013). Reinvención de marcas territorio a través de la organización de eventos: Cuenca y su riqueza paleontológica. *Arte y Ciudad*, *3*(1), 153–170.

Hunt, J. D. (1975). Image as a factor in tourism development. *Journal of Travel Research*, *13*(3), 1–7. doi:10.1177/004728757501300301

IAB Spain. (2020). *Estudio Redes Sociales 2020*. IAB Spain. Retrieved from https://iabspain.es/estudio/estudio-redes-sociales-2020/

Jacobsen, J. K. S., & Munar, A. M. (2012). Tourist information search and destination choice in a digital age. *Tourism Management Perspectives*, *1*, 39–47. doi:10.1016/j.tmp.2011.12.005

Jadhav, V., Raman, S., Patwa, N., Moorthy, K., & Pathrose, J. (2018). Impact of Facebook on leisure travel behavior of Singapore residents. *International Journal of Tourism Cities*, *4*(2), 6–20. doi:10.1108/IJTC-06-2017-0032

Jeong, Y., & Kim, S. (2019). Exploring a suitable model of destination image: The case of a small-scale recurring sporting event. *Asia Pacific Journal of Marketing and Logistics*, *31*(5), 1287–1307. doi:10.1108/APJML-10-2018-0441

Jorrín, J. (2017). *Sin sol y playa no hay turismo: España copa también las zonas menos visitadas de Europa*. El Confidencial. Retrieved from https://www.elconfidencial.com/economia/2017-08-16/turismo-comunidades-menos-visitadas-turismofobia-extremadura-castilla-mancha-leon-aragon_1429101/

Kane, G. C., Fichman, R. G., Gallaugher, J., & Glaser, J. (2009). Community relations 2.0. *Harvard Business Review*, *87*, 45–50. PMID:19891388

Kazak, L. (2016). *The impact of social media on the tourism industry*. Retrieved from https://www.linkedin.com

Kent, M., & Ellis, K. (2015). People with disability and new disaster communications: Access and the social media mash-up. *Disability & Society*, *30*(3), 419–431. doi:10.1080/09687599.2015.1021756

Kim, J., & Fesenmaier, D. R. (2017). Sharing tourism experiences: The posttrip experience. *Journal of Travel Research*, *56*(1), 28–40. doi:10.1177/0047287515620491

La Vanguardia. (2016). *Cuenca celebra su declaración como Ciudad Patrimonio de la Humanidad con una "fiesta de cumpleaños" el 13 de diciembre*. La Vanguardia. Retrieved from https://www.lavanguardia.com/vida/20161206/412438221880/cuenca-celebra-su-declaracion-como-ciudad-patrimonio-de-la-humanidad-con-una-fiesta-de-cumpleanos-el-13-de-diciembre.html

Lai, L. S., & To, W. M. (2015). Content analysis of social media: A grounded theory approach. *Journal of Electronic Commerce Research*, *16*, 138.

Litvin, S. W., Goldsmith, R. E., & Pan, B. A. (2018). Retrospective view of electronic word-of-mouth in hospitality and tourism management. *International Journal of Contemporary Hospitality Management*, *30*(1), 1–26. doi:10.1108/IJCHM-08-2016-0461

Llodrá-Riera, I. (2014). *Gestión de la imagen del destino en el contexto del turismo 2.0: Recomendaciones estratégicas para las Organizaciones de Marketing de los Destinos (OMD)* (Doctoral dissertation). Universidad de Castilla-La Mancha, Spain.

Llodrá-Riera, I., Martínez-Ruiz, M., Jiménez-Zarco, A., & Izquierdo-Yusta, A. A. (2015). multidimensional analysis of the information sources construct and its relevance for destination image formation. *Tourism Management*, *48*, 319–328. doi:10.1016/j.tourman.2014.11.012

Lo, I. S., McKercher, B., Lo, A., Cheung, C., & Law, R. (2011). Tourism and online photography. *Tourism Management*, *32*(4), 725–731. doi:10.1016/j.tourman.2010.06.001

Luo, Q., & Zhong, D. (2015). Using social network analysis to explain communication characteristics of travel-related electronic word-of-mouth on social networking sites. *Tourism Management*, *46*, 274–282. doi:10.1016/j.tourman.2014.07.007

MacKay, K. J., & Fesenmaier, D. R. (2000). An exploration of cross-cultural destination image assessment. *Journal of Travel Research*, *38*(4), 417–423. doi:10.1177/004728750003800411

Mariussen, A., Von Ibenfeldt, C., & Vespestad, M. K. (2014). The Typology and Role of Online Information Sources in Destination Image Formation: An Eye-Tracking Study. *The International Journal of Digital Accounting Research*, *14*, 141–164. doi:10.4192/1577-8517-v14_6

McNamara, K. E., & Prideaux, B. (2011). Experiencing 'natural' heritage. *Current Issues in Tourism*, *14*(1), 47–55. doi:10.1080/13683500.2010.492852

Molina, A., Gómez, M., & Martín-Consuegra, D. (2010). Tourism marketing information and destination image management. *African Journal of Business Management*, *4*, 722–728.

Montes, D. (2020). *Las redes sociales, vitales para las agencias durante el coronavirus*. Agenttravel. Retrieved from https://www.agenttravel.es/noticia-039142_Las-redes-sociales-vitales-para-las-agencias-durante-el-coronavirus.html

Moutinho, L. (1987). Consumer behaviour in tourism. *European Journal of Marketing*, *21*(10), 5–44. doi:10.1108/EUM0000000004718

Munar, A. M., & Ooi, C. S. (2012). *What social media tell us about the heritage experience. CLCS Working*. Copenhagen Business School.

Organization for Economic Cooperation and Development. (2007). *Working party of the Information Economy*. OECD. Retrieved from https://www.oecd.org/sti/38393115.pdf

Palacio, A.B., Santana, J.D.M., & Gil, S.M. (2012). Los Agentes que conforman la imagen de los destinos turísticos. *Universidad de Las Palmas de Gran Canaria*, 1-22.

Piramanayagam, S., Rathore, S., & Seal, P. P. (2020). Destination image, visitor experience, and behavioural intention at heritage centre. *Anatolia*, *31*(2), 211–228. doi:10.1080/13032917.2020.1747234

Remoaldo, P., Ribeiro, J. C., Da Cruz Vareiro, L. M., & Santos, J. (2014). Tourists' perceptions of world heritage destinations: The case of Guimarães (Portugal). *Tourism and Hospitality Research*, *14*(4), 206–218. doi:10.1177/1467358414541457

Ricou, J. (2018). *El turismo vende el destino*. La Vanguardia. Retrieved from https://www.lavanguardia.com/ocio/viajes/20180328/441996593656/turistas-fotos-redes-sociales-marketing-visual.html

Rodríguez, G. R., & Roget, F. M. (2009). *Nuevos retos para el turismo*. Netbiblo S.L. doi:10.4272/978-84-9745-402-5

Shen, S., Sotiriadis, M., & Zhou, Q. (2020). Could Smart Tourists Be Sustainable and Responsible as Well? The Contribution of Social Networking Sites to Improving Their Sustainable and Responsible Behavior. *Sustainability*, *12*(4), 1470. doi:10.3390u12041470

Smith, K. (2016). *37 estadísticas en Instagram*. Brandwatch. Retrieved from https://www.brandwatch.com/es/blog/37-estadisticas-de-instagram/

Smith, W. W., Li, X. R., Pan, B., Witte, M., & Doherty, S. T. (2015). Tracking destination image across the trip experience with smartphone technology. *Tourism Management*, *48*, 113–122. doi:10.1016/j.tourman.2014.04.010

Sotiriadis, M. D. (2017). Sharing tourism experiences in social media. *International Journal of Contemporary Hospitality Management*, *29*(1), 179–225. doi:10.1108/IJCHM-05-2016-0300

Statista. (2020). *Number of monthly Facebook users worldwideas of 3rd quarter 2020*. Retrieved from https://www.statista.com/statistics/264810/number-of-monthly-active-facebook-users-worldwide/

TecnoHotelNews. (2018). *Las redes sociales buscan la alianza del sector turístico*. TecnoHotelNews. Retrieved from https://tecnohotelnews.com/2018/01/21/redes-sociales-turismo-fitur/

The Social Media Family. (2020). *V Estudio sobre los usuarios de Facebook, Twitter e Instagram en España*. Retrieved from https://thesocialmediafamily.com/wp-content/uploads/92020/02/vi-informe-rrss-2020.pdf

TourSpain. (2020). *Plan del Turismo Español Horizonte 2020*. TourSpain. Retrieved from https://www.tourspain.es/es/Conozcanos/Documents/HistoricoPoliticaTuristica/PlanTurismoEspanolHorizonte2020.pdf

World Tourism Organization. (2020). *UNWTO*. Retrieved from https://www.unwto.org/

Xiang, Z., & Gretzel, U. (2010). Role of social media in online travel information search. *Tourism Management*, *31*(2), 179–188. doi:10.1016/j.tourman.2009.02.016

Yacout, O. M., & Hefny, L. I. (2015). Use of Hofstede's cultural dimensions, demographics, and information sources as antecedents to cognitive and affective destination image for Egypt. *Journal of Vacation Marketing*, *21*(1), 37–52. doi:10.1177/1356766714538444

KEY TERMS AND DEFINITIONS

Depopulation: The decrease of the population in a territory during a certain period of time.

Destination Image: Individual perceptions, ideas, and impressions that an individual has about a place. It influences tourist decision to choose a destination.

Social Media: Communication channels that allow users to create and share content on the Web 2.0.

Sustainability: The balance between economic growth, environment, and consumer's needs.

Tourism Marketing: Marketing strategies applied by businesses in the tourism industry.

Tourist Information Source: Online and offline channels where tourists search for tourist-related information before, during and after a trip.

World Heritage City: It is a distinction name for cities in the world with a rich value for humanity.

ENDNOTE

[1] The review of the Facebook and Instagram pages was carried out on October 10, 2020.

Chapter 15
Determination of Guest Satisfaction by Text Mining:
Case of Turkey Hotels

Ozan Çatir
Usak University, Turkey

ABSTRACT

The satisfaction of guests is of paramount importance to ensure the continuity and profitability of hotels. This study aims to determine guests' satisfaction with hotels by analyzing the online comments of guests. The text mining method has been utilized in this study. 58,193 Turkish comments about 5-star hotels in Turkey have been examined. These comments have been subjected to frequency and association analysis by models with Rapid Miner program. It may be stated that the guests are satisfied with 5-star hotel management in Turkey, and they are also satisfied with hotels in general and the services provided by hotels.

INTRODUCTION

Since online travel agencies and online reservation media have emerged, many Guests share their experiences about hotels and journeys in these media. Therefore, these media may regard as effective marketing instruments that provide superior benefits (Su, Reynolds and Sun, 2015). Hotel managers were using traditional methods to determine guests' satisfactions and their behavioral intention. There was survey in the hotel rooms and guests were filling satisfaction surveys after their accommodation in the hotels. However, guests were not willing to give feedback (Ekiz and Au, 2011).

The guests can easily express not only their satisfactions but also their dissatisfactions and they can also use these social media when they decide and select (García-Pablos, Cuadros and Linaza, 2016). In addition, guests certainly use these online platforms when they decide their vacations (Schuckert, Liu and Law, 2015). Analysis of online comments is important for understanding online sales and guest satisfaction.

DOI: 10.4018/978-1-7998-8165-0.ch015

Since internet media has become an important information source on vacation decisions of guests, the need of research has increased in this field (Spark and Browning, 2011). It is important to analyze guests' own Comment to understand the guests better and to provide better services.

On the other hand, this chapter uses text mining analysis to analyze text and obtain important results, as it is difficult to analyze large amounts of data on online platforms (Turban, Sharda and Delen, 2010). This study will provide better results compared to previous studies, as it analyzes more data than traditional methods and relies on recommendations from guests (Jannach, Zanker and Fuchs, 2014; Lu and Stepchenkova, 2015; Wang, Chan and Pan, 2015; Gursoy, 2019). There are also specific studies that analyze online comments, determine guests' attitudes, behavioral intentions and lifestyles, and provide viable marketing strategies (Ghosh, 2018; Moro, Rita and Oliveiar, 2018). Hence this chapter is important to determine guest profile, properties and satisfaction statues of 5-star hotels in Turkey. Besides this study differs from prior studies because it uses a developed emotional analogy method to understand the hotel experiences of hotel guests.

This study aims to determine satisfaction conditions of guests by considering whether guests are satisfied or not by analyzing comments of user about 5-star hotels in Turkey. The text mining method has been selected as the methodology of this study by supposing that significant results can be obtained by huge amount of data from online comments hotel guests. This study consists of four parts. In the first section, the literature on satisfaction and big data analysis in the tourism sector is examined. The second section describes how part of the text mining method works. In the third section, the results obtained for guest satisfaction are presented. In the fourth and final section, results, discussions and suggestions are given.

BACKGROUND

Guests' Satisfaction in Tourism Sector by Text Mining Analysis

The subject of satisfaction has been tried to be explained with the two-factor theory of Herzberg, Mausner and Snyderman (1959). The theory put forward for the job satisfaction of the employees stated that job satisfaction can be achieved by two factors: continuity of motivation and continuity of hygiene. Later, Cadotte and Turgeon (1988) proposed a model for guest satisfaction, taking this theory into account. According to this model, regarding satisfaction, hotel properties are divided into 4 categories: satisfiers, dissatisfiers, criticals and neutrals. Satisfiers are defined as traits whose absence does not lead to dissatisfaction, but whose presence provides satisfaction. Dissatisfiers, on the other hand, are traits that cause dissatisfaction when not found or poorly done, but not satisfaction when provided. Criticals are traits that can cause dissatisfaction or satisfaction depending on the situation. Neutrals is defined as the features of a service that do not cause compliments or complaints (Cadotte and Turgeon, 1988).

When the prior studies are examined in the literature, it has been stated that the evaluations of the guests about hotels have a significant influence on vacation decision process and hotel preference of the guests (O'Connor, 2008; Gretzel and Yoo, 2008; Xie, Miao, Kuo and Lee, 2011). According to Stringam, Gerdes and Vanleeuwen (2010), about %90 of the guests has stated hotels' comments are precious. The summaries of the studies on guest satisfaction are as follows.

Ruan (2020) aimed to examine the effect of social relations between guest and host on guest satisfaction in secondary residences. He analyzed the hypotheses he formed in his study using the questionnaire technique by performing regression analysis. According to the results obtained from the study, it has been determined that the relationship between the guest and the host has a positive effect on guest satisfaction. However, while the sociability relationship between the host and the guest has a positive effect on renting the room, it has been concluded that if the whole house is rented, it is not welcomed by other residents. The study presented important findings in terms of revealing the effect of social relationships on satisfaction for home sharing platforms and hosts.

Customer satisfaction is an issue that is constantly on the agenda of tourism research (Dolnicar and Otter, 2003). Variables that affect customers' satisfaction with hotels are determined as staff quality, room quality, value for money, diverse and effective services, business-related services and security (Qu, Ryan and Chu, 2000). Price and service quality are also determined as factors affecting customer satisfaction (Tse, 2001). Although these factors affect the satisfaction of customers, they may differ in the factors that affect the satisfaction of customers who have different cultural backgrounds and who speak different languages (Dolcinar and Grün, 2007; Tse and Ho, 2009).

Tourism research in recent years has focused on user-generated reviews to conduct research. Zhou et al. (2014); Researchers such as Rhee and Yang (2015), Banerjee and Chua (2016) examined the reviews and their importance ratings on travel sites such as Agoda.com and TripAdvisor. It has been emphasized that big data analytics can be used to better understand and gain insights into the tourism industry. (Marine-Roig and Clave, 2015). Studies have also emphasized that the points made by the customers and given about the hotels are an excellent tool to understand customer satisfaction (Hargreaves, 2015; Schuckert et al., 2015).

Zhu, Lin and Chen (2020) analyzed the relationship between guest emotions and online ratings in their study and examined its effect on guest satisfaction. 4602 Airbnb records in San Francisco were examined in the study. Tobit and sequential logit models are used to give consistent estimation results. As a result, it has been stated that the positive or negative sensitivity of guest feelings affects guest satisfaction at a high level. It was also stated that the sensitivity of guest feelings and the correlation between ratings were high.

Padma and Ahn (2020) aimed to reveal the main characteristics of luxury hotel services in Malaysia by subjecting the online comments presented on Tripadvisor to big data analysis. In addition, features related to service quality, room-related features, personnel-related features and travel-related features were revealed with word frequencies. In addition, by using the critical event technique, the premises and consequences of the satisfaction and dissatisfaction of the hotel guests were determined. As a result of the study, it was stated that the quality of the rooms and the communication of the employees affected the satisfaction of the guests, word of mouth marketing and their intention to visit again.

Sann and Lai (2020) aimed to analyze online complaints to synthesize specific service failure items and group them into hotel guest cycle and related transactions. It was also aimed to determine the expression models used by Asian and non-Asian guests regarding their hotel experiences. 390,236 online complaints of approximately 353 hotel guests in the UK from 63 countries were analyzed. It was stated that Asian guests complained more about the physical aspects of the hotel services, while non-Asian guests complained about the cleanliness. It has been found that complaints generally increase during periods of 80% occupancy. It was emphasized that these complaints should be resolved for guest satisfaction.

Li and Ryan (2020) aimed to examine the perceptions of guests about North Korea hotels in their study. As a result of the study, it was stated that hotel evaluation criteria do not provide complete information about the satisfaction levels and opinions of the guests due to a limited selection set. While the comments about hotels remain within a certain limit on the evaluation sites, it has been determined that regret and joy are presented more transparently in social media. In this respect, it was stated that it would be useful to examine social media and evaluation sites together in examining satisfaction.

Villenuve and O'Brien (2020) examined the relationship between the indoor environmental quality of the residences and the general satisfaction levels of the guests. 1.35 million comments in Canada on the Airbnb platform were analyzed by text mining method. As a result of the study, it was stated that the indoor environmental quality constitutes 5% of all complaints and has a significant effect on general guest satisfaction.

Merli, Preziosi, Acampora, Lucchetti and Ali (2019) aimed to determine how the green practices implemented by the environmentally friendly Italian Beach Club are perceived by the guests and how they affect guest satisfaction and loyalty. PLS-SEM was used in the study. In the study, guest environmental concern positively affects the attitude of guests towards green practices and their evaluations about green practices, the environmental concern of guests is not an important precursor of guest satisfaction, guest attitude towards green practices positively affects the evaluation of green practices, guest attitude towards environmental practices, guest satisfaction and the green practices of the beach club affect the guest satisfaction and loyalty positively.

Nunkoo, Teeroovengadum, Ringle and Sunnassee, (2019) aimed to reveal the effect of the quality of the services offered by hotel businesses operating in South Africa on customer satisfaction according to different star ratings. By using multi-group analysis, importance performance map analysis and service quality performance scores through PLS-SEM, the rating of hotels with different stars and their effect on guest satisfaction were tried to be determined. It has been determined that one and two star hotels attach importance to the accommodation structure and employee expertise of their guests in terms of satisfaction. The determinants of satisfaction in three-star hotels are determined as safety and room quality. Satisfaction determinants of four and five star hotels emerged as waiting time and guest interaction factors.

Sukhu, Choi, Bujisic and Bilgihan (2019) aimed to examine the effect of various hotel elements on the satisfaction levels of the guests in their study. In the study, justified action theory and planned behavior theory are based. It was tried to determine the differences in the beliefs and attitudes of the guests about the common areas, rooms, ambiance, social and green areas of the hotels. According to the results of the study performed on 310 people in 4-star hotel enterprises; It was stated that guests who are emotionally connected to hotels do more word of mouth marketing than satisfied guests. It was emphasized that hotel managers should focus more on guests who are emotionally attached to the hotels.

Jin, Nicely, Fan and Adler (2019) examined the effect of service recovery time and completion of service recovery life cycle on guest satisfaction in their study. Data were collected through a scenario-based online survey with 495 participants. Joint service improvement within 30 minutes according to the results of the study; The fact that it has the greatest positive effect on the satisfaction of hotel guests, the shorter the duration, the more positively affected the satisfaction.

Merli, Preziosi, Acampora and Ali (2019) aimed to determine how hotel guests perceive "green hotel" practices and what kind of relationship is between their behavioral intentions. In addition, how the guest's environmental commitment affects guest satisfaction and loyalty was examined. According to the results of the study performed using PLS-SEM analysis; It was stated that guests perceive the environmental commitment of the hotels positively and significantly affect guest satisfaction and loyalty. In addition, it has been concluded that guests staying in a green hotel are more likely to develop loyalty towards green hotels.

Radojevic, Satinisic and Stanic (2019) examined the effect of the national culture of hotel employees and the services provided by the employees on the satisfaction of the guests. According to the results of the study; It has been stated that employees from countries with a low cultural dimension, Hofstede's Individuality and Tolerance, are particularly skilled in providing high quality hotel services. It has advantageous cultural profiles that are consistent with depictions of the hospitality culture of Asian countries such as Japan, Pakistan, Hong Kong, China, Lebanon, India, and the Philippines. For this, it has been emphasized that it is of great importance for the satisfaction of the guests.

Sánchez-Franco, Navarro-García and Rondán-Cataluña (2019) examined how terms related to guest experiences can be used to improve hospitality services and classify guest satisfaction. 47,172 reviews of 33 hotels operating in Las Vegas, registered on Yelp, a social networking site, were discussed. As a result of the study, it was emphasized that staff experience, professionalism and gambling-based attractions have an effect on customer satisfaction and how managers can make improvements in these matters.

Lin, Lai and Morrison (2019) examined the impact of physical environment and personal interactions on satisfaction and intention to visit again. The study was carried out using a survey technique for visitors staying in small hotels operating in Taiwan. As a result of the study, it was stated that personal interactions positively affect satisfaction, and that it affects the intention to visit again. Physical environment, on the other hand, has been found to have little effect on satisfaction and intention to revisit.

Tung, Chen and Schckert (2017) examined the effect of employee sensitivity towards customer citizenship behavior and corporate assurance on guest satisfaction, loyalty and perceived value creation. The study is based on attachment theory, self-adaptation theory, emotion infusion model and social change theories. An experimental design based on the scenario was applied in the study. As a result of the study, it was concluded that both employee sensitivity and organizational assurance significantly reduced guest satisfaction, loyalty and perceived value.

Furenes, Øgaard and Gjerald (2017) examined whether using face-to-face feedback would increase guest satisfaction or not. In the study, feedback was given to the guests, both verbally and in writing, and they were asked what kind of feedback affected the satisfaction. According to the results of the study, it was stated that verbal feedback is more sincere and valuable for the satisfaction of the guests.

Han and Hyun (2017) examined the effect of general image, physical environment, service and food quality on the satisfaction of the guests and their intention to visit the restaurant again. As a result of the study, it was stated that the quality dimensions have an effect on the guest satisfaction, the general image on the guest's decision making and the intention to visit the restaurant again.

Tussyadiah (2016) aimed to determine the factors that affect guests' satisfaction and their intention to visit again. According to the results of the study carried out using the online survey technique on 644 visitors in the USA; It has been determined that guest satisfaction is affected by entertainment factors, monetary advantages and accommodation opportunities. Entertainment factors and monetary benefits have also been shown to positively affect revisit intention.

Zhang and Cole (2016) aimed to determine the level of satisfaction of people with mobility difficulties with accommodation services. 543 comments on travel websites have been analyzed. As a result of the study, it was stated that room access, staff attitude, luggage and equipment support and general accommodation features have positive effects on the satisfaction of the guests.

Su, Swanson and Chen (2016) examined the relationship between perceived service quality, repeat purchase intention, subjective well-being and general customer satisfaction. According to the results of the study conducted on 451 Chinese hotel guests; The relationship between perceived service quality, repeat purchase intention, subjective well-being and guest satisfaction has been determined.

Chen, Yang, Li and Liu (2015) examined the effect of hotel price on guest satisfaction in their study. As a result of the study, it was stated that room prices and food and beverage prices at low price level increase customer satisfaction, while high price level has the opposite effect. It has been determined that there is an inverse U-shaped relationship between price level and guest satisfaction.

Berezan, Raab, Yoo and Love (2013) examined how sustainable hotel practices affect the satisfaction of hotel guests of different nationalities and their intention to return. Data were obtained from a popular tourism destination in Mexico using a survey technique. As a result of the study, it was stated that green practices of hotels have a positive relationship for Mexicans, Americans and other nations on the satisfaction levels and return intentions of the guests.

Ariffin (2013) determined the general aspects of hospitality for hotel services and examined the effects of these aspects on guest satisfaction. The data obtained from 305 hotel guests by structural equation modeling were analyzed. The hospitality aspects of the hotel were determined as personalization, comfort and warm welcome, and it was stated that personalization and warm welcome had an effect on guest satisfaction.

Mikulić and Prebežac (2011) examined the effects of animation programs on guest satisfaction in their studies. According to the results of the study conducted on 994 guests in Croatian hotels and holiday villages, it was stated that among the animation activities, sports activities, evening entertainment and entertainment programs for children differ from the satisfaction levels of the guests according to their accommodation type and demographic characteristics.

Lee, Kim, Kim and Lee (2010) examined the effect of the location of five-star hotels on guest satisfaction in their study. According to the results of the study conducted on guests staying in 17 five-star hotels operating in Korea, it has been determined that the guests care about the location of the hotels and having good access to security and transportation channels is important for their satisfaction.

Matzler, Pechlaner, Abfalter and Wolf (2005) examined the effects of correct responses to online questions on both booking behavior and guest satisfaction. As a result of the study, it was stated that the response rate, response time, and the quality of the answers have an effect on guest satisfaction. It was also concluded that the feedback was good even in the low season.

Heo, Jogaratnam and Buchanan (2004) examined how services such as menus, magazines and hotel guides in their own languages affect the satisfaction of American, Japanese and Korean guests. As a result of the study, it was emphasized that such personalized product adaptations have positive effects on satisfaction.

Choi and Chu (2001) examined the general satisfaction levels of guests from Hong Kong hotels and their intention to visit again. As a result of the study, it was stated that the personnel service quality, room qualities, general facilities, value and security factors affect the general satisfaction level of the guests and their intention to visit again.

Spinelli and Canavos (2000) examined the relationship between employee satisfaction and guest satisfaction in their study. The study was carried out on 240 hotel employees and 600 hotel guests. At the end of the study, it was stated that monetary factors negatively affect employee satisfaction, and appreciation of employees positively affects satisfaction. In addition, it was concluded that the fast, competent and friendly staff positively affected the satisfaction of the guests.

King and Garey (1997) examined the effect of employees' interactions with customers on guest satisfaction. According to the results of the study carried out using the survey technique, it was stated that while bureaucratic climate, excessive workload and stress-related factors reduce employee satisfaction, they also negatively affect guest satisfaction rates.

Gundersen, Haide and Olsson (1996) aimed to determine what aspects of the hotel experience guests consider important, what their perception of the hotel is about the quality of the hotel and what its effect on guests' satisfaction. It was stated that the tangible and intangible elements of the reception, housekeeping and food and beverage departments affect the general satisfaction level of the guests.

Some studies for analyzing the guests' experiences, examining the prior templates and determining future tendencies by text mining have been found in tourism sector. Garci, Barriocanal, Sicilia and Korfiatis (2010) have analyzed guests' positive and negative comments by text mining method in their study. It has been stated in the study that online comments are important for hotel quality assessment. It has been determined in the study, which have been conducted with online comments for the hotels of London, that hotel location, room size, stuff, cleanness, comfort, temperature, pollution and maintenance are taken into consideration (O'Connor, 2010). It has been shown that hotel cleaned is important for guests in this study which aims to determine motivation factors about guests' hotel evaluation. In addition, it has been stated in the study that the location, the transportation and proximity to malls provide more positive comments (Barreda and Bilgihan, 2013). Xiang, Schwartz and Gerdes (2015) has analyzed the association between guests' experiences and satisfactions by text mining and an association has been found. Another study has developed marketing strategies for cruise sector by analyzing Twitter comments (Park, Ok and Chae, 2016). Online examination about prices can be shown as concrete evidence which shows the influence of the online comments on potential guests (Moro, Rita and Oliveira, 2018). Similarly, Ghosh (2018) has determined the impact on booking intentions. These studies are important to reveal the efficiency to improve marketing strategies and to analyze online comments by analyzing guests' expectations.

METHODOLOGY

This study aims to determine satisfaction conditions of guests by considering whether guests are satisfied or not by analyzing comments of user about 5-star hotels in Turkey. The text mining method has been selected as the methodology of this study by supposing that significant results can be obtained by huge amount of data from online comments hotel guests. With the text mining method, words are grouped and their relations with each other are determined. (Aggarwal, 2012).

Sample and Data

The comments that have been used in this study have been gained from TripAdvisor site which is the most popular travel site with 250 billion of guests' comments (see; www.tripadvisor.com). This site is a popular web site in which guests can express their ideas and experiences freely with positive or negative comments. This site includes important benefits since guests can examine the comments and experiences when they decide to have a holiday. The online comments about hotels have been transferred from web media by an automatic web browser. This study has been conducted in Turkey which is regarded as an important destination in Mediterranean and it welcomes tourists from variety of the World. It has been determined from travel site that there are 116 of 5-star hotels in Turkey. Total 58.193 online comments about 5-star hotels in Turkey have been analyzed from the travel site. The comments have been obtained between February and March in 2020. The comments about the hotels have been downloaded with a Webharvy program that is used for Web mining. The data have been transferred to the Excel program and they have prepared for the text mining application. Research population has in Tripadvisor comments of the 5 star hotels in Turkey. All reviews of hotels have been obtained from Tripadvisor. Table 1 shows the sample data set about hotel comments.

Table 1. Sample Data Set about Hotel Comments

ID	Hotel Name	Comment
1	A	"I'm very happy about your service. It was fairly well, thanks a lot for your attention. Actually, I liked the breakfast in Adana. Really enjoyed that, and finally. Personnel are so good. pleasant. I will most definitely be back when I next visit Istanbul"
2	B	"A great hotel with great services. The food is excellent and the staff is very friendly and helpful. The view from the hotel is very beautiful and calm. The prices are very normal, and the hotel location is good because it's near all the useful places. I'm so happy that i was their guest in Adana, and if I will come back, I will choose this hotel again and again."
3	C	"I stayed at Sea Mansion Suites in April together with my family. We have been given a suite with s wonderful sea view! The accommodation was first class in terms of bed comfort, bathroom facilities and suite size. Breakfast was nice. Location is very good since it is closed to Topkapi Palace, blue mosque is near also. Good choice for families! Recommend !!"

Data Analysis

After the comments about hotels had been downloaded, text mining step was passed. RapidMiner program has been preferred for text mining analysis. RapidMiner is a program with "open source software" which is written in Java language and which is easily used in academic studies. Hence, this program has been used. RapidMiner works by operator functions that are linked with drag and drop method to each other and required parameters may be determined easily by clicking operator functions. Coding knowledge is not required thanks to this property. Many data can be processed and many significant information can be obtained by these data thanks to this program (Çelik, Akçetin and Gök, 2017, pp.1-5). Obtained excel file have been transferred to RapidMiner program. A model has been prepared to separate the words in the comments one by one, to extract word frequencies and for association analysis (Antonio et. al., 2018). Fig 1 shows the design of the model that has been developed during the data pre-processing step.

Fig 1 shows the operator of the model formed in RapidMiner program. These operators work to realize "transform cases", "tokenize", "filter stop words" and "stem" and "combination of similar words in a unique word stem". Table 2 shows descending sort of word frequencies obtained from comments about 5-star hotels and hotel rooms in Turkey.

Figure 1. View of data pre-processing design

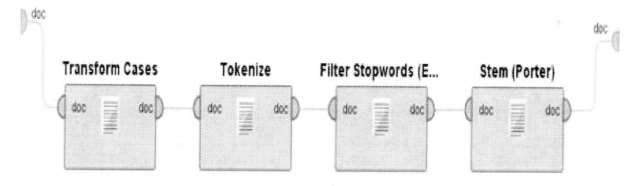

Association Analysis (Market Basket Analysis)

Association analysis is a kind of analysis, which determined the relationship between the objects in a data set and which explains the relationship of an object with another. The words stem, which have been obtained when the word frequency analysis was made, have been subjected to the association analysis and the association rules of the words in the comments have been revealed. Therefore, frequencies of the words in the comments about 5-star hotels in Turkey have been determined with reliance parameters and the visitors' perceptions about hotel image have been established.

The model, which was used in the application of association analysis, is shown in Fig 2.

Figure 2. Research model

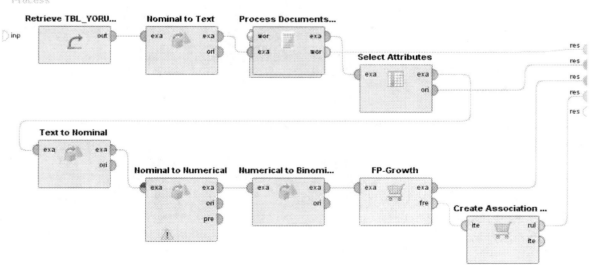

According to Fig 2, the frequencies obtained in the Process Documents file have been turned into certain properties by Select Attributes. The presence of a word in a comment should be known in order to extract the association rules of the words. Thus the document term matrix has been formed initially. The word matrix has been formed by passing the 'Text to Nominal, Nominal to Numerical, Numerical to Binominal' steps in the formed attributes. Table 2 shows the sample of word matrix.

Table 2. Sample of Document Term Matrix

No	Hotel	Breakfast	Location	Restaurant	Room	Pool	Clean	Delicious	Amazing
1	False	True	False	True	False	True	True	False	True
2	True	False	True	False	True	False	False	True	False
3	True	True	False	True	True	False	True	True	True
4	True	True	True	True	False	True	False	False	False
5	False	True	True	False	True	True	True	True	True

As it is seen in Table 2, the words which are used in the comments get "true" figure and the words which aren't used in the comment get "false" figure. The association rules (Market Basket Analysis) have been obtained then by subjecting the word matrix obtained to association analysis. As it is seen in Fig 2, the algorithm, which has been used in rule formation, is Fp-Growth algorithm. The Fp-Growth algorithm is an algorithm, which is used to determine the most frequently used objects in a data set. This algorithm which uses the divide and rule strategy scans the objects in the data set and it forms the rules with data tree by calculating the backup figures (Ikhwan, Yetri, Syahra, Halim, Siahaan, Aryza and Yacob 2018, p.1663). Association analysis benefits from confidence criteria when it forms the rules. In accordance with the established model, the confidence figure has been determined as 0.678. The rules, which have been obtained because of analysis, are presented in this context.

SOLUTIONS AND RECOMMENDATIONS

This part presents the positive and negative adjective and association analysis outcomes obtained from the comments about hotels.

Word Frequencies about Positive and Negative Adjectives

Table 3 shows data binning of frequencies and percentages about positive adjectives in the comments that were made about 5-star hotels in Turkey.

When Table 3 is examined it is seen that 48,38% of good, 46,97% of great, 33,48% of nice, 23,50% of excellent adjectives are used as positive adjectives in the comments about 5-star hotels in Turkey. It may be stated that guests use positive adjectives in high incidence in the comments. Since guests have used "helpful" adjectives (22,14%) for staff, it may be an evidence that shows staff is generally helpful. The adjectives of amazing, beautiful, perfect, wonderful, spacious, fantastic, enjoyed have been used commonly so it may be inferred that hotel guests think positive about the hotels and the services provided by the hotels. The usage of "comfortable" and "modern" adjectives may be the evidence that shows hotels are modern comfortable. The rare adjectives are; generous (0,59%), delightful (0, 66%)

Determination of Guest Satisfaction by Text Mining

and luckily (0, 67%) in the comments. Table 4 shows data binning of frequencies and percentages about negative adjectives in the comments that were made about 5-star hotels in Turkey.

Table 3. Word Frequencies and Percentages of Positive Adjectives from 5-Star Hotels in Turkey

Words	f	%	Words	f	%
good	28151.0	48.38%	smile	1347.0	2.31%
great	27336.0	46.97%	efficient	1255.0	2.16%
nice	19484.0	33.48%	incredible	1216.0	2.09%
excellent	13677.0	23.50%	pretty	1216.0	2.09%
helpful	12884.0	22.14%	plenty	1144.0	1.97%
amazing	12117.0	20.82%	gorgeous	1047.0	1.80%
comfortable	9075.0	15.59%	courteous	1022.0	1.76%
beautiful	8512.0	14.63%	quick	918.0	1.58%
perfect	7866.0	13.52%	elegant	890.0	1.53%
wonderful	6416.0	11.03%	tasty	886.0	1.52%
spacious	5192.0	8.92%	breathtaking	873.0	1.50%
fantastic	4529.0	7.78%	unique	811.0	1.39%
enjoyed	4050.0	6.96%	nicely	786.0	1.35%
modern	3893.0	6.69%	impressive	718.0	1.23%
professional	3561.0	6.12%	comfy	681.0	1.17%
delicious	3226.0	5.54%	magnificent	671.0	1.15%
quiet	2574.0	4.42%	brilliant	658.0	1.13%
luxury	2314.0	3.98%	impeccable	636.0	1.09%
huge	2236.0	3.84%	surprised	628.0	1.08%
attentive	2190.0	3.76%	charming	618.0	1.06%
happy	2157.0	3.71%	famous	616.0	1.06%
pleasant	1971.0	3.39%	renovated	604.0	1.04%
super	1937.0	3.33%	priced	480.0	0.82%
fresh	1835.0	3.15%	trained	478.0	0.82%
expensive	1791.0	3.08%	cozy	452.0	0.78%
luxurious	1702.0	2.92%	peaceful	409.0	0.70%
fabulous	1508.0	2.59%	calm	397.0	0.68%
stunning	1484.0	2.55%	lucky	390.0	0.67%
relaxing	1454.0	2.50%	delightful	385.0	0.66%
smile	1347.0	2.31%	generous	343.0	0.59%
awesome	1304.0	2.24%			

Table 4 shows that the negative adjectives of 2, 10% of noise, 1, 53% of disappointed, 1,22% of negative have been commonly used in the comments. The negative adjectives of regret (0,45%), worst

(0, 57%), dirty (0,63%) have been rarely used in the comments instead. It may be said that the most disturbing point is noise for guests. It may be referred that certain services have disappointed the guests since the adjective of "disappointed" have presented in the comments. The adjective of "negative" may show that negative emotions have been experienced in certain services.

Table 4. Word Frequencies and Percentages of Negative Adjectives from 5-Star Hotels in Turkey

Words	f	%
noise	1220.0	2.10%
disappointed	893.0	1.53%
negative	709.0	1.22%
limited	670.0	1.15%
crowded	527.0	0.91%
wrong	448.0	0.77%
lack	396.0	0.68%
dirty	365.0	0.63%
worst	332.0	0.57%
regret	259.0	0.45%

Compared to negative and positive adjectives in general, it can be said that positive adjectives are more commonly used than negative adjectives. It can also be expressed that guests generally think positively about hotels and hotel services.

Association Analysis Results

Table 5 shows the words used in conjunction with the word "hotel". A review of Table 5 found that the words "Good, beautiful, wonderful, beautiful, spacious, excellent, amazing, beautiful, wonderful, pleasure, fantastic, pleasant, excellent, Super" were used together with the word "hotel"." When these words are examined, we can express that guests are extremely happy with 5-star hotels in Turkey. In addition, the words" luxury, quality, variety, access, large and quiet "were also used with the word" hotel". Therefore, it can be concluded that hotels are clean, high quality, comfortable, luxurious, affordable, variable and large. Since the words "helpful and friendly" are used for hotel staff, it seems that the hotel staff is helpful and friendly. The use of the word" delicious " suggests that the food and beverage services of hotels are delicious. Since guests use the words" Thank you and happy", it can be concluded that guests are thankful and happy for the services of hotels and hotels.

The positive comments have been generally used with the word of "hotel". Therefore, it may be stated that guests have positive opinion and that they are satisfied with the hotels.

Table 5. Association Rules Related to the Word of "Hotel" obtained from 5-Star Hotel Managements in Turkey

Words	Result	Reliability Value
good	hotel	0.899
nice	hotel	0.888
clean	hotel	0.876
great	hotel	0.876
helpful	hotel	0.866
modern	hotel	0.863
beautiful	hotel	0.862
friendly	hotel	0.855
comfortable	hotel	0.855
luxury	hotel	0.842
spacious	hotel	0.842
excellent	hotel	0.837
amazing	hotel	0.832
lovely	hotel	0.826
problem	hotel	0.813
wonderful	hotel	0.812
quality	hotel	0.811
quiet	hotel	0.810
enjoyed	hotel	0.801
variety	hotel	0.800
fantastic	hotel	0.795
pleasant	hotel	0.795
access	hotel	0.795
perfect	hotel	0.793
huge	hotel	0.792
super	hotel	0.777
delicious	hotel	0.775
thank	hotel	0.766
happy	hotel	0.760

Table 6 presents the words used with "staff, bed and breakfast". Looking at Table 6, it seems that the word "staff" is used with the words "friendly, helpful, wonderful, clean, good, amazing, excellent, beautiful and professional". Therefore, it can be said that guests perceive the staff as "friendly, helpful, wonderful, good, amazing and pleasant". It can also be added that guests see staff as clean and staff provide professional services in accordance with guests' perception. The word "room" was also used with the words "appearance and comfort". It can be concluded that guests are satisfied with the view and comfort of the rooms in the hotels. The word " breakfast" was used with the words "buffet, great, good

Table 6. Association Rules related to the Words of "Staff, Room and Breakfast" Obtained from 5-Star Hotel Managements in Turkey

Words	Result	Reliability Value
friendly, helpful	staff	0.880
great	staff	0.862
clean	staff	0.831
good	staff	0.818
amazing	staff	0.813
excellent	staff	0.807
nice	staff	0.774
professional	staff	0.706
Words	**Result**	**Reliability Value**
view	room	0.770
comfortable	room	0.678
Words	**Result**	**Reliability Value**
great, buffet	breakfast	0.853
good	breakfast	0.827
variety	breakfast	0.765

Figure 3. Association rules for staff, breakfast and room words

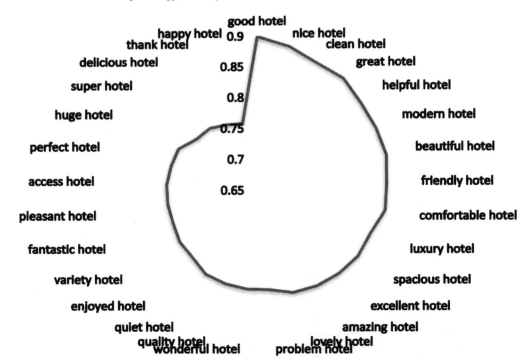

and varied". According to this finding, it can be stated that guests are satisfied with the hotels' buffet breakfast services and consider these services to be "excellent, good and variable". Chart 3 shows the comparison of the words "hotel, staff, bed and breakfast" with other words of hotel guests.

Figure 4.

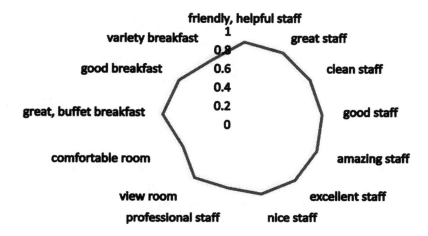

When Fig 3 and 4 is examined it is seen that guests have used positive adjective about "hotel, staff, room and breakfast". Therefore, it may be stated that they are satisfied with the services provided. It is determined by the association analysis conducted that no negative adjective has been used. This state shows the high satisfaction level. Although certain negative adjectives have been determined in frequency analysis, it may not affect the satisfaction level of the guests since they have been rarely used.

FUTURE RESEARCH DIRECTIONS

It is expected that the outcomes of this study will encourage many other researches in this field. The next studies may be conducted with different hotels in different classes. Besides, the guests' satisfaction may be measured with other online comments about different destinations in other countries like Greece or Spain.

CONCLUSION

This study aims to examine hotel guests' online comments about hotels by analyzing them to understand their satisfaction with hotels. This study was conducted using the text mining technique and determined whether hotel guests were satisfied with the hotel, staff, bed and breakfast factors. In addition, positive and negative adjectives were extracted from the comments and an attempt was made to determine the overall level of satisfaction. From the data obtained, it can be concluded that guests are generally satisfied with hotels. We can clearly infer this result with the positive adjectives used by guests and the words "hotel, staff, rooms and breakfast." Since no negative adjectives are used in the relationship analysis, it can also be concluded that the hotel guests are satisfied.

According to the results of the research, it is concluded that the guests are satisfied with the staff being helpful and friendly. The results of the study coincide with the results of Padma and Ahn (2020), Nunkoo et. al (2019), Zhang and Cole (2016), Ariffin (2013), Choi and Chu (2001), Spinelli and Canavos (2000).

Another thing that guests are satisfied with is that the hotels and rooms are modern, comfortable, clean, high quality, luxurious, accessible, diverse and large. The results of the study are Lin, Lai and Morrison (2019), Tussyadiah (2016), Lee et. al. (2010), Choi and Chu (2001), Padma and Ahn (2020), Nunkoo et. al. (2019), Sánchez-Franco et. al (2019), Zhang and Cole (2016) show similarities with the results of their studies. Another result is that guests report their dissatisfaction with the noise in the hotels. This result of the study also supports the results of the study conducted by Villenuve and O'Brien (2020).

When the study's findings were examined, it was found that guests used positive adjectives for a high proportion of hotels. On the other hand, negative reviews are low-incidence, and the words "noise, frustration, and negative" have been used prominently. However, these negative adjectives did not appear in the association analysis. In terms of low incidence rate and lack of association analysis, it can be said that these negative adjectives have no effect on the satisfaction level of hotel guests. In accordance with the association analysis of the word" hotel "and other words, the word" hotel " is good, beautiful and perfect, etc.it has been used in conjunction with other positive adjectives, including. It can be said that hotel guests are generally satisfied with hotels. The results of the study include: guests see staff as "helpful and friendly," they see breakfast as "variable and excellent, and rooms as comfortable."

If the results of the study are considered in terms of contributions to operational management, it is important to analyze guest feedback, study these feedback, and develop marketing strategies for guests. Analysis of travel booking systems by text mining method is particularly valuable for understanding the profile of guests and developing effective activities in holiday decisions.

This study provides two contributions. Firstly, it supports the decisions about quality of the hotel services and assessment of the satisfaction that have been examined in the previous studies. Unlike the traditional methods that are used to measure the service quality, this method has conducted a study in which both concrete and abstract factors are evaluated. This study has also provided contributions about service quality theory in addition to concrete analysis findings about the services like rooms, breakfast and abstract analysis findings about staff. The second contribution of the study is that it has used text mining method. This approach provides opportunity to hotel managers and researchers to study with huge data and to obtain significant patterns. Text mining approach provides positive contributions to understand and to perceive the guests better and to design and to market the services better. The hotel managers and researchers can determine the trends and the factors about their guests and can determine the satisfaction levels of the guests by using text mining method since online comments are becoming wider day by day. Therefore, it may be suggested that online comments may be evaluated by text mining method regularly. Hotel managers should examine online comments determine weak and strong aspects of the rivals and to compare and to analyze the differences between their services provided. The examination of the comments obtained will provide opportunity to understand their state in the sector and to improve action plan accordingly. The manager may also follow the rivals' reputation and their activities. The hotel managers may improve their marketing plans and strategies by using the text mining methods.

This study contains certain restrictions. This study has only been conducted in the sample frame which includes only online comments about 5-star hotels in Turkey in a travel site. Taking into account all of these factors, findings may vary according to different hotel types.

REFERENCES

Aggarwal, C. C., & Zhai, C. (2012). An introduction to text mining. *Mining Text Data*, 1–10. doi:10.1007/978-1-4614-3223-4_1

Antonio, N., de Almeida, A., Nunes, L., Batista, F., & Ribeiro, R. (2018). Hotel online reviews: Different languages, different opinions. *Information Technology & Tourism*, *18*(1), 157–185. doi:10.100740558-018-0107-x

Ariffin, A. A. M. (2013). Generic dimensionality of hospitality in the hotel industry: A host–guest relationship perspective. *International Journal of Hospitality Management*, *35*, 171–179. doi:10.1016/j.ijhm.2013.06.002

Banerjee, S., & Chua, A. Y. K. (2016). In search of patterns among travellers' hotel ratings in TripAdvisor. *Tourism Management*, *53*, 125–131. doi:10.1016/j.tourman.2015.09.020

Barreda, A., & Bilgihan, A. (2013). An analysis of user generated content for hotel experiences. *Journal of Hospitality and Tourism Technology*, *4*(3), 263–280. doi:10.1108/JHTT-01-2013-0001

Berezan, O., Raab, C., Yoo, M., & Love, C. (2013). Sustainable hotel practices and nationality: The impact on guest satisfaction and guest intention to return. *International Journal of Hospitality Management*, *34*, 227–233. doi:10.1016/j.ijhm.2013.03.010

Cadotte, E. R., & Turgeon, N. (1988). Key factors in guest satisfaction. *The Cornell H.R. AQ (Balmain, N.S.W.)*, *28*(4), 44–51.

Çelik, U., Akçetin, E., & Gök, M. (2017). RapidMiner ile Uygulamalı Veri Madenciliği. Pusala Yayınevi.

Chen, C. M., Yang, H. W., Li, E. Y., & Liu, C. C. (2015). How does hotel pricing influence guest satisfaction by the moderating influence of room occupancy? *International Journal of Hospitality Management*, *49*, 136–138. doi:10.1016/j.ijhm.2015.06.006

Choi, T. Y., & Chu, R. (2001). Determinants of hotel guests' satisfaction and repeat patronage in the Hong Kong hotel industry. *International Journal of Hospitality Management*, *20*(3), 277–297. doi:10.1016/S0278-4319(01)00006-8

Dolnicar, S., & Grün, B. (2007). Assessing analytical robustness in cross-cultural comparisons. *International Journal of Culture, Tourism and Hospitality Research*, *1*(2), 140–160. doi:10.1108/17506180710751687

Dolnicar, S., & Otter, T. (2003). Which hotel attributes matter? A review of previous and a framework for future research. *Proceedings of the 9th annual conference of the Asia Pacific tourism association*, 176-188.

Ekiz, E., & Au, N. (2011). Comparing Chinese and American attitudes towards complaining. *International Journal of Contemporary Hospitality Management, 23*(3), 327–343. doi:10.1108/09596111111122514

Furenes, M. I., Øgaard, T., & Gjerald, O. (2017). How face-to-face feedback influences guest outcome evaluation of co-production: Changing or shaping guest experiences? *Tourism Management Perspectives, 21*, 59–65. doi:10.1016/j.tmp.2016.11.004

García-Barriocanal, E., Sicilia, M.-A., & Korfiatis, N. (2010). Exploring hotel service quality experience indicators in user-generated content: A case using Tripadvisor data. In *Mediterranean Conference on Information Systems (MCIS) 2010 Proceedings* (Paper No. 33). Tel Aviv, Israel: AIS Electronic Libary (AISeL).

García-Pablos, A., Cuadros, M., & Linaza, M. T. (2016). Automatic analysis of textual hotel reviews. *Information Technology & Tourism, 16*(1), 45–69. doi:10.100740558-015-0047-7

Ghosh, T. (2018). Predicting hotel book intention: The influential role of helpfulness and advocacy of online reviews. *Journal of Hospitality Marketing & Management, 27*(3), 299–322. doi:10.1080/19368623.2017.1364198

Gretzel, U., & Yoo, H. K. (2008). Use and impact of online travel reviews. *Information and Communication Technologies in Tourism, 2008*(2), 35–46. doi:10.1007/978-3-211-77280-5_4

Gundersen, M. G., Heide, M., & Olsson, U. H. (1996). Hotel guest satisfaction among business travelers: What are the important factors? *The Cornell Hotel and Restaurant Administration Quarterly, 37*(2), 72–81. doi:10.1177/001088049603700222

Gursoy, D. (2019). A critical review of determinants of information search behavior and utilization of online reviews in decision making process. *International Journal of Hospitality Management, 76*, 53–60. doi:10.1016/j.ijhm.2018.06.003

Han, H., & Hyun, S. S. (2017). Impact of hotel-restaurant image and quality of physical-environment, service, and food on satisfaction and intention. *International Journal of Hospitality Management, 63*, 82–92. doi:10.1016/j.ijhm.2017.03.006

Hargreaves, C. A. (2015). Analysis of hotel guest satisfaction ratings and reviews: An application in Singapore. *American Journal of Marketing Research, 1*(4), 208–214.

Heo, J. K., Jogaratnam, G., & Buchanan, P. (2004). Customer-focused adaptation in New York City hotels: Exploring the perceptions of Japanese and Korean travelers. *International Journal of Hospitality Management, 23*(1), 39–53. doi:10.1016/j.ijhm.2003.07.003

Herzberg, F., Mausner, B., & Snyderman, B. B. (1959). *The motivation to work*. John Wiley and Sons.

Ikhwan, A., Yetri, M., Syahra, Y., Halim, J., Siahaan, A. P. U., Aryza, S., & Yacob, Y. M. (2018). A Novelty of Data Mining for Promoting Education based on FP-Growth Algorithm. *International Journal of Civil Engineering and Technology, 9*(7), 1660–1669.

Jannach, D., Zanker, M., & Fuchs, M. (2014). Leveraging multi-criteria customer feedback for satisfaction analysis and improved recommendations. *Information Technology & Tourism, 14*(2), 119–149. doi:10.100740558-014-0010-z

Jin, D., Nicely, A., Fan, A., & Adler, H. (2019). Joint effect of service recovery types and times on customer satisfaction in lodging. *Journal of Hospitality and Tourism Management, 38*, 149–158. doi:10.1016/j.jhtm.2019.01.005

King, C. A., & Garey, J. G. (1997). Relational quality in service encounters. *International Journal of Hospitality Management, 16*(1), 39–63. doi:10.1016/S0278-4319(96)00045-X

Lee, K. W., Kim, H. B., Kim, H. S., & Lee, D. S. (2010). The determinants of factors in FIT guests' perception of hotel location. *Journal of Hospitality and Tourism Management, 17*(1), 167–174. doi:10.1375/jhtm.17.1.167

Li, F. S., & Ryan, C. (2020). Western guest experiences of a Pyongyang international hotel, North Korea: Satisfaction under conditions of constrained choice. *Tourism Management, 76*, 103947. doi:10.1016/j.tourman.2019.07.001

Lin, Y. C., Lai, H. J., & Morrison, A. M. (2019). Social servicescape and Asian students: An analysis of spring break island bed and breakfast experiences in Taiwan. *Tourism Management Perspectives, 31*, 165–173. doi:10.1016/j.tmp.2019.04.005

Lu, W., & Stepchenkova, S. (2015). User-generated content as a research mode in tourism and hospitality applications: Topics, methods, and software. *Journal of Hospitality Marketing & Management, 24*(2), 119–154. doi:10.1080/19368623.2014.907758

Marine-Roig, E., & Clave, S. A. (2015). Tourism analytics with massive usergenerated content: A case study of Barcelona. *Journal of Destination Marketing & Management, 4*(3), 162–172. doi:10.1016/j.jdmm.2015.06.004

Matzler, K., Pechlaner, H., Abfalter, D., & Wolf, M. (2005). Determinants of response to customer e-mail enquiries to hotels: Evidence from Austria. *Tourism Management, 26*(2), 249–259. doi:10.1016/j.tourman.2003.10.001

Merli, R., Preziosi, M., Acampora, A., & Ali, F. (2019). Why should hotels go green? Insights from guests experience in green hotels. *International Journal of Hospitality Management, 81*, 169–179. doi:10.1016/j.ijhm.2019.04.022

Merli, R., Preziosi, M., Acampora, A., Lucchetti, M. C., & Ali, F. (2019). The impact of green practices in coastal tourism: An empirical investigation on an eco-labelled beach club. *International Journal of Hospitality Management, 77*, 471–482. doi:10.1016/j.ijhm.2018.08.011

Mikulić, J., & Prebežac, D. (2011). Evaluating hotel animation programs at Mediterranean sun-and-sea resorts: An impact-asymmetry analysis. *Tourism Management, 32*(3), 688–696. doi:10.1016/j.tourman.2010.05.026

Moro, S., Rita, P., & Oliveira, C. (2018). Factors influencing hotels' online prices. *Journal of Hospitality Marketing & Management, 27*(4), 443–464. doi:10.1080/19368623.2018.1395379

Nunkoo, R., Teeroovengadum, V., Ringle, C. M., & Sunnassee, V. (2019). Service quality and customer satisfaction: The moderating effects of hotel star rating. *International Journal of Hospitality Management*, 102–414. doi:10.1016/j.ijhm.2019.102414

O'Connor, P. (2008). User-generated content and travel: A case study on TripAdvisor.com. *Information and Communication Technologies in Tourism*, *2008*(2), 47–58. doi:10.1007/978-3-211-77280-5_5

O'Connor, P. (2010). Managing a hotel's image on TripAdvisor. *Journal of Hospitality Marketing & Management*, *19*(7), 754–772. doi:10.1080/19368623.2010.508007

Padma, P., & Ahn, J. (2020). Guest satisfaction and dissatisfaction in luxury hotels: An application of big data. *International Journal of Hospitality Management*, *84*, 102–318. doi:10.1016/j.ijhm.2019.102318

Park, S. B., Ok, C. M., & Chae, B. K. (2016). Using twitter data for cruise tourism marketing and research. *Journal of Travel & Tourism Marketing*, *33*(6), 885–898. doi:10.1080/10548408.2015.1071688

Qu, H., Ryan, B., & Chu, R. (2000). The importance of hotel attributes in contributing to travelers' satisfaction in the Hong Kong hotel industry. *Journal of Quality Assurance in Hospitality & Tourism*, *1*(3), 65–83. doi:10.1300/J162v01n03_04

Radojevic, T., Stanisic, N., & Stanic, N. (2019). The culture of hospitality: From anecdote to evidence. *Annals of Tourism Research*, *79*, 102789. doi:10.1016/j.annals.2019.102789

Rhee, H. T., & Yang, S.-B. (2015). Does hotel attribute importance differ by hotel? Focusing on hotel star-classifications and customers' overall ratings. *Computers in Human Behavior*, *50*, 576–587. doi:10.1016/j.chb.2015.02.069

Ruan, Y. (2020). Perceived host-guest sociability similarity and participants' satisfaction: Perspectives of airbnb guests and hosts. *Journal of Hospitality and Tourism Management*, *45*, 419–428. doi:10.1016/j.jhtm.2020.09.009

Sánchez-Franco, M. J., Navarro-García, A., & Rondán-Cataluña, F. J. (2019). A naive Bayes strategy for classifying customer satisfaction: A study based on online reviews of hospitality services. *Journal of Business Research*, *101*, 499–506. doi:10.1016/j.jbusres.2018.12.051

Sann, R., & Lai, P. C. (2020). Understanding homophily of service failure within the hotel guest cycle: Applying NLP-aspect-based sentiment analysis to the hospitality industry. *International Journal of Hospitality Management*, *91*, 102–678. doi:10.1016/j.ijhm.2020.102678

Schuckert, M., Liu, X., & Law, R. (2015). A segmentation of online reviews by language groups: How English and non-English speakers rate hotels differently. *International Journal of Hospitality Management*, *48*, 143–149. doi:10.1016/j.ijhm.2014.12.007

Schuckert, M., Liu, X., & Law, R. (2016). Insights into suspicious online ratings: Direct evidence from TripAdvisor. *Asia Pacific Journal of Tourism Research*, *21*(3), 259–272. doi:10.1080/10941665.2015.1029954

Sparks, B. A., & Browning, V. (2011). The impact of online reviews on hotel booking intentions and perception of trust. *Tourism Management*, *32*(6), 1310–1323. doi:10.1016/j.tourman.2010.12.011

Spinelli, M. A., & Canavos, G. C. (2000). Investigating the relationhip between employee satisfaction and guest satisfaction. *Cornell Hotel and Restaurant Administration Quarterly*, *41*(6), 29-33.7

Stringam, B. B., & Gerdes, J. (2010). An analysis of word-of-mouse ratings and guest comments of online hotel distribution sites. *Journal of Hospitality Marketing and Management, 19*(7), 773–796.

Su, L., Swanson, S. R., & Chen, X. (2016). The effects of perceived service quality on repurchase intentions and subjective well-being of Chinese tourists: The mediating role of relationship quality. *Tourism Management, 52*, 82–95. doi:10.1016/j.tourman.2015.06.012

Su, N., Reynolds, D., & Sun, B. (2015). How to make your Facebook posts attractive: A case study of a leading budget hotel brand fan page. *International Journal of Contemporary Hospitality Management, 27*(8), 1772–1790. doi:10.1108/IJCHM-06-2014-0302

Sukhu, A., Choi, H., Bujisic, M., & Bilgihan, A. (2019). Satisfaction and positive emotions: A comparison of the influence of hotel guests' beliefs and attitudes on their satisfaction and emotions. *International Journal of Hospitality Management, 77*, 51–63. doi:10.1016/j.ijhm.2018.06.013

TripAdvisor. (2020). *Fact sheet*. Retrieved on from https://tripadvisor.mediaroom.com/US-about-us

Tse, A. C. B. (2001). How much more are consumers willing to pay for a higher level of service? A preliminary survey. *Journal of Services Marketing, 15*(1), 11–17. doi:10.1108/08876040110381328

Tse, E. C.-Y., & Ho, S.-C. (2009). Service quality in the hotel industry: When cultural contexts matter. *Cornell Hospitality Quarterly, 50*(4), 460–474. doi:10.1177/1938965509338453

Tung, V. W. S., Chen, P. J., & Schuckert, M. (2017). Managing customer citizenship behaviour: The moderating roles of employee responsiveness and organizational reassurance. *Tourism Management, 59*, 23–35. doi:10.1016/j.tourman.2016.07.010

Turban, E., Sharda, R., & Delen, D. (2010). *Decision support and business intelligence systems* (9th ed.). Prentice Hall.

Tussyadiah, I. P. (2016). Factors of satisfaction and intention to use peer-to-peer accommodation. *International Journal of Hospitality Management, 55*, 70–80. doi:10.1016/j.ijhm.2016.03.005

Villeneuve, H., & O'Brien, W. (2020). Listen to the guests: Text-mining Airbnb reviews to explore indoor environmental quality. *Building and Environment, 169*, 106–555. doi:10.1016/j.buildenv.2019.106555

Wang, D., Chan, H., & Pan, S. (2015). The impacts of mass media on organic destination image: A case study of Singapore. *Asia Pacific Journal of Tourism Research, 20*(8), 860–874. doi:10.1080/10941665.2014.948464

Xiang, Z., Schwartz, Z., Gerdes, J. H. Jr, & Uysal, M. (2015). What can big data and text analytics tell us about hotel guest experience and satisfaction? *International Journal of Hospitality Management, 44*, 120–130. doi:10.1016/j.ijhm.2014.10.013

Xie, H., Miao, L., Kuo, P.-J., & Lee, B.-Y. (2011). Consumers' responses to ambivalent online hotel reviews: The role of perceived source credibility and pre-decisional disposition. *International Journal of Hospitality Management, 30*, 178–183. doi:10.1016/j.ijhm.2010.04.008

Zhang, Y., & Cole, S. T. (2016). Dimensions of lodging guest satisfaction among guests with mobility challenges: A mixed-method analysis of web-based texts. *Tourism Management*, *53*, 13–27. doi:10.1016/j.tourman.2015.09.001

Zhou, L., Ye, S., Pearce, P. L., & Wu, M.-Y. (2014). Refreshing hotel satisfaction studies by reconfiguring customer review data. *International Journal of Hospitality Management*, *38*, 1–10. doi:10.1016/j.ijhm.2013.12.004

Zhu, L., Lin, Y., & Cheng, M. (2020). Sentiment and guest satisfaction with peer-to-peer accommodation: When are online ratings more trustworthy? *International Journal of Hospitality Management*, *86*, 102369. doi:10.1016/j.ijhm.2019.102369

ADDITIONAL READING

Chen, Y., & Xie, J. (2008). Online consumer review: Word-of-mouth as a new element of marketing communication mix. *Management Science*, *54*(3), 477–491. doi:10.1287/mnsc.1070.0810

De Wever, B., Schellens, T., Valcke, M., & Van Keer, H. (2006). Content analysis schemes to analyze transcripts of online asynchronous discussion groups: A review. *Computers & Education*, *46*(1), 6–28. doi:10.1016/j.compedu.2005.04.005

Jo, Y., & Oh, A. H. (2011, February). Aspect and sentiment unification model for online review analysis. In *Proceedings of the fourth ACM international conference on Web search and data mining* (pp. 815-824). 10.1145/1935826.1935932

King, R. A., Racherla, P., & Bush, V. D. (2014). What we know and don't know about online word-of-mouth: A review and synthesis of the literature. *Journal of Interactive Marketing*, *28*(3), 167–183. doi:10.1016/j.intmar.2014.02.001

Liu, Z., & Park, S. (2015). What makes a useful online review? Implication for travel product websites. *Tourism Management*, *47*, 140–151. doi:10.1016/j.tourman.2014.09.020

Mayzlin, D., Dover, Y., & Chevalier, J. (2014). Promotional reviews: An empirical investigation of online review manipulation. *The American Economic Review*, *104*(8), 2421–2455. doi:10.1257/aer.104.8.2421

Morahan-Martin, J. M. (2004). How internet users find, evaluate, and use online health information: A cross-cultural review. *Cyberpsychology & Behavior*, *7*(5), 497–510. doi:10.1089/cpb.2004.7.497 PMID:15667044

KEY TERMS AND DEFINITIONS

Big Data: Large-scale data, often obtained from online environments.
Guest: Customers arriving at the hotel.
Online Review: Expressing feelings and thoughts about an institution, person, or product on online websites.

Satisfaction: Feelings and behaviors after purchasing a product or service.

Text Mining: It is an analysis in which the word frequencies and hidden meanings of the texts are revealed.

TripAdvisor: A comprehensive website where tourists get information and write reviews about hotels and destinations.

Turkey: It is a developed country in terms of tourism, with an important geographical position between Europe and Asia.

Compilation of References

Abbate, C. S., & Di Nuovo, S. (2013). Motivation and personality traits for choosing religious tourism. Research on the case of Medjugorje. *Current Issues in Tourism*, *16*(5), 501–506. doi:10.1080/13683500.2012.749844

ABC. (2016). *Cuenca, 20 años como Ciudad Patrimonio de la Humanidad*. ABC. Retrieved from https://www.abc.es/espana/castilla-la-mancha/abci-cuenca-20-anos-como-ciudad-patrimonio-humanidad-201612061402_noticia.html

Abou-Shouk, M., Lim, W. M., & Megicks, P. (2013). Internet Adoption by Travel Agents: A Case of Egypt. *International Journal of Tourism Research*, *15*(3), 298–312. doi:10.1002/jtr.1876

Adame, M. (2019). *Redes sociales más usadas en el mundo hispano: tips para crecer tu presencia y alcance social*. Hootsuite. Retrieved from https://blog.hootsuite.com/es/redes-sociales-mas-usadas/

Adeola, O., & Evans, O. (2019). Digital tourism: Mobile phones, internet and tourism in Africa. *Tourism Recreation Research*, *44*(2), 190–202. doi:10.1080/02508281.2018.1562662

Adeola, O., & Evans, O. (2020). ICT, infrastructure, and tourism development in Africa. *Tourism Economics*, *26*(1), 97–114. doi:10.1177/1354816619827712

Adeyemi, T. O., & Olaleye, F. O. (2010). Information Communication and Technology (ICT) for the Effective Management of Secondary Schools for Sustainable Development in Ekiti State, Nigeria. *American-Eurasian Journal of Scientific Research*, *5*(2), 106–113.

Aggarwal, C. C., & Zhai, C. (2012). An introduction to text mining. *Mining Text Data*, 1–10. doi:10.1007/978-1-4614-3223-4_1

Agostino, D., & Sidorova, Y. (2016). A performance measurement system to quantify the contribution of social media: New requirements for metrics and methods. *Measuring Business Excellence*, *20*(2), 38–51. doi:10.1108/MBE-05-2015-0030

Ahmad, N. L., Rashid, W. E. W., Razak, N. A., Yusof, A. N. M., & Shah, N. S. M. (2013). Green Event Management and Initiatives for Sustainable Business Growt. *International Journal of Trade, Economics and Finance*. doi:10.7763/IJTEF.2013.V4.311

Ahmad, J., & Daud, N. (2016). Determining Innovative Tourism Event Professional Competency for Conventions and Exhibitions Industry: A Preliminary Study. *Procedia: Social and Behavioral Sciences*, *219*, 69–75. doi:10.1016/j.sbspro.2016.04.041

Ahmad, N. L., Mohd. Yusuf, A. N., Mohamed Shobri, N. D., & Wahab, S. (2012). The Relationship between Time Management and Job Performance in Event Management. *Procedia: Social and Behavioral Sciences*, *65*, 937–941. doi:10.1016/j.sbspro.2012.11.223

Compilation of References

Akbas, Y. E., Senturk, M., & Sancar, C. (2013). Testing for causality between the foreign direct investment, current account deficit, GDP and total credit: Evidence from G7. *Panoeconomicus*, *60*(6), 791–812. doi:10.2298/PAN1306791A

Albayrak, T., Caber, M., & Sigala, M. (2020). A quality measurement proposal for corporate social network sites: The case of hotel Facebook page. *Current Issues in Tourism*, 1–16. doi:10.1080/13683500.2020.1854199

Alcántara, B. (2017). *Instagram Stories llega a los 150 millones de usuarios diarios*. Xombit. Retrieved from https://xombit.com/2017/01/instagram-stories-150-millones-usuarios-diarios

Alford, P., & Clarke, S. (2009). Information technology and tourism a theoretical critique. *Technovation*, *29*(9), 580–587. doi:10.1016/j.technovation.2009.05.006

Ali, A., & Frew, A. J. (2014). ICT and sustainable tourism development: An innovative perspective. *Journal of Hospitality and Tourism Technology*, *5*(1), 2–16. doi:10.1108/JHTT-12-2012-0034

Alivizatou-Barakou, M., Kitsikidis, A., Tsalakanidou, F., Dimitropoulos, K., Giannis, C., Nikolopoulos, S., Al Kork, S., Denby, B., Buchman, L., Adda-Decker, M., Pillot-Loiseau, C., Tillmane, J., Dupont, S., Picart, B., Pozzi, F., Ott, M., Erdal, Y., Charisis, V., Hadjidimitriou, S., ... Grammalidis, N. (2017). Intangible Cultural Heritage and New Technologies: Challenges and Opportunities for Cultural Preservation and Development. In M. Ioannides, N. Magneant-Thalmann, & G. Papagiannakis (Eds.), *Mixed Reality and Gamification for Cultural Heritage* (pp. 129–158). Springer. doi:10.1007/978-3-319-49607-8_5

Ali, Y. (2017). *Challenge and prospect of ethiopian tourism policy*. Global J Manag Bus Res.

Alizadeh, A., & Isa, R. M. (2015). The use of social media in destination marketing: An exploratory study. *Tourism (Zagreb)*, *63*(2), 175–192.

Allport, G. (1954). *The nature of prejudice*. Addison-Wesley.

Al-Masud, T. M. M. (2015). Tourism Marketing in Bangladesh: What, Why and How. Asian Business Review, 5(1), 13–19. doi:10.18034/abr.v5i1.47

Almula, M. A. (2020). The Effectiveness of the Project-Based Learning (PBL) Approach as a Way to Engage Students in Learning. *SAGE Open*, 1–15. https://journals.sagepub.com/doi/full/10.1177/2158244020938702

Alonso, A. (2020). *El turismo rural se crece frente al coronavirus*. 20 minutos. Retrieved from https://www.20minutos.es/opinion/opinion-turismo-rural-crece-frente-coronavirus-20200927-4396171/

Al-Thoblany, M. S., & Alyuosef, M. I. (2021). The role of digital management in improving the performance of tourism sectors in the Kingdom of Saudi Arabia in the light of the 2030 vision. *Journal of Sustainable Finance & Investment*, 1-15.

Álvarez-García, J., del Río Rama, M. D. L., & Gómez-Ullate, M. (Eds.). (2018). *Handbook of research on socio-economic impacts of religious tourism and pilgrimage*. IGI Global.

Alves, G. M., Sousa, B. M., & Machado, A. (2020). The Role of Digital Marketing and Online Relationship Quality in Social Tourism: A Tourism for All Case Study. In J. Santos & O. Silva (Eds.), Digital Marketing Strategies for Tourism, Hospitality, and Airline Industries (pp. 49–70). IGI Global. doi:10.4018/978-1-5225-9783-4.ch003

American Psychiatric Association (APA). (2013). Diagnostic and Statistical Manual of Mental Disorders (5th ed.). American Psychological Association Press.

Amichai-Hamburger, Y., & Furnham, A. (2007). The Positive Net. *Computers in Human Behavior*, *23*(2), 1033–1045. doi:10.1016/j.chb.2005.08.008

Amichai-Hamburger, Y., Hasler, B. S., & Shani-Sherman, T. (2015). Structured and unstructured intergroup contact in the digital age. *Computers in Human Behavior*, *52*, 515–522. doi:10.1016/j.chb.2015.02.022

Anderson, P. (2007). What is Web 2.0? Ideas, technologies and implications for education. *JISC Technology and Standards Watch*, 2-64. Retrieved from http://www.jisc.ac.uk/media/documents/ techwatch/tsw0701b.pdf

Anderson, C. K. (2012). The impact of social media on lodging performance. *Cornell Hosp Rep*, *12*(5), 4–12.

Andreu, L., Aldás, J., Bigné, J. E., & Mattila, A. S. (2010). An analysis of e-business adoption and its impact on relational quality in travel agency–supplier relationships. *Tourism Management*, *31*(6), 777–787. doi:10.1016/j.tourman.2009.08.004

Anne Coussement, M., & Teague, T. (2013). The new customer-facing technology: Mobile and the constantly-connected consumer. *Journal of Hospitality and Tourism Technology*, *4*(2), 177–187. doi:10.1108/JHTT-12-2011-0035

Annex 2. Tourism as an Economic Development Tool. (n.d.). Retrieved February 12, 2021, Retrieved From http://www.oas.org/dsd/publications/unit/oea78e/ch10.htm

Antonio, N., de Almeida, A., Nunes, L., Batista, F., & Ribeiro, R. (2018). Hotel online reviews: Different languages, different opinions. *Information Technology & Tourism*, *18*(1), 157–185. doi:10.100740558-018-0107-x

Appadurai, A. (1990). Disjuncture and difference in the global cultural economy. *Theory, Culture & Society*, *7*(2–3), 295–310. doi:10.1177/026327690007002017

Appel, G., Grewal, L., Hadi, R., & Stephen, A. T. (2019). The future of social media in marketing. *Journal of the Academy of Marketing Science*, *48*(1), 79–95. doi:10.100711747-019-00695-1 PMID:32431463

Aramendia-Muneta, M. E., & Ollo-Lopez, A. (2013). ICT Impact on tourism industry. *International Journal of Management Cases*, *15*(2), 87–98.

Aranda, J. L., & Salvatierra, J. (2020). *Covid-19 crisis devastates Spain's tourism industry*. El País. Retrieved from https://english.elpais.com/economy_and_business/2020-08-05/covid-19-crisis-devastates-spains-tourism-industry.html

Arcodia, C., & Barker, T. (2002). A review of web-based job advertisements for australian event management positions. *Journal of Human Resources in Hospitality & Tourism*, *1*(4), 1–18. doi:10.1300/J171v01n04_01

Arharmid, A., Anuar, K., Fauzi, I., & Wee, H. (2017). Mycrowd: Mobile Application For Event Tourism. In Creative Innovation without Boundaries (pp. 146–150). MNNF Publisher.

Ariffin, A. A. M. (2013). Generic dimensionality of hospitality in the hotel industry: A host–guest relationship perspective. *International Journal of Hospitality Management*, *35*, 171–179. doi:10.1016/j.ijhm.2013.06.002

Arnett, J. J. (2002). The psychology of globalization. *The American Psychologist*, *57*(10), 774–783. doi:10.1037/0003-066X.57.10.774 PMID:12369500

Asadi, M. M., Heidari, M., & Asadian, F. (2016). Forecasting religious tourism demand using an artificial intelligence case study: Mashhad city. *International Journal of Humanities and Cultural Studies*, 1597-1617.

AslanD. (2021). Retrieved from www.dailysabah.com: https://www.dailysabah.com/business/tourism/turkey-develops-new-promotion-platform-strategy-to-enhance-tourism-minister-ersoy-says

Asplet, M., & Cooper, M. (2000). Cultural designs in New Zealand souvenir clothing: The question of authenticity. *Tourism Management*, *21*(3), 307–312. doi:10.1016/S0261-5177(99)00061-8

Assenov, I., & Khurana, N. (2012). *Social Media Marketing and the Hospitality Industry: Evidence from Thailand*. Academic Press.

Compilation of References

Aytun, C., Akın, C. S., & Akın, S. (2018). Turizm ve Bilgi İletişim Teknolojileri İlişkisi. *İzmir International Congress on Economics and Administrative Sciences*, 2633–2643.

Aziz, A. A., Bakhtiar, M., Syaquif, M., Kamaruddin, Y., & Ahmad, N. (2012). Information and communication technology application's usage in hotel industry. *Journal of Tourism, Hospitality, and Culinary Arts*, *4*(2), 34–48.

Azuma, R., Baillot, Y., Behringer, R., Feiner, S., Julier, S., & MacIntrye, B. (2001, Nov.). Article. Recent Advances in Augmented Reality, 34-47.

Azuma, R. T. (1997). A survey of augmented reality. *Presence (Cambridge, Mass.)*, *6*(4), 355–385. doi:10.1162/pres.1997.6.4.355

Azuma, R., Baillot, Y., Behringer, R., Feiner, S., Julier, S., & MacIntyre, B. (2001). Recent advances in augmented reality. *IEEE Computer Graphics and Applications*, *21*(6), 34–47. doi:10.1109/38.963459

Bachleitner, R., & Zins, A. H. (1999). Cultural tourism in rural communities: The residents' perspective. *Journal of Business Research*, *44*(3), 199–209. doi:10.1016/S0148-2963(97)00201-4

Backman, K. F. (2018). Event management research: The focus today and in the future. *Tourism Management Perspectives*, *25*, 169–171. doi:10.1016/j.tmp.2017.12.004

Bagaturi, G., & Johnson, M. (2014). The Impact of Social Media in Marketing Management. *The Journal of Business*, *3*(1), 5.

Bahrini, R., & Qaffas, A. A. (2019). Impact of Information and Communication Technology on Economic Growth: Evidence from Developing Countries. *Economies 2019*, *7*(1), 21. doi:10.3390/economies7010021

Baker, B. (2007). *Destination Branding for small cities: the essentials for successful place branding*. Creative Leap Books.

Baloglu, S., & McCleary, K. W. (1999). A model of destination image formation. *Annals of Tourism Research*, *26*(4), 868–897. doi:10.1016/S0160-7383(99)00030-4

Bandura, A. (2002). Social cognitive theory in cultural context. *Applied Psychology*, *51*(2), 269–290. doi:10.1111/1464-0597.00092

Banerjee, S., & Chua, A. Y. K. (2016). In search of patterns among travellers' hotel ratings in TripAdvisor. *Tourism Management*, *53*, 125–131. doi:10.1016/j.tourman.2015.09.020

Bansal, R., Masood, R., & Dadhich, V. (2008). Social Media Marketing-A tool of Innovative Marketing. An International Journal HATAM Publishers J. *Org. Management*, *9*(3), 2014.

Barber, R. (1991). *Pilgrimages*. Boydell & Brewer Ltd.

Barger, V. A., & Labrecque, L. (2013). An integrated marketing communications perspective on social media metrics. *International Journal of Integrated Marketing Communications*, (Spring), 64–76.

Barich, H., & Kotler, P. (1991). A framework for marketing image management. *MIT Sloan Management Review*, *32*, 94. PMID:10111301

Barile, S., Ciasullo, M. V., Troisi, O., & Sarno, D. (2017). The role of technology and institutions in tourism service ecosystems: Findings from a case study. *The TQM Journal*, *29*(6), 811–833. doi:10.1108/TQM-06-2017-0068

Barreda, A., & Bilgihan, A. (2013). An analysis of user generated content for hotel experiences. *Journal of Hospitality and Tourism Technology*, *4*(3), 263–280. doi:10.1108/JHTT-01-2013-0001

Barreiro, T., Breda, Z., & Dinis, G. (2019). Marketing de Influência e Influenciadores Digitais: aplicação do conceito pelas DMO em Portugal. *Marketing & Tourism Review, 4*(1).

Bartsch, F., Riefler, P., & Diamantopoulos, A. (2016). A Taxonomy and Review of Positive Consumer Dispositions toward Foreign Countries and Globalization. *Journal of International Marketing, 24*(1), 82–110. doi:10.1509/jim.15.0021

Bataller, A. (2011). *La ruta literaria como actividad universitaria vinculada al territorio y al patrimonio*. Revista Asabranca.

Bauman, Z., & Lyon, D. (2013). *Liquid Surveillance: A Conversation*. John Wiley & Sons. https://www.wiley.com/en-us/Liquid+Surveillance%3A+A+Conversation-p-9780745662824

Bec, V., Moyle, B., Schaffer, V., & Timms, K. (2021). Virtual reality and mixed reality for second chance tourism. *Tourism Management, 83*, 104256. doi:10.1016/j.tourman.2020.104256

Beerli, A., & Martín, J. D. (2004). Factors influencing destination image. *Annals of Tourism Research, 31*(3), 657–681. doi:10.1016/j.annals.2004.01.010

Belk, R. W. (2013). Extended Self in a Digital World. *The Journal of Consumer Research, 40*(3), 477–500. doi:10.1086/671052

Belk, R. W. (2014). Digital consumption and the extended self. *Journal of Marketing Management, 30*(11–12), 1101–1118. doi:10.1080/0267257X.2014.939217

Belk, R. W. (2016). Extended self and the digital world. In *Current Opinion in Psychology* (Vol. 10, pp. 50–54). Elsevier., doi:10.1016/j.copsyc.2015.11.003

Bell, S. (2010). Project-based learning for the 21st century: Skills for the future. *The Clearing House: A Journal of Educational Strategies, Issues and Ideas, 83*(2), 39–43. doi:10.1080/00098650903505415

Benko, H., Wilson, A. D., & Zannier, F. (2014, October). Dyadic projected spatial augmented reality. In *Proceedings of the 27th annual ACM symposium on User interface software and technology* (pp. 645-655). 10.1145/2642918.2647402

Berezan, O., Raab, C., Yoo, M., & Love, C. (2013). Sustainable hotel practices and nationality: The impact on guest satisfaction and guest intention to return. *International Journal of Hospitality Management, 34*, 227–233. doi:10.1016/j.ijhm.2013.03.010

Berné, C., García-González, M., García-Uceda, M. E., & Múgica, J. M. (2015). The effect of ICT on relationship enhancement and performance in tourism channels. *Tourism Management, 48*, 188–198. doi:10.1016/j.tourman.2014.04.012

Berno, T. (1999). When a guest is guest: Cook islanders view tourism. *Annals of Tourism Research, 26*(3), 656–675. doi:10.1016/S0160-7383(99)00002-X

Berno, T., & Ward, C. (2005). Innocence abroad: A pocket guide to psychological research on tourism. *The American Psychologist, 60*(6), 593–600. doi:10.1037/0003-066X.60.6.593 PMID:16173892

Berry, J. W. (1997). Immigration, acculturation, and adaptation. *Applied Psychology, 46*(1), 5–34. doi:10.1111/j.1464-0597.1997.tb01087.x

Berry, J. W. (2008). Globalisation and acculturation. *International Journal of Intercultural Relations, 32*(4), 328–336. doi:10.1016/j.ijintrel.2008.04.001

Berry, J. W., Kim, U., Power, S., Young, M., & Bujaki, M. (1989). Acculturation Attitudes in Plural Societies. *Applied Psychology, 38*(2), 185–206. doi:10.1111/j.1464-0597.1989.tb01208.x

Berry, J. W., Phinney, J. S., Sam, D. L., & Vedder, P. (2006). Immigrant Youth: Acculturation, Identity, and Adaptation. *Applied Psychology*, *55*(3), 303–332. doi:10.1111/j.1464-0597.2006.00256.x

Bethapudi, A. (2013). The role of ICT in tourism industry. *Journal of Applied Economics and Business*, *1*(4), 67–79.

Bhat, S. A., & Shah, M. A. (2014). *Diffusion of Internet Technology in the Tourism Sector: An Empirical Study*. doi:10.1080/15475778.2014.904674

Bigne, J. E., Sanchez, M. I., & Sanchez, J. (2001). Tourism image, evaluation variables and after purchase behaviour: Inter-relationship. *Tourism Management*, *22*(6), 607–616. doi:10.1016/S0261-5177(01)00035-8

Bilgihan, A., Peng, C., & Kandampully, J. (2014). Generation Y's dining information seeking and sharing behavior on social networking sites: An exploratory study. *International Journal of Contemporary Hospitality Management*, *26*(3), 349–366. doi:10.1108/IJCHM-11-2012-0220

Bimber, O., & Raskar, R. (2005). *Spatial augmented reality: merging real and virtual worlds*. CRC Press. doi:10.1201/b10624

Bloom Consulting. (2019). *Portugal City Brand Ranking*. Available at https://www.bloomconsulting.com/pt/pdf/rankings/Bloom_Consulting_City_Brand_Ranking_Portugal.pdf

Boh, W., De-Haan, U., & Strom, R. (2016). University technology transfer through entrepreneurship: Faculty and student spinoffs. *The Journal of Technology Transfer*, *41*(4), 661–669. doi:10.100710961-015-9399-6

Bojanic, D., & Xu, Y. (2006). An investigation of acculturation and the dining-out behavior of Chinese living in the United States. *International Journal of Hospitality Management*, *25*(2), 211–226. doi:10.1016/j.ijhm.2005.06.002

Bolotaeva, V. A. (2011). Marketing Opportunities with Social Networks. *Journal of Internet Social Networking and Virtual Communities*.

Bonson, E., & Ratkai, M. (2013). A set of metrics to assess stakeholder engagement and social legitimacy on a corporate Facebook page. *Online Information Review*, *37*(5), 787–803. doi:10.1108/OIR-03-2012-0054

Borowiecki, K. J., & Castiglione, C. (2014). Cultural participation and tourism flows: An empirical investigation of Italian provinces. *Tourism Economics*, *20*(2), 241–262. doi:10.5367/te.2013.0278

Bosma, N. D., & Onna, K. (2018). Global Entrepreneurship Monitor, Global Report 2018/2019. *GEM: International Journal on Geomathematics*.

Botelho, M. L., Rosas, L., & Barreira, H. (2017). Designing exhibitions at Google Cultural Institute: between pedagogical experiences and the creation of heritage diffusion products. *Libro de Actas V Congresso Internacional Cidades Criativas, CITCEM / Icono14*, 128-138.

Botsman, R. (2013). *The sharing economy lacks a shared definition*. http://www.collaborativeconsumption.com/2013/11/22/the-sharing-economy-lacks-a-shared-definition/

Bourdieu, P., & Wacquant, L. J. (1992). *An invitation to reflexive sociology*. University of Chicago Press.

Boutillier, S. (2019). Small Entrepreneurship, Knowledge and Social Resources in a Heavy Industrial Territory. The Case of Eco-Innovations in Dunkirk, North of France. *Journal of the Knowledge Economy*, *10*(3), 997–1018. Advance online publication. doi:10.100713132-017-0511-z

Bowden, J. L.-H. (2009). The process of customer engagement: A conceptual framework. *Journal of Marketing Theory and Practice*, *17*(1), 63–74. doi:10.2753/MTP1069-6679170105 boyd, d. m., & Ellison, N. B. (2007). Social Network Sites: Definition, History, and Scholarship. *Journal of Computer-Mediated Communication, 13*(1), 210–230. doi:10.1111/j.1083-6101.2007.00393.x

Bozkurt, A., Koseoglu, S., & Singh, L. (2019). An analysis of peer reviewed publications on openness in education in half a century: Trends and patterns in the open hemisphere. *Australian Journal of Educational Technology, 35*(4), 78–97. doi:10.14742/ajet.4252

Breazeale, M. (2009). Word of mouse-An assessment of electronic word-of-mouth research. *International Journal of Market Research, 51*(3), 1–19. doi:10.1177/147078530905100307

Bredican, J., & Vigar-Ellis, D. (2014). Smartphone applications-idea sourcing and app development: implications for firms. *South African Journal of Economic and Management Sciences=SuidAfrikaanse Tydskrifvir Ekonomiese en Bestuur swetenskappe, 17*(3), 232-248.

Brodie, R. J., Ilic, A., Juric, B., & Hollebeek, L. (2013). Consumer engagement in a virtual brand community: An exploratory analysis. *Journal of Business Research, 66*(1), 105–114. doi:10.1016/j.jbusres.2011.07.029

Brown, B., & Chalmers, M. (2003). Tourism and mobile technology. In *ECSCW 2003* (pp. 335–354). Springer. doi:10.1007/978-94-010-0068-0_18

Bryman, A. (2016). *Social Research Methods* (5th ed.). Oxford University Press.

Bryon, J. (2012). Tour Guides as Storytellers – From Selling to Sharing. *Scandinavian Journal of Hospitality and Tourism, 12*(1), 27–43. doi:10.1080/15022250.2012.656922

Budeanu, A. (2013). Sustainability and Tourism Social Media. In Tourism Social Media: Transformations in Identity, Community and Culture (pp. 87-103). Emerald Group Publishing Limited. doi:10.1108/S1571-5043(2013)0000018008

Buhalis, D., & Amaranggana, A. (2013). Smart Tourism Destinations. In Information and Communication Technologies in Tourism 2014 (pp. 553–564). doi:10.1007/978-3-319-03973-2_40

Buhalis, D. (1998). Strategic use of information technologies in the tourism industry. *Tourism Management, 19*(5), 409–421. doi:10.1016/S0261-5177(98)00038-7

Buhalis, D., & Kaldis, K. (2008). eEnabled Internet Distribution for Small and Medium Sized Hotels: The Case of Athens. *Tourism Recreation Research, 33*(1), 67–81. doi:10.1080/02508281.2008.11081291

Buhalis, D., & Law, R. (2008). Progress in information technology and tourism management: 20 years on and 10 years after the Internet-The state of eTourism research. *Tourism Management, 29*(4), 609–623. doi:10.1016/j.tourman.2008.01.005

Buhalis, D., & O'Connor, P. (2005). Information communication technology revolutionizing tourism. *Tourism Recreation Research, 30*(3), 7–16. Advance online publication. doi:10.1080/02508281.2005.11081482

Buhalis, D., & Sinarta, Y. (2019). Real-time co-creation and nowness service: Lessons from tourism and hospitality. *Journal of Travel & Tourism Marketing, 36*(5), 563–582. doi:10.1080/10548408.2019.1592059

Burns, P. M. (1999). *An Introduction to Tourism and Anthropology*. Routledge. https://books.google.com.tr/books?hl=tr&lr=&id=d9un9bkVkrkC&oi=fnd&pg=PP11&dq=an+introduction+to+tourism+anthropology&ots=ZWxleh-_RR&sig=_mDGSMKbUvWjSAvnmXlWUs_JuKo&redir_esc=y#v=onepage&q=anintroductiontotourismanthropology&f=false

Burton, E. P., Frazier, W., Annetta, L., Lamb, R., Cheng, R., & Chmiel, M. (2011). Modeling Augmented Reality Games with Preservice. *Journal of Technology and Teacher Education, 19*(3), 303–329.

Compilation of References

Bustamante, S. (2015). *Algunas "apps" muy útiles para viajar este verano*. ABC. Retrieved from https://www.abc.es/viajar/top/20150713/abci-apps-diez-viajero-201507072030.html

Bustard, J. R. T., Bolan, P., Devine, A., & Hutchinson, K. (2019). The emerging smart event experience: An interpretative phenomenological analysis. *Tourism Review*, *74*(1), 116–128. doi:10.1108/TR-10-2017-0156

Buzinde, C. N., Kalavar, J. M., Kohli, N., & Manuel-Navarrete, D. (2014). Emic understandings of Kumbh Mela pilgrimage experiences. *Annals of Tourism Research*, *49*, 1–18. doi:10.1016/j.annals.2014.08.001

Cadotte, E. R., & Turgeon, N. (1988). Key factors in guest satisfaction. *The Cornell H.R. AQ (Balmain, N.S.W.)*, *28*(4), 44–51.

Cai, W., Richter, S., & McKenna, B. (2019). Progress on technology use in tourism. In Journal of Hospitality and Tourism Technology (Vol. 10, Issue 4, pp. 651–672). doi:10.1108/JHTT-07-2018-0068

Çakmak, F., & Dilek, S. (2019). Religion and Tourism in Turkey: An Economically Empirical Study. *Uluslararası İktisadi ve İdari İncelemeler Dergisi*, (22), 209–224.

Calvaresi, D., Leis, M., Dubovitskaya, A., Schegg, R., & Schumacher, M. (2019). Trust in Tourism via Blockchain Technology: Results from a Systematic Review. In *Information and Communication Technologies in Tourism 2019* (pp. 304–317). Springer International Publishing., doi:10.1007/978-3-030-05940-8_24

Canalis, X. (2019). *Marketing en Instagram ¿el nuevo embudo para el turismo?* Hosteltur. Retrieved from https://www.hosteltur.com/127353_marketing-en-instagram-el-nuevo-embudo-para-el-turismo.html

Capterra. (2021). *The 7 most popular hotel management software for hotel chains compared. Software Buying Tips and Advice for Businesses*. Retrieved from: https://blog.capterra.com/most-popular-hotel-management-software-for-hotel-chains/

Carmigniani, J., Furht, B., Anisetti, M., Ceravolo, P., Damiani, E., & Ivkovic, M. (2011). Augmented reality technologies, systems and applications. *Multimedia Tools and Applications*, *51*(1), 341–377. doi:10.100711042-010-0660-6

Carr, C. T., & Hayes, R. A. (2015). Social media: Defining, developing, and divining. *Atlantic Journal of Communication*, *23*(1), 46–65. doi:10.1080/15456870.2015.972282

Carter, R. W., & Beeton, R. J. S. (2008). Managing cultural change and tourism: A review and Perspective. In Cultural and heritage tourism in Asia and the Pacific. Routledge.

Casanova, M. B., Kim, D. Y., & Morrison, A. M. (2006). The relationships of meeting planners' profiles with usage and attitudes toward the use of technology. In Journal of Convention and Event Tourism (Vol. 7, Issues 3–4, pp. 19–43). doi:10.1300/J452v07n03_02

Castilla-La Mancha Media. (2018). *Frenar la despoblación: el reto de la provincia de Cuenca*. Castilla-La Mancha Media. Retrieved from https://www.cmmedia.es/noticias/castilla-la-mancha/frenar-la-despoblacion-el-reto-de-la-provincia-de-cuenca/

Castro, C., Ferreira, F. A., & Nunes, P. (2020). Digital Technologies and Tourism as Drivers of Economic Growth in Europe and Central Asia. *Smart Innovation. Systems and Technologies*, *209*, 341–350. doi:10.1007/978-981-33-4260-6_30

Çelik, U., Akçetin, E., & Gök, M. (2017). RapidMiner ile Uygulamalı Veri Madenciliği. Pusala Yayınevi.

Cerqueira, C. S., & Kirner, C. (2012). Developing Educational Applications with a Non-Programming Augmented Reality Authoring Tool. *Proceedings of World Conference on Educational Multimedia, Hypermedia and Telecommunications*, 2816-2825.

Cerutti, S., & Piva, E. (2016). The role of tourists' feedback in the enhancement of religious tourism destinations. *International Journal of Religious Tourism and Pilgrimage, 4*(3), 6-16.

Chalip, L., & Costa, C. A. (2005). Sport event tourism and the destination brand: Towards a general theory. Sport in Society. doi:10.1080/17430430500108579

Chappel, S., & Brown, L. (2006). Literary Tourism Beyond the City. In P. A. Whitelaw & G. Barry O'Mahoney (Eds.), *CAUTHE 2006: To the City and Beyond* (pp. 1764–1772). Victoria University School of Hospitality, Tourism and Marketing.

Chari, S. (2011). The Impact of Hinduism on the West. *India Currents*. https://indiacurrents.com/the-impact-of-hinduism-on-the-west/

Chaulagain, S., Wiitala, J., & Fu, X. (2019). The impact of country image and destination image on US tourists' travel intention. *Journal of Destination Marketing & Management, 12*, 1–11. doi:10.1016/j.jdmm.2019.01.005

Chayes, S. (2015). *Thieves of state: Why corruption threatens global security*. WW Norton & Company.

Chen, C. M., Yang, H. W., Li, E. Y., & Liu, C. C. (2015). How does hotel pricing influence guest satisfaction by the moderating influence of room occupancy? *International Journal of Hospitality Management, 49*, 136–138. doi:10.1016/j.ijhm.2015.06.006

Chernova, D. V., Sharafutdinova, N. S., Novikova, E. N., Nasretdinov, I. T., Xametova, N. G., & Valeeva, Y. S. (2020). Evaluation of Event Marketing in IT Companies. In Lecture Notes in Networks and Systems (Vol. 84, pp. 487–493). doi:10.1007/978-3-030-27015-5_59

Cheung-Blunden, V. L., & Juang, L. P. (2008). Strategies generalizable in a colonial context? Expanding acculturation theory: Are acculturation models and the adaptiveness of acculturation. *International Journal of Behavioral Development, 32*(1), 21–33. doi:10.1177/0165025407084048

Cheung, C. M. K., & Lee, M. K. O. (2009). Understanding the sustainability of a virtual community: Model development and empirical test. *Journal of Information Science, 35*(3), 279–298. doi:10.1177/0165551508099088

Chevers, D. A. (2015). Evaluating the Impact of ICT Usage on the Performance of Jamaican Hotels: A Conceptual Perspective. *Journal of Tourism and Hospitality Management, 3*(1–2), 22–31.

Chiang, I. (2019). Exploring the benefits of social media marketing for brands and communities. *International Journal of Electronic Commerce Studies, 10*(2), 113–140. doi:10.7903/ijecs.1547

Choi, S., Lehto, X. Y., & Morrison, A. M. (2007). Destination image representation on the web: Content analysis of Macau travel related websites. *Tourism Management, 28*(1), 118–129. doi:10.1016/j.tourman.2006.03.002

Choi, T. Y., & Chu, R. (2001). Determinants of hotel guests' satisfaction and repeat patronage in the Hong Kong hotel industry. *International Journal of Hospitality Management, 20*(3), 277–297. doi:10.1016/S0278-4319(01)00006-8

Choney, S. K., Berryhill-Paapke, E., & Robbins, R. R. (1995). The acculturation of American Indians: developing frameworks for research and practice. In *Handbook of multicultural counseling* (pp. 73–92). Sage Publications.

Chou, C. H., Chang, N. W., Shrestha, S., Hsu, S. D., Lin, Y. L., Lee, W. H., & Huang, H. D. (2016). miRTarBase 2016: Updates to the experimentally validated miRNA-target interactions database. *Nucleic Acids Research, 44*(D1), D239–D247. doi:10.1093/nar/gkv1258 PMID:26590260

Chu, K., & Tseng, C. (2013). Research of Service Innovation on Event Marketing Performance. *International Journal on Advances in Information Sciences and Service Sciences, 5*(12), 97–104. doi:10.4156/aiss.vol5.issue12.11

Compilation of References

Chung, J. Y., & Buhalis, D. (2008). Information needs in online social networks. *Information Technology & Tourism*, *10*(4), 267–281. doi:10.3727/109830508788403123

Cico, O. (2019). The Impact of IT Bootcamp on Student Learning - Experience from ICT Enabled Experiential-Based Course. Software Business, 430-435. doi:10.1007/978-3-030-33742-1_37

Ciolfi, L. (2005). *Proceedings of the International Workshop Re-Thinking Technology in Museums: Towards a new understanding of people's experience in museums*. Academic Press.

Clark, L., & Roberts, S. (2010). Employer's use of social networking sites: A socially irresponsible practice. *Journal of Business Ethics*, *95*(4), 507–525. doi:10.100710551-010-0436-y

Clarysse, B., Wright, M., Lockett, A., Van de Velde, E., & Vohora, A. (2005). Spinning out new ventures: A typology of incubation strategy from European research institutions. *Journal of Business Venturing*, *20*(2), 183–216. doi:10.1016/j.jbusvent.2003.12.004

Cleveland, M., & Bartsch, F. (2018). Global consumer culture: Epistemology and ontology. *International Marketing Review*. Advance online publication. doi:10.1108/IMR-10-2018-0287

Cleveland, M., & Laroche, M. (2007). Acculturation to the global consumer culture: Scale development and research paradigm. *Journal of Business Research*, *60*(3), 249–259. doi:10.1016/j.jbusres.2006.11.006

CLM24. (2017). *Las pernoctaciones en Cuenca alcanzan por primera vez las dos noches de duración*. CLM24. Retrieved from https://www.clm24.es/articulo/cuenca/pernoctaciones-cuenca-alcanzan-primera-vez-noches-duracion/20170917193928173394.html

CMST – Câmara Municipal de Santo Tirso. (2017). *MIEC já é uma referência nacional e internacional*. Available at: https://www.cm-stirso.pt/noticia/miec-e-ja-uma-referencia-nacional-e-internacional

Cohen, E. (1984). The sociology of tourism: Approaches, issues, and findings. *Annual Review of Sociology*, *10*(1), 373–392. doi:10.1146/annurev.so.10.080184.002105

Cohen, E. (1985). The Tourist Guide: The Origins, Structure and Dynamics of a Role. *Annals of Tourism Research*, *12*(1), 5–29. doi:10.1016/0160-7383(85)90037-4

Correia, A., Oliveira, M., Leal, M., Roque, M. I., Forte, M. J., & Rodrigues de Sousa, S. (2016). *The Mediating Role of Literary Tour Guides: Saramago versus Mafra's National Palace. In New Challenges and Boundaries in Tourism: Policies, Innovations and Strategies*. International Association of Tourism Policy.

Costa, H. (2018). *Designing a Virtual Exhibitions for Google Arts & Culture: Public Art, Tecnhology and Intercultural Communication* (Master's thesis). Available at https://recipp.ipp.pt/bitstream/10400.22/12646/1/Hugo_Costa_MISB_2018.pdf

Cox, C., Burgess, S., Sellitto, C., & Buultjens, J. (2009). 'The Role of User-Generated Content in Tourists' Travel Planning Behavior'. *Journal of Hospitality Marketing & Management*, *18*(8), 743–764. doi:10.1080/19368620903235753

Creswell, J. W. (2009). *Research design: Qualitative, quantitative, and mixed methods approaches* (3rd ed.). Sage Publications, Inc.

Crowther, P. (2011). Marketing event outcomes: From tactical to strategic. *International Journal of Event and Festival Management*, *2*(1), 68–82. doi:10.1108/17582951111116623

Cuenca News. (2018). *La provincia de Cuenca ha perdido más del 34% de su población desde 1900*. Periódico Digital CuencaNews.es. Retrieved from https://www.cuencanews.es/noticia/57770/provincia/la-provincia-de-cuenca-ha-perdido-mas-del-34--de-su-poblacion-desde-1900.html

Cuenin, F. (2011). *Patrimonio cultural y desarrollo socioeconómico: la recuperación de áreas centrales históricas.* BID – Banco Interamericano de Desarrollo. Available at: https://publications.iadb.org/es/publicacion/13208/patrimonio-cultural-y-desarrollo-socioeconomico-la-recuperacion-de-areas

Cunill, O. M., & Forteza, C. M. (2010). The franchise contract in hotel chains: A study of hotel chain growth and market concentrations. *Tourism Economics, 16*(3), 493–515.

Da Cruz Vareiro, L. M., & De Sousa Pinheiro, T. C. (2017). A Influência Da Crise Na Escolha Pelo Consumidor Entre Agências De Viagens Ou Operadores On-Line. *Turismo - Visão e Ação, 19*(2), 220.

Daniel, M., Bogdan, G., & Daniel, Z. (2012). The Use of Event Marketing Management Strategies. *Procedia: Social and Behavioral Sciences, 46*, 5409–5413. doi:10.1016/j.sbspro.2012.06.448

Das, S., & Lall, G. (2016). Traditional marketing VS digital marketing: An analysis. *International Journal of Commerce and Management Research, 2*(8), 5-11.

Data Reportal. (2020). *Digital 2020: Bangladesh.* Retrieved from: https://datareportal.com/reports/digital-2020-bangaldesh

De Ascaniis, S., Bischof, N., & Cantoni, L. (2013). Building destination image through online opinionated discourses. the case of swiss mountain destinations. In Information and Communication Technologies in Tourism (pp. 94-106). Academic Press.

De Ascaniis, S., & Cantoni, L. (2016). Information and communication technologies in religious tourism and pilgrimage. *International Journal of Religious Tourism and Pilgrimage, 4*(3).

De Oliveira Magalhães, M. (2017). *Estudo da utilização de vídeos 360º na experiência turística.* Academic Press.

De Oliveira, R. K., & Correa, C. (2017). Virtual Reality como estratégia para o marketing turístico. *Virtual Reality, 10*(23).

de Zúñiga, H. G., Barnidge, M., & Scherman, A. (2017). Social Media Social Capital, Offline Social Capital, and Citizenship: Exploring Asymmetrical Social Capital Effects. *Political Communication, 34*(1), 44–68. doi:10.1080/10584609.2016.1227000

Dedeoglu, B. B. (2018). Are information quality and source credibility really important for shared content on social-media? The moderating role of gender. *International Journal of Contemporary Hospitality Management, 31*, 513–534. doi:10.1108/IJCHM-10-2017-0691

Desligar: "detox digital" em 8 alojamentos livres de wi-fi. (2020). Retrieved 10 November 2020, from https://boacamaboamesa.expresso.pt/boa-cama/2019-08-05-Desligar-detox-digital-em-8-alojamentos-livres-de-wi-fi

Deuze, M. (2006). Participation, remediation, bricolage: Considering principal components of a digital culture. *The Information Society, 22*(2), 63–75. doi:10.1080/01972240600567170

Dey, B. L., Alwi, S., Yamoah, F., Agyepong, S. A., Kizgin, H., & Sarma, M. (2019). Towards a framework for understanding ethnic consumers' acculturation strategies in a multicultural environment: A food consumption perspective. *International Marketing Review, 36*(5), 771–804. doi:10.1108/IMR-03-2018-0103

Dey, B. L., Yen, D., & Samuel, L. (2020). Digital consumer culture and digital acculturation. *International Journal of Information Management, 51*, 102057. doi:10.1016/j.ijinfomgt.2019.102057

Díaz-Plaja, A., Prats, M., & Ramos, J. M. (n.d.). *Dracs literaris.* https://sites.google.com/site/dracsliteraris/home

Dickinson, J. E., Hibbert, J. F., & Filimonau, V. (2016). Mobile technology and the tourist experience:(Dis) connection at the campsite. *Tourism Management, 57*, 193–201. doi:10.1016/j.tourman.2016.06.005

Compilation of References

Digital Travel, A. P. A. C. (2020). *The Role of Social Media in Tourism Marketing*. Retrieved from: https://digitaltravela-pac.wbresearch.com/blog/social-media-in-tourism-marketing

Dolnicar, S., & Grün, B. (2007). Assessing analytical robustness in cross-cultural comparisons. *International Journal of Culture, Tourism and Hospitality Research*, *1*(2), 140–160. doi:10.1108/17506180710751687

Dolnicar, S., & Otter, T. (2003). Which hotel attributes matter? A review of previous and a framework for future research. *Proceedings of the 9th annual conference of the Asia Pacific tourism association*, 176-188.

Donath, J., & Boyd, D. (2004). Public displays of connection. *BT Technology Journal*, *22*(4), 71–82. doi:10.1023/B:BTTJ.0000047585.06264.cc

Draper, J. (2016). An exploratory study of the differences in prior travel experience and tourist information sources. *Tourism and Hospitality Research*, *16*(2), 133–143. doi:10.1177/1467358415600216

Dumitrescu, E. I., & Hurlin, C. (2012). Testing for Granger non-causality in heterogeneous panels. *Economic Modelling*, *29*(4), 1450–1460. doi:10.1016/j.econmod.2012.02.014

Dumitrescu, G., Lepadatu, C., & Ciuera, C. (2014). Creating virtual Exhibitions for Educational and Cultural Development. *Informações Econômicas*, *18*(1/2014), 102–110. doi:10.12948/issn14531305/18.1.2014.09

Dunne, Á., Lawlor, M. A., & Rowley, J. (2010). Young people's use of online social networking sites - a uses and gratifications perspective. *Journal of Research in Interactive Marketing*, *4*(1), 46–58. doi:10.1108/17505931011033551

Durgee, J. F., & Colarelli O'Connor, G. (1995). An exploration into renting as consumption behavior. *Psychology and Marketing*, *12*(2), 89–104. doi:10.1002/mar.4220120202

Dwivedi, A. (2015). A higher-order model of consumer brand engagement and its impact on loyalty intentions. *Journal of Retailing and Consumer Services*, *24*, 100–109. doi:10.1016/j.jretconser.2015.02.007

Echtner, C. M., & Ritchie, J. B. (1991). The meaning and measurement of destination image. *Journal of Tourism Studies*, *2*, 2–12.

Edgett, S. J., & Cullen, C. W. (1993). Service Organization Selection: A Cross-cultural Analysis of the Role of Involvement. *European Journal of Marketing*, *27*(2), 33–45. doi:10.1108/03090569310026844

Egger, I., Lei, S. I., & Wassler, P. (2020). Digital free tourism – An exploratory study of tourist motivations. *Tourism Management*, *104098*, 1–10. doi:10.1016/j.tourman.2020.104098

Ekiz, E., & Au, N. (2011). Comparing Chinese and American attitudes towards complaining. *International Journal of Contemporary Hospitality Management*, *23*(3), 327–343. doi:10.1108/09596111111122514

El Digital de Albacete. (2019). *El turismo sigue batiendo récords en Castilla-La Mancha*. El Digital de Albacete. Retrieved from https://www.eldigitaldealbacete.com/2019/06/18/el-turismo-sigue-batiendo-records-en-castilla-la-mancha/

Eley, B., & Tilley, S. (2009). *Online Marketing Inside Out*. Sitepoint Pty. Ltd.

Elhadidi, M. F., & City, Z. (2018). Beyond access to social media: A comparison of gratifications, interactivity, and content usage among Egyptian adults. *Global Media Journal*, *16*(30), 108.

Elmo, C. G., Arcese, G., Valeri, M., Poponi, S., & Pacchera, F. (2020). Sustainabiliy in tourism as a innovation driver: An analysis of familiy business reality. *Sustainability*, *12*(15), 6149. doi:10.3390u12156149

El-Said, O., & Aziz, H. (2021). *Virtual Tours a Means to an End: An Analysis of Virtual Tours' Role in Tourism Recovery Post COVID-19*. Https://Doi.Org/10.1177/0047287521997567 doi:10.1177/0047287521997567 eMarketer. (2016). *Worldwide Ad Spending: eMarketer's Updated Estimates and Forecast for 2015–2020*. Author.

Ergen, F. D. (2021). Artificial Intelligence Applications for Event Management and Marketing. In *Impact of ICTs on Event Management and Marketing* (pp. 199–215). IGI Global. doi:10.4018/978-1-7998-4954-4.ch012

Ernestad, V. H. R. (2010). *Social media marketing from a bottom-up perspective - the social media transition*. Retrieved from http:// www.carphonewarehouse.com

Etzkowitz, H., & Leydesdorff, L. (2001). Universities and the Global Knowledge Economy. *Continuum*.

EU – European Commission. (n.d.). *Culture*. Available at: https://ec.europa.eu/regional_policy/en/policy/themes/culture/

Expreso. (2020). *Cuenca, camino de convertirse en Destino Turístico Inteligente*. Expreso. Retrieved from https://www.expreso.info/noticias/espana/77938_cuenca_camino_de_convertirse_en_destino_turistico_inteligente

Falk, J. H., & Dierking, L. D. (2008). Enhancing visitor interaction and learning with mobile technologies. *Digital technologies and the museum experience: Handheld guides and other media*, 19-33.

Fan, D. X., Buhalis, D., & Lin, B. (2019). A tourist typology of online and face-to-face social contact: Destination immersion and tourism encapsulation/decapsulation. *Annals of Tourism Research*, *78*, 102757. doi:10.1016/j.annals.2019.102757

Fayos-Solà, E., & Cooper, C. (2019). Conclusion: The future of tourism: innovation and sustainability. The Future of Tourism, 325-337.

Felix, R., Rauschnabel, P. A., & Hinsch, C. (2017). Elements of strategic social media marketing: A holistic framework. *Journal of Business Research*, *70*, 118–126. doi:10.1016/j.jbusres.2016.05.001

Ferguson, G. M., & Bornstein, M. H. (2012). Remote acculturation: The "Americanization" of Jamaican Islanders. *International Journal of Behavioral Development*, *36*(3), 167–177. doi:10.1177/0165025412437066

Ferguson, G. M., & Bornstein, M. H. (2015). Remote acculturation of early adolescents in Jamaica towards European American culture: A replication and extension. *International Journal of Intercultural Relations*, *45*, 24–35. doi:10.1016/j.ijintrel.2014.12.007 PMID:25709142

Ferguson, G. M., Tran, S. P., Mendez, S. N., & van de Vijyer, F. J. R. (2017). Remote acculturation: Conceptualization, measurement, and implications for health outcomes. In S. J. Schwartz & J. B. Unger (Eds.), *The Oxford Handbook of Acculturation and Health*. Oxford University Press.

Fernandes, F. A. R. (2015). A indústria hoteleira e as reclamações online: o caso TripAdvisor (Master). FEP, Porto.

Fernandez-Serrano, J., Martinez-Román, J., & Romero, I. (2019). The entrepreneur in regional innovation system. The comparative study for high- and low income regions. *Entrepreneurship and Regional Development*, *31*(5-6), 5–6, 337–356. doi:10.1080/08985626.2018.1513079

Ferrara, E., Varol, O., Davis, C., Menczer, F., & Flammini, A. (2016). The rise of social bots. *Communications of the ACM*, *59*(7), 96–104. doi:10.1145/2818717

Ferreira, A. (2018). *A Influência dos Social Media e dos Digital Influencers na intenção de visita e na imagem do destino*. Vila Nova de Famalicão: Universidade Lusíada.

Ferreira, J., & Sousa, B. (2020) Experiential Marketing as Leverage for Growth of Creative Tourism: A Co-creative Process. In Advances in Tourism, Technology and Smart Systems. Smart Innovation, Systems and Technologies (vol 171. pp 567-577). Springer. doi:10.1007/978-981-15-2024-2_49

Figueira, L. M. (2013). *Manual para elaboração de roteiros de turismo cultural*. Instituto Politécnico de Tomar.

Fiore, F. (2001). *E-marketing Estratégico*. Academic Press.

Firat, A. F., & Venkatesh, A. (1995). Liberatory Postmodernism and the Reenchantment of Consumption. *The Journal of Consumer Research*, *22*(3), 239. doi:10.1086/209448

Firoiu, D., & Croitoru, A. (2013). Tourism And Tourism Infrastructure From The Perspective Of Technological Changes. *Romanian Economic Business Review, Romanian-American University*, *8*(2), 93–103.

Fisher, D. (2004). The Demonstration Effect Revisited. *Annals of Tourism Research*, *31*(2), 428–446. doi:10.1016/j.annals.2004.01.001

Flannery, W. P., Reise, S. P., & Yu, J. (2001). An Empirical Comparison of Acculturation Models. *Personality and Social Psychology Bulletin*, *27*(8), 1035–1045. doi:10.1177/0146167201278010

Fleacă, E., Fleacă, B., & Maiduc, S. (2016). Fostering Organizational Innovation based on modeling the Marketing Research Process through Event-driven Process Chain (EPC). *TEM Journal*, *5*(4), 460–466.

Foo, S. (2008). Online virtual exhibitions: Concepts and design considerations. *Bulletin of Information Technology*, *28*(4), 22–34.

Formica, S. (2015). *Digital detox: 7 Steps to find your inner balance*. Sandro Formica.

Fotis, J. N., Buhalis, D., & Rossides, N. (2012). Social media use and impact during the holiday travel planning process. Springer-Verlag. doi:10.1007/978-3-7091-1142-0_2

FPRM. (2009). *Social Media Tools, What You Need to Know*. The Firm of Public Relations and Marketing. Retrieved from: https://www.scribd.com/doc/16536112/Social-Media-for-the-Hospitality-Industr

Freeman, C., & Louçã, F. (2001). *As time goes by. From the industrial revolutions to the information revolution*. Oxford University Press.

Furenes, M. I., Øgaard, T., & Gjerald, O. (2017). How face-to-face feedback influences guest outcome evaluation of co-production: Changing or shaping guest experiences? *Tourism Management Perspectives*, *21*, 59–65. doi:10.1016/j.tmp.2016.11.004

Gallarza, M. G., Saura, I. G., & García, H. C. (2002). Destination image: Towards a conceptual framework. *Annals of Tourism Research*, *29*(1), 56–78. doi:10.1016/S0160-7383(01)00031-7

Galvez-Rodriguez, M. D., Alonso-Canadas, J., Haro-de-Rosario, A., & Caba-Perez, C. (2020). Exploring best practices for online engagement via Facebook with local destination management organisations (DMOs) in Europe: A longitudinal analysis. *Tourism Management Perspectives*, *34*, 100636. Advance online publication. doi:10.1016/j.tmp.2020.100636

García, A. (2016). *Radiografía del perfil del viajero: Del turista tradicional al 3.0*. Hosteltur. Retrieved from https://www.hosteltur.com/comunidad/nota/004536_radiografia-del-perfil-del-viajero-del-turista-tradicional-al-30.html

García-Barriocanal, E., Sicilia, M.-A., & Korfiatis, N. (2010). Exploring hotel service quality experience indicators in user-generated content: A case using Tripadvisor data. In *Mediterranean Conference on Information Systems (MCIS) 2010 Proceedings* (Paper No. 33). Tel Aviv, Israel: AIS Electronic Libary (AISeL).

García-Pablos, A., Cuadros, M., & Linaza, M. T. (2016). Automatic analysis of textual hotel reviews. *Information Technology & Tourism*, *16*(1), 45–69. doi:10.100740558-015-0047-7

Garoz, J. (2020). *19 municipios de la Serranía para disfrutar de las próximas lluvias de estrellas*. Voces de Cuenca. Retrieved from https://www.vocesdecuenca.com/provincia/serrania/19-municipios-de-la-serrania-para-disfrutar-de-las-proximas-lluvias-de-estrellas/

Gere, C. (2008). *Digital Culture* (2nd ed.). Reaktion Books.

Getz, D. (2008). Event tourism: Definition, evolution, and research. *Tourism Management*, *29*(3), 403–428. doi:10.1016/j.tourman.2007.07.017

Getz, D., & Page, S. J. (2014). Progress and prospects for event tourism research. *Tourism Management*, *52*, 593–631. doi:10.1016/j.tourman.2015.03.007

Ghosh, T. (2018). Predicting hotel book intention: The influential role of helpfulness and advocacy of online reviews. *Journal of Hospitality Marketing & Management*, *27*(3), 299–322. doi:10.1080/19368623.2017.1364198

Gjerald, O. (2008). *Sociocultural Impacts of Tourism: A Case Study from Norway.* Http://Dx.Doi.Org/10.1080/14766820508669095 doi:10.1080/14766820508669095

Glazier, A. (2011). *Searchial Marketing: How Social Media Drives Search Optimization in Web 3.0.* https://www.amazon.com/Searchial-MarketingSocial-Drives-Optimization/dp/1456738925

Goffman, E. (1959). *The presentation of self in everyday life.* Anchor Book.

Gökçearslan, Ş., Yildiz Durak, H., Berikan, B., & Saritepeci, M. (2021). Smartphone Addiction, Loneliness, Narcissistic Personality, and Family Belonging Among University Students: A Path Analysis. *Social Science Quarterly*, *102*(1), 1–18. doi:10.1111squ.12949

Goldfarb, B., & Henrekson, M. (2002). *Bottom-up versus top-down policies towards the commercialization of university intellectual property.* Elsevier Science BV.

Gombault, A. (2003). La nouvelle identité organisationnelle des musées. Le cas du Louvre. *Revue française de gestion*, *142*, 189-203. Available at https://www.cairn.info/revue-francaise-de-gestion-2003-1.html

González, C. M., & Herrero, J. L. C. (2014). *Aplicaciones de tecnología 3D para el turismo cultural y la difusión del patrimonio: realidad aumentada vs realidad virtual.* Paper presented at the TuriTec 2014, X Congreso Nacional Turismo y Tecnologías de la Información y las Comunicaciones, Universidad de Málaga (UMA).

González-Oñate, C., & Martínez-Bueno, S. (2013). Reinvención de marcas territorio a través de la organización de eventos: Cuenca y su riqueza paleontológica. *Arte y Ciudad*, *3*(1), 153–170.

Google. (2018). *Partners.* Available at Google Cultural Institute: https://www.google.com/culturalinstitute/about/partners/

Gordon, M. (1964). *Assimilation in American Life: The Role of Race.* Religion and National Origin.

Gössling, S. (2021). Tourism, technology and ICT: A critical review of affordances and concessions. *Journal of Sustainable Tourism*, *29*(5), 733–750. doi:10.1080/09669582.2021.1873353

Graburn, N. H. (1983). The anthropology of tourism. *Annals of Tourism Research*, *10*(1), 9–33. doi:10.1016/0160-7383(83)90113-5

Graham, P. (2005). *Web 2.0 and Why?* Retrieved from: http//:www.fossbox.org.uk

Gravari-Barbas, M. (2018). Arquitectura, museos, turismo: la guerra de las marcas (A. Ávila-Gómez & D.C. Ruiz-Robayo, Trans.). *Revista de Arquitectura*, *20*(1), 102-114. Available at: https://www.researchgate.net/publication/325978618_Arquitectura_museos_turismo_la_guerra_de_las_marcas

Grave, J. F. (2019). What KPIs are key? Evaluating performance metrics for social media influencers. *Social Media + Society*, *5*(3). Advance online publication. doi:10.1177/2056305119865475

Gretzel, U. (2006). Consumer Generated Content -Trends and Implications for Branding. *Ereview of Tourism Research*.

Compilation of References

Gretzel, U. (2007). *Online travel review study: role and impact of online travel reviews. Texas A&M University*. Laboratory for Intelligent Systems in Tourism.

Gretzel, U., & Jamal, T. (2009). Conceptualizing the Creative Tourist Class: Technology, Mobility, and Tourism Experiences. *Tourism Analysis*, *14*(4), 471–481. doi:10.3727/108354209X12596287114219

Gretzel, U., Sigala, M., Xiang, Z., & Koo, C. (2015). Smart tourism: Foundations and developments. *Electronic Markets*, *25*(3), 179–188. doi:10.100712525-015-0196-8

Gretzel, U., & Yoo, H. K. (2008). Use and impact of online travel reviews. *Information and Communication Technologies in Tourism*, *2008*(2), 35–46. doi:10.1007/978-3-211-77280-5_4

Grimaldi, Kenney, Siegel, & Wright. (2011). 30 years after Bayh-Dole: reassessing academic entrepreneurship. *Research Policy, 40*, 1045-1057.

Gubbi, J., Buyya, R., Marusic, S., & Palaniswami, M. (2013). Internet of things (IoT). *Future Generation Computer Systems*, *29*(7), 1645–1660. doi:10.1016/j.future.2013.01.010

Gundersen, M. G., Heide, M., & Olsson, U. H. (1996). Hotel guest satisfaction among business travelers: What are the important factors? *The Cornell Hotel and Restaurant Administration Quarterly*, *37*(2), 72–81. doi:10.1177/001088049603700222

Gursoy, D. (2019). A critical review of determinants of information search behavior and utilization of online reviews in decision making process. *International Journal of Hospitality Management*, *76*, 53–60. doi:10.1016/j.ijhm.2018.06.003

Guttentag, D. A. (2010). Virtual reality: Applications and implications for tourism. *Tourism (Zagreb)*.

Hadad, S., Hadad, Y., Malul, M., & Rosenboim, M. (2012). The economic efficiency of the tourism industry: A global comparison. *Tourism Economics*, *18*(5), 931–940. doi:10.5367/te.2012.0165

Hamari, J., Sjöklint, M., & Ukkonen, A. (2016). The sharing economy: Why people participate in collaborative consumption. *Journal of the Association for Information Science and Technology*, *67*(9), 2047–2059. doi:10.1002/asi.23552

Hammady, R., Ma, M., Strathern, C., & Mohamad, M. (2020). Design and development of a spatial mixed reality touring guide to the Egyptian museum. *Multimedia Tools and Applications*, *79*(5), 3465–3494. doi:10.100711042-019-08026-w

Han, H., & Hyun, S. S. (2017). Impact of hotel-restaurant image and quality of physical-environment, service, and food on satisfaction and intention. *International Journal of Hospitality Management*, *63*, 82–92. doi:10.1016/j.ijhm.2017.03.006

Han, W., McCabe, S., Wang, Y., & Chong, A. Y. L. (2018). Evaluating user-generated content in social media: An effective approach to encourage greater pro-environmental behavior in tourism? *Journal of Sustainable Tourism*, *26*(4), 600–614. doi:10.1080/09669582.2017.1372442

Harb, A. A., Fowler, D., Chang, H. J., Blum, S. C., & Alakaleek, W. (2019). Social media as a marketing tool for events. *Journal of Hospitality and Tourism Technology*, *10*(1), 28–44. doi:10.1108/JHTT-03-2017-0027

Hargreaves, C. A. (2015). Analysis of hotel guest satisfaction ratings and reviews: An application in Singapore. *American Journal of Marketing Research*, *1*(4), 208–214.

Harrigan, P., Evers, U., Miles, M., & Daly, T. (2017). Customer engagement with tourism social media brands. *Tourism Management*, *59*, 597–609. doi:10.1016/j.tourman.2016.09.015

Harrison, R., Byrne, S., & Clarke, A. (2013). *Reassembling the collection: ethnographic museums and indigenous agency*. SAR Press.

Hassanien, A., & Dale, C. (2012). Drivers and barriers of new product development and innovation in event venues: A multiple case study. *Journal of Facilities Management*, *10*(1), 75–92. doi:10.1108/14725961211200414

Hays, S., Page, S. J., & Buhalis, D. (2013). Social Media as a destination marketing tool: Its use by national tourism organization. *Current Issues in Tourism*, *16*(3), 211–239. doi:10.1080/13683500.2012.662215

Hede, A. M., & Kellett, P. (2012). Building online brand communities: Exploring the benefits, challenges and risks in the Australian event sector. *Journal of Vacation Marketing*, *18*(3), 239–250. doi:10.1177/1356766712449370

Henderson, J. C. (2011). Religious tourism and its management: The hajj in Saudi Arabia. *International Journal of Tourism Research*, *13*(6), 541–552. doi:10.1002/jtr.825

Heo, J. K., Jogaratnam, G., & Buchanan, P. (2004). Customer-focused adaptation in New York City hotels: Exploring the perceptions of Japanese and Korean travelers. *International Journal of Hospitality Management*, *23*(1), 39–53. doi:10.1016/j.ijhm.2003.07.003

Herbert, D. (2001). Literary Places, Tourism and the Heritage Experience. *Annals of Tourism Research*, *28*(2), 312–333. doi:10.1016/S0160-7383(00)00048-7

Herzberg, F., Mausner, B., & Snyderman, B. B. (1959). *The motivation to work*. John Wiley and Sons.

Hiller, H. H., & Franz, T. M. (2004). New ties, old ties and lost ties: The use of the internet in diaspora. *New Media & Society*, *6*(6), 731–752. doi:10.1177/146144804044327

Hinterholzer, T., & Jooss, M. (2013). *Social Media Marketing und Management im Tourismus*. Springer Verlag. doi:10.1007/978-3-642-37952-9

Hoffman, D. L., & Fodor, M. (2010). Can You Measure the ROI of Your Social Media Marketing? *Mit Sloan Management Review*, *52*(1).

Hollebeek, L. D., Glynn, M. S., & Brodie, R. J. (2014). Consumer brand engagement in social media: Conceptualization, scale development and validation. *Journal of Interactive Marketing*, *28*(2), 149–165. doi:10.1016/j.intmar.2013.12.002

Hossain, A., Suchana, J. J., & Avi, A. R. (2020). Promoting Bangladesh Tourism through the Internet: Theoretical Perspectives and Empirical Evidence. *Canadian Journal of Business and Information Studies*, *2*(5), 87–95. doi:10.34104/cjbis.020.087095

Hoving, K. (2017). *Digital Detox Tourism: Why disconnect? What are the motives of Dutch tourists to undertake a digital detox holiday?* Academic Press.

Huang, C. Y., Chou, C. J., & Lin, P. C. (2010). Involvement theory in constructing bloggers' intention to purchase travel products. *Tourism Management*, *31*(4), 513–526. doi:10.1016/j.tourman.2009.06.003

Hudson, S., & Gilbert, D. (2006). The Internet and small hospitality businesses: B&B marketing in Can-ada. *Journal of Hospitality & Leisure Marketing*, *14*(1), 99–116. doi:10.1300/J150v14n01_06

Hughes, K., & Moscardo, G. (2019). ICT and the future of tourist management. *Journal of Tourism Futures*, *5*(3), 228–240. doi:10.1108/JTF-12-2018-0072

Hunt, J. D. (1975). Image as a factor in tourism development. *Journal of Travel Research*, *13*(3), 1–7. doi:10.1177/004728757501300301

Husain, W., & Dih, L. Y. (2012). A framework of a personalized location-based traveler recommendation system in mobile application. *International Journal of Multimedia and Ubiquitous Engineering*, *7*(3), 11–18.

Compilation of References

Hwang, B., & He, Z. (1999). Media Uses and Acculturation Among Chinese Immigrants in the USA. *Gazette (Leiden, Netherlands)*, *61*(1), 5–22. doi:10.1177/0016549299061001001

IAB Spain. (2020). *Estudio Redes Sociales 2020*. IAB Spain. Retrieved from https://iabspain.es/estudio/estudio-redes-sociales-2020/

Ikhwan, A., Yetri, M., Syahra, Y., Halim, J., Siahaan, A. P. U., Aryza, S., & Yacob, Y. M. (2018). A Novelty of Data Mining for Promoting Education based on FP-Growth Algorithm. *International Journal of Civil Engineering and Technology*, *9*(7), 1660–1669.

INDICATE. (2012, August). *Handbook on virtual exhibitions and virtual performances*. Available at: www.indicate-project.eu/getFile.php?id=412

Iriobe, O., & Abiola-Oke, E. (2019). Moderating effect of the use of eWOM on subjective norms, behavioural control and religious tourist revisit intention. *International Journal of Religious Tourism and Pilgrimage*, *7*(3).

Islam, F., & Islam, N. (2006). *Tourism in Bangladesh: An Analysis of Foreign Tourist arrivals*. http://stad.adu.edu.tr/TURKCE/makaleler/stadbah2004/makale040103.asp

Ivanov, S., & Webster, C. (2019). Conceptual framework of the use of robots, artificial intelligence and service automation in travel, tourism, and hospitality companies. In *Robots, artificial intelligence, and service automation in travel, tourism and hospitality*. Emerald Publishing Limited. doi:10.1108/978-1-78756-687-320191002

Jacobsen, J. K. S., & Munar, A. M. (2012). Tourist information search and destination choice in a digital age. *Tourism Management Perspectives*, *1*, 39–47. doi:10.1016/j.tmp.2011.12.005

Jacobson, J., Gruzd, A., & Hernández-García, Á. (2020). Social media marketing: Who is watching the watchers? Journal of Retailing and Consumer Services.

Jadhav, V., Raman, S., Patwa, N., Moorthy, K., & Pathrose, J. (2018). Impact of Facebook on leisure travel behavior of Singapore residents. *International Journal of Tourism Cities*, *4*(2), 6–20. doi:10.1108/IJTC-06-2017-0032

Jafari, J., & Scott, N. (2014). Muslim world and its tourisms. In Annals of Tourism Research (Vol. 44, Issue 1, pp. 1–19). Pergamon. doi:10.1016/j.annals.2013.08.011

Jafari, J., & Aaser, D. (1988). Tourism as the subject of doctoral dissertations. *Annals of Tourism Research*, *15*(3), 407–429. doi:10.1016/0160-7383(88)90030-8

Jain, S., & Mishra, S. (2020). Luxury fashion consumption in sharing economy: A study of Indian millennials. *Journal of Global Fashion Marketing*, *11*(2), 171–189. doi:10.1080/20932685.2019.1709097

Jalilvand, M. R., Ebrahimi, A., & Samiei, N. (2013). Electronic word of mouth effects on tourists' attitudes toward Islamic destinations and travel intention: An empirical study in Iran. *Procedia: Social and Behavioral Sciences*, *81*, 484–489. doi:10.1016/j.sbspro.2013.06.465

Jannach, D., Zanker, M., & Fuchs, M. (2014). Leveraging multi-criteria customer feedback for satisfaction analysis and improved recommendations. *Information Technology & Tourism*, *14*(2), 119–149. doi:10.100740558-014-0010-z

Januszewska, M., Jaremen, D. E., & Nawrocka, E. (2015). The effects of the use of ICT by tourism enterprises. *The Effects of the Use of ICT by Tourism Enterprises*, *16*(2), 65–73. doi:10.18276mt.2015.16-07

Jashi, C. (2013). Significance of Social Media Marketing in Tourism. *8th Silk Road International Conference "Development of Tourism in Black and Caspian Seas Regions,"* 37–40

JB B, M. P., Thulasi, P. C., & Philip, J. (2013). Nomophobia-do we really need to worry about. *Reviews of Progress*, *1*(1), 1–5.

Jeong, M., & Oh, H. (1998). Quality function deployment: An extended framework for service quality and customer satisfaction. *Journal on Information Systems in Developing Countries*, *36*(1), 1–21.

Jeong, M., & Shin, H. H. (2020). Tourists' Experiences with Smart Tourism Technology at Smart Destinations and Their Behavior Intentions. *Journal of Travel Research*, *59*(8), 1464–1477. doi:10.1177/0047287519883034

Jeong, Y., & Kim, S. (2019). Exploring a suitable model of destination image: The case of a small-scale recurring sporting event. *Asia Pacific Journal of Marketing and Logistics*, *31*(5), 1287–1307. doi:10.1108/APJML-10-2018-0441

Jiang, Y., & Balaji, M. S. (2021). Getting unwired: What drives travellers to take a digital detox holiday? *Tourism Recreation Research*, ●●●, 1–17.

Jin, D., Nicely, A., Fan, A., & Adler, H. (2019). Joint effect of service recovery types and times on customer satisfaction in lodging. *Journal of Hospitality and Tourism Management*, *38*, 149–158. doi:10.1016/j.jhtm.2019.01.005

Jorrín, J. (2017). *Sin sol y playa no hay turismo: España copa también las zonas menos visitadas de Europa.* El Confidencial. Retrieved from https://www.elconfidencial.com/economia/2017-08-16/turismo-comunidades-menos-visitadas-turismofobia-extremadura-castilla-mancha-leon-aragon_1429101/

Juang, L. P., & Syed, M. (2019). The Evolution of Acculturation and Development Models for Understanding Immigrant Children and Youth Adjustment. *Child Development Perspectives*, *13*(4), 241–246. doi:10.1111/cdep.12346

Jung, T. H., & Han, D. I. (2014). Augmented Reality (AR) in Urban Heritage Tourism. *e-Review of Tourism Research*, *5*.

Jun, J. W., Ham, C.-D., & Park, J. H. (2014). Exploring the Impact of Acculturation and Ethnic Identity on Korean U.S. Residents' Consumption Behaviors of Utilitarian versus Hedonic Products. *Journal of International Consumer Marketing*, *26*(1), 2–13. doi:10.1080/01924788.2013.848077

Kahn, W. A. (1990). Psychological conditions of personal engagement and disengagement at work. *Academy of Management Journal*, *33*(4), 692–724. doi:10.5465/256287

Källbäck, J. (2019). *Examines the benefits of social media marketing in contrast to traditional advertising*. Academic Press.

Kamal, S. (2017). Social Media Usage and Impact: A Study on Bangladesh Tourism Industry. *International Journal of Case Studies*. Retrieved from https://www.academia.edu/36958530/Social_media_usage_and_impact_a_study_on_Bangladesh_Tourism_Industry

Kamel, S., Rateb, D., & El-Tawil, M. (2009). The impact of ICT investments on economic development in Egypt. *The Electronic Journal on Information Systems in Developing Countries*, *36*(1), 1–21. doi:10.1002/j.1681-4835.2009.tb00248.x

Kampf, R., & Cuhadar, E. (2015). Do computer games enhance learning about conflicts? A cross-national inquiry into proximate and distant scenarios in Global Conflicts. *Computers in Human Behavior*, *52*, 541–549. doi:10.1016/j.chb.2014.08.008

Kane, G. C., Fichman, R. G., Gallaugher, J., & Glaser, J. (2009). Community relations 2.0. *Harvard Business Review*, *87*, 45–50. PMID:19891388

Kaplan, A. M., & Haenlein, M. (2010). Users of the world, unite! The challenges and opportunities of Social Media. *Business Horizons*, *53*(1), 59–68. doi:10.1016/j.bushor.2009.09.003

Kaya, T. (2020). *Tarımsal alanda bilgi ve iletişim teknolojilerinin kullanımı: Adana ili örneği*. Çukurova Üniversitesi.

Compilation of References

Kazak, L. (2016). *The impact of social media on the tourism industry*. Retrieved from https://www.linkedin.com

Keil, J., Pujol, L., Roussou, M., Engelke, T., Schmitt, M., Bockholt, U., & Eleftheratou, S. (2013, October). A digital look at physical museum exhibits: Designing personalized stories with handheld Augmented Reality in museums. In *2013 Digital Heritage International Congress (Digital Heritage)* (Vol. 2, pp. 685-688). IEEE. 10.1109/DigitalHeritage.2013.6744836

Kendzerski, P. (2005). *Web Marketing E Comunicação Digital*. Academic Press.

Kenteris, M., Gavalas, D., & Economou, D. (2009). An innovative mobile electronic tourist guide application. *Personal and Ubiquitous Computing*, *13*(2), 103–118. doi:10.100700779-007-0191-y

Kent, M., & Ellis, K. (2015). People with disability and new disaster communications: Access and the social media mash-up. *Disability & Society*, *30*(3), 419–431. doi:10.1080/09687599.2015.1021756

Kesgin, M., & Murthy, R. S. (2019). Consumer engagement: The role of social currency in online reviews. *Service Industries Journal*, *39*(7-8), 609–636. doi:10.1080/02642069.2018.1553237

Khaliq, R. u. (2019). *Turkey ranks 3rd 'halal tourist' destination: Report*. Retrieved from https://www.aa.com.tr/en/turkey/turkey-ranks-3rd-halal-tourist-destination-report/1449385

Khan, M. Y. H., & Hossain, A. (2018). *The Effect of ICT Application on the Tourism and Hospitality Industries in London*. doi:10.21272ec.4(2).60-68.2018

Khatri, I. (2019). Information Technology in Tourism & Hospitality Industry: A Review of Ten Years' Publications. *Journal of Tourism and Hospitality Education*, *9*, 74–87. doi:10.3126/jthe.v9i0.23682

Kim, B., & Kim, S. S. (2018). Hierarchical value map of religious tourists visiting the Vatican City/Rome. *Tourism Geographies*.

Kim, D. B., & Lee, K. H. (2011). Computer-aided appearance design based on BRDF measurements. *Computer Aided Design*, *43*(9), 1181–1193. doi:10.1016/j.cad.2011.04.015

Kim, D. Y., Jang, S., & Morrison, A. M. (2011). Factors affecting organizational information technology acceptance: A comparison of convention and visitor bureaus and meeting planners in the United States. *Journal of Convention & Event Tourism*, *12*(1), 1–24. doi:10.1080/15470148.2010.551291

Kim, D., & Kim, S. (2017). The Role of Mobile Technology in Tourism: Patents, Articles, News, and Mobile Tour App Reviews. *Sustainability*, *9*(11), 2082. doi:10.3390u9112082

Kim, J. W., & Chock, T. M. (2017). Personality traits and psychological motivations predicting selfie posting behaviors on social networking sites. *Telematics and Informatics*, *34*(5), 560–571. doi:10.1016/j.tele.2016.11.006

Kim, J., & Fesenmaier, D. R. (2015). Sharing Tourism Experiences: The Posttrip Experience. *Journal of Travel Research*, *56*(1), 28–40. doi:10.1177/0047287515620491

Kim, N. S., & Chalip, L. (2004). Why travel to the FIFA World Cup? Effects of motives, background, interest, and constraints. *Tourism Management*, *25*(6), 695–707. doi:10.1016/j.tourman.2003.08.011

Kim, S., Kim, J., Badu-Baiden, F., Giroux, M., & Choi, Y. (2021). Preference for robot service or human service in hotels? Impacts of the COVID-19 pandemic. *International Journal of Hospitality Management*, *93*, 102807. doi:10.1016/j.ijhm.2020.102795

Kim, Y., Wang, Y., & Oh, J. (2016). Digital media use and social engagement: How social media and smartphone use influence social activities of college students. *Cyberpsychology, Behavior, and Social Networking*, *19*(4), 264–269. doi:10.1089/cyber.2015.0408 PMID:26991638

King, C. A., & Garey, J. G. (1997). Relational quality in service encounters. *International Journal of Hospitality Management*, *16*(1), 39–63. doi:10.1016/S0278-4319(96)00045-X

Kiráľová, A., & Pavlíčeka, A. (2015). Development of Social Media Strategies in Tourism Destination. *Procedia: Social and Behavioral Sciences*, *175*, 358–366. doi:10.1016/j.sbspro.2015.01.1211

Kizgin, H., Jamal, A., Dey, B. L., & Rana, N. P. (2018). The Impact of Social Media on Consumers' Acculturation and Purchase Intentions. *Information Systems Frontiers*, *20*(3), 503–514. doi:10.100710796-017-9817-4

Kizgin, H., Jamal, A., Dwivedi, Y. K., & Rana, N. P. (2020). The impact of online vs. offline acculturation on purchase intentions: A multigroup analysis of the role of education. *Journal of Business Research*. Advance online publication. doi:10.1016/j.jbusres.2020.05.011

Kızılcık, O., & Taştan, H. (2019). Mağara turizminin motivasyon faktörlerinin belirlenmesi: Karaca Mağarası Örneği. *Çukurova Üniversitesi Sosyal Bilimler Enstitüsü Dergisi*, *28*(3), 240–251.

Kline, S. L., & Liu, F. (2005). The influence of comparative media use on acculturation, acculturative stress, and family relationships of Chinese international students. *International Journal of Intercultural Relations*, *29*(4), 367–390. doi:10.1016/j.ijintrel.2005.07.001

Kokkossis, H., Tsartas, P., & Grimba, E. (2011). *Special and alternative forms of tourism*. Kritiki.

Konok, V., Gigler, D., Bereczky, B. M., & Miklósi, Á. (2016). Humans' attachment to their mobile phones and its relationship with interpersonal attachment style. *Computers in Human Behavior*, *61*, 537–547. doi:10.1016/j.chb.2016.03.062

Kónya, L. (2006). *Exports and growth: Granger causality analysis on OECD countries with a panel data approach*. doi:10.1016/j.econmod.2006.04.008

Koo, C., Shin, S., Gretzel, U., Hunter, W. C., & Chung, N. (2016). Conceptualization of Smart Tourism Destination Competitiveness. *Asia Pacific Journal of Information Systems*, *26*(4), 561–576. doi:10.14329/apjis.2016.26.4.561

Kozhevnikov, M., & Thornton, R. (2006). Real-Time Data Display, Spatial Visualization Ability, and Learning Force and Motion Concepts. *Journal of Science Education and Technology*, *15*(1), 1. doi:10.100710956-006-0361-0

Krauß, M., & Bogen, M. (March 31, 2010). Conveying Cultural Heritage and Legacy with Innovative AR-based Solutions. In J. Trant & D. Bearman (Eds.), *Museums and the Web 2010: Proceedings*. Archives & Museum Informatics. Available at https://www.archimuse.com/mw2010/papers/krauss/krauss.html

Küçük, M. A. (2013). *İnanç turizmi açısından Türkiye'de dinî mekânlar:(Yahudilik-Hıristiyanlık örneği)*. Berikan Yayınevi.

Kumar, S., & Sharma, D. (2017). Study of ICT and tourism led growth in India and Thailand. *Social Science Asia*, *3*(3), 24–31. https://socialscienceasia.nrct.go.th/index.php/SSAsia/article/view/17

Kumar, N., & Kumar, R. R. (2020). Relationship between ICT and international tourism demand: A study of major tourist destinations. *Tourism Economics*, *26*(6), 908–925. doi:10.1177/1354816619858004

Kumar, R. R., & Kumar, R. (2012). Exploring the nexus between information and communications technology, tourism and growth in Fiji. *Tourism Economics*, *18*(2), 359–371. doi:10.5367/te.2012.0117

Kumar, R. R., Stauvermann, P. J., Kumar, N., & Shahzad, S. J. H. (2019). Exploring the effect of ICT and tourism on economic growth: A study of Israel. *Economic Change and Restructuring*, *52*(3), 221–254. doi:10.100710644-018-9227-8

Kwok, A. O. J., & Koh, S. G. M. (2020). COVID-19 and extended reality (XR). *Current Issues in Tourism*, 1–6. doi:10.1080/13683500.2020.1798896

Compilation of References

La Vanguardia. (2016). *Cuenca celebra su declaración como Ciudad Patrimonio de la Humanidad con una "fiesta de cumpleaños" el 13 de diciembre*. La Vanguardia. Retrieved from https://www.lavanguardia.com/vida/20161206/412438221880/cuenca-celebra-su-declaracion-como-ciudad-patrimonio-de-la-humanidad-con-una-fiesta-de-cumpleanos-el-13-de-diciembre.html

Lai, L. S., & To, W. M. (2015). Content analysis of social media: A grounded theory approach. *Journal of Electronic Commerce Research*, *16*, 138.

Landey, J., & Silvers, J. R. (2005). The miracle of training in event management. *Journal of Convention & Event Tourism*. Advance online publication. doi:10.1300/J452v06n03_03

Landström, H., Aström, F., & Harirchi, G. (2013). *Innovation and Entrepreneurship Studies: One or Two Fields of Research?* Springer + Business Media.

Lange-Faria, W., & Elliot, S. (2012). Understanding the role of social media in destination marketing. Tourismos. *An International Multidisciplinary Journal of Tourism*, *7*(1), 193–211.

Laperche, B., Sommers, P., & Uzunidiols, D. (Eds.). (2010). Innovation and Cluster Networks. In The Knowledge Backbone. Peter Lang.

Laporte, A. (2013). Estructuración, comercialización y comunicación de casas museo como productos de turismo cultural. In A. Cardona (Coord.), Casas museo: museología y gestión. Actas de los Congresos sobre Casas Museo (2006, 2007, 2008) (pp. 22-27). Ministerio de Educación, Cultura y Deporte.

Law, R., Chan, I. C. C., & Wang, L. (2018). A comprehensive review of mobile technology use in hospitality and tourism. *Journal of Hospitality Marketing & Management*, *27*(6), 626–648. doi:10.1080/19368623.2018.1423251

Lebbe, A., & Aslam, M. (2020). Long-run relationship between ICT and Tourism Demand in Sri Lanka. *Journal of Information Systems & Information Technology*, *5*(1), 68–74. http://ir.lib.seu.ac.lk/handle/123456789/5435

Lee, B. C., & Wicks, B. (2010). Tourism technology training for destination marketing organisations (DMOs): Need-based content development. *Journal of Hospitality, Leisure, Sport and Tourism Education*, *9*(1), 39–52. doi:10.3794/johlste.91.241

Lee, H., & Kelley, D. (2008). Building dynamic capabilities for innovation: An exploratory study of Key Management Practices. *R & D Management*, *38*(2), 155–168. doi:10.1111/j.1467-9310.2008.00506.x

Lee, K. W., Kim, H. B., Kim, H. S., & Lee, D. S. (2010). The determinants of factors in FIT guests' perception of hotel location. *Journal of Hospitality and Tourism Management*, *17*(1), 167–174. doi:10.1375/jhtm.17.1.167

Lee, S. S., & Lee, C. H. (2014). An Exploratory Study of Convention Specific Social Media Usage by Attendees: Motivations and Effect of Generations on Choice of Convention Information Source and Intention to Use Mobile Application. *Journal of Convention & Event Tourism*, *15*(2), 135–149. doi:10.1080/15470148.2013.862514

Lehmann, J., Lalmas, M., Yom-Tov, E., & Dupret, G. (2012). Models of user engagement. In *International Conference on User Modeling, Adaptation, and Personalization* (Vol. 7379, pp. 164-175). Springer. 10.1007/978-3-642-31454-4_14

Leite, B. S. (2020). Aplicativos de realidade virtual e realidade aumentada para o ensino de Química. *Revista de Estudos e Pesquisas sobre Ensino Tecnológico*, *6*.

Lessig, L. (2008). *Remix: Making art and commerce thrive in the hybrid economy*. Penguin Press. doi:10.5040/9781849662505

Levinson, J., & Gibson, S. (2010). *Guerrilla social media marketing* (1st ed.). Entrepreneur Press.

Levitt, T. (1983). The globalization of markets. *Harvard Business Review*, *61*(3), 92–102.

Li, W., & Darban, A. (2012). *The impact of online social networks on consumers' purchasing decision: The study of food retailers*. Academic Press.

Li, Y. (2012). *ICT, the single greatest force affecting change in the hospitality industry*. Academic Press.

Li, C., Guo, S., Wang, C. L., & Zhang, J. (2019). Veni, vidi, vici: The impact of social media on virtual acculturation in tourism context. *Technological Forecasting and Social Change*, *145*, 513–522. doi:10.1016/j.techfore.2019.01.013

Li, C., & Tsai, W.-H. S. (2015). Social media usage and acculturation: A test with Hispanics in the U.S. *Computers in Human Behavior*, *45*, 204–212. doi:10.1016/j.chb.2014.12.018

Li, F. S., & Ryan, C. (2020). Western guest experiences of a Pyongyang international hotel, North Korea: Satisfaction under conditions of constrained choice. *Tourism Management*, *76*, 103947. doi:10.1016/j.tourman.2019.07.001

Li, F., & Du, T. C. (2017). The effectiveness of word of mouth in offline and online social networks. *Expert Systems with Applications*, *88*, 338–351. doi:10.1016/j.eswa.2017.07.004

Li, J., Xu, L., Tang, L., Wang, S., & Li, L. (2018). Big data in tourism research: A literature review. *Tourism Management*, *68*, 301–323. doi:10.1016/j.tourman.2018.03.009

Lindridge, A., Henderson, G. R., & Ekpo, A. E. (2015). (Virtual) ethnicity, the Internet, and well-being. *Marketing Theory*, *15*(2), 279–285. doi:10.1177/1470593114553328

Lin, K. Y., & Lu, H. P. (2011). Why people use social networking sites: An empirical study integrating network externalities and motivation theory. *Computers in Human Behavior*, *27*(3), 1152–1161. doi:10.1016/j.chb.2010.12.009

Lin, Y. C., Lai, H. J., & Morrison, A. M. (2019). Social servicescape and Asian students: An analysis of spring break island bed and breakfast experiences in Taiwan. *Tourism Management Perspectives*, *31*, 165–173. doi:10.1016/j.tmp.2019.04.005

Li, T. E., McKercher, B., & Chan, E. T. H. (2020). Towards a conceptual framework for diaspora tourism. *Current Issues in Tourism*, *23*(17), 2109–2126. doi:10.1080/13683500.2019.1634013

Litvin, S. W., Goldsmith, R. E., & Pan, B. A. (2018). Retrospective view of electronic word-of-mouth in hospitality and tourism management. *International Journal of Contemporary Hospitality Management*, *30*(1), 1–26. doi:10.1108/IJCHM-08-2016-0461

Llodrá-Riera, I. (2014). *Gestión de la imagen del destino en el contexto del turismo 2.0: Recomendaciones estratégicas para las Organizaciones de Marketing de los Destinos (OMD)* (Doctoral dissertation). Universidad de Castilla-La Mancha, Spain.

Llodrá-Riera, I., Martínez-Ruiz, M., Jiménez-Zarco, A., & Izquierdo-Yusta, A. A. (2015). multidimensional analysis of the information sources construct and its relevance for destination image formation. *Tourism Management*, *48*, 319–328. doi:10.1016/j.tourman.2014.11.012

Lo, I. S., McKercher, B., Lo, A., Cheung, C., & Law, R. (2011). Tourism and online photography. *Tourism Management*, *32*(4), 725–731. doi:10.1016/j.tourman.2010.06.001

López García, J. J., Lizcano, D., Ramos, C. M., & Matos, N. (2019). Digital marketing actions that achieve a better attraction and loyalty of users: An analytical study. *Future Internet*, *11*(6), 130. doi:10.3390/fi11060130

Loureiro, S. M. C., Guerreiro, J., & Ali, F. (2020). 20 years of research on virtual reality and augmented reality in tourism context: A text-mining approach. *Tourism Management*, *77*, 104028. doi:10.1016/j.tourman.2019.104028

Luo, Q., & Zhong, D. (2015). Using social network analysis to explain communication characteristics of travel-related electronic word-of-mouth on social networking sites. *Tourism Management*, *46*, 274–282. doi:10.1016/j.tourman.2014.07.007

Compilation of References

Lu, W., & Stepchenkova, S. (2015). User-generated content as a research mode in tourism and hospitality applications: Topics, methods, and software. *Journal of Hospitality Marketing & Management*, *24*(2), 119–154. doi:10.1080/19368623.2014.907758

MacKay, K. J., & Fesenmaier, D. R. (2000). An exploration of cross-cultural destination image assessment. *Journal of Travel Research*, *38*(4), 417–423. doi:10.1177/004728750003800411

MacLeod, D. V. L. (2004). *Tourism, globalisation and cultural change: an island community perspective*. Channel View Publications.

Magano, J., & Cunha, M. (2020). Digital marketing impact on tourism in Portugal: A quantitative study. *African Journal of Hospitality, Tourism and Leisure*, *9*.

Mainolfi, G., & Marino, V. (2020). Destination beliefs, event satisfaction and post-visit product receptivity in event marketing. Results from a tourism experience. *Journal of Business Research*, *116*, 699–710. doi:10.1016/j.jbusres.2018.03.001

Makiwa, J. (2018). Developing and validating an ICT adoption framework for SMES in developing countries: A case of Zimbabwe. *Management Journal*, *17*(1), 7–28.

Manap KhairulHilmi, A. A. N. (2013). *The Role of User Generated Content (UGC) in Social Media for Tourism Sector*. Retrieved from http://www.westeastinstitute.com/wp-content/uploads/2013/07/Khairul-Hilmi-A-Manap.pdf

Manap, K., & Adzharudin, N. (2013). *The Role of User Generated Content (UGC) in Social Media for Tourism Sector*. Academic Press.

Mandić, A., & Garbin Praničević, D. (2019). Progress on the role of ICTs in establishing destination appeal: Implications for smart tourism destination development. *Journal of Hospitality and Tourism Technology*, *10*(4), 791–813. doi:10.1108/JHTT-06-2018-0047

Mangold, W. G., & Faulds, D. J. (2009). Social media: The new hybrid element of the promotion mix. *Business Horizons*, *52*(4), 357–365. doi:10.1016/j.bushor.2009.03.002

Mansfield, C. (2017). Travel Writing in Place Branding. A Case Study on Nantes. *Journal of Tourism. Heritage & Services Marketing*, *3*(2), 1–7.

Manyika, J., Chiu, M., Bughin, J., Dobbs, R., Bisson, P., & Marrs, A. (2013). *Disruptive Technologies*. McKinsey Global Institute.

Marcussen, C. (1999). *Internet Distribution of European Travel and Tourism Services*. Research Centre of Bornholm.

Marine-Roig, E., & Clave, S. A. (2015). Tourism analytics with massive usergenerated content: A case study of Barcelona. *Journal of Destination Marketing & Management*, *4*(3), 162–172. doi:10.1016/j.jdmm.2015.06.004

Mariussen, A., Von Ibenfeldt, C., & Vespestad, M. K. (2014). The Typology and Role of Online Information Sources in Destination Image Formation: An Eye-Tracking Study. *The International Journal of Digital Accounting Research*, *14*, 141–164. doi:10.4192/1577-8517-v14_6

Marques, A. (2020). *Using Storytelling and Creative writing for the virtual promotion of Arts & Culture* (Master's thesis). Available at: https://recipp.ipp.pt/handle/10400.22/17528

Marques, L., & Borba, C. (2017). Co-creating the city: Digital technology and creative tourism. *Tourism Management Perspectives*, *24*, 86–93. doi:10.1016/j.tmp.2017.07.007

Marras, I., Nikolaidis, N., Mikrogeorgis, G., Lyroudia, K., & Pitas, I. (2008). A virtual system for cavity preparation in endodontics. *Journal of Dental Education*, *72*(4), 494–502. doi:10.1002/j.0022-0337.2008.72.4.tb04514.x PMID:18381855

Marsilio, M., & Vianna, S. L. G. (2015). Agências de Viagens e Turismo e o Impacto da Internet: um Estudo Bibliométrico. *Turismo - Visão e Ação, 16*(2), 450–476.

Marty, P. F. (2008). Museum websites and museum visitors: Digital museum resources and their use. *Museum Management and Curatorship, 23*(1), 81–99. doi:10.1080/09647770701865410

Matzler, K., Pechlaner, H., Abfalter, D., & Wolf, M. (2005). Determinants of response to customer e-mail enquiries to hotels: Evidence from Austria. *Tourism Management, 26*(2), 249–259. doi:10.1016/j.tourman.2003.10.001

Maudlin, L. (2019). *Weekly Travel News*. Retrieved from www.tourism-review.com: https://www.tourism-review.com/turkey-could-increase-its-tourism-revenues-news11070

McCabe, S., Sharples, M., & Foster, C. (2012). Stakeholder engagement in the design of scenarios of technology-enhanced tourism services. *Tourism Management Perspectives, 4*, 36–44. doi:10.1016/j.tmp.2012.04.007

McEwen, W. (2004). Why satisfaction isn't satisfying. *Gallup Management Journal Online, 11*, 1–4.

McNamara, K. E., & Prideaux, B. (2011). Experiencing 'natural' heritage. *Current Issues in Tourism, 14*(1), 47–55. doi:10.1080/13683500.2010.492852

Mehdizadeh, S. (2010). Self-Presentation 2.0: Narcissism and Self-Esteem on Facebook. *Cyberpsychology, Behavior, and Social Networking, 13*(4), 357–364. doi:10.1089/cyber.2009.0257 PMID:20712493

Mehrotra, A., & Lobo, J. (2020). Technology Driving Event Management Industry to the Next Level. *ICRITO 2020 - IEEE 8th International Conference on Reliability, Infocom Technologies and Optimization (Trends and Future Directions)*, 436–441. 10.1109/ICRITO48877.2020.9198025

Mendoza, M. L. (n.d.). *Museo y Ocio. Nuevos paradigmas para el museo del siglo XXI*. Biblioteca Digital da Faculdade de Letras da Universidade do Porto. Available at: https://ler.letras.up.pt/uploads/ficheiros/10372.pdf

Merli, R., Preziosi, M., Acampora, A., & Ali, F. (2019). Why should hotels go green? Insights from guests experience in green hotels. *International Journal of Hospitality Management, 81*, 169–179. doi:10.1016/j.ijhm.2019.04.022

Merli, R., Preziosi, M., Acampora, A., Lucchetti, M. C., & Ali, F. (2019). The impact of green practices in coastal tourism: An empirical investigation on an eco-labelled beach club. *International Journal of Hospitality Management, 77*, 471–482. doi:10.1016/j.ijhm.2018.08.011

Miksch, L., & Schulz, C. (2018). *Disconnect to reconnect: The phenomenon of digital detox as a reaction to technology overload*. Academic Press.

Mikulić, J., & Prebežac, D. (2011). Evaluating hotel animation programs at Mediterranean sun-and-sea resorts: An impact-asymmetry analysis. *Tourism Management, 32*(3), 688–696. doi:10.1016/j.tourman.2010.05.026

Milano, R., Baggio, R., & Piattelli, R. (2011). *The effects of online social media on tourism websites*. Academic Press.

Minghetti, V., & Buhalis, D. (2010). Digital divide in tourism. *Journal of Travel Research, 49*(3), 267–281. doi:10.1177/0047287509346843

Mistiaen, V. (2013). Converting to Islam: British women on prayer, peace and prejudice. *The Guardian*. https://www.theguardian.com/world/2013/oct/11/islam-converts-british-women-prejudice

Moaven, Z., Khajenoori, B., Forooghan Geransaieh, Z., & Rayanpour, R. (2017). Globalization of Culture and Religious Tourism. *European Online Journal of Natural and Social Sciences: Proceedings, 6*(1), 1.

Compilation of References

Mohsin, A. (2005). Tourist attitudes and destination marketing—The case of Australia's Northern Territory and Malaysia. *Tourism Management*, *26*(5), 723–732. doi:10.1016/j.tourman.2004.03.012

Moita, P. (2017). e-Business em Turismo. In F. Silva & J. Umbelino (Eds.), Planeamento e Desenvolvimento Turístico (pp. 159-171). Lisboa: Lidel.

Molina, A., Gómez, M., & Martín-Consuegra, D. (2010). Tourism marketing information and destination image management. *African Journal of Business Management*, *4*, 722–728.

Montes, D. (2020). *Las redes sociales, vitales para las agencias durante el coronavirus.* Agenttravel. Retrieved from https://www.agenttravel.es/noticia-039142_Las-redes-sociales-vitales-para-las-agencias-durante-el-coronavirus.html

Moro, S., Rita, P., & Oliveira, C. (2018). Factors influencing hotels' online prices. *Journal of Hospitality Marketing & Management*, *27*(4), 443–464. doi:10.1080/19368623.2018.1395379

Moutinho, L. (1987). Consumer behaviour in tourism. *European Journal of Marketing*, *21*(10), 5–44. doi:10.1108/EUM0000000004718

Muhammedrisaevna, T. M., Mubinovna, R. F., & Kizi, M. N. U. (2020). The role of information technology in organization and management in tourism. *Academy*, *4*(55).

Muhammedrisaevna, T. M., Mubinovna, R. F., & U Kizi, M. N. (2020). The role of information technology in organization and management in tourism. *Academy*, *4*(55).

Munar, A. M., & Ooi, C. S. (2012). *What social media tell us about the heritage experience. CLCS Working.* Copenhagen Business School.

Ndivo, R. M., & Cantoni, L. (2016). Rethinking local community involvement in tourism development. *Annals of Tourism Research*, *57*, 275–278. doi:10.1016/j.annals.2015.11.014

Nelson, R. R., & Winter, S. G. (1982). *An Evolutionary theory of Economic Change.* The Belknap Press of Harvard University Press.

Neuhofer, B., & Buhalis, D. (2014). *Issues, challenges and trends of technology enhanced tourism experience. The Routledge Handbook of Tourism Marketing.*

Nolan, M. L., & Nolan, S. (1992). Religious sites as tourism attractions in Europe. *Annals of Tourism Research*, *19*(1), 68–78. doi:10.1016/0160-7383(92)90107-Z

Noone, B. M., McGuire, K. A., & Rohlfs, K. V. (2011). Social media meets hotel revenue management: Opportunities, issues and unanswered questions. *Journal of Revenue and Pricing Management*, *10*(4), 293–305. doi:10.1057/rpm.2011.12

Nunez, T. A. (1963). Tourism, Tradition, and Acculturation: Weekendismo in a Mexican Village. *Ethnology*, *2*(3), 352. doi:10.2307/3772866

Nunkoo, R., Teeroovengadum, V., Ringle, C. M., & Sunnassee, V. (2019). Service quality and customer satisfaction: The moderating effects of hotel star rating. *International Journal of Hospitality Management*, 102–414. doi:10.1016/j.ijhm.2019.102414

Nyandro, C. K. (2016). *Factors Influencing Information Communication Technology (ICT) Acceptance and Use in Small and Medium Enterprise (SMEs) in Kenya.* Capella University.

O'Brien, H. L., & Toms, E. G. (2010). The development and evaluation of a survey to measure user engagement. *Journal of the American Society for Information Science and Technology*, *61*(1), 50–69. doi:10.1002/asi.21229

O'Connor, P. (2008). User-generated content and travel: A case study on TripAdvisor.com. *Information and Communication Technologies in Tourism, 2008*(2), 47–58. doi:10.1007/978-3-211-77280-5_5

O'Connor, P. (2010). Managing a hotel's image on TripAdvisor. *Journal of Hospitality Marketing & Management, 19*(7), 754–772. doi:10.1080/19368623.2010.508007

Odabaş, H., & Akkaya, M. A. (2017). *Bilişim Teknolojilerinin Bilgi Merkezlerine ve Hizmetlerine Etkileri*. Hiperlink Publisher.

OECD. (2020). *OECD Tourism Trends and Policies 2020*. Retrieved from https://www.oecd-ilibrary.org/sites/f3b16239-en/index.html?itemId=/content/component/f3b16239-en

Oğrak, A. (2010). *Bilgi Teknolojilerinin Kobi'lerin Rekabet Gücü Üzerindeki Etkileri: İnegöl Mobilya İşletmelerinde Bir Uygulama*. Selçuk University.

Okuyucu, A., & Somuncu, M. (2013, May). Türkiye'de inanç turizmi: bugünkü durum, sorunlar ve gelecek. In *International Conference on Religious Tourism and Tolerance* (pp. 9-12). Academic Press.

Organization for Economic Cooperation and Development. (2007). *Working party of the Information Economy*. OECD. Retrieved from https://www.oecd.org/sti/38393115.pdf

Ozcan, C. C., Aslan, M., & Nazlioglu, S. (2017). Economic freedom, economic growth and international tourism for post-communist (transition) countries: A panel causality analysis. *Theoretical & Applied Economics, 24*(2).

Özekici, Y. K., & Ünlüönen, K. (2019b). Reflection of acculturation in tourism: A systematic literature review. In International Journal of Tourism Anthropology (Vol. 7, Issues 3–4, pp. 284–308). Inderscience Publishers. doi:10.1504/IJTA.2019.107322

Özekici, Y. K., & Ünlüönen, K. (2019a). Bir Küresel Tüketim Kültürü Aracı: Turizm. *Sosyal. Beşeri ve İdari Bilimler Dergisi, 2*(7), 508–524. doi:10.26677/TR1010.2019.196

Özekici, Y. K., & Ünlüönen, K. (2019c). Turizm Odaklı Kültürel Dönüşümü Açıklayıcı Bir Temel: Kültürleşme Teorisi. *Seyahat ve Otel İşletmeciliği Dergisi, 16*(3), 470–492. doi:10.24010oid.539666

Ozer, S. (2013). Theories and Methodologies in Acculturation Psychology: The Emergence of a Scientific Revolution? *National Academy of Psychology, 58*(3), 339–348. doi:10.100712646-013-0203-0

Ozer, S. (2019). Towards a Psychology of Cultural Globalisation: A Sense of Self in a Changing World. *Psychology and Developing Societies, 31*(1), 162–186. doi:10.1177/0971333618819279

Öztamur, D., & Karakadılar, İ. S. (2014). Exploring the role of social media for SMEs: As a new marketing strategy tool for the firm performance perspective. *Procedia: Social and Behavioral Sciences, 150*, 511–520. doi:10.1016/j.sbspro.2014.09.067

Ozturk, A. B., Wei, W., Hua, N., & Qi, R. (2021). Factors affecting attendees continued use of mobile event applications. *Journal of Hospitality and Tourism Technology*. doi:10.1108/JHTT-03-2020-0058

Padma, P., & Ahn, J. (2020). Guest satisfaction and dissatisfaction in luxury hotels: An application of big data. *International Journal of Hospitality Management, 84*, 102–318. doi:10.1016/j.ijhm.2019.102318

Palacio, A.B., Santana, J.D.M., & Gil, S.M. (2012). Los Agentes que conforman la imagen de los destinos turísticos. *Universidad de Las Palmas de Gran Canaria*, 1-22.

Papalexandri, N., & Lymperopoulos, D. (2014). *Public Relations: The function of communication in modern organizations*. Benou.

Paris, C. M., Lee, W., & Seery, P. (2010). The role of social media in promoting special events: Acceptance of Facebook Events. *Information and Communication Technologies In Tourism*, *14*, 531–541. doi:10.1007/978-3-211-99407-8_44

Park, S. B., & Park, K. (2017). Thematic trends in event management research. In International Journal of Contemporary Hospitality Management (Vol. 29, Issue 3, pp. 848–861). doi:10.1108/IJCHM-09-2015-0521

Park, S. B., Ok, C. M., & Chae, B. K. (2016). Using twitter data for cruise tourism marketing and research. *Journal of Travel & Tourism Marketing*, *33*(6), 885–898. doi:10.1080/10548408.2015.1071688

Paryani, K., Masoudi, A., & Cudney, E. A. (2010). *QFD application in the hospitality industry: A hotel case study*. Quality.

Pascoal, S., Tallone, L., & Furtado, M. (2021). The Impact of COVID-19 on Cultural Tourism: Virtual Exhibitions, Technology and Innovation. In *Advances in Tourism, Technology and Smart Systems - Proceedings of ICOTTS'20* (vol. 2). Singapore: Springer.

Pascoal, S., Tallone, L., Furtado, M., & Ribeiro, S. (2018). Marketing public Art: using project based learning to teach creativity and entrepreneurship. In *Polissema 18 Revista de Letras do ISCAP, S. Mamede Infesta*. Instituto Superior de Contabilidade e Administração do Porto. Available at: https://parc.ipp.pt/index.php/Polissema/article/view/3203

Pascoal, S., Tallone, L., Furtado, M., & Ribeiro, S. (2019), Promover o património cultural através do empreendedorismo e da criatividade: o projeto Google Arts & Culture. In *Sensos-E, Revista Multimédia de Investigação em Educação*. InED - Centro de Investigação e Inovação em Educação, da Escola Superior de Educação do Instituto Politécnico do Porto. Available at: https://parc.ipp.pt/index.php/sensos/article/view/3038/1497

Pascoal, S., Tallone, L., & Furtado, M. (2020). Cultural Tourism: using Google Arts & Culture platform to promote a small city in the North of Portugal. In *Advances in Tourism, Technology and Smart Systems, Smart Innovations, Systems and Technology 171* (pp. 47–56). Springer Nature Singapore. doi:10.1007/978-981-15-2024-2_5

Pawłowska-Legwand, A., & Matoga, Ł. (2020). Disconnect from the Digital World to Reconnect with the Real Life: An Analysis of the Potential for Development of Unplugged Tourism on the Example of Poland. *Tourism Planning & Development*, 1–24. doi:10.1080/21568316.2020.1842487

Pearce, L. (2013). *The social psychology of tourist behaviour: International series in experimental social psychology*. Elsevier.

Pedrosa, S. M., & Zappala-Guimarães, M. A. (2019). *Realidade Virtual e Realidade Aumentada: refletindo sobre usos e benefícios na educação*. Academic Press.

Penaloza, L. (1994). Atravesando Fronteras/Border Crossings: A Critical Ethnographic Exploration of the Consumer Acculturation of Mexican Immigrants. *The Journal of Consumer Research*, *21*(1), 54. doi:10.1086/209381

Pereira, N. (2016). *Fazer turismo no passado, com uma aplicação de realidade virtual*. Euronews.

Perez, P., Gonzalez-Sosa, E., Kachach, R., Ruiz, J., Benito, I., Pereira, F., & Villegas, A. (2019, March). Immersive gastronomic experience with distributed reality. In *2019 IEEE 5th Workshop on Everyday Virtual Reality (WEVR)* (pp. 1-6). IEEE. 10.1109/WEVR.2019.8809591

Pergolino, M., Rothman, D., Miller, J., & Miller, J. (2012). *The Definitive Guide to Social Marketing. A Marketo Workbook*. Retrieved from: https://www.slideshare.net/ntdlife/definitive-guidetosocialmarketing-32648238

Perinotto, A., Mota, D., & Ferreira, H. (2018). *As Mídias Sociais e os Influenciadores Digitais na Promoção de Destinos Turísticos*. Anais Brasileiros de Estudos Turísticos.

Perreault, M.-C., & Mosconi, E. (2018). Social media engagement: Content strategy and metrics research opportunities. *Proceedings of the 51st Hawaii International Conference on System Sciences.*

Pesaran, M. H., Pesaran, M. H., Shin, Y., & Smith, R. P. (1999). Pooled Mean Group Estimation of Dynamic Heterogeneous Panels. *Journal of the American Statistical Association, 94*(446), 621–634. doi:10.1080/01621459.1999.10474156

Pesonen, J., Komppula, R., & Riihinen, A. (2015). Typology of senior travellers as users of tourism information technology. *Information Technology & Tourism, 15*(3), 233–252. doi:10.100740558-015-0032-1

Peters, K., Chen, Y. B., Kaplan, A. M., Ognibeni, B., & Pauwels, K. (2013). Social media metrics: A framework and guidelines for managing social media. *Journal of Interactive Marketing, 27*(4), 281–298. doi:10.1016/j.intmar.2013.09.007

Petkova, L., Ryabokon, M., & Vdovychenko, Y. (2019). Modern systems for assessing the informatization of countries in the context of global sustainable development. *Baltic Journal of Economic Studies, 5*(2), 158–170. doi:10.30525/2256-0742/2019-5-2-158-170

Pfaffenberger, B. (1983). Serious pilgrims and frivolous tourists the chimera of tourism in the pilgrimages of Sri Lanka. *Annals of Tourism Research, 10*(1), 57–74. doi:10.1016/0160-7383(83)90115-9

Pham, M. H. T. (2015). "I click and post and breathe, waiting for others to see what i see": On #feministselfies, outfit photos, and networked vanity. *Fashion Theory, 19*(2), 221–241. doi:10.2752/175174115X14168357992436

Phinney, J. (2003). Ethnic identity and acculturation. In K. Chun, P. Organista, & G. Marin (Eds.), *Acculturation: Advances in theory, measurement, and applied research* (pp. 63–81). American Psychological Association Inc. doi:10.1037/10472-006

Phinney, J. S. (1990). Ethnic identity in adolescents and adults: Review of research. *Psychological Bulletin, 108*(3), 499–514. doi:10.1037/0033-2909.108.3.499 PMID:2270238

PhoCusWright. (2013a). *Optimizing the mobile travel experience.* Retrieved from https://www.phocuswright.com/free_reports/optimizing-the-mobile-travel-experience

Phua, J., Jin, S. V., & Kim, J. (2017). Uses and gratifications of social networking sites for bridging and bonding social capital: A comparison of Facebook, Twitter, Instagram, and Snapchat. *Computers in Human Behavior, 72*, 115–122. doi:10.1016/j.chb.2017.02.041

Pine, B. J., & Gilmore, J. H. (1999). *The experience economy: work is theatre & every business a stage.* Harvard Business School.

Piramanayagam, S., Rathore, S., & Seal, P. P. (2020). Destination image, visitor experience, and behavioural intention at heritage centre. *Anatolia, 31*(2), 211–228. doi:10.1080/13032917.2020.1747234

Pırnar, İ., & Miral, A. C. (2000). EU tourism policy and Turkey's situation during the adaptation process. *Management, 12*(7), 436.

Polyzos, S. (2015). *Urban development.* Kritiki Publications.

Poon, A. (1993). *Tourism, Technology and Competitive Strategies.* CAB International.

Porter, M. E. (1996). What is strategy? *Harvard Business Review, 74*(6), 61–78. PMID:10158475

Pujol-Tost, L. (2011). Integrating ICT in exhibitions. *Museum Management and Curatorship, 26*(1), 63–79. doi:10.1080/09647775.2011.540127

Purohit, A. K., Barclay, L., & Holzer, A. (2020). Designing for digital detox: Making social media less addictive with digital nudges. In *Extended Abstracts of the 2020 CHI Conference on Human Factors in Computing Systems* (pp. 1-9). ACM.

Qu, H., Ryan, B., & Chu, R. (2000). The importance of hotel attributes in contributing to travelers' satisfaction in the Hong Kong hotel industry. *Journal of Quality Assurance in Hospitality & Tourism*, *1*(3), 65–83. doi:10.1300/J162v01n03_04

Quinn, B. (2009). Festivals, events, and tourism. In The SAGE Handbook of Tourism Studies (pp. 483–503). doi:10.4135/9780857021076.n27

Quinquiolo, N. C., Santos, C. A., & Souza, M. A. (2020). Uso dos softwares de Realidade Aumentada como Ferramenta Pedagógica: Apresentação do Aplicativo Virtual TEE. Academic Press.

Quinteiro, S., & Baleiro, R. (2017). *Estudos em literatura e turismo*. Universidade de Lisboa. Faculdade de Letras. Centro de Estudos Comparatistas.

Quinteiro, S. (2020). Link up with Technology Application in Literary Tourism. In A. Hassan & A. Sharma (Eds.), *The Emerald Handbook of ICT in Tourism and Hospitality* (pp. 379–389). Emerald Publishing Limited. doi:10.1108/978-1-83982-688-720201024

Qurashi, J., & Sharpley, R. (2018). The impact of Smart Media Technologies on the spiritual experience of Hajj pilgrims. *International Journal of Religious Tourism and Pilgrimage*, *6*(3), 37–48.

Radojevic, T., Stanisic, N., & Stanic, N. (2019). The culture of hospitality: From anecdote to evidence. *Annals of Tourism Research*, *79*, 102789. doi:10.1016/j.annals.2019.102789

Raedersdorf Bollinger, S. (2019). Creativity and forms of managerial control in innovation processes: Tools, viewpoints and practices. *European Journal of Innovation Management*, *32*(2), 214–229. doi:10.1108/EJIM-07-2018-0153

Rafael, C., & Almeida, A. (2017). Impacto da informação online na formação da imagem de destino virtual. *Dos Algarves: A Multidisciplinary E-Journal*, (23), 27-50.

Rahman, Z., Suberamanian, K., Zanuddin, H., Moghavvemi, S., & Nasir, M. H. N. M. (2016). Social media engagement metric analysis: Study on fan page content. *Journal of Telecommunication Electronic and Computer Engineering*, *8*(8), 71–76.

Rajesh, R. (2014). Issues and Trends of Event Tourism Promotion in Destinations: Puducherry, an empirical Study. *IJSSTH*, *1*(6), 25–41.

Raj, R., & Griffin, K. A. (Eds.). (2015). *Religious tourism and pilgrimage management: An international perspective*. Cabi. doi:10.1079/9781780645230.0000

Ramalho, B. (2019). *O Papel dos Influenciadores Digitais Portugueses na Promoção de um Destino Turístico*. Vila do Conde: Politécnico do Porto.

Ramos, C. M., Henriques, C., & Lanquar, R. (2016). Augmented reality for smart tourism in religious heritage itineraries: Tourism experiences in the technological age. In Handbook of Research on Human-Computer Interfaces, Developments, and Applications (pp. 245-272). IGI Global.

Ramos, J. M., & Prats, M. (2019). Procés de creació d'un protocol d'anàlisi de rutes literàries des de la perspectiva de la recerca de didàctica de la literatura. *Didacticae*, *3*, 99–114.

Raskar, R., Welch, G., Cutts, M., Lake, A., Stesin, L., & Fuchs, H. (1998). The office of the future: a unified approach to image-based modeling and spatially immersive displays. *SIGGRAPH 1998 Proceedings of the 25th Annual Conference on Computer Graphics and Interactive Techniques*, 179–188. 10.1145/280814.280861

Raskar, R., Welch, G., & Fuchs, H. (1998). Spatially augmented reality. *Proceeding of the First IEEE Workshop on Augmented Reality*, 63–72.

Rasmussen, E., & Wright, M. (2015). *How can universities facilitate academic spin-offs? An entrepreneurial competency perspective*. Springer Science, Business Media New York. doi:10.100710961-014-9386-3

Redfield, R., Linton, R., & Melville, J. H. (1936). Memorandum for the Study of Acculturation. *American Anthropologist*, *38*(1), 149–152. doi:10.1525/aa.1936.38.1.02a00330

Remoaldo, P., Ribeiro, J. C., Da Cruz Vareiro, L. M., & Santos, J. (2014). Tourists' perceptions of world heritage destinations: The case of Guimarães (Portugal). *Tourism and Hospitality Research*, *14*(4), 206–218. doi:10.1177/1467358414541457

REVFINE. (2020). *11 key technology trends emerging in the travel industry in 2020*. Retrieved From: https://www.revfine.com/technology-trends-travel-industry/

Rhee, H. T., & Yang, S.-B. (2015). Does hotel attribute importance differ by hotel? Focusing on hotel star-classifications and customers' overall ratings. *Computers in Human Behavior*, *50*, 576–587. doi:10.1016/j.chb.2015.02.069

Richard, L. (2013). The role of ICT in the hospitality industry. *International Journal of Scientific Research*, *2*(9), 49–51. doi:10.15373/22778179/SEP2013/17

Richards, G. (2011). Creativity and tourism: The state of the art. *Annals of Tourism Research*, *38*(4), 1225–1253. doi:10.1016/j.annals.2011.07.008

Ricou, J. (2018). *El turismo vende el destino*. La Vanguardia. Retrieved from https://www.lavanguardia.com/ocio/viajes/20180328/441996593656/turistas-fotos-redes-sociales-marketing-visual.html

Rieke, R., Coppolino, L., Hutchison, A., Prieto, E., & Gaber, C. (2012). Security and reliability requirements for advanced security event management. Lecture Notes in Computer Science (Including Subseries Lecture Notes in Artificial Intelligence and Lecture Notes in Bioinformatics), 7531 LNCS, 171–180. doi:10.1007/978-3-642-33704-8_15

Rinschede, G. (1992). Forms of religious tourism. *Annals of Tourism Research*, *19*(1), 51–67. doi:10.1016/0160-7383(92)90106-Y

Robertson, M., Yeoman, I., Smith, K. A., & Mcmahon-Beattie, U. (2015). Technology, society, and visioning the future of music festivals. *Event Management*, *19*(4), 567–587. doi:10.3727/152599515X14465748774001

Robinson, P., Lück, M., & Smith, S. (2013). *Tourism* (1st ed.). CABI. doi:10.1079/9781780642970.0000

Rodrigues, R. A. C. S. (2018). *Realidade virtual e realidade aumentada: o papel das tecnologias nas estratégias de marketing em Portugal* (Doctoral dissertation).

Rodriguez, A., & Rodriguez, S. (2018). Impacto de las tic en el turismo: Caso colombiano. *Cuadernos de Turismo*, *41*, 399–418.

Rodríguez, G. R., & Roget, F. M. (2009). *Nuevos retos para el turismo*. Netbiblo S.L. doi:10.4272/978-84-9745-402-5

Rosenfeld, K. N. (2015). *Digital online culture, identity, and schooling in the twenty-first century*. Palgave Macmillan. doi:10.1057/9781137442604

Ruan, Y. (2020). Perceived host-guest sociability similarity and participants' satisfaction: Perspectives of airbnb guests and hosts. *Journal of Hospitality and Tourism Management*, *45*, 419–428. doi:10.1016/j.jhtm.2020.09.009

Russell, R., Atchinson, M., & Brooks, R. (2008). Business plan competition in tertiary institutions: Encouraging entrepreneurship education. *Journal of Higher Education Policy and Management*, *30*(2), 123–138. doi:10.1080/13600800801938739

Ruta la Sombra del Viento. Ruta de arte y cultura. (n.d.). https://www.catalunya.com/ruta-laposombra-del-vent-24-1-22?language=es

Ruta Mercè Rodoreda. Ruta de arte y cultura. (n.d.). https://www.catalunya.com/rutas-merce-rodoreda-barcelona-24-1-62?language=es

Rutten, R., & Boekema, F. (2009). Universities and Regional Development. Regional Studies, 43(5), 771-775.

Ryan, T., & Xenos, S. (2011). Who uses Facebook? An investigation into the relationship between the Big Five, shyness, narcissism, loneliness, and Facebook usage. *Computers in Human Behavior*, 27(5), 1658–1664. doi:10.1016/j.chb.2011.02.004

Saayman, A., Saayman, M., & Gyekye, A. (2014). Perspectives on the regional economic value of a pilgrimage. *International Journal of Tourism Research*, 16(4), 407–414. doi:10.1002/jtr.1936

Sahoo, D. S. S., & B.G., M. M. (2017). Role of Social Media in Promoting Tourism Business - A Study on Tourism Promoting in Odisha. *International Journal of Creative Research Thoughts*, 23(9), 272–281.

Salavati, S., & Hashim, N. H. (2015). Website adoption and performance by Iranian hotels. *Tourism Management*, 46, 367–374. doi:10.1016/j.tourman.2014.07.017

Sam, D. L., & Berry, J. W. (2010). *Acculturation: When Individuals and Groups of Different Cultural Backgrounds Meet*. Https://Doi.Org/10.1177/1745691610373075 doi:10.1177/1745691610373075

Sambhanthan, A., & Good, A. (2013). *A virtual world model to enhance tourism destination accessibility in developing countries*. Cornell University.

Sánchez-Franco, M. J., Navarro-García, A., & Rondán-Cataluña, F. J. (2019). A naive Bayes strategy for classifying customer satisfaction: A study based on online reviews of hospitality services. *Journal of Business Research*, 101, 499–506. doi:10.1016/j.jbusres.2018.12.051

Sandip, S. (2014). Competitive Marketing Strategies for Tourism Industry in the Light of Bangladesh. *Vision (Basel)*.

SanMiguel, P. (2020). *Influencer Marketing*. Editorial Almazura.

Sann, R., & Lai, P. C. (2020). Understanding homophily of service failure within the hotel guest cycle: Applying NLP-aspect-based sentiment analysis to the hospitality industry. *International Journal of Hospitality Management*, 91, 102–678. doi:10.1016/j.ijhm.2020.102678

Santos, A. (2014). *Visitas imersivas em contexto turístico* (Doctoral dissertation). Instituto Politécnico do Porto. Instituto Superior de Engenharia do Porto.

Santos, V., Ramos, P., Sousa, B., & Valeri, M. (2021). Towards a Framework for the Global Wine Tourism System. *Journal of Organizational Change Management*. Advance online publication. doi:10.1108/JOCM-11-2020-0362

Saprikis, V., Markos, A., Zarmpou, T., & Vlachopoulou, M. (2018). Mobile shopping consumers' behavior: An exploratory study and review. *Journal of Theoretical and Applied Electronic Commerce Research*, 13(1), 71–90. doi:10.4067/S0718-18762018000100105

Sarı, Y., & Kozak, M. (2005). Turizm Pazarlamasına İnternetin Etkisi: Destinasyon Web Siteleri İçin Bir Model Önerisi. *Akdeniz İİBF Dergisi, 5*(9), 248–271. http://acikerisim.mu.edu.tr/xmlui/handle/20.500.12809/8606

Schaeffer & Mirelle. (2016). Development of an academic entrepreneurship in the non-mature context: the role of the University of the hub organisation. *Entrepreneurship & Regional Development*, 28(9-10), 724-745.

Schertler, G. F., & Hargrave, P. A. (1995). Projection structure of frog rhodopsin in two crystal forms. *Proceedings of the National Academy of Sciences of the United States of America*, 92(25), 11578–11582. doi:10.1073/pnas.92.25.11578 PMID:8524807

Schuckert, M., Liu, X., & Law, R. (2015). A segmentation of online reviews by language groups: How English and non-English speakers rate hotels differently. *International Journal of Hospitality Management*, *48*, 143–149. doi:10.1016/j.ijhm.2014.12.007

Schuckert, M., Liu, X., & Law, R. (2016). Insights into suspicious online ratings: Direct evidence from TripAdvisor. *Asia Pacific Journal of Tourism Research*, *21*(3), 259–272. doi:10.1080/10941665.2015.1029954

Schumpeter, J. A. (2008). *Capitalism, socialism and democracy*. Harper Perennial. (Original work published 1942)

Schumpeter, J. A. (2008). *The theory of economic development*. Transaction Publishers. (Original work published 1911)

Scott, A. (1998). *Regions and the World Economy*. Oxford University Press.

Senouci, D. (2021).*The importance of social media in tourism: Facebook and Twitter, Amara ingenieria de Marketing*. Retrieved from: https://www.amara-marketing.com/travel-blog/social-media-tourism-facebook-twitter

Seth, G. (2012). *Analyzing the Effects of Social Media on the Hospitality Industry*. Academic Press.

Shao, G. (2009). Understanding the appeal of user-generated media: A uses and gratification perspective. *Internet Research*, *19*(1), 7–25. doi:10.1108/10662240910927795

Sharma, G., Qiang, Y., Wenjun, S., & Qi, L. (2013). Communication in virtual world: Second life and business opportunities. *Information Systems Frontiers*, *15*(4), 677–694. doi:10.100710796-012-9347-z

Sheldon, P. (1997). *Tourism information technology*. CAB International.

Shen, S., Sotiriadis, M., & Zhou, Q. (2020). Could Smart Tourists Be Sustainable and Responsible as Well? The Contribution of Social Networking Sites to Improving Their Sustainable and Responsible Behavior. *Sustainability*, *12*(4), 1470. doi:10.3390u12041470

Shereni, N. C., & Chambwe, M. (2020). Hospitality Big Data Analytics in Developing Countries. *Journal of Quality Assurance in Hospitality & Tourism*, *21*(3), 361–369. doi:10.1080/1528008X.2019.1672233

Sheresheva, M. Y. (2018). The Russian tourism and hospitality market: new challenges and destinations. In Worldwide Hospitality and Tourism Themes (Vol. 10, Issue 4, pp. 400–411). Emerald Group Publishing Ltd. doi:10.1108/WHATT-04-2018-0027

Siegel, D. S., & Wright, M. (2015). Academic entrepreneurship: Time for a rethink? *British Journal of Management*, *26*(4), 582–595. doi:10.1111/1467-8551.12116

Sigala, M. (2003). Developing and benchmarking Internet marketing strategies in the hotel sector in Greece. *Journal of Hospitality & Tourism Research (Washington, D.C.)*, *27*(4), 375–401. doi:10.1177/10963480030274001

Sigala, M. (2018). New technologies in tourism: From multi-disciplinary to anti-disciplinary advances and trajectories. *Tourism Management Perspectives*, *25*, 151–155. doi:10.1016/j.tmp.2017.12.003

Silberberg, T. (1995). Cultural tourism and business opportunities for museums and heritage sites. *Tourism Management*, *16*(5), 361–365. doi:10.1016/0261-5177(95)00039-Q

Silva, J. (2018). *Marketing digital e Redes Sociais no Turismo: O caso do Municipio de Ovar*. Universidade de Aveiro.

Simas, D., & Júnior, A. (2018). Sociedade em Rede: Os Influencers Digitais e a Publicidade Oculta nas Redes Sociais. *Revista de Direito. Governança e Novas Tecnologias*, *4*(1), 17–32. doi:10.26668/IndexLawJournals/2526-0049/2018.v4i1.4149

Singh, R. P. (2006). 15 Pilgrimage in Hinduism. *Tourism, religion and spiritual journeys*, 220.

Compilation of References

Singh, S. (2008). *Social Media Marketing for Dummies*. John Wiley and Sons.

Sirirak, S., Islam, N., & Khang, D. B. (2015). Does ICT adoption enhance hotel performance? *Journal of Hospitality and Tourism Technology, 2*(1). doi:10.1108/17579881111112403

Slocum, S. L., & Lee, S. (2014). Green ICT practices in event management: Case study approach to examine motivation, management and fiscal return on investment. *Information Technology & Tourism, 14*(4), 347–362. doi:10.100740558-014-0019-3

Smith, K. (2016). *37 estadísticas en Instagram*. Brandwatch. Retrieved from https://www.brandwatch.com/es/blog/37-estadisticas-de-instagram/

Smith, W. W., Li, X. R., Pan, B., Witte, M., & Doherty, S. T. (2015). Tracking destination image across the trip experience with smartphone technology. *Tourism Management, 48*, 113–122. doi:10.1016/j.tourman.2014.04.010

So, K. K. F., King, C., & Sparks, B. (2014). Customer engagement with tourism brands: Scale development and validation. *Journal of Hospitality & Tourism Research (Washington, D.C.), 38*(3), 304–329. doi:10.1177/1096348012451456

Soldevila, L. (2009). *Geografia literària: Comarques Barcelonines*. Pòrtic.

Soldevila, L. (2010). Les rutes literàries. Algunes pautes organitzatives i logístiques a tenir en compte. In G. Bordons (Ed.), *Manual de gestió del patrimoni literari de l'Alt Pirineu i Aran*. Garsineu – CAN.

Soldevila, L., & San Eugenio, J. (2012). Geografia literària dels Països Catalans. El cas de la comarca d'Osona. *AUSA, 170*, 979–1001.

Song, S. J., & Yoo, M. (2016). The Role of Social Media during the Pre-purchasing Stage. *Journal of Hospitality and Tourism Technology, 7*(1), 84–99. doi:10.1108/JHTT-11-2014-0067

Sood, A. (2011, February 1). *Explore museums and great works of art in the Google Art Project*. Available at: https://googleblog.blogspot.com/2011/02/explore-museums-and-great-works-of-art

Soren, B. J. (2005). Best practices in creating quality online experiences for museum users. *Museum Management and Curatorship, 20*(2), 131–148. doi:10.1080/09647770500402002

Sotiriadis, M. D. (2017). Sharing tourism experiences in social media. *International Journal of Contemporary Hospitality Management, 29*(1), 179–225. doi:10.1108/IJCHM-05-2016-0300

Sousa, B. B., Magalhães, F. C., & Soares, D. B. (2021). The Role of Relational Marketing in Specific Contexts of Tourism: A Luxury Hotel Management Perspective. In Building Consumer-Brand Relationship in Luxury Brand Management (pp. 223-243). IGI Global. doi:10.4018/978-1-7998-4369-6.ch011

Sousa, B., & Rodrigues, S. (2019). The role of personal brand on consumer behaviour in tourism contexts: The case of madeira. *Enlightening Tourism. A Pathmaking Journal, 9*(1), 38-62. doi:10.33776/et.v9i1.3597

Sousa, B., & Silva, M. (2019). Creative tourism and destination marketing as a safeguard of the cultural heritage of regions: The case of sabugueiro village. *Revista Brasileira de Gestão e Desenvolvimento Regional, 15*(5), 78–92.

Sox, C. B., Campbell, J. M., Kline, S. F., Strick, S. K., & Crews, T. B. (2016). Technology use within meetings: A generational perspective. *Journal of Hospitality and Tourism Technology, 7*(2), 158–181. doi:10.1108/JHTT-09-2015-0035

Sparks, B. A., & Browning, V. (2011). The impact of online reviews on hotel booking intentions and perception of trust. *Tourism Management, 32*(6), 1310–1323. doi:10.1016/j.tourman.2010.12.011

Spencer, A. (2019). ICT and Caribbean Tourism. In *In: Travel and Tourism in the Caribbean*. Palgrave Macmillan.

Spencer, A. J. (2014). Tourism and technology in the global economy: Challenges for small island states. *Worldwide Hospitality and Tourism Themes, 6*(2), 152–165. doi:10.1108/WHATT-12-2013-0047

Spigel, B. (2015). The relational organization of entrepreneurial ecosystems. *Entrepreneurship Theory and Practice, 12*, 1-24.

Spinelli, M. A., & Canavos, G. C. (2000). Investigating the relationhip between employee satisfaction and guest satisfaction. *Cornell Hotel and Restaurant Administration Quarterly, 41*(6), 29-33.7

St. John, J., St. John, K., & Han, B. (2021). Entrepreneurial crowdfunding backer motivations: A latent Dirichlet allocation approach. *European Journal of Innovation Management*. Advance online publication. doi:10.1108/EJIM-05-2021-0248

Stamboulis, Y., & Skayannis, P. (2003). Innovation strategies and technology for experience-based tourism. *Tourism Management, 24*(1), 35–43. Advance online publication. doi:10.1016/S0261-5177(02)00047-X

Standing, C., Tang-Taye, J.-P., & Boyer, M. (2014). *The Impact of the Internet in Travel and Tourism: A Research Review 2001–2010*. doi:10.1080/10548408.2014.861724

Statista. (2020). *Number of monthly Facebook users worldwideas of 3rd quarter 2020*. Retrieved from https://www.statista.com/statistics/264810/number-of-monthly-active-facebook-users-worldwide/

Stebbins, R. (2001). Serious Leisure. *Society, 38*(4), 53–57. doi:10.100712115-001-1023-8

Stefani, U., Schiavone, F., Laperche, B., & Burger-Helmchen, T. (2020). New tools and practices for financing novelty: A research agenda. *European Journal of Innovation Management, 23*(2), 314–328. doi:10.1108/EJIM-08-2019-0228

Stelzner, M. (2011). *2011 Social Media Marketing Industry Report How Marketers Are Using Social Media To Grow Their Businesses*. Retrieved from http://www.socialmediaexaminer. com/SocialMediaMarketingReport2011.pdf

Stokes, R. (2006). Network-based strategy making for events tourism. *European Journal of Marketing, 40*(5–6), 682–695. doi:10.1108/03090560610657895

Stringam, B. B., & Gerdes, J. (2010). An analysis of word-of-mouse ratings and guest comments of online hotel distribution sites. *Journal of Hospitality Marketing and Management, 19*(7), 773–796.

Stuart, J., & Kurek, A. (2019). Looking hot in selfies: Narcissistic beginnings, aggressive outcomes? *International Journal of Behavioral Development, 43*(6), 500–506. doi:10.1177/0165025419865621

Submitted, T., & Policy, P. (2020). *Effectiveness of Social Media in Promoting Tourism in Bangladesh By TARANNUM*. Tasnim Effectiveness of Social Media in Promoting Tourism in Bangladesh By.

Sukhu, A., Choi, H., Bujisic, M., & Bilgihan, A. (2019). Satisfaction and positive emotions: A comparison of the influence of hotel guests' beliefs and attitudes on their satisfaction and emotions. *International Journal of Hospitality Management, 77*, 51–63. doi:10.1016/j.ijhm.2018.06.013

Su, L., Swanson, S. R., & Chen, X. (2016). The effects of perceived service quality on repurchase intentions and subjective well-being of Chinese tourists: The mediating role of relationship quality. *Tourism Management, 52*, 82–95. doi:10.1016/j.tourman.2015.06.012

Su, N., Reynolds, D., & Sun, B. (2015). How to make your Facebook posts attractive: A case study of a leading budget hotel brand fan page. *International Journal of Contemporary Hospitality Management, 27*(8), 1772–1790. doi:10.1108/IJCHM-06-2014-0302

Sussamann, S., & Vanhegan, H. J. (2000). Virtual Reality and the Tourism Product: Substitution or Complement? Realidade Virtual no Turismo: Entretenimento ou Mudança de Paradigma? *Rosa dos Ventos, 11*(4), 908-921.

Compilation of References

Syvertsen, T., & Enli, G. (2020). Digital detox: Media resistance and the promise of authenticity. *Convergence*, *26*(5-6), 1269–1283. doi:10.1177/1354856519847325

Tajfel, H. (1982). *Social Psychology of Intergroup Relations*. Http://Dx.Doi.Org/10.1146/Annurev.Ps.33.020182.000245 doi:10.1146/annurev.ps.33.020182.000245

Talantis, S., Shin, Y. H., & Severt, K. (2020). Conference mobile application: Participant acceptance and the correlation with overall event satisfaction utilizing the technology acceptance model (TAM). *Journal of Convention & Event Tourism*, *21*(2), 100–122. doi:10.1080/15470148.2020.1719949

Tam, S. (2015). Entrepreneurial Ecosystems and Regional Policy: Sympathetic A Critique. *European Planning Studies*, *23*(9), 1759–1769. doi:10.1080/09654313.2015.1061484

Tarutė, A., & Gatautis, R. (2014). ICT Impact on SMEs Performance. *Procedia: Social and Behavioral Sciences*, *110*, 1218–1225. doi:10.1016/j.sbspro.2013.12.968

Tavakoli, R., & Mura, P. (2015). "Journeys in Second Life" - Iranian Muslim women's behaviour in virtual tourist destinations. *Tourism Management*, *46*, 398–407. doi:10.1016/j.tourman.2014.07.015

Taylor, J. (2001). Authenticity and Sincerity in Tourism. *Annals of Tourism Research*, *28*(1), 7–26. doi:10.1016/S0160-7383(00)00004-9

TecnoHotelNews. (2018). *Las redes sociales buscan la alianza del sector turístico*. TecnoHotelNews. Retrieved from https://tecnohotelnews.com/2018/01/21/redes-sociales-turismo-fitur/

TFEU - Treaty on the Functioning of the European Union. (2011). Available at: https://eur-lex.europa.eu/legal-content/EN/TXT/HTML/?uri=CELEX:12012E/TXT&from=EN

Thakur, K. (2020). *Importance of Tourism & Economic Values*. Retrieved from: https://market-width.com/blogs/Importance-Tourism-Industry-Economic-Value.htm

The Smart City Journal. (2020). *Smart Tourism*. Retrieved from www.thesmartcityjournal.com: https://www.thesmartcityjournal.com/en/articles/smart-cities-and-smart-tourism-a-narrative-on-tourism-in-turkey

The Social Media Family. (2020). *V Estudio sobre los usuarios de Facebook, Twitter e Instagram en España*. Retrieved from https://thesocialmediafamily.com/wp-content/uploads/92020/02/vi-informe-rrss-2020.pdf

Thomas, P. C., & David, W. M. (1992). Augmented reality: An application of heads-up display technology to manual manufacturing processes. In Hawaii international conference on system sciences (pp. 659-669). Academic Press.

Thomas, B. H., Von Itzstein, G. S., Vernik, R., Porter, S., Marner, M. R., Smith, R. T., ... Schumacher, P. (2011, March). Spatial augmented reality support for design of complex physical environments. In *2011 IEEE International Conference on Pervasive Computing and Communications Workshops (PERCOM Workshops)* (pp. 588-593). IEEE. 10.1109/PERCOMW.2011.5766958

Thomson, A., Proud, I., Goldston, A. L. J., & Dodds-Gorman, R. (2021). Virtual Reality for Better Event Planning and Management. In *Impact of ICTs on Event Management and Marketing* (pp. 177–198). IGI Global. doi:10.4018/978-1-7998-4954-4.ch011

Tidbits, T. (2014). *The importance of the Religious Tourism Marke*. Retrieved from /www.travelmole.com

Tokunaga, R. S., & Rains, S. A. (2010). An Evaluation of Two Characterizations of the Relationships Between Problematic Internet Use, Time Spent Using the Internet, and Psychosocial Problems. *Human Communication Research*, *36*(4), 512–545. doi:10.1111/j.1468-2958.2010.01386.x

Töllinen, A., & Karjaluoto, H. (2011). Marketing communication metrics for social media. *International Journal of Technology Marketing*, *6*(4), 316–330. doi:10.1504/IJTMKT.2011.045911

TourSpain. (2020). *Plan del Turismo Español Horizonte 2020*. TourSpain. Retrieved from https://www.tourspain.es/es/Conozcanos/Documents/HistoricoPoliticaTuristica/PlanTurismoEspanolHorizonte2020.pdf

TripAdvisor. (2020). *Fact sheet*. Retrieved on from https://tripadvisor.mediaroom.com/US-about-us

Tse, A. C. B. (2001). How much more are consumers willing to pay for a higher level of service? A preliminary survey. *Journal of Services Marketing*, *15*(1), 11–17. doi:10.1108/08876040110381328

Tse, E. C.-Y., & Ho, S.-C. (2009). Service quality in the hotel industry: When cultural contexts matter. *Cornell Hospitality Quarterly*, *50*(4), 460–474. doi:10.1177/1938965509338453

Tsokota, T., Solms, R., & Greunen, D. (2019). The reticent effect of ICT on tourism: A case study of Zimbabwe. *African Journal of Hospitality, Tourism and Leisure*, *8*(3).

Tung, V. W. S., Chen, P. J., & Schuckert, M. (2017). Managing customer citizenship behaviour: The moderating roles of employee responsiveness and organizational reassurance. *Tourism Management*, *59*, 23–35. doi:10.1016/j.tourman.2016.07.010

Turban, E., Sharda, R., & Delen, D. (2010). *Decision support and business intelligence systems* (9th ed.). Prentice Hall.

Türker, N. (2016). Religious Tourism in Turkey. In *Alternative Tourism in Turkey* (pp. 151–172). Springer. doi:10.1007/978-3-319-47537-0_10

Turkish Statistical Institute (TurkStat). (2012). *Tourism statistics*. http://www.turkstat.gov.tr/Start.do;jsessionid=0TgbWtyF6hxbQF2MhVZ9L4b60H8SWBrFr3dj7HrpfLwfyJMSTLTc!- 982956404

Turkle, S. (2011). *Alone Together: why we expect more from technology and less from each other*. Basic Books.

Turner, J., & Shah, R. (2011). *How to Make Money with Social Media*. F.T. Press.

Tussyadiah, I. P. (2016). Factors of satisfaction and intention to use peer-to-peer accommodation. *International Journal of Hospitality Management*, *55*, 70–80. doi:10.1016/j.ijhm.2016.03.005

Tussyadiah, I. P. (2017). Technology and Behavioral Design in Tourism. In *Design science in tourism* (pp. 173–191). Springer. doi:10.1007/978-3-319-42773-7_12

Twain, M. (2017). *The Traveling Public and Tourism Promoters*. https://www.pearsonhighered.com/assets/samplechapter/0/1/3/4/0134484487.pdf

Udell, M. K. (2019). *The Museum of the Infinite Scroll: Assessing the Effectiveness of Google Arts and Culture as a Virtual Tool for Museum Accessibility* (Master's thesis). University of San Francisco. Available at: https://repository.usfca.edu/capstone/979

Ulusu, Y. (2010). Determinant factors of time spent on facebook: Brand community engagement and usage types. *Journal of Yasar University*, *18*(5), 2949–2957.

Ungerman, O., Dedkova, J., & Gurinova, K. (2018). the Impact of Marketing Innovation on the Competitiveness of Enterprises in the Context of Industry 4.0. *Journal of Competitiveness*, *10*(2), 132–148. doi:10.7441/joc.2018.02.09

UNWTO. (2020). *International Tourism Highlights, 2020 Edition*. UNWTO.

UNWTO. (n.d.). *Glossary of tourism terms*. Retrieved from: https://www.unwto.org/glossary-tourism-terms

Compilation of References

Van Ouytsel, J., Van Gool, E., Walrave, M., Ponnet, K., & Peeters, E. (2016). Exploring the role of social networking sites within adolescent romantic relationships and dating experiences. *Computers in Human Behavior*, *55*, 76–86. doi:10.1016/j.chb.2015.08.042

Van Winkle, C., Cairns, A., MacKay, K., & Halpenny, E. (2016). Mobile device use at festivals: Opportunities for value creation. *International Journal of Event and Festival Management*, *7*(3), 201–218. doi:10.1108/IJEFM-04-2016-0025

Van Winkle, C. M., Bueddefeld, J. N. H., Halpenny, E. A., & MacKay, K. J. (2019). The unified theory of acceptance and use of technology 2: Understanding mobile device use at festivals. *Leisure Studies*, *38*(5), 634–650. doi:10.1080/02614367.2019.1618895

Vargas La Rosa, M. (2019). *Application of digital detox hotels for digital detoxification*. Academic Press.

Veloutsou, C., & Guzmán, F. (2017). The evolution of brand management thinking over the last 25 years as recorded in the Journal of Product & Brand Management. *Journal of Product and Brand Management*, *26*(1), 2–12. doi:10.1108/JPBM-01-2017-1398

Veloutsou, C., & Mafe, C. R. (2019). Brands as relationship builders in the virtual world: A bibliometric analysis. *Electronic Commerce Research and Applications*, *39*, 100901. Advance online publication. doi:10.1016/j.elerap.2019.100901

Vicentt, P. S. (2010). The economic impacts of academic spin-off companies and their implications for public policy. *Research Policy*, *39*(6), 736–747. doi:10.1016/j.respol.2010.02.001

Vilaseca i Requena, J., Lladós i Masllorens, J., Garay Tamajon, L., & Torrent i Sellens, J. (2007). Tecnologías de la Información y Comunicación, innovación y actividad turística: Hacia la empresa en red. *Cuadernos de Turismo*, *19*, 217–240.

Villamediana, J., Kuster, I., & Vila, N. (2019). Destination engagement on Facebook: Time and seasonality. *Annals of Tourism Research*, *79*, 102747. Advance online publication. doi:10.1016/j.annals.2019.102747

Villamediana-Pedrosa, J. D., Vila-Lopez, N., & Kuster-Boluda, I. (2019). Secrets to design an effective message on Facebook: An application to a touristic destination based on big data analysis. *Current Issues in Tourism*, *22*(15), 1841–1861. doi:10.1080/13683500.2018.1554625

Villeneuve, H., & O'Brien, W. (2020). Listen to the guests: Text-mining Airbnb reviews to explore indoor environmental quality. *Building and Environment*, *169*, 106–555. doi:10.1016/j.buildenv.2019.106555

Vukonic, B. (1997). Targeted tourism destinations. *Tourism, development and growth. Challenges in Sustainability*, 86.

Vukonic, B. (2002). Religion, tourism and economics: A convenient symbiosis. *Tourism Recreation Research*, *27*(2), 59–64. doi:10.1080/02508281.2002.11081221

Vural, Z. B. A. (2005). Enformasyon iletişim teknolojileri: Gelişimi, doğası ve ahlaki konular. *Yeni Düşünceler*, *1*(1), 125–136.

Wagaw, M., & Mulugeta, F. (2018). Integration of ICT and tourism for improved promotion of tourist attractions in Ethiopia. *Applied Informatics 2018*, *5*(1), 1–12. doi:10.1186/s40535-018-0053-x

Wahyono, I. D., Asfani, K., Mohamad, M. M., Aripriharta, A., Wibawa, A. P., & Wibisono, W. (2020, August). New smart map for tourism using artificial intelligence. In *2020 10th Electrical Power, Electronics, Communications, Controls and Informatics Seminar (EECCIS)* (pp. 213-216). IEEE.

Waitt, G. (2000). Consuming heritage: Perceived historical authenticity. *Annals of Tourism Research*, *27*(4), 835–862. doi:10.1016/S0160-7383(99)00115-2

Wang, D., Chan, H., & Pan, S. (2015). The impacts of mass media on organic destination image: A case study of Singapore. *Asia Pacific Journal of Tourism Research*, *20*(8), 860–874. doi:10.1080/10941665.2014.948464

Wang, S., Kirillova, K., & Lehto, X. (2016). Travelers' food experience sharing on social network sites. *Journal of Travel & Tourism Marketing*, *34*(5), 680–693. doi:10.1080/10548408.2016.1224751

Ward, C., & Szabo, A. (2019). Affect, behaviour, cognition and development: Adding to the alphabet of acculturation. In D. Matsumoto & H.-S. Hwang (Eds.), Handbook of culture and psychology (2nd ed., pp. 640–692). Oxford University Press.

Ward, C. (2008). Thinking outside the Berry boxes: New perspectives on identity, acculturation and intercultural relations. *International Journal of Intercultural Relations*, *32*(2), 105–114. doi:10.1016/j.ijintrel.2007.11.002

Ward, C., & Geeraert, N. (2016). Advancing acculturation theory and research: The acculturation process in its ecological context. *Current Opinion in Psychology*, *8*, 98–104. doi:10.1016/j.copsyc.2015.09.021 PMID:29506811

Wassler, P., & Talarico, C. (2021). Sociocultural impacts of COVID-19: A social representations perspective. *Tourism Management Perspectives*, *38*(100813), 1–10. doi:10.1016/j.tmp.2021.100813

Weber, L. (2009). *Marketing to the Social Web: How Digital Customer Communities Build Your Business*. Wiley Inc. doi:10.1002/9781118258125

Weinreich, P. (2009). "Enculturation", not "acculturation": Conceptualising and assessing identity processes in migrant communities. *International Journal of Intercultural Relations*, *33*(2), 124–139. doi:10.1016/j.ijintrel.2008.12.006

Weking, A. N., & Ndala, S. (2018, November). Analysis Of Mobile Application Smart Religious Tourism. In *2018 3rd International Conference on Information Technology, Information System and Electrical Engineering (ICITISEE)* (pp. 69-73). IEEE. 10.1109/ICITISEE.2018.8720958

Weking, A. N., & Santoso, A. J. (2020). A Development of Augmented Reality Mobile Application to Promote the Traditional Indonesian Food. *International Journal of Interactive Mobile Technologies*, *14*(9), 248. doi:10.3991/ijim.v14i09.11179

Wellman, B. (2001). Physical Place and Cyberplace: The Rise of Personalized Networking. *International Journal of Urban and Regional Research*, *25*(2), 227–252. doi:10.1111/1468-2427.00309

Wilcockson, T. D., Osborne, A. M., & Ellis, D. A. (2019). Digital detox: The effect of smartphone withdrawal on mood, anxiety, and craving. *Addictive Behaviors*, *99*, 106013. doi:10.1016/j.addbeh.2019.06.002 PMID:31430621

Willett, W. C., Sacks, F., Trichopoulou, A., Drescher, G., Ferro-Luzzi, A., Helsing, E., & Trichopoulos, D. (1995). Mediterranean diet pyramid: A cultural model for healthy eating. *The American Journal of Clinical Nutrition*, *61*(6), 1402S–1406S. doi:10.1093/ajcn/61.6.1402S PMID:7754995

Williams, P., & Hobson, J. P. (1995). Virtual reality and tourism: Fact or fantasy? *Tourism Management*, *16*(6), 423–427. doi:10.1016/0261-5177(95)00050-X

Wong, I. K. A. (2011). Using Destination Attributes to Promote Event Travel: The Case of Macau. *Journal of Convention & Event Tourism*, *12*(4), 241–252. doi:10.1080/15470148.2011.619884

World Tourism Organization (UNWTO). (2014). *Tourism highlights 2013*. UNWTO.

World Tourism Organization. (2020). *UNWTO*. Retrieved from https://www.unwto.org/

Wright, M., Clarysse, B., Mustar, P., & Lockett, A. (Eds.). (2007). Academic entrepreneurship in Europe. Edward Elgar.

WTTC. (2021). *Travel & Tourism*. Retrieved From: https://wttc.org/

Compilation of References

Xiang, Z., & Gretzel, U. (2010). Role of social media in online travel information search. *Tourism Management*, *31*(2), 179–188. Advance online publication. doi:10.1016/j.tourman.2009.02.016

Xiang, Z., Schwartz, Z., Gerdes, J. H. Jr, & Uysal, M. (2015). What can big data and text analytics tell us about hotel guest experience and satisfaction? *International Journal of Hospitality Management*, *44*, 120–130. doi:10.1016/j.ijhm.2014.10.013

Xie, H., Miao, L., Kuo, P.-J., & Lee, B.-Y. (2011). Consumers' responses to ambivalent online hotel reviews: The role of perceived source credibility and pre-decisional disposition. *International Journal of Hospitality Management*, *30*, 178–183. doi:10.1016/j.ijhm.2010.04.008

Xu, F., Weber, J., & Buhalis, D. (2013). Gamification in Tourism. *Information and Communication Technologies in Tourism 2014: Proceedings of the International Conference*.

Yacout, O. M., & Hefny, L. I. (2015). Use of Hofstede's cultural dimensions, demographics, and information sources as antecedents to cognitive and affective destination image for Egypt. *Journal of Vacation Marketing*, *21*(1), 37–52. doi:10.1177/1356766714538444

Yamin, M. (2019). Managing crowds with technology: cases of Hajj and Kumbh Mela. *International Journal of Information Technology*, *11*(2), 229-237.

Yang, F. X., & Tan, S. X. (2017). Event innovation induced corporate branding. *International Journal of Contemporary Hospitality Management*, *29*(3), 862–882. doi:10.1108/IJCHM-09-2015-0512

Yazdanifard, R., & Yee, L.T. (2014). Impact of Social Networking Sites on Hospitality and Tourism Industries. *Global Journal of Human-Social Science: E Economics*, *14*(8).

Ye, J. (2006). An Examination of Acculturative Stress, Interpersonal Social Support, and Use of Online Ethnic Social Groups among Chinese International Students. *The Howard Journal of Communications*, *17*(1), 1–20. doi:10.1080/10646170500487764

Yen, D. A., & Dey, B. L. (2019). Acculturation in the social media: Myth or reality? Analysing social-media-led integration and polarisation. *Technological Forecasting and Social Change*, *145*, 426–427. doi:10.1016/j.techfore.2019.04.012

Youtie, J., & Shapira, P. (2008). Building an Innovation Hub: A Case Study of the Transformation of University Roles in Regional Technological and Economic Development. *Research Policy*, *37*(8), 1188–1204. doi:10.1016/j.respol.2008.04.012

Yovcheva, Z., Buhalis, D., & Gatzidis, C. (2013). Engineering augmented tourism experiences. In *Information and communication technologies in tourism 2013* (pp. 24–35). Springer. doi:10.1007/978-3-642-36309-2_3

Yulia, C., Hasbullah, H., Nikmawati, E. E., Mubaroq, S. R., Abdullah, C. U., & Widiaty, I. (2018). Augmented reality of traditional food for nutrition education. In *MATEC Web of Conferences* (Vol. 197, p. 16001). EDP Sciences.

Zaidan, E. (2016). *Analysis of ICT usage patterns, benefits and barriers in tourism SMEs in the Middle Eastern countries: The case of Dubai in UAE*. doi:10.1177/1356766716654515

Zakarevičius, P. & Lionikaitė, J. (2013). An Initial Framework for Understanding the Concept of Internal Place Branding. *Organizacijų vadyba: sisteminiai tyrimai*, *67*, 143-160.

Zellner, A. (1962). An Efficient Method of Estimating Seemingly Unrelated Regressions and Tests for Aggregation Bias. *Journal of the American Statistical Association*, *57*(298), 348–368. doi:10.1080/01621459.1962.10480664

Zeng, B., & Gerritsen, R. (2014). What Do We Know about Social Media in Tourism? A Review. *Tourism Management Perspectives*, *10*, 27–36. doi:10.1016/j.tmp.2014.01.001

Zeng, Z., Chen, P.-J. J., & Lew, A. A. (2020). From high-touch to high-tech: COVID-19 drives robotics adoption. *Tourism Geographies*, *22*(3), 724–734. doi:10.1080/14616688.2020.1762118

Zhang, C. X., Wang, L., & Rickly, J. M. (2021). Non-interaction and identity change in Covid-19 tourism. *Annals of Tourism Research*, *89*, 1–14. doi:10.1016/j.annals.2021.103211

Zhang, Y., & Cole, S. T. (2016). Dimensions of lodging guest satisfaction among guests with mobility challenges: A mixed-method analysis of web-based texts. *Tourism Management*, *53*, 13–27. doi:10.1016/j.tourman.2015.09.001

Zhou, L., Ye, S., Pearce, P. L., & Wu, M.-Y. (2014). Refreshing hotel satisfaction studies by reconfiguring customer review data. *International Journal of Hospitality Management*, *38*, 1–10. doi:10.1016/j.ijhm.2013.12.004

Zhu, Z., Ma, W., & Leng, C. (2021). *ICT adoption and tourism consumption among rural residents in China*. doi:10.1177/13548166211000478

Zhu, L., Lin, Y., & Cheng, M. (2020). Sentiment and guest satisfaction with peer-to-peer accommodation: When are online ratings more trustworthy? *International Journal of Hospitality Management*, *86*, 102369. doi:10.1016/j.ijhm.2019.102369

Ziyadin, S., Koryagina, E., Grigoryan, T., Tovma, N., & Ismail, G. Z. (2019). Specificity of using information technologies in the digital transformation of event tourism. *International Journal of Civil Engineering and Technology*, *10*(1), 998–1010.

Zucconi, F. (2018). Heritage and Digital Technology: Google Arts & Culture. Cartaditalia, Rivista di cultura italiana contemporanea, 9(2), 350-361.

About the Contributors

Célia M. Q. Ramos graduated in Computer Engineering from the University of Coimbra, obtained her Master in Electrical and Computers Engineering from the Higher Technical Institute, Lisbon University, and the PhD in Econometrics in the University of the Algarve (UALG), Faculty of Economics, Portugal. She is Associate Professor at School for Management, Hospitality and Tourism, also in the UALG, where she lectures computer science. Areas of research and special interest include conception and development of information systems, tourism information systems, big data, etourism, econometric modeling and panel-data models. Célia Ramos has published in the fields of information systems and tourism, namely, she has authored a book, six book chapters, conference papers and journal articles. At the level of applied research, she has participated in several funded projects.

Sílvia Quinteiro is Associate Professor at University of the Algarve – School of Management, Hospitality and Tourism, where she teaches since 1994 and, among other positions and functions, was President of the Technical and Scientific Council. She holds a first degree in Modern Languages and Literatures (Portuguese and German Studies) from New University of Lisbon, a Master's and a PhD degree in Comparative Literature from the University of Lisbon. She founded and coordinated the Research Cluster in Literature and Tourism Studies: LIT&TOUR (2012-2020). Her research interests include Comparative Literature, and the relation between Literature and Tourism. She is a full member of CIAC – Centre for Research in Arts and Communication (University of the Algarve) member of the Rede Entremeio: Geography, Tourism and Literature Research Network of the Federal University of Rio de Janeiro and collaborates with project LITESCAPE. PT Literary Atlas of Continental Portugal. She cocoordinates the Literary Route of the Algarve, and has authored several national and international scientific publications.

Alexandra R. Gonçalves is Assistant Professor at the University of the Algarve, School of Management, Hospitality and Tourism. Integrated Researcher of the Research Centre for Tourism, Sustainability and Well-being (CinTurs) for the areas of Tourism, Sustainability, Territory, Heritage, Museums, Cultural Management and Creative Industries. PhD Degree in Tourism. Master's Degree in Cultural Heritage Management. Post-graduate degree in Cultural Heritage Law. Graduate in Marketing. Regional Director of Culture of the Algarve from December 16, 2013 to December 15, 2018; councilor of the Municipality of Faro (Oct. 2009-Oct. 2013). Since October 30th, 2019, is the Director of the School of Management, Hospitality and Tourism (University of Algarve). Has several published research in the areas of tourism, cultural experiences, cultural and creative tourism, cultural heritage management and museums, events evaluation. Was the regional researcher responsible for the project funded by the Portuguese Science and Tecnology Foundation -CREATOUR-Creative Tourism Destination Development in Small Cities and Rural Areas (2016-2020). Currently is the UALG coordinator for the iHERITAGE project, ENI CBC MED Program (2020-2023).

* * *

Tanvir Abir is an experienced researcher with a demonstrated history of working in the area of business research, health management and the higher education industry. He is currently working as an Associate Professor at the College of Business Administration (CBA) of IUBAT—International University of Business Agriculture and Technology, Dhaka, Bangladesh. Dr. Abir is skilled in Negotiation, Management, Marketing, Leadership, Microsoft Excel, and Data Analysis. He is a strong research professional with a Doctor of Philosophy - PhD focused in Health Management and Applied statistics from Western Sydney University.

Volkan Altıntaş is Associate Professor at Izmir Katip Celebi University.

Belem Barbosa is Assistant Professor at the University of Porto, Portugal. She received her PhD in Business and Management Studies – specialization in Marketing and Strategy from the University of Porto. Her research interests lie primarily in the area of internet marketing and consumer behavior.

Selman Bayrakcı is a Ph.D. researcher in research areas tourism economics, tourism sociology, tourism psychology, cultural tourism, and tourism marketing in the Department of Tourism Management.

Jordi Chumillas holds a PhD in Translation, Languages and Literatures and a degree on Translation and Interpretation. He is a professor in the Department of Philology and Didactics of Language and Literature (UVic-UCC), where he teaches at degree and master's degree levels. Member of the Research Group "Contemporary Literary Texts: study, editing and translation" (TEXLICO), his major research topics are literary reception, publishing houses, literary translation and literary geographies.

Muhammad Farooq is a PhD student at Yasar University.

Marco António Furtado has a University Degree in Modern Languages and Literatures – English and German Studies – by the Faculty of Letters of Porto University, Portugal. He has a Master's Degree in Bilingual and Intercultural German-Portuguese Studies by Minho University, Braga, Portugal, and a PhD Degree in Interpreting Studies by Vigo University, Spain. He is currently a Senior Lecturer at the Porto Accounting and Business School ISCAP-P.Porto. His research work is mainly focused on Interpreting Studies. Furthermore, he is developing additional research work on Intercultural Studies, German Contemporary History and Culture, and German Culture for Business. Marco Furtado is in charge of CEI's (Centre for Intercultural Studies) Research Line in "Intercultural Studies in Business" since September 2019.

Mia Güell holds a PhD in Translation, Languages and Literatures and she is a philologist and professor at the University of Vic - Central University of Catalonia. Her major fields of research are Literary Geographies, Didactics of Literature and Literature as a resource for language learning. Editor of

About the Contributors

Endrets.cat, she is a member of the Research Group "Contemporary Literary Texts: study, editing and translation" (TEXLICO), where she coordinates a line of research devoted to Didactics of Literature.

Md Yusuf Hossein Khan is currently working as an Assistant Professor at the College of Tourism and Hospitality Management (CTHM) of IUBAT—International University of Business Agriculture and Technology, Dhaka, Bangladesh. He is also a PhD Researcher at the faculty of Economics at the University of Algarve, Portugal. He has a good number of experience working within the tourism and hospitality industry in several countries. Yusuf H Khan has completed his MSc in International Tourism Management from the Cardiff Metropolitan University, UK, and MBA International from the Anglia Ruskin University, UK. Besides, Yusuf H Khan is an expert in curriculum design and currently is an active member of CTHM curriculum task force team of IUBAT. His current research interests are in particular, Safety and Risk in Tourism, Travelers loyalty, Tourist motivation and behavior, and Tourism destination image and development. He has a good number of publications on these areas.

Ricardo Martinez-Cañas is an Associate Professor in Business Management at Castilla-La Mancha University (Spain). His research interest are Social Capital; Science Parks; Business Ethics; Wine Tourism; Innovation; Pay Satisfaction; Ethical Leadership; Educational Research; Entrepreneurial Intention; Value Co-creation.

María Pilar Martínez-Ruiz is Ph.D. in Economics and Business Administration, and currently Associate Professor at the Department of Marketing of the University of Castilla-La Mancha, Albacete (Spain). She has participated in different Conferences and Seminars worldwide, has written different book chapters and numerous research articles in prestigious journals such as European Journal of Marketing, International Journal of Market Research, Journal of the Operational Research Society and Decision Support Systems. Her main research lines are marketing communications, retailing, and product and service innovation.

Ceyhun Can Ozcan is an Associate Professor in research areas tourism economics, economic development, and applied econometrics, economics growth, and macroeconomics in the Department of Tourism Management.

Sara Pascoal is an Adjunct Professor at the Polytechnic Institute of Porto (ISCAP- P.Porto), Portugal, since 1997. She has an undergraduate degree in Modern Languages and Literatures, a Master's degree in Portuguese Culture and a PHD in Romanic Languages and Cultures. She is currently doing research on Literary geography and Literary tourism and she's involved in the SAICT – 23447, 2016 (MCTES, Portugal 2020 e FCT) Project "TheRoute – Tourism and Heritage Routes including Ambient Intelligence with Visitants' Profile Adaptation and Context Awareness", led by ISEP – P. Porto. She is a researcher and member of the Scientific Board of the Centre for Intercultural Studies of IPP, a researcher at the Institute for the Study of Literature and Tradition (IELT). Her research interests range from Literary Geography and Geocriticism, Cultural Tourism, Intercultural Communication, Portuguese Culture and Translation.

Pere Quer holds a PhD in Catalan Philology and he is a professor at the University of Vic - Central University of Catalonia. He is a member of the Contemporary Literary Texts Research Group (TEXLICO) and also of the Literary Geographies 3.0 Innovation Project. His research areas include Literary

Reception in Catalonia, History of Publishing Houses, History of Translation and Cultural Relations and the study of Literary Heritage; in particular, he works on Literary Routes applied to Education.

Rayane Ruas is a specialist in Planning and Public Policy in Tourism. Ph.D. student in Tourism at the University of Aveiro, focusing on the use of technologies and big data for tourism. Has a Master's degree in Tourism from the University of Brasília (2013), an Executive MBA in Project Management from AVM (2015), an MBA in Digital Marketing from AVM (2016), a postgraduate degree in Heritage Management, Culture and Sustainable Tourism from the Ortega y Gasset Foundation. (2011) and Degree in Tourism from IESB (2010). Is a Co-Funder and Head of intelligence of Up Soluções, a startup company for collaborative and intelligent tourist destinations and technological development of tourist destinations.

Pablo Ruiz-Palomino is Associate Professor of Business Management at University of Castilla-La Mancha, Spain. He earned a Ph.D. in Business Administration at this same University in November, 2008, which was awarded the 1st Prize in the 2010 (IV) Edition of FORETICA-MSD for Business Ethics and Corporate Social Responsibility Research (International Call). Since then, he has acted as visiting scholar in a number of prestigious universities such as Bentley University, University of Arizona, IESE Business School, Alliant International University and University of Edinburgh, among others. His research interests are ethical leadership, organizational behaviour, and social capital in business, tourism, and hospitality contexts.

Bruno Sousa is a Professor in Polytechnic Institute of Cavado and Ave (IPCA, Portugal) Head of Master Program - Tourism Management - PhD Marketing and Strategy. He was Market Analist at Sonae Distribuição – Modelo e Continente, S.A. (2006 to 2009) and he was Marketing Assistant - Jornal O Jogo at Controlinveste (2005) - Best Paper Award in Strategic Marketing & Value Creation (International Conference on Innovation and Entrepreneurship in Marketing and Consumer Behaviour 2020) Teaching Award of the School of Economics and Management of the University of Minho 2015/2016 - Best Thesis in Tourism Award - ICIEMC 2015 - Management Graduation, University of Minho Award - Best performance (2006) - Merit Scholarship for Students in Public Higher Education Awards of Merit Scholarship by University of Minho in 2001/02 - 2002/03 - 2003/04 Rresearch centre: CiTUR and Applied Management Research Unit (UNIAG). He is author or co-author of several papers and her research interests include tourism management, marketing and strategy. Editorial board member of several peer reviewed scientific journals and ad-hoc reviewer of several peer-reviewed scientific journals. Member of the scientific committee of several national and international congresses and conferences.

Laura Tallone has a BA in Philology and BA in Literary, Technical and Scientific Translation. MA in Specialised Translation and Interpreting. Translation Specialist Degree granted by Porto Polytechnic Institute. Editor of the volumes Do signo ao texto: Contributos Pedagógicos para a Tradução Técnica em Quatro Línguas (De Facto Editores, 2016) and Do texto ao Contexto: Novos Contributos Pedagógicos para a Tradução Técnica em Quatro Línguas (CEI, 2020). Currently, senior translation lecturer at ISCAP Instituto Superior de Contabilidade e Administração do Porto. Member of the Direction of ISCAP's Master in Specialised Translation and Interpreting. Researcher at CEI Centro de Estudos Interculturais (ISCAP). Member of the editorial committee of POLISSEMA – Revista de Letras do ISCAP.

About the Contributors

Tuba Türkmendağ works at Atatürk University. She graduated from Balıkesir University School of Tourism and Hotel Management, Department of Hospitality Management with a Bachelor's and Master's Degree and from Gazi University with a doctoral degree. Her research areas are tourism marketing, innovation management, human resources management, and recreation management.

Zafer Türkmendağ works at Atatürk University in Turkey. He graduated from Akdeniz University with a Bachelor's Degree and Gazi University with a master's and doctoral degree. His main research areas are tourism management systems, artificial intelligence and big data in tourism management and marketing.

Sofia Vairinho received her MS in Law from Universidad de Huelva (Spain) where she is finishing her PhD studies, and holds a degree and a pos-graduation in Law from Universidade de Coimbra (Portugal). She is a law practitioner with relevant experience in the fields of Intellectual Property, Technology Transfer, Entrepreneurship and spin-off support, Regional Innovation Strategy and management with international experience as Manager for Business Development and Licensing due to her work at the Center for Technology Transfer and Enterprise Creation at Carnegie Mellon University (U.S.A.). Currently she is Head of the IP and Licensing Unit (GAPI/PATLIB Centre) and also works as invited professor at Universidade do Algarve (Portugal). She writes and presents widely on the above mentioned fields, and is the co-author of, for example, 'The Single Patent for Portuguese or Spanish Language Countries' (2015, S. Vairinho et al.) and of 'Le rôle du transfert de connaissances dans l'affirmation scientifique des petites et moyennes universités - Le cas de l'Université d'Algarve (Portugal)' (2021, J. Guerreiro et S. Vairinho).

Index

A

acculturation 42-52, 54-65
application 2-3, 6-7, 13, 16, 18, 26-28, 34, 39-40, 71-74, 76, 78, 80, 82, 104, 109-110, 116, 119-120, 123, 129, 139-140, 142, 167, 169, 183, 194-195, 206, 208, 211, 221, 254-255, 264, 266
applications 6, 9, 11-12, 17-18, 21, 23-24, 30, 32, 40, 54, 67-68, 73, 76, 79, 106-115, 117, 119, 121, 135, 137, 139-140, 145, 181, 213, 216, 218, 222-223, 227, 234, 236, 265
artificial intelligence 49, 53, 74, 76-78, 80, 84, 104, 106-107, 109, 112-113, 115-117, 120-121, 180, 187

B

Bangladesh 30, 32, 38, 213-215, 217-218, 222-229
big data 34, 40, 104-106, 110, 112-113, 115, 119, 121, 211, 248-249, 266-268
Blockchain 112, 117, 121
business 2, 5, 7, 11, 13, 30, 32-35, 38-39, 60, 62, 64, 74, 77, 82-84, 93, 100, 108, 111-113, 115-116, 118-119, 123-127, 129, 139-141, 160, 164, 166, 171-175, 177-178, 180-190, 193, 196, 206, 209, 213-216, 218, 220-222, 224-229, 241-245, 264, 266-267

C

challenges 12, 27-28, 31, 35, 79, 100, 108, 118, 122-123, 126, 152, 165, 172, 174, 177-178, 194, 197, 200, 207, 211, 220, 226, 234, 268
communication 1, 4-5, 12-13, 18, 30-32, 34-35, 37-40, 42-43, 53, 55-56, 59-60, 64-65, 67, 71-73, 75-76, 78, 82, 87, 91, 98, 104, 108-113, 116-117, 121-123, 125, 127-129, 137-142, 150, 152-153, 155-161, 163-164, 166, 174, 181, 186, 193, 208, 211-212, 214, 216-218, 227, 230, 232-233, 242, 244, 246, 249, 264, 266, 268

connected loneliness 42-43, 53, 57, 65
Consumer Behavior Online 137, 169
COVID-19 48-49, 55, 60, 62, 65, 82, 94, 96, 99, 122-124, 130, 132-133, 167, 171, 174, 231, 241
Cuenca City 230, 236
cultural tourism 4-5, 7, 11, 13, 15-16, 18, 23, 29, 57, 81-83, 85, 91-92, 98-99, 106
culture 1-5, 7, 20, 30, 40, 43-58, 60-61, 64-65, 69, 71, 74-75, 78, 81-87, 91-94, 96-101, 126, 132, 175, 182, 184, 232-233, 238, 240-241, 251, 263, 266
Culture Commoditization 100
customer engagement 125, 192-196, 209-211, 219

D

depopulation 231-232, 246
destination image 108-109, 211, 230, 232-234, 241-246, 267
detox 155-158, 160, 163-169
developing country 30, 32, 35, 40
development 1-5, 7, 9-10, 12-14, 25, 27, 30, 34-41, 44-49, 53, 55-57, 60-61, 64-65, 74, 79, 83-84, 87, 91, 93, 98-99, 104, 107-108, 111-112, 115-119, 123-125, 129, 132, 138-144, 148, 150-157, 161, 164-166, 168, 172, 174-183, 185, 187-190, 194-195, 210-211, 213, 225-226, 229, 231-235, 243, 245
digital 2-4, 6-10, 12, 18, 42-44, 46-61, 64, 71, 76-77, 84, 86, 91, 97, 99-100, 106-107, 109, 111, 113, 119, 121-123, 125-128, 131-132, 134-137, 140, 150-151, 153-169, 194-195, 208, 214, 218, 221, 223, 225, 228, 234, 236, 242-244
digital acculturation 42-43, 46-52, 54-58, 60
digital marketing 113, 125-128, 134-135, 137, 169, 194, 208, 218, 221, 223, 225
DMO 128, 134, 192-194, 196, 200

E

education 1, 4-5, 11-12, 14-15, 39, 52, 59, 62, 81, 109, 119, 149, 170, 173, 176-177, 181, 183-187, 189, 208, 224, 264, 268
enculturation 42-43, 49, 56-57, 65
entrepreneurship 82-83, 87, 94, 97, 99, 101, 170, 172-178, 180, 186-190
E-Satisfaction 137, 169
Event 4, 72, 104-121, 243, 249
E-WOM 51, 72-73, 137, 169

F

Facebook 47, 63-64, 109, 125-126, 128, 160, 201, 206, 209-211, 214, 216-224, 227-228, 230, 233, 235-237, 240, 243, 245-246, 267
followers 19, 46, 56, 69, 109, 128, 198, 201-203, 206-207, 212, 214, 217-218, 236-238, 240

G

gastronomic tourism 1, 4
Google Arts and Culture 81, 85, 100
Greece 1, 4-6, 8-10, 144, 228, 261
Green Communication 112, 121
guest 48, 59, 115, 165, 247-252, 262-268
guest satisfaction 247-252, 263-264, 266, 268

H

hotel 30-31, 33-34, 38-40, 93, 119, 132, 136, 164, 167, 209, 214, 218-219, 228, 231, 238, 247-256, 258-268
Hotel Managements 247, 259-260
hybrid 62, 114, 137, 227

I

ICT 5-8, 10, 13-16, 18-21, 23-40, 42, 47-48, 71, 81-83, 85, 91, 107-108, 113, 116, 120, 122-124, 126, 129, 135, 138-144, 147-153, 155, 157-159, 163, 171, 176, 179-181, 187-188
ICT Integration in Museums 14
ICT tools 15, 21, 23-27, 29, 34, 47, 140
impression 108-109, 212
information and communication 1, 5, 13, 30-32, 34, 38-40, 42, 67, 71, 76, 78, 111, 116-117, 122-123, 137-141, 150, 153, 155, 157, 163, 174, 181, 186, 227, 242, 264, 266
Information and Communication Technologies 1, 5, 13, 32, 40, 42, 71, 78, 111, 116-117, 123, 137, 139, 141, 153, 155, 157, 163, 174, 181, 227, 242, 264, 266
information and communication technology 30-32, 34, 38-40, 76, 138-140, 150, 186
Information Tourist Sources 230
innovation 4, 83, 89, 93, 99, 104-105, 107-112, 115-118, 120-121, 124, 135, 139, 151, 159, 170-182, 184-190, 208, 221, 231, 242
Innovation Leader 108, 121
Innovation Networks 170, 190
Instagram 64, 201, 203, 214, 218, 220-221, 230, 233, 235-236, 238-241, 245-246
intellectual property 171-172, 174, 178-179, 183-188, 190
interactions 5, 42, 47-48, 77, 110, 156, 161-163, 193-196, 198, 201-204, 206-207, 212, 219, 233, 237-238, 240, 251-252
Interculturalism 82, 100
international tourism 138, 143, 151-154
Interpretative Role 29

L

level of engagement 193
Literary Education 15
Literary Place 29
Literary Places 15, 18, 28
literary route 15-17, 21, 23, 26, 29
literary tourism 15-21, 27-29

M

marketing 12, 28, 30-32, 34, 38-40, 54, 58-63, 68, 77, 81-85, 93, 99, 104-113, 115-120, 122-123, 125-138, 141-142, 144, 149, 155-156, 166-167, 169, 171-172, 179, 186, 192-195, 207-211, 213-215, 217-230, 232-233, 240-250, 253, 262, 264-268
MIEC 81-82, 85, 87-88, 91-98, 100-101
multiculturalism 43, 82, 100
museum 1-3, 6-10, 12-13, 81-82, 84-87, 91, 93-95, 97, 100, 131-132
Mushroom Museum 8-9

N

novel culture 43, 46-51, 57

O

online acculturation 42-43, 47, 49

Online Relationship 134, 137, 169
online review 268

P

panel data 138, 144-145, 151, 153-154
PANEL GRANGER CAUSALITY TEST 138, 145
PBL 81-82, 85, 87-92, 94, 97-98, 100-101
pilgrimage 4, 67-69, 71, 77-79, 165
process 2-3, 6, 9, 31-32, 38, 41-58, 65, 74, 79, 83, 90, 94, 100, 104, 108, 113, 115, 117, 128, 135, 139-140, 149, 157, 171, 173, 176, 178-181, 183, 186-187, 190, 192-193, 195, 208-209, 219-220, 223, 229, 232, 234-235, 240, 243, 248, 255, 264
promotion 6, 31, 71, 73, 81-82, 86, 89, 91, 93, 97, 99, 109, 111, 115, 119, 125-127, 129-130, 148-149, 153, 173-176, 178, 180, 198, 202, 213, 215, 218, 220, 222-223, 227, 229, 231-232, 238, 240

R

reach 2, 7, 49, 106, 113, 125-128, 144, 165-166, 194, 198, 201-202, 204, 206, 209, 212, 222, 224, 232
Real-Time Service 106, 121
religious tourism 4, 67-80
remote acculturation 43-46, 60-61, 65

S

satisfaction 32, 34, 38-39, 71-72, 94, 111, 119-120, 131, 156, 159-160, 162, 195, 210, 212, 219, 229, 234, 247-253, 261-269
Second Life 55, 64-65
security 35, 77, 104, 112-113, 120, 249, 252
segmentation 155, 266
service industry 35, 126, 141, 213, 217, 229
sharing economy 43, 51-52, 59, 61, 65
smart event tourism 104, 113-115
social capital 42-43, 54, 57, 60, 64, 66, 83
Social Identity 44, 66
social media 38, 43, 55-56, 60-62, 65, 68, 71, 73, 76, 82, 105, 109-110, 118-119, 121, 125, 127-128, 131, 135, 137, 141, 153, 160-162, 168-169, 192-201, 206-230, 232-236, 240-247, 250
social media engagement 192-194, 197-199, 206-208, 210-212
Social Media Interaction 192
Social Media Profiles 212
social networking sites 42, 46, 60, 62-64, 73, 192, 196, 198, 200-201, 203, 212, 214, 216-218, 221, 224-225, 228, 244-245

social networks 23, 43, 109-110, 123, 125-128, 137, 157, 162, 166-167, 169, 214, 216-218, 221, 224-225, 227, 230, 232-237, 240
Spatial Augmented Reality 1-3, 9, 11, 13-14
special and alternative forms of tourism 1-3, 12
Special and Alternative Tourism 14
storytelling 15, 20, 29, 91, 99
sustainability 3, 54, 79, 84, 98, 108, 117-118, 132-134, 211, 231-232, 234, 240-242, 245-246

T

teaching 17, 21-22, 81, 83, 100, 179
technology 2-13, 28, 30-35, 38-40, 45-55, 57, 59, 61, 64, 67-69, 71-77, 80-81, 84, 86-87, 90-91, 93-94, 97-100, 102, 104-106, 109-113, 115-121, 123, 125, 127-129, 132-133, 135, 138-141, 143, 150-153, 156-168, 170-173, 176-179, 181-182, 185-188, 190, 210-211, 213, 216, 221, 223-225, 227-228, 234-235, 240, 245, 263-264
Technology Transfer and Commercialization 170, 190
Technology-supported 113
text mining 247-248, 250, 253-254, 261-263, 269
time 1-4, 6-10, 16, 20, 36, 51-53, 56-57, 64, 72, 83-84, 91, 93-94, 98, 104, 106-111, 113, 116, 123, 130-132, 140, 145, 157-163, 166, 171, 175, 188-189, 193, 196, 203, 208, 211, 217-218, 228, 232-234, 236-237, 240, 246, 250, 252
tourism 1-5, 7, 10-21, 23, 27-44, 47-54, 56-65, 67-85, 91-93, 98-100, 104-144, 147-156, 164-165, 167-168, 172-173, 176, 181, 188, 192-194, 196, 198, 202, 207-211, 213-219, 221-238, 240-246, 248-249, 252-253, 263-269
tourism and hospitality 28, 30-34, 36, 38-39, 41, 78, 109-110, 116, 151-152, 213-215, 222-223, 229, 242, 245, 263, 265
tourism and hospitality industries 31-32, 38-39, 213-214, 222-223
tourism and hospitality industry 30, 32, 34, 38, 41, 213-215
tourism demand 44, 77, 138, 143-144, 148, 151, 153-154, 215
tourism destination 68, 118, 136, 144, 151, 192, 226, 252
tourism development 30, 41, 79, 116, 139, 143, 150, 153, 243
Tourism Marketing 12, 85, 107, 116, 123, 133, 223-225, 228, 230, 232, 240, 244, 246, 266
tourism sector 3, 5, 7, 10, 35, 52, 67-74, 77, 84, 107, 110, 112, 123-125, 129-130, 134, 139, 141-142, 144, 148-150, 154, 172, 176, 196, 213-214, 221,

Index

    227, 232-233, 235, 240, 248, 253
tourist experience 19, 26, 48, 93, 97, 124, 164, 168, 193
Tourist Guide 15, 19-20, 28-29, 78
Tourist Information Source 246
touristic destinations 47, 76, 170, 178, 190
trends 2, 5, 10, 12, 22-23, 40, 52, 59, 69, 79, 85, 93, 100, 108, 119, 123, 126-127, 155-156, 214-215, 262
TripAdvisor 109, 125-126, 131, 135, 141, 249, 253-254, 263-264, 266-267, 269
TSM Engagement Framework 192, 194, 197, 199, 206-208
Turkey 42, 48, 67-71, 74-79, 104, 138, 144, 147, 247-248, 253-260, 263, 269

U

university spin-off 170-172, 179, 182, 184-185, 187, 190

V

viral 131, 198, 204, 212
virtual 2-3, 6-8, 10-14, 18, 34, 42-43, 46-47, 51-52, 54-56, 60, 62-66, 71, 76, 81-87, 91-101, 105, 107, 109-110, 112-115, 117, 120-123, 125-126, 128-137, 169, 180, 182, 187, 193, 209, 221, 224, 229, 235, 243
virtual exhibition 81-85, 87, 91, 93-94, 97, 100-101
Virtual Social Places 109, 121
virtual tourism 122-123, 129-134, 137
virtual tours 60, 82, 109, 121, 134

W

WDI (World Development Indicators) 144, 154
World Heritage City 230, 235, 246

Recommended Reference Books

IGI Global's reference books are available in three unique pricing formats:
Print Only, E-Book Only, or Print + E-Book.

Shipping fees may apply.

www.igi-global.com

ISBN: 978-1-7998-1048-3
EISBN: 978-1-7998-1049-0
© 2020; 605 pp.
List Price: US$ **285**

ISBN: 978-1-5225-8933-4
EISBN: 978-1-5225-8934-1
© 2020; 667 pp.
List Price: US$ **295**

ISBN: 978-1-7998-0357-7
EISBN: 978-1-7998-0359-1
© 2020; 451 pp.
List Price: US$ **235**

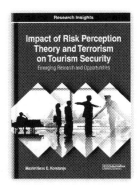

ISBN: 978-1-7998-0070-5
EISBN: 978-1-7998-0071-2
© 2020; 144 pp.
List Price: US$ **175**

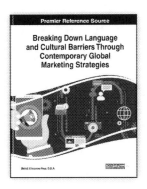

ISBN: 978-1-5225-6980-0
EISBN: 978-1-5225-6981-7
© 2019; 339 pp.
List Price: US$ **235**

ISBN: 978-1-5225-5390-8
EISBN: 978-1-5225-5391-5
© 2018; 125 pp.
List Price: US$ **165**

Do you want to stay current on the latest research trends, product announcements, news, and special offers?
Join IGI Global's mailing list to receive customized recommendations, exclusive discounts, and more.
Sign up at: **www.igi-global.com/newsletters.**

Publisher of Peer-Reviewed, Timely, and Innovative Academic Research

www.igi-global.com ✉ Sign up at www.igi-global.com/newsletters f facebook.com/igiglobal t twitter.com/igiglobal in linkedin.com/igiglobal

Ensure Quality Research is Introduced to the Academic Community

Become an Evaluator for IGI Global Authored Book Projects

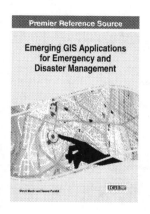 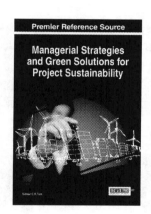  

The overall success of an authored book project is dependent on quality and timely manuscript evaluations.

Applications and Inquiries may be sent to:
development@igi-global.com

Applicants must have a doctorate (or equivalent degree) as well as publishing, research, and reviewing experience. Authored Book Evaluators are appointed for one-year terms and are expected to complete at least three evaluations per term. Upon successful completion of this term, evaluators can be considered for an additional term.

If you have a colleague that may be interested in this opportunity, we encourage you to share this information with them.

IGI Global Author Services

Providing a high-quality, affordable, and expeditious service, IGI Global's Author Services enable authors to streamline their publishing process, increase chance of acceptance, and adhere to IGI Global's publication standards.

Benefits of Author Services:

- **Professional Service:** All our editors, designers, and translators are experts in their field with years of experience and professional certifications.
- **Quality Guarantee & Certificate:** Each order is returned with a quality guarantee and certificate of professional completion.
- **Timeliness:** All editorial orders have a guaranteed return timeframe of 3-5 business days and translation orders are guaranteed in 7-10 business days.
- **Affordable Pricing:** IGI Global Author Services are competitively priced compared to other industry service providers.
- **APC Reimbursement:** IGI Global authors publishing Open Access (OA) will be able to deduct the cost of editing and other IGI Global author services from their OA APC publishing fee.

Author Services Offered:

English Language Copy Editing
Professional, native English language copy editors improve your manuscript's grammar, spelling, punctuation, terminology, semantics, consistency, flow, formatting, and more.

Scientific & Scholarly Editing
A Ph.D. level review for qualities such as originality and significance, interest to researchers, level of methodology and analysis, coverage of literature, organization, quality of writing, and strengths and weaknesses.

Figure, Table, Chart & Equation Conversions
Work with IGI Global's graphic designers before submission to enhance and design all figures and charts to IGI Global's specific standards for clarity.

Translation
Providing 70 language options, including Simplified and Traditional Chinese, Spanish, Arabic, German, French, and more.

Hear What the Experts Are Saying About IGI Global's Author Services

"Publishing with IGI Global has been *an amazing experience* for me for sharing my research. The *strong academic production* support ensures quality and timely completion." – **Prof. Margaret Niess, Oregon State University, USA**

"The service was *very fast, very thorough, and very helpful* in ensuring our chapter meets the criteria and requirements of the book's editors. I was *quite impressed and happy* with your service." – **Prof. Tom Brinthaupt, Middle Tennessee State University, USA**

Learn More or Get Started Here: For Questions, Contact IGI Global's Customer Service Team at cust@igi-global.com or 717-533-8845

www.igi-global.com

Celebrating Over 30 Years of Scholarly Knowledge Creation & Dissemination

InfoSci®-Books

A Database of Nearly 6,000 Reference Books Containing Over 105,000+ Chapters Focusing on Emerging Research

GAIN ACCESS TO **THOUSANDS** OF REFERENCE BOOKS AT **A FRACTION** OF THEIR INDIVIDUAL LIST **PRICE**.

InfoSci®-Books Database

The **InfoSci®-Books** is a database of nearly 6,000 IGI Global single and multi-volume reference books, handbooks of research, and encyclopedias, encompassing groundbreaking research from prominent experts worldwide that spans over 350+ topics in 11 core subject areas including business, computer science, education, science and engineering, social sciences, and more.

Open Access Fee Waiver (Read & Publish) Initiative

For any library that invests in IGI Global's InfoSci-Books and/or InfoSci-Journals (175+ scholarly journals) databases, IGI Global will match the library's investment with a fund of equal value to go toward **subsidizing the OA article processing charges (APCs) for their students, faculty, and staff** at that institution when their work is submitted and accepted under OA into an IGI Global journal.*

INFOSCI® PLATFORM FEATURES

- Unlimited Simultaneous Access
- No DRM
- No Set-Up or Maintenance Fees
- A Guarantee of No More Than a 5% Annual Increase for Subscriptions
- Full-Text HTML and PDF Viewing Options
- Downloadable MARC Records
- COUNTER 5 Compliant Reports
- Formatted Citations With Ability to Export to RefWorks and EasyBib
- No Embargo of Content (Research is Available Months in Advance of the Print Release)

*The fund will be offered on an annual basis and expire at the end of the subscription period. The fund would renew as the subscription is renewed for each year thereafter. The open access fees will be waived after the student, faculty, or staff's paper has been vetted and accepted into an IGI Global journal and the fund can only be used toward publishing OA in an IGI Global journal. Libraries in developing countries will have the match on their investment doubled.

To Recommend or Request a Free Trial:
www.igi-global.com/infosci-books

eresources@igi-global.com • Toll Free: 1-866-342-6657 ext. 100 • Phone: 717-533-8845 x100

www.igi-global.com

Publisher of Peer-Reviewed, Timely, and Innovative Academic Research Since 1988

IGI Global's Transformative Open Access (OA) Model:
How to Turn Your University Library's Database Acquisitions Into a Source of OA Funding

Well in advance of Plan S, IGI Global unveiled their OA Fee Waiver (Read & Publish) Initiative. Under this initiative, librarians who invest in IGI Global's InfoSci-Books and/or InfoSci-Journals databases will be able to subsidize their patrons' OA article processing charges (APCs) when their work is submitted and accepted (after the peer review process) into an IGI Global journal.

How Does it Work?

Step 1: Library Invests in the InfoSci-Databases: A library perpetually purchases or subscribes to the InfoSci-Books, InfoSci-Journals, or discipline/subject databases.

Step 2: IGI Global Matches the Library Investment with OA Subsidies Fund: IGI Global provides a fund to go towards subsidizing the OA APCs for the library's patrons.

Step 3: Patron of the Library is Accepted into IGI Global Journal (After Peer Review): When a patron's paper is accepted into an IGI Global journal, they option to have their paper published under a traditional publishing model or as OA.

Step 4: IGI Global Will Deduct APC Cost from OA Subsidies Fund: If the author decides to publish under OA, the OA APC fee will be deducted from the OA subsidies fund.

Step 5: Author's Work Becomes Freely Available: The patron's work will be freely available under CC BY copyright license, enabling them to share it freely with the academic community.

Note: This fund will be offered on an annual basis and will renew as the subscription is renewed for each year thereafter. IGI Global will manage the fund and award the APC waivers unless the librarian has a preference as to how the funds should be managed.

Hear From the Experts on This Initiative:

"I'm very happy to have been able to make one of my recent research contributions *freely available* along with having access to the *valuable resources* found within IGI Global's InfoSci-Journals database."

– **Prof. Stuart Palmer**, Deakin University, Australia

"Receiving the support from IGI Global's OA Fee Waiver Initiative *encourages me to continue my research work without any hesitation*."

– **Prof. Wenlong Liu**, College of Economics and Management at Nanjing University of Aeronautics & Astronautics, China

For More Information, Scan the QR Code or Contact: IGI Global's Digital Resources Team at eresources@igi-global.com.

Are You Ready to Publish Your Research?

IGI Global — PUBLISHER of TIMELY KNOWLEDGE

IGI Global offers book authorship and editorship opportunities across 11 subject areas, including business, computer science, education, science and engineering, social sciences, and more!

Benefits of Publishing with IGI Global:

- Free one-on-one editorial and promotional support.
- Expedited publishing timelines that can take your book from start to finish in less than one (1) year.
- Choose from a variety of formats, including: Edited and Authored References, Handbooks of Research, Encyclopedias, and Research Insights.
- Utilize IGI Global's eEditorial Discovery® submission system in support of conducting the submission and double-blind peer review process.
- IGI Global maintains a strict adherence to ethical practices due in part to our full membership with the Committee on Publication Ethics (COPE).
- Indexing potential in prestigious indices such as Scopus®, Web of Science™, PsycINFO®, and ERIC – Education Resources Information Center.
- Ability to connect your ORCID iD to your IGI Global publications.
- Earn honorariums and royalties on your full book publications as well as complimentary copies and exclusive discounts.

Join Your Colleagues from Prestigious Institutions, Including:

Australian National University · MIT Massachusetts Institute of Technology · Johns Hopkins University · Harvard University · Tsinghua University · Columbia University in the City of New York

Learn More at: www.igi-global.com/publish
or Contact IGI Global's Aquisitions Team at: acquisition@igi-global.com